THEOLOGICAL

GUIDE TO

CALVIN'S

INSTITUTES

ESSAYS AND ANALYSIS

EDITED BY

DAVID W. HALL

and

PETER A. LILLBACK

PUBLISHING
P.O. BOX 817 • PHILLIPSBURG • NEW JERSEY 08865-0817

Printed in the United States of America

Library of Congress Cataloging-in-Publication Data

A theological guide to Calvin's Institutes : essays and analysis / edited by David W. Hall and Peter A. Lillback.
    p. cm. — (The Calvin 500 series)
Includes bibliographical references and index.
ISBN 978-1-59638-091-2 (cloth)
1. Calvin, Jean, 1509-1564. Institutio Christianae religionis. 2. Reformed Church—Doctrines. 3. Theology, Doctrinal. I. Hall, David W., 1955- II. Lillback, Peter A.
BX9420.I69T44 2008
230'.42—dc22

                                    2008005073

Historiam esse vitae magistram, vere dixerunt ethnicic
—Calvin on Romans 4:23–24

The editors wish to echo the author that all the following authors seek to honor by acknowledging not only that the world of unbelief occasionally joins Calvin in referring to history as the teacher of life (*vitae magistram*) but also that in our own lives, those who have preceded us have been marvelous teachers of life, precisely because they valued history so highly. For centuries, little-known (but faithful) professors have sought to enlighten young minds with the knowledge that John Calvin profferred. Our lives have been enriched by such, and we are profoundly grateful for those who taught us Calvin's *Institutes* and an appreciation for Calvin's insights. We wish to thank and dedicate this volume to all those who have been our seminary professors and life instructors, especially to those below who kindly and wisely inculcated a love for Calvin in us during our formative years:

Dr. William S. Barker
Dr. Robert L. Reymond
Dr. David C. Jones
Dr. Joseph H. Hall
Dr. David C. Calhoun
Dr. D. Clair Davis
Dr. Sinclair B. Ferguson
Dr. S. Lewis Johnson
Dr. Richard B. Gaffin Jr.

Contents

FOREWORD

Calvin's *Institutes* (5th edition, 1559) is one of the wonders of the literary world—the world, that is, of writers and writing, of digesting and arranging heaps of diverse materials, of skillful proportioning and gripping presentation; the world, as Dorothy L. Sayers described it in *The Mind of the Maker*, of the Idea, the Word, and the Power. In the days before blurbs and dust jackets, authors had to state on the title page whatever they wanted readers and bookshop browsers to be aware of regarding their book's contents. This explains why, with what might strike us as self-promoting grandiloquence, Calvin titled the first edition (1536) *Basic instruction* (institutio) *in the Christian religion, embracing just about* (fere) *the whole sum of godliness* (summa pietatis), *and all that needs to be known in the doctrine of salvation; a work very well worth reading by everyone zealous for godliness*; and why in 1539 this became *Basic instruction in the Christian religion, now at last truly answering to its description* (nunc vere demum suo titulo respondens); and why the 1559 edition announced itself as *Basic instruction in the Christian religion, freshly set out in four books, and divided into chapters according to the fittest method, and so greatly enlarged that it can almost be regarded as a new work*. Plainly, Calvin was at last content with what he had done, and the verdict of history is that he was entitled to be. Simply, as grand-scale exposition of a very large body of integrated thought, the *Institutio* is truly a marvel.

Through its five editions, Calvin's *summa pietatis* grew to five times its original length and from six to eighty chapters, divided into four books of which the fourth matches for length the first three put together. It began as a catechetical account of foundational Protestant Christianity, loosely modeled on Luther's Smaller Catechism, covering in sequence the Decalogue, the Apostles' Creed, the Lord's Prayer, the gospel sacraments and the five rites incorrectly so called, and the life of freedom under the Word of God in church and state; all with an apologetic cast, in hope of gaining respect and acceptance from the King of France, to whom Calvin addressed a courteous dedicatory letter. New material mutated the second edition (1539) into a sort of *summa theologiae*, a theological student's preparation and *vade mecum* for Bible study, and this trebled the book's length. In the third and fourth editions the amplifying process continued, and by 1559 the *Institutio* was twice as long again as in 1539. It was now a full-scale declaration of biblical Christianity as Calvin saw it—who and what God is, and what he was, is, and will be doing in and for the human race, according to his Word. The titles of the four books reflect the four-part division of the Creed and, behind this, the order of things in Paul's letter to the Romans. They run thus: "of the knowledge of God in his works and qualities ... as Creator and sovereign Governor of the world"; "of the knowledge of God the Redeemer as he has shown himself in Jesus Christ"; "of the manner of participating in the grace of Jesus Christ"; and "of the external means of aids which God uses to draw us to Jesus Christ his Son and to keep us in him" (church, sacraments, and civil order, all viewed as a means of grace).

The readability of the *Institutio*, considering its size, is remarkable. Calvin's pacing is steady and urgent throughout. Just about every sentence contains concentrated thought expressed in elegant, fast-moving, colorful, punchy Latin rhetoric. (No English translation fully matches Calvin's Latin; that of the Elizabethan, Thomas Norton, perhaps gets closest; Beveridge gives us Calvin's feistiness but not always his precision; Battles gives us the precision but not always the punchiness, and fleetness of foot; Allen is smooth and clear, but low-key.) Calvin's combative streak and lawyer's training impelled him to argue his opponents under the table, as we might put it, and sixteenth-century controversial manners, or lack of them, led him to bad-mouth his opponents personally as he argued against their ideas, and the 1559 *Institutio* is disfigured by some over-arguings and satirical brutalities. All in all, however, the book remains a literary masterpiece, a triumph of the didactic writer's art, and when read seriously it makes a very winning impact on the mind and heart, even today.

Nor is that all.

The *Institutio* is also one of the wonders of the spiritual world—the world of doxology and devotion, of discipleship and discipline, of Word-through-Spirit illumination and transformation of individuals, of the Christ-centered mind and the Christ-honoring heart. Shaping all its elaborate doctrinal discussions, with their rigorous biblicism, their strong assertions of divine sovereignty, and their sharply focused trinitarianism, is a persistent orientation to the conscience, a contagious awareness that we do and must live our lives *coram Deo*, in the presence and sight of the searcher of hearts, and a drumbeat insistence that sound belief must express itself in *pietas*, faithful—that is, faith-full—obedience to, and worship of, the Father and the Son through the Spirit. Though the *Institutio* became more than a catechism in that it reached beyond the basics of the discipling process, it nowhere became less than a catechism by losing its discipling focus as the permanent bottom line. The exposition of Jesus Christ as set forth in the Creed, and of the Christian life, of the Ten Commandments, and of praying the Lord's Prayer, stands out in the ongoing flow as (to change the image) jewels in the crown

Catechizing, a ministry neglected and needing to be recovered in the modern church, is the work of systematically teaching children and adults the truths that Christians live by, and the way of actually living by them. The catechizing process may take different forms, from the familiar question-and-answer, repeat-after-me style of children's catechisms, to the lecture-for-discussion method of such as Cyril of Jerusalem in the fourth century and Nicky Gumbel in the Alpha course of today. Real, intelligent commitment to Jesus Christ as Savior, Lord, and God, to the fellowship of the church as one's proper milieu for life, and to self-identification as pilgrims through a world that is not our home to a heaven that is, must ever be catechizing's direct goal. This practical discipling purpose runs all through the *Institutio*. I doubt there is any other treatise of comparable length of which that can be said. Still today, one simply cannot read it receptively without being searched, humbled, and challenged regarding one's sincerity and progress (Calvin's favorite word), or lack of it, in one's personal Christian life.

And there is yet more to be said.

Calvin's *Institutio* is one of the wonders of the theological world, too—that is, the world of truth, faithfulness, and coherence in the mind regarding God; of combat, regrettable but inescapable, with intellectual insufficiency and error in believers and unbelievers alike; and of vision, valuation, and vindication of God as he presents himself through his Word to our fallen and disordered minds. Refusing to affirm anything that does not echo explicit biblical teaching, and refusing too to separate things God has joined, Calvin spells out Christ-centered faith and life with a sure touch. Justification by faith, "the mainstay for upholding religion" (3.11.1), is central, both spatially and theologically, occupying chapters 11–18 of book 3. What precedes it is what must first be known before we can grasp it—that God is triune, holy, and just yet good and gracious, Lord of history and disposer of all things (1.10–18); that godliness means humble love, gratitude, reverence, submission, and dependence God-ward (1.2); that we humans are by nature guilty, blind, and helpless in sin (2.1–5); that both Testaments witness to Jesus Christ, the divine-human Mediator, whose death gained salvation for us (2.6–17); what the law requires (2.8); what faith is (3.2); how God gives faith (3.1); how faith begets repentance (3.3–5); and Christian living (3.6–10). What follows justification is, in effect, a program for our spiritual health as justified sinners. We must know that our freedom from the law is for obedience to it (3.19); that we cannot go on without prayer (3.20); that God's election guarantees our final salvation (3.21–24, the "predestination chapters"); that we have a sure hope of resurrection in glory (3.25); that we must wait on the ministry of Word and sacrament in the church for our soul's growth (4.1–19); and that we must be good citizens, since civil government exists to protect the church (4.20). Such is personal Christianity, with justification as the framing notion, as Calvin's giant catechism—overgrown, perhaps, but a catechism still—sets it forth.

For Calvin, the angle of these pastoral presentations was just as important as their substance. Doxological theocentrism shaped everything. His compassionate concern that everyone should know God's grace was rooted in a deeper desire, namely that everyone should glorify God by a life of adoring worship for the wonder of his work in creation, providence, and salvation, fully recognizing the realities that the Reformational slogans *sola Scriptura, solo Christo, sola fide, sola gratia*, and *soli Deo gloria*, were put in place to guard. Knowledge of God as Creator and Redeemer, holy, just, wise, and good, comes to us by Scripture *alone*, not by our own independent insight or guesswork. The blessings of redemption—reconciliation with God, the gift of righteousness and sonship, regeneration, glory—come to us by Christ *alone*, not by any fancied personal merit or any priestly mediation on the part of the church. Christ and his gifts are received by faith *alone*, not earned by effort. That very faith is given to us and sustained in us by grace *alone*, so that our own contribution to our salvation is precisely nil; all the glory for it must go to God *alone*, and none be diverted to us. We are simply the sinners whose need of salvation is met by the marvelous mercy of him who "did not spare his own Son but gave him up for us all" (Rom. 8:32 ESV). The 1559 *Institutio* is, as we have seen, Calvin's swan song, in which he speaks his last word on everything, including the errors he constantly battled—anti-trinitarianism, illuminism, Pelagianism, antinomianism, autosoterism, sacerdotalism; wrong ideas about justification, ecclesiastical authority, the eucharist, and so on—and the roughness of his polemic as he works over these deviant views for what he expects to be the last time is an index of the intensity of his sense that the mistakes rob God of the praise that is his due.

Great theology, like the Bible in which all great theology is soaked, is essentially transhistorical and transcultural, and interprets us, joltingly sometimes, as we seek to interpret it. The 1559 *Institutio* is great theology, and it is uncanny how often, as we read and re-read it, we come across passages that seem to speak directly across the centuries to our own hearts and our own present-day theological debates. You never seem to get to the book's bottom; it keeps opening up as a veritable treasure trove of biblical wisdom on all the main themes of the Christian faith. Do you, I wonder, know what I am talking about? Dig into the *Institutio*, and you soon will.

This book celebrates the five hundredth anniversary of John Calvin's birth and is the work of a team of scholars to whom different sections of the *Institutio* were parceled out. Full advantage is taken of the current cottage industry of Calvin studies, which has achieved already notable insights in many areas. The essays vary in technical level, but are all strong and clear for the wayfaring man, and some are outstanding. They add up to a very valuable volume, which I commend with enthusiasm. For making Calvin known today as well as once he was, and in every age deserves to be, this really is a major step forward. *Soli Deo gloria!*

J. I. PACKER

PREFACE

Over the centuries various ways have been found to gather some of the finest authorities for conversations. Whether one thinks of the ancient Athenian agora where citizen philosophers held forth, or an Arthurian round table which was an early form of a polis, or Luther's table talks with disciples in German common houses, or a French salon heady with eighteenth-century Enlightenment ideals, or today's blog, which provides instant access for an international community, we often find that excellent ideas are further sharpened with infusions of commentary from others. This volume is best viewed as a conversation among informed friends.

The common topic is textual matter from John Calvin's *Institutes of the Christian Religion*. The common commitment is to honor the text and to, perhaps, elucidate the topic in some fashion. The scholarship contained is uncommon.

The editors are quite happy to present to the reading public this collection of commentaries on Calvin's *Institutes*. We think that John Calvin would certainly approve of the hearty discussion, amplification, and reflection upon his work such as we offer herein. He certainly recognized that his first edition (1536) could be improved, for he revised this magnum opus in 1539, 1545, 1554, and 1559.

One can observe how widely his work spread in a relatively short time. By 1578, Oxford undergraduates were required to read Calvin's *Institutes* and his Catechism. Moreover, if English sermons in the next (seventeenth) century were still referencing Calvin's *Institutes* as a vital source for opposing governmental abuse, American colonial sermons conveyed his sentiments even more. "Probably no other theological work," wrote Herbert Foster, "was so widely read and so influential from the

Reformation to the American Revolution. . . . In England [it] was considered 'the best and perfectest system of divinity' by both Anglican and Puritan until [Archbishop William] Laud's supremacy in the 1630s."[1] "Most colonial libraries seem to contain some work by Calvin"; indeed, "scarcely a colonial list of books from New Hampshire to South Carolina appears to lack books written by Calvinists."[2]

For centuries, this robust theological classic has remained must-reading for ministerial students, informed Christians, and various academic disciplines. The fact that this work is still available in multiple editions via the leading online book service is a further tribute to its value.

Prior to this present work, other individuals have set forth their own commentaries or summaries of Calvin's *Institutes*. What this volume offers is a chorale with many voices; we believe that the chorale is superior to a solo.

Expert commentators were chosen for this volume with three criteria in mind: (1) their sympathetic readings of Calvin's work, although not uncritically so; (2) their teaching of this material for a considerable span of time, normally in seminaries or universities; and (3) their willingness to meet a rigid publication schedule to have this material form part of the commemorative corpus for the Calvin Quincentenary in 2009.

The editors wish to thank each of our overextended contributors who prioritized this work. The end product reflects the years of preparation and contemplation of these topics that each of them brings to this volume. We wish to thank them, their families, and their

---

1. Robert M. Kingdon, *Calvin and Calvinism: Sources of Democracy* (Lexington, MA: D. C. Heath and Company, 1970), 37. See also the *Collected Papers of Herbert D. Foster* (privately printed, 1929), 116.

2. Kingdon, *Calvin and Calvinism*, 37. Other historians argue that the Puritanism of New England was "patterned after the Westminster Catechism and embodied the type of Calvinistic thought current in all of New England at that time." See Peter De Jong, *The Covenant Idea in New England Theology, 1620–1847* (Grand Rapids: Eerdmans, 1945), 85. Foster, *Papers*, 79, lists numerous Americans who owned copies of Calvin's *Institutes*. Patricia Bonomi has also firmly established that the majority of seventeenth-century Americans followed "some form of Puritan Calvinism, which itself was divided into a number of factions." See Patricia U. Bonomi, *Under the Cope of Heaven: Religion, Society, and Politics in Colonial America* (New York: Oxford University Press, 1986), 14.

institutions for allowing them to lend a hand to a once-in-a-lifetime festschrift, one that we cheerfully albeit posthumously offer to the Protestant Reformer who offered so many tributes to the theological exemplars who shaped his life. We do so with the prayer that five hundred years from now, perhaps an even larger audience will be working similarly.

DAVID W. HALL
PETER A. LILLBACK

I

The Historical Context of the *Institutes* as a Work in Theology

William S. Barker

John Calvin was twenty-six years old when he drafted the first edition of his *Institutes of the Christian Religion*, which was published in the following year, 1536. His fifth and final Latin edition, published in 1559 (there were also several French editions published in his own lifetime), was almost five times as long, yet it still bore his "Prefatory Address to King Francis I of France" even though that monarch had died in 1547. Calvin made a few modifications to this Preface in his editions of 1539 and 1543, but he evidently believed that his address to King Francis provided an appropriate introduction to his work, which he intended both as a defense of the Protestant Reformation movement, begun by Martin Luther less than two decades before Calvin's first edition, and as an instruction to the followers of the Reformers in the basic tenets of the Christian faith, so that they could study the Bible with greater facility. The Latin word *institutio*, sometimes in the plural form *institutiones*, was used frequently in sixteenth-century titles, with the meaning of "instruction" or "education." Hence Calvin's title means instruction in the Christian religion.

To understand the unique place of this influential work in the history of theology we must first inquire as to the role of Francis I, then grasp the context of persecution, next see the Reformers' relation to Scripture and the early church, also their relation to the radical Anabaptist wing of the Reformation, and then see more fully the purpose of the *Institutes*.

Who Was Francis I (1515–47)?

A quintessential Renaissance monarch, Francis was twenty-one when he became king of France. Over six feet tall, he was a promoter of scholarship and loved magnificent clothing. Almost exactly contemporary with Henry VIII of England (1509–1547), Francis won a wrestling match with Henry in June of 1520 on the "Field of the Cloth of Gold" outside Calais to settle some of the disputes between their two realms. Not unlike Henry, Francis was a philanderer. In May 1517 he and his courtiers rode incognito through the streets of Paris at night, visiting houses of ill-repute. By 1522 his court comprised 540 officials, more than twice that of his predecessor, Louis XI, in 1480. During Francis's reign the population of France grew to be more than double that of Spain and five times that of England. The Concordat of Boulogne with Pope Leo X in 1516 gave the French church the freedom to nominate its own bishops, thus gaining for Francis the church finances of 10 archbishoprics, 82 bishoprics, 527 abbeys, and multitudes of priories and canonries, and therefore no need to break from the papacy.[1]

1. Information on Francis I can be found in R. J. Knecht, "Francis I: Prince and Patron of the Northern Renaissance," in A. G. Dickens, ed., *The Courts of Europe: Politics, Patronage, and Royalty, 1400–1800* (New York: McGraw-Hill, 1977), 99–119; Alistair Horne, *La Belle France: A Short History* (New York: Alfred A. Knopf, 2005); Marshall B. Davidson, *The Horizon Concise History of France* (New York: American Heritage, 1971); Edith Simon, *The Reformation* (New York: Time-Life Books, 1966); and Lewis W. Spitz, *The Protestant Reformation, 1517–1559* (New York: Harper & Row, 1987).

Early success in pursuing French interests in Italy tempted Francis into repeated military adventures with less happy outcomes. For a time he was even held prisoner in Spain. Concerned about potential encirclement by the Hapsburg ring (Spanish, Dutch, Italian, and Austrian territories united in the person of Holy Roman Emperor Charles V), Francis's treatment of Protestants depended on shifting political circumstances. Although a Catholic whose practice was to attend daily mass before ten o'clock, he was not above making an alliance with the Protestant princes of Germany, or even with the Turks, when it served his interests.

Francis did, however, have sincere interests in the new learning of the Renaissance era, including the sphere of religious thought. In March of 1530 he established four royal professorships, two for Greek and two for Hebrew. His sister, Margaret of Angoulême, being influenced by the evangelical Catholic Jacques Lefèvre d'Etaples, wrote devotional poetry and also provided haven for some who were persecuted for religion. Francis twice, in 1523 and 1526, gained release from prison for the follower of Erasmus and Luther, Louis de Berquin, who was hastily condemned and burned as a heretic in 1529 while Francis was away from Paris. The chrism with which Francis was anointed at his coronation was believed to make the French king "the most Christian king," whose touch could heal the skin disease scrofula. In 1530 Francis so touched some 1,730 people. Such was the one whom John Calvin addressed as "Most Mighty and Illustrious Monarch, Francis, Most Christian King of the French."

The Context of Persecution

While Calvin might entertain some hope of appealing to the scholarly and religious interests of his Renaissance monarch, the immediate context of his writing is one of persecution. Indeed by his third paragraph he is denouncing the injustice of the French regime. He himself had gone into exile from his native France, apparently being implicated in the reforming inaugural address of Nicolas Cop, the new rector of the University of Paris, on November 1, 1533. Then, on October 18, 1534, the incident of the Placards, crude posters denouncing the idolatry of the mass, appearing on many public buildings and even in the king's bedchamber, led to severe repression and burnings, including some of Calvin's personal friends and associates. Clearly, Francis's toleration for reform extended only up to the point of public disruption of society. To Calvin, however, those put to death were true martyrs of the Christian faith. And so, addressing the king on August 23, 1535,[2] he makes clear that he is not writing a personal defense, for although still loving his country, "as things now stand I do not much regret being excluded. Rather, I embrace the common cause of all believers, that of Christ himself." Appealing to the king to find the leisure to read "this our confession," Calvin states that "a very great question is at stake: how God's glory may be kept safe on earth, how God's truth may retain its place of honor, how Christ's Kingdom may be kept in good repair among us."[3] Feeling that he and his fellow Reformers are falsely accused of heresy and sedition, Calvin seeks to demonstrate the orthodoxy and orderly conduct of the Protestant movement.

The Reformers' Relationship to Scripture, the Early Fathers, and the Church

Claiming that the true religion is that which has been handed down in the Scriptures, and arguing against implicit faith in "the authority of Holy Mother Church" and "the primacy of the Apostolic See,"[4] Calvin answers the charge of newness on the part of the Protestant Reformers by citing their agreement with many of the early church fathers on various of the doctrines and practices at issue. In a section running five pages on the "Misleading Claim That the Church Fathers Oppose the Reformation Teaching," he states, "If the contest were to be determined by patristic authority, the title of victory—to put it very modestly—would turn to

2. For the correct date of Calvin's address, see "Prefatory Address to King Francis I of France," in *Calvin: Institutes of the Christian Religion*, 2 vols., Library of Christian Classics 20–21, ed. John T. McNeill, trans. Ford Lewis Battles (Philadelphia: Westminster, 1960), 1:31 and n. 51.

3. "Prefatory Address," 11. References to the king's finding opportunity to read the *Institutes* are on pp. 27 and 31. There is no evidence that Francis ever read the *Institutes* or even the "Prefatory Address" although it is certainly possible that he was made aware of Calvin's work.

4. "Prefatory Address," 14.

our side."[5] Calvin acknowledges that one cannot agree with the Fathers in everything, which is an allegiance owed only to Christ. But then he cites a litany of the Fathers to show that the Church of Rome has imposed many things that the ancient church did not accept (such as abstaining from meat, the begging of monks, images of Christ or saints, transubstantiation, participating in only one kind in the mass, many canons and doctrines without any word of God, laws of fasting, and celibacy of the clergy. Among those cited are Jerome; various bishops mentioned in Eusebius or in the histories by Socrates, Sozomen, and Theodoret (late fourth and fifth centuries); Ambrose (twice); Augustine (four times); Epiphanius, bishop of Salamis; the Council in Spain (c. 305); Gelasius (twice); John Chrysostom; Cyprian (twice); and Tertullian.[6]).

In October of 1536 Calvin, by now recruited by Guillaume Farel for the reform of Geneva, participated as a junior partner with Farel and Pierre Viret in a disputation with Roman Catholic churchmen at Lausanne. Remaining silent through the early part of the debate, Calvin leapt into action at the charge of one of the Catholic disputants that the Protestants despised antiquity. Calvin's response shows once again that he had diligently studied the Fathers, and he was able to cite key passages from memory, referring off the cuff to Tertullian, Chrysostom, and six passages in Augustine, practically giving chapter and verse.[7] This display of patristic scholarship confirmed Calvin's claim that the early fathers tended to support the Reformation: "After Calvin had spoken, the Franciscan brother Jean Tandy stood up to announce his conversion to the gospel."[8]

Calvin made the same sort of claim to support from the church fathers in his "Reply to Cardinal Sadoleto" on September 1, 1539. After Farel and Calvin had been expelled from Geneva in 1538, Cardinal Jacopo Sadoleto sought to bring Geneva back into the Roman Catholic Church. Calvin responded from Strasbourg to Sadoleto's treatise. Focusing on what constitutes the true church, Calvin cited

5. Ibid., 18.
6. Ibid., 18–23.
7. *Calvin: Theological Treatises*, ed. J. K. S. Reid, Library of Christian Classics 22 (Philadelphia: Westminster, 1954), 40–42.
8. Anthony N. S. Lane, *John Calvin, Student of the Fathers* (Grand Rapids: Baker, 1999), 28.

Chrysostom for emphasizing "the simple doctrine of the gospel." Then he claimed the support of the ancient fathers:

> But here you bring a charge against me. For you teach that all that has been approved for fifteen hundred years or more by the uniform consent of the faithful, is by our rashness torn up or destroyed.... You know, Sadolet, ... not only that our agreement with antiquity is far closer than yours, but that all we have attempted has been to renew the ancient form of the church which, at first distorted and stained by illiterate men of indifferent character, was afterward criminally mangled and almost destroyed by the Roman pontiff and his faction.
>
> I shall not press you so closely as to call you back to that form which the apostles instituted, though in it we have the only model of a true Church, and whosoever deviates from it in the smallest degree is in error. But to indulge you so far, I ask you to place before your eyes the ancient form of the Church as their writings prove it to have been in the ages of Chrysostom and Basil among the Greeks, and of Cyprian, Ambrose, and Augustine among the Latins; and after so doing, to contemplate the ruins of that Church which now survive among yourselves.... Will you here declare one an enemy of antiquity who, zealous for ancient piety and holiness and dissatisfied with the corrupt state of matters existing in a dissolute and despised Church, attempts to ameliorate its condition and restore it to pristine splendour?[9]

In his "Prefatory Address to King Francis" Calvin says, "Surely the church of Christ has lived and will live so long as Christ reigns at the right hand of his Father. . . . Against this church we now have no quarrel." But whereas his opponents "contend that the form of the church is always apparent and observable" and "they set this form in the see of the Roman Church and its hierarchy," he states that "it has quite another mark: namely, the pure preaching of God's Word and the lawful administration of the sacraments."[10] Although the church, as in the Old Testament time of Elijah, is not always to be identified with external, visible institutions, Calvin's citations of the church fathers

9. *Calvin: Theological Treatises*, 231–32.
10. "Prefatory Address," 24–25.

shows that he readily identified with the church of the fourth and fifth centuries as representing classical Christianity, 60 percent of his citations in the *Institutes* and his Commentaries coming from Western fathers between the Councils of Nicaea (A.D. 325) and Chalcedon (A.D. 451).[11]

The Reformers' Relation to the Anabaptists

Having refuted the Roman Catholic charge of newness by showing the consistency of the Protestant Reformers with the orthodox ancient church, Calvin next answers the charge of seditious tumults resulting from the Reformation. In the contexts both of Martin Luther in Saxon Wittenberg and also of Ulrich Zwingli in Zurich and German-speaking Switzerland, ecclesiastical reform approved by the civil magistrate had been soon accompanied by more radical reform usually characterized by believer's baptism and a separation of church and state. In the Dutch/northwestern German city of Münster, however, radical reform gained control of both ecclesiastical and civil government, and in the period 1533–35 produced a theocracy with community of goods and polygamy and resulted in a violent end.[12]

Writing his first edition of the *Institutes* in the year that the revolutionary theocracy of Münster was overturned and restored to order by Lutheran and Catholic forces, Calvin ascribes such tumults to the work of Satan, who always through history seeks to oppose the true faith with false religion. As was the case in the day of the apostles, so now in the Reformation there are movements that Satan has inspired in order to discredit the genuine Reformers. For his own part, Calvin disclaims to King Francis any effort to overthrow kingdoms: "we, from whom not one seditious word was ever heard . . . we, who do not cease

11. Lane, *John Calvin*, 41 n. 198, cites statistics from the work (in Dutch) of R. J. Mooi, *Het Kerk—en Dogmahistorisch Element in de Werken van Johannes Calvijn* (Wageningen: Veenman, 1965).

12. A detailed account is given in George Huntston Williams, *The Radical Reformation*, 3d ed. (Kirksville, MO: Sixteenth Century Journal, 1992), 553–82. See also Thomas M. Lindsay, *A History of the Reformation*, 2 vols., 2d ed. (Edinburgh: T. & T. Clark, 1907–8), 2:451–69.

to pray for yourself and your kingdom, although we are now fugitives from home."[13]

The Purpose of the "Institutes"

As the "Prefatory Address to King Francis I" shows, therefore, the purpose of the first edition of the *Institutes* in 1536 was both apologetic and instructional. In his rare autobiographical account, the "Author's Preface" to his Commentary on the Psalms, dated July 22, 1557, Calvin describes how "whilst I lay hidden at Basle, and known only to a few people, many faithful and holy persons were burnt alive in France," and how these martyrs were falsely identified with "Anabaptists and seditious persons." In this context,

> it appeared to me, that unless I opposed them [the ones making false charges] to the utmost of my ability, my silence could not be vindicated from the charge of cowardice and treachery. This was the consideration which induced me to publish my Institute of the Christian Religion. My objects were, first, to prove that these reports were false and calumnious, and thus to vindicate my brethren, whose death was precious in the sight of the Lord; and next, that as the same cruelties might very soon after be exercised against many unhappy individuals, foreign nations might be touched with at least some compassion towards them and solicitude about them. When it was then published, it was not that copious and laboured work which it now is, but only a small treatise containing a summary of the principal truths of the Christian religion; and it was published with no other design than that men might know what was the faith held by those whom I saw basely and wickedly defamed by those flagitious and perfidious flatterers.[14]

As the "Prefatory Address to King Francis I" was primarily apologetic, defending the Reformation against charges of newness and sedition, the

---

13. "Prefatory Address," 30. See also Willem Balke, *Calvin and the Anabaptist Radicals,* trans. William Heynen (Grand Rapids: Eerdmans, 1981).
14. John Calvin, *Commentary on the Book of Psalms,* trans. James Anderson, 3 vols. (Grand Rapids: Baker, 1979), 1:xli–xlii.

1536 first edition of the *Institutes* was a basic manual educating Calvin's followers in the Christian faith. By the final edition of 1559 the instructional purpose had expanded into the more systematic two volumes most familiar to readers today.

While the final 1559 edition evidently satisfied Calvin with its more systematic arrangement of doctrine, his purpose was still not speculative, but rather practical. As he said in "John Calvin to the Reader" introducing his 1559 edition, "God has filled my mind with zeal to spread his Kingdom and to further the public good," and "since I undertook the office of teacher in the church, I have had no other purpose than to benefit the church by maintaining the pure doctrine of godliness."[15] And thus, after the 1536 edition, which he regarded as almost catechetical in treating the rudiments of the faith (the law, the Apostles' Creed, the Lord's Prayer, and the sacraments), was replaced by his own Geneva Catechism of 1537, his second edition of the *Institutes* (1539) was directed more to theological students preparing for ministry, rather than ordinary lay people. As he says in his introductory word to the 1559 edition, it

> has been my purpose in this labor to prepare and instruct candidates in sacred theology for the reading of the divine Word, in order that they may be able both to have easy access to it and to advance in it without stumbling.[16]

He was concerned to the end, nevertheless, not only for the theological student, but also for the ordinary Christian. In his "Subject Matter of the Present Work" introducing his final French edition of 1560 he wrote: "Perhaps the duty of those who have received from God fuller light than others is to help simple folk at this point, and as it were to lend them a hand, in order to guide them and help them to find the sum of what God meant to teach us in his Word."[17]

Two things should especially be noted in these statements of Calvin's purpose in producing the *Institutes*. One is that, whether he is thinking of theological students or of ordinary lay Christians, his

---

15. "John Calvin to the Reader," in *Calvin: Institutes of the Christian Religion*, 1:4.
16. Ibid.
17. "Subject Matter of the Present Work," in *Calvin: Institutes of the Christian Religion*, 1:6.

purpose is to provide a basis for the study of the Scriptures. As he appended to his 1560 French edition:

> I can at least promise that it can be a key to open a way for all children of God into a good and right understanding of Holy Scripture. Thus, if henceforth our Lord gives me the means and opportunity of writing some commentaries, I shall use the greatest possible brevity, because there will be no need for long digressions, seeing that I have here treated at length almost all the articles pertaining to Christianity.[18]

The second thing to be noticed is that the ultimate purpose is godliness. The long title of the first edition underscores this point: "Institutes of the Christian Religion, Embracing Almost the Whole Sum of Piety, and Whatever Is Necessary to Know of the Doctrine of Salvation: A Work Most Worthy to Be Read by All Persons Zealous for Piety. . . ."[19] The goal, then, of use of the *Institutes* is study of God's Word, which in turn is to produce godliness, a piety characterized by gratitude, love for God, and obedience to his revealed will.

The Place of the *Institutes* in the History of Theology

John T. McNeill claimed, "Calvin's *Institutes of the Christian Religion* is one of the few books that have profoundly affected the course of

18. Ibid., 1:7. These words appeared in an earlier edition, before Calvin's first commentary, on Romans, published in 1540. See also his statement in "John Calvin to the Reader," 5 (and n. 4): "If . . . I shall publish any interpretations of Scripture, I shall always condense them, because I shall have no need to undertake long doctrinal discussions, and to digress into commonplaces. In this way the godly reader will be spared great annoyance and boredom, provided he approach Scripture armed with a knowledge of the present work, as a necessary tool."

19. Ford Lewis Battles, "Introduction" to the 1536 edition of the *Institutes* (Grand Rapids: Eerdmans, 1986), reprinted in Richard C. Gamble, ed., *Articles on Calvin and Calvinism*, 14 vols., vol. 2: *Calvin's Early Writings and Ministry* (New York: Garland, 1992), 265. This entire article, 245–87, is very helpful in understanding Calvin's purpose, as is I. John Hesselink, "The Development and Purpose of Calvin's Institutes," *Reformed Theological Review* 24 (1964): 65–72, reprinted in Gamble, ed., vol. 4, *Influences Upon Calvin and Discussion of the 1559 "Institutes,"* 209–16.

history."[20] Philip Schaff similarly said: "This book is the masterpiece of a precocious genius of commanding intellectual and spiritual depth and power. It is one of the few truly classical productions in the history of theology, and has given its author the double title of the Aristotle and Thomas Aquinas of the Reformed Church."[21] Schaff goes on to describe how Roman Catholics called it "the Koran and Talmud of heresy" and had it burned by order of the Sorbonne at Paris and other places "and more fiercely and persistently persecuted than any book of the sixteenth century; but . . . it has found also great admirers among Catholics who . . . freely admit its great merits in the nonpolemical parts."[22] Indeed, a more modern Roman Catholic scholar describes how Calvin drew on the work of other Reformers, saying that "it is indisputable that Calvin was from the start superior to Luther in his careful biblical and patristic documentation":

> As a young theologian, Calvin cannot be compared to a musical per-former or to an orchestra conductor whose task is limited to interpreting faithfully a piece of music; rather, he is like a composer who borrows several themes and then orchestrates them according to his personal inspiration. Calvin makes the themes of Luther, Melanchthon, Zwingli, and Bucer resound at times *forte* and at other times *piano* and interprets them into a composition that is his own.[23]

Another modern interpreter, Protestant but outside the Reformed tradition, gives this assessment:

> Almost certainly Calvin's great reputation is due to his personal passion and leadership and his magnificent systematic mind as it is expressed in his magnum opus, *Institutes of the Christian Religion*, published in several editions over his lifetime. It became *the* textbook

20. John T. McNeill, *The History and Character of Calvinism* (New York: Oxford University Press, 1967), 119.
21. Philip Schaff, *History of the Christian Church*, 8 vols., 3d rev. ed. (Grand Rapids: Eerdmans, 1953), 8:329.
22. Ibid.
23. Alexandre Ganoczy, *The Young Calvin*, trans. David Foxgrover and Wade Provo (Philadelphia: Westminster, 1987), 232.

for Reformed theology for centuries and is still published, analyzed, interpreted and debated.[24]

The *Institutes* did indeed gain immediate acceptance among Reformed Protestants. As Schaff reports: "The Evangelicals greeted the *Institutes* at once with enthusiastic praise as the clearest, strongest, most logical, and most convincing defence of Christian doctrines since the days of the apostles." A few weeks after its publication Martin Bucer wrote to the author: "It is evident that the Lord has elected you as his organ for the bestowment of the richest fulness of blessing to his Church."[25] McNeill adds, "The *Institutes* . . . was a pronounced success. Within a year the publisher informed him that the stock was exhausted and that a revised edition was called for."[26]

How is one to account for this impact of the *Institutes?* Schaff rightly contrasts it with the "rousing power" of Luther's "Appeal to the German Nobility" or his "On Christian Liberty" upon German readers, "but it is a book for scholars of all nations, and had a deeper and more lasting effect upon them than any work of the Reformers." He comments on how it "combines dogmatics and ethics in organic unity," how it is planted "on the immovable rock of the Word of God, as the only safe guide in matters of faith and duty," how it makes "judicious and discriminating use of the fathers," and how its "style is luminous and forcible."[27] More modern scholars have put the greater emphasis on Calvin's rhetoric. McNeill concludes: "It is not Calvin's logic but the vigor of his rhetoric and his rarely matched powers of communication, under the sway of religious conviction and emotion, that constitute him, through the *Institutes*, one of the makers of the modern mind."[28]

One of the most recent biographers of Calvin has viewed the *Institutes* through an architectural analogy:

24. Roger E. Olson, *The Story of Christian Theology: Twenty Centuries of Tradition & Reform* (Downers Grove, IL: InterVarsity, 1999), 408.

25. Schaff, *History,* 8:329.

26. McNeill, *History and Character,* 125.

27. Schaff, *History,* 8:330–31.

28. McNeill, *History and Character,* 128.

One enters into the *Institutes* as though into a cathedral, a sort of gigantic edifice where the succession of words, paragraphs, and chapters testifies to the glory of God and the enterprise of man. . . .

The *Institutes* is a stone structure, built to last. . . .

The *Institutes* is built over time, a cathedral in which every pillar, every pilaster is endowed with a history. A primitive cord goes back to 1536; it has the charm, the sturdiness of the Romanesque churches. . . .

The edition of 1539–41 adds to this structure a patristic, or more precisely Augustinian, porch. . . .

The third great version was completed in 1559, after several intermediate stages. The text is now four and a half times longer than the original. While preserving the grand architectural principles of 1539, this internal remodeling establishes books, distinguished according to their content. This increasing complexity already takes on a baroque character, expansion conflicting with strict order.[29]

Calvin himself saw the *Institutes* as embodying his theological thought in its original and also its most mature form:

"The whole of Calvinism is in the *Institutes*—a work of capital importance, the work most valued by Calvin, who spent all his life revising and reshaping as well as enriching it. All his other works— commentaries, controversies, smaller dogmatic or moral treatises—are related to it like advanced redoubts meant to defend the heart of the place against the enemy." Not only do the *Institutes* occupy the central place in Calvin's literary production. . . . Whatever interest and value may attach to his other theological writings, the *Institutes* are the faithful summary of the ideas he expounded in them. Moreover, the *Institutes*—at least in their final form—purport to give a complete account of Christian teaching. They therefore present a synthesis of Calvinist thought, and one that is sufficient in itself; whereas to define the positions of a Luther or a Zwingli, one must have recourse to writings very different from one another.[30]

29. Bernard Cottret, *Calvin, A Biography*, trans. M. Wallace McDonald (Grand Rapids: Eerdmans, 2000), 309–10.

30. François Wendel, *Calvin: The Origins and Development of His Religious Thought*, trans. Philip Mairet (New York: Harper & Row, 1963), 111, quoting Imbart de la Tour, *Calvin et l'Institution chrétienne*, 55.

And yet, as we have seen, Calvin's purpose in producing the *Institutes* was to provide a foundation for the study of the Bible, whether by theological students or by lay Christians—in other words, a platform on which his commentaries could build. And as a result his commentaries could be concise and to the point, not as wordy and voluminous as those of Martin Bucer, nor organized by commonplaces as in the works of Philipp Melanchthon.

It is this relation between theology and exegesis of Scripture that gives distinctive character to the Reformed faith. And the Reformed faith is aptly termed "Calvinism" because it is Calvin's *Institutes* that establishes this relation between theology and exegesis. Richard C. Gamble suggests the connection between the *duplex cognitio dei* (the interrelatedness of knowledge of God and knowledge of self) in the *Institutes* and *brevitas et facilitas* (comprehensive brevity) in the commentaries. He argues that Calvin's method was distinct from such predecessors as Luther, Zwingli, John Oecolampadius, and Bucer, and from such contemporaries as Henry Bullinger and Theodore Beza in that he maintained a consciousness of the Creator/creature distinction in his theology and sought in his commentaries to imitate the apostle Paul in using the "simple and rude" style of the Scriptures just as the Creator had accommodated to the unlearned creatures in his revealed Word.[31]

Zwingli and Oecolampadius, leaders of the German-speaking Swiss Reform in Zurich and Basel, died in 1531. Before Luther died in 1546 he is reported by Melanchthon's son-in-law to have applauded Calvin's 1540 "Short Treatise on the Holy Supper of Our Lord Jesus Christ," even though it described candidly how Luther and Zwingli had failed to understand each other on the one point (out of fifteen) of the Lord's Supper at the Marburg Colloquy of 1529.[32] The Strasbourg Reformer Martin Bucer taught at Cambridge University from 1549 until his death in 1551; his enthusiastic approval of Calvin's *Institutes* has already been

---

31. Richard C. Gamble, "Calvin as Theologian and Exegete: Is There Anything New?" *Calvin Theological Journal* 23 (1988): 178–94, reprinted in Gamble, ed., *Articles on Calvin and Calvinism*, vol. 7, *The Organizational Structure of Calvin's Theology*, 44–60; see especially 54–58.

32. *John Calvin: Selections from His Writings*, ed. John Dillenberger (Garden City, NY: Doubleday, 1971), 507.

noted. By the time of the publication of the 1559 edition of the *Institutes* Calvin was recognized as the chief theologian of the Protestant Reformation. That reputation would continue in Reformed circles because of the distinctive relation between theology and the exegesis of Scripture as propounded and lived out in the context of the church. Particularly in the English-speaking world this would be apparent in such subsequent theologians as John Owen in the seventeenth century, Jonathan Edwards in the eighteenth century, Charles Hodge and Benjamin B. Warfield in the nineteenth century, and J. Gresham Machen, J. Oliver Buswell Jr., and John Murray in the twentieth century. Like Calvin, these theologians were expositors of Scripture and also preachers of the Word in the context of the church.

In his "Address to King Francis I" John Calvin's eloquent apology is not unlike those of Justin Martyr and Irenaeus in the second century. They had to establish Christianity's continuity with the true faith of ancient Judaism in the Old Testament and also to distinguish true New Testament Christianity from the bizarre and false claims of Gnosticism. In like manner Calvin needed to defend Protestantism as consistent with the orthodox Christian church of the early fathers and the church councils of the fourth and fifth centuries while also distancing the Reformers from the polygamous, seditious, and violent acts of certain Anabaptists. Whether the Renaissance king of France heard him or not, generations of followers in France, Switzerland, the Netherlands, Scotland, England, America, and around the world have listened, studied, and claimed to be Calvinists because the theology of the *Institutes* is based upon, and points to, the Scriptures as the very Word of the living and true God, whom to know is life eternal.

2

A PRIMAL AND
SIMPLE KNOWLEDGE

INSTITUTES 1:1–5
K. SCOTT OLIPHINT

For at the same time as we have enjoyed a slight taste of the divine from contemplation of the universe, having neglected the true God, we raise up in his stead dreams and specters of our own brains, and attribute to anything else than the true source the praise of righteousness, wisdom, goodness, and power. Moreover, we so obscure or overturn his daily acts by wickedly judging them that we snatch away from them their glory and from their Author his due praise.[1]

This statement, in sum, concisely lays out for us the main elements in chapters 1–5 of book 1 of Calvin's *Institutes*. With this, Calvin ends his discussion of God's revelation to us in nature, and, from there, begins to

1. John Calvin, *Institutes of the Christian Religion*, ed. John T. McNeill, trans. Ford Lewis Battles, 2 vols., Library of Christian Classics 20–21 (Philadelphia: Westminster, 1960), 1.5.15.

discuss the necessity of Scripture for that knowledge of God that leads to salvation.

Our concern in this chapter will be the topic of natural revelation and its effects, as Calvin expresses it in these opening chapters. For those familiar with this topic, controversies, debates, anachronisms, and misunderstandings may come immediately to mind.[2] Though Calvin spends relatively little time on it in the *Institutes*, the implications of just what natural revelation is, and how it is received and applied, move way beyond its word count in his work. Our task will be to attempt to understand just what it is that Calvin is saying in these five short chapters, and also to suggest certain central and important implications of what Calvin says on this topic for a Reformed understanding of natural revelation and natural theology. In order to understand what Calvin is saying, it is first necessary for us to note several important contextual matters.

Organization—Method and Structure[3]

One of the primary purposes of Calvin's *Institutes* is to develop and explicate a series of theological topics that would help and guide students of theology in their approach to Scripture.[4] But Calvin's explication of

2. Among controversies, most famous would surely be that between Brunner and Barth on natural theology, as both saw themselves in Calvin's line. See Emil Brunner and Karl Barth, *Natural Theology: Comprising "Nature and Grace"* (London: G. Bles, The Centenary Press, 1946); and Karl Barth, *Nein! Antwort an Emil Brunner*, Theologische Existenz Heute 14 (Munich: C. Kaiser, 1934).

3. These two points are central to our exposition of this section of the *Institutes* and so need to be set forth and kept in mind in this chapter.

4. John Calvin, "John Calvin to the Reader, 1559," in *Institutes of the Christian Religion*, 1:4. See Richard A. Muller, *Prolegomena to Theology* (Grand Rapids: Baker, 2003), 56ff. Note also: "One might fairly argue that Calvin never set out to produce a theological system in the modern sense of the term. At the same time, it must be emphasized (against several modern accommodations of his work) that he certainly did intend to produce a theological system or body of doctrine in and for his own time. Specifically, he determined in his *Institutes* to develop a fairly cohesive set of theological topics and disputations that would guide *theological students* in their approach to Scripture—and he expanded the text in the light of insights gained in his work of preaching and exegesis and in the course of his polemical defense of the Reformation." Richard A. Muller, *The Unaccommodated Calvin: Studies in the Foundation of a Theological Tradition* (New York: Oxford University Press, 2000), 5 (emphasis added).

natural revelation and its effects is not created in a vacuum. Like us all, Calvin was a man of his time. His influences, goals, and content will be, therefore, to a greater or lesser degree, reflective of that time. It should help us, then, to note some significant contours of Calvin's thinking. In this regard, we will focus, albeit briefly, on two important aspects of Calvin's thought in order better to understand the content and development of chapters 1–5 of book 1 of the *Institutes*.[5]

Despite Alister McGrath's contention that some editions of the *Institutes* were "poorly organized,"[6] there seems to be little question that Calvin was consciously developing and deepening the *Institutes* from the beginning.[7] From 1539 on, according to Muller, Calvin organized the *Institutes* according to the then-popular idea of "common places" (*loci communes*)[8] and disputations (*disputationes*).[9] The *Institutes*, therefore, contain the doctrinal elaborations that flow from the exegetical work that Calvin undertook in his commentaries.

5. We will not focus on *all* or *most* of the influences of Calvin's thinking, but will instead pick out two of the ones most centrally related to our topic. For a fuller understanding of Calvin's context and influences, see, for example, Muller, *Unaccommodated Calvin*; idem, *Prolegomena to Theology*, 273ff.; idem, *The Divine Essence and Attributes* (Grand Rapids: Baker, 2002), 173f.; idem, "Duplex Cognitio Dei in the Theology of Early Reformed Orthodoxy," *Sixteenth Century Journal* 10.2 (1979); Peter J. Leithart, "The Eminent Pagan: Calvin's Use of Cicero in *Institutes* I:1–5," *Westminster Theological Journal* 52 (1990); Egil Grislis, "Calvin's Use of Cicero in the Institutes I:1–5—A Case Study in Theological Method," *Archiv für Reformationsgeschichte* 62 (1971).

6. Alister E. McGrath, *Reformation Thought: An Introduction*, 2d ed. (Oxford: Blackwell, 1993), 246.

7. According to Muller, what we find in successive editions (after the 1536 edition, which was patterned after Luther's Small Catechism) of the *Institutes* in Calvin is the development of a more formal, doctrinal theology. See Muller, *Prolegomena to Theology*, 56–57.

8. Calvin, "John Calvin to the Reader, 1559," 1:5. *Loci communes* was an organizational term indicating that Christian doctrine was explained according to different *loci* in Scripture. In this sense, the *Institutes* depends, at least in part, on Melanchthon's methodology in his *Loci Communes*. "The order of *loci* identified by Melanchthon in Paul's Epistle to the Romans thus established a standard for the organization of Protestant theology." Muller, *Unaccommodated Calvin*, 129.

9. Calvin, "John Calvin to the Reader, 1559," 1:5. "That Calvin, from 1539 on, did understand his *Institutes* as a gathering of *loci communes* and *disputationes* appears also from the even more explicit statements presented in his introductory 'Argument' to the French translation of 1541. . . . In this 'argument,' Calvin once again indicates the purpose of the *Institutes* and, this time, omits all reference to piety, identifying his purpose, first, as providing a 'sum of Christian doctrine' and, second, as offering a point of entry into the study of the Old and New Testaments." Muller, *Unaccommodated Calvin*, 105.

Important and central for our purposes, given this general organizational method, is the fact that the *Institutes* are developed, more specifically, according to the *loci* of the Epistle to the Romans. Book 1 of the *Institutes* should be seen, therefore, as an explication of Paul's own order as he wrote the book of Romans. Specifically, what we find in the beginning of book 1 is "the relationship of God to humanity, the character of the human predicament, and the fact that humanity is left 'without excuse' in the presence of the revelation of God in nature."[10]

So the first point to be made with respect to our particular section of the *Institutes* is that, while Calvin no doubt refers to a number of humanist and Renaissance sources, and while there are similarities at points between, for example, the arguments of Cicero and Calvin's own arguments,[11] the driving force, or impetus, behind the content and arguments set forth by Calvin resides in the order of argumentation set forth by the apostle Paul in Romans. This is an important interpretive point that must be kept in mind. It is a fine distinction to make, but one that is central to understanding what Calvin is saying, and why he is saying it.

For example, Edward Dowey notes that Calvin's notion of the *sensus divinitatis* (about which, more below) is "much dependent" on Cicero in the latter's *Nature of the Gods*.[12] There can be no question that Calvin refers to Cicero and others in his elaboration of the *sensus*. However, to think that Calvin's concept of that notion derives, in the main, from sources other than Scripture is to miss the point of Calvin's argument, as we shall see below.

The second contextual point, which again will bolster our hermeneutical method as we peruse chapters 1–5 of the *Institutes*, and which goes hand in hand with the first point above, has to do with Calvin's organizing *structure* in these initial chapters.[13]

---

10. Muller, *Unaccommodated Calvin*, 137.

11. Note again the references to Leithart and Grislis in n. 5.

12. "The *sensus divinitatis* in man is not very closely defined in Calvin's thought, although he uses it widely, and with much dependence on Cicero." Edward A. Dowey, *The Knowledge of God in Calvin's Theology*, 3d ed. (Grand Rapids: Eerdmans, 1994), 51.

13. We are making a distinction in this section, somewhat artificial, between Calvin's organizing method and his organizing structure. The point to be made is that, as we have noted, the way that Calvin chose the topics presented, and the order of those topics, is dependent on Paul's order in Romans. The general headings under which he chose to

First, as much in the fashioning of the universe as in the general teaching of Scripture the Lord shows himself to be simply the Creator. Then in the face of Christ he shows himself the Redeemer. Of the resulting twofold knowledge of God (*hinc duplex emergit eius cognitio*) we shall now discuss the first aspect; the second will be dealt with in its proper place.[14]

This *duplex cognitio* is oftentimes hailed as the organizing principle of Calvin's *Institutes*.[15] Calvin states plainly, in the citation just quoted, that he will be discussing this *duplex* throughout the *Institutes*. Certainly, given the four books as a whole, this *duplex* is easily seen. This organizing structure is not original with Calvin, but has its precedent both in Luther, and in the Christian tradition generally.[16]

More pertinent to our particular discussion in this chapter, however, is that the *duplex* is not the organizing structure of our particular section. That structure is articulated clearly in the first sentence of the *Institutes*: "Nearly all the wisdom we possess, that is to say, true and sound wisdom, consists of two parts: the knowledge of God and of ourselves."[17]

Before proceeding to the overall *duplex cognitio Dei*, Calvin needs first to flesh out the relationship of our knowledge of God to our knowledge of ourselves. Hence, as Muller notes,

[T. H. L.] Parker is certainly correct in arguing against Dowey that the initial and most basic twofold knowledge in the *Institutes* is not the

---

structure those topics, and that serve to frame them, as we will see, have their source in the theological tradition on which Calvin depended. See Muller, *Unaccommodated Calvin*, 127–30, 134, 138.

14. Calvin, *Institutes of the Christian Religion*, 1.2.1.

15. "The really significant ordering principle of the *Institutes* in the 1559 edition is the *duplex cognitio Domini*, not the Apostles' Creed." Dowey, *Knowledge of God*, 42.

16. "Luther's theology, specifically his exegesis of Galatians, may also be the proximate source of the theme of twofold knowledge of God that became so prominent a feature of Calvin's *Institutes* in 1559." Muller, *Prolegomena to Theology*, 99. "The *duplex cognitio* in Calvin is not original with him, but probably also reflects the medieval Augustinian identification of the *obiectum theologiae* as God the Creator and Redeemer (Giles of Rome) or God the Creator, Redeemer, and Glorifier (Gregory of Rimini)." Muller, *Unaccommodated Calvin: Studies in the Foundation of a Theological Tradition* (New York, Oxford: Oxford University Press, 2000), 73.

17. Calvin, *Institutes of the Christian Religion*, 1.1.1.

"twofold knowledge of God" but the "knowledge of God and ourselves," the knowledge of God and self that was identified as basic to Calvin's thought in the first sentence of the 1536 text and that became the two foundational introductory chapters in 1539: this introductory structure remains in 1559.[18]

We have now before us two organizing principles that will provide the backdrop for our understanding of the first five chapters of the *Institutes*. Our explication of Calvin in these chapters will depend on the above two points. We will take for granted that behind all that Calvin is saying in chapters 1–5 is the apostle Paul's discussion in Romans (specifically, for us, in Rom. 1), and that at the heart of Calvin's concern in these initial chapters is the relationship of our knowledge of God to our self-knowledge.

How then does Calvin initiate the training of theological students in these beginning chapters? What matters are central and important for Calvin if his readers are to think biblically about the relationship of our knowledge of God and man? These seem to be the central questions to ask as we look at Calvin's argumentation.

Chapters 1–5—Knowledge of God and of Ourselves

We should not pass over too quickly the radical and penetrating way in which Calvin begins his discussion in the *Institutes*. He is not concerned, first of all, with elaborating a biblical doctrine of God. Neither is he intent, in the first place, on defending a biblical doctrine of Scripture. Instead, Calvin begins *covenantally*.[19] His primary and initial concern is to establish that all men are related to the God who created them, and that this relationship has everything to do with the way that we all think and act. Given the impetus of Calvin's thinking (i.e., Paul's order of topics in Romans), what we have in these initial chapters is the foundation for a Reformed, Christian apologetic.

According to Benjamin Warfield (speaking of Calvin):

18. Muller, *Unaccommodated Calvin*, 134.
19. This is not to say that Calvin uses the term "covenant." It is only to note that Calvin begins with man's relationship to God, his Creator, first of all.

But we can attribute to nothing but his theological genius the feat by which he set a compressed apologetical treatise in the forefront of his little book—for the "Institutes" were still in 1539 a little book, although already expanded to more than double the size of their original form (edition of 1536). Thus he not only for the first time supplied the constructive basis for the Reformation movement, but even for the first time in the history of Christian theology drew in outline the plan of a complete structure of Christian Apologetics. For this is the significance in the history of thought of Calvin's exposition of the sources and guarantee of the knowledge of God, which forms the opening topic of his "Institutes."[20]

Though we will need, below, to lodge some disagreements with Warfield about this very structure, there can be little question that his analysis is correct. Calvin's chosen organizational method provided for the Protestant church a rich and deep foundation from which a Reformed apologetic could be developed.

It may help at this point to offer a brief summary of the five chapters that inaugurate Calvin's *Institutes*, after which we can look at each chapter in a bit more detail. One way to summarize these opening chapters, in Calvin's own words, would be this:

It is certain that man never achieves a clear knowledge of himself unless he has first looked upon God's face, and then descends from contemplating him to scrutinize himself [1.1.2]. . . . Our knowledge should serve first to teach us fear and reverence; secondly, with it as our guide and teacher, we should learn to seek every good from him [1.2.2]. . . . Since, therefore, men one and all perceive that there is a God and that he is their Maker, they are condemned by their own testimony because they have failed to honor him and to consecrate their lives to his will [1.3.1]. . . . Miserable men do not rise above themselves as they should, but measure him by the yardstick of their own carnal stupidity, and neglect sound investigation; thus out of curiosity they fly off into empty speculations [1.4.1]. . . . Yet hence it appears that if men were taught only by nature, they would hold to

20. Benjamin B. Warfield, "Calvin's Doctrine of the Knowledge of God," in *Calvin and Calvinism* (New York: Oxford University Press, 1931), 30.

nothing certain or solid or clear-cut, but would be so tied to confused principles as to worship an unknown god. [1.5.1]

If we read the subject matter of chapters 1–5 of the *Institutes* through the lens of Romans, it is evident that Romans 1:18–25 determines the order and content of these chapters. In attempting to lay out Calvin's concerns, it may help us to have the key passages from Romans before us:

> For the wrath of God is revealed from heaven against all ungodliness and unrighteousness of men, who by their unrighteousness suppress the truth. For what can be known about God is plain to them, because God has shown it to them. For his invisible attributes, namely, his eternal power and divine nature, have been clearly perceived, ever since the creation of the world, in the things that have been made. So they are without excuse. (Rom. 1:18–20)

Why, given these verses, does Calvin begin with the mutual dependence of knowledge of God and knowledge of self? One explanation would be that Calvin has in mind here, implicitly, just exactly what the apostle Paul has in mind, implicitly, in these verses, that is, the image of God. This point seems clear enough, especially since Calvin reiterates this twofold knowledge later in the *Institutes* as he begins to discuss the image of God:

> We must now speak of the creation of man: not only because among all God's works here is the noblest and most remarkable example of his justice, wisdom, and goodness; but because, as we said at the beginning, *we cannot have a clear and complete knowledge of God unless it is accompanied by a corresponding knowledge of ourselves* [emphasis added].[21]

The reason, in other words, that God's wrath is revealed, and that all people know God, is that man is made in the image of God. Though Paul does not state this explicitly in this section of Romans, there can be little doubt that what Paul is describing here is an essential part

21.Calvin, *Institutes of the Christian Religion*, 1.15.1.

of what it means to be the image of God.[22] It is just because we are image that we know God, and it is our reaction to that knowledge that motivates God's wrath toward those who remain in Adam. As image, it is impossible to know ourselves aright without, at the same time, knowing the One whose image we are. Calvin reiterates this point in his comments on Acts 17:28: "Now, we see that all those who know not God know not themselves; because they have God present with them not only in the excellent gifts of the mind, but in their very essence; because it belongeth to God alone to be, all other things have their being in him."[23]

Thus, the necessary affirmation of Calvin that the two knowledges are inextricably linked. They are inextricably linked because man is ineradicably and eternally image of God.[24]

In the first two chapters, noted by Richard Muller to be "foundational introductory" chapters, Calvin elaborates on what it means that true knowledge of self depends on knowledge of God. Here, it seems, he is pouring content into what it means to be image of God. As soon as we think that we are not image, but independent reality, we have a skewed and illusory vision of who we are. "As long as we do not look beyond the earth, being quite content with our own righteousness, wis-

22. Allusions in this section of Romans to the creation account are numerous, such that there can be no question that Paul has that account in mind. Note, for example, Calvin's comment on Rom. 1:18: "And he brings, as the first proof of condemnation, the fact,—that though the structure of the world, and the most beautiful arrangement of the elements, ought to have induced man to glorify God, yet no one discharged his proper duty." John Calvin, *Commentaries on the Epistle of Paul the Apostle to the Romans*, ed. John Owen, Calvin's Commentaries 19 (Grand Rapids: Baker, 1979), 67. And on 1:19, "By saying, that *God has made it manifest*, he means, that man was created to be a spectator of this formed world, and that eyes were given him, that he might, by looking on so beautiful a picture, be led up to the Author himself." Calvin, *Romans*, 70. For a discussion of Paul's allusions to creation, see K. Scott Oliphint, "The Irrationality of Unbelief," in *Revelation and Reason: New Essays in Reformed Apologetics*, ed. K. Scott Oliphint and Lane G. Tipton (Phillipsburg, NJ: P&R, 2007).

23. John Calvin, *Commentary on the Acts of the Apostles*, vol. 2, ed. Henry Beveridge, Calvin's Commentaries 19 (Grand Rapids: Baker, 1979), 168–69.

24. If we think, to use one example, of a mirror image, the image in the mirror is dependent for its very being and existence on the reality that stands before it. Not only so, but it is defined and its properties are determined according to that reality. So it is with man. If, *per impossible*, the reality (God) were ever removed from us, we would cease to exist. Conversely, our reality is such only in the light of his.

dom, and virtue, we flatter ourselves most sweetly, and fancy ourselves all but demigods."[25]

Calvin seems to be indicating, in these initial two chapters, what the knowledge of self and of God means for those who respond properly to natural revelation. "Thus from the feeling of our own ignorance, vanity, poverty, infirmity, and—what is more—depravity and corruption, we recognize that the true light of wisdom, sound virtue, full abundance of every good, and purity of righteousness rest in the Lord alone."[26] This could be true only of those whose hearts have been changed by the Holy Spirit. So Calvin's concern at the beginning is to explain what it means that knowledge of God and knowledge of self are so closely intertwined. What it means is that, unless we see ourselves against the backdrop of God's holiness, we will never see ourselves for what and who we truly are. This is the principle that will underlie the rest of what Calvin wants to say in book 1, and especially in the following three chapters.

Having discussed the mutual relationship of knowledge of God and of self, Calvin begins, in chapter 3, to discuss, first, the knowledge of God. This is in keeping with the order of topics taken up by the apostle Paul beginning in Romans 1:18.[27] As Paul begins his discussion of the wrath of God revealed, he introduces two notions, each of which needs its own explanation. God's wrath is revealed, according to Paul, because all of us, in Adam, suppress (first notion) the truth (second notion). Paul then goes on, beginning in verse 19, to explain, first of all, just what that truth is that we have (vv. 19–21a), and then, afterward (21b–23), what the suppression of that truth looks like in us. Beginning in chapter 3, Calvin follows the logic of Paul's argument.

In chapter 3, Calvin is interested in arguing Paul's point in Romans 1:18. He wants to set forth the notion that all men know God. Thus, he begins, "There is within the human mind, and indeed by natural instinct,

---

25. Calvin, *Institutes of the Christian Religion*, 1.1.2.

26. Calvin, *Institutes of the Christian Religion*, 1.1.1.

27. Calvin notes at the end of chapter 1 that "however the knowledge of God and of ourselves may be mutually connected, the order of right teaching (*ordo recte docendi*) requires that we discuss the former first, then proceed afterward to treat the latter." This "order of right teaching," we should remember here, discussed in detail by Richard Muller, relies on Paul's arrangement of topics in the Epistle to the Romans. See "Establishing the *Ordo docendi*," in Muller, *Unaccommodated Calvin*, 118–39.

an awareness of divinity (*divinitatis sensum*)."[28] This *sensus divinitatis* is not, as we noted above, a notion which Calvin takes from Cicero. Calvin does, however, depend heavily on Cicero in much of this and the following chapters. The reason for that, we should make clear, is Calvin's chosen method of argumentation in this section. Because this knowledge of God is universal—that is, it is seen in all men everywhere—Calvin's argumentation seeks to show just how that is the case. In that sense, though his argument presupposes the truth of Scripture, in that it has its focus in Paul's affirmations in Romans 1:18, Calvin takes the truth of Scripture and demonstrates that it is, as a matter of fact, the case in practice. His method, then, is to show from nature what Scripture says is true.

That same method is seen, for example, in Calvin's exposition of Paul's encounter on Mars Hill. In his comments on Paul's use of the Greek poet Aratus, Calvin notes:

> He citeth half a verse out of Aratus, not so much for authority's sake, as that he may make the men of Athens ashamed; for such sayings of the poets came from no other fountain save only from nature and common reason. Neither is it any marvel if Paul, who spake unto men who were infidels and ignorant of true godliness, do use the testimony of a poet, wherein was extant a confession of that knowledge which is naturally engraven in men's minds.[29]

As with Paul and his use of Aratus, so also with Calvin. He seeks to show, by way of Cicero's account of religion, just how the truth of Romans 1:18 is practiced; he gives the application of that truth. Calvin's use of Cicero (and others), then, has more to do with his method of argumentation than with his source. Commenting on the same section (Acts 17:16–34), Calvin notes of Paul that "because he hath to deal with profane men, he draweth proofs from nature itself; for in vain should he have cited testimonies of Scripture."[30] Calvin, like Paul (though Calvin's audience is different), seeks to show "from nature itself" just how this universal knowledge of God is made manifest. Or, as Calvin himself says,

28. Calvin, *Institutes of the Christian Religion*, 1.3.1.
29. Calvin, *Acts*, 169.
30. Calvin, *Acts*, 158.

"Therefore, since from the beginning of the world there has been no region, no city, in short, no household, that could do without religion, there lies in this a tacit confession of a sense of deity (*divinitatis sensum*) inscribed in the hearts of all."[31]

We need to be clear here. Calvin is not saying that we know there is a sense of deity because of the universal testimony to such. Rather, he is saying that the universal testimony is evidence, a "tacit confession," that the biblical position set forth by Paul is true. The universal testimony is, in that sense, supportive of the truth and not constitutive of it. Idolatry in all its forms, according to Calvin, is "ample proof (*documentum*)"[32] that this *sensus divinitatis* is implanted in us all by God.

Calvin seems to use the two notions of *sensus divinitatis* and *semen religionis* in a similar way. McNeill thinks that both terms "refer generally to a numinous awareness of God."[33] Warfield, on the other hand, seems to see the two designations as two sides of the same coin:

> The phraseology by which Calvin designates this "natural instinct" (*naturalis instinctus*; iii. 1, *ad init.*) varies from *sensus divinitatis* or *sensus deitatis* to such synonyms as: *numinis intelligentia, dei notio, dei notitia.* It is the basis on the one hand of whatever *cognitio dei* man attains to and on the other of whatever *religio* he reaches; whence it is called the *semen religionis.*[34]

Whatever the case with respect to these two ideas, at least two things are true of them both.

First, they both constitute a knowledge of God. Calvin, again following Paul (Rom. 1:18–21), discusses man's general culpability before God on the basis that man does, as a matter of fact and because of

---

31. Calvin, *Institutes of the Christian Religion*, 1.3.1.
32. Calvin, *Institutes of the Christian Religion*, 1.3.1.
33. Calvin, *Institutes of the Christian Religion*, 1:43 n. 2.
34. Warfield, "Calvin's Doctrine of the Knowledge of God," 34 n. 3. Without being overly pedantic here, it seems to me that the better understanding of Calvin is with Warfield here. Though there is certainly much continuity between the way Calvin thinks of the *sensus divinitatis* and his use of the *semen religionis*, it does seem to be the case that, as two sides of the same coin, it is the *sensus*, as knowledge, that works itself out in terms of religious practice, which practice is motived by the *semen religionis*.

being created, know God. That is to say, whatever else may be said of this *sensus divinitatis*, it is surely the case that it is no mere capacity for knowledge which may or may not be filled in and by us. Rather, the *sensus is* knowledge itself.

This again is consistent with the apostle Paul's argument in Romans 1:18–21, wherein Paul makes clear, that, because we all know God, not only some, who by their own reasoning process and comprehension stand without excuse before God, but all of us, by virtue of the knowledge of God implanted in us by God, stand without excuse before him.

A few select quotations from Calvin's commentaries will suffice here to demonstrate what he had in mind as he elaborated on the *sensus divinitatis* in the *Institutes*. In his comments on Romans 1:18–23, Calvin notes that "*the truth of God* means, the true knowledge of God."[35] This true knowledge of God is "sufficiently clear" that we "cannot plead our ignorance as an excuse for our perverseness."[36] "But this knowledge of God, which avails only to take away excuse, differs greatly from that which brings salvation."[37] With regard to Romans 1:21, Calvin notes that Paul "plainly testifies here, that God has presented to the minds of all the means of knowing him, having so manifested himself by his works, that they *must necessarily see* what of themselves they seek not to know—that there is some God."[38] Because of this "right notion of God" we ought to praise him.[39] Calvin goes on to argue that the unrighteousness of men is demonstrated in that "they quickly choked by their own depravity the seed of right knowledge, before it grew up to ripeness."[40]

One more important point should be noted here with respect to Calvin's notion of the *sensus*, a point perhaps more relevant to us than it would have been to Calvin. In *Institutes* 1.4.2 Calvin refers to this *sensus* as "the light of nature." Specifically, Calvin says, "David's statement that ungodly men and fools feel in their hearts that there is no God must first, as we

35. Calvin, *Romans*, 69.
36. Calvin, *Romans*, 71.
37. Calvin, *Romans*, 71.
38. Calvin, *Romans*, 71.
39. Calvin, *Romans*, 72.
40. Calvin, *Romans*, 73.

shall see again a little later, be limited to those who, by extinguishing the light of nature (*suffocata naturae luce*), deliberately befuddle themselves."

The notion of a "light of nature" has a long and complex history in philosophy and theology, a history that relates directly (among other things) to one's understanding of theology and its relationship to apologetic methodology.[41] Without replaying that history here, we would suggest that the reason Calvin is able easily to exchange the language of a *sensus divinitatis* for the language of a "light of nature" is that for him, the two were identical.

In his Commentary on the Gospel of John, Calvin notes this concerning John's phrase (in 1:5) that "the darkness did not comprehend" the Logos: "The light which still dwells in corrupt nature consists chiefly of two parts; for, first, all men naturally possess some seed of religion; and, secondly, the distinction between good and evil is engraven on their consciences."[42]

The language that Calvin uses here is identical to the language used in our present section of the *Institutes*. It is obvious that Calvin sees an identity between that which God implants in us and the notion of the light of nature. He sees this identity because the idea of a light of nature is taken directly from Scripture itself, and its content is, therefore, not a faculty of man generally, but that faculty as grounded in the power of Christ.

One contemporary example of this view should be mentioned here, if for no other reason than to show continuity, in a contemporary Reformed context, with Calvin's understanding of this passage in John. Geerhardus Vos, in working through the exegetical and redemptive-historical aspects of John's prologue, makes the following observation with respect to John 1:4:

> When the light of men is derived from the Logos not directly, but mediately through the life that He supplies, this is a representation which suits the natural relation of mankind to the Logos far better

41. The phrase itself, for example, is used ten times in the Westminster Standards (Westminster Confession 1:1, 6; 10:4; 20:4; 21:1; Westminster Larger Catechism 2, 60 (2 times), 121, 151).

42. John Calvin, *Commentary on the Gospel according to John* (CD-ROM: Books for the Ages: Ages Digital Software, 1998), 23.

than the redemptive relation. The Gospel of John everywhere makes a point of it that in the soteriological process the light of revelation comes first in order, as supplied by Christ after an objective, supernatural fashion, and not as something that emerges out of the new life of man, and passes through his subjectivity.... Here the Logos-revelation is actually mediated through the subjective life which man in dependence on the Logos possesses. The life here naturally produces the light. The meaning is not that in man life assumes the form of light, which would savor of idealism, but that the life which man receives carries in itself and of itself kindles in him, the *light of the knowledge of God*.[43]

In other words, it is the revelation of God in Christ that grounds whatever understanding remains in us after the fall. So, says Calvin,

As he is the eternal Speech of God, by him the world was made; by his power all things continue to possess the life which they once received; man especially was endued with an extraordinary gift of understanding; and though by his revolt he lost the light of understanding, yet he still sees and understands, so that what he naturally possesses from the grace of the Son of God is not entirely destroyed.[44]

This is an important historical point, as the notion of the light of nature in Arminianism, for example, came to be seen as equivalent to human reason. As equivalent, it was then thought that a scriptural theology could be built on, or perhaps itself would require, a reasonable theology as its foundation. The phrase "light of nature," then, lost its revelational underpinnings as that which was implanted in us by God, and came to refer, simply, to our innate cognitive capacity, rather than something that is ours by way of God's revelation implanted in us.[45] For

43. Geerhardus Vos, "The Range of the Logos Title in the Prologue to the Fourth Gospel," in *Redemptive History and Biblical Interpretation: The Shorter Writings of Geerhardus Vos*, ed. Richard B. Gaffin Jr. (Phillipsburg, NJ: P&R, 1980), 76 (emphasis added).
44. John Calvin, *John*, 24.
45. For a historical evaluation of the devolution of revelation as fundamental *principium*, see Muller, *Prolegomena to Theology*, 270–310.

Calvin, it was equivalent to the *sensus divinitatis* that is ours by virtue of God's, not our, activity.[46]

Secondly, having looked at the notion of truth as it is introduced by the apostle Paul in Romans 1:18, Calvin then begins to deal with the second important concept: suppression. That is, once Calvin establishes the fact of a *sensus divinitatis* or *semen religionis*, as that which is ours because of what God does, he then goes on to spell out what happens when we, in our sins, get hold of it. What happens, in a word, is perversion.

There seem to be two primary and related points that Calvin wants to make here. Once we get hold of the truth that God gives to each of us, in our sins we fashion a god of our own image. In so doing, we proceed to build a religion around the false god(s) that we have created. Each of these responses is the inevitable reaction, for those who remain in Adam, to the knowledge of God implanted in us, and these responses follow, again, Paul's presentation in Romans 1. Speaking of just how it is that we suppress the truth given, Paul says,

> For although they knew God, they did not honor him as God or give thanks to him, but they became futile in their thinking, and their foolish hearts were darkened. Claiming to be wise, they became fools, and exchanged the glory of the immortal God for images resembling mortal man and birds and animals and reptiles. Therefore God gave them up in the lusts of their hearts to impurity, to the dishonoring of their bodies among themselves, because they exchanged the truth about God for a lie and worshiped and served the creature rather than the Creator, who is blessed forever! Amen. (Rom. 1:21–25)

We will return to this point below, when we attempt to flesh out the apologetic implications of Calvin's understanding of natural revelation, but for now we should see that Calvin, like Paul, sees no reaction (by those in Adam) to natural revelation that would provide a foundation for a true biblical theology.

Commenting on verse 22, Calvin notes:

46. For a discussion of the philosophical implications of the *sensus divinitatis*, see K. Scott Oliphint, *Reasons for Faith: Philosophy in the Service of Theology* (Phillipsburg, NJ: P&R, 2006), 122–66.

It is commonly inferred from this passage, that Paul alludes here to those philosophers, who assumed to themselves in a peculiar manner the reputation of wisdom.... But they seem to me to have been guided by too slender a reason; for it was not peculiar to the philosophers to suppose themselves wise in the knowledge of God, but it was equally common to all nations, and to all ranks of men. There were indeed none who sought not to form some ideas of the majesty of God, and to make him such a God as they could conceive him to be according to their own reason. This presumption I hold is not learned in the schools, but is innate, and comes with us, so to speak, from the womb.... The arrogance then which is condemned here is this—that men sought to be of themselves wise, and to draw God down to a level with their own low condition, when they ought humbly to have given him his own glory. For Paul holds this principle, that none, except through their own fault, are unacquainted with the worship due God.[47]

In our rebelliousness, therefore, according to Calvin, sinners culpably commit idolatry. Not only so, but instead of fearing the God they know, "they do not desist from polluting themselves with every sort of vice, and from joining wickedness to wickedness, until in every respect they violate the holy law of the Lord and dissipate all his righteousness."[48]

In chapter 5, Calvin moves from his elaboration of Paul's notion of suppression, to a discussion of just what Paul means when he says that God's "invisible attributes, namely, his eternal power and divine nature, have been clearly perceived, ever since the creation of the world, in the things that have been made. So they are without excuse" (Rom. 1:20). This chapter, the longest of the five we have surveyed, is concerned with explaining just how it is that the knowledge of God is revealed through that which God has made.

At the beginning of this chapter, Calvin makes a distinction between that which is sown in men's minds, already discussed, and that which is revealed to us externally:

47. Calvin, *Romans*, 73.
48. Calvin, *Institutes of the Christian Religion*, 1.4.4.

Lest anyone, then, be excluded from access to happiness, he not only sowed in men's minds that seed of religion (*religionis semen*) of which we have spoken but revealed himself and daily discloses himself in the whole workmanship of the universe. As a consequence, men cannot open their eyes without being compelled to see him.[49]

Thus, Calvin introduces the subject matter of this chapter by distinguishing what he has said previously (the *semen religionis*) and that which he will now discuss.

The distinction, however, should not be overstated. It is not as though Calvin is moving now from that which is ours immediately, to that which is ours mediately.[50] His major point in this chapter is not that all human beings have an implanted knowledge of God, on the one hand, and a derived knowledge of God, on the other. Rather, Calvin is discussing in this chapter another mode of the same kind of knowledge that he has discussed in chapter 3.

At the end of chapter 5, Calvin concludes,

Therefore we are justly denied every excuse when we stray off as wanderers and vagrants even though everything points out the right way. But, however that may be, yet the fact that men soon corrupt the seed of the knowledge of God (*semen notitiae Dei*), *sown in their minds out of the wonderful workmanship of nature* (thus preventing it from coming to a good and perfect fruit), must be imputed to their own failing.[51]

That which is sown in the mind, the seed of religion, which is the knowledge of God, is implanted there, via both internal and external modes, by God himself.

Here it seems we cannot follow Dowey's analysis of Calvin. Though admittedly, the knowledge situation which Calvin describes in these

49. Calvin, *Institutes of the Christian Religion*, 1.5.1.
50. Though the language of "mediate" and "immediate" is not altogether clear, we can limit our understanding of the two in terms of a common distinction between "perceptual," "derived," or "reasoned" knowledge (mediate), and "conceptual," "direct," or "intuited" knowledge (immediate).
51. Calvin, *Institutes of the Christian Religion*, 1.5.15 (emphasis added).

initial chapters is difficult precisely to define and delineate (of which, more below), it does not seem to be the case, in this fifth chapter of the *Institutes*, that Calvin is explicating a rational process for acquisition of the knowledge of God different from what he was discussing in previous chapters. According to Dowey,

> What we are now about to point to is the philosophic and rational quality of the process by which man derives the content of the objective revelation from his experience of the world. Man empirically observes the order of nature and from this draws conclusions about its Maker and Governor. Rather than an immediate *sensus divinitatis*, we have immediate experience of the world as the raw material or sense data on the basis of which the mind of man says "therefore" about God. Thus, certain attributes of God appear in the form of predicates to human experience, so far as the knowing process is concerned. The fact that mental processes rather than immediacy are involved, seems in no way to detract in Calvin's mind from the revelatory character of what is known or to make it less compelling.[52]

The points of agreement with respect to Dowey's analysis here would be (1) that the revelation of God given to man is immediate and (2) that the knowledge of God given is revelatory. However, it does not seem to be the case that Calvin is arguing for a process of ratiocination or inference, out of which would come the true knowledge of God. Any "therefore" with respect to our experience of the world (and the knowledge of God entailed thereby), Calvin would argue, would inevitably lead to idolatry, not truth. According to Dowey, "The commonest phenomena of the world are not self-explanatory, and we must rise above them to their Author."[53] Even if Dowey is noting here the substance of Calvin's argument (i.e., that it is our duty to recognize God in what he has made), the fact of the matter seems to be that Calvin thinks the works of God are self-explanatory, and in this he follows Paul.

For example, Calvin seems clear enough about our lack of ability to conclude for truth on the basis of God's revelation in creation:

52. Dowey, *Knowledge of God*, 74.
53. Ibid., 75.

And where Paul teaches that what is to be known of God is made plain from the creation of the universe, he does not signify such a manifestation as men's discernment can comprehend; but, rather, shows it not to go farther than to render them inexcusable.[54]

And,

Although we lack the natural ability to mount up unto the pure and clear knowledge of God, all excuse is cut off because the fault of dullness is within us.[55]

In his comment on Paul's Areopagus address, Calvin notes,

After their boldness they fashion him so as they may comprehend him. By such inventions is the sincere and plain knowledge of God corrupt; yea, his truth, as saith Paul, is turned into a lie (Romans 1:25).[56]

Therefore, as Calvin argues, it cannot be the case that sinful man is able to take God's revelation in nature and, by process of inference, conclude for the true God.

There is, however, some sense in which sinful man can arrive at a semblance of the truth from creation. This is a difficult matter precisely to articulate, and it is made difficult because of the irrationality that sin brings with it. As we saw above, in his comment on Paul's use of Aratus in his Areopagus address, Calvin attempts to explain why such use contains a legitimate appeal to those who are outside of Christ, and have no knowledge of Scripture:

Now, that I may return unto this sentence which I have in hand, it is not to be doubted but that Aratus spake of Jupiter; neither doth Paul, in applying that unto the true God, which he spake unskillfully of his Jupiter, wrest it unto a contrary sense. For because men are imbued with

54. Calvin, *Institutes of the Christian Religion*, 1.5.14.
55. Calvin, *Institutes of the Christian Religion*, 1.5.15.
56. Calvin, *Acts*, 159.

some knowledge of God (*aliquo Dei sensu imbuti sunt*), they draw true principles from that fountain.[57]

What might Calvin mean here when he speaks of the Greeks "drawing true principles" from the fountain of the implanted revelatory knowledge of God? At this point, we can begin to address that question as we move from exposition to some implications of Calvin's thinking in these five chapters.

Implications

Without question, the most controversial subject of Calvin's discussion in this section is that of natural theology. The controversy reached its peak in the twentieth century, in the debate between Karl Barth and Emil Brunner. The crux of the debate can be seen in one quote from Barth:

> Brunner's interpretation of Calvin has one fault which vitiates everything. He has, with amazing cold blood and consistency, left out the very important brackets within which Calvin always speaks of the natural knowledge of God. They are the expression *si integer stetisset* Adam [if Adam had remained upright—from *Institutes* 1.2.1].[58]

In other words, Barth's understanding of Calvin was that the natural knowledge of God was obliterated at the fall. Since Adam did not remain upright, there can be no natural knowledge of God.

Numerous problems arise in this understanding of Calvin, not the least of which is that Barth seems to make no distinction between natural revelation and natural theology.[59] The distinction is a crucial one, and one that must be kept in mind here. Natural revelation is that which God gives to man. As Calvin notes, it is that which God implants in us. Natural theology is that which man does with that natural revelation that God implants.

57. Calvin, *Acts*, 169. We have used the alternative translation of the Latin, as in n. 1 of the same page.
58. Brunner and Barth, *Natural Theology*, 109.
59. Muller, *Prolegomena to Theology*, 275.

There are a few central notions in this regard that may help us to understand Calvin's relationship to current debates. First, "Calvin, Bullinger, Vermigli, and Musculus all discuss the naturally available 'knowledge of God,' but they nowhere construct a 'natural theology' and nowhere discuss either the advisability or inadvisability of constructing one."[60] Not only so, but Calvin does not even use the term *theologia naturalis*.[61] In this sense, Calvin's concerns with respect to natural revelation are not identical to later concerns, particularly, though certainly not exclusively, since the Enlightenment.

Second, that having been said, it is surely not the case that Calvin said nothing about natural theology and its usefulness, or lack thereof. According to Muller,

> Calvin, in fact, consistently assumes the existence of false, pagan natural theology that has warped the knowledge of God available in nature into gross idolatry. Calvin must argue in this way because he assumes the existence of natural revelation which *in se* is a true knowledge of God. If natural theology were impossible, idolatrous man would not be left without excuse. The problem is that sin takes the natural revelation of God and fashions, in fact, an idolatrous and sinful theology. The theology exists and man is to blame because it is sin and sin alone that stands in the way of a valid natural theology.[62]

For Calvin, then, there is a natural theology that is idolatrous. But there is also a legitimate natural theology. Calvin "testifies not only to the existence of natural revelation and to the fact of pagan, idolatrous, natural theology, but to the real possibility of a natural theology of the regenerate."[63] This dual aspect of natural theology in Calvin's thought provided the background for a fuller development and articulation of the subject in the seventeenth century.[64]

60. Ibid., 271.
61. Ibid., 273.
62. Ibid., 274.
63. Ibid., 276.
64. For this, see ibid., 278–310. We should note here that one of Calvin's contemporaries, Peter Martyr Vermigli, was also influential in the development and classification of natural revelation and natural theology. See also Jeffrey K. Jue, "*Theologia Naturalis*: A Reformed

It seems clear that Calvin was not optimistic about any attempt by an unbeliever to move from the knowledge of the truth given in natural revelation, and implanted by God, to a theology of the true God based on that revelation. Rather, he viewed all pagan attempts at natural theology as corrupt, and as a perversion of that which is given by God. In this way, as we have seen, he follows the apostle Paul's reasoning.

For example, at his Areopagus address in Acts 17, Paul can utilize and refer to the quotation from Aratus ("For we are indeed his offspring"), but not because Aratus got it right; Calvin admits that Aratus was referring to Jupiter, not to the true God. Paul uses the quotation, having already poured the proper content, earlier in his address, into the notion of "him" in that quote. For Aratus, the "principle" (as Calvin puts it) of truth may remain, but the content makes the proposition false. Only if the proper "matter" is given to the skeletal "form" (or "principle") of the statement does the statement itself reflect the truth. The truth "in principle," according to Calvin, flows from the truth given in natural revelation. The perversion of the content is what we do with that truth—it is one mode of suppression—once we take hold of the revelation that God implants in us. So, says Calvin, "so soon as they begin to think upon God, they vanish away in wicked inventions, and so the pure seed doth degenerate into corruptions; yet the first general knowledge of God doth nevertheless remain still in them."[65]

For Calvin, therefore, there is no natural theology on the part of an unbeliever that serves to do anything but render him without excuse. Every unbelieving attempt to construct a true natural theology will inevitably lead to condemnation.

It would seem, therefore, that with respect to the theistic proofs, which Barth, due to his misreading of Calvin, would have rejected, Warfield is correct. Speaking of Calvin, Warfield notes,

> His special interest in the theistic argument is, accordingly, due less to the consideration that it rounds out his systematic view of truth than to the fact that it helps us to the vital knowledge of God.... In and of itself,

---

Tradition," in *Revelation and Reason: New Essays in Reformed Apologetics*, ed. K. Scott Oliphint and Lane G. Tipton (Phillipsburg, NJ: P&R, 2007), 168–89.

65. Calvin, *Acts*, 169–70.

indeed, it has no limitations; Calvin is fully assured of its validity and analyses its data with entire confidence. . . . But Calvin cannot content himself with an intellectualistic contemplation of the objective validity of the theistic argument. So dominated is he by practical interests that he actually attaches to the chapter in which he argues this objective validity a series of sections in which he equally strongly argues the subjective inability of man to receive its testimony. Objectively valid as the theistic proofs are, they are ineffective to produce a just knowledge of God in the sinful heart.[66]

Worth noting here is the agreement of Cornelius Van Til with Warfield's (and Calvin's) assessment:

To say that the argument for Christianity and for the existence of God is absolutely valid I am merely applying the idea that God's revelation without and within man is perspicuous. If then man rightly interprets this revelation he has an absolutely valid argument for the truth. But the sinner, so far as he works from his adopted principle which rests in himself as autonomous, does not interpret the facts of the universe rightly. How could he? He assumes himself to be ultimate. He therefore assumes also that the facts of the universe are not created but exist in themselves. . . . Therefore . . . , we presuppose that man is of necessity confronted with the truth about himself as the creature of God. This objective truth about man himself, the ineradicable truth, this inescapable confrontation by God, man, *so far as he thinks from his sinful principle*, seeks to suppress. But he cannot suppress it. It comes to him with the pressure of God, the inescapable One. God's revelation is everywhere, and everywhere perspicuous. Hence the theistic proofs are absolutely valid.[67]

The proofs are valid, but the subjective aspect of those proofs—that which man takes and applies to himself—will always, more or less, pervert and distort that validity, so long as man remains in Adam. It is likely for this reason that Calvin sought to present his arguments, in these initial

66. Warfield, "Calvin's Doctrine," 41–42.
67. Cornelius Van Til, *Common Grace and the Gospel* (Phillipsburg, NJ: P&R, 1972), 180–81.

chapters, not as formal demonstrations of God's existence, but rather as *persuasions*. This is true of Calvin's method generally.

According to Muller, Calvin was more engaged in persuasion than in demonstration.[68] This is not to say that persuasion is opposed to demonstration; quite the contrary. Persuasion is a methodology that has implicitly what logical demonstration (for example, in the form of a syllogism) has explicitly. Moreover, persuasion has imbedded within it the recognition that, fundamental to the debate, the problem is not, at root, so much a lack of knowledge as it is a refusal to be convinced. In that sense, with respect to God's clear revelation, the problem is one of irrationality, not ignorance.[69]

The methodological point, however, should not be underestimated. It is a methodological point that has sweeping ramifications for apologetic method. While there may certainly be instances when syllogistic demonstration is warranted in apologetic discussions (so long as, with Calvin, revelation is presupposed as the point of contact, and not some neutral notion of reason), it may be that the persuasive approach, appealing as it does to the knowledge of God implanted in us all, is often a better way to bridge the gap between believer and unbeliever.[70]

Conclusion

These first five chapters of Calvin's *Institutes* are a gold mine for Christian theology generally, and for Christian apologetics more specifically. Given that Calvin's choice of topics follows closely the topics that Paul gives us in Romans, there can be little question that Calvin's initial concern was the relation of God to man generally, a relationship that has at its core the fact of man as God's image, and of God as constantly confronting

---

68. Muller, *Unaccommodated Calvin*, 110–11.

69. Note, for example, Calvin's assessment of the rejection of God's revelation; it is "madness" (*vesania*, 1.5.4) and "stupid" (*stupor*, 1.5.11). The problem is not that man doesn't know the truth, it is that he will not accept the truth for what it is, and thus has a built-in propensity, by virtue of sin, to reject the world as it really is.

70. For a look at the value of persuasion in apologetic argument, with reference to Paul's Areopagus address, see K. Scott Oliphint, *The Battle Belongs to the Lord* (Phillipsburg, NJ: P&R, 2003), 143–73.

man by way of his clear, and clearly understood, revelation in and through all of creation. The commonality that all of us share, as God's creatures, is that we all will never, because we can never, escape the presence (and knowledge of that presence) of God.[71]

For this reason, Calvin's argumentation with respect to this general and natural knowledge of God is to set forth the obvious, and to point out the irrationality of a rejection of it. He presses the point that any accounting of man must recognize the necessity of a Creator (1.5.2–3, 5). He reiterates the fact of God's sovereignty and providence over his creation as the only possible way of accounting for the complexity of it all (1.5.6–7). These "enthymemes"[72] offered by Calvin are of persuasive value, in that the implicit premise in all of them is that we know that God, and he alone, is the Creator and Sustainer of all that he has made. In other words, the presupposition behind all that Calvin says, and all of his argumentation with respect to the unbelieving assessments of creation, is that God exists, that he is known truly, and that the true knowledge of him is inevitably perverted and distorted because of sin. It is that true knowledge, and man's reaction to it, that renders him eternally inexcusable. But Calvin also appeals to that true knowledge in order to argue for the true worship and adoration of God.[73] Such worship and adoration can be ours only when we see the knowledge of God the Creator inextricably tied to the knowledge (gleaned alone from Scripture) of God the Redeemer.

Bibliography

Barth, Karl. *Nein! Antwort an Emil Brunner*. Theologische Existenz Heute 14. Munich: C. Kaiser, 1934.

Brunner, Emil, and Karl Barth. *Natural Theology: Comprising "Nature and Grace."* London: G. Bles, The Centenary Press, 1946.

71. As Calvin says, "It is, accordingly, clear that there is no one to whom the Lord does not abundantly show his wisdom." Calvin, *Institutes of the Christian Religion*, 1.5.2.

72. Note again the discussion in Muller, *Unaccommodated Calvin*, 108–11.

73. "Knowledge of this sort, then, ought not only to arouse us to the worship of God but also to awaken and encourage us to the hope of the future life." Calvin, *Institutes of the Christian Religion*, 1.5.10.

Calvin, John. *Commentaries on the Epistle of Paul the Apostle to the Romans.* Edited by John Owen. Calvin's Commentaries 19. Grand Rapids: Baker, 1979.

―――. *Commentary on the Acts of the Apostles.* Vol. 2. Edited by Henry Beveridge. Calvin's Commentaries 19. Grand Rapids, Baker, 1979.

―――. *Commentary on the Gospel according to John.* CD-ROM: Books for the Ages: Ages Digital Software, 1998.

―――. *Institutes of the Christian Religion.* Edited by John T. McNeill. Translated by Ford Lewis Battles. 2 vols. Library of Christian Classics 20–21. Philadelphia: Westminster, 1960.

Dowey, Edward A. *The Knowledge of God in Calvin's Theology.* 3d ed. Grand Rapids: Eerdmans 1994.

Grislis, Egil. "Calvin's Use of Cicero in the Institutes I:1–5—A Case Study in Theological Method." *Archiv für Reformationsgeschichte* 62 (1971): 5–37.

Jue, Jeffrey K. "*Theologia Naturalis*: A Reformed Tradition." In *Revelation and Reason: New Essays in Reformed Apologetics,* edited by K. Scott Oliphint and Lane G. Tipton, 168–89. Phillipsburg, NJ: P&R, 2007.

Leithart, Peter J. "The Eminent Pagan: Calvin's Use of Cicero in *Institutes* I:1–5." *Westminster Theological Journal* 52 (1990): 1–12.

McGrath, Alister E. *Reformation Thought: An Introduction.* 2d ed. Oxford: Blackwell, 1993.

Muller, Richard A. *The Divine Essence and Attributes.* Grand Rapids: Baker, 2002.

―――. "*Duplex Cognitio Dei* in the Theology of Early Reformed Orthodoxy." *Sixteenth Century Journal* 10. 2 (1979): 51–61.

―――. *Prolegomena to Theology.* Grand Rapids: Baker, 2003.

―――. *The Unaccommodated Calvin: Studies in the Foundation of a Theological Tradition.* New York: Oxford University Press, 2000.

Oliphint, K. Scott. *The Battle Belongs to the Lord.* Phillipsburg, NJ: P&R, 2003.

―――. "The Irrationality of Unbelief." In *Revelation and Reason: New Essays in Reformed Apologetics,* edited by K. Scott Oliphint and Lane G. Tipton, 59–73. Phillipsburg, NJ: P&R, 2007.

———. *Reasons for Faith: Philosophy in the Service of Theology*. Phillipsburg, NJ: P&R, 2006.

Van Til, Cornelius. *Common Grace and the Gospel*. Phillipsburg, NJ: P&R, 1972.

Vos, Geerhardus. "The Range of the Logos Title in the Prologue to the Fourth Gospel." In *Redemptive History and Biblical Interpretation: The Shorter Writings of Geerhardus Vos*, edited by Richard B. Gaffin Jr., xxiii, 559. Phillipsburg, NJ: P&R, 1980.

Warfield, Benjamin B. "Calvin's Doctrine of the Knowledge of God." In *Calvin and Calvinism*, 29–130. New York: Oxford University Press, 1931.

3

CALVIN'S DOCTRINE
OF HOLY SCRIPTURE

INSTITUTES I.6–10
ROBERT L. REYMOND

The original Strasbourg editors of Calvin's complete works stated about Calvin and his *Institutes of the Christian Religion* in the mid-nineteenth century:

Calvin may justly be called the leader and standard-bearer of theologians. For who will not marvel at his command of language and letters, at his control of the entire sphere of learning? The abundance of his learning, the admirable disposition of his material, the force and validity of his reasoning in dogmatics, the acuteness and subtlety of his mind, and the alternating gay and biting saltiness of his polemics, the felicitous perspicuity, sobriety and sagacity of his exegetics, the nervous eloquence and freedom of his paraenetics, his incomparable legislative prudence and wisdom in the constitution, ordering and governing of the churches—all this is fully recognized among men of learning and candor. . . . All these qualities are, of course, present in his other writings, but they are especially striking in that immortal *Institutes of the Christian Religion*, which beyond all controversy far excels all expositions of the kind that have been written from the days of the apostles. . . .[1]

In his incomparable *Institutes of the Christian Religion* Calvin treats the doctrine of Holy Scripture in book 1, chapters 6–10, particularly chapters 7–9, with 1.6 and 1.10 serving as introductory and concluding bookends to the three central chapters. While Calvin presupposes the teaching of Scripture in 1.1–5 where he treats man's knowledge of God from creation,[2] it is at 1.6 that Scripture begins to function formally and officially in the *Institutes*.

1. *Corpus Reformatorum: Johannis Calvini Opera quae supersunt omnia*, ed. by N. W. Baum, E. Cunitz, E. Reuss, P. Lobstein, and A. Erichson (Brunswick and Berlin: C. A. Schwetschke, 1863–1900), xxix, xxi.

2. Calvin argues that man's knowledge of God apart from Scripture comes from God's internal and external revelation to him (*Institutes*, 1.3–5). The former—God's internal revelation—he speaks of as man's *sensus divinitatis, sensus deitatis*, and *semen religionis*:

"There is within the human mind . . . an *awareness of divinity (divinitatis sensum)*. . . . They who in other aspects of life seem least to differ from brutes still continue to retain some seed of religion *(semen religionis)*. . . . [There is] a sense of deity *(sensus deitatis)* inscribed in the hearts of all [1.3.1]."

"The sense of divinity, which they greatly wished to have extinguished, thrives and presently burgeons. From this we conclude that [man's knowledge of God] is not a doctrine that must first be learned in school, but one of which each of us is master from his mother's womb and which nature itself permits no one to forget, although many strive with every nerve to this end [1.3.3]."

"God has sown a seed of religion in all men. But scarcely one man in a hundred is met with who fosters it, once received, in his heart, and none in whom it ripens—much less shows fruit in season [1.4.1]."

"[Men] entangle themselves in such a huge mass of errors that blind wickedness stifles and finally extinguishes those sparks which once flashed forth to show them God's glory. Yet that seed remains which can in no wise be uprooted: that there is some sort of divinity; but this seed is so corrupted that by itself it produces only the worst fruits [1.4.4]."

This internal knowledge of God is instinctive (1.3.1) and ineradicable (1.3.3); hence no real atheists exist (1.3.2), but it is ineffective (1.4.1), producing in the ungodly "only the worst fruits," namely, all the false religions of the world (1.4.4) that are marked by superstition (1.4.1–3) and by hypocrisy (1.4.4).

The latter—God's external revelation—comes to man both in and by the natural creation itself ("this skillful ordering of the universe is for us a sort of mirror in which we can contemplate God who is otherwise invisible," 1.5.1) and in providence (1.5.7–10), both comprising

The Necessity of Holy Scripture for
a True Knowledge of God (1.6)

Because natural revelation will never bring the fallen creature to a knowledge of the one living and true God, "Scripture Is Needed as Guide and Teacher for Anyone Who Would Come to God the Creator" (title of 1.6). Alongside natural revelation ("this most glorious theater," 1.6.2) God has placed the Scriptures as "another and better help" to direct us to God (1.6.1).

Calvin employs three metaphors to make his point. First, the Scriptures are spectacles placed upon blind eyes that enable men properly to interpret God's revelation in creation and the light of nature in man:

> Just as old or bleary-eyed men and those with weak vision, if you thrust before them a most beautiful volume, even if they recognize it to be some sort of writing, yet can scarcely construe two words, but with the aid of spectacles will begin to read distinctly; so Scripture, gathering up the otherwise confused knowledge of God in our minds, having dispersed our dullness, clearly shows us the true God. [1.6.1; see also 1.14.1]

Second, the Scriptures are a thread running through a labyrinth. Man by nature is sinfully wrong-minded, according to Calvin, and is faced with the "inexplicable labyrinth" of the "splendor of the divine countenance." We cannot comprehend it, and it will ever remain a puzzle to us "unless we are conducted into it by the thread of the Word; so that it is better to limp along this path than to dash with all speed outside it" (1.6.3).

Third, *the Scriptures are our teacher*: "in order that true religion may shine upon us, we ought to hold that it must take its beginning from heav-

---

a "dazzling theater." But "however much the glory of God shines forth, scarcely one man in a hundred is a true spectator of it!" (1.5.8). So these external revelational means are also ineffective, due to the corruption of the human heart (1.5.11–12). The actual effect of natural theology then is man's inexcusability before God (1.5.13–15). By this point Calvin has, in effect, crossed out all natural theology as in any way being able to help fallen man to know God. This is the profound argument Calvin gives for the necessity of Scripture (see his title of 1.6.1 and Westminster Confession 1.1)!

enly doctrine and that no one can get even the slightest taste of right and sound doctrine unless he be *a pupil of Scripture*" (1.6.2, emphasis added). Therefore, Calvin states,

> In order that truth might abide forever in the world with a continuing succession of teaching and survive through all ages, the same oracles he gave the patriarchs it was his pleasure to have recorded, as it were, on public tablets. [1.6.2]

> Without Scripture we fall into error . . . [since] his likeness imprinted upon the most beautiful form of the universe [is] insufficiently effective. . . . [But] Scripture can communicate to us what the revelation in the creation cannot. . . . Since God in vain calls all peoples to himself by the contemplation of heaven and earth, [his Word] is *the very school of God's children.* [1.6.3–4, emphasis added]

According to Calvin, then, because "daily oracles are not sent from heaven, for it pleased the Lord to hallow his truth to everlasting remembrance in the Scriptures alone . . . the Scriptures obtain full authority among believers only when men regard them as having sprung from heaven, as if there the living words of God were heard" (1.7.1).

The Authority of Holy Scripture (1.7)

Book 1, chapters 7–9 comprise the heart of Calvin's view of Holy Scripture. For Calvin the Bible is the divinely inspired Word of God: "Scripture is from God . . . it has flowed to us from the very mouth of God by the ministry of men" (1.7.5). "The Sacred Scriptures, which so far surpass all gifts and graces of human endeavor, breathe something divine" (1.8.1). While he acknowledged that the Scripture writings reflect the diverse styles of their several writers, Calvin argued that this fact in no way impinges upon the full divinity of Scripture in the whole and in the part:

> I admit that some of the prophets had an elegant and clear, even brilliant, manner of speaking, so that their eloquence yields nothing to

secular writers . . . while [the Holy Spirit] elsewhere used a rude and unrefined style. But whether you read David, Isaiah, and the like, whose speech flows sweet and pleasing, or Amos the herdsman, Jeremiah, and Zechariah, whose harsher style savors of rusticity, that majesty of the Spirit . . . will be evident everywhere. [1.8.2]

The Bible's Authority Not Dependent on the Church

Calvin argues that the church is not the Christian's final and ultimate authority in matters of faith and life as the Roman Catholic Church claimed in his day and still claims today:

A most pernicious error widely prevails that Scripture has only so much weight as is conceded to it by the consent of the church. As if the eternal and inviolable truth of God depended upon the decision of man! For they mock the Holy Spirit when they ask: Who can convince us that these writings came from God? Who can assure us that Scripture has come down whole and intact to our very day? . . . Thus these sacrilegious men, wishing to impose an unbridled tyranny under the cover of the church, do not care with what absurdities they ensnare themselves and others, provided that they can force this one idea upon the simpleminded: that the church has authority in all things. Yet, if this is so, what will happen to miserable consciences seeking firm assurance of eternal life if all promises of it consist in and depend upon the judgment of men? [1.7.1]

But such wranglers are neatly refuted by just one word of the apostle. He testifies that the church is "built upon the foundation of the prophets and apostles." If the teaching of the prophets and the apostles is the foundation, this must have had an authority before the church began to exist. Groundless, too, is their subtle objection that, although the church took its beginning here, the writings to be attributed to the prophets and apostles nevertheless remain in doubt until decided by the church. . . . Thus, while the church receives and gives its seal of approval to the Scriptures, it does not thereby render authentic what is otherwise doubtful or controversial. But because the church recognizes Scripture to be the truth of its own God, as a pious duty it unhesitatingly venerates Scripture. . . . Scripture exhibits fully as clear evidence of its own truth as white and black things do of their color, or sweet and bitter things do of their taste. [1.7.2]

The Bible's Authority Dependent upon God, Its Author, Who Is Truth Itself (see Westminster Confession of Faith 1.4)

The Holy Spirit speaking in Holy Scripture is the believer's final and ultimate authority in all matters of belief and behavior. But the inner witness of the Holy Spirit, working by and with the Word in his heart, Calvin argued, confirms to the believer that the Bible is God's Word. That is to say, the Christian's confidence in Holy Scripture as the Word of God is produced by the Holy Spirit who graciously bears witness in the believer's heart at regeneration to the truthfulness of God's Word being proclaimed to him. Calvin writes that the "credibility of doctrine is not established until we are persuaded beyond doubt that God is its Author. Thus, the highest proof of Scripture derives in general form from the fact that God in person speaks in it." He continues,

> If we desire to provide in the best way for our consciences—that they may not be perpetually beset by the instability of doubt or vacillation, and that they may not also boggle at the smallest quibbles—*we ought to seek our conviction in a higher place than human reason, judgments, or conjectures, that is, in the secret testimony of the Spirit.* True, if we wished to proceed by arguments, we might advance many things that would easily prove ... that the law, the prophets, and the gospel come from [God]. Indeed, ever so learned men, endowed with the highest judgment, rise up in opposition and bring to bear and display all their mental powers in this debate. Yet, unless they become hardened to the point of hopeless impudence, this confession will be wrested from them: that they see manifest signs of God speaking in Scripture.[3] From this it is clear that the teaching of Scripture is from heaven. [1.7.4, emphasis added]

3. The Westminster Confession of Faith, 1.5 describes these internal divine *indicia*, specifically, "the heavenliness of the matter, the efficacy of the doctrine, the majesty of the style, the consent of all the parts, the scope of the whole (which is to give all glory to God), the full discovery [disclosure] it makes of the only way of man's salvation, the many other incomparable excellencies, and the entire perfection thereof," as "arguments whereby [the Scripture] doth abundantly *evidence itself* to be the Word of God" (emphasis added).

Calvin called it "backward" to attempt to prove Scripture's authority "through disputation." He forsook "dexterity or eloquence," even though the "clamourous voices" of skeptics could be easily silenced. His reasoning was that even with superior debating ability, until God "imprint[ed] upon their hearts that certainty that piety requires," unbelievers would "stand by opinion alone." Calvin argued, however, that

> the testimony of the Spirit is more excellent than all reason. For as God alone is a fit witness of himself in his Word, so also the Word will not find acceptance in men's hearts before it is sealed by the inward testimony of the Spirit. The same Spirit, therefore, who has spoken through the mouths of the prophets must penetrate into our hearts to persuade us that they faithfully proclaimed what had been divinely commanded. [1.7.4]

Calvin believed that it was not

> right to subject [Scripture] to proof and reasoning. And the certainty it deserves with us, it attains by the testimony of the Spirit. For even if it wins reverence for itself by its own majesty, it seriously affects us only when it is sealed upon our hearts through the Spirit. Therefore, illumined by his power, we believe neither by our own nor by anyone else's judgment that Scripture is from God; but above human judgment we affirm with utter certainty (just as if we were gazing upon the majesty of God himself) that it has flowed to us from the very mouth of God by the ministry of men. [1.7.5]

He concludes this topic by stating:

> Such, then, is a conviction that requires no reasons; such, a knowledge with which the best reason agrees—in which the mind truly reposes more securely and constantly than in any reasons; such, finally, a feeling that can be born only of heavenly revelation. I speak of nothing other than what each believer experiences within himself—though my words fall far beneath a just explanation of the matter. [1.7.5]

50

The Self-Authenticating Character
of Holy Scripture (1.7.5)

> Let this point therefore stand: that . . . Scripture indeed is self-authenticated [*autopiston*]; hence, it is not right to subject it to proof and reasoning. [1.7.5]

By asserting that Scripture is *autopiston*, that is, "self-authenticated,"[4] Calvin asserted the self-attesting character of Holy Scripture. He not only clearly understood that the Bible is man's only foundation for the certainty of knowledge, but also recognized that the Word of God would, of necessity, have to be self-attesting, carrying within itself its own divine *indicia* (see Westminster Confession of Faith 1.5), for if it needed anyone or anything other than itself to authenticate and validate its divine character—based on the principle that the validating source is always the higher and final authority (see Heb. 6:13)—it would not be the Word of God because the validating source would be the higher authority.[5]

The Credibility of Holy Scripture (1.8)

Some scholars have contended that Calvin, having vigorously argued in 1.7 that "we ought to seek our conviction in a higher place than human reason, judgments, or conjectures, that is, in the secret testimony of the Spirit," reversed himself when he wrote 1.8, titled "So Far as Human

---

4. In his French translation of the *Institutes*, Calvin's words here are *porte avec soi sa créance*, that is, "carries with[in] itself its [own] credentials."

5. When Christ as the incarnate Son of God authenticated the Scriptures, he was authenticating his own Word, and he was doing it according to his own declared authority in keeping with the principle he enunciated in John 8:14: "if I do bear witness about myself, my testimony is true, for I know where I came from and where I am going." The point to note is that Jesus validated his claims by appealing to his knowledge of himself, unintimidated by the charge of *petitio principii* or begging the question (Jesus' appeal to self-knowledge here accords with the divine procedure stipulated in Heb. 6:13: "When God made a promise to Abraham, since he had no one greater by whom to swear, he swore by himself"). Since then the words of Scripture are the words of Christ, one must never separate the words of Scripture from the Christ of Scripture. It is the same self-attesting Word speaking in and through both.

Reason Goes, Sufficiently Firm Proofs Are at Hand to Establish the Credibility of Scripture." While the chapter may contain some ambiguities with reference to his doctrine of *sola scriptura* as man's only rule in matters of belief and behavior, Calvin prepared his reader for this chapter both by his earlier comment, "if we wished to proceed by arguments, we might advance many things that would easily prove—if there is any God in heaven—that the law, the prophets, and the gospel come from him," and by his caveat in the chapter's title, "So Far as Human Reason Goes." So he obviously did not feel the reversal that some scholars have ascribed to him.

Rather, a careful reading of this much-discussed chapter, which in my opinion Calvin would have been better advised to title "Self-Evidencing Arguments from Scripture for the Credibility of Scripture," will show, I think, that Calvin is in the main presenting *biblical* data in favor of the Bible's truthfulness. Virtually all of his argumentation for the credibility of Scripture—the "very heavenly majesty," the "beautiful agreement of all the parts," the "incontestable miracles" and the "confirmed prophecy" of the Old Testament (1.8.3–10) and the "heavenly character of its doctrine" and the "simplicity" and "authority" of the New Testament (1.8.11)—is drawn from the Bible. What little evidence he advances that is not drawn directly from Scripture—the indestructibility of Scripture through the ages, its wide acceptance by the nations, martyrs willing to die for it (1.8.12–13)—is not the primary thrust of his chapter by any means. And in my opinion, this evidence not drawn from Scripture is not compelling since the same could be said of other books such as the Koran. And to the degree that he used it, he compromised his own *sola scriptura* principle.

Benjamin Warfield, heir as he was to the empirical apologetic based on Thomas Reid's Scottish common sense realism that ruled at Princeton Seminary, understood 1.8 as setting forth a list of evidentiary proofs by which the witnessing Spirit leads us to conclude that the Bible is divine, and therefore these proofs, taken up by Warfield into a "probability argument," become the direct ground of our faith in Scripture.[6] His view relates the Spirit's testimony directly to the *indicia* of the Scripture as proofs and

---

6. See my *Faith's Reasons for Believing* (Ross-shire, Scotland: Christian Focus, 2008), chapter 8, for my fuller discussion of Warfield's apologetic method.

not to the divine authorship of Scripture.[7] I would argue that the Holy
Spirit illumines the human mind, that is, brings conviction to it, directly
by means of the Word of God as such, with the proofs being "secondary
aids to our feebleness":

> There are other reasons [than the ones mentioned in 1.8], neither few
> nor weak, for which the dignity and majesty of Scripture are not only
> affirmed in godly hearts, but brilliantly vindicated against the wiles of
> its disparagers; yet of themselves these are not strong enough to provide
> firm faith, until our Heavenly Father, revealing his majesty there, lifts
> reverence for Scripture beyond the realm of controversy. Therefore
> Scripture will ultimately suffice for *a saving knowledge* of God only
> when its certainty is founded upon the inward persuasion of the Holy
> Spirit. [1.8.13, emphasis added]

By saying these things in 1.8.13, Calvin affirms the same view that he
espoused in 1.7. So there is no contradiction between the two sections.
In short, Calvin's view relates the Spirit's testimonial work directly to the
authority of the Word of God and not to its proofs, a view that I personally think is truer to Scripture than is Warfield's.

After underscoring the two facts that this special testimony of the
Spirit neither brings a new revelation, for then this new revelation would
call for further attestation ad infinitum, nor is it identical with the faith

---

7. Warfield argues in "The Westminster Doctrine of Scripture" in *Selected Shorter Writings
of Benjamin B. Warfield* (Nutley, N J: P&R, 1973), 2:560–87, that because the Confession
of Faith lists the sixty-six books of the Bible in 1.2a and declares in 1.2b, "all which are given
by inspiration of God," the evidentiary issues of canonics and inspiration were being presupposed when it stated what it did in 1.4 about the Bible's authority. In other words, asserts
Warfield, the Confession of Faith is teaching that "the authority of a book of Scripture rests
on its being of divine inspiration and part of the canon as previously settled facts" (565),
and that "the order of procedure in ascertaining Scripture is to settle first the canon, then
its inspiration, and then, as a corollary, its authority" (565). This procedure, while it accords
with Warfield's apologetic method, does not agree with Calvin's position. Moreover, it is a
stretch to derive an apologetic method from the order in which the Confession logically
presents its confessional data. Before the issue of canonics was ever addressed in the early
church, the Old Testament and the individual books of the New, being immediately inspired
by God, were already at work in the church, growing and nurturing the church. They were
both recognized as inspired Scripture and authoritative and received the church's submission
to them long before the issue of canonics was addressed in any formal sense.

experience per se inasmuch as the Spirit's testimony is the efficient cause (*causa efficiens*) of faith, Louis Berkhof elaborates:

> The Testimony of the Holy Spirit is simply the work of the Holy Spirit in the heart of the sinner by which he removes the blindness of sin, so that the erstwhile blind man, who had no eyes for the sublime character of the Word of God, now clearly sees and appreciates the marks of its divine nature, and receives immediate certainty respecting the divine origin of Scripture. . . . The Christian believes the Bible to be the Word of God in the last analysis on the testimony which God Himself gives respecting this matter in His Word, and recognizes that Word as divine by means of the testimony of God in his heart. The testimony of the Holy Spirit is therefore . . . not so much the final ground of faith, but rather the means of faith. The final ground of faith is Scripture only, or better still, the authority of God which is impressed upon the believer in the testimony of Scripture. The ground of faith is identical with its contents, and cannot be separated from it. But the testimony of the Holy Spirit is the moving cause of faith. We believe Scripture, not because of, but through the testimony of the Holy Spirit.[8]

The Unity of the Holy Scripture and the Holy Spirit (1.9)

In 1.9 Calvin deals with those whom he calls fanatics—here he has in mind such Anabaptists as B. Hubmaier, H. Denck, and L. Haetzer, such rationalists as Sebastian Franck, and such spiritualists as Thomas Muenzer, A. B. Karlstadt, and K. Schwenkfeld—who separate the Spirit of God from the Word of God and elevate the former in their experience over the latter:

> I should like to know from them what this spirit is by whose inspiration they are borne up so high that they dare despise the Scriptural doctrine as childish and mean . . . by a heinous sacrilege these rascals tear apart those things which [Isaiah 59:21] joined together with an inviolable bond. [1.9.1]

8. Louis Berkhof, *Introductory Volume to Systematic Theology* (Grand Rapids: Eerdmans, 1932), 182–85.

We ought zealously to apply ourselves both to read and to hearken to Scripture if indeed we want to receive any gain and benefit from the Spirit of God. [1.9.2]

The Holy Spirit so inheres in His truth, which He expresses in Scripture, that only when its proper reverence and dignity are given to the Word does the Holy Spirit show forth His power. . . . By a kind of mutual bond the Lord has joined together the certainty of his Word and of his Spirit so that the perfect religion of the Word may abide in our minds when the Spirit, who causes us to contemplate God's grace, shines. [1.9.3]

In sum, Calvin argues in 1.9 that the Spirit without the Word is a delusion and the Word without the Spirit is dead. Word and Spirit ever belong together and must never be separated.

The Agreement between the Knowledge of God Revealed in Creation and the Knowledge of God Revealed in Holy Scripture (1.10)

Chapter 1.10 might best be titled "The Agreement between the Knowledge of God Revealed in Creation and the Knowledge of God Revealed in Holy Scripture," for in a certain sense 1.10 attaches to 1.6 ("Scripture Is Needed as Guide and Teacher for Anyone Who Would Come to God the Creator") and forms a conclusion to Calvin's whole treatment of Scripture, with chapters 7–9 in which he sets forth his view of sacred Scripture nestled between them. Calvin begins this section by stating that "the knowledge of God, otherwise clearly set forth in the system of the universe and in all creatures, is nonetheless more intimately and also more vividly revealed in his Word. But now it is worthwhile to ponder whether the Lord represents himself to us in Scripture as we previously saw him delineate himself in his works" (1.10.1).

In 1.10.2 Calvin argues that "the attributes of God according to Scripture agree with those known in his creatures," but with Scripture describing God's attributes more clearly. Interestingly, however, perhaps because he believed that God "speaks sparingly of his essence" in Scripture (1.13.1), Calvin hardly treats in any systematic fashion at all God's attributes, the nearest thing to a treatment of them by him in the *Institutes* occurring here in 1.10.2 where, basing his comment on Jeremiah 9:24, he speaks of God's justice, mercy, and judgment as the "three things [that] are especially necessary for us to know" about God, although he immediately declares:

> Neither [God's] truth, nor power, nor holiness, nor goodness is thus overlooked. For how could we have the requisite knowledge of his justice, mercy, and judgment unless that knowledge rested upon his unbending truth? And without understanding his power, how could we believe that he rules the earth in judgment and justice? But whence comes his mercy save from his goodness? If, finally, "all his paths are mercy," judgment, justice, in these also is his holiness visible. [1.10.2]

This is largely the sum and substance of Calvin's systematic exposition of God's attributes in his *Institutes*, if one can even call it that. I do not intend to suggest that Calvin did not mention other attributes of God, for he often speaks in his *Institutes* of God as a self-existent, simple, invisible, incomprehensible Spirit who is infinite, immense, eternal, and perfect in his being, power, knowledge, wisdom, righteousness, justice, holiness, goodness, and truth; who is severe, clement, merciful, pitying, gracious, beneficent, and benign; who is our Lord, Creator, Sustainer, Governor, and Judge, and who as our defender and protector is our Father.[9] Such a list of attributes, however, hardly supports Calvin's contention that God speaks sparingly in Scripture of his essence.

Of course, when Calvin said this, I think that what he also intended to say is that Scripture reveals God "not as he is in himself, but as he is toward us" (1.10.2). Calvin believed that God accommodated the revelation of himself in Scripture to "our slight capacity." Accordingly, we do not know God as he is in himself (*in se*) but only as he revealed himself to us. Elsewhere Calvin makes the same point:

> Who even of slight intelligence does not understand that, as nurses commonly do with infants, God is wont in a measure to "lisp" in speaking to us? Thus such forms of speaking do not so much express clearly what

9. See Benjamin Warfield, "Calvin's Doctrine of God," in *The Works of Benjamin B. Warfield* (Grand Rapids: Baker, 1991), 168–69, for the specific locations in the *Institutes* where he speaks of these attributes.

God is like as accommodate the knowledge of him to our slight capacity. To do this he must descend far beneath his loftiness. [1.13.1]

Because our weakness does not attain to his exalted state, the description of him that is given to us [in and by Scripture] must be accommodated to our capacity so that we may understand it. Now the mode of accommodation is for him to represent himself to us *not as he is in himself, but as he seems to us.* Although he is beyond all disturbance of mind, yet he testifies that he is angry toward sinners. Therefore whenever we hear that God is angered, we ought not to imagine any emotion in him, but rather to consider that this expression has been taken from our own human experience; because God, whenever he is exercising judgment, exhibits the appearance of one kindled and angered. [1.17.13]

Calvin appears to mean by these statements that because of our finitude God could not give to us a univocal verbal depiction of himself as he is in himself. Rather, what we possess is at best only a finite representation of God, and thus ours is an understanding of him "as he seems to us" and not as he is in himself. I would counsel that we should not follow Calvin here since we can know on the basis of God's verbal self-revelation many things about him in the same sense that he knows them. That is why God gave us the Bible in the first place—that we might know him. Of course, we will not know God exhaustively, but we can know him truly as he is in himself.

The Inerrancy of Holy Scripture

One final issue yet remains to be addressed: Did Calvin regard the Bible's autographs[10] as inerrant in all that they taught? Of course, the church had always held

10. Some critical scholars argue that the distinction that evangelicals make between inerrant autographs and errant apographs is of fairly recent vintage. Indeed, it is an evangelical ploy, they say, to minimize the impact of the "assured results" of textual criticism. This is erroneous. Augustine, who represents generally the opinion of the patristic age, drew this same distinction in his Epistle (82) to Jerome:

I have learned to defer this respect and honor to the canonical books of Scripture alone, that I most firmly believe that no one of their authors has committed any error in

that the Bible is the Word of God in such a sense that its words, though written by men and bearing indelibly impressed upon them the marks of their human origin, were written, nevertheless, under such an influence of the Holy Spirit as to be also the words of God, the adequate expression of His mind and will.... The Spirit's superintendence extends to the choice of the words by the human authors (verbal inspiration), and preserves its product from everything inconsistent with a divine authorship—thus securing, among other things, that entire truthfulness which is everywhere presupposed in and asserted for Scripture by the Biblical writers (inerrancy).[11]

In spite of Calvin's careful exegesis of Scripture in his commentaries, Calvin scholars today hotly debate whether Calvin believed in biblical inerrancy as the church has always confessed. Warfield contended:

Calvin held [the sixty-six books of canonical Scripture] to be the very Word of God. This assertion he intended in its simplest and most literal sense. He was far from overlooking the fact that the Scriptures were written by human hands: he expressly declares that, though we have received them from God's own mouth, we have nevertheless received them "through the ministry of men" (1.7.5). But he was equally far from conceiving that the relation of their human authors to their divine author resembled to any degree that of free intermediaries, who, after receiving the divine word, could do with it what they listed. On the contrary, he thought of them rather as notaries (4.8.9), who set down in authentic registers (1.6.3) what was dictated to them. They wrote, therefore, merely as the organs of the Holy Ghost.... The diversity of the human authors thus disappears for Calvin before the unity of the Spirit, the sole responsible author of Scripture, which ... is *a Deo*; it has "come down to us from the very mouth of God" (1.7.5). It has "come down to us from heaven as if the living words of God themselves were heard in it" (1.7.1); and "we owe it therefore the same reverence which

---

writing. And if in their writings I am perplexed by anything that seems to me contrary to truth, I do not doubt that it is nothing else than either that the [copied] manuscript is corrupt, or that the translator has not followed what was said, or that I have myself failed to understand it.

11. Benjamin Warfield, "The Real Problem of Inspiration," in *The Inspiration and Authority of the Bible* (Philadelphia: P&R, 1948), 173.

we owe to God Himself, since it has proceeded from Him alone, and there is nothing human mixed with it" (commentary on 2 Timothy 3:16). According to this declaration the Scriptures are altogether divine, and in them, as he puts it energetically in another place, "it is God who speaks with us and not mortal men" (commentary on 2 Peter 1:20). Accordingly, he cites Scripture everywhere not as the word of man but as the pure word of God.[12]

While he did not accept the inerrancy of the Bible's autographs himself, Edward A. Dowey Jr. acknowledged that Calvin not only "conceived the Scriptures as literally dictated by God"[13] but also as inerrant in the autographs: "There is no hint anywhere in Calvin's writings that the original text contained any flaws at all.... According to Calvin the Scriptures were so given that—whether by 'literal' or 'figurative' dictation—the result was a series of documents errorless in their original form."[14]

Kenneth S. Kantzer argued as well that the evidence supporting the view that Calvin held to the

> rigidly orthodox verbal type of inspiration ... is so transparent that any endeavor to clarify his position seems almost to be a work of supererogation.... the merest glance at Calvin's commentaries will demonstrate how seriously the Reformer applied his rigid doctrine of verbal inerrancy to his exegesis of Scripture.... Attempts to discover a looser view of inspiration in Calvin's teaching fall flat upon examination.[15]

John Murray further corroborated this conclusion:

> [Calvin] affirms most explicitly that the Scripture is from God, that it comes to us from the very mouth of God, and that in believing the Scripture we feel the firmest conviction that we hold an invincible truth. To insinuate that this conviction has respect simply to the heavenly

12. Benjamin Warfield, "Calvin's Doctrine of the Knowledge of God," in *The Works of Benjamin B. Warfield* (Grand Rapids: Baker, 1991), 5:60–62.
13. Edward A. Dowey Jr., *The Knowledge of God in Calvin's Theology* (Grand Rapids: Eerdmans, 1994), 99.
14. Ibid., 100–102.
15. Kenneth S. Kantzer, "Calvin and the Holy Scriptures," in *Inspiration and Interpretation*, ed. John F. Walvoord (Grand Rapids: Eerdmans, 1957), 137, 142ff.

doctrine, as distinct from Scripture as the depository, is to interject a distinction of which there is no suggestion in the relevant passages. In other words, Calvin identifies the doctrine of which he speaks with the Scripture itself. . . . His jealousy for the original text cannot be dissociated from his estimate of Scripture as the oracles of God, that Scripture has nothing human mixed with it, and in all its parts it is as if we heard the mouth of God speaking from heaven.[16]

J. I. Packer also affirmed: "The attribution to [Calvin] of a willingness to admit error in Scripture rests on a superficial mis-reading of what he actually says."[17]

Other American scholars, however, such as Charles Augustus Briggs of Union Seminary, New York,[18] have urged that, while Calvin believed that the Bible is the authoritative Word of God, his view of inspiration "was not the high doctrine of plenary, verbal inspiration, espoused by the Reformed dogmaticians of the seventeenth century";[19] more specifically, he did not espouse the inerrancy of the Bible's original autographs. For example, John T. McNeill writes: "The authority of the Bible as God's Word and the source of indisputable truth is never called in question by Calvin. . . . Yet he is not concerned to assert what in later controversy has been spoken of as 'verbal inerrancy.'"[20] Jack B. Rogers and Donald K. McKim urged the same view.[21] This latter contention is based not on remarks in Calvin's *Institutes* but on statements Calvin makes in his commentaries. But if these scholars who say that Calvin occasionally admitted the presence of errors in the auto-graphs—which I deny he did—are correct, they should, at least, acknowledge

16. John Murray, "Calvin's Doctrine of Scripture," in *Calvin on Scripture and Divine Sovereignty* (Philadelphia: P&R, 1960), 21, 28.

17. James I. Packer, "Calvin's View of Scripture," in *God's Inerrant Word*, ed. John Warwick Montgomery (Minneapolis: Bethany Fellowship, 1974), 105.

18. Charles Augustus Briggs, *The Bible, Church, and Reason* (New York: Scribner, 1892), 110ff., 219ff.

19. Murray, "Calvin's Doctrine of Scripture," 11. Murray, as we noted, does not share this view.

20. John T. McNeill, "Introduction" to John Calvin, *Institutes of the Christian Religion*, 2 vols., trans. Ford Lewis Battles, Library of Christian Classics 20–21 (Philadelphia: Westminster, 1960), 1:liv.

21. Jack B. Rogers and Donald K. McKim, *The Authority and Interpretation of the Bible* (New York: Harper and Row, 1979), 89–116.

that these admissions were a case of "Homer nodding" (Packer) since it is apparent that over his long career Calvin uncompromisingly and everywhere argued to the contrary for biblical inerrancy. His classic statements in this regard deserve extended quotation:

> Where it pleased the Lord to raise up a more visible form of the church, he willed to have his Word [in the context he is referring to the law] set down and sealed in writing. . . . He commanded that the prophecies also be committed to writing and be accounted part of his Word. At the same time, histories were added to these, also the labor of the prophets, but composed under the Holy Spirit's dictation.[22] I include the psalms with the prophecies, since what we attribute to the prophecies is common to them.
>
> Therefore, that whole body, put together out of law, prophecies, psalms, and histories, was the Lord's Word for the ancient people. . . . *All perfection was contained in it.*
>
> Let this be a firm principle: No other word is to be held as the Word of God, and given place as such in the church, than what is contained first in the Law and the Prophets, then in the writings of the apostles [who] were to expound the ancient Scripture and to show that what is taught there has been fulfilled in Christ. Yet they were not to do this except from the Lord, that is, with Christ's Spirit as precursor in a certain measure dictating the words (*verba quodammodo dictante Christi Spiritu*) [the adverb *quodammodo* would be better translated "in a certain sense"[23]]. [The apostles] were sure and genuine scribes

22. Calvin's occasional references to the Spirit's "dictating" Scripture and using the biblical writers as his "amanuenses" should be viewed as a theological metaphor meaning simply that what is written in Scripture bears the same relation to the mind of God, its ultimate source, as a letter written by a good secretary bears to the mind of the person from whom he or she took it (Packer), for Calvin did not deny, as we have already seen, the variations of style among the penmen themselves.

23. McNeill, basing his remarks on material supplied primarily by Dowey and Battles, with incidental contributions from other sources, in his comment on Calvin's phrase (*Institutes*, 2:1155–576 n. 7) goes beyond the evidence when he states that the adverb is a "*deliberate* qualification, *discounting* any doctrine of exact verbal inspiration. The context has reference to teaching, not words merely, showing that Calvin's point is not verbal inerrancy, but the authoritative message of Scripture" (emphasis added).

McNeill will not face the fact that a biblical document's authority depends upon its inerrant truthfulness. Anyone who affirms on the one hand that the Bible is God's authoritative Word and on the other that its autographs contained errors has a major epistemological

of the Holy Spirit (*certi et authentici Spiritus sancti amanuenses*[24]), and their writings are therefore to be considered the oracles of God; and the sole office of others is to teach what is provided and sealed in the Holy Scriptures. [4.8.6, 8–9]

Commenting on 2 Timothy 3:16 he writes:

[Paul] commends the Scripture, first, on account of its authority, and, second, on account of the utility that springs from it. In order to uphold the authority of Scripture, he declares it to be divinely inspired (*divinitus inspiratam*): for if it be so, it is beyond all controversy that men should receive it with reverence. . . . Whoever then wishes to profit in the Scriptures, let him first of all lay down as a settled point this—that the law and the prophecies are not teaching delivered by the will of men, but dictated (*dictatam*) by the Holy Spirit. . . . Moses and the prophets did not utter at random what we have from their hand, but, since they spoke by divine impulse, they confidently and fearlessly testified, as was actually the case, that it was the mouth of the Lord that spoke (*os Domini locutum esse*). . . . We owe to the Scripture the same reverence that we owe to God, because it has proceeded from him alone, and has nothing of man mixed with it (*nec quicquam humani habet admixtum*).

Scholars who deny that Calvin held to inerrancy for the autographs do so, as I have already stated, on the basis of certain remarks that he makes in his commentaries on Genesis 1:16; Matthew 8:23–27 (compare Mark 4:35–41; Luke 8:22–25); Matthew 27:9; Acts 7:14–16; Romans 3:4; 9:10; 11:12; 14:1; Ephesians 4:8; and Hebrews 11:21. But Kantzer in his essay "Calvin and the Holy Scriptures," Murray in

---

problem on his hands, namely, to explain how the Spirit of truth, in order to provide mankind with guidance into all truth, could move men to write propositions in Scripture that contain errors, the very opposite of truth.

24. McNeill affirms on page 1157, footnote 9: "This passage has been held to support the view that Calvin's doctrine of the inspiration of Scripture was one of verbal inerrancy. Yet he has no explicit support of such a view anywhere else, and here he immediately makes it clear that his interest is in the teaching rather than in the form of expression." But Murray is correct when he observed: "To insinuate that [Calvin's assertions have] respect simply to the heavenly doctrine, as distinct from Scripture as the depository, is to interject a distinction of which there is no suggestion in the relevant passages. In other words, Calvin identifies the doctrine of which he speaks with the Scripture itself" (see n.16 above).

his essay "Calvin's Doctrine of Scripture," and J. I. Packer in his essay "Calvin's View of Scripture," all address every one of these remarks and demonstrate that they do not undermine Calvin's high view of Scripture's inerrancy for the biblical autographs. The minute handful of passages in his commentaries—like "a few raindrops in the oceans of the world" (Packer)—where negative questions have been raised may be divided into the following categories:

+ Some are simply places where God has accommodated himself to ordinary forms of human language and is not concerned to speak with the degree of accuracy that goes beyond what these forms of speech would naturally require.
+ Some show signs of having been altered in the course of transmission. In Matthew 27:9, for instance, Calvin tells us that "by mistake" Jeremiah's name has somehow "crept in *(obrepserit)*."
+ Some deal with cases where apostolic writers quote Old Testament texts loosely or paraphrastically in order to bring out the true sense and to make their application.
+ Some constitute what we might call only "formal but not real inaccuracies" in which, since no assertion is intended, therefore no real error can fairly be said to have been made. For example, Calvin denies that the Evangelists meant at every point to write narratives that are chronologically ordered. Therefore, since they did not intend to connect everything in precise chronological order but on occasion preferred to follow a topical or theological principle of arrangement, they cannot be said to contradict each other when they narrate the same event in a different sequence.[25]

It will be apparent to and acknowledged by every fair-minded interpreter that in every one of these cited cases Calvin's concern was to show that the biblical writers did *not* commit error. In conclusion, we must in fairness to Calvin declare that he stood with the church of all ages and did

25. See Murray, "Calvin's Doctrine of Scripture," 12–31, and Packer, "Calvin's View of Scripture," 95–114.

in fact believe that the Bible's original autographs were inerrant. Murray quite properly declares:

> In Calvin we have a mass of perspicuous statement and of length-
> ened argument to the effect that Scripture is impregnable and
> inviolable, and it would be the resort of desperation to take a few
> random comments, wrench them from the total effect of Calvin's
> teaching, and build upon them a thesis which would run counter
> to his own repeated assertions respecting the inviolable character
> of Scripture as the oracles of God, and as having nothing human
> mixed with it.[26]

---

26. Murray, "Calvin's Doctrine of Scripture" in *Calvin on Scripture and Divine Sovereignty*, 31.

4

THE TRUE AND TRIUNE GOD: CALVIN'S DOCTRINE OF THE HOLY TRINITY

INSTITUTES I.II–I3
DOUGLAS F. KELLY

The theology of John Calvin has rightly been called theocentric. He began both the first (1536) and the final (1559) edition of his *Institutes* by noting that to be a human means that we are immediately confronted by knowledge of God, along with knowledge of self, and that these two are so closely intertwined that we can never untangle them.[1] The purpose of our created life is that we may live for the glory of this God, and in so doing find the joy of eternal salvation.

The joy of salvation always follows zeal for the glory of God. As Calvin wrote to Cardinal Sadoleto (who sought to draw back Geneva to

1. John Calvin, *Institutes of the Christian Religion*, ed. John T. McNeill, trans. Ford Lewis Battles, 2 vols., *Library of Christian Classics* 20–21 (Philadelphia: Westminster, 1960), 1.1.1.

the Roman Church after Calvin had been expelled):"It is not very sound theology to confine a man's thoughts so much to himself, and not to set before him as the prime motive of his existence zeal to show forth the glory of God. For we are born first of all for God and not for ourselves. As all things flowed from him and subsist in him, as Paul says (Rom. 11:36), they ought to be related to him."[2]

Calvin's theological methodology follows this theocentric emphasis (though always with a keen eye to the joy of human salvation.)[3] Early on in the first edition of his *Institutes* (1536), Calvin sets forth the one true God as triune.[4] In his final, 1559 edition, the exposition of the doctrine of the Trinity is still placed early in the much-enlarged volume.[5] As B. B. Warfield noted, Calvin's trinitarian teaching increased about fourfold between 1536 and 1559 (slightly more than the increase of the other parts of the *Institutes*).[6] Thus, in terms both of priority and of sheer amount of content, Calvin holds the being of God to be of utmost importance.

The one true God for whose glory we were created, and whom to know is life eternal (cf. John 17:3), is (1) infinitely spiritual in being and (2) triune in person.

God's Infinite Spirituality

In *Institutes* book 1, chapter 10, God's infinite spirituality is taught, and in the following two chapters, the consequence of that spirituality

2. John Calvin,"Reply to Sadoleto," in *Calvin: Theological Treatises*, Library of Christian Classics 22 (London: SCM, 1954), 228.

3. For instance, Calvin immediately adds to his emphasis on the primacy of God's glory these words in his response (quoted directly above) to Sadoleto:"I acknowledge indeed that the Lord, to recommend the glory of his name to men the better, has tempered zeal for its advance and extension by uniting it indissolubly with our salvation" ("Reply to Sadoleto," 228).

4. Chapter 2—"Containing an Explanation of the Creed (Called Apostolic)." See the translation and annotation by Ford Lewis Battles, *Institutes of the Christian Religion: 1536 Edition* (Grand Rapids: Eerdmans, 1975), 42–58.

5. 1.13 (120–59 in the Battles edition). This section on the Trinity is preceded by two chapters (11 and 12) that deal with the spirituality of God and requisite purity of worship.

6. B. B. Warfield, "The Doctrine of the Trinity," in *Calvin and Augustine* (Philadelphia: P&R, 1956), 219 n. 48.

is applied to the prime duty of God's image-bearers: pure worship that excludes images and pictorial representations of God.

Auguste Lecerf calls "the doctrine of the infinity of God the foundation of Calvinism,"[7] and James H. Thornwell, the nineteenth-century Southern Presbyterian theologian, considered the spirituality and holiness of God absolutely basic to Christian theology,[8] and thus "the foundation of all religious worship; the foundation of all the divine attributes."[9]

In terms of John Calvin's own time, there can be no doubt that his beginning with God's infinitude and spirituality in the various editions of his *Institutes* was related to the sixteenth-century Reformer's desire to purge the Roman Catholic Church of crucial aspects of its worship which he considered to be idolatrous, and thereby not only to dishonor God,[10] but also to "obscure the gospel."[11] But such a reformation could be brought about only by a penitent rethinking of the central doctrine of God, back to its patristic and biblical roots. Who God truly is in his revelation to us profoundly shapes our life, thought, and worship, and hence, above all else, we must seek to know who he is.

Calvin teaches that the reality of God is understood to be, as we have just noted, (1) eternally spiritual and (2) eternally triune. Calvin never disconnects these two interrelated realities (for—with Gregory Nazianzus, whom he quotes—he thinks that to meet the one God is to meet the three persons),[12] but at least he begins his discussion of God in his *Institutes* with God's spirituality, and what it means for worship.

---

7. Auguste Lecerf, *An Introduction to Reformed Dogmatics* (London: Lutterworth, 1949), 379.

8. James H. Thornwell, *The Collected Writings of James Henley Thornwell*, vol. 1, *Theological* (Edinburgh: Banner of Truth, 1974), Lecture VII, 173–88.

9. Ibid., 173.

10. Calvin quotes Isaiah as teaching "that God's majesty is sullied by an unfitting and absurd fiction, when the incorporeal is made to resemble corporeal matter, the invisible a visible likeness, the spirit an inanimate object" (*Institutes* 1.11.2).

11. See Calvin's discussion of how worship is to be purged of anything "that overthrows the chief thing in religion," in his "The True Method of Giving Peace and of Reforming the Church," in *Selected Works of John Calvin: Tracts and Letters*, ed. by Henry Beveridge and Jules Bonnet (Grand Rapids: Baker, 1983), 3:262. Also see James I. Packer's discussion of "ceremonies that obscure the Gospel" in his *A Quest for Godliness: The Puritan Vision of the Christian Life* (Wheaton, IL: Crossway, 1990), ch. 15.

12. See Calvin's *Institutes* 1.13.7, quoting Gregory Nazianzus, *Oratio* 40.41.

So we shall consider God's spirituality, and then go on more fully to speak of his eternal triune existence.

Calvin stated: "For nothing excludes the view that the whole essence of God is spiritual, in which are comprehended Father, Son, and Spirit. This is made plain from Scripture. For as we there hear God called Spirit, so also do we hear the Holy Spirit, seeing that the Spirit is a hypostasis of the whole essence, spoken of as of God and from God."[13] Because of the spirituality of God, Calvin is concerned that "we imagine nothing earthly or carnal of him":

> The Scriptural teaching concerning God's infinite and spiritual essence ought to be enough. . . . But even if God to keep us sober speaks sparingly of his essence, yet by those two titles that I have used [immeasurable and spiritual], he banishes stupid imaginings and restrains the boldness of the human mind. Surely, his infinity ought to make us afraid to try to measure him by our own senses. Indeed, his spiritual nature forbids our imagining anything earthly or carnal of him.[14]

Reflecting on the words of Jesus to the woman of Samaria that "God is spirit" (John 4:24), T. F. Torrance writes in his study of the patristic doctrine of the Trinity:

> God *is* Spirit and is truly known and worshipped as such, for *Spirit* is the specific nature of God's eternal being (*ousia*), whether as Father, Son or Holy Spirit, and therefore . . . their interrelations are to be understood and expressed only in an essentially *spiritual* way. . . . We have to think of the terms [Father and Son] as referring *imagelessly* to the Father and the Son without the intrusion of creaturely images or material forms of thought. It is by linking together in our minds the imaging of the Father by the Son and the imaging of the Son by the Spirit that we are enabled to refer images taken from our human relationships to the Godhead in a spiritual and not in a material or creaturely way.[15]

13. *Institutes* 1.13.20.
14. *Institutes* 1.13.1.
15. T. F. Torrance, *The Trinitarian Faith* (Edinburgh: T. & T. Clark, 1988), 194–95.

We can think of God in a properly spiritual way only by taking our thoughts from his revealed Word, with the assistance of the Holy Spirit who inspired that Word.[16] So, Calvin states: "Indeed, the knowledge of God set forth for us in Scripture is destined for the very same goal as the knowledge whose imprint shines in his creatures, in that it invites us first to fear God, then to trust in him."[17] To attain this goal of glorifying God in human life, Calvin believes that God requires of us humility and restraint in our thoughts and speech of God, so that we never go beyond or against the clear teaching of Holy Scripture:

> Let us use great caution that neither our thoughts nor our speech go beyond the limits to which the Word of God itself extends. For how can the human mind measure off the measureless essence of God according to its own little measure? ... And let us not take it into our heads either to seek out God anywhere else than in his Sacred Word, or to think anything about him that is not prompted by his Word [18]

Of great significance here is the restoration by the Calvinist wing of the sixteenth-century Reformation of the second commandment, which prohibits graven images. (This commandment had been set aside by both Roman Catholics and Lutherans. The Lutherans held that it pertained only to Jews.) T. F. Torrance comments on "the epistemological implications" of Calvin's restoration of the second commandment in his 1536 *Institutes*:

> God is not imaginable. All the images we invent are idols of the mind, products of our own imagination, for God ever remains like himself and is not a spectre or phantasm to be transformed according to our desires. It is a fact, however, that the mind of fallen man remains a perpetual factory of idols and false imaginations of God, so that he is always projecting his own inventions or figments upon God. That is to say, he is constantly tempted to corrupt the knowledge of the truth

16. Calvin writes: "For by a kind of mutual bond the Lord has joined together the certainty of his Word and of his Spirit so that the perfect religion of the Word may abide in our minds when the Spirit, who causes us to contemplate God's face, shines" (*Institutes* 1.9.3).
17. *Institutes* 1.10.2.
18. Ibid., 1.13.21.

through the creations of his own brain. True knowledge is objectively derived and cuts against the speculations and imaginations of the human mind.[19]

But on the contrary, the very fact that we are enabled to speak of and to know truly (though never exhaustively)[20] who God is by means of his Word and Spirit has required an infinite condescension on the part of God. Calvin often speaks of this infinitely gracious condescension to our limited human understanding as God's "lisping" to us, as he accommodates himself massively beneath his infinite loftiness to our frail capacities.[21] God has accommodated himself to us in his written Word and supremely in his incarnate Word—his Son,[22] both of whom we meet (i.e., the Father and the Son) by the divine ministrations of the Holy Spirit.[23] That is why

19. T. F. Torrance, *The Hermeneutics of John Calvin* (Edinburgh: Scottish Academic Press, 1988), 91–92.

20. See *Institutes* 3.2.14: "When we call faith 'knowledge' we do not mean comprehension of the sort that is commonly concerned with those things which fall under human sense perception. . . . Even where the mind has attained, it does not comprehend what it feels." T. F. Torrance has explicated this distinction between apprehension and comprehension in his *Theological Science* (London: Oxford University Press, 1969): "There are acts of conception in which, as it were, we can get our fingers round something and enclose it in our grasp, but there are other acts of conception in which what we are grasping at is too big to get our fingers round, for as we grasp or conceive it, it transcends us, so that even in genuine apprehension there cannot be full comprehension" (p. 15). Saint Hilary, whom Calvin so often followed, had stated in the mid-fourth century the all-important distinction between *apprehension* of God (which is possible for humans) and *comprehension* of God (which for us is impossible): "The perfect knowledge of God is so to know Him that we are sure we must not be ignorant of Him, yet cannot describe Him. We must believe, must apprehend, must worship; and such acts of devotion must stand in lieu of definition . . . the proper service of faith is to grasp and confess the truth that it is incompetent to comprehend its Object" (*On the Trinity* 2.7.11).

21. *Institutes* 1.13.1. Also note the important article by Ford Lewis Battles, "God Was Accommodating Himself to Human Capacity," in Robert Benedetto, *Interpreting John Calvin: Ford Lewis Battles* (Baker, 1996), 117–37.

22. "God is comprehended in Christ alone" (*Institutes* 2.6.4).

23. See Calvin's Sermon on Luke 2:50–52, in *Calvini Opera* 46:477, where he discusses how the Holy Spirit applies to us all that Christ accomplished for us, thus bringing us into the very presence of God the Father. See also *Institutes* 3.2.34: "It is through the Spirit that we come to grasp 'the mind of Christ' [1 Cor. 2:16]. . . . Indeed, the Word of God is like the sun, shining upon all those to whom it is proclaimed, but with no effect among the blind. Now, all of us are blind by nature in this respect. Accordingly, it cannot penetrate into our minds unless the Spirit, as the inner teacher, through his illumination makes entry for it."

the spirituality of the triune God, and not our human philosophy and imagination, is to control the thought and worship of the church.[24]

God's Triune Personhood

Therefore, the one true God, who is infinite in his spirituality, has revealed himself to us as Father in his written Word, in his incarnate Word, and in his Holy Spirit. It is there that we know who God is. For that reason John Calvin gladly follows Gregory Nazianzus in his insight that once we meet the one true God, we immediately meet the three persons, and that when we meet the three, we meet the one:

> And that passage in Gregory of Nazianzus vastly delights me: "I cannot think on the one without quickly being encircled by the splendor of the three; nor can I discern the three without being straightway carried back to the one."[25] Let us not, then, be led to imagine a trinity of persons that keeps our thoughts distracted and does not at once lead them back to that unity. Indeed, the words "Father," "Son," and "Spirit" imply a real distinction—let no one think that these titles, whereby God is variously designated from his works, are empty—but a distinction, not a division.[26]

In order reverently to explicate the biblical doctrine of the triune God, Calvin—in company with the whole Christian tradition both East and West—finds it necessary to employ a few crucial nonbiblical terms to set forth and safeguard the biblical truth. Such words as "person" and *homoousios* ("of the same substance or reality") were developed by the church to provide an accurate and balanced explication of the scriptural truth of who God is. Significantly, it was the heretics themselves who most loudly decried the usage of such "nonbiblical" terms. There were good reasons for their opposition, as Calvin states.

---

24. For the sake of space, I shall not expand upon Calvin's criticisms of the impure worship that came into medieval Catholicism through pictorial and graven images. For details see chapters 11 and 12 of book 1.
25. Gregory of Nazianzus, *Oration* 40.41.
26. Calvin, *Institutes* 1.13.17.

First, Calvin rightly asks: "But what prevents us from explaining in clearer words those matters in Scripture which perplex and hinder our understanding, yet which conscientiously and faithfully serve the truth of Scripture itself, and are made use of sparingly and modestly and on due occasion?" As illustrations, he then mentions the words "Trinity" and "person."[27]

Calvin then notes that the proper use of such ancient theological terms exposes the errors of both Arians (who deny the deity of Christ) and Sabellians (who make God an evolving unitarian monad that turns from Father into Son into Spirit, and thus is not three persons):

> Arius says that Christ is God, but mutters that he was made and had a beginning. . . . Say "consubstantial" [*homoousios*] and you will tear off the mask of this turncoat, and yet you add nothing to Scripture. Sabellius says that Father, Son, and Spirit signify no distinctions in God. Say that they are three, and he will scream that you are naming three Gods. Say that in the one essence of God there is a trinity of persons; you will say in one word what Scripture states, and cut short empty talkativeness.[28]

As for the validity of these and other theological terms historically used to teach trinitarian truth, Calvin does not overrate them, nor does he underrate them. Although they are not as such scriptural (with the exception of "person" or "hypostasis"), yet "it has been proved that the church is utterly compelled to make use of the words "Trinity" and "persons."[29] We shall later discuss how Calvin himself is critical of some terms in the ancient Christian tradition, without however totally denying them. Calvin appreciates Hilary's insight that the false teaching of heretics in the church forced its orthodox leaders to say more (about "things inexpressible") than they might otherwise wish to have said.[30] And in this context he refers to Saint Augustine on the insufficiency of human language to express the Trinity: "And Augustine's excuse is similar: on account of the poverty of

27. *Institutes* 1.13.3.
28. Ibid., 1.13.5.
29. Ibid., 1.13.3.
30. He refers to Hilary's *De Trinitate* 2.2 in *Institutes* 1.13.5.

human speech in so great a matter, the word 'hypostasis' ('person') had been forced upon us by necessity, not to express what it is, but only not to be silent on how Father, Son, and Spirit are three."[31]

Well over a century before Augustine's time, Athanasius had written about the necessity of the usage of nonbiblical words to safeguard biblical truth. As G. L. Prestige summarizes:

> Thus [Athanasius] writes (*de decret.* 20) that, owing to the evasive atti-
> tude of the Conservative sympathizers with Arianism, the bishops were
> compelled to go outside the word of Scripture in order to enforce its
> substance, and to say that the Son is homoousios with the Father, in
> order to indicate that the Son is not merely similar to the Father from
> whom he proceeds, but identical in similarity.[32]

With intentions of truest biblical fidelity, Calvin therefore makes use of these crucial theological terms in order to express as best he can (in company with the church fathers) the basic teaching of Scripture on who God is. After agreeing with Gregory Nazianzus that when we meet the one God, we meet the three persons (and vice versa), he notes how something like the term "person" (in Greek, *hypostasis*) is required to make sense of the way the one God presents himself to us in Scripture as three distinct persons.

Calvin defines person in a way as closely related to scriptural truth as possible:

> "Person," therefore, I call a "subsistence" in God's essence, which, while
> related to the others, is distinguished by an incommunicable quality.
> By that term "subsistence" we would understand something different
> from "essence." For if the Word were simply God, and yet possessed
> no other characteristic mark, John would wrongly have said that the
> Word was always with God [John 1:1]. When immediately after he
> adds that the Word was also God himself, he recalls us to the essence
> as a unity. But because he could not be with God without residing

31. In *Institutes* 1.13.5, Calvin refers to Augustine's *De Trinitate* 7.4.7, 9.
32. G. L. Prestige, *God in Patristic Thought* (London: SPCK, 1952), 214. See similarly Torrance, *Trinitarian Faith*, 42, 57, 128.

in the Father, hence emerges the idea of a subsistence, which, even though it has been joined with the essence by a common bond and cannot be separated from it, yet has a special mark whereby it is distinguished from it. Now, of the three subsistences I say that each one, while related to the others, is distinguished by a special quality. This "relation" is here distinctly expressed: because where simple and indefinite mention is made of God, this name pertains no less to the Son and the Spirit than to the Father. But as soon as the Father is compared with the Son, the character of each distinguishes the one from the other. Thirdly, whatever is proper to each individually, I maintain to be incommunicable, because whatever is attributed to the Father as a distinguishing mark cannot agree with, or be transferred to, the Son. Nor am I displeased with Tertullian's definition . . . that there is a kind of distribution or economy in God which has no effect on the unity of essence.[33]

Calvin argues that "person" (or "hypostasis"), since it is used of Christ in Hebrews 1:3 (the Son is the very image [or *hypostasis*] of the Father), is therefore biblical.[34] This is true, although as Warfield points out *hypostasis* is used in Hebrews 1:3 to point out the full deity of Christ, not really to deal with relations within the Trinity.[35] But Calvin's main point about the scriptural necessity of speaking of the one God as three persons is well grounded: "three are spoken of, each of which is entirely God, yet . . . there is not more than one God."[36]

Further on in this thirteenth chapter, Calvin summarizes the biblical position: "when we profess to believe in one God, under the name of God is understood a single, simple essence, in which we comprehend three persons, or hypostases."[37] This statement, Calvin believes, concisely expresses the truth of Scripture about the Trinity: "For nothing excludes the view that the whole essence of God is spiritual, in which are comprehended Father, Son, and Spirit. This is made plain from Scripture. For as we there hear God called Spirit, so also do we hear the Holy Spirit,

33. *Institutes* 1.13.6, where he refers to Tertullian, *Against Praxeas* 2.9.
34. Ibid., 1.13.2.
35. Warfield, "Doctrine of the Trinity," 214–15.
36. *Institutes* 1.13.3.
37. Ibid., 1.13.20.

seeing that the Spirit is a hypostasis of the whole essence, spoken of as of God and from God."[38]

Calvin's Contribution to Trinitarian Theology

It is precisely here in Calvin's clear distinction (though not division) between God's essence and God's personhood—and in how he applies it to the full deity of the Son and the Spirit—that his great contribution to trinitarian theology lies. Some of our best modern interpreters of the trinitarian thought of John Calvin have pointed to this as the strongest point of his strong teaching. B. B. Warfield extensively comments on Calvin's "very great service" in this regard:

> It was, therefore, a very great service to Christian theology which Calvin rendered when he firmly asserted for the second and third persons of the Trinity their *autotheos* ["self-existence" or "aseity"]. . . . If we will glance over the history of the efforts of the Church to work out for itself an acceptable statement of the great mystery of the Trinity, we shall perceive that it is dominated from the beginning to the end by a single motive—to do full justice to the absolute deity of Christ. . . . [Warfield then mentions the names of three of the greatest contributors to this effort: Tertullian, Augustine, and Calvin.] It is into this narrow circle of elect spirits that Calvin enters by the contribution he made to the right understanding of the doctrine of the Trinity. That contribution is summed up in his clear, firm, and unwavering assertion of the *autotheotes* of the Son. By this assertion the *homoousiotes* of the Nicene Fathers at last came to its full right, and became in its fullest sense the hinge of the doctrine.[39]

T. F. Torrance brings out much the same point on Calvin's notable clarification of the full deity of Christ and the Holy Spirit, against the lingering semisubordinationism of some who followed one line of thought of several (though not all) of the Nicene fathers. He speaks of:

38. Ibid.
39. Warfield, "Doctrine of the Trinity," 273, 284.

Calvin's account of the manifold of interpenetrating personal relations or subsistences within the one indivisible Godhead, which is in many respects his most significant contribution to the doctrine of the Triunity of God. Here it becomes clear that his biblical approach has led him to offer a more unreserved account of the Deity of the Son and of the Spirit both in their distinguishing properties and in their consubstantial relations with God the Father than that offered by most of his theological predecessors.[40]

A careful reading of book 1, chapter 13 of the *Institutes*, as well as other related material of Calvin, will indicate that Warfield and Torrance are certainly right in noting the great clarity Calvin brought to the expression of the full deity of the Son and the Holy Spirit in his trinitarian doctrine. Calvin particularly clarified the issue of the full deity (or *autotheotes*) of Christ and the Holy Spirit by emphasizing the distinction between God's one essence and his triune personhood (without this distinction ever being regarded as a division or separation).

It is important to note here that Calvin clarifies the trinitarian teaching of the Christian tradition, but he does not innovate. In explicating this distinction between God's one essence and his threefold personhood, Calvin cites Augustine: "By these appellations which set forth the distinction is signified their mutual relationships, and not the very substance by which they are one."[41] Augustine and one whole line of the Eastern fathers had long recognized the significant distinction between God's essence and his personhood for appreciating the full deity of the Son and the Spirit. We must first deal with this distinction, and then with its historical/theological background.

The Distinction between Essence and Person

The One Divine Essence

Calvin, in line with Augustine and many of the Eastern orthodox fathers (as we shall see below), shows that the full deity of the Son and

---

40. T. F. Torrance, "Calvin's Doctrine of the Trinity," in *Trinitarian Perspectives* (Edinburgh: T. & T. Clark, 1994), 54.
41. *Institutes* 1.13.19, citing Augustine's *Epistula ad Pascentium*, 174.

that of the Holy Spirit are anchored in the one essence of God that they share equally with the Father. Warfield expresses it well:

> [Calvin's] conception involved, of course, a strongly emphasized distinction between the essence and the Personality. In essence the three Persons are numerically one; the whole essence belongs to each Person; the whole essence, of course, with all its properties, which are only its peculiarities as an essence and are inseparable from it just because they are not other substances but only qualities.[42]

Calvin writes: "It remains that the essence is wholly and perfectly common to Father and Son. If this is true, then there is indeed with respect to the essence no distinction of one from the other."[43] And earlier he had explained the shared absolute Godness of the Father, the Son, and the Spirit:

> For since the essence of God is simple and undivided, and he contains all in himself, without portion or derivation, but in integral perfection, the Son will be improperly, even foolishly, called his "stamp" [referring to Heb. 1:3]. But because the Father, although distinct in his proper nature, expresses himself wholly in the Son, for a very good reason is it said that he has made his hypostasis visible in the latter. In close agreement with this are the words immediately following, that the Son is "the splendor of his glory" [Heb. 1:3]. Surely we infer from the apostle's words that the very hypostasis that shines forth in the Son is in the Father. From this we also easily ascertain the Son's hypostasis, which distinguishes him from the Father.
>
> The same reasoning applies to the Holy Spirit: for we shall presently prove that he is God, and yet it is necessary for him to be thought of as other than the Father. Indeed, this is not a distinction of essence, which it is unlawful to make manifest.[44]

Calvin then summarizes the significance of the all-important distinction between essence and person: "they [the heretics] cannot shake our conviction that three are spoken of, each of which is entirely God,

42. Warfield, "Doctrine of the Trinity," 243.
43. *Institutes* 1.13.23.
44. Ibid., 1.13.2.

yet that there is not more than one God. What wickedness, then, it is to disapprove of words that explain nothing else than what is attested and sealed by Scripture!"[45]

All of this is to say that speaking of the one essence of God refers to the absolute "Godness" of God, which is eternal, self-existent, and underived (*autotheotes* or *a se esse*). The biblical revelation presents the one, eternal, and self-existent God in three persons. As Gregory of Nazianzus says, we never meet the one without finding the three; we never meet the three without going back to the one. Various texts of Holy Scripture can now speak of one of the three persons as God, and now another. It is only when the three persons are spoken of in relationship to each other that a certain "order" is in view (first, the Father, then the Son, then the Spirit). But any one of the three divine persons can be referred to "without particulariza-tion" in Scripture simply as God in and of himself (*autotheos* and thus *a se esse*), especially as long as the relationship to the other coequal persons is not directly in view in the text.

Calvin explicates this distinction:

> When we profess to believe in one God, under the name of God is understood a single, simple essence, in which we comprehend three persons, or hypostases. Therefore, whenever the name of God is men-tioned without particularization, there are designated no less the Son and the Spirit than the Father; but where the Son is joined to the Father, then the relation of the two enters in; and so we distinguish among the persons. But because the peculiar qualities in the persons carry an order within them, e.g., in the Father is the beginning and the source, so often as mention is made of the Father and the Son together, or the Spirit, the name of *God* is peculiarly applied to the Father. In this way, unity of essence is retained, and a reasoned order is kept, which yet takes nothing away from the deity of the Son and the Spirit.[46]

The Three Divine Persons

Calvin, drawing upon the church's patristic and medieval exegetical tradition (and strengthened by the historico-linguistic advances of recent

45. Ibid., 1.13.3.
46. Ibid., 1.13.20.

Renaissance and Reformation scholarship), proves the full deity of the Son and the Spirit, so that they are on the same high level of being as God the Father Almighty. Perhaps Calvin's most fundamental proof of the absolute deity of the Christ is in the New Testament application to him of the covenant divine name revealed by God to Moses in the burning bush of Exodus 3:14: "I AM WHO I AM," or the tetragrammaton—*jhvh* ("Yahweh," or in older versions of Scripture, "Jehovah").

"I AM WHO I AM" means that God is absolutely self-existent; he depends on nothing else for his existence, while everything else depends directly upon him. He has no need of an origin, while all other realities require an origin outside themselves. Thus, in Exodus 3, the God of the covenant assured Moses that God himself, who was sending Moses, was well able to handle Pharaoh, the world's most powerful ruler. "I AM WHO I AM" would accomplish all his divine will through Moses (who felt keenly his own human weakness and inability for such a task).

In the Septuagint (third-century B.C. Greek translation of the Hebrew Old Testament), the word *kyrios* (something like "sovereign master") is used to render *jhvh*. Thus, the self-existent God Almighty of the covenant of grace is *kyrios*. When we come to the New Testament period, we find that its inspired writers are heavily influenced by the Septuagint translation in their employment of Greek words to express the gospel revelation. Particularly, the apostles (and the "apostolic men" who joined them in writing the NT Scriptures) apply this word for Almighty Self-Existent God (or "Sovereign Master") to the Lord Jesus Christ. This means that the incarnate Son is of the very same high being—absolute deity—as the heavenly Father who sent him. There is no difference in their Godhead or essence.

Calvin comments: "Now, that the name of Jehovah taken without specification corresponds to Christ is also clear from Paul's words [he quotes 2 Cor. 12:8–9]. . . . For it is certain that the name 'Lord' was put there in place of 'Jehovah' [or *Yahweh—jhvh*]. . . . And we know from the common custom of the Greeks that the apostles usually substitute the name *kyrios* [Lord] for Jehovah. . . . When Paul calls upon God in an absolute sense he immediately adds the name of Christ."[47]

47. Ibid., 1.13.20.

A bit later, Calvin adds: "Therefore whenever mention is made of deity, we ought by no means to admit any antithesis between Son and Father, as if the name of the true God applied to the latter alone. For of course the God who manifested himself to Isaiah [Isa. 6:1] was the true and only God, the God whom nevertheless John affirms to have been Christ [John 12:41]."[48] And in his work against Peter Caroli, Calvin states that "for the reason that Christ is said to be the one eternal God, he is said to be self-existent."[49]

Calvin uses many other traditional patristic proofs from both Old and New Testament to demonstrate the full deity of Christ (such as the OT appearances of "the Angel of the Lord,"[50] the significance of "Word' in John's Gospel,[51] etc.). Calvin also supports the full deity of Christ on the basis of his saving work, such as eternal forgiveness. After quoting Isaiah 43:25 and Matthew 9:6, Calvin says: "We therefore perceive that he possesses not only the administration merely but the actual power of remission of sins, which the Lord says will never pass from him to another."[52] But for the purposes of this essay, these details are not necessary here, since they are readily accessible in the *Institutes*.

Calvin, again in common with many church fathers, demonstrates from the Old and New Testaments the full deity of the Holy Spirit. It is especially in light of the divine works wrought by the Spirit that Calvin shows him to be fully God. The Holy Spirit brings about regeneration and immortality by his own (not a derived) power. Many of the same works attributed to the Son are also attributed to the Spirit. He could not work in this way if he were not a person subsisting in the very essence of God, and thus as fully God as the Father and the Son.

> Now, Scripture teaches in many places that he is the author of regeneration not by borrowing but by his very own energy. . . . In short, upon him, as upon the Son, are conferred functions that especially belong to divinity. . . . Thus, through him we come into communion with God, so that we in a way feel his life-giving power toward us. . . . For if the

48. Ibid., 1.13.23. See also Calvin's Commentary on Ex. 3:4.
49. Calvin, *Adversus Calumnias P. Caroli*, in *Opera Calvini* 11:560.
50. *Institutes* 1.13.10.
51. Ibid., 1.13.7.
52. Ibid., 1.13.12.

Spirit were not an entity subsisting in God, choice and will [referring to 1 Cor. 12:11] would by no means be conceded to him. Paul, therefore, very clearly attributes to the Spirit divine power, and shows that he resides hypostatically in God.[53]

The "Principle" of Godness

If, therefore, one accepts the full divinity (or aseity) of the three divine persons whom we meet in Holy Scripture and in salvation, then what is their mysterious relationship to one another that makes them one essence (or Godhead) rather than three Gods? Or to ask it another way, where does the "monarchy" or the "principle" of the Trinity lie? Different answers were given to this question by ancient and medieval church teachers. This leads us to consider briefly the principle's historical and theological background.

The Historical/Theological Background concerning the Principle of the Trinity

It is here above all that John Calvin made his greatest contribution toward clarifying this issue on a firm biblical basis, although as we shall immediately see, he followed one theological line of the ancient church (while rejecting another) in doing so. For our purposes here, we may simplify a most complex matter in the very long history of Christian theology by suggesting that there were basically two types of answers to the question of where the one monarchy of God finally reposed, or what was the principle involved in determining precisely who was God. One kind of approach or answer may be termed (a) subordinationism (of which there were many variations), and the other, opposing approach or answer could be termed something like (b) full equalitarianism of all three divine persons.

Subordinationism

In the relatively brief compass of this essay, it is not really possible to trace out the necessary details found in the writings of those

53. Ibid., 1.13.14.

who followed the subordinationist line. But we will refer to some recent works which provide the background (on subordinationism as well as on full equalitarianism). B. B. Warfield fairly and luminously discusses subordinationist concerns during the controversies of the sixteenth-century Reformation down through the eighteenth century.[54] Thomas F. Torrance has contributed several volumes to the study of this issue, especially during the patristic era.[55] Standing on the shoulders of these men, I have sought to give an account of these issues in a forthcoming volume, with reference to patristic, medieval, Reformational, and contemporary periods in both the Greek East and Latin West.[56] All we can do here is to (a) mention the main point of the subordinationists and then (b) explain why and how Calvin follows the equalitarian fathers in a very different direction from the subordinationists.

Some of the earlier, and relatively weaker, theologians (as concerns the coherence of trinitarian theology)[57] such as several of the second- and third-century apologists (like Justin Martyr, Theophilus of Antioch, etc.) sought to anchor the unity of the Godhead in the person of the Father, whereby he alone was considered eternally self-existent, so that somehow before and beyond the categories of time and space, the Father in some sense "caused" the Son and then the Spirit. That is, the Father was the principle of their deity, so that their deity was derived; they were therefore not thought of as self-existent.

This approach was also taken by some of the truly great theologians of the ages, not least by two of the three Cappadocians—that is, Basil the Great and his brother, Gregory of Nyssa, and by the famous summarizer of theology, John of Damascus in the eighth century.

54. Warfield, "Doctrine of the Trinity," 233–84.
55. T. F. Torrance, *Trinitarian Faith*, especially chs. 4, 5, and 8; *The Christian Doctrine of God: One Being, Three Persons* (Edinburgh: T. & T. Clark, 1996), especially chs. 4–7; and two chapters in *Trinitarian Perspectives*, 2 and 3.
56. Douglas F. Kelly, *The God Who Is: The Holy Trinity* (Fearn, Ross-shire: Christian Focus, 2008), especially chs. 8 and 9.
57. Although their intentions were orthodox, it must be remembered that they were pioneers, at the beginning of a tradition, and thus feeling their way forward without the exegetical and theological advantages that were available by the fourth century.

The account they rendered was in general far more satisfactory than that of most of the apologists, and yet they finally did not advance beyond the concept of causation, origin, or principle concerning the persons of the Son and the Spirit. Illustrations of their approach are not hard to find.

While the Cappadocians definitely hold that the Son and the Spirit are equally eternal with the Father,[58] still they work with the concept of cause within the Trinity. Basil speaks of the Father as "the cause of the cause of all things": "On the other hand there is a certain power subsisting without generation and without origination, which is the cause of the cause of all things. . . . But God, who is over all, alone has, as one special mark of his own hypostasis, his being Father, and his deriving his hypostasis from no cause."[59] And Gregory of Nyssa writes: "While we confess the invariable character of the nature, we do not deny the difference in respect of cause, and that which is caused, by which alone we apprehend that one Person is distinguished from another—by our belief, that is, that one is the Cause, and another is of the Cause; and again in that which is of the Cause we recognize another distinction. For one is directly from the first Cause."[60]

Following them, John of Damascus says:

> But if we say that the Father is the origin of the Son, and greater than the Son, we do not suggest any precedence in time or superiority in nature of the Father over the Son (for through his agency He made the ages) or superiority in any other respect save causation. And we mean by this that the Son is begotten of the Father and not the Father of the Son, and that the Father naturally is the cause of the Son: just as we say in the same way not that the fire proceedeth from light, but rather light from fire. So then, whenever we hear it said that the Father is the origin of the Son, and greater than the Son, let us understand it to mean in respect of causation.[61]

58. See Basil, *On the Holy Spirit* 14, and Gregory of Nyssa, *Against Eunomius* 1.42.
59. Basil, *Letter* 38.4.
60. Gregory of Nyssa, *That There Are Not Three Gods* (*Nicene and Post-Nicene Fathers*, 5:336).
61. John of Damascus, *De Fide Orthodoxa* 1.8.

Thus we see that these fathers seek to secure the oneness, monarchy, or principle of the Godhead in the person of the Father (rather than the one essence of God), so that the deity of the Father is said to be uncaused or underived, whereas that of the Son and that of the Spirit are eternally derived or caused. These fathers have thereby introduced a sort of causal series within the persons of the Trinity, making the deity of Son and Spirit dependent upon the person of the Father. It was not this line of patristic thought that Calvin followed, but rather one that is equally ancient, and—he believed—more biblical.

Full Equalitarianism

We can only make brief reference to three of the greatest of the Fathers who were full equalitarians as concerns the absolute deity of all three persons of the Trinity: Gregory of Nazianzus (one of the three Cappadocians), Cyril of Alexandria, and Epiphanius. They rejected the causal or principial subordinationism held by their close colleagues and friends. And we see from the *Institutes* that it was this line of thought that Calvin accepted and developed.

These theologians understood the unity of the substance of God to be anchored in the being of the Father, the Son, and the Holy Spirit, rather than in the person of the Father. Hence Gregory of Nazianzus came to deny

> the application of the concept of "principle" or *arche* to the Father *alone* in distinguishing him from the Son and the Spirit, for that appeared to import the impossible idea of precedence in honour and even of unequal degrees of Deity within the Holy Trinity. Gregory Nazianzus felt strongly that to subordinate any of the three divine Persons to another was to overthrow the doctrine of the Trinity. He was thus returning to the more unified conception of the divine *arche* advocated by Athanasius, who had also rejected any idea of degrees of Deity in the Trinity.[62]

So, Gregory of Nazianzus wrote that each of the three persons of the Trinity is fully God himself:

62. Torrance, *Trinitarian Perspectives*, 30.

neither increased nor diminished by superiorities or inferiorities; in every respect equal, in every respect the same; just as the beauty and the greatness of the heavens is one; the infinite conjunction of the three infinite Ones. Each God when considered in Himself; as the Father so the Son, as the Son so the Holy Ghost; the Three One God when contemplated together; each God because consubstantial; one God because of the Monarchia.[63]

Gregory refused to use the word "origin" for any of the trinitarian persons,[64] and taught that to subordinate any person of the three is "to overthrow the Trinity."[65] Thus he held that the monarchy is not limited to any one of the three divine persons.[66]

It is the same with Cyril of Alexandria (d. 444), who denied the subordination of one person to another within the Trinity, but instead held to a full coequality.[67] Cyril clearly rejected the teaching of Basil and Gregory of Nyssa that, in order to avoid tritheism, one must affirm a causal status of the Father that subordinates the other two triune persons.[68] Instead, he held that the entire Godhead is a completely personal being in himself; that is, God is a communion of personal being, so that the whole undivided being of God is in each person, without any sort of causal priority or subordination.[69] He taught that the Father can be held to be greater than the Son only *economically*, and thus excluded any *ontological* subordination.[70] We will see that John Calvin follows him in this understanding.[71]

Epiphanius, whose teaching preceded that of Cyril of Alexandria, and apparently influenced his, held that each person of the Trinity is whole

63. Gregory of Nazianzus, *Oration* 40.41,

64. Ibid., 40.43.

65. Ibid., 43.29.

66. Ibid., 29.2.

67. E.g., see his discussion of the names in the baptismal formula of Matt. 28, in Cyril's *Dialogues sur la Trinité*, vol. 1, "Dialogue 2," Sources Chrétiennes, 239–41.

68. Cyril of Alexandria, *Thesaurus de Trinitate* in Migne, *Patrologia Graeca*, 75:128.

69. Cyril of Alexandria, *In Joannis Evangelium* 15.1.

70. Cyril, *Thesaurus*, 144, 177.

71. See Warfield, "Doctrine of the Trinity," 283, on Calvin's references at this point to Cyril, and also Calvin's references to Cyril's *De Trinitate* 3 and *Thesaurus* 10.2 in *Adversus Calumnias P. Caroli*, in *Opera Calvini* 7:322.

and perfect God.[72] Against subordinationism, he affirmed that the being of the persons of the Trinity is "beyond beginning and beyond time" with no "before" or "after" in God.[73] Unlike Basil, Gregory of Nyssa, and John of Damascus, Epiphanius refers the monarchy to the entire Trinity, not just to the person of the Father: "In proclaiming the *Monarchia* ... we do not err, but confess the Trinity, Unity in Trinity and Trinity in Unity, one Godhead of the Father, Son and Holy Spirit."[74]

Calvin Follows the Full Equalitarian Fathers

In a colloquy at Neuchâtel with other Reformed ministers, Calvin speaks of Cyril's teaching that "the Father has nothing of himself which the Son does not have of himself."[75] And in the line of Epiphanius,[76] Calvin attributes self-existence (*autousia*) to Christ.[77] In his *Institutes*, he argues against Valentine Gentile, who held that the Father "gave essence" to the Son and the Spirit, so that they had merely a derived deity. Calvin answers:

> For if we consider no one but the Father to be God, we definitely cast the Son down from this rank. Therefore whenever mention is made of deity, we ought by no means to admit any antithesis between Son and Father, as if the name of the true God applied to the latter alone. For of course the God who manifested himself to Isaiah (Isa. 6:1) was the true and only God, the God whom nevertheless John affirms to have been Christ (John 12:41).[78]

Thus Calvin affirms the full deity and *autotheos* of Christ.

Here we find the contribution of Calvin to trinitarian theology in the luminous way he clarifies the full deity of the Son and the Spirit (who are distinct persons from the Father), while at the same time affirming the

72. Epiphanius, *Haereses* 62.3ff.
73. Epiphanius, *Ancoratus* 46.
74. Epiphanius, *Haereses* 62.3.
75. Cyril of Alexandria, *De Trinitate* 3, referred to by Calvin in *Opera Calvini* 11:560.
76. As above, Epiphanius, *Haereses* 69.
77. Calvin, *Opera Calvini* 7:322 and 323.4.
78. *Institutes* 1.13.20.

absolute oneness and simplicity of the essence the three persons share in common from all eternity. Calvin shows that the personal distinctions of the three always refer to their personal relationships within the one essence, in which there is a certain "economic order," according to which the Father has priority.[79] This order of personal relationship "takes nothing away from the deity of the Son and the Spirit."[80] Calvin holds that the Scriptures teach that "God is one in essence, and hence that the essence both of the Son and of the Spirit is unbegotten.… Thus God without particularization is unbegotten; and the Father also in respect to his person is unbegotten."[81]

In sum, Calvin shows that three persons are distinct from one another (though not divided), in which Father is first, Son is second, and Spirit is third, in the order of revelatory and redeeming activity.[82] "The Father is the fountain of Deity, with respect, not to Being, but to order."[83] That is to say, for instance, sonship is a relation so that the Son differs from the Father only by this property of sonship (or being begotten), but as to his own being it is the same essence as that of the Father.[84] Calvin writes:

> Therefore we say that deity in an absolute sense exists of itself; whence likewise we confess that the Son since he is God, exists of himself, but not in respect of his Person; indeed, since he is the Son, we say that he exists from the Father. Thus his essence is without beginning; while the beginning of his Person is God himself. Those orthodox writers who formerly spoke concerning the Trinity applied this name only to the persons.[85]

And the same is true of the "proceeding of the Spirit" by which he is personally distinguished from the Father and the Son. But as to his own being or essence, it is *homoousios* with the Son, as the Son is *homoousios* with the Father.[86]

---

79. Ibid., 1.13.25.
80. Ibid.
81. Ibid.
82. Ibid., 1.13.18.
83. Ibid., 1.13.26.
84. Ibid., 1.13.6.
85. Ibid., 1.13.25.
86. Gregory Nazianzus applies *homoousios* to the Spirit as well as to the Son in *Oration* 31.9. Calvin says: "Paul [with reference to 1 Cor. 12:11], therefore, very clearly attributes to the Spirit divine power, and shows that He resides hypostatically in God" (*Institutes* 1.13.14).

In other words, considered as to their one Godness, they share absolutely and simply one and the same eternal essence as *autotheos* or self-existent, underived deity. Hence, the Father, the Son, and the Holy Spirit are each *autotheos* or *a se esse*, because they are the one true and triune God.[87] Each of them possesses the whole essence of the Godhead, and yet this does not make them more than one God, nor remove their personal distinctions.[88] "Hence it is quite clear that in God's essence reside three persons in whom one God is known."[89]

This obviously means that the essence of God is totally beyond our human conceptions of it. His being may reverently be thought of as something like a being which is always personal and never impersonal, so that for God to exist is always to exist within personal relationship, which constitutes no division of his being.[90]

But if that is the case, why did Calvin demur at some of the Nicene terminology, such as "God of God" and "eternally begotten"? I believe that both Warfield and Torrance are correct in stating that during some of the debates with subordinationists, Calvin criticized these ancient terms (without ever fully rejecting them) in the interests of showing that biblical exegesis must be the final determiner of our theology of the Trinity.[91] As Calvin says: "And let us not take it into our heads either to seek out God anywhere else than in his Sacred Word, or to think anything about him that is not prompted by his Word, or to speak anything that is not taken from that Word."[92]

As concerns the Nicene phrase "God of God, Very God of Very God," Calvin did not finally deny its validity as such, but preferred to state more clearly that it should not be taken to import that there is any causation or principle in the person of the Father which gives deity to the Son and the Spirit. Thus Calvin terms it "a hard saying"[93] (but not a false saying, when taken in the right

87. *Institutes* 1.13.20.
88. "This is made plain from Scripture. For as we there hear God called Spirit, so also do we hear the Holy Spirit, seeing that the Spirit is a hypostasis of the whole essence, spoken of as of God and from God" (ibid., 1.13.20).
89. Ibid., 1.13.16.
90. Ibid., 1.13.17.
91. Warfield, "Doctrine of the Trinity," 245–50, and Torrance, *Trinitarian Perspectives*, 62–65.
92. *Institutes* 1.13.21.
93. Calvin, Preface to *Expositio impietatis Valent. Gentilis, Opera Calvini* 9:368.

way—i.e., of personal distinction, without notions of derived deity or division or inequality of essence). That is, this phrase must not imply that the Father alone is "the essence giver" to the other two persons (or "the essentiator").[94] So Calvin rejects only the subordinationist interpretation of "God of God," not the right understanding of it, or as Warfield states it: "this is a criticism of the form, not of the content of this statement [i.e., 'God of God']."[95]

Calvin's hesitancy at the ancient term which affirms that the Son is "eternally begotten" of the Father has the same motive as above. He never denies that in one sense the Son is indeed eternally begotten of the Father. That is, as regards the distinct personal relationship between Father and Son, the Son is eternally begotten, since the divine intertrinitarian relations are eternal. But what Calvin denies is the theory of the eternal genera-tion of the Son as a sort of continuing communication of essence, or a continuing emanation from the Father. "Therefore [in light of John 1:1 and 1:3] we again state that the Word, conceived beyond the beginning of time by God, has perpetually resided with him. By this, his eternity, his true essence, and his divinity are proved."[96]

Some sort of continuous communication of divine essence from the Father to the Son cannot be the case, for the Son possesses his own *auto-theos* as to his essence, as does the Father. Instead of any concept of com-munication of essence from the person of the Father to those of the Son and the Spirit, all three of them are self-existent; all three divine persons eternally subsist in the one being (or essence) of God.[97]

In summary, Calvin's criticism of certain interpretations of ancient terms from the Christian theological tradition is only intended to strengthen the biblical doctrine of the church that the one true God exists eternally as three coequal persons in one infinitely spiritual being. To know this God is to pos-sess eternal life (John 17:3). And thus to seek to know, to speak of, and to love this God in humble and thoughtful accordance with his revealed Word are worth the best efforts of our lives, as they have been worth the best efforts of God's saints through the ages.

---

94. *Institutes* 1.13.23.

95. Warfield, "Doctrine of the Trinity," 249.

96. *Institutes* 1.13.6.

97. See Calvin's rejection of this theory in his *Refutatio errorum M. Serveti, Opera Calvini* 7:563.

5

Election and Predestination: The Sovereign Expressions of God

---

INSTITUTES 3.21–24
R. Scott Clark

N o person in the history of Christianity, with the possible exception of Augustine of Hippo (354–430), has been so identified with the doctrine of election as John Calvin (1509–64) has been. This is a remarkable fact for a variety of reasons. First, it is remarkable since in his own summary of this doctrine, he did not come to teaching it formally and explicitly until book 3 of the *Institutes*.[1] As Richard Muller notes, much ahistorical mischief has been perpetrated in

---

1. Brian Gerrish says provocatively, "if you begin with predestination, it becomes virtually impossible to hear Calvin say anything else." B. A. Gerrish, *Grace and Gratitude: The Eucharistic Theology of John Calvin* (Edinburgh: T. & T. Clark, 1993), 170.

Calvin studies on this point.[2] For Calvin, the location of his discussion of predestination has more to do with what he regarded as the order of right teaching than any peculiarity of Calvin's theology. Second, that Calvin should be considered the predestinarian theologian par excellence says more about the success of anti-Calvin Lutheran polemics and the effect of the Enlightenment on historiography than it does about Calvin's exegesis, theology, or preaching.[3] The doctrine of predestination is a catholic doctrine. Augustine taught a robust doctrine of predestination against the Pelagians and semi-Pelagians.[4] Prosper of Aquitaine (c. 390–c. 460) followed Augustine's predestination. It is true that the Second Council of Orange (529) rejected the doctrine of reprobation, but the doctrine of double predestination persisted into the early medieval period in Godescalc of Orbais (c. 804–c. 869) and his supporters (e.g., Ratramnus of Corbie) and throughout the entire medieval period.[5] Predestination was "one of the central issues in medieval theology" so that nearly every medieval theologian discussed it to one extent or another.[6] The question whether " 'it is possible or not for the predestined to be damned' and whether 'it is possible for the reprobate to be saved' "[7] was a standard

2. "Calvin did not, as has often been stated, remove the doctrine of predestination from the doctrine of God and place it in an a posteriori position in order to avoid the theological problems of the *'Deus nudus absconditus,'* speculative determinism, and central *dogmas.*" Richard A. Muller, *The Unaccommodated Calvin*, Oxford Studies in Historical Theology (New York: Oxford University Press, 2000), 129. Rather, as Muller notes, the organization of the *Institutes* was influenced by Melanchthon's *Loci Communes* and the structure of Romans.

3. On the Lutheran view of Calvin see R. Scott Clark, "Calvin: A Negative Boundary Marker in American Lutheran Self-Identity 1871–1934," in *The Modern Calvin: John Calvin in Nineteenth- and Twentieth-Century Memory Cultures*, ed. Johann de Niet, et al. (Leiden: E. J. Brill, 2008).

4. E.g., *De praedestinatione sanctorum* in J. P. Migne, ed., *Patrologia Latina*, 221 vols. (Paris: Garnier Bros., 1844), 44:955–92.

5. Godescalc, *Oeuvres Theologiques et Grammaticales de Godescalc d' Orbais*, Spicilegium Sacrum Lovaniense Etudes et Documents 20 (Louvain: Spicilegium Sacrum Lovaniense, 1945), 52–78, 180–258, 338–46.

6. Russell L. Friedman, "The *Sentences* Commentary, 1250–1320. General Trends, the Impact of the Religious Orders, and the Test Case of Predestination," in *Mediaeval Commentaries on the Sentences of Peter Lombard: Current Research*, ed. G. R. Evans (Leiden: Brill, 2002), 43.

7. " . . . ut cum dicitur: 'Praedestinatus potest vel non potest damnari' et 'reprobatus potest salvari.'" Peter Lombard, *Magistri Petri Lombardi Parisiensis Episcopi Sententiae in IV*

theological topic that Peter Lombard (c. 1100–1160) discussed in his *Sentences* (1.40–41), the standard theology textbook until the middle of the sixteenth century.

In the high medieval period, Thomas Aquinas (c. 1224–74) taught double predestination as clearly and unequivocally as anyone in the history of the church.[8] His contemporary, Bonaventure (c. 1217–74), minister general of the Franciscans, discussed election and reprobation under the heading of the divine wisdom (*sapientia*).[9] The doctrine of predestination was developed and elaborated in the late medieval period in response to the perception that William of Ockham's construction of the divine will and human freedom was Pelagian.[10] Indeed, Heiko Oberman warned against the "fallacy of the long-defended thesis that, on the eve of the Reformation, St. Augustine had been forgotten except for some isolated 'Augustinian lights in a Pelagian night.'"[11] Thomas Bradwardine (c. 1295–1349) vigorously championed double predestination against Ockham and his followers.[12] Gregory of Rimini (c. 1300–1358) and Marsilius von Inghen (c. 1340–96) "defended the authority of Augustine just as passionately as Thomas Bradwardine had done half a century before." Rimini, whose formulations would influence the leading Reformed theologian Peter Martyr Vermigli (1499–1562),[13] was responding to an argument by Peter Auriol (c. 1280–1322) that God, by his will of complacency, wills all and none

---

Libris Distinctae. Sententiarum, 2 vols. (Grottaferrata: Editiones Collegii S. Bonaventurae ad Claras Aquas, 1971–81), 1:285.

8. E.g., see Thomas Gilby, ed., *Summa Theologiae*, 60 vols. (London and New York: Blackfriars, 1963), 1a 23 [all], 83.1.

9. Bonaventure, *Tria Opuscala: Breviloquium, Itinerarium Mentis in Deum & De Reductione Artium ad Theologiam* (Florence: St. Bonaventure College Press, 1911), 52.

10. On Ockham's doctrine of predestination see Marilyn McCord Adams and Norman Kretzmann, eds., *Predestination, God's Foreknowledge, and Future Contingents*, 2d ed. (Indianapolis: Hackett, 1983).

11. Heiko A. Oberman, ed., *Forerunners of the Reformation: The Shape of Late Medieval Thought Illustrated by Key Documents*, trans. Paul L. Nyhus (London: Lutterworth, 1967), 131.

12. Thomas Bradwardine, *De Causa Dei contra Pelagianorum* (London, 1618). Portions of this work are translated into English in Oberman, ed., *Forerunners*, 151–64.

13. Frank A. James, *Peter Martyr Vermigli and Predestination: The Augustinian Inheritance of an Italian Reformer*, Oxford Theological Monographs (Oxford: Oxford University Press, 1998), 128–48.

in particular to be saved.[14] Luther's father confessor Johann von Staupitz preached an equally muscular doctrine of predestination, which
he described as the covenant of grace between God and the elect.[15]
From a different philosophical approach (realism), John Wycliffe (c.
1320–84) augmented his political theory with the doctrine of double
predestination.[16]

Double or absolute predestination was not only a catholic doctrine,
that is, taught throughout the history of the church, but also a pan-
Protestant doctrine through much of the sixteenth century. Warfield
was quite right to say,

> And so little is it a peculiarity of the Reformed theology, that it
> underlay and gave its form and power to the whole Reformation
> movement. . . . There was accordingly no difference among the
> Reformers on this point: Luther and Melanchthon and the com-
> promising Butzer were no less jealous for absolute predestination
> than Zwingli and Calvin. Even Zwingli could not surpass Luther

14. Heiko A. Oberman, *The Harvest of Medieval Theology: Gabriel Biel and Late Medieval Nominalism*, 3d ed. (Durham, NC: Labyrinth, 1983), 196. See also 204–6; Chrus Schabel, "Parisian Commentaries from Peter Auriol to Gregory of Rimini, and the Problem of Pre-destination," in *Mediaeval Commentaries on the Sentences of Peter Lombard*, vol. 1, ed. G. R. Evans (Leiden: Brill, 2002), 223. James L. Halverson is right to say that there is considerable ambiguity in the way historians use the word "predestination" in this discussion. He challenges the assumption that what he calls the doctrine of "double-particular election" was the dominant anti-Pelagian view in the late medieval church. He argues that Rimini was among the few who taught the "strong" doctrine of double predestination by which God actively elects and reprobates. See James L. Halverson, *Peter Auriol on Predestination: A Challenge to Late Medieval Thought*, Studies in the History of Christian Thought 88 (Leiden: Brill, 1998), 7–8.

15. Johann von Staupitz, *Libellus de executione eterne praedestinationis* (Nuremberg, 1517). Selections of this work are translated into English in Oberman, ed., *Forerunners*, 139, 175–203. On the relations between Staupitz and Luther see David C. Steinmetz, *Misericordia Dei: The Theology of Johannes von Staupitz in Its Late Medieval Setting* (Leiden: Brill, 1968); idem, *Luther and Staupitz: An Essay in the Intellectual Origins of the Protestant Reformation* (Durham, NC: Labyrinth, 1980).

16. Marcia L. Colish, *Medieval Foundations of the Western Intellectual Tradition, 400–1400* (New Haven: Yale University Press, 1997), 256–57. See also Jaroslav Pelikan, *The Reforma-tion of the Church and Dogma (1300–1700)*, vol. 4, of *The Christian Tradition: A History of the Development of Doctrine* (Chicago: University of Chicago Press, 1985), 32–33. There is disagreement, however, among medievalists. G. R. Evans argues that Wycliffe rejected double predestination and "was not a forerunner of Calvin." See G. R. Evans, *John Wycliffe: Myth and Reality* (Downers Grove, IL: IVP Academic, 2005), 218.

in sharp and unqualified assertion of it: and it was not Calvin but Melanchthon who gave it a formal place in his primary scientific statement of the elements of the Protestant faith.[17]

Among the magisterial Protestants, contrary to some popular presentations, the doctrine of double predestination was taught virtually without exception. Philipp Melanchthon (1497–1560) published his *Loci Communes*, the first Protestant system, in 1521. The first thing he discussed after the distinction between law and gospel was the doctrine of predestination:

> And still, what does it matter whether I take up first or last in my compendium that which will intrude into all parts of our disputation? And since free will had to be discussed in the very first topic, how could I conceal the position of Scripture when it deprives our will of freedom by the necessity of predestination? I think it makes considerable difference that young minds are immediately imbued with this idea that all things come to pass, not according to the plans and efforts of men but according to the will of God.[18]

Clearly, Melanchthon was carried away with enthusiasm for what was, for him, a newly discovered doctrinal treasure that he regarded as both revolutionary and fundamental. In later editions of his *Common Places* (from 1533) he would relocate his doctrine of predestination away from soteriology, discussing it under ecclesiology and focusing more on what he called external freedom, but he never abandoned it completely.[19]

17. Benjamin Breckinridge Warfield, "Calvinism," in *Calvin and Calvinism* (New York: Oxford University Press, 1931), 357–58.

18. Wilhelm Pauck, ed., *Melanchthon and Bucer*, Library of Christian Classics 19 (Philadelphia: Westminster, 1969), 25–26. "Quamquam quid attinet in compendio, primo an prostremo loco id agam, quod in omnes disputationis nostrae partes incidet? Et cum de libero arbitrio omnino primo loco agendum esset, qui potui dissimulare sententiam scripturae de praedestinatione, quando voluntati nostrae libertatem per praedestinationis necessitatem adimit scriptura? Quamquam non omnino nihil puto referre statim pueriles mentes hac sententia imbui, quod omnia eveniant, non iuxta hominum consilia et conatus, sed iuxta dei voluntatem." Philipp Melanchthon, *Melanchthons Werke in Auswahl*, 7 vols. (Gütersloh: Gütersloher Verlagshaus Mohn, 1955), 2./1.27–12.6.

19. See R. Scott Clark, *Caspar Olevian and the Substance of the Covenant: The Double Benefit of Christ*, Rutherford Studies in Historical Theology (Edinburgh: Rutherford House, 2005),

One of the most striking and rhetorically powerful statements of double predestination was Luther's 1525 *De servo arbitrio* (*On the Bondage of the Will*) written and published in response to Erasmus's critique of Luther's doctrine of predestination.[20] Among the English Protestants, William Tyndale's (c. 1494–1536) doctrine of predestination focused, in his preface to Romans, on the comfort it brings to the believer.[21] On the continent, Huldrych Zwingli (1484–1531) taught clearly the doctrine of double predestination in his 1530 treatise *On Providence*.[22] Calvin's sometime colleague Martin Bucer (1491–1551) defended the doctrine of double predestination in his massive commentary on Romans.[23] It has been claimed that Heinrich Bullinger (1504–1575), Zwingli's successor in Zurich, rejected double predestination.[24] Cornelis Venema has shown, however, that Bullinger's concerns about double predestination were not theological but homiletical and practical.[25]

It is evident that the doctrines of predestination and double predestination were not unique to Calvin at all but the common property since

---

172–73. See also Randall Zachman's helpful discussion of Calvin's relations to Melanchthon in Randall C. Zachman, *John Calvin as Teacher, Pastor, and Theologian: The Shape of His Writings and Thought* (Grand Rapids: Baker Academic, 2006), 36–44.

20. Martin Luther, *Luthers Werke Kritische Gesamtausgabe* (Weimar: H. H. Böhlau, 1883), 18:600–787; Martin Luther, *Luther's Works*, 55 vols. (St. Louis: Concordia, 1958), vol. 33 (hereafter, *WA*).

21. William Tyndale, *The Works of William Tyndale*, 2 vols., Parker Society for the Publication of the Works of the Fathers and Early Writers of the Reformed English Church (Cambridge: University Press, 1848), 1:504–5. Dewey D. Wallace Jr. argues that, though it was subdued, there is a strong organic connection between the early English Protestant doctrine of predestination and that taught by Calvin later. See Dewey D. Wallace Jr., "The Doctrine of Predestination in the Early English Reformation," *Church History* 43 (1974): 201–15.

22. Huldrych Zwingli, *Huldrici Zuingli Opera Completa*, 8 vols., ed. M. Schuler and J. Schultess (Zurich: F. Schultess, 1828–42), 4:79–144. Ulrich Zwingli, *On Providence and Other Essays* (Durham, NC: Labyrinth, 1983), 180–92. See also W. P. Stephens, *The Theology of Huldrych Zwingli* (Oxford: Oxford University Press, 1986), 97–107.

23. Martin Bucer, *Metaphrases et Enarrationes Perpetuae. In Epistolam ad Romanos* (Strasbourg, 1536). See also Joel Edward Kok, "The Influence of Martin Bucer on John Calvin's Interpretation of Romans: A Comparative Case Study" (Duke University, 1993); David C. Steinmetz, *Calvin in Context* (New York: Oxford University Press, 1995), 141–50.

24. J. Wayne Baker, *Heinrich Bullinger and the Covenant: The Other Reformed Tradition* (Athens: Ohio University Press, 1980).

25. Cornelis P. Venema, *Heinrich Bullinger and the Doctrine of Predestination: Author of "the Other Reformed Tradition,"* Texts and Studies in Reformation and Post-Reformation Thought (Grand Rapids: Baker Academic, 2002).

Augustine. Why then is Calvin so closely identified with this complex of doctrines? There are several reasons. First, during the confessional period, from the 1550s, the doctrine of double predestination became a point of contention between Lutheran and Reformed orthodox theologians. Most of the confessional Lutheran theologians taught unconditional predestination to salvation but denied the doctrine of reprobation.[26] It was in this context, and in the context of Jerome Bolsec's (d. 1584) opposition to Calvin's doctrine of predestination, that Theodore Beza (1519–1605), Calvin's successor and close colleague, defended the propriety and pastoral use of teaching and preaching the doctrine of election in his *Summa totius christianismi* in 1555.[27] The nearly thirty-year controversy between the Reformed and the Remonstrants, culminating in the Canons of the Synod of Dort (1619), focused on the doctrine of predestination, giving the appearance to the critics of the Reformed churches that the Calvinists were obsessed with predestination. The Reformed orthodox contested vehemently the rise of biblicism and rationalism in the Socinians and subsequent related movements. These precursors of modernity have become heroes in Enlightenment and post-Enlightenment historiography. The theological underpinnings of modernity and postmodernity are the autonomy of human persons with respect to all other persons (including God), the universal fatherhood of God, and the universal fraternity of humanity. Calvin's doctrine of predestination contained within it the antitheses of each of these modernist fundamentals. Thus, it is not surprising that the honest modernists simply dismissed Calvin's doctrine as a relic of an unenlightened age, and others have sought to make it palatable to late modern sensibilities.

It will surprise no one to learn that the secondary literature surrounding Calvin's doctrine of predestination is immense, defying adequate survey here. It must suffice to say that for much of the nineteenth and twentieth

26. See Heinrich Schmid, *The Doctrinal Theology of the Evangelical Lutheran Church*, trans. Charles A. Hay and Henry E. Jacobs, 4th ed. (Philadelphia: Lutheran Publication Society, 1889), 273–92.

27. See Richard A Muller, "The Use and Abuse of a Document: Beza's *Tabula Praedestinationis*, the Bolsec Controversy, and the Origins of Reformed Orthodoxy," in *Protestant Scholaticism: Essays in Reassessment*, ed. Carl R. Trueman and R. Scott Clark (Carlisle, UK: Paternoster, 1999), 33–61.

centuries, driven by the "Kerygma to Dogma" historiography, there was an unfortunate scholarly consensus that where Luther's *Zentraldogma* (i.e., that principle from which the rest of his theology was deduced) was justification, [28] Calvin's was said to be predestination. [29] According to Richard Gamble, "this outdated view of Calvin has been rejected. As a matter of fact, most leading scholars today maintain that there is no one single key to unlock the door of Calvin's theology." [30] In 1998 Richard Muller was more concerned that, though there are positive signs in Calvin studies, there are also unhappy trends. Some scholars seem to be "moving backward or down various pre-established *cul-de-sacs*." [31]

Whereas in the nineteenth and early twentieth centuries, and even today among certain Lutheran schools of thought, it was common to see Calvin described as a rationalist, dogmatic theologian, in two recent accounts, the pendulum has swung in the opposite direction. [32] The degree to which the pendulum has swung is illustrated by the recent biographies by Suzanne Selinger and William J. Bouwsma describing an anxious, antidogmatic Calvin. [33] This view of Calvin staring into the abyss is complemented by a recent trend to focus on Calvin as a relational

28. Richard A. Muller, *Christ and the Decree: Christology and Predestination in Reformed Theology from Calvin to Perkins* (Durham, NC: Labyrinth, 1986), 180. See also idem, *Post-Reformation Reformed Dogmatics*, 2d ed., 4 vols. (Grand Rapids: Baker Academic, 2003), 1:123–32. Warfield's objection to the "central dogma" method is notable for its uniqueness. See Warfield, "Calvinism," 357.

29. E.g., I. A. Dorner, *History of Protestant Theology*, trans. George Robson and Sophia Taylor, 2 vols. (Edinburgh: T. & T. Clark, 1871), 1:415–17. This view has persisted and been modified in modern scholarship. David N. Wiley argues that Calvin's doctrine of predestination was "primarily a soteriological doctrine" (as opposed to being a subset of his doctrine of providence). Wiley denies that predestination was Calvin's central dogma but "it was something close to this within his soteriology." David Neeld Wiley, "Calvin's Doctrine of Predestination: His Principal Soteriological and Polemical Doctrine" (Ph.D. diss., Duke University, 1971), iii, 3, 171.

30. Richard C. Gamble, "Current Trends in Calvin Research, 1982–90," in *Calvinus Sacrae Scripturae Professor*, ed. Wilhelm H. Neuser (Grand Rapids: Eerdmans, 1994), 106.

31. Richard A. Muller, "Directions in Current Calvin Research," in *Calvin Studies IX: Papers Presented at the Ninth Colloquium on Calvin Studies*, ed. John H. Leith and Robert A. Johnson (Davidson, NC: 1998), 87. Muller expands on these themes in idem, *The Unaccommodated Calvin*.

32. See Clark, "Calvin: A Negative Boundary Marker," for documentation of this claim.

33. Suzanne Selinger, *Calvin against Himself: An Inquiry in Intellectual History* (Hamden, CT: Archon Books, 1984); William J. Bouwsma, *John Calvin: A Sixteenth Century*

theologian or as a theologian of union with Christ, even ontological union with Christ. Thomas L. Wenger describes this move as the "New Perspective on Calvin."[34]

In contrast with the Enlightenment picture of Calvin where his doctrine of predestination served as a metaphor for or a corollary to his alleged tyranny over Geneva, and in distinction from the frequently ahistorical neoorthodox approach to Calvin which has focused almost exclusively on the *Institutes*, and in opposition to the partisan confessional Lutheran account of Calvin's allegedly rationalist doctrine of election, this essay will argue that Calvin's doctrine of predestination was exegetical, theological, and pastoral in character.

Following the example of François Wendel, T. H. L. Parker, David Steinmetz, Anthony N. S. Lane, and Richard Muller, by making a good-faith effort to understand Calvin's doctrine of predestination in its historical context,[35] and in line with the methodological agenda sketched by Muller to pursue "careful historical and contextual study of Calvin's exegesis, preaching, and theology," this essay will survey Calvin's exegesis on Romans 9, his theological formulations in the *Institutes* and his *Bondage and Liberation of the Will*, and conclude with a brief account of Calvin's preaching of the doctrine of predestination.[36]

The Context

It is commonplace in Enlightenment-inspired accounts of Calvin that he was the tyrant of Geneva.[37] In his appallingly unhistorical account,

---

Portrait (New York: Oxford University Press, 1988). See also Muller, *The Unaccommodated Calvin*, 79–98.

34. Thomas L. Wenger, "The New Perspective on Calvin: Responding to Recent Calvin Interpretations," *Journal of the Evangelical Theological Society* 50 (2007): 311–28.

35. François Wendel, *Calvin: The Origin and Development of His Religious Thought*, trans. Philip Mairet (New York: Harper and Row, 1950); T. H. L. Parker, *John Calvin: A Biography* (Philadelphia: Westminster, 1975); Steinmetz, *Calvin in Context*; A. N. S. Lane, *John Calvin: Student of the Fathers* (Grand Rapids: Baker, 1999); Muller, *Unaccommodated Calvin*.

36. Muller, "Directions in Current Calvin Research," 87. See also idem, *Unaccommodated Calvin*, 29, 105.

37. Timothy George, "Introduction," in *John Calvin and the Church: A Prism of Reform*, ed. Timothy George (Louisville: Westminster/John Knox, 1990), 15.

Stefan Zweig writes of Calvin's seizure of power in Geneva.[38] As a matter of fact, forced to flee Paris after the Affair of the Placards, Calvin arrived in Geneva as a refugee in 1536, was expelled once to a sabbatical of sorts in Strasbourg, and returned reluctantly primarily out of an exaggerated sense of guilt and duty. He spent the remainder of his life as an alien in a frequently hostile city.[39] Of Calvin's second tenure in Geneva, only the last ten years can be considered settled, and even then he was unable to control the city.[40] This is not to suggest that he exercised no influence in the city. He exercised enormous influence, but his authority was primarily moral, persuasive, and ecclesiastical, that is to say, ministerial.[41]

When Calvin first arrived in Geneva, the independence of the republic was precarious. Having been invaded by Savoy in 1535, the city relied on the protection of the king of France and the Swiss canton (county) of Bern. Thus, to a significant degree, Geneva was not her own. Theological controversy was necessarily a civil affair. As Steinmetz reminds us, when Calvin first arrived in Geneva, "the Reformation was still a fresh experiment."[42] Intolerant of the very sort of controversy swirling around Calvin (who was involved in controversies with Anabaptists and a violent argument with Pierre Caroli in which the latter charged Calvin with Arianism) and bent on satisfying their protectors in Bern, who were making demands of the Genevan churches that Calvin and the pastors were opposing, the larger council of two hundred discharged Calvin during Easter week of 1538.[43]

38. Stefan Zweig, *The Right to Heresy: Castellio against Calvin*, trans. Eden Paul and Cedar Paul (London: Cassell, 1936), 29–56.

39. H. A. Oberman, "*Europa Afflicta*: The Reformation of the Refugees," *Archiv für Reformationsgeschichte* 83 (1992): 91–111.

40. William G. Naphy, *Calvin and the Consolidation of the Genevan Reformation* (Manchester: Manchester University Press, 1994), 213–14.

41. On Calvin's life in Geneva see Steinmetz, *Calvin in Context*, 9–20; Wendel, *Calvin*, 69–107; Parker, *John Calvin*, 51–66, 82–132; Robert M. Kingdon, *Geneva and the Coming Wars of Religion, 1555–1563* (Geneva: Droz, 1956); William Monter, *Calvin's Geneva* (New York: Wiley, 1967); Gillian Lewis, "Calvinism in Geneva in the Time of Calvin and Beza, 1541–1605," in *International Calvinism 1541–1715*, ed. Menna Prestwich (Oxford: Oxford University Press, 1985); Naphy, *Calvin and the Consolidation of the Genevan*.

42. Steinmetz, *Calvin in Context*, 11.

43. Parker, *John Calvin*, 64–66.

Having been recalled by Geneva in 1541, he returned reluctantly, taking up his sermon in St. Pierre where he had ended it earlier, "indicating by this that I had only temporarily interrupted my office of preaching and had not given it up entirely."[44] Through the 1540s he and the pastors went about instituting Reformed worship, catechesis, and church order. He was faced with the regular problems that burden any pastor in addition to his remarkable schedule of preaching, writing, correspondence, lecturing, leadership of the consistory and the company of pastors, and his de facto leadership of the francophone Reformed churches.

His theology was not without challenge. His second tenure in Geneva was "filled with theological controversy" requiring him to dispute with internal critics (Sebastian Castellion, Jerome Bolsec), Lutheran theologians (Andreas Osiander, Joachim Westphal, Tilemann Heshussen), rationalists (Miguel Servetus, Laelius Socinus), Anabaptists (Menno Simons), and "a host of nameless figures he somewhat imprecisely categorized as Epicureans, Libertines, Anabaptists, Nicodemites, Sorbonnists, and Sophists."[45] When the reorganized and expanded edition of the *Institutes* appeared in 1539, chapter 8, "De Praedestinatione et Providentia Dei,"[46] was forwarded to the Dutch Roman theologian Albert Pigge (Pighius) (c. 1490–1542), who published a scathing critique, *De libero hominis arbitrio et divina gratia*, in ten books.[47] In his *Defense of the Sane and Orthodox Doctrine concerning the Bondage and Liberation of the Human Will against the Calumnies of Albert Pigge of Kampen* (1543), Calvin was able to reply to the first six chapters of Pigge's treatise in time for the Frankfurt book fair in the fall of

44. "Locum explicandum assumpsi in quo substitutoram." John Calvin, *Opera Quae Supersunt Omnia*, 59 vols., Corpus Reformatorum (Brunswick: C. A. Schwetschke and Sons, 1863), 11:365.49–366.14 (hereafter *CO*); T. H. L. Parker, *Calvin's Preaching* (Louisville: Westminster/John Knox, 1992), 59–60.

45. Steinmetz, *Calvin in Context*, 18.

46. This was chapter 8 in the 1539 edition but in later editions (to 1554) it was chapter 14. Thus in the *CO* it is given as XIV (VIII). See Richard F. Wevers, ed., *Institutes of the Christian Religion of John Calvin, 1539: Text and Concordance*, 4 vols. (Grand Rapids: Meeter Center for Calvin Studies, 1988), 1:216; *CO* 1:861–62. This section became 3.21–24 in the 1559 edition.

47. Cologne, 1542. For a brief survey of Pigge's life and work see F. L. Schulze, *Calvin's Reply to Pighius*, vol. 9, Human Sciences Research Council (Potchefstroom: Pro Rege, 1971), 11–18.

1543.[48] He intended to reply to the remaining chapters in 1544 but, since Pigge died in 1542, Calvin was distracted from finishing the task.[49]

Another controversy over predestination erupted in 1551 when Jerome Bolsec, a former Carmelite monk turned physician, who had vacillated between the Reformation and Rome, attacked Calvin's doctrine of predestination during a meeting of the congregation.[50] Bolsec, "a poor theologian technically" and "particularly weak on the history doctrines," charged Calvin with making God the author of sin.[51] Absent for the first part of Bolsec's complaint, Calvin arrived unseen and stood to reply extempore for one hour.[52] He replied to Bolsec in print in 1552 with *De aeterna dei praedestinatione*.[53] We must read the development of Calvin's theology in the light of his own personal development (he was a young man when he arrived in Geneva) and in the light of the various challenges to his doctrine of predestination.

Commentarius in Epistolam ad Romanos (1540)

There is some uncertainty as to the exact origins of Calvin's commentary on Romans. He was appointed "doctor of the sacred letters" (*sacrarum litterarum doctor*) "with the task of expounding Scripture in lectures."[54] There is some evidence that he began his lectures in the Pauline epistles by lecturing through Romans. According to T. H. L. Parker, these lectures

48. *Defensio sanae et orthodoxae doctrinae de servitute et liberatione humani arbitrii adversus calumnias alberti pighii campensis* (Geneva, 1543). CO 6:225–404. A. N. S. Lane, ed., *The Bondage and Liberation of the Will: A Defence of the Orthodox Doctrine of Human Choice against Pighius* (Grand Rapids: Baker, 1996), xiv.

49. Lane, ed., *The Bondage and Liberation of the Will*, xv. See also idem, *John Calvin: Student of the Fathers* (Grand Rapids: Baker, 1999), 179–89.

50. Bernard Cottret, *Calvin: A Biography*, trans. M. Wallace McDonald (Grand Rapids: Eerdmans, 2000), 209–212.

51. Parker, *John Calvin*, 113.

52. After which Bolsec was arrested and taken to prison to await trial.

53. *De aeterna dei praedestinatione qua in salutem alios ex hominibus elegit, alios suo exitio reliquit: item de providentia qua res humanas gubernat, consensus pastorum geneyensis ecclesiae* (Geneva, 1552) in CO 8:257–366. The modern critical English translation is John Calvin, *Concerning the Eternal Predestination of God*, trans. J. K. S. Reid (London: James Clarke, 1961).

54. CO 21:126.

likely formed the basis of the commentary that he completed in Strasbourg in 1539.[55] It was revised in 1551 and again in 1556 for style and to reflect the controversies over predestination with Bolsec and Pighius.[56]

In his dedicatory epistle to the great humanist Simon Grynée (1493–1541), Erasmus's successor in Basel, dated November 15, 1539,[57] Calvin revealed to the public that they had been discussing for some time the best method for commenting on Scripture and had agreed upon "perspicuous brevity" (*perspicua brevitate*).[58] Melanchthon's focus on disputed points in his 1532 commentary left too much of Paul's argument untouched,[59] and Bucer's lengthy discourses made his commentary unwieldy. In his argumentum, Calvin made it clear that he regarded Romans as carefully constructed, and thus, by implication, his own work would follow Paul's example.[60] The whole epistle was not only "*methodica*," but the "principal question of the whole epistle is our justification by faith."[61] When he had hardly begun commenting, Calvin was compelled to make clear that our "only righteousness" is "the mercy of God in Christ, offered in the gospel, apprehended by faith."[62] These comments by Calvin recommend that, from the outset, we consider Calvin's doctrine of predestination to be both exegetical and theological. Any account of Calvin's doctrine of predestination must reckon with the fact that he developed it out of his exegetical

55. T. H. L. Parker, ed., *Commentarius in Epistolam Pauli ad Romanos*, Ioannis Calvini Opera Omnia, Series II: Ioannis Calvini Opera Exegetica 13 (Geneva: Droz, 1999), xiii (hereafter, *OE* 13 followed by page and line numbers). Bernard Cottret speculates that the commentary arose out his lectures in Johann Sturm's gymnasium. Cottret, *Calvin*, 143.

56. Ibid., xiii–xix.

57. This is the date, under the Julian calendar, given in the Latin text (ibid., 6.9).

58. Ibid., 3.9.

59. G. C. Bretschneider, ed., *Corpus Reformatorum* (Brunswick: Schwetschke et Sons, 1834), 15:495–796. The modern critical edition is *Melanchthons Werke*, vol. 5. The English translation is Philipp Melanchthon, *Commentary on Romans*, trans. Fred Kramer (St. Louis: Concordia, 1992). For more on sixteenth-century commentaries on Romans see Clark, *Caspar Olevian*, 141–48; idem, "Olevianus and Paul," in *Paul in the Reformation*, ed. R. Ward Holder (Leiden: Brill, 2008).

60. *OE* 13.7.12–13.

61. "Atque ingreditur principalem totius epistolae quaestionem, fide nos iustificari." Ibid., 7.19–20.

62. "Unicam esse hominibus iustitiam, Dei misericordiam in Christo, dum per Euangelium oblata, fide apprehenditur." Ibid., 7.22–23.

work in Romans, which book he read to be chiefly about the material doctrine of the Reformation: justification *sola fide*.

Given his overtly theological reading of the epistle, his reading of Romans 9 is not surprising but is striking nonetheless. He begins where the chapter begins, with the historical and rhetorical problem that Paul faced: How to account for the fact that the Jews, the *primarios custodes* and *haeredes* of the covenant (*foederis*), have "turned away from Christ" (*a Christo abhorrere*).[63] Is it the case that the covenant has been transferred (*translatum*) from the "posterity of Abraham" (*ab Abrahae posteritate*) or that Christ is not the promised Redeemer?[64] Having accounted for Paul's rhetorical move to disarm his critics, Calvin turned to Paul's doctrine of election as the source of explanation. The *genus* of the sons of Abraham was *duplex*.[65] Not everyone who was *secundum carnem* was to be reckoned (*censeri*) "in the seed with respect to participating in the covenant of grace."[66] There were some who were *extraneos* and who "through faith were engrafted, to be reckoned in the position of sons."[67] This fact can be explained only by recourse to the *exemplum* of Jacob and Esau.[68] "So then, Paul here recalls us to the election of God," and it is this doctrine on which (*unde*) we are to regard "the whole business" (*totum negotium*) necessarily to depend.[69] "Further, since this election depends on the mercy of God alone," it is "vain" (*frustra*) to seek its cause "in human worth."[70] For most of the church through most of its history, Calvin's position of the gracious, unconditional election of Jacob is relatively uncontroversial. Accounting for Esau, however, was another matter. Here we come to the "other side" (*ex adverso*) of the question, the *reiectio* (of Esau).[71] Even though (*tametsi*) the righteousness (*iustitia*)

63. Ibid., 10.31–32.
64. Ibid., 10.33–35.
65. Ibid., 10.40.
66. "In semine ad participandam foederis gratiam." Ibid., 11.1.
67. "Per fidem inserantur, filiorum haberi loco." Ibid., 11.2.
68. Ibid., 11.3.
69. "Proinde hic nos ad electionem Dei revocat, unde totum negotium dependere necessario reputandum est." Ibid., 11.3–4.
70. "Porro quum haec electio sola Dei misericordia nitatur, frustra eius causa quaeritur in hominum dignitate." Ibid., 11.4–5.
71. Ibid., 11.6.

of God's decree of reprobation is certain (*certa*), the implication is clear that a problem remains since "there exists no cause superior to the will of God."[72]

Calvin unfolded these lines of argumentation in the commentary proper. However concerned Paul was to remove unnecessary obstacles to faith in Christ, he will not "concede a whit to them" if it results in the *detrimentum Euangelii*.[73] Paul shows "no lack of skill" (*non caret artificio*) in beginning with his own grief (*cruciavit*) at the unbelief among the Jews and at the "destruction of the Jews."[74] Nevertheless, Paul knew that their unbelief must be explained by "God's will and disposing."[75] For Calvin, there is no conflict between grieving (*ingemiscamus*) over the reprobate (*ad perditorum hominum ruinam*) and recognizing that they are "destined by the righteous judgment of God."[76] Paul's invocation of the divine anathema upon himself was genuine. He did this, not with his own sure election, but with the salvation of his own people in view.[77] He spoke out of love. The "scope of Paul's entire prayer" is that, in spite of their "impious separation" from God, nevertheless the "light of grace was not extinct" among them.[78] They had the advantage of being the adopted, national, covenant people of God, through whom the Messiah had come.

Nevertheless, for Calvin, Paul's *propositio* is that the promise was given to Abraham and to his seed, but there is a more important determinant in reckoning the stability of the covenant promise and the seed of Abraham: election.[79] The Lord willed that his covenant be sealed (*obsignari*) no less in Ishmael and Esau than it is in Isaac and Jacob.[80] Calvin was careful to note that Esau and Ishmael were both *promissionis filios* (quoting Gal. 4:28) and *filii pactorum* (quoting Acts 3:25).[81] They had this status, "even

72. "Causa tamen Dei voluntate superior non extat." Ibid., 11.7.
73. Ibid., 186.19–20.
74. Ibid., 11.27.
75. "Deo volente atque ita disponente." Ibid., 187.27–28.
76. "Sciemus iusto Dei iudicio destinatos." Ibid., 187.29–30.
77. Ibid., 188.6–15.
78. "Ad hunc scopum dirigitur tota Pauli oratio, utcunque defectione sua Iudaei impium cum Deo divortium fecerint, non tamen prorsus extinctam in illis esse lucem gratiae Dei." Ibid., 189.34–36.
79. Ibid., 192.31–193.4.
80. Ibid., 193.6.
81. Ibid., 193.4, 10.

though they were *infidels*," because they were physically descended from Abraham.[82] He cited Ezekiel 16:20–21 as evidence that the Lord called them sons.[83] Indeed, Calvin was pointed about the reality of the administration of the covenant of grace. In language that he repeated almost verbatim in the *Institutio* (see below), he warned against speaking of the covenant of grace with *contumelia*.[84]

Calvin, however, qualified his account of the administration of the covenant of grace with a second (*alterum*) point.[85] This sealing, however, does not mean that Esau and Ishmael had the same relation to God, salvation, and grace that Isaac and Jacob enjoyed. The sons of the promise "properly" or narrowly reckoned are those in whom the "power and efficacy" of the covenant of grace are found.[86] "For this reason," Calvin reminds his readers, "Paul denies that all the sons of Abraham are sons of God, even though the covenant was initiated with them by the Lord."[87]

The distinction (*differentia*) that Calvin made here, between those who are genuinely a part of the administration of the covenant of grace, recipients of the offer (*oblata*) of salvation confirmed by the "symbol of circumcision," and those who actually receive what has been offered and sealed is election.[88] "Paul denies that they were included in the true election of God."[89] He restated the distinction this way, which he described in *Institutio* 3.21.7 as the distinction between *electio generalis* and *electio specialis*,[90] as a distinction between "the election common to the Israelite people" (*communis populi Israelitici electio*), which he also described as a *foedus vitae*, and God's free choosing (*deligat*) by his "secret counsel"

---

82. Ibid., 193.9–10.

83. Ibid., 193.14–16.

84. "Quod sine Dei contumelia dici non potest." Ibid., 196.8. "Quod non sine foederis contumelia diceretur." Petrus Barth and Wilhelm Niesel, eds., *Joannis Calvini Opera Selecta*, 5 vols. (Munich: Christian Kaiser, 1926), 4:368 (hereafter *OS*, followed by page and line numbers), 4.378.26–27.

85. *OE* 13.193.11.

86. "Filios promissionis proprie nuncupari in quibus ipsius virtus et efficacia extet." Ibid., 193.11–12.

87. "Ea ratione hic negat Paulus, omnes Abrahae filios esse filios Dei, etiamsi pactum cum illis initum esset a Domino." Ibid., 193.12–14.

88. Ibid., 193.18–19, 20–21.

89. "Paul eos esse comprehensos in vera Dei electione negat." Ibid., 193.23.

90. *OS* 4.377.34–378.5.

(*arcano suo consilio*) whom he will.[91] For Calvin, this distinction was only an application of the same distinction that he made in his comments on Romans 2:28. A "true Jew is not to be reckoned either by family descent, or by title of profession, or from eternal symbol." It is not circumcision (or baptism, as he made clear in his comments on Rom. 2:25) that "constitutes" one a Jew, that is, a believer, but one must be so internally.[92]

In the same way, in his comments on Romans 9:6, Calvin wrote that Paul "denies that 'all who are of Israel and all who are of the seed of Abraham are Israelites.'"[93] He did not accuse Paul of equivocating on election, but he described Paul's usage as paronomasia whereby in the first clause he included all who are physically Israelite, and in the second clause he referred only to "true sons" (*tantum filios*) who demonstrated their election by remaining faithful.[94] Paul shows that the "external call" (*externam vocationem*) is controlled by the "hidden election" (*electionem arcanam*).[95]

He made this point even clearer in his comments on Romans 9:11. Even though all the circumcised are adopted (*adoptati*) into the *foederis societatem*, nevertheless grace is not efficacious in all.[96] "Therefore those who enjoy the benefit of God are the sons of the promise."[97] The distinction between those who receive the benefits of Christ and those who do not is determined solely by election. "The whole cause is referred to the election of God."[98] "And," Calvin adds, "that election is gracious."[99] "Nothing superior to the goodness of God is to be sought in the salvation of the pious, in the destruction of the reprobate, nothing higher is to be sought than his righteous severity."[100]

91. *OE* 13.193.23–25, 27.

92. Ibid., 54.24–33. For more on how this distinction has functioned in Reformed theology, see R. Scott Clark, "Baptism and the Benefits of Christ: The Double Mode of Communion," *Confessional Presbyterian Journal* 2 (2006): 3–19.

93. "Quod autem *omnes qui sunt ex Israele*, negat *esse Israelitas, et omnes qui sunt ex semini Abrahae, esse filios.*" Ibid., 193.29–30.

94. S.v. "paronomazo," in Henry George Liddell et al., eds., *A Greek-English Lexicon*, rev. ed. (Oxford: Clarendon, 1996).

95. *OE* 13.193.33–34.

96. Ibid., 195.17–18.

97. "Eos ergo qui fruantur Dei beneficio, esse promissionis filios." Ibid., 195.18–19.

98. "Causam totam ad electionem Dei refert." Ibid., 195.20–21.

99. "Eamque gratuitam." Ibid., 195.21.

100. "Nihil superius quaeratur Dei bonitate, in salute piorum, in reproborum exitio, nihil superius iusta eius severitate." Ibid., 195.22–23.

As he continued working clause by clause through verses 11 and 12, Calvin was at pains to reiterate the gracious character of election, salvation, and justification over against the "sophists," that is, the theologians of the Sorbonne. "Therefore," he concludes, "we have the whole stability of our election confined only in the purpose of God."[101]

As he did in the *Institutio*, having laid out his fundamental view, his reading of Paul's doctrine of election, in his commentary on the remainder of Romans 9, he elaborated on the same basic themes and distinctions, working carefully through the Greek text clause by clause and word by word,[102] at every turn reasserting this fundamental distinction between the sovereign decree (election and reprobation) and its administration among the visible people of God.

The *Institutes of the Christian Religion* (1559) 3.21–24

It is beyond the scope of this essay to address the development of Calvin's doctrine of election in the *Institutes*, so it must do to say that his account of election developed chiefly in response to the sort of external challenges already described, and partly because of Calvin's own growth as a pastor and theologian, but his doctrine of election did not change fundamentally in the twenty-three years from the first Latin edition to the last.[103] He always taught an unequivocal doctrine of double predestination.

Where in his commentary on Romans the discussion of election is firmly situated in the concrete historical setting of Paul's proclamation of the gospel and the problem of the Jewish national covenant, in *Institutio* 3.21.1, the question is more generic, although the language is analogous (both have to do with covenants): "The covenant of life (*foedus vitae*) is not preached equally to all men, and among those to whom it is preached it does not find the same place equally or perpetually."[104] How does one

---

101. "Habemus ergo, totam electionis nostrae firmitudinem in solo Dei proposito esse conclusam." Ibid., 196.36–38.

102. Parker, "Introduction," in ibid., xxxii.

103. E.g., CO 1:73–77.

104. "Iam vero quod non apud omnes peraeque homines foedus vitae praedicatur, et apud eos quibus praedicatur, non eundem locum vel aequaliter vel perpetuo reperit." OS 4.368.33–35.

explain how it is that not all hear the gospel or that not all who hear it believe? The answer is in the heading for the chapter in the 1559 edition: "Concerning Eternal Election by Which God Has Predestined Some to Salvation and Others to Perdition."[105] In this diversity the "marvelous height of the divine judgment discloses itself."[106]

Calvin's theological agenda was not only to explain why things are as they are, why some come to faith and others do not, but also to give assurance to those who do believe. "We shall never be persuaded clearly that our salvation flows from the font of God's gracious mercy, until his eternal election is made clear to us: which by this comparison illustrates the grace of God, which does not adopt all promiscuously into the hope of salvation, but gives to some what it denies to others."[107] In other words, given that, in the end, some do not believe, and that unbelief is traceable to the divine will, the fact that one does believe is a source of great encouragement, for it means that one has been unconditionally elected by Christ's sovereign grace. Ignorance of this doctrine has two effects: First, it diminishes (*imminuat*) the glory of God. Second, it detracts from true humility.[108] Those who would refuse to teach this doctrine are tearing up the "root of humility."[109] Those who cover up this doctrine deny to Christians a ground of "solid confidence" (*solidae fiduciae*).[110]

From the very outset of his discussion of the *locus* of predestination it is clear that this is not a mere academic exercise. Calvin writes about predestination with pastoral care for the spiritual well-being of his readers and of those to whom they would preach and counsel. This pastoral concern becomes even clearer when, in his introduction of the question, he warns about a potential problem. "The curiosity of men" makes "disputation about predestination, already a difficult thing in itself, perplexing

105. "De electione aeterna, qua Deus alios ad salutem, alios ad interitum praedestinavit." OS 4.368.31–32.
106. "In ea diversitate mirabilis divini iudicii altitudo se profert." Ibid., 4.368.35–36.
107. "Nunquam liquido ut decet persuasi erimus salutem nostram ex fonte gratuitae misericordiae Dei fluere, donec innotuerit nobis aeterna eius electio: quae hac comparatione gratiam Dei illustrat, quod non omnes promiscue adoptat in spem salutis, sed dat aliis quod aliis negat." Ibid., 4.369.10–14.
108. Ibid., 4.369.15–16.
109. "Humilitatis radicem evellunt." Ibid., 4.369.27.
110. Ibid., 4.369.35.

and hazardous."[111] If unbridled, this curiosity will lead one straight into a labyrinth.[112] The only safe path, therefore, when inquiring into predestination, is to give oneself over to those "secrets of his will" (*voluntatis suae arcana*) that he has determined to reveal in his Word.[113]

In 3.21.2–3, Calvin elaborates on the themes established in section 1. In 3.21.4, however, he addresses the problem of those "profane men" (*profani homines*) who "take hold" (*arripiunt*) of the doctrine of predestination in order to mock it.[114] Their mocking, however, should not discourage the pious. These same fellows will also mock creation, the Trinity, and other *dogmata fidei*.[115]

There is another danger, however, that is more subtle. Those who would be regarded as pious do not openly reject "predestination by which God adopts some to life and sentences others to eternal death"[116] Rather, instead of the unconditioned divine will, they make election conditional upon divine foreknowledge (*praescientiam faciunt eius causam*).[117] There is no question whether God has foreknowledge and whether he predestines. The question is the relation between the two. To make God's foreknowledge the cause of election is to move the ground of election from God to the creature. For Calvin, in such a case, election would no longer be a free divine act, grounded in the free divine will. It would condition the divine will by something outside of God, and this, for Calvin, was almost unthinkable.

Further, such a construal of the relations between foreknowledge and predestination entails a redefinition of foreknowledge. When Calvin said *praescientia* he meant that "all things are and remain perpetually before his

111. "Disputationem de praedestinatione, quam per se sit aliquantum impedita, valde perplexam atque adeo periculosam reddit hominum curiositas." Ibid., 4.370.12–14. See also *Institutes* 3.23.12–15.

112. Ibid., 4.370.23.

113. Ibid., 4.370.28–29.

114. Ibid., 4.372.1–2.

115. Ibid., 4.372.4.

116. "Praedestinationem, qua Deus alios in spem vitae adoptat, alios adiudicat aeternae morti." Ibid., 4.373.31–34. The verb *adiudicat* is difficult to translate. Ford Lewis Battles's choice of "sentence" seems apt. John Calvin, *Institutes of the Christian Religion*, trans. Ford Lewis Battles, 2 vols., Library of Christian Classics 20–21 (Philadelphia: Westminster, 1960), 3.21.5 (hereafter, *Institutes*).

117. *OS* 4.374.2.

eyes."[118] To God, nothing is "future or past" (*futurum aut praeteritum*).[119] Thus he defined predestination as "the eternal decree of God, by which he held as constituted with himself what he wills to be concerning each man."[120] Some are predestined to life, others to death. This decree of election "remains inviolable" (*inviolabilis manet*), even in the administration of the temporary, typological election of national Israel, and even when the *signa* do not always appear.[121]

The cases of Ishmael and Isaac and of Jacob and Esau offered to Calvin incontrovertible evidence of the nature of particular election (3.21.6). Both Ishmael and Isaac were "of the same race of Abraham" (*ex eodem genere Abrahae*), the *spirituale foedus* was sealed (*obsignatum*) to both of them by circumcision, but Ishmael was "cut off" (*exciditur*).[122] Calvin observed the same pattern in Saul, Jacob, and throughout the *sacra historia*.[123] They were all a part of the visible people of God and recipients of certain benefits; nevertheless, God repudiated some (*repudiavit*), favoring (*fovendo*) others.[124] This is the outworking of the "second, more restricted degree" of election which manifests God's *gratia magis specialis*.[125]

Gracious election is only "half exposited" (*ex parte exposita*) by the case of national Israel. One must account for the election of "individual persons" (*singulas personas*). The explanation is that God, by his *occulto consilio*, freely elects those whom he will and rejects others (3.21.7).[126] God not only "offers" (*offert*) salvation, he actually assigns (*assignat*) so that it is not (as it is in the Roman view) a matter of doubt or suspense.[127] Because God has made an "eternal covenant of life" (*vitae eternae pacto*),[128] particular election is certain. Because the Father has "collected" his elect

---

118. "Omnia semper fuisse ac perpetuo manere sub eius oculis." Ibid., 4.374.5–6.
119. Ibid., 4.374.6.
120. "Praedestinationem vocamus aeternum Dei decretum, quo apud se constitutum habuit quid de unoquoque homine fieri vellet." Ibid., 4.374.11–13.
121. Ibid., 4.376.21–22.
122. Ibid., 4.376.27–28.
123. Ibid., 4.376.34.
124. Ibid., 4.376.25.
125. "Secundus gradus restrictior." Ibid., 4.376.23–24.
126. Ibid., 4.377.19–22.
127. Ibid., 4.377.23.
128. Ibid., 4.377.34–35.

and bound (*devinxit*) them to himself with an "insoluble nexus,"[129] they receive a "special mode of election."[130] Grace does not elect all promiscuously and efficaciously.[131]

As in the commentary on Romans 9, Jacob and Esau provide the definitive case study.[132] "Jacob have I loved" refers both to a class of people and also to particular individuals.[133] The prophet juxtaposes (*opponit*) the class of those who are identified with Jacob with the class of those identified with Esau. The *electio generalis* is not always "firm."[134] All those who participate in the covenant have an *externa mutatio*, but they do not all receive the "interior efficacious grace" (*interiori gratiae efficacia*) and the "Spirit of regeneration," and therefore they do not persevere to the end.[135] It was not "worthless and unfruitful" (*inanis et infructuosa*) to be a part of the visible image (*imago*) and seed (*seminis*) of Abraham, to participate in the administration of the covenant of grace—to say that would dishonor the covenant—but the administration of the covenant is subject to the *immutabile Dei consilium*.[136] By this immutable counsel, God has predestined some to salvation and damned others.[137]

"Scripture shows clearly" that election to life is not conditioned by human dignity (*nullo humanae dignitatis respectu*), but rather by God's "eternal and immutable counsel."[138] His election to salvation is grounded in "his gracious mercy" (*in gratuita eius misericordia*), and his reprobation is a "holy, irreproachable but incomprehensible judgment."[139] For those who are elect, prior to glorification there are two testimonies of election. The first is efficacious, inward *vocatio*. The second is *iustificatio*.[140]

---

129. "Electos suos caelestis Pater inter se colligavit, et sibi insolubili nexu devinxit." Ibid., 4.377.28–29.

130. "Specialem electionis modum." Ibid., 4.377.34–35.

131. Ibid., 4.377.35–36.

132. See also *Institutes* 3.22.4–6.

133. *OS* 4.377.36–378.1.

134. Ibid., 4.378.4–5.

135. Ibid., 4.378.6–9.

136. Ibid., 4.378.21–27.

137. Ibid., 4.378.28–29.

138. Ibid., 4.378.32.

139. "Iusto quidem et irreprehensibili, sed incomprehensibili ipsius iudicio." Ibid., 4.379.1–3.

140. Ibid., 4.379.3–4. See also *Institutes* 3.22.10.

"By vocation and justification the Lord seals the elect" and excludes the reprobate "from the knowledge of his name and from his Spirit of sanctification."[141] These comments, as Calvin summarizes his doctrine of election and reprobation, validate Wiley's conclusion that, through his doctrine of justification, Calvin "defended the theological validity of the Reformation's doctrine of gratuitous justification apart from meritorious works."[142]

The basic lines of Calvin's theology of the decree are clear enough. The following chapters, 22–24, merely elaborate and defend the arguments already laid out in the commentary on Romans and in *Institutio* 3.21. In 3.22.2 he makes clear that, when he rejected making foreknowledge the ground of election, that rejection included the notion of *merita fore praevidet*.[143] By this commitment to unconditional election, he rejected the notion that we are elected because of foreseen sanctity (3.22.3). For Calvin, such a claim "inverts Paul's order."[144]

In 3.23.1 his apology (*Refutatio calumniarum*) for double predestination addressed the possibility of a doctrine of election without a doctrine of reprobation.[145] Some "acknowledge election as they deny that anyone is reprobated."[146] Election can only be understood in the light of reprobation. Calvin was not opposed to saying that God passes by (*praeterit*) some so long as it is understood that, by preterition, God reprobates (*reprobat*) them.[147] God wills (*vult*) to exclude the reprobate.[148] As Calvin saw it, the problem the critics have with the doctrine of reprobation is that they will not be "curbed" (*fraenari*) by the Word of God.[149] Calvin recognized that Paul ascribes to the reprobate "the guilt of perdition who bring it on

141. "Quemadmodum autem vocatione et iustificatione electos suos Dominus signat, ita reprobos vel a notitia sui nominis, vel a Spiritu sui sanctificatione excludendo." Ibid., 4.379.6–8.

142. Wiley, "Calvin's Doctrine of Predestination," iv.

143. OS 4.379.22. The references to Aquinas's *Summa Theologiae* in the Battles edition are provided by the editor and not embedded in the Latin text.

144. "Et ordinem Pauli invertes." Ibid., 4.382.12.

145. OS 4.393.34.

146. "Electionem ita fatentur ut negent quenquam reprobari." Ibid., 4.394.1–2.

147. Ibid., 4.394.6.

148. Ibid., 4.394.8.

149. Ibid., 4.394.9.

themselves by their own will."[150] Paul employed a variety of ways of speaking (*diversa loquendi*) to mitigate (*lenire*) the severity (*asperitatem*) of this doctrine,[151] but his rhetorical strategy does not change the fact that the *praeparationem ad interitum* (preparation for condemnation) cannot be transferred to any other place than the *arcanum consilium Dei* (the secret counsel of God).[152]

As has become evident throughout this survey, Calvin turned repeatedly to the divine will as the ultimate explanation. Nowhere is that clearer than in the next section (3.23.2) where he raises the question whether such a doctrine makes God capricious. His answer: the pious will recognize the shamelessness (*improbitas*) of investigating (*percontari*) the "causes of the divine will" (*causas divinae voluntatis*).[153]

> For his will is, and rightly ought to be, the cause of all things that are.
> For if it has any cause, something must precede it, to which it is, as it
> were, bound; this is unlawful to imagine. For God's will (*Dei voluntas*)
> is so much the highest (*summa*) rule of righteousness that whatever
> he wills, by the very fact that he wills it, must be considered righteous.
> When, therefore, one asks why God has so done, we must reply: because
> he has willed it.[154]

There is nothing behind God's will to which one may appeal. Nevertheless, Calvin is not arguing for a sort of Ockhamist voluntarism. "Neither do we agree with the fiction of 'absolute power,' as this is profane and rightly ought to be detestable to us."[155] The *commentum* he rejected was certainly the claim that, theoretically, God the Son could have become incarnate as a donkey. Neither, however, was Calvin an intellectualist. God does not will according to some

---

150. "Perditionis culpam reiicit in eos qui proprio arbitrio ipsam sibi accersunt." Ibid., 4.395.7–8.

151. Ibid., 4.395.9–10.

152. Ibid., 4.395.10–11.

153. Ibid., 4.395.33–34.

154. *Institutes*, 3.24.2; OS 4.395–96.5.

155. "Neque tamen commentum ingerimus absolutae potentiae: quod sicuti profanum est, ita merito detestabile nobis esse debet." Ibid., 4.396.16–18. On Calvin's relations to voluntarism see R. Scott Clark, "Calvin on the *Lex Naturalis*," *Stulos Theological Journal* 6 (1998): 13–14.

external norm, but he wills according to his own nature. It is not given to creatures to bring reproach (3.23.4) upon God. Calvin appealed again to Romans 9:20–21, "O homo, tu quis est . . . ?"[156] Paul calls God's judgments "inscrutable" (3.25.5).[157]

As to the question why God "imputes" (*imputaret*) as sin those things that necessarily happened (e.g., the fall) according to the decree:[158] having rejected a couple of possible solutions as inadequate, Calvin concluded that God foreknows (*praevideat*) future contingents only because (*quia*) he has "decreed them to be" (*fierent decrevit*).[159] Nor will it do to appeal to the distinction between the will and permission (*voluntatis et permissionis*, 3.23.8).[160] Calvin was not opposed to all talk of permission, but he did reject the notion of things occurring *sola Dei permissione* (only by the divine permission) if that mere permission excludes the divine ordination,[161] since predestination is nothing else but the dispensation of the justice of God.[162] There is, however, a useful way of speaking about permission. The perdition of the reprobate "depends upon the predestination of God, so that the cause and occasion (*materia*) are to be found in themselves."[163] In other words, for Calvin, though there is no cause or occasion in anyone for his election to salvation, and despite his strong emphasis on the freedom and inscrutability of the divine will, the decree of reprobation is not exactly parallel, in every respect, to the decree of election. There is, in the reprobate, at least an occasion of damnation.

In the last chapter on predestination (3.24) Calvin spends seventeen sections answering objections and restating earlier points in answer to the variations on earlier criticisms. In 3.24.4, however, he touches on a new theme for these chapters, namely, the question of how not to think about election. Just as they err who make the power of election contingent upon

156. OS 3.397.30.
157. Ibid., 3.399.22.
158. Ibid., 3.399.33.
159. Ibid., 3.401.3–4.
160. Ibid., 3.402.12.
161. Ibid., 3.402.15–16.
162. Ibid., 3.402.27–28.
163. "Adhoc, sic ex Dei praedestinatione pendet eorum perditio, ut causa et materia in ipsis reperiatur." Ibid., 4.402.31–32.

faith,[164] so too Satan has no more "grave or dangerous temptation" by which he discourages and disquiets the faithful with doubts about their election than to lead them to inquire "with cupidity" about their election "outside the way."[165] It is going "outside the way" (*extra viam*) when a "little man" (*homuncio*) seeks to "break through" (*perrumpere*) into the recesses of the "hidden divine wisdom" (*abditos divinae sapientiae recessus*) to find out what the tribunal of God has constituted with respect to himself.[166] By such attempts at knowing the hidden decree one only covers oneself in "an abyss of darkness."[167] The way to assurance and peace is to avoid being dashed against the rock of destruction by asking directly about one's election. We are all tempted to ask, "What revelation is there of your election?"[168] The answer instead is to give oneself to the promises of the Word. "Therefore let this be our way of inquiring, that we might make a beginning from the call of God, and that we might end in the same place."[169]

The call in view here is the external call of the preached gospel (*Evangelii praedicationem*).[170] To find assurance, to find "the mercy and favor of the Father, we must turn our eyes to Christ, in whom alone the Spirit of the Father rests" (3.24.5).[171] After all, the elect are not chosen "in themselves" (*in ipsis*) but "*in Christo suo*" (in his Christ).[172] If we are "elect in him," then we do not discover (*reperiemus*) the certainty of our election in ourselves," as if we had access to God the Father apart from Christ. "Christ, therefore, is the mirror in whom it is appropriate to regard our election, and without deception."[173]

---

164. "Ergo ut perperam faciunt qui electionis vim suspendunt a fide Evangelii." Ibid., 4.414.6–7.

165. "Nulla tentatione vel gravius vel periculosius fideles percellit Satan, quam dum ipsos suae electionis dubitatione inquietans, simul prava eius extra viam inquirendae cupiditate sollicitat." Ibid., 4.414.10–13.

166. Ibid., 4.414.3–15.

167. "Caliginis abysso se adobruit." Ibid., 4.414.19.

168. "Electionis porro quae tibi revelatio?" Ibid., 4.414.25.

169. "Sit igitur haec nobis inquirendi via, ut exordium sumamus a Dei vocatione, et in ipsam desinamus." Ibid., 3.415.3–4.

170. Ibid., 4.416.10.

171. "Primum, si paternam Dei clementiam propitiumque animum quaerimus, ad Christum convertendi sunt oculi, in quo solo Patris anima acquiescit." Ibid., 4.415.27–29.

172. Ibid., 4.415.27–37.

173. "Quod si in eo sumus electi, non in nobis ipsis reperiemus electionis nostrae certitudinem: ac ne in Deo quidem Patre, si nudum illum absque Filio imaginamur. Christus

Calvin accepted as a given Luther's dictum that God in himself (*in se*) is hidden (*absconditus*) and unknowable (*Institutes* 1.17.2).[174] We know him only as he reveals himself to us in Christ. Thus, for Calvin to invoke Christ as the mirror is to say that he is "God revealed" (*Deus revelatus*) to us. Therefore, Calvin is not here being merely poetic, but quite precise. There is a very important theological point here. He means to say, "Christ is the point at which God's election pierces, as it were, through the cloud of secrecy in which God's decree is normally veiled."[175] In short, the question for Calvin is not "Am I elect?" but "Do I believe the good news of Christ crucified and raised for me?" The syllogism is clearly implied: only the elect believe the gospel, I believe the gospel, *ergo* I am elect. The source of assurance, however, is the revealed gospel promise to believing sinners.

Having considered Calvin's exegetical and theological approach to predestination, we may turn briefly to notice how he preached the same to his congregation.

The Sermons on Ephesians (1558)

Calvin had the highest possible view of Scripture. The text of Scripture is God's Word and therefore inherently authoritative. The proclamation of that word to the congregation carries with it "the authority of the Word of God" and possesses "the authority of God himself."[176] Thus, we cannot understand fully his doctrine of predestination in his commentary on Romans and in the *Institutes* until we reckon with the way he preached it. The two sermons to be considered below were the first two in a series on the book of Ephesians preached

---

ergo speculum est in quo electionem nostram contemplari convenit, et sine fraude licet." Ibid., 4.415.34–416.4.

174. OS 3.204.15, 23, 25. Luther said, "Theologus gloriae dicit malum bonum et bonum malum, Theologus crucis dicit id quod res est." WA, 1.354. See also ibid., 17.684–85. See Herman Selderhuis, *Calvin's Theology of the Psalms*, Texts and Studies in Reformation and Post-Reformation Thought (Grand Rapids: Baker Academic, 2007), 179–94.

175. Jonathan H. Rainbow, *The Will of God and the Cross: An Historical and Theological Study of John Calvin's Doctrine of Limited Redemption*, Princeton Theological Monograph Series 22 (Allison Park, PA: Pickwick, 1990), 87.

176. T. H. L. Parker, *Calvin's Preaching* (Louisville: Westminster/John Knox, 1992), 41.

on Sunday mornings to a lay congregation in Saint Peter's Cathedral from May 1558 to March 1559.[177]

The first sermon, on Ephesians 1:1–3, sets the tone for the rest. Calvin spent much of it establishing the nature of the book, of sermons in general, but also of the Christ whom he was preaching. The first lesson to be learned is that "our faith must not waver one way or another, but have a sure and immovable foundation to rest on, namely, God's truth, even as it is contained in the gospel."[178] We ought not "doubt that God's Spirit speaks to us at this day by his mouth."[179]

In the second sermon (1:3–4), Calvin came to one of the gospel doctrines for which he had worked to prepare the congregation in the first. He begins with Pauline doxology, but now it is reckoned, not relative to the obligations of the law upon the Christian (*tertius usus legis*), but relative to the gospel. Though we are "subject to much misery in this world, yet there is good reason for us to content ourselves with God's choosing of us after that fashion and with his calling of us to himself, for it is witnessed to us by the gospel that he is our Father . . . inasmuch as he has joined us to our Lord Jesus Christ as members to their head."[180]

The "principal cause" of this rejoicing is not just that the gospel has been made known, and not that with it having been revealed, it is within every man's power to believe—if that were the case then we would have merit before God—but rather it is that "there is no distinction between men except that some receive God's grace and others refuse it."[181] To exclude human merit and to show that "all comes from God's pure goodness and grace," Paul says that God has "blessed us according to his election beforehand." This explains why it is that when the gospel is preached, "some will be affected with lively faith in their hearts and others will go away as they came without benefiting at all or else they harden themselves

---

177. Ibid., 152; Wendel, *Calvin*, 53–56. These sermons were published as *Sermons de Iean Caluin sur epistre S. Paul apostre aux Ephesiens* (Geneva, 1562). The English translation is, John Calvin, *Sermons on Ephesians*, trans. Arthur Golding (Edinburgh: Banner of Truth Trust, 1973).

178. Calvin, *Sermons on Ephesians*, 10.

179. Ibid.

180. Ibid., 22.

181. Ibid.

against God. . . . What is the reason for this difference? Even this, that God directs the one sort by his Holy Spirit and leaves the other sort in their natural corruption."[182]

The preaching of the gospel is the "thing in which God's goodness shines forth most to us," but when "it is received by us with heart and affection, that is yet a further and more special token by which we perceive" God's fatherly adoption of us.[183] We will never know where our salvation comes from until we have "lifted up our minds to God's eternal counsel by which he has chosen us . . . and left the remainder in their confusion and ruin."[184] It is significant that in more academic settings, for example, in the *Institutes* (and treatises against Pigge and Bolsec) and in the commentary on Romans, Calvin was willing to speak of reprobation as "passing by" so long as it was clearly understood as a way of speaking about God's willing. In this sermon, however, he seems content to speak of reprobation with less precision and force and in terms of the divine preterition. Where the emphasis in the academic settings was on the role of the divine will in reprobation, in the pulpit the emphasis was upon the fallen condition of the reprobate.

Calvin recognized that some think this doctrine "strange and hard," because it "does not fit in at all with man's natural understanding."[185] The natural tendency and that of the philosophers is to try to correlate God's love and human worth. Calvin warns the congregation against measuring God "by our own yardstick" and against the presumption of imposing a law upon God. The reason that some find the doctrine of predestination difficult is not the doctrine itself, but that they are "too much wedded to their own opinion" and they are arrogant.[186] He also warns against those who grant the truth of predestination but want it "buried so that it might never be spoken of." If this were granted, we would deprive ourselves of a great source of consolation. They must be Manichees who would so mutilate the gospel.[187]

182. Ibid., 23.
183. Ibid.
184. Ibid.
185. Ibid., 23–24.
186. Ibid., 24.
187. Ibid., 25.

The preaching of God's Word to his people is a "singular benefit" but the preaching of election is a "double grace" because we will not believe the word that is preached unless God reveals himself to us by his Holy Spirit and speaks thereby to our hearts. That some believe and others do not "makes God's grace more apparent to us."[188]

Calvin warned against those who would overturn Paul's doctrine that we were elected before the world began and therefore have nothing to offer to God. The "papists," however, "show much subtlety on this point," because they affirm unconditional election on one hand and on the other teach that God elects on the basis of foreseen merits or that "he did it to make them deserve it."[189] Such a view does not account for the nature of human corruption in Adam. If God waited a century, "it is certain that we should never come to him nor do anything else but increase the mischief continually to our own condemnation."[190] Rather we are to regard election as a "token of his free grace." As is typical, Calvin returns to Romans 9, to Jacob and Esau, as proof of the unconditioned nature of election.[191]

As in the *Institutes*, Calvin pressed the point that we were not elected in ourselves, but in Christ. God did not first of all have "an eye to us" when he "vouchsafed to love us," but he must have had "before him his pattern and mirror in which to see us, that is to say, he must have first looked on our Lord Jesus Christ before he could choose us and call us."[192] God's election is the "book of life," and "Jesus Christ serves as a register. It is in him that we are written down and acknowledged by God as his children."[193]

For Calvin, preaching entailed not only gospel preaching, including election, but also moral application. In this sermon (and it is typical of the other sermons on election), knowing that we are God's children, in Christ, and loved by God from eternity out of free grace, we ought to "walk in all righteousness before God." The gracious election by God "does not provide us with license to do evil and to lead a disordered life, or to run

188. Ibid., 26.
189. Ibid., 31.
190. Ibid., 31–32.
191. In 1579 the English Presbyterian John Field issued a translation of thirteen of Calvin's sermons on Jacob and Esau. See John Calvin, *Sermons on Election and Reprobation*, trans. John Field (Audubon, NJ: Old Paths, 1996 reprint).
192. Calvin, *Sermons on Ephesians*, 33.
193. Ibid.

amok."[194] The morally, logically necessary change in our lives ought to flow from this electing grace. God's election and vocation "to holiness are things joined inseparably together."[195] This being a preparatory sermon before the Lord's Supper, "which is a pledge to us of our election, as well as the hope of our salvation and of all the spiritual benefits that come forth from this source and fountain of God's free love," Calvin called the congregation to refuse to abuse such privileges but to use them to glorify God.

In the *Institutes*, Calvin had argued for the necessity and pastoral benefits of preaching the doctrines of election and reprobation. Calvin took his own advice. He preached the doctrines of election and reprobation as sources of comfort to believers (and as a source of discomfort to unbelievers) but the tenor is different. In this sermon particularly, he elaborated on the metaphor of the mirror and used other equally powerful images to point the congregation to Christ as the revelation of God's grace to sinners and the sole mediator between God and his people. For Calvin, the doctrine of election was not an inducement to moral sloth, but inasmuch as election is an expression of free grace in Christ to needy sinners, it is a powerful inducement to piety.

Conclusions

The one thing that most know about Calvin is that he taught the doctrine of predestination, and from this "knowledge" people are wont to make assumption and deductions about what must also be true about Calvin's doctrines of election and predestination.

A close contextual reading of Calvin's doctrine of election, however, reveals a multilayered approach to a difficult set of questions. The first, diachronic, aspect of his context is the historical development of the doctrine of double predestination. Calvin was not only an heir of centuries

194. Ibid.
195. Ibid., 33–34. On this theme in Calvin's theology see Cornelis P. Venema, "The Twofold Nature of the Gospel in Calvin's Theology: The *Duplex Gratia Dei* and the Interpretation of Calvin's Theology" (Ph.D. diss., Princeton Theological Seminary, 1985); R. Scott Clark, "The Benefits of Christ: Double Justification in Protestant Theology before the Westminster Assembly," in *The Faith Once Delivered: Essays in Honor of Wayne R. Spear*, ed. Anthony T. Selvaggio (Phillipsburg, NJ: P&R, 2007), 107–34.

of theological reflection on the Genesis narratives, texts such as Malachi 1:2, and Romans 9:13. He was also heir to centuries of anti-Pelagian rhetoric beginning with Augustine and running through Godescalc and into the neo-Augustinians of the late medieval church. Moreover, he was also heir to a broad Protestant consensus on these doctrines. The formal principle of the Reformation was *sola scriptura,* and whether it was Luther's *Bondage of the Will* or Melanchthon's *Loci Communes* (1521), or Bucer's commentary on Romans, Calvin's influences and colleagues were all reading the same passages the same way and saying essentially the same thing on election and predestination. Thus, however strange this doctrine may seem to late modern readers steeped in assumptions about human autonomy and freedom, Calvin, though aware of such notions, lived largely in a world where repudiation of double predestination was a form of unbelief and apostasy.

The second or synchronic context for his doctrine of predestination was the Reformation of the Genevan congregations and the controversies which stimulated the development of his doctrine of predestination. Just as his reaction to Andreas Osiander stimulated a massive expansion of his explanation of his doctrine of justification, so too his arguments with Pigge, Bolsec, and others prodded him to elaborate upon what began as a brief discussion in 1536 until it became the expansive, detailed, and sometimes polemical discussion of predestination in the 1559 edition.

Certainly there is no support either in modern Calvin studies or in the text of Calvin's writings, for the old caricature that Calvin invented the doctrine of double predestination out of his head. Rather, it is clear from his commentary on Romans—forgetting for the moment his commentaries on Genesis, Ephesians, and others—that Calvin was driven to his doctrine of double predestination by his reading of Scripture. It is a remarkable feature of Calvin's exegetical work that it still stands up to critical scrutiny after 450 years. This fact is a testimony to the care with which he handled the text of Scripture and the grammar, art, and theology of the text of Scripture. At every turn in his commentary on Romans, Calvin was asking and answering the question: What does the text intend that we think?

How Calvin viewed the doctrines of election and predestination pastorally is evident in his sermons on Ephesians. He was conscious that these were difficult doctrines to accept. Perhaps the most striking feature of his sermons on predestination is their gospel orientation. Though he did not refuse to preach the doctrine of reprobation, he presented the election to salvation as good news for sinners and a source of encouragement to believers. Christians may have confidence because they have been awakened to faith, and shall be kept in the same, by the same sovereign grace which elected them from all eternity.

Finally, his *Institutio* must be read in the context of his exegetical and homiletical work with the doctrine. The *Institutes* (and other treatises) was the place where he harvested the theological reflections that grew out of his preaching and lecturing on Scripture. The *Institutio* was to be a preliminary text, a starting point for students and pastors. Calvin intended his *Institutio* to be read along with his biblical commentaries and, in the case of those who were able, along with the daily and weekly expositions of Scripture and the administration of the sacraments on the Lord's Day.

As this essay has tried to follow the method Calvin intended, it has tried to understand Calvin's doctrine of double predestination as he intended, as an exegetical, theological, and pastoral doctrine. Derived from Scripture, developed and advanced in relation to other key doctrines such as the doctrines of God, sin, grace, justification, Christ, and the church, the doctrine of predestination is understood by Calvin to teach that God has, in Christ, elected to salvation a certain number from all eternity and reprobated others, or decreed that they remain in the state of sin, and that this decree must be traced finally to the unquestionable and inscrutable will of God. He understood this doctrine to be biblical *and* theologically necessary, and he understood it as a pastoral doctrine, a source of comfort and assurance for those tempted to doubt their own salvation.

6

CREATION AND PROVIDENCE

INSTITUTES I.14, 16–18
JOSEPH A. PIPA JR.

Creation

In the earlier editions of the *Institutes*, Calvin dealt with the doctrine of creation under his exposition of the Apostles' Creed and the doctrine of providence in connection with his discussion of the decree and election. In the 1559 edition, he moves the discussion of election to book 3, where he develops it in the context of salvation, and elaborates on creation and providence after his discussion of the Trinity in book 1, chapters 14–18.[1] In this chapter, we will consider Calvin's understanding of the work of creation (ch. 14) and the work of providence (chs. 16–18).[2] Calvin's methodology in these chapters is consistent with his manner of doing theology.

1. See Ford Lewis Battles. *Analysis of the Institutes of the Christian Religion of John Calvin* (Phillipsburg, NJ: P&R, 2001), 15.
2. Chapter 15 will be dealt with in chapter 7 of this book.

He is guided by two great principles: (1) all theology must be rooted in Scripture and (2) the purpose of theology is experiential—to lead men to trust in and worship God. With respect to his scriptural model, Robert Schneider writes that John Calvin returned the language of creation theology to its biblical roots.[3]

In chapter 14, Calvin says little about the mode of creation and does not give a detailed account of the process. He focuses his attention on the creation from man's point of view and needs. In his commentary on Genesis 1, however, Calvin explores the topic in much greater detail. Richard Muller suggests that since Calvin dealt extensively with the history of creation in the Genesis commentary, there was no need for him to elaborate in the *Institutes*. Calvin viewed the commentaries as a complement to the *Institutes* in the development of doctrine.[4]

Purpose of the History of Creation

Calvin's overarching purpose in chapter 14 is for men to see the goodness of God toward them in creation.[5] He begins his discussion with two stated purposes. First, he says the account of creation is necessary to establish the Creator-creature distinction. Genesis 1 clearly spells out that God is separate from his creation and thus refutes all forms of pantheism.[6] He writes in his commentary, "The intention of Moses, in beginning his Books with the creation of the world, is, to render God, as it were, visible to us in his works."[7] Second, the creation account establishes that Jehovah is the true God: "Therefore it was his will that the history of Creation be made manifest, in order that the faith of the church, resting upon this, might seek no other God but him who was put forth by Moses as the Maker and Founder of the universe."[8]

3. Robert Schneider, "Essay II: Theology of Creation: Historical Perspectives and Fundamental Concepts," http://community.berea.edu/scienceandfaith/essay02.asp.

4. Richard A. Muller, *The Unaccommodated Calvin: Studies in the Foundation of a Theological Tradition* (New York: Oxford University Press, 2000), 154.

5. 1.14.2, 12, 18, 20–22.

6. 1.14.1.

7. John Calvin, *Calvin's Commentaries: Genesis*, vol. 1, trans. John King (Grand Rapids: Eerdmans. 1948), 58. See also p. 59. Earlier he states that creation reveals God's knowledge, wisdom, and creative artistry, 1.5.1–2; *Genesis*, 63.

8. 1.14.1.

The Work of Creation

Calvin defines the work of creation in this fashion:

> From this history we shall learn that God by the power of his Word and Spirit created heaven and earth out of nothing; that thereupon he brought forth living beings and inanimate things of every kind, that in a wonderful series he distinguished an innumerable variety of things, that he endowed each kind with its own nature, assigned functions, appointed places and stations; and that, although all were subject to corruption, he nevertheless provided for the preservation of each species (kinds) until the Last Day.[9]

By this definition, Calvin asserts that creation is the work of the triune God. In the previous chapter, he asserts the role of the Son and Spirit in creation in order to prove their deity.[10] His definition also asserts that the work of creation was *ex nihilo*. By this he means that the original act of creation was God's making all things out of nothing. Calvin argues for creation out of nothing on the basis of the Hebrew word *bara'* in Genesis 1:1: "He moreover teaches by the word 'created,' that what before did not exist was now made; for he has not used the term *yatsar*, which signifies to frame or form, but *bara'*, which signifies to create."[11]

Benjamin Warfield was one of the first to attempt to adjust Calvin's thought with modern theories. Using Calvin's distinction between the first created act of God being *ex nihilo* and the subsequent acts as merely the forming of things, he asserts:

9. 1.14.20. He refers his readers to the works of Basil and Ambrose for a fuller exposition of the work of creation.

10. 1.13.7–14. He expands on their role in the Godhead in his comments on Genesis 1:1–2, Calvin, *Genesis*, 73–74. See also *Calvin's Commentaries: The Gospel according to St. John 1–10*, ed. David and Thomas Torrance and trans. T. H. L. Parker (Grand Rapids: Eerdmans, 1959), 7–9. For an intriguing discussion of the role of God the Son see Peter Wyatt, *Jesus Christ and Creation in the Theology of John Calvin*, Princeton Theological Monograph Series (Allison Park, PA: Pickwick, 1996).

11. Calvin, *Genesis*, 70. Although he presses the meaning of *bara'* too far, the verb does express the concept of extraordinary and supernatural. Francis Brown, S. R. Driver, and Charles A. Briggs, *Hebrew and English Lexicon of the Old Testament* (Oxford: Clarendon, 1962), 185; see also 1.14.20, n. 29.

What concerns us here is that he ascribed the entire series of modifications by which the primal "indigested mass," called "heaven and earth,"
has passed into the form of the ordered world which we see, including
the origination of all forms of life, vegetable and animal alike, inclusive
doubtless of the bodily form of man, to second causes as their proximate
account. And this, we say, is a very pure evolutionary scheme. He does
not discuss, of course, the factors of the evolutionary process, nor does
he attempt to trace the course of the evolutionary advance, nor even
expound the nature of the secondary cause by which it was wrought. It
is enough for him to say that God said, "Let the waters bring forth. . . .
Let the earth bring forth," and they brought forth. Of the interaction of
forces by which the actual production of forms was accomplished, he
had doubtless no conception: he certainly ventures no assertions in this
field. . . . Calvin doubtless had no theory whatever of evolution; but he
teaches a doctrine of evolution. . . . Accordingly his doctrine of evolution
is entirely unfruitful. The whole process takes place in the limits of six
natural days. That the doctrine should be of use as an explanation of the
mode of production of the ordered world, it was requisite that these six
days should be lengthened out into six periods—six ages of the growth
of the world. Had that been done Calvin would have been precursor
of the modern evolutionary theorists. As it is, he only forms a point of
departure for them to this extent—that he teaches, as they teach, the
modification of the original world-stuff, by the instrumentality of second
causes—or as a modern would put it, of its intrinsic forces.[12]

Warfield's use of the term "evolution" is improper. Evolution as a theory
demands long ages of time and the term (scientifically) has no meaning
divorced from time. Moreover, since Calvin held to the order of the six
days, his view could not be a point of departure for evolutionary theories,
since the evolutionary order is very different from that of Genesis 1.

Warfield, in fact, misunderstood Calvin's views. Although Calvin
will argue that the Hebrew term *bara'* should be used exclusively for the
creation *ex nihilo*, he does not depict the subsequent acts as results of

12. Benjamin Warfield, *The Works of Benjamin Warfield*, vol. 5, *Calvin and Calvinism*
(Grand Rapids: Baker, 1981), 305–6. After quoting Bavinck in note 45, Warfield makes
the statement, "Calvin accordingly very naturally thought along the lines of a theistic evo-
lutionism" (306).

second causes. Rather, the creative word of God works in the primal mass to bring forth the things that God created.[13] Calvin uses the verb "create" and the noun "creation" to refer to these acts of God.[14]

Calvin's definition also highlights God's eternity and self-existence.[15] Calvin says that time is first marked in Genesis 1:1 so that men might know the source of all things.[16] In this manner God asserts his eternity. With respect to God's eternity, he argues that it is not proper to speculate on why God created when he did: "For it is neither lawful nor expedient for us to inquire why God delayed so long, because if the human mind strives to penetrate thus far, it will fail a hundred times on that way. And it would not even be useful for us to know what God himself, to test our moderation of faith, on purpose willed to be hidden."[17] In his commentary, he writes, "As for ourselves, it ought not to seem so very absurd that God, satisfied in himself, did not create a world which he needed not, sooner than he thought good."[18]

Calvin makes a similar observation with respect to space. Space is a created, finite entity, and we ought not to inquire what lies outside it or why God chose to make a finite amount of space.[19] We must be content with revelation. We have more than sufficient matter with which to occupy our minds contemplating the work of God in the almost six thousand years since creation.[20] He concludes, "Therefore let us willingly remain enclosed within these bounds to which God has willed to confine us, and as it were, to pen up our minds that they may not, through their very freedom to wander, go astray."[21]

Calvin held to a literal six days of creation and rejects speculation as to why God did not create instantaneously. He states that God chose to create in a gradual progression rather than instantaneously for our sake

13. Calvin, *Genesis*, 90.
14. Ibid., 74–90.
15. 1.14.1, 3.
16. 1.14.1.
17. Ibid.
18. Calvin, *Genesis*, 61. See also Heb. 11:3.
19. 1.14.1.
20. As seen by his allusion to six thousand years, he also believed that the Genesis genealogies are chronologies.
21. 1.14.1.

in order to draw our minds away from all fictitious accounts of creation and that we might fulfil our calling in contemplating God's great work.[22] The ordered progression of creation demonstrates God's love for man.[23] Since man thinks in time, God observed the laws of time to provide man with the material for holy meditation. Neither is God's power diminished by taking six days; his wisdom dictates the exercise of his power.[24] Calvin adds in his commentary:

> Let us rather conclude that God himself took the space of six days, for the purpose of accommodating his works to the capacity of men. We slightingly pass over the infinite glory of God, which here shines forth; whence arises this but from our excessive dullness in considering his greatness? In the meantime, the vanity of our minds carries us away elsewhere. For the correction of this fault, God applied the most suitable remedy when he distributed the creation of the world into successive portions, that he might fix our attention, and compel us, as if he had laid his hand upon us, to pause and to reflect.[25]

Calvin also asserts the importance of the order of the six days; the order, he says, demonstrates God's fatherly love for mankind:

> For if he had put him [Adam] in an earth as yet sterile and empty, if he had given him life before light, he would have seemed to provide insufficiently for his welfare. Now when he disposed the movements of the sun and stars to human uses, filled the earth, waters, and air with living things, and brought forth an abundance of fruits to suffice as foods, in thus assuming the responsibility of a foreseeing and diligent father of the family he shows his wonderful goodness toward us.[26]

Furthermore, with respect to the order of creation Calvin explains the importance of the origin of light before the creation of the sun. Although the sun is necessary for the sustenance of life on the earth, God made the

22. 1.14.2.
23. Ibid. See also 1.14.22.
24. 1.14.22.
25. Calvin, *Genesis*, 78.
26. 1.14.2.

light first and then plants before he made the sun. "Therefore the Lord, by the very order of the creation, bears witness that he holds in his hand the light, which he is able to impart to us without the sun and moon."[27]

Calvin's commitment to six days and the order of the days stands in bold contrast to modern theories such as the framework hypothesis and the analogical view of Genesis 1. He emphatically insists on the order of the six days as both advantageous to man and instructive about the character of God; for example, his insistence on God's creating light and plants before he created the sun. He directly counters the modern views and repudiates the notion that ordinary providence was the process by which God did his creative work.[28] Moreover, he rejects the notion that Moses divides the work of creation into six days simply for instruction.[29]

Calvin concludes this section with two assertions. First, with respect to the reliability of the creation account, "Moses was a sure witness and herald of the one God, the creator."[30] Second, Moses ascribes the work of creation to the Trinity so "that we may not conjure up some other god than him who would have himself recognized in that clear image."[31]

The Creation of Angels and Devils

Calvin devotes the greater part of his discussion of creation in this chapter to the spiritual part of creation. Although he was pressing on to discuss the creation of man (ch. 15), he felt compelled to discuss angelic beings for two reasons. First, they are noble examples of God's work from whom we learn a great deal about God.[32] Second, he counters errors that surround these holy beings; some apply divinity to them, and others, like Mani,[33] make the devil eternal, since a good God would create only good and not evil. Such madness, claims Calvin, would rob God of his glory, because to ascribe to the devil the

27. Calvin, *Genesis*, 76. See also 1.16.2.
28. Meredith G. Kline, "Because It Had Not Rained," *Westminster Theological Journal* 20 (1957–58): 146–57.
29. Calvin, *Genesis*, 78.
30. 1.14.2. See *Genesis*, 58–59.
31. Ibid.
32. 1.14.3.
33. Ibid. Mani was Manichaeus (d. 277), who founded the dualistic sect of the Manicheans.

creation of evil would declare him to be eternal. God alone is eternal and self-existent. Moreover, the doctrine of dualism robs God of his sovereignty and omnipotence. Calvin counters the problem of a good God creating evil by asserting, along with Augustine, that no created nature is evil: "For the depravity and malice both of man and of the devil, or the sins that arise therefrom, do not spring from nature, but rather from corruption of nature."[34]

Although Genesis 1 does not specifically describe the creation of angels, Calvin asserts that the Bible clearly teaches that God created the angels within the six days of creation, but does not tell us on which day.[35] He adds that since Scripture refers to them as God's ministers (Ps. 103:20–21), "there should be no question that they are also his creatures."[36]

Angels (1.14.4–12)

In sections 4–12, Calvin expounds the doctrine of good angels. He begins his discussion by reasserting the principle of being governed by the Bible alone. If it were for our edification, God would have told us more. Here Calvin gives a useful note on how we are to read Scripture: we are to seek and study those things that are for our edification. He also comments on the task of the theologian, which is to teach those things that are "true, sure, and profitable."[37]

He addresses the speculations on the nature, order, and number of angels, specifically referring to *De coelesti hierarchia* (*The Celestial and Ecclesiastical Hierarchy* of Dionysius the Areopagite.[38] This book is a discourse on the order of the angelic hosts. With respect to Dionysius, Calvin writes:

> If you read that book, you would think a man fallen from heaven recounted, not what he had learned, but what he had seen with his

34. 1.14.3.
35. 1.14.3–4.
36. 1.14.4.
37. Ibid.
38. A fifth-century book discussing angels, their nature, and order. The medieval church ascribed this work to Dionysius the Areopagite, who joined himself to Paul in Acts 17:34. Renaissance textual criticism proved that the work was written in the fifth century. By the seventeenth century it was universally recognized to be late fifth century. This work was popularized by Thomas Aquinas.

own eyes. Yet Paul, who had been caught up beyond the third heaven [2 Cor. 12:2], not only said nothing about it, but also testified that it is unlawful for any man to speak of the secret things that he has seen [2 Cor. 12:4]. Therefore, bidding farewell to that foolish wisdom, let us examine in the simple teaching of Scripture what the Lord would have us know of his angels.[39]

Calvin affirms that angels are real, personal beings. Although they are agents through whom God acts, we are not to think of them as a figurative expression of God's power and work. He proves this point from a number of Scripture references: they are a great host (Rev. 5:11; Matt. 26:53); they have emotions (Luke 15:10); they lift believers and carry their souls to heaven (Ps. 91:11; Luke 16:22); they look on the face of God (Matt. 18:10); they administered the law (Acts 7:53; Gal. 3:19); believers in heaven will be like them in certain respects (Matt. 22:30); they will come with Christ on the last day (Matt. 25:31); Paul calls on them as witnesses (1 Tim. 5:21); and Christ is more excellent than they (Heb. 1:4; 2:5, 16).[40]

The name "angel" is derived from the word "messenger" and refers to their primary task, to serve as messengers of God. They are called hosts, because they are God's army that surrounds his throne and makes his majesty conspicuous. They are called dominions, principalities, and powers because God exercises his dominion through them. They are called thrones, probably because God's glory resides in them. Finally, they are called gods because God in some manner manifests his divinity through them. Calvin concurs with the interpretation that the angel of God was Christ in a preincarnate appearance.[41]

Although they are given these names, we are unable to determine the orders and numbers of the angels.[42] There are two references to the archangel (Jude 9; 1 Thess. 4:16), and the Scripture names Michael, who is called the great prince (Dan. 12:1), and Gabriel, and assigns to them important roles in revelation. There is, however, no clear evidence as to their relations and hierarchies. Although the Bible reveals that

39. 1.14.4.
40. 1.14.9.
41. 1.14.5.
42. 1.14.8.

they are a great multitude (Matt. 26:53; Dan. 7:10; 2 Kings 6:17), it never gives the tally.[43]

With respect to their form, angels are spirits. Although Scripture depicts them with wings, under the names of cherubim and seraphim, this was a figure to depict their swiftness in serving God.[44] Again Calvin reminds his readers not to speculate: "Whatever besides can be sought of both their number and order, let us hold it among those mysteries whose full revelation is delayed until the Last Day. Therefore let us remember not to probe too curiously or talk too confidently."[45]

The Bible primarily teaches about their work: they are "dispensers and administrators of God's beneficence toward us."[46] They watch over us for our safety and defense, direct our ways (delivering messages from God in the time before the canon was completed), and administer comfort to us. What the angels did for Christ (Ps. 91:11–12), they do for all those who are in Christ.[47]

Calvin denies the doctrine that each person has a personal guardian. He maintains that all the angels are assigned the care of God's elect.[48] He answers three arguments for individual guardian angels. First, that particular angels have been assigned to serve as guardians over kingdoms (Dan. 10:13, 20; 12:1) does not imply that each individual has a specific guardian angel. Second, the reference to children's angels beholding the face of the Father (Matt. 18:10) does hint that certain angels have been assigned to look after the safety of children, but this is not sufficient ground to assert a guardian angel. Third, with respect to Peter's angel (Acts 12:15), it is possible the servant girl believed that Peter had a particular guardian angel, but nothing prevents the interpretation that an angel was appointed care of him in prison.[49] Calvin also rejects the specious belief

43. Ibid. In his sermons on Deuteronomy he states that their number is infinite. *The Sermons of John Calvin upon the Fifth Booke of Moses Called Deuteronomie*, trans. Arthur Golding (Edinburgh: Banner of Truth Trust, 1987), 1187.

44. 1.14.8.

45. Ibid.

46. 1.14.6.

47. Ibid.

48. 1.14.7.

49. Ibid.

that each person has a good and evil angel warring over him.[50] For Calvin the bottom line was, Why settle for one when in fact we have the hosts of heaven watching over us?[51]

Because angels are such glorious creatures, men are tempted to worship them. Paul addresses this problem in Colossians 1:16, 20, and John confesses his confusion in Revelation 19:10; 22:8–9. Calvin points out that their work is ministerial, and God uses them for our sake. Although he is not bound to work through them, he freely chooses to do so.[52] God who alone is our protector teaches that he cares for us through a multitude of angels to prop our weak faith. Calvin gives the example of Elisha's servant whose faith is greatly strengthened by the revelation of the angelic army (2 Kings 6:17).[53] Therefore, if we think of angels as other than those who "lead us by the hand straight to him [God],"[54] we shall fall into idolatry. We must not divide our trust between angels and God.[55]

Devils (1.14.13–19)

Although a discussion of devils does not belong here chronologically, Calvin includes this section, since they were fallen angels. He warns of the danger of Satan and his demons (he calls them devils) and the necessity of vigilance in spiritual warfare until our death. Like the angels from whom they declined, devils are real beings. Calvin offers a number of proofs from Scripture that devils are real, personal creatures and not some malignant force in the world.[56]

God created Satan and the devils as holy angels; their evil natures are a perversion of the created order.[57] Calvin offers two proofs for this statement: "he abode not in the truth," implying he once was in the truth; and he is "the father of lies," implying he may impute to God his deceit

---

50. Ibid.
51. Ibid.
52. 1.14.10.
53. Ibid.
54. 1.14.12.
55. Ibid.
56. 1.14.19.
57. 1.14.16. See also 1.14.3.

and malice.[58] Calvin insists we must be content with the relative silence of Scripture with respect to the details of the fall of the devils and refuse to speculate.[59]

He was well aware of the power of the evil fiend and reminds his readers that Satan is called the god and prince of this world, a strong-armed man, the spirit who exercises power over the air, and a prowling lion.[60] Our task is to resist him. Calvin gives an eloquent warning:

> We have been forewarned that an enemy relentlessly threatens us, an enemy who is the very embodiment of rash boldness, of military prowess, of crafty wiles, of untiring zeal and haste, of every conceivable weapon and of skill in the science of warfare. We must, then, bend our every effort to this goal: that we should not let ourselves be overwhelmed by carelessness or faintheartedness, but on the contrary, with courage rekindled stand our ground in combat. Since this military service ends only at death, let us urge ourselves to perseverance. Indeed, conscious of our weakness and ignorance, let us especially call upon God's help, relying upon him alone in whatever we attempt, since it is he alone who can supply us with counsel and strength, courage and armor.[61]

We must be mindful of their power. Like the angelic hosts from which they declined, the devils are an innumerable host.[62] When Satan or the devil is mentioned in the singular, it refers to the wicked kingdom that opposes the kingdom of righteousness.[63]

Satan and his demons set themselves in opposition to God and all that he wills. They are the epitome of depravity, "the author, leader, and architect of all malice and iniquity."[64] Calvin cautions that, if we care about God's glory, the advance of Christ's kingdom, and our own salvation, we must ceaselessly struggle against the dark kingdom.[65]

58. Ibid.
59. Ibid.
60. 1.14.13.
61. Ibid.
62. 1.14.14.
63. Ibid.
64. 1.14.15.
65. Ibid.

Although the devil is powerful, he is under the control of God and can do nothing apart from God's will.[66] Calvin illustrates this from the account of Job (1:6, 12; 2:1, 6)[67] and from the false spirit commissioned by God to deceive Ahab (1 Kings 22:20–22). Moreover, God sent him to torment Saul (1 Sam. 16:14; 18:10) and to destroy the Egyptians (Ps. 78:49). Even the blinding of unbelievers, which is of God, is ascribed to Satan (2 Thess. 2:9–10; 2 Cor. 4:4). So although he resists God and God's work, his "resistance and opposition are dependent upon God's sufferance."[68]

Anticipating what he would write on providence and sin, Calvin points out that the devil acts of his own evil nature, but God by his sovereign power binds him so that he can only accomplish God's will.[69]

God, by his sovereign good pleasure, allows the devils to attack and afflict his people, at times grievously wounding and defeating them, yet Satan will not ultimately conquer them. Because of our union with Christ, we will be victorious, although we may suffer many a defeat in the battle.[70] Christ conquered Satan in his death and resurrection. As Christ's kingdom advances, Satan's falls. Christ has dominion over the wicked and will carry them to perdition.[71]

Spiritual Lessons from Creation (1.14.20–22)

Calvin concludes his discussion of creation by directing our attention to its lessons. We, he says, are "to take pious delight in the works of God open and manifest in this most beautiful theater."[72] It is important that we firmly believe the creation account of Genesis 1 and 2, since the creation teaches us clearly about God. Creation, he says, is an evidence for faith.[73]

66. 1.14.17.
67. See Calvin's sermons on Job for amplification. John Calvin, *Sermons on Job*, trans. Arthur Golding (Edinburgh: Banner of Truth Trust, 1993).
68. 1.14.17.
69. Ibid.; 1.18.3–4.
70. 1.14.18.
71. Ibid.
72. 1.14.20.
73. Ibid.

He summarizes the work of creation: God made all things from nothing and nourishes and preserves all that he created so that each species will be preserved until the last day. (He does not use "species" in the modern sense, but for all the various kinds that God created.) From time to time he reinvigorates some, and on others confers the gift of propagation so that they will not die off; he has adorned all with great beauty and order, and he crowns the whole with the creation of man.[74]

Man then should carefully study all creatures in order to learn God's "wisdom, justice, goodness, and power."[75] Particularly, believers are to observe "the conspicuous powers which God shows forth in his creatures, and then learn so to apply it to themselves that their very hearts are touched."[76]

Such meditations will compel us "to trust, invoke, praise, and love him."[77] God made all things for man; what ingratitude and impiety to think that he will not care for us perfectly.[78] We then should petition him for what we desire and give thanks for all his benefits. Calvin concludes: "So invited by the great sweetness of his beneficence and goodness, let us study to love and serve him with all our heart."[79]

Calvin's Doctrine in the Modern Church

Calvin's doctrine of creation went unchallenged until the middle of the nineteenth century. The challenges that have arisen are not against his exegesis, but his naiveté. It is asserted that if he knew what we know (implying the claims of many modern scientists about the age of the earth and the order of creation), he would not have held to a literal six-day creation and a world that is only about six thousand years old. Of course, one cannot dogmatically prove such an assertion wrong, but one can examine the implications and trajectory of Calvin's thought.

We have noted that, methodologically, he was bound to Scripture. He recognized creation as an extraordinary, unrepeatable work of God.

74. Ibid.
75. 1.14.21.
76. Ibid.
77. 1.14.22.
78. Ibid.
79. Ibid.

He insisted that we must rely on revelation to understand what God did. Moreover, contrary to modern assertions,[80] he never placed general revelation on a par with special revelation. Calvin clearly asserts that we can understand natural revelation only by the spectacles of Scripture and that creation can be properly understood only by the believer.[81] Scripture, in fact, corrects the observation of nature.[82] Furthermore, although he commends the work of the scientist (for example, the astronomer), he says the account of creation is written for the layman and describes the creation from man's perspective, and thus we do not need scientific investigation to understand Moses' account.[83]

Providence—Chapters 16–18

Calvin begins his discussion of providence by establishing the inseparable relationship between creation and providence. If we neglect God's role in governing what he created, we do not truly understand his role as Creator.[84] Although some see no more than a general divine energy bestowed on creation for the sustenance of all things, Scripture demands we recognize God's active preservation and governance of all things (Ps. 33:6, 13; 104:27–30; Acts 17:28).[85]

Calvin defines providence: "to conclude he is also everlasting Governor and Preserver—not only in that he drives the celestial frame as well as its several parts by a universal motion, but also in that he sustains, nourishes, and cares for, everything he has made, even to the least sparrow [cf. Matt. 10:29]."[86] Calvin's discussion of providence presupposes that God has eternally foreordained all that comes to pass.

80. Pattle P. T. Pun, "A Theology of Progressive Creationism," *Perspectives on Science and Christian Faith: Journal of the American Scientific Affiliation* 39. 1 (March 1987): 9–19.
81. Calvin, *Genesis*, 63.
82. Battles, *Analysis*, 74.
83. Calvin, *Genesis*, 86–87.
84. 1.16.1.
85. Ibid.
86. Ibid. See also Wilhelm Niesel, *The Theology of Calvin*, trans. Harold Knight (Philadelphia: Westminster, 1956), 70.

He begins by rejecting various pagan notions of providence. In our own day we hear a great deal about mother nature or the laws of nature affecting the weather. Bad or good luck is associated with death or success in an enterprise. Calvin declares that all such notions are pagan concepts. He says that in times of sudden calamity or unexpected deliverance we ought to ascribe all to God's providence.[87] All events, as well as the actions of inanimate objects, are governed by God's secret plan and ordered by his power.[88]

For example, Calvin points out that the sun is necessary for the sustenance of life on the earth, but God made the light first and then plants before he made the sun. "Therefore a godly man will not make the sun either the principal or the necessary cause of these things which existed before the creation of the sun, but merely the instrument that God uses because he so wills."[89] Moreover, the sun's standing still (Josh. 10:13) or moving backward (2 Kings 20:11) teaches that the sun does not operate by blind instinct; it is governed by God.[90]

Calvin explains that, if God is omnipotent, he must govern all things. His omnipotence is not an empty, vague thing nor a general principle of random motion that sets things in motion, but "is directed toward individual and particular motions."[91] Omnipotence means much more than that God can act when he wishes; it means he governs all things and nothing occurs apart from his divine power.[92] When the Bible declares that he does whatever he wills (Ps. 115:3), it does not mean that he is only the first cause of all general effects, but that his will is the "certain and deliberate" cause of all things.[93] Therefore nothing in the universe operates on the basis of universal natural law, divorced from divine activity.

Calvin points out that the biblical doctrine of providence has two practical results: a great motive to obey the one who has so wonderfully provided for us, and a sense of security under God's protection, freeing

87. 1.16.2.
88. Ibid.
89. Ibid.
90. Ibid. He further illustrates this point from the progression and diversity of the seasons.
91. 1.16.3.
92. Ibid.
93. Ibid.

138

us from superstition.[94] He applies this deliverance from superstition to "judicial astrology." Our trust and fear must be directed toward God and not to the heavenly bodies: "Remember that there is no erratic power, or action, or motion in creatures, but that they are governed by God's secret plan in such a way that nothing happens except what is knowingly and willingly decreed by him."[95]

Calvin begins section 4 by reminding the reader that providence is much more than foreknowledge. By providence God actively governs all things. When Abraham told Isaac that "God will provide" (Gen. 22:8), he referred not only to God's foreknowledge, but also to God's provision.[96]

Calvin addresses a number of errors. First, he dismisses the doctrine that providence is a universal, not a specific determination: "that the universe, men's affairs, and men themselves are governed by God's might, but not by His determination."[97] Providence, he writes, involves the real agency of God; it involves God's will.[98] Those who hold to a universal, nonspecific providence teach that man acts by his own free will and may be moved contingently or by his free choice, without any determination on God's part.[99]

Second, he rejects the Epicurean concept that God is idle in the affairs of the universe.

Third, he dismisses those who imagine that God rules inanimate objects above the middle region, but leaves the lower regions to be ruled by fortune.[100]

Fourth, he exposes the notion of general providence as opposed to special providence. By general providence he refers to those who grant God a general, blind motion over the general operations of the universe, but not the direct governance of all things. Calvin does not deny that God's power sets in motion specific relations, and that laws in the

94. Ibid.
95. Ibid.
96. Ibid., 1.16.4.
97. Ibid.
98. Ibid.
99. Ibid.
100. Ibid.

universe operate as he determined. Yet we must affirm that everything "proceeds from his set plan, that nothing takes place by chance."[101] Calvin explains that Scripture clearly teaches the active involvement of God in the sustenance and governance of the world (John 5:17; Acts 17:28; Heb. 1:3).[102]

Calvin demonstrates from Scripture that God's providence directs all individual occurrences in the world. If providence were only general, there would be no room for understanding that adverse things may be acts of God's judgment, and that beneficial things are his fatherly blessing (Lev. 26:3–4, 19; Deut. 11:12–14; 28:12, 22; Isa. 28:2; Hag. 2:18–19).[103] The Bible also attributes the regular acts of nature to God; he feeds the birds sometimes abundantly and sometimes sparsely (Ps. 147:9), and not one bird falls to the ground apart from God's will (Matt. 10:29).[104]

Moreover, Calvin proves special providence from the actions of men. If providence applied only generally to men, they would ultimately be in control of their fate. But man, in fact, is the special object of providence; his actions are under the absolute disposal of God (Jer. 10:23; Prov. 20:24). His willing, choosing, and acting all are ordered (Prov. 16:1); God determines all of men's acts (Prov. 16:1, 9). Scripture also teaches that apparently fortuitous events are of God (Ex. 21:13; Prov. 16:33). Even man's condition as rich or poor is determined by God (Prov. 29:13; Ps. 75:6–7).[105]

Natural occurrences also prove special providence. The Bible attributes these peculiar natural occurrences to God—the weather (Ps. 107:25–29), conception (Gen. 30:2), provision of food (Deut. 8:3; Matt. 4:4; Isa. 3:1; Matt. 6:11; Ps. 136:25). God alone makes the earth fruitful or barren.[106] Our asking him for our daily bread (Matt. 6:11) and God's gracious response to the prayers of the righteous and his punishment of the wicked further prove that his providential care is specific and not general.[107]

101. Ibid.
102. Ibid.
103. 1.16.5.
104. Ibid.
105. 1.16.6.
106. 1.16.7.
107. Ibid.

Having established the specific nature of providence, Calvin distinguishes providence from fate. Since the days when Pelagius accused Augustine of holding to fate,[108] those who reject the doctrine of God's sovereignty have confused the doctrine of providence with fate. Fate is the impersonal, natural necessity of events, while providence is the intelligent act of God:

> But we make God the ruler and governor of all things, who in accordance with his wisdom has from the farthest limit of eternity decreed what he was going to do, and now by his might carries out what he has decreed. From this we declare that not only heaven and earth and the inanimate creatures, but also the plans and intentions of men, are so governed by his providence that they are borne by it straight to their appointed end.[109]

Calvin anticipates the question: does anything happen by chance or contingency?[110] He rejects the concept of fortune or chance as pagan. He says that what men mean by a "chance occurrence" is something "of which the reason and cause are secret."[111]

Moreover, he, along with Augustine, rejects all contingent events as occurring apart from God's providence. A contingent event is that which is unforeseen, a result of some occurrence or free choice of men. He admits that many events, although ordained by God, according to our perspective appear to be fortuitous. "But since the order, reason, end, and necessity of those things which happen for the most part lie hidden in God's purpose, and are not apprehended by human opinion, those things which it is certain take place by God's will, are in a sense fortuitous. For they bear on the face of them no other appearance, whether they are considered in their own nature or weighed according to our knowledge and judgment."[112]

The same holds true for the contingency of future events. Although they appear uncertain to us, they are planned and executed by God.[113] To

108. 1.16.8 n. 15.
109. Ibid.
110. Ibid.
111. Ibid.
112. 1.16.9.
113. Ibid.

make his point, Calvin uses the scholastic distinction of relative necessity and absolute necessity and of consequent and consequence. Relative necessity means that a thing is not of itself necessary, but so determined by the decree of God.[114] Absolute necessity refers to the known effects of causes; we drop a book and it falls. "Consequent" (*necessitas consequentis*) refers to those things that are the automatic effects of causes. They cannot be other than they are.[115] By "consequence" Calvin refers to *necessitas consequentiae*, events arising from contingent circumstances or from hypothetical necessity.[116] Consequently, when God decrees something, it necessarily comes to pass, even contingent circumstances.

Calvin notes three ends or objects we are to keep before our minds when interpreting providence: providence extends equally to future events as to past ones; it works by, without, or against an intermediary; God, in his providential acts, reveals his concern for mankind, but especially the church.[117] He adds that although the causes may be hidden from us, we rest in the reality that God has foreordained whatsoever comes to pass.[118] God always has a purpose—adversity is for reproof, for chastisement, for prevention of sin, for humility, or to punish the wicked; and although the design is often concealed, we are not to condemn; consequently, we must repress all rash judgments and confess that God is always wise and good.[119]

Calvin insists that we must approach the doctrine of providence with reverence and humility; reason must be tethered to Scripture.[120] All that happens is governed by God's eternal decree, "incomprehensible plans."[121]

114. None of Christ's bones will be broken is an example offered in 1.16.9.

115. Richard A. Muller, *Dictionary of Latin and Greek Theological Terms* (Grand Rapids: Baker, 1998), 200.

116. Ibid. Turretin explains "consequence": "nothing prevents those things (which as to mode of production take place contingently with respect to second causes) from still having a necessity of consequence or of the infallible futurition of the event from the order of providence." Francis Turretin, *Institutes of Elenctic Theology*, ed. James T. Dennison Jr. and trans. George Musgrave Giger (Phillipsburg, NJ: P&R, 1992) 1:500. An example would be the hypothetical necessity of the atonement.

117. 1.17.1.

118. Ibid.

119. Ibid.

120. 1:17, 2.

121. Ibid.

Although many reject this doctrine as dangerous, it is sufficient that God reveals it. Here Calvin distinguishes between God's holy will and his precepts (Deut. 29:29).[122] Some, like Sebastian Castellio, accused Calvin of teaching that God has two wills. Calvin insists that God has one simple will: "Yet God's will is not therefore at war with itself, nor does it pretend not to will what he wills. But even though his will is one and simple in him, it appears manifold to us because, on account of our mental incapacity, we do not grasp how in divers ways it wills and does not will something to take place."[123] By his secret decree he accomplishes the moral ends he reveals in his law. Calvin compares God's hidden will to a deep abyss. We then must submit to God's supreme authority and adore his plan.[124] Calvin does not mean that God's absolute authority is arbitrary or divorced from justice. God's will is an absolute law, but it is not arbitrary. Thus he rejects the doctrine of the nominalist who maintained that God could act in any way he determined.[125]

Calvin asserts that providence does not annul human responsibility. Our duty is to obey God as he has revealed his will in Scripture. Calvin counters two errors. First, he rebuts those who murmur against God because of their adversities or who blame him for their sins. Man's duty is to obey God.[126] Second, he answers those who claim that the use of means is vain.[127] He particularly has in mind the sect of the Libertines.[128]

Expanding on the use of means, Calvin teaches that providence does not excuse the need for prudence, or the necessity to plan for the future, or the use of means that are consistent with God's Word.[129] He demonstrates that God's rule connects means and end:

> For this reason, God pleased to hide all future events from us, in order
> that we should resist them as doubtful, and not cease to oppose them

122. Ibid.
123. 1.18.3.
124. 1.17.2.
125. 1.17.2; see also n. 7.
126. 1.17.3.
127. Ibid.
128. Ibid, n. 10.
129. 1.17.4.

with ready remedies, until they are either overcome or pass beyond all care. I have therefore already remarked that God's providence does not always meet us in its naked form, but God in a sense clothes it with the means employed.[130]

Calvin further rejects the doctrine of the Libertines by pointing out that God's ordering of all things does not exculpate the guilt of the perpetrators.[131] He touched on this doctrine when he dealt with devils. If wicked men are serving God's will, why should they be punished? Calvin answers that if they do not obey God's law, they are not serving his will. God's will is revealed in his law. Although God's purposes were fulfilled in the sinful acts, we do his will only when we submit to his Word.[132]

Calvin writes that God uses men without being party to their wickedness. He illustrates this principle from the activity of the sun in the putrefaction of a corpse. One does not blame the sun because the heat of its rays causes a carcass to putrefy and smell.[133]

The best guard against such errors is to meditate on the benefits of providence to believers. Calvin points out four things: God has ordered all events; God orders all things for the well-being of his people; God uses all agents, good and evil; and God exercises special care for his people.[134] He summarizes: "As far as men are concerned, whether they are good or evil, the heart of the Christian will know that their plans, wills, efforts, and abilities are under God's hand; that it is his choice to bend them whither he pleases and to constrain them whenever he pleases."[135]

Calvin proves this point with a number of scriptural promises with respect to God's particular care of his people.[136] He holds to the medieval distinction of hierarchical causes: God is the primary cause, but man and the devil are secondary causes. By this distinction, he frees God from the accusation of being the author of sin.

130. Ibid.
131. 1.17.5.
132. Ibid.
133. Ibid.
134. 1.17.6.
135. Ibid.
136. Ibid.

Calvin applies the doctrine of special providence to prosperity. All our affairs are in God's hands; therefore, we should be grateful for all good things, patient in adversity, and free of worry about the future.[137] Consequently, in times of prosperity, we give all glory to God.[138]

Moreover, in times of adversity, the believer will raise his mind to God and wait patiently on him, looking for his good purposes (Gen. 45:5, 7–8; 50:20). We then ought not to lash out against those who wickedly abuse us or grumble at the affairs of our lives. Rather, Calvin says, "If there is no more effective remedy for anger and impatience, he has surely benefited greatly who has so learned to meditate upon God's providence that he can always recall his mind to this point: the Lord has willed it; therefore it must be borne, not only because one may not contend against it, but also because he wills nothing but what is just and expedient."[139]

Such an attitude, however, does not rule out expressing gratitude to human agents for our blessings. The recipient of blessing will honor God and thank those who have been his instruments.[140] On the other hand, if one experiences loss because of one's own negligence or imprudence, one will recognize God's sovereignty, but will make no excuse for oneself. The same holds true if someone else suffers because of one's negligence.[141]

With respect to the future, we are to make use of human helps and other creatures capable of enabling us to pursue righteous ends.[142] But our confidence and trust are in the Lord.[143]

Calvin reminds us of the uncertainty of living in a world out of control; there is no end to possible calamities. Without the certainty of a good, all-powerful God directing our lives, life would be intolerable.[144] Belief in providence gives us great equanimity of mind even in the face of the attacks of the wicked and the afflictions that arise apart from human agency.[145]

137. 1.17.7.
138. Ibid.
139. 1.17.8.
140. 1.17.9.
141. Ibid.
142. Ibid.
143. Ibid.
144. 1.17.10.
145. Ibid.; 1.17.8.

By the proper consideration of providence, the believer is delivered from all care and worry, because he knows that his Father carefully directs his life.[146] Calvin summarizes: "In short, not to tarry any longer over this, if you pay attention, you will easily perceive that ignorance of providence is the ultimate of all miseries; the highest blessedness lies in the knowledge of it."[147]

At this point Calvin anticipates two objections: the repentance of God and the abrogation of God's decree. With respect to God's repenting of something, he teaches that because God is immutable, he cannot change his mind.[148] The repentance of God is a figure of speech by which he accommodates himself to our capacity. By this language God reveals his anger and that his subsequent acts are the manifestation of righteous judgment.[149]

With respect to broken decrees (Nineveh, the death of Hezekiah, King Abimelech), God used threats to bring about repentance.

> For the Lord, when by warning of punishment he admonishes to repentance those whom he wills to spare, paves the way for his eternal ordinance, rather than varies anything of his will, or even his Word, although he does not express syllable by syllable what is nevertheless easy to understand. That saying of Isaiah must indeed remain true: "the Lord of Hosts has purposed, and who will annul it? His hand is stretched out, and who will turn it back?" [Isa. 14:27][150]

Before leaving the doctrine of providence, Calvin addresses the difficult subject of the relation of God to acts of Satan and sinful acts of men. How can he will these things and not contract some defilement or participate in some blame? Some answer this question with the doctrine of permission. God permits men to do these things by directing their wickedness to the ends he determines to be good and using their wicked deeds to accomplish his purposes, but he does not actively will

146. 1.17.11.
147. Ibid.
148. 1.17.12.
149. 1.17.13.
150. 1.17.14.

those things.[151] Although such an attempt is noble, it is clearly in violation of Scripture. Calvin offers Satan's attacks on Job as an example: God compelled Satan to report to him, and he could not undertake anything that was not God's will. Although Satan is the primary culprit and then the Sabeans and Chaldeans, Job recognized that God was the one who stripped him of all.[152]

The clearest statement in the Bible of God's decree of evil being more than bare permission is the death of Christ, which God predetermined, but men were held responsible (Acts 4:28; 2:23). After a number of other examples, Calvin concludes, "Those who are moderately versed in the Scriptures see that for the sake of brevity I have put forward only a few of many testimonies. Yet from these it is more than evident that they babble and talk absurdly who, in place of God's providence, substitute bare permission—as if God sat in a watchtower awaiting chance events, and his judgments thus depended upon human will."[153]

Calvin resorts to the doctrine of concurrence to explain how God orders sinful acts.[154] Calvin states, "Whatever we conceive of in our minds is directed to his own end by God's secret inspiration." He adds, "As if these two statements did not perfectly agree, although in divers ways, that man, while he is acted upon by God, yet at the same time himself acts!"[155] He illustrates this interaction from a number of passages.[156] Particularly, he shows how God actively blinds and hardens the hearts of men; he bends the wills of men to execute his judgments.[157]

151. 1.18.1. This seems to be Barth's understanding. Karl Barth, *Church Dogmatics: A Selection* (Louisville: Westminster/John Knox, 1994), 134ff.

152. Ibid.

153. Ibid.

154. Berkhof defines concurrence as "the cooperation of the divine power with all subordinate powers, according to the pre-established laws of their operation, causing them to act and to act precisely as they do." Louis Berkhof, *Systematic Theology*, 4th ed. (Grand Rapids: Eerdmans, 1965), 171. For a more detailed discussion of Calvin's views see *Calvin's Calvinism: Treatises on the Eternal Predestination of God & the Secret Providence of God* (Grand Rapids: Reformed Free, 1987). Paul Helm has an excellent discussion of this book in *John Calvin's Ideas* (Oxford: Oxford University Press, 2004), ch. 4.

155. 1.18.2.

156. Ibid.

157. Ibid.

Satan also plays a role in God's acting in the wicked. "I confess, indeed, that it is often by means of Satan's intervention that God acts in the wicked, but in such a way that Satan performs his part by God's impulsion and advances as far as he is allowed."[158] Calvin summarizes his position thus: "To sum up, since God's will is said to be the cause of all things, I have made his providence the determinative principle for all human plans and works, not only in order to display its force in the elect, who are ruled by the Holy Spirit, but also to compel the reprobate to obedience."[159]

Calvin again answers the objection that if God foreordains all things, there are two wills in him. He asserts that God's will is one, but it appears to be manifold to us on account of our finite understanding.[160] As he states above, we must hold to the unity of God's will by faith, as it is revealed in Scripture.

He answers a second objection that if God wills and governs the work of the ungodly, he is the author of sin. Calvin says that, ultimately, the wicked are only carrying out what God decrees. Those who accuse Calvin of the monstrous error making God the author of sin are confusing God's will with his precept. "While God accomplishes through the wicked what he has decreed by his secret judgment, they are not excusable, as if they had obeyed his precept which out of their own lust they deliberately break."[161] He illustrates this truth by the events leading to the split between Israel and Judah and Judas's betrayal of Christ.[162]

By not seeking answers beyond the clear statements of Scripture, Calvin avoids the error of some who teach the doctrine of concurrence. He concludes:

> Let those for whom this seems harsh consider for a little while how bearable their squeamishness is in refusing a thing attested by clear

158. Ibid.
159. Ibid. Charles Hodge opposes this doctrinal formulation. See *Systematic Theology*, 3 vols. (Grand Rapids: Eerdmans 1975), 1:598ff. See also G. C. Berkouwer, *Studies in Dogmatics: The Providence of God*, trans. Lewis B. Smedes (Grand Rapids: Eerdmans, 1974), ch. 5. For a defense of concurrence see Berkhof and Morton H. Smith, *Systematic Theology* (Greenville, SC: Greenville Seminary Press, 1994), 219–21.
160. 1.18.3.
161. 1.18.4.
162. Ibid.

Scriptural proofs because it exceeds their mental capacity, and find fault that things are put forth publicly, which if God had not judged useful for men to know, he would never have bidden his prophets and apostles to teach. For our wisdom ought to be nothing else than to embrace with humble teachableness, and at least without finding fault, whatever is taught in Sacred Scripture.[163]

Bibliography

Barth, Karl. *Church Dogmatics: A Selection*. Louisville: Westminster/John Knox, 1994.

Battles, Ford Lewis. *Analysis of the Institutes of the Christian Religion of John Calvin*. Phillipsburg, NJ: P&R, 2001.

Berkhof, Louis. *Systematic Theology*. 4th ed. Grand Rapids: Eerdmans, 1965.

Berkouwer, G. C. *Studies in Dogmatics: The Providence of God*. Translated by Lewis B. Smedes. Grand Rapids: Eerdmans, 1974.

Brown, Francis, S. R. Driver, and Charles A. Briggs, *Hebrew and English Lexicon of the Old Testament*. Oxford: Clarendon, 1962.

Calvin, John. *Calvin's Calvinism: Treatises on the Eternal Predestination of God & the Secret Providence of God*. Grand Rapids: Reformed Free, 1987.

———. *Calvin's Commentaries: Genesis*. Vol. 1. Translated by John King. Grand Rapids: Eerdmans, 1948.

———. *Calvin's Commentaries: The Gospel according to St. John 1–10*. Edited by David and Thomas Torrance. Translated by T. H. L. Parker. Grand Rapids: Eerdmans, 1959.

———. *The Sermons of John Calvin upon the Fifth Booke of Moses Called Deuteronomie*. Translated by Arthur Golding. Edinburgh: Banner of Truth Trust, 1987.

———. *Sermons on Job*. Translated by Arthur Golding. Edinburgh: Banner of Truth Trust, 1993.

Helm, Paul. *John Calvin's Ideas*. Oxford: Oxford University Press, 2004.

---

163. Ibid.

Hodge, Charles. *Systematic Theology*. 3 vols. Grand Rapids: Eerdmans, 1975.

Kline, Meredith G. "Because It Had Not Rained." *Westminster Theological Journal* 20 (1957–58): 146–57.

Richard A. Muller. *Dictionary of Latin and Greek Theological Terms*. Grand Rapids: Baker, 1998.

———. *The Unaccommodated Calvin: Studies in the Foundation of a Theological Tradition*. New York: Oxford University Press, 2000.

Niesel, Wilhelm. *The Theology of Calvin*. Translated by Harold Knight. Philadelphia: Westminster, 1956.

Pun, Pattle P. T. "A Theology of Progressive Creationism." *Perspectives on Science and Christian Faith: Journal of the American Scientific Affiliation* 39.1 (March 1987): 9–19.

Schneider, Robert. "Essay II: Theology of Creation: Historical Perspectives and Fundamental Concepts." http://community.berea.edu/scienceandfaith/essay02.asp.

Smith, Morton H. *Systematic Theology*. Greenville, SC: Greenville Seminary Press, 1994.

Turretin, Francis. *Institutes of Elenctic Theology*. Edited by James T. Dennison Jr. Translated by George Musgrave Giger. Phillipsburg, NJ: P&R, 1992.

Warfield, Benjamin. *The Works of Benjamin Warfield*. Vol. 5, *Calvin and Calvinism*. Grand Rapids: Baker, 1981.

Wyatt, Peter. *Jesus Christ and Creation in the Theology of John Calvin*. Princeton Theological Monograph Series. Allison Park, PA: Pickwick, 1996.

7

A Shattered Vase: The Tragedy of Sin in Calvin's Thought

INSTITUTES 1.15; 2.1–4
Michael S. Horton

The Enlightenment had high hopes for humanity. Emancipated from the church, tradition, and Scripture, the self-made individual aspired to attain intellectual or at least (after Kant) moral perfection. For this realization of the moral kingdom, Christ was not absolutely necessary. Not only is there no such thing as original sin in the Enlightenment perspective, but also the example or model of a life well-pleasing to God is already innate in our minds. Therefore, we may advance simply on the basis of the moral law within. However, Pelagianism—the religion of self-salvation—is the default setting of the fallen heart ever since the fall. We find it even in the nineteenth-century American evangelist Charles Finney, and it remains a potent theology in practice even in many places where it is denied in theory. Accordingly, the emphasis falls on human activity and striving, self-improvement, and the moral transformation of society. In many ways, modernity represents a theological and spiritual movement: a Christian heresy that could arise only as the negation of the faith that offended its moral sensibilities.

Turning his back even on the supposed givens of nature, Friedrich Nietzsche insisted that truth is not discovered, but made—by us. Our lives do not have any purpose, given their accidental origin, but we can create a destiny for ourselves. Preserving the emphasis on blind willing, many of Nietzsche's postmodern heirs have also deconstructed the sovereign self presupposed by their mentor. Michel Foucault realized that it was, to borrow a term from Nietzsche, "bad fiction." In reality, the self is no more a fixed and stable entity than other notions, such as truth, being, God, or the world. We are not sovereign over our own lives, but are shaped by constantly changing power structures.[1] From the sovereign self, emancipated from all authorities, to the vanishing self, imprisoned in a network of power-relations, humanity is unsure of itself now more than ever.

For a variety of reasons, John Calvin's treatment of humanity provokes a host of questions and answers that remind us how powerfully Scripture still speaks to our condition. Wherever the realism of the biblical account of the human condition is taken seriously, the gospel is seen more clearly and embraced more deeply. Calvin would likely agree with Foucault that there is no such thing as an autonomous self that first exists and then enters into power-relations (i.e., social structures). Rather, human beings are inherently covenantal. That is, they are always already participants in a web of relationships. First of all, they are "in Adam"—both sinners and sinned-against, caught up in the paradox of being image-bearers of God accountable to God for their obedience or transgression. No one is an island of pure subjectivity, alone determining what one is or will be. Rather, we are conditioned by our relatedness to each other as children of Adam. Second, as they are "in Christ," the elect are not only accountable and therefore liable to condemnation, but are chosen, redeemed, called, justified, sanctified, and glorified. They belong to the covenant community, including its practices of baptism, catechesis, discipline, communion, and

---

1. Michel Foucault, "The Subject and Power" in *Was ist Aufklarung?* (*What Is Enlightenment?*), in *The Foucault Reader*, ed. Paul Rabinow (New York: Pantheon Books), 32–50; cf. Barry Cooper, *Michel Foucault: An Introduction to the Study of His Thought*, Studies in Religion and Society 2 (New York: Edwin Mellen, 1981).

so forth. There is no abstract self hovering above these two networks of power-relations. One is either a covenant-keeper in Christ or a covenant-breaker in Adam. Like Jesus' generation, which he compared to children who did not know either how to mourn or dance properly, we—even in the church—seem to regard the verdict of the law as too severe and the verdict of the gospel as too good to be true. Our age does not seem to know either the grandeur of creation or the tragedy of the fall.

The Paradox in Calvin's Anthropology

Not only Calvin's critics, but sometimes admirers, are surprised to discover in his writings such lavish descriptions of the majesty of creation in general and the dignity of human beings in particular. Absent from Calvin is the traditional Augustinian and medieval notion of a *donum superadditum*—a gift of grace added to nature in order to orient human beings toward God, righteousness, and life.[2] This view depended largely on a Platonic/Neoplatonic cosmology, with the intellect at the highest rung of the ladder, participating in divinity, and the body toward the lower rungs, with the soul ranged midway. Thus, with the superadded gift, Adam could either raise himself above the realm of the body and its passions, following the image of God imprinted on his mind, or allow his lower nature to drag him down.

In Calvin's understanding, created nature was excellent simply by virtue of being generated by God's unfailing word. "For not only did a lower appetite seduce him, but unspeakable impiety occupied the very citadel of his mind, and pride penetrated to the depths of his heart. Thus it is pointless and foolish to restrict the corruption that arises thence only to what are called the impulses of the senses; or to call it the 'kindling wood' that attracts, arouses, and drags into sin only that part which they term 'sensuality.'"[3] Human fallenness cannot be attributed to any weakness in

---

2. John Calvin, *Institutes* 1.16.8. Calvin simply refuses to speculate about why Adam did not persevere in holiness. All references are from *Institutes of the Christian Religion* (1559), 2 vols., ed. John T. McNeill, trans. Ford Lewis Battles, Library of Christian Classics 20–21(Philadelphia: Westminster, 1960).

3. Ibid., 2.1.9.

human nature as created, which would place blame ultimately at God's feet. Rather, it was the inexplicable apostasy from true righteousness and holiness. Calvin put it this way:

> Now away with those persons who dare write God's name upon their faults, because we declare that men are vicious by nature! They perversely search out God's handiwork in their own pollution, when they ought rather to have sought it in that unimpaired and uncorrupted nature of Adam. Our destruction, therefore, comes from the guilt of our flesh, not from God, inasmuch as we have perished solely because we have degenerated from our original condition."[4]

To God alone is attributed human dignity. The *imago dei* can be properly defined only in relation to its renewal in Christ by the Spirit (1.15.4). "In this integrity man by free will had the power, if he so willed, to attain eternal life. Here it would be out of place to raise the question of God's secret predestination because our present subject is not what can happen or not, but what man's nature was like. Therefore Adam could have stood if he wished, seeing that he fell solely by his own will." His faculties

> were rightly composed to obedience, until in destroying himself he corrupted his own blessings. Hence the great obscurity faced by the philosophers, for they were seeking in a ruin for a building, and in scattered fragments for a well-knit structure. They held this principle, that man would not be a rational animal unless he possessed free choice of good and evil; also it entered their minds that the distinction between virtues and vices would be obliterated if man did not order his life by his own planning. Well reasoned so far—if there had been no change in man. But since this was hidden from them, it is no wonder they mix up heaven and earth![5]

Not abstract metaphysical speculation, but the concrete history of the covenant as interpreted by divine revelation, was Calvin's way of approaching the tragedy of human corruption. Not nature as fashioned by the hand

4. Ibid., 2.1.10.
5. Ibid. 1.15.8.

of God, but the willful decision of the covenant partner to violate the commission entrusted to him, was the locus of misery in the world. Ranged, like Irenaeus, against the Gnostic identification of evil with the warp and woof of creation itself—a view that has returned with a vengeance among Nietzsche's heirs—Calvin emphasized the fall as the historical event of willful human transgression that spoiled a glorious theater.

This paradox of human dignity and human tragedy is apparent throughout Calvin's treatment of sin, and it is far from unique to the Geneva Reformer. Especially among the younger reformers such as Calvin, humanism had made a deep impression. Although differences are sometimes exaggerated, in material terms humanism exhibited greater interest in human dignity, and in terms of method was more concerned with history and the interpretation of texts than with the more speculative approach characteristic of medieval scholasticism. When Calvin heaped scorn on the "school-men," he was simply echoing Erasmus, Lefèvre, Valla, and other humanists of his day. The Reformed scholasticism that followed in the wake of Bucer, Calvin, Vermigli, Musculus, and numerous other important figures, was imbued with this humanist spirit, however much it seems to have followed the more traditional method of scholastic systems. However, it is Scripture that shaped their anthropology, so that it could simultaneously affirm human nature as such and reckon with the gruesome reality of human misery.[6] Much like our own day, there were humanists such as Pico della Mirandola who exalted the divinity of the human soul, and those whom Calvin identified as new Epicureans, who could scarcely distinguish humans from brute animals.

Of course, this somewhat paradoxical anthropology of what we might call simultaneously dignified and deranged is not always apparent in the work of everyone who claims Calvin's legacy. Especially in more popular renditions, the summary often begins with total depravity. This may be due in part to the famous acronym "TULIP," which is itself a shorthand summary of the Canons of the Synod of Dort (1618–19). However, it must be remembered that Dort was a response to the Five Points of the Remonstrants (Arminians) and as such never intended to offer a sum-

---

6. This characteristic emphasis of Reformed anthropology can be found among many of Calvin's students, as in J. I. Packer's *Christianity: The True Humanism* (Waco: Word, 1986).

mary of Calvinism per se, but a defense of Reformed doctrines at stake in that controversy. Furthermore, even there, under the topic of human corruption, the canons begin, "Man was originally formed after the image of God. His understanding was adorned with a true and saving knowledge of his Creator, and of spiritual things; his heart and will were upright, all his affections pure, and the whole man was holy." Only after saying this did the divines assembled at Dort think it possible to add, "But, revolting from God by the instigation of the devil and by his own free will, [man] forfeited these excellent gifts; and in the place thereof became involved in blindness of mind, horrible darkness, vanity, and perverseness of judgment; became wicked, rebellious, and obdurate in heart and will, and impure in his affections."[7]

The same dual emphasis is found in the Belgic Confession, where, after commenting on the *imago dei*, it is added, "But being in honor, he understood it not, neither knew his excellency, but willfully subjected himself to sin and consequently to death and the curse, giving ear to the words of the devil." Transgressing "the commandment of life," he "corrupted his whole nature" and "lost all his excellent gifts which he had received from God, and retained only small remains thereof, which, however, are sufficient to leave man without excuse."[8] The same affirmation of created dignity and total corruption appears in the Heidelberg Catechism (Q. 6) as well as the Westminster Confession (4.2) and catechisms (Shorter, Q. 10, 15–19).

If we begin with total depravity rather than creation, the former can easily lose the tragic element; sin too easily then becomes confused with our humanity as such rather than with its corruption. This is the popular caricature of Calvin's critics, where human existence itself is a fate that must be endured with extreme reluctance and dissatisfaction, breeding an asceticism that makes its medieval versions seem appealing by comparison.

7. The Canons of Dort, Third and Fourth Heads of Doctrine, Art. 1, in the *Psalter Hymnal: Doctrinal Standards and Liturgy of the Christian Reformed Church* (Grand Rapids: Board of Publications for the Christian Reformed Church, 1976), 102. See also Michael S. Horton, "Post-Reformation Reformed Anthropology," in Richard Lints, Michael Horton, and Mark Talbot, eds., *Personal Identity in Theological Perspective* (Grand Rapids: Eerdmans, 2006), 45ff. I treat this historical development at greater length in *Lord and Servant* (Louisville: Westminster/John Knox, 2005), chs. 4 and 5.
8. The Belgic Confession, Art.14, in the *Psalter Hymnal*, 75.

However, for Calvin and Reformed theology, it is not our humanity with its magnificent endowments, but the perversity of our willful suppression of the truth in unrighteousness, employing those gifts as weapons against a good Creator, that introduces the tragic element in nature and history. "This is the inherited corruption, which the church fathers termed 'original sin,' meaning by the word 'sin,' the depravation of a nature previously good and pure."[9] Calvin explicitly appeals to the double imputation in Romans 5—that is, the parallel between Adam and Christ. If human corruption is simply a matter of imitating Adam's trespass, then salvation comes by imitating Christ's good example.[10] Calvin refuses to become mired in the finer historical debates over the transmission of the soul from one generation to another, content to assert with Scripture that Adam stood as the covenantal representative for the human race.[11] Original sin includes both guilt and corruption.[12]

How *Total* Is Total Depravity?

Calvin and Reformed theology generally differed from Luther and Lutheranism on the question of the effect of the fall on the image of God. For the latter tradition, the fall so corrupted human nature that there is no vestige of the image of God; it has been entirely lost and can be restored only by redemption in Jesus Christ.[13] Again Calvin's concern to uphold the integrity of God's creation is exhibited in his refusal to accept a total eradication of the divine image. In fact, particularly against the radical Anabaptists, Calvin offers a challenge that is worth quoting at length:

Whenever we come upon these matters in secular writers, let that admirable light of truth shining in them teach us that the mind of man, though fallen and perverted from its wholeness, is nevertheless clothed

9. Calvin, *Institutes* 2.1.5.
10. Ibid., 2.1.6.
11. Ibid., 2.1.7.
12. Ibid., 2.1.8.
13. See Edmund Schlink, *Theology of the Lutheran Confessions*, trans. Paul F. Koehneke and Herbert J. A. Bouman (Philadelphia: Fortress, 1961), 47 and 59, with ample citations from the Book of Concord and Lutheran orthodoxy.

and ornamented with God's excellent gifts. If we regard the Spirit of God as the sole fountain of truth, we shall neither reject the truth itself, nor despise it wherever it shall appear, unless we wish to dishonor the Spirit of God. For by holding the gifts of the Spirit in such slight esteem, we condemn and reproach the Spirit himself. What then? Shall we deny that the truth shone upon the ancient jurists who established civic order and discipline with such great equity? Shall we say that the philosophers were blind in their fine observation and artful description of nature? Shall we say that those men were devoid of understanding who conceived the art of disputation and taught us to speak reasonably? Shall we say that they are insane who developed medicine, devoting their labor to our benefit? What shall we say of all the mathematical sciences? Shall we consider them the ravings of madmen? No, we cannot read the writings of the ancients on these subjects without great admiration. . . . Those men whom Scripture calls "natural men" were, indeed, sharp and penetrating in their investigation of inferior things. Let us, accordingly, learn by their example how many gifts the Lord left to human nature even after it was despoiled of its true good.[14]

The Spirit is at work savingly in the elect, but also in common grace toward the reprobate.[15]

Luther too, of course, spoke of the potential for unregenerate humanity in "things earthly," but Calvin saw this as evidence not of the neutrality or indifference of earthly things in relation to God and his kingdom, but of the ineradicable and indelible imprint of God's image. Indeed, it is this fact that humanity remains in some sense God's image-bearer and covenant partner that motivates human beings in their sinfulness to idolatry and sophisticated schemes of religious distortion. Fallen human beings are not irreligious, but idolatrous. The image must be suppressed because it is still there. Like a mirror that reveals a reflection that we do not want to see, it must be distorted, covered over, smeared with mud. Because it reflects the God whose existence stands over against us in judgment, the image of God is no longer redolent of high office, but is a burden to be cast off. Precisely because it cannot be eradicated, it is disfigured beyond recognition.

14. Calvin, *Institutes* 2.2.15.
15. Ibid., 2.2.16.

Again, this gives to Calvin's doctrine of sin an irreducibly ethical determination. In the fall, humanity lost nothing of its created nature. There is no missing part, no weak faculty, that could account for disobedience.

> Because of the bondage of sin by which the will is held bound, it cannot move toward good, much less apply itself thereto; for a movement of this sort is the beginning of conversion to God, which in Scripture is ascribed entirely to God's grace.... Nonetheless the will remains, with the most eager inclination disposed and hastening to sin. For man, when he gave himself over to this necessity, was not deprived of will, but of soundness of will.... Therefore simply to will is of man; to will ill, of a corrupt nature; to will well, of grace.[16]

This requires a distinction between necessity and compulsion. Just as God's immunity to sin derives from his own natural goodness rather than any external compulsion, so the reverse is true for sinners. Calvin appeals to Bernard's argument that human beings are "oppressed by no other yoke than that of a kind of voluntary servitude."

> Surely my readers will recognize that I am bringing forth nothing new, for it is something that Augustine taught of old with the agreement of all the godly, and it was still retained almost a thousand years later in monastic cloisters. But Lombard, since he did not know how to distinguish necessity from compulsion, gave occasion for a pernicious error.[17]

Reformed scholastics would invoke the distinction between natural and moral ability, which makes the same point perhaps more precisely. Yet the two sets of terms are related: depravity is natural in the sense that it is universally inherited, not in the sense that it is inherent in human nature as created; human beings retain the natural ability to contemplate God in his works because the image of God has not been completely lost, yet the moral ability to render gratitude, true worship, and obedience to God is entirely surrendered to the bondage of sin. Everyone still retains a *sensus*

16. Ibid., 2.3.5.
17. Ibid.

divinitatis: "a sense of divinity which can never be effaced is engraved upon men's minds."[18] In fact, superstition and idolatry are evidence both of this general revelation and its distortion in the fallen heart.[19]

Some Calvinists may be embarrassed by Calvin's repeated affirmations of the persistence of the divine image, particularly with the Reformer's appeal to metaphors such as embers, lamps, and remnants. Indeed, total depravity is sometimes represented even by advocates as requiring something closer to the Lutheran view, with every vestige of original righteousness, holiness, and love extinguished in the unregenerate heart. However, Calvin is closer to Augustine in this respect. Although he does not attach himself (at least explicitly) to the theory of sin as mere privation of the good, he typically understands sin as parasitical. It cannot create, but can only undo; it cannot bring about its own state of affairs, but can only corrupt, distort, disfigure, and suppress an original state of affairs determined by God's goodness. Ugliness is the marring of beauty; stupidity and foolishness are the derangement of an original intelligence and wisdom; injustice is, as its prefix suggests, the undoing of justice; error is the distortion of the truth. Sin and evil cannot create, but only destroy.

But not destroy *completely.* The rays of God's glory in creation still manage to penetrate through the mud that human beings have smeared onto the mirror, and God's gracious providence (what later Reformed theology would call common grace) enables humanity even in its perversity to arrive at some semblance of truth, goodness, and beauty in things earthly. For Calvin, then, depravity was total in its extensiveness, not in its intensiveness. In other words, there is no foothold of goodness anywhere in us—in our mind, will, emotions, or body—where we could rise up to God. Sin has corrupted the whole person, like a poison that works its way in greater or lesser intensity throughout the entire stream. Yet, despite ourselves, this does not eliminate the possibility of reflecting God's glory. Humanity is therefore not as bad as it could possibly be, but as badly off as it could possibly be. There is no residue of obedient piety in us, but only a *sensus divinitatis* that we exploit for

18. Ibid., 1.3.3.
19. Ibid.

idolatry, self-justification, and superstition. Thus the same remnants of original righteousness that allow even pagans to create a reasonably equitable civic order in things earthly provoke them in their corruption to false religion in things heavenly.

As Calvin sees things, medieval theology had compromised both the integrity of creation and the sovereignty of grace. With respect to the former, creation lacked genuine integrity apart from a superadded gift of grace that elevated nature beyond itself. Yet with respect to God's tribunal, general revelation yielded some saving truth to which at least the relatively unfallen intellect could assent and, as the will cooperated with grace, conversion could ensue. Calvin took creation and the fall more seriously. He took issue with the popular notion that God simply holds out his hand in an offer of pardon to those who turn themselves toward him—and that this constitutes the grace of God in regeneration. "We admit that man's condition while he still remained upright was such that he could incline to either side. But inasmuch as he has made clear by his example how miserable free will is unless God both wills and is able to work in us, what will happen to us if he imparts his grace to us in this small measure?"[20] Again, it is not that the will is rendered inactive by sin, but that it is bound by sin until grace restores it in a one-sided, unilateral, and unassisted divine act (2.3.14).

God's revelation in creation renders us all inexcusable. "Yet let this difference be remembered," Calvin adds, "that the manifestation of God, by which he makes his glory known in his creation, is, with regard to the light itself, sufficiently clear; but that on account of our blindness, it is not found to be sufficient."[21] Only by the light of faith can we properly discern even the revelation of God in creation, Calvin argues, appealing to Hebrews 11:3.[22]

Calvin's repeated images are vivid: the burning lamps shine, but we immediately leap to extinguish them; embers continue to smolder, but we smother them; wherever rays of God's glory break through, we smear the mirror with our filth; the tree is chopped down before it can bear the

20. Ibid., 2.3.10.
21. John Calvin, *Commentaries on the Epistle of Paul the Apostle to the Romans*, trans. John Owen (Grand Rapids: Baker, 1996), 71.
22. Ibid.

fruit of true righteousness." Their unrighteousness was this—they quickly choked by their own depravity the seed of right knowledge, before it grew up to ripeness."[23] "As experience shows," he says, "God has sown a seed of religion (*semen religionis*) in all men. But scarcely one man in a hundred is met with who fosters it, once received, in his heart, and none in whom it ripens—much less shows fruit in season." Whether they explicitly deny God or embrace their own superstitions, "all degenerate from the true knowledge of him."[24] Creation is "a glorious theater"; indeed, "wherever you cast your eyes, there is no spot in the universe wherein you cannot discern at least some sparks of his glory," especially in "this most vast and beautiful system of the universe in its wide expanse."[25] Even the most uneducated person can recognize this, but how much more can those who daily engage in "astronomy, medicine, and all natural science," not to mention "the liberal arts."[26]

Another popular analogy is that of a labyrinth.[27] In the theater of this world, "so many burning lamps shine for us in the workmanship of the universe to show forth the glory of its Author. Although they bathe us wholly in their radiance, yet they can of themselves in no way lead us into the right path. Surely they strike some sparks, but before their fuller light shines forth these are smothered."[28]

In his Romans commentary, Calvin follows Paul's logic closely: the consequence of human wickedness and suppression of the truth in unrighteousness is not atheism, but idolatry, speculation, and the measuring of God's majesty according to human standards.[29] "[Paul] then intimates, that they, making a depraved choice, preferred their own vanities to the true God; and thus the error, by which they were deceived, was voluntary."[30] Romans 1 targets the obvious vices of the Gentiles, but chapter 2 "is directed against hypocrites, who dazzle the eyes of men by displays of outward sanctity, and even think themselves to be accepted before God,

23. Ibid., 73.
24. Calvin, *Institutes* 1.4.1.
25. Ibid., 1.5.1.
26. Ibid., 1.5.2.
27. Ibid., 1.5.12.
28. Ibid., 1.6.14.
29. Calvin, *Romans*, 73–74.
30. Ibid., 80.

as though they had given him full satisfaction. Hence Paul, after having stated the grosser vices, that he might prove that none are just before God, now attacks saintlings (*sanctulos*) of this kind, who could not have been included in the first catalogue."[31] If "the Lord sings to the deaf as long as he does not touch inwardly their hearts," it is only because of our own perversity.[32]

God continues to give general or common graces to the wicked. "For this reason, we are not afraid, in common parlance, to call this man wellborn, that one depraved in nature. Yet we do not hesitate to include both under the universal condition of human depravity."[33] Therefore, in the court of human justice and opinion, there is great diversity. Some people are more vicious, others more virtuous; some more intelligent, artful, just, and generous than others. Yet before God's tribunal, all mouths are stopped.

Calvin's distinctions between God's general gifts in providence and God's saving grace in the church, necessity and compulsion, nature-as-created and the corruption of nature, things heavenly and things earthly, a righteousness before God and a righteousness before humanity, allow him to continue to affirm the goodness of creation as such alongside the most unflinching appraisal of human wickedness. So although we are swimming in revelation, our minds are drowning in self-imposed ignorance and vanity. Not until God speaks in the Scriptures is there a proper knowledge of God.[34] Only with the Scriptures as our spectacles are we able to recognize truly what before we had seen only confusedly and distortedly.[35] Now, we apprehend God's works, "while these very works are appraised not by our depraved judgment but by the rule of eternal truth." To be sure, even here we see through a glass darkly, but "it is better to limp along this path than to dash with all speed outside it."[36] Human beings are the loftiest examples of divine wisdom,[37] which makes their willful ingratitude in turning away from God all the more culpable.[38]

31. Ibid., 83–84.
32. Ibid., 88.
33. Calvin, *Institutes* 2.3.4.
34. Ibid., 1.6.1.
35. Ibid.
36. Ibid., 1.6.3.
37. Ibid., 1.5.3.
38. Ibid., 1.5.4.

Is God the Author of Sin?

As the quote above from the Canons of Dort attests, Calvinism in its official expressions attributes original sin to the transgression of Adam, "by his own free will." It is not God's sovereignty that holds human freedom in bondage, but sin. Here too, confessional Reformed theology is obliged to hold together two apparently conflicting theses: God has decreed whatever comes to pass, yet this in no way infringes on creaturely freedom. It would be easier, of course, for finite intellects to resolve this dilemma in the direction of either human autonomy or fatalism, but the Bible does not allow these options.

Calvin's theological heirs are therefore simply affirming with their mentor the futility of speculation, which can only lead finally to error and ultimately to idolatry. God is not the author of sin, since he does not directly cause or bring it about. (In his treatment in the *Institutes*, Calvin freely employs the Aristotelian categories of primary and secondary causality.) That is, God does not make, create, or coerce creatures toward evil. This conclusion, in fact, Calvin regards as blasphemy.[39] At the same time, the fall did not catch God by surprise. From all eternity, God had elected a people from the human race in Christ for eternal life. Supralapsarians and infralapsarians have both found statements in Calvin to support their positions (that God's decree of election was made with regard to humanity either as created or as fallen, respectively). However, this is a later debate that can only be anachronistically inserted into Calvin's thinking.

The important thing for Calvin is simply to affirm simultaneously that God is neither the author nor the passive victim of creaturely aggression. He cautions,

> Let no one grumble here that God could have provided better for our salvation if he had forestalled Adam's fall. Pious minds ought to loathe this objection, because it manifests inordinate curiosity. . . . Let us accordingly remember to impute our ruin to depravity of nature, in order that we may not accuse God himself, the Author of nature.[40]

39. Ibid., 3.23.4–5.
40. Ibid., 2.2.11.

In fact, we call this corruption natural only "in order that no man may think that anyone obtains it through bad conduct, since it holds all men fast by hereditary right." Thus, it is not nature itself but its corruption that is in view.[41]

Sin and Grace

We have seen that for Calvin human dignity rather than depravity must be the starting point for anthropology. It should be added that his stark appraisal of sin was but a prelude to the gospel. Just as creation measured the tragedy of the fall, redemption in Christ measured the triumph of grace. Throughout Calvin's discussion of the first chapters of Romans, it is repeatedly observed that the apostle's grave commentary on human depravity is calculated to drive the sinner to God's mercy in Christ. The purpose was not simply to expose human perversity, but "Paul's object was to teach us where salvation is to be found," namely, "in the grace of God alone"—in Christ rather than in us.[42]

The targets of Calvin's polemics are "the Pelagians of our own age, that is, the Sophists of the Sorbonne."[43] At the heart of this heresy, even in its more moderate forms, was the failure to distinguish the nature of humanity as originally created from the state of humanity after the fall. Before the fall, humanity was indeed oriented toward God and righteousness, capable of doing all that God had commanded. "Law" is humanity's native tongue. After the fall, however, at least if there is to be any hope of rescue, another word must be announced. The gospel is not innate. It must be revealed from heaven as good news. "In this ruin of mankind no one now experiences God either as Father or as Author of salvation or favorable in any way, until Christ the Mediator comes forward to reconcile him to us."[44]

The natural order was that the frame of the universe should be the school in which we were to learn piety, and from it pass over to eternal

41. Ibid.
42. Calvin, *Romans*, 68.
43. Calvin, *Institutes* 2.3.13.
44. Ibid., 1.2.1.

life and perfect felicity. But after man's rebellion, our eyes—wherever they turn—encounter God's curse.... For even if God wills to manifest his fatherly favor to us in many ways, yet we cannot by contemplating the universe infer that he is Father. Rather, conscience presses us within and shows in our sin just cause for his disowning us and not regarding or recognizing us as his sons. Dullness and ingratitude follow, for our minds, as they have been blinded, do not perceive what is true.... Therefore, although the preaching of the cross does not agree with our human inclination, if we desire to return to God our Author and Maker, from whom we have been estranged, in order that he may again begin to be our Father, we ought nevertheless to embrace it humbly. Surely, after the fall of the first man no knowledge of God apart from the Mediator has had power unto salvation.[45]

It was this faith in Christ, directed by the shadows of the law and the prophetic promises, that kept a remnant in Israel looking toward the future in hope.[46] God can be considered the object of faith only with the qualification that "unless God confronts us in Christ, we cannot come to know that we are saved." And "in this sense Irenaeus writes that the Father, himself infinite, becomes finite in the Son, for he has accommodated himself to our little measure lest our minds be overwhelmed by the immensity of his glory.... Actually, it means nothing else than that God is comprehended in Christ alone."[47]

Apart from Christ, then, there can be only a "fleeting knowledge of God" that quickly turns to the vinegar of idolatry and superstition, however much "they [Calvin refers to Moslems here] proclaim at the top of their lungs that the Creator of heaven and earth is God"[48]

According to surveys, most professing evangelicals, along with the wider culture, deny original sin.[49] In his recent study, sociologist Christian Smith has characterized religion in America as "moralistic, therapeutic deism," with no distinction between those who have been raised in evan-

45. Ibid., 2.6.1.
46. Ibid., 2.6.2–3.
47. Ibid., 2.6.4.
48. Ibid.
49. See the statistics offered in David F. Wells, *Above All Earthly Pow'rs: Christ in a Postmodern World* (Grand Rapids: Eerdmans, 2005), 299.

gelical churches and those reared in liberal, Unitarian, or unchurched backgrounds.[50] Having witnessed the baneful effects of Pelagianism on mainline Protestantism, the evangelical movement in North America seems increasingly to be reaping the whirlwind of the seeds sown by its revivalist legacy. Pragmatism, consumerism, self-help moralism, and narcissism are simply the symptoms of a disease that is, at its heart, theological: namely, the drift toward Pelagianism. Whatever the formal creed, and regardless of whether it appears in the form of a rigorous legalism or a sentimental antinomianism, a seriously deficient appraisal of sin surely lies at the heart of the church's lack of confidence in the gospel to create and empower the church's life, worship, and witness.

I leave it to the reader to evaluate this gloomy appraisal, which is increasingly observed with considerable alarm even by mainline theologians. If it is indeed accurate, or even partly accurate, then the condition of at least American Christianity may actually be worse than that of the medieval church. In any case, it is hoped that the richly biblical wisdom that Calvin offers—both in the speculations that he eschews and the frank if unpleasant exegesis that he so vividly expounds—will prove its worth again in our faith and practice today.

---

50. Christian Smith with Melinda Lundquist Denton, *Soul Searching: The Religious and Spiritual Lives of American Teenagers* (New York: Oxford University Press, 2005).

8

CALVIN'S INTERPRETATION OF THE HISTORY OF SALVATION: THE CONTINUITY AND DISCONTINUITY OF THE COVENANT

INSTITUTES 2.10–11
PETER A. LILLBACK

With the Reformation's emphasis on Scripture, the covenant became an important theological concern in the Reformed tradition.[1] Huldrych Zwingli, for example, emphasized

1. J. W. Baker, *Heinrich Bullinger and the Covenant: The Other Reformed Tradition* (Athens: Ohio University Press, 1980); L. D. Bierma, "The Covenant Theology of Caspar Olevian" (Ph.D. diss., Duke University, 1980); idem, "Federal Theology in the Sixteenth Century: Two Traditions?" *Westminster Theological Journal* 45 (1983): 304–21; idem, *German Calvinism in the Confessional Age: The Covenant Theology of Caspar Olevianus* (Grand Rapids: Baker, 1996); idem, "Covenant or Covenants in the Theology of Olevianus," *Calvin Theological Journal* 22 (1987): 228–50; idem, "The Role of Covenant Theology in Early Reformed Orthodoxy,"

the covenant with Abraham and identified Genesis 17 as the model of the relationship of the Christian with God. In 1534, Heinrich Bullinger wrote the first treatise in church history on the covenant: *Of the One and Eternal Testament or Covenant of God.* Bullinger argued that all of Scripture must be seen in light of the Abrahamic covenant in which God graciously offers himself to man, and in turn, demands that man "walk before him and be blameless."

John Calvin also employed the covenant idea extensively. In various ways he can be considered the forerunner of covenant and federal theology. He made extensive use of the covenant idea in his *Institutes* (1559) and other writings in the following areas: the unity of the Old and New Testament, the mutuality and conditionality of the covenant, the benefits of salvation, the Christian life (law, prayer, repentance, assurance), predestination (predestination explains why the covenant works as it does), the Reformation of the church (the Roman Church has broken the covenant, and therefore may be and must be resisted), and the sacraments. Even an elementary form of the covenant of works appears in Calvin's writings.[2]

Students of Calvin further developed his thought and formulated the ideas of a prefall covenant of works and a pretemporal covenant of redemption. In 1562, Zacharias Ursinus (1534–83) spoke of a prefall covenant of law between God and Adam in the garden that demanded perfect obedience

---

Sixteenth Century Journal 21. 3 (1990): 453–62; Peter A. Lillback, *The Binding of God: Calvin's Role in the Development of Covenant Theology* (Grand Rapids: Baker Academic, 2001); idem, "Calvin's Covenantal Response to the Anabaptist View of Baptism," *Christianity and Civilization* (1982): 185–232; idem, "The Continuing Conundrum: Calvin and the Conditionality of the Covenant," *Calvin Theological Journal* 29.1 (1994): 42–74; idem, "The Early Reformed Covenant Paradigm: Vermigli in the Context of Bullinger, Luther & Calvin," in *Peter Martyr Vermigli and the European Reformations*, ed. Frank A. James III (Leiden: Brill, 2004), 70–96; idem, "Ursinus' Development of the Covenant of Creation: A Debt to Melanchthon or Calvin?" *Westminster Theological Journal* 43 (1981): 247–88; C. S. McCoy and J. W. Baker, *Fountainhead of Federalism: Heinrich Bullinger and the Covenantal Tradition* (Louisville: Westminster/John Knox, 1991), 23–26; S. Preus, *From Shadow to Promise* (Cambridge, MA: Harvard University Press); S. Strehle, *Calvinism, Federalism, and Scholasticism: A Study of the Reformed Doctrine of Covenant* (Bern: Peter Lang, 1988); G. Vos, "The Doctrine of the Covenant in Reformed Theology," in R. B. Gaffin Jr., ed., *Redemptive History and Biblical Interpretation* (Phillipsburg, NJ: P&R, 1980), 234–67; D. A. Weir, *The Origins of the Federal Theology in Sixteenth-Century Reformation Thought* (Oxford: Clarendon, 1990).

2. See Peter A. Lillback, "The Binding of God: Calvin's Role in the Development of Covenant Theology" Ph.D. diss. (Westminster Theological Seminary, 1985).

with the promise of life and threatened disobedience with the penalty of death. In 1585, Caspar Olevianus (1536–87) presented the idea of a pretemporal covenant between God the Father and God the Son for the salvation of man. The covenants of works and grace received credal status in the Westminster Confession and Catechisms (1643–49).[3]

Interpretations of Calvin's Covenant Theology

Scholars have largely disagreed over Calvin's understanding and use of the covenant. As we prepare to consider his covenantal thought in book 2, chapters 10–11 of the *Institutes*, a brief summary of these interpretations will be helpful.

Calvin's Theological System Is in Tension with Covenant Theology and Especially with Fully Developed Federalism

Some scholars have alleged that Calvin stood in tension with covenantal thought in general and federalism in particular. Scholars from this perspective have highlighted three conflicts. The first conflict is that Calvin's teaching on grace seems to be opposed to the Melanchthonian law/gospel distinction employed in the development of the covenant of works. The second conflict is that Calvin's predestinarianism seems to be incompatible with the conditional covenant of the Rhineland Reformers. The third conflict is that Calvin's reformational theology seems to be irreconcilable with the rehabilitated medieval scholastic covenant theology found in the federalism of Protestant scholasticism.

Scholars who hold the first perspective believe that the covenant of works is the result either of the intrusion of Melanchthonian natural law and law-gospel distinction conceptions into Calvin's system, or of a later influx of Puritan legalism. It is claimed that Calvin's perspective on the covenant was exclusively grace-oriented, and so no legal covenant could stand in tandem with it. The conception of the merging of Melanchthonian and Calvinian theology to produce the hybrid doctrine of the covenant of works is argued

---

3. For an overview of the history of the covenant, see Peter A. Lillback, "The Covenant (Biblical and Historical)," in *New Dictionary of Theology* (Downers Grove, IL: InterVarsity, 1988), 173–76.

primarily by continental scholars. In fact, this idea appears to have gained near axiomatic status among many scholars as is indicated by the host of eminent authors who support it.[4] Karl Barth summarizes this view: "In Calvin there can be no question of the Law destroying the character of the covenant as a covenant of grace, nor can we find any combination of the covenant concept with a primitive *lex naturae*. This idea came in as a result of the influence which Melanchthon came to exercise on Reformed theology."[5]

English-speaking scholars who can be placed in this category of inter-pretation have tended to see this "intrusion" into true Calvinism as a result of Puritan theology.[6] For example, Holmes Rolston writes of the Puritan theology in the Westminster Confession of Faith, "That it is by name a covenant of works has a very deadening effect on anything said about grace." A little later he adds, "Of all this Calvin knew nothing, for these theological innovations were the work of his successors."[7] Michael McGiffert explains, "Although nurtured by Calvinists, the Adamic covenant was in critical

---

4. Paul Althaus, *Die Prinzipien der deutschen reformierten Dogmatik* (Leipzig: Deichert, 1914), 148–52; Karl Barth, *Church Dogmatics*, trans. G. W. Bromiley (Edinburgh: T. & T. Clark, 1974), 4/1:54ff.; August Lang, *Der Heidelberger Katechismus* (Leipzig: n.p., 1907), lxiv–lxvii; *Lexikon für Theologie und Kirche* (1960), s.v. "Föderaltheologie," by J. Moltmann; Otto Ritschl, "Die Entwicklung des Bundesgedankens in der reformierten Theologie des 16. und des 17. Jahrhunderts," in *Dogmengeschichte des Protestantismus* (Göttingen: Van-denhoeck & Ruprecht, 1926), 3:416–18; Gottlob Schrenk, *Gottesreich und Bund im alteren Protestantismus vornehmlich bei Johannes Cocceius* (Gütersloh: C. Bertelsmann, 1923), 48–49; Erdmann Sturm, *Der junge Zacharias Ursin* (Neukirchen-Vluyn: Neukirchener Verlag, 1972), 253–56.

5. Barth, *Dogmatics*, 4/1:58.

6. Representative scholars of this viewpoint include: Michael McGiffert, "Grace and Work: The Rise and Division of Covenant Divinity in Elizabethan Puritanism," *Harvard Theological Review* 75.4 (1982): 463–502; idem, "The Perkinsian Moment of Federal Theology," *Calvin Theological Journal* 29.1 (1994): 117–48; Holmes Rolston III, *John Calvin versus the Westminster Confession* (Richmond: John Knox, 1972); idem, "Responsible Man in Reformed Theology: Calvin versus the *Westminster Confession*," *Scottish Journal of Theology* 23 (1970): 129–56; James B. Torrance, "Strengths and Weaknesses of the Westminster Theology," in *The Westminster Confession*, ed. Alisdair Heron (Edinburgh: St. Andrews, 1982), 40–53; idem, "Covenant or Contract? A Study of the Theological Background of Worship in Seventeenth-Century Scot-land," *Scottish Journal of Theology* 23 (1970): 51–76; idem, "Calvin and Puritanism in England and Scotland—Some Basic Concepts in the Development of 'Federal Theology,'" in *Calvinus Reformator* (Potchefstroom: Potchefstroom University for Christian Higher Education, 1982), 264–77; David N. J. Poole, *The History of the Covenant Concept from the Bible to Johannes Cloppenburg's "De Foedere Dei"* (San Francisco: Mellen Research University Press, 1992).

7. Rolston, *John Calvin versus the Westminster Confession*, 17, 23.

respects an alien and anomalous idea that disturbed the balance of the Calvinist system and shook the relationships of older components."[8]

Donald J. Bruggink is another who perceives the federal system with its covenant of works as a "perversion of great seriousness" with respect to the theology of Calvin. Pointing to the neonomian doctrine of justification in Richard Baxter, Bruggink warns that Calvin's emphasis on grace is distorted when such a federal scheme is followed. Bruggink concludes his study by asserting that this form of covenant theology damaged Calvin's theology by introducing a covenant of works as a valid relationship between man and God, and then carrying works into the very covenant of grace. Bruggink also argues that Calvin's high view of the church is detrimentally affected by the doctrines of the federal theologians. In his view, federal theology ought to be abandoned rather than refurbished as the church follows Calvin in the study of the Scriptures.[9] Whether the covenant of works is "absent," or "alien," or an "amplification," or an "innovation" of Calvin's covenantal thought, none of these views sees a prelapsarian covenant to be authentic primal Calvinism.[10]

Other scholars such as Leonard J. Trinterud, J. Wayne Baker, Charles S. McCoy, and Joseph C. McLelland have also recognized that Calvin

8. McGiffert, "Perkinsian Moment," 118.

9. Donald J. Bruggink, "Calvin and Federal Theology," *Reformed Review* 13 (1959–60): 15–22.

10. Studies of significance with respect to the origins of the Reformed concept of the covenant of works include: George Park Fisher, "The Augustinian and Federal Theories of Original Sin Compared," in *Discussions in History and Theology* (New York: Scribner, 1880), 355–409; N. Diemer, *Het Scheppingsverbond met Adam bij de Theologen der 16e, 17e, en 18e Eeuw in Zwitserland, Duitschland, Nederland en Engeland* (Kampen: J. H. Kok, 1935); Mark W. Karlberg, "The Mosaic Covenant and the Concept of Works in Reformed Hermeneutics: A Historical-Critical Analysis with Particular Attention to Early Covenant Eschatology" (Ph.D. diss., Westminster Theological Seminary, 1980); idem, "Reformed Interpretation of the Mosaic Covenant," *Westminster Theological Journal* 43 (Fall 1980): 1–57; Robert W. A. Letham, "The *Foedus Operum*: Some Factors Accounting for Its Development," *Sixteenth Century Journal* 14 (1983): 457–67; Peter Alan Lillback, "Ursinus' Development of the Covenant of Creation: A Debt to Melanchthon or Calvin?" *Westminster Theological Journal* 43 (1981): 247–88; Michael McGiffert, "From Moses to Adam: The Making of the Covenant of Works," *Sixteenth Century Journal* 19.2 (1988): 131–55; Mark Muller, "The Covenant of Works and the Stability of Divine Law in Seventeenth-Century Reformed Orthodoxy: A Study in the Theology of Herman Witsius and Wilhelmus A. Brakel," *Calvin Theological Journal* 29.1 (1994): 75–100; W. J. Van Asselt, "The Doctrine of the Abrogations in the Federal Theology of Johannes Cocceius (1603–1669)," *Calvin Theological Journal* 29.1 (1994): 101–16; David A. Weir, *The Origins of the Federal Theology in Sixteenth-Century Reformation Thought* (Oxford: Clarendon, 1990).

employs the covenant idea.[11] From their standpoint, however, Calvin's utilization of the covenant is not that of the majority of the Reformed theologians. Thus the Rhineland theologians such as Bullinger and Oecolampadius developed a bilateral conditional covenant that was not possible for Calvin because of his predestinarianism. To remain consistent with his unyielding views of election, Calvin was compelled to teach an unconditional unilateral covenant.[12] The differences between the two approaches are to be found in the Rhinelanders' milder form of predestination that accommodates itself to the idea of a mutual covenant between God and man, and Calvin's stern double predestinarianism that resisted the notion of human response in the covenant of grace. Trinterud claims that the interpretation given to the term "covenant" in Calvin's writings can "in no manner be compatible with [the] meaning" of such terms as "treaty," "alliance," "mutual agreement," and "reciprocal agreement" as used in the Rhineland-Puritan covenant theology.[13] Lyle D. Bierma summarizes Trinterud's perspective as follows:

> Calvin and the Genevan theologians:
> The covenant is unilateral.
> The covenant is God's unconditional promise to man.
> The burden of fulfilling the covenant rests on God.
> The covenant is fulfilled in Christ's Incarnation, Crucifixion, and
>   Resurrection.

11. Leonard J. Trinterud, "The Origins of Puritanism," *Church History* 20 (1951): 37–57; J. Wayne Baker, *Heinrich Bullinger and the Covenant* (Athens: Ohio University Press, 1980), xxi–xxiii, 193–98; Charles S. McCoy and J. Wayne Baker, *Fountainhead of Federalism: Heinrich Bullinger and the Covenantal Tradition* (Louisville: Westminster/John Knox, 1991), 23–26; Joseph C. McLelland, "Covenant Theology—A Re-Evaluation," *Canadian Journal of Theology* 3 (1957): 184–85. A related viewpoint held by some scholars is that Johannes Cocceius's covenantal theology was developed explicitly to blunt Calvinistic predestinarianism. See J. A. Dorner, *History of Protestant Theology*, trans. G. Robson and S. Taylor (Edinburgh: T. & T. Clark, 1871), 2:39–42; Ludwig Diestel, "Studien zur Föderaltheologie," *Jahrbuch fur Deutsche Theologie* 10 (1865): 266ff.; Otto Ritschl, "Entwicklung des Bundesgedankens in der reformierten Theologie des 16. und des 17. Jahrhunderts," in *Dogmengeschichte des Protestantismus* (Göttingen: Vandenhoeck & Ruprecht, 1926), 3:430–35.

12. I have chosen not to place Jens Møller in this category even though his view can fit here because he softens the differences between Zurich and Geneva because of his more careful presentation of both parties' views in comparison with Trinterud.

13. Trinterud, "Origins of Puritanism," 56 n. 27.

> Zwingli, Bullinger, and the Rhineland theologians:
> The covenant is bilateral.
> The covenant is God's conditional promise to man and man's response
>   (a mutual pact or treaty).
> The burden of fulfilling the covenant rests on man.
> The covenant is fulfilled in the obedience of the individual.[14]

J. Wayne Baker's study of Heinrich Bullinger's covenant theology is clearly the most thorough and best-argued presentation of the differing approaches outlined by Trinterud in his evaluation of the early roots of covenant theology. It is Baker's contention that Bullinger's idea of the covenant differed from Luther's and Calvin's, since his was a mutual covenant while theirs was a unilateral testament. While many Reformers used the terms *testamentum* and *foedus* interchangeably and indiscriminately, they invariably meant a unilateral testament. On the other hand, Bullinger used both terms to refer to a mutual pact or covenant. Even Zwingli, Bullinger's mentor, did not clearly articulate a conditional covenant beacause of the blunting of conditional elements in his thought by his doctrine of election. Thus Calvin's theology of testament was a necessary corollary to his doctrine of double predestination. Bullinger, however, held to a conditional covenant encased within a carefully stated doctrine of single predestination. This, Baker argues, is a crucial distinction that must be recognized if one is to comprehend the development of Reformed Protestantism. It was never a unitary tradition, but rather was an outgrowth of the differing theologies established in Zurich by Bullinger and in Geneva by Calvin.

Baker concludes that Trinterud is correct in asserting that the contractual element is missing from Calvin's covenant idea. Perry Miller is wrong for overlooking Calvin's clear use of the covenant. Anthony A. Hoekema claims too much for Calvin when he develops an idea of conditionality in Calvin's thought.[15] George Marsden is correct to criticize Miller's view of Calvin, yet Miller is correct "in his suggestion that the later Puritan idea of covenant as contract weakened God's sovereignty and thus eroded election in a way that Calvin never allowed."[16] Calvin's development of

14. Bierma, "Covenant Theology of Caspar Olevian," 25.
15. Hoekema's views are considered below.
16. Baker, *Bullinger and the Covenant*, xxi–xxiii, 193–98.

the covenant according to Trinterud and Baker is thus not the viewpoint of the Zurich Reformers, and thus is not the view that ultimately was embodied in the Puritans. Ultimately, the Puritans had more in common with Zurich than they did with Geneva because the Puritans embodied the mutual conditional covenantal thought of Bullinger.[17]

Stephen Strehle is a representative of those scholars who see an inherent tension between Calvin's reformational theology and the rehabilitated medieval scholastic covenant theology found in the federalism of Protestant scholasticism.[18] Strehle's survey of the federal theologians thoroughly demonstrates their emphasis on a conditional covenant.[19] But such covenantal thought is alleged to be alien to Calvin's theology partly because of the paucity of the covenant concept in Calvin's thought:

17. Ibid. See also McCoy and Baker, *Fountainhead of Federalism*, 24: "The differences between Bullinger and Calvin formed the basis for the two alternative, though related, strands within the Reformed tradition—Federalism and Calvinism. It has become usual among historians to reduce Reformed thought in the sixteenth and seventeenth centuries to Calvinism. This reductionism has even led many to refer to the Westminster Confession as a Calvinist theological statement. It is a Reformed confession, but it is most certainly much more a product of the federal tradition than of the Calvinist element." This perspective has been challenged by the following: Everett H. Emerson, "Calvin and Covenant Theology," *Church History* 25 (June 1956): 136–44; Lyle D. Bierma, "Federal Theology in the Sixteenth Century," 304–21; idem, "Covenant or Covenants," 228–50; idem, "The Role of Covenant Theology," 453–62; Lillback, "The Continuing Conundrum, 42–74. See also David C. Steinmetz, "Heinrich Bullinger (1504–1575): Covenant and the Continuity of Salvation History," in *Reformers in the Wings*, ed. David C. Steinmetz (Philadelphia: Fortress, 1971), 133–42.

18. Strehle, *Calvinism*, 149–56. Strehle's efforts to show continuity between medieval scholasticism and Reformed federalism flow out of the research and questions raised by Heiko Oberman, *Forerunners of the Reformation* (Philadelphia: Fortress, 1981), 136–37; idem, "Wir sind Pettler. Hoc est Verum: Bund und Gnade in der Theologie des Mittelalters und der Reformation," *Zeitschrift für Kirchengeschichte* 78.3 (1967): 247–48; idem, *The Harvest of Medieval Theology: Gabriel Biel and the Late Medieval Nominalism* (Cambridge: Harvard University Press, 1963), and idem, "The Shape of Late Medieval Thought: The Birthpangs of the Modern Era," in *The Pursuit of Holiness in Late Medieval and Renaissance Religion*, ed. Charles E. Trinkaus, Studies in Medieval and Reformation Thought 10 (Leiden: E. J. Brill, 1974), 3–25. For other relevant studies, see William J. Courtenay, *Covenant and Causality in Medieval Thought: Studies in Philosophy, Theology, and Economic Practice* (London: Variorum Reprints, 1984); Berndt Hamm, *Promissio, Pactum, Ordinatio: Freiheit und Selbstbindung Gottes in der scholastischen Gnadenlehre*, Beiträge zur historischen Theologie 54 (Tübingen: J. C. B. Mohr [Paul Siebeck], 1977), 390; Francis Oakley, *Omnipotence, Covenant, and Order: An Excursion in the History of Ideas from Abelard to Leibnitz* (Ithaca, NY: Cornell University Press, 1984).

19. For a few examples among many others, see Strehle, *Calvinism*, 159, 162, 164, 170–71, 175–76, 182–88.

"In accordance with Zurich theology, Calvin does incorporate as well a conception of covenant in his *Institutio*, even though it can hardly be considered a constitutive factor, being intercalated rather sparingly and delimited basically to sacramental and testamental discussions."[20] But the absence of the scholastic covenantal thought in Calvin can also be attributed to doctrinal considerations:

> The covenant thus becomes here in essence a bilateral commitment, and as such must incorporate and depend upon some human contribution toward its fulfillment. The Calvinists of the upcoming chapters will inherit this *confoederatio*, even unabashedly declaring it to be a *mutua pactio mutuis obligationibus*. The tension between such a doctrine and other orthodox standards such as unconditional election, irresistible grace, and *sola fides*—doctrines which speak solely of God—will provide those Calvinists with an opportunity to summon their most ingenious creative devices to concoct a synthesis.[21]

The precise relationship of Reformed covenant theology to the medieval development continues to be a focus of scholarly debate.[22] That there was an important connection between the two has also been asserted by Heiko Oberman and Berndt Hamm. Oberman explains:

> In the centuries to come Covenant theology would continue to provide a structure for the understanding of revelation. Elaborated in many different directions, it became an even more basic and explicit theme in the theology of Ulrich Zwingli, John Calvin, and Johannes Cocceius, and was carried from the Dutch to the English shores. It finally came into full bloom in New England Puritan theology.[23]

In similar terms, Hamm states, "Lines led from the medieval tradition of the self-binding of God into the era of the Reformation and

20. Ibid., 149.
21. Ibid., 137.
22. Bierma, "Caspar Olevian," 221 n. 3 states, "That raises a prior and more pressing question, however, concerning the relationship between the covenant doctrine of the late medieval nominalists and the first and second generation Reformed theologians. No one to date has examined this problem in any depth." See Greschat, "Bundesgedanke," 44, for a similar admission of inadequate research.
23. Oberman, *Forerunners of the Reformation*, 136–37.

Counter-Reformation."[24] A possible link between medieval and Reformed varieties of covenant theology has been conjectured by Oberman. He has pointed out that Luther's break with nominalistic covenant theology did not altogether remove his own perspective on the covenant notion. Luther's early thought on this subject can be characterized by a great difference between the Old and New Testaments in that the Old was a covenant of works which could be ended if the covenant pledge was not kept, while the New Testament was a one-sided covenant out of God's mercy which continued even if the covenanter fell into sin. This, he suggests, is anticipatory of the later Reformed theology.[25] Strehle, however, sees no connection between Luther or Calvin and the later federalists.[26]

The strongest case for the continuity between the early reformational theology and later Reformed scholastic orthodoxy has been made by Richard A. Muller.[27] This has been denominated the Muller Thesis by Martin

24. Hamm, *Promissio*, 390 (my translation).

25. Oberman, "Wir sind Pettler," 247–48.

26. See Strehle, *Calvinism*, 83–97. Strehle claims that Melanchthon and Beza are to be blamed for the introduction of medieval scholastic covenantal theology into Reformational thought. "In addition to Melanchthon, Theodore de Beze should also be exposed for vitiating the positive insights of the early Reformers through Scholastic aberrations. John Calvin, the predecessor of Beze at Geneva, had earlier spurned such theology as impious. . . . All of these statements betray a legacy in Scotism, not Calvin" (97–98, 102–3). Examples of other scholars who see a cleavage between Calvin and the later Calvinists are Ernst Bizer, *Frühorthodoxie und Rationalismus* (Zurich: EVZ, 1963), and Basil Hall, "Calvin against the Calvinists," in *John Calvin*, ed. G. E. Duffield (Appleford: Sutton Courtenay, 1966), 18–37. For helpful discussions of this point see John W. Beardslee III, *Reformed Dogmatics* (Grand Rapids: Baker, 1977), 17–19; Paul Jacobs, *Prädestination und Verantwortlichkeit bei Calvin* (Neukirchen: Buchhandlung des Erziehungsvereins, 1937), 41ff.; Richard A. Muller, *Post-Reformation Reformed Dogmatics*, Vol. 1, *Prolegomena to Theology* (Grand Rapids: Baker, 1987), 93–96, 309–10; Wilhelm Niesel, *The Theology of Calvin*, trans. Harold Knight (Grand Rapids: Baker, 1980), 159ff.; François Wendel, *Calvin*, trans. Philip Mairet (Glasgow: Collins, 1963), 269ff.; Brian G. Armstrong, *Calvinism and the Amyraut Heresy* (Madison: University of Wisconsin Press, 1969), 198–202.

27. Richard A. Muller, "Scholasticism Protestant and Catholic: Francis Turretin and the Object and Principles of Theology," *Church History* 55 (June 1986): 193–205; idem, "*Vera Philosophia cum sacra Theologia nusquam pugnat*: Keckermann on Philosophy, Theology, and the Problem of Double Truth," *Sixteenth Century Journal* 15 (Fall 1984): 341–65; idem, "'Duplex cognitio dei' in the Theology of Early Reformed Orthodoxy," *Sixteenth Century Journal* 10 (1979): 51–62; idem, "Perkins' A Golden Chaine: Predestinarian System or Schematized *Ordo Salutis?*" *Sixteenth Century Journal* 9 (April 1978): 69–81; idem, "Christ in the Eschaton: Calvin and Moltmann on the Duration of the *Munus Regium*," *Harvard Theological Review* 74 (1981): 31–59; idem, "Covenant and Conscience in English Reformed Theology: Three Variations on a

Klauber.[28] The Muller Thesis provides an excellent context in which to consider another group of scholars, namely, those who see a substantial continuity between the theology of Calvin and the federalists.

Calvin Develops an Extensive If Incomplete Covenant Theology

The studies by W. Vanden Bergh, W. H. Van der Vegt, Anthony A. Hoekema, Elton M. Eenigenburg, and Peter A. Lillback argue that Calvin's covenant theology is extensive even if it is not complete.[29] Vanden Bergh's *Calvijn over het Genadeverbond* is now over a century old.[30]

Vanden Bergh develops Calvin's covenantal thought in terms of his close association with Bullinger. He claims that no one before Calvin except for Bullinger treated the covenant as seriously as did Calvin, and the basic lines of thought of Bullinger are all present in Calvin's covenantal ideas.[31] The significance of Vanden Bergh's study is in its insistence that there is extensive continuity between Calvin's covenantal views and those of the later federalists.

The more recent studies of Hoekema and Eenigenburg both limit Calvin's covenantal thought only to the covenant of grace to the exclusion of the covenants of works and redemption. These scholars demonstrate that

---

Seventeenth Century Theme," *Westminster Theological Journal* 42 (1980) 308–34; idem, "The Debate over the 'Vowel Points' and the Crisis in Seventeenth Century Hermeneutics," *Journal of Medieval and Renaissance Studies* 10 (Spring 1980): 53–72; idem, "The Spirit and the Covenant: John Gill's Critique of the *Pactum Salutis*," *Foundations: A Baptist Journal of History and Theology* 24 (January 1981): 4–14; idem, *Christ and the Decree: Christology and Predestination from Calvin to Perkins* (Grand Rapids: Baker, 1988); idem, *Prolegomena to Theology*; idem, *Dictionary of Latin and Greek Theological Terms* (Grand Rapids: Baker, 1985).

28. Martin I. Klauber, "Continuity and Discontinuity in Post-Reformation Reformed Theology: An Evaluation of the Muller Thesis," *Journal of the Evangelical Theological Society* 33.4 (Dec. 1990): 467–75.

29. W. Vanden Bergh, *Calvijn over het Genadeverbond* ('s Gravenhage: W. A. Beschoor, 1879); W. H. Van der Vegt, *Het Verbond der Genade bij Calvijn* (Aalten: De Graafschap, 1939); Elton M. Eenigenburg, "The Place of the Covenant in Calvin's Thinking," *Reformed Review* 10 (1957): 1–22; Anthony A. Hoekema, "Calvin's Doctrine of the Covenant of Grace," *Reformed Review* 15 (1962): 1–12; idem, "The Covenant of Grace in Calvin's Teaching," *Calvin Theological Journal* 2 (1967): 133–61; Lillback, "Ursinus' Development of the Covenant of Creation"; idem, "Calvin's Covenantal Response," 185–232; idem, "The Binding of God"; idem, "The Continuing Conundrum."

30. Van der Vegt's *Het Verbond der Genade bij Calvijn* is less ambitious even though written after Vanden Bergh, but he does develop the question of covenant and election more fully than does Vanden Bergh.

31. Vanden Bergh, *Calvijn*, v, 10.

Calvin applies the covenant not only to his task of organizing the theology of Scripture, but also to his exegesis and to his preaching. Thus the covenant was an idea that Calvin encountered in several spheres of his work—the *Institutes*, his commentaries, and his sermons. The primary areas are the unity of Scripture, the sacraments, and the doctrine of election. Eenigenburg's study sees the covenant and election as coterminous in Calvin's thought, while Hoekema argues that Calvin developed a middle position between the reprobate and the elect.[32] This middle position was composed of nonelect members of the covenant of grace. A fourth area identified is the question of how the believer's good works enter into his salvation in light of the doctrine of the free forgiveness of sins in justification by faith.

Both Eenigenburg and Hoekema insist on the conditionality of the covenant in Calvin. In keeping with this, they underscore the mutuality as well as the reality of apostasy and covenant-breaking in Calvin's exposition of the covenant of grace. Eenigenburg says, "The covenant itself is unconditional, as we have observed, but the place of the participants in it is conditional upon their effective observance of the stipulations."[33] Hoekema makes this same point when he writes, "The covenant of grace can be broken by man but not by God."[34] This Hoekema believes to be Calvin's method of emphasizing the priority of God's grace—the covenant is monopleuric or unilateral in origin. It also serves to underscore man's solemn responsibility—the covenant is dipleuric or bilateral in its fulfilment.[35] As a result, the warnings of Scripture take on deep seriousness, and signal the importance of self-examination for all who belong to the covenant of grace.[36]

In summary, this viewpoint not only recognizes the importance of the covenant in Calvin's development of the history of redemption, the sacraments, election, and the interrelationship between faith and obedience in salvation, it also insists that there is no discontinuity between Calvin and

---

32. Van der Vegt advances the position held by Hoekema. See *Verbond*, 5–41. Van der Vegt's work in 1939 prompted a critique in 1940 by A. D. R. Polman, "Het Verbond der Genade bij Calvijn," in *Gereformeerd Theologisch Tijdschrift*. Polman claims that the covenantal middle ground between the elect and nonelect was intended by Calvin only for the Old Testament context.

33. Eenigenburg, "Covenant in Calvin's Thinking," 13.

34. Hoekema, "Calvin's Doctrine of the Covenant," 9.

35. Idem, "Covenant of Grace in Calvin's Teaching," 140.

36. Idem, "Calvin's Doctrine of the Covenant," 10.

the theology of a conditional covenant. For Hoekema and Eenigenburg, Calvin just as much as Zwingli's descendants beginning with Bullinger insisted on a mutual covenant of grace.

From this survey, it is evident there is substantial interest in the subject of Calvin's covenantal perspective. Moreover, there is no scholarly consensus on the place of the covenant in Calvin's theology, nor is there scholarly agreement with regard to Calvin's role in the development of covenant theology.

The Parties of the Covenant and the Centrality of the Abrahamic Covenant in the *Institutes*

Before we consider Calvin's exposition of the covenant in the *Institutes*, found in chapters 10 and 11, these chapters must be placed in the broader context of Calvin's understanding of the parties of the covenant in the *Institutes* themselves, as well as in terms of Calvin's emphasis on the Abrahamic covenant.

The Parties of the Covenant

For Calvin, the parties of the covenant in the *Institutes* are Adam,[37] Adam and Eve,[38] Abel,[39] Noah,[40] Abraham,[41] Abraham's children,[42] Jacob,[43] Esau,[44] Ishmael[45] and Isaac,[46] the patriarchs (fathers),[47] Moses,[48] Levi,[49]

37. Calvin, *Institutes* 2.10.7, 20; 4.1.17; 4.14.12, 18. See also the following references to Adam in *Calvin's Commentaries*, 22 vols. (Grand Rapids: Baker, 1979): Heb. 1:2 (22:33–34); Heb. 2:5 (22:57); Heb. 5:9 (22:124–25); 1 John 1:1 (22:158–59).
38. *Institutes* 4.14.18.
39. *Institutes* 2.10.7.
40. *Institutes* 2.10.7; 4.14.18.
41. *Institutes* 1.6.1; 1.8.3; 1.10.1; 2.6.2; 2.7.1; 2.10.7; 3.20.25; 3.21.6, 7; 4.14.5; 4.16.3, 6, 12, 14, 15, 24.
42. *Institutes* 3.21.7; 3.22.4.
43. *Institutes* 3.20.25; 3.21.6; 3.22.4, 6; 4.16.14.
44. *Institutes* 3.21.6; 4.16.14.
45. *Institutes* 3.21.6; 3.24.8; 4.16.14.
46. *Institutes* 3.20.25; 3.21.6, 7; 4.16.14, 24.
47. *Institutes* 2.7.1; 2.10.1, 2, 7, 17, 23; 2.11.9, 10; 3.20.25; 4.1.24; 4.14.5; 4.15.9; 4.16.3, 6, 11, 12, 15.
48. *Institutes* 2.5.12; 2.7.1; 2.11.4.
49. *Institutes* 4.2.3; 4.7.30; 4.8.2; 4.9.2.

Levitical priests,[50] Israel (the Jews),[51] David,[52] prophets,[53] Christ,[54] the apostles and the prophets,[55] the church,[56] the church and kingdom,[57] Christians,[58] Rome, the papists,[59] European nations,[60] any people,[61] all men adopted by God,[62] believers,[63] families,[64] babies and children,[65] the Lord's servants,[66] the holy generation,[67] Gentiles or any people,[68] spiritual sons or children,[69] posterity, descendants, and successors,[70] the elect,[71] adult converts,[72] infants of Israel and of Christians,[73] the communicant,[74] "Us," that is, New Testament Christians,[75] and those who keep the covenant.[76] Thus, for Calvin, the covenant encompasses the entire scope of salvation history.

50. *Institutes* 4.9.2.
51. *Institutes* 2.5.9; 2.8.15, 23, 29; 2.10.1, 2, 4, 5, 19, 23; 2.11.3, 4, 8, 11; 3.2.22; 3.21.5, 6, 7; 3.22.4, 6; 4.2.7, 11; 4.15.17; 4.16.6, 11, 14, 15, 23. See also the following references to the covenant with the Jews in *Calvin's Commentaries*: Heb. 6:17 (22:150); Heb. 8:10 (22:188–91); Jude 5 (22:434–35); 1 Peter 2:9 (22:74–75).
52. *Institutes* 2.6.3, 4; 2.10.17; 3.20.25; 4.1.17.
53. *Institutes* 2.10.15.
54. *Institutes* 3.4.32 (the true Solomon); 3.20.25 (David as a type of Christ); Christ, the true Solomon: 1.6.1; 2.10.4; 3.4.32; 3.6.2; 3.20.45; 4.1.27.
55. *Institutes* 4.9.2.
56. *Institutes* 2.8.21; 3.20.45; 3.21.7; 4.1.24; 4.2.7; 4.16.10 (implied).
57. *Institutes* 4.1.20. See also the following reference to the kingdom and the covenant in *Calvin's Commentaries*: Heb. 8:10 (22:188–91).
58. *Institutes* 2.10.5; 4.14.19.
59. *Institutes* 3.22.4; 4.2.7, 11.
60. *Institutes* 4.2.11.
61. *Institutes* 3.21.7.
62. *Institutes* 2.10.1.
63. *Institutes* 1.6.1; 1.9.3; 2.10.23; 3.21.7; 4.1.27; 4.13.6; 4.16.6.
64. *Institutes* 2.8.21.
65. Babies: *Institutes* 4.15.20; 4.16.5, 7, 12, 15, 17, 21, 23, 24, 30. Children: *Institutes* 4.15.22; 4.16.6, 9, 10, 12.
66. *Institutes* 2.10.8.
67. *Institutes* 4.16.14.
68. *Institutes* 2.11.12; 3.2.22; 3.21.7; 4.16.23.
69. *Institutes* 3.21.7; 3.22.4, 7; 3.24.5; 4.15.22.
70. *Institutes* 3.20.25; 3.21.7; 4.2.3; 4.14.18.
71. *Institutes* 2.11.4; 3.21.5.
72. *Institutes* 4.16.23, 24.
73. *Institutes* 4.16.5, 6, 9, 12, 21.
74. *Institutes* 4.17.1, 6.
75. *Institutes* 2.5.10; 2.10.1, 5; 3.4.32; 4.1.20; 4.16.6.
76. *Institutes* 3.2.7; 3.17.1, 3, 5, 6, 15.

First, Calvin insists on the unity and eternity of the covenant. He writes:

> The covenant made with all the patriarchs is so much like ours in substance and reality that the two are actually one and the same. Yet they differ in the mode of dispensation.[77]

> The spiritual covenant was also common to the patriarchs. . . . Adam, Abel, Noah, Abraham, and other spiritual patriarchs cleaved to God by such illumination of the Word.[78]

Similarly, Calvin describes the covenant as "one and eternal." The covenant is "everlasting" or "eternal,"[79] "forever inviolable,"[80] "firm and inviolable,"[81] and "still in force."[82] It has been established "once and for all"[83] and "keeps itself alive by its own strength."[84]

Second, Calvin explains the differences between the various biblical covenants in terms of progressive revelation:

> The Lord held to this orderly plan in administering the covenant of his mercy: as the day of full revelation approached with the passing of time, the more he increased each day the brightness of its manifestation. Accordingly, at the beginning when the first promise of salvation was given to Adam it glowed like a feeble spark. Then, as it was added to, the light grew in fullness, breaking forth increasingly and shedding its radiance more widely. At last—when all the clouds were dispersed—Christ, the Sun of Righteousness, fully illumined the whole earth.[85]

Third, Calvin sees the covenant with Abraham as the actual establishment of God's covenant. Calvin states, "For what else does he [Moses]

77. *Institutes* 2.10.2.
78. *Institutes* 2.10.7.
79. *Institutes* 2.6.3, 4; 2.11.4, 10; 2.17.4; 3.4.32; 3.20.25.
80. *Institutes* 4.1.27; 4.2.11.
81. *Institutes* 4.15.17; 4.16.5.
82. *Institutes* 4.16.6.
83. *Institutes* 4.16.14; 4.17.1.
84. *Institutes* 4.2.11. See also the following references in *Calvin's Commentaries*: Ps. 105:6–11 (6:176–79); Jer. 31:3 (10:57–58); and Jer. 32:40 (10:215).
85. *Institutes* 2.10.20.

do but call them back to the covenant begun with Abraham?" Calvin believes that the covenant was in existence before Abraham. Yet, in a very real sense, the covenant's formal establishment was with Abraham in the words of Genesis 17. Here one may observe the harmony between Calvin's *Institutes* and Bullinger's *Of the One and Eternal Testament or Covenant of God.*

Calvin's Understanding of the Abrahamic Covenant in the Institutes

Given Zwingli's and Bullinger's view of the centrality of the Abrahamic covenant, it is significant to see Calvin's full support for this perspective. There appear to be five aspects of the Abrahamic covenant that are emphasized by Calvin in the *Institutes* that are also in harmony with the covenantal theology of the Reformers of Zurich.

First, the covenant is the divine means of separating the world into those who are believers in Christ and those who are not. Calvin asserts:

> My readers therefore should remember that I am not yet going to discuss that covenant by which God adopted to himself the sons of Abraham, or that part of doctrine which has always separated believers from unbelieving folk, for it was founded in Christ.[86]

> I do not yet touch upon the special covenant by which he distinguished the race of Abraham from the rest of the nations. For, even then in receiving by free adoption as sons those who were enemies, he showed himself to be their Redeemer.[87]

Second, the Abrahamic covenant is the source of salvation for Israel, as they are the offspring of Abraham. Calvin avers:

> He [Jacob] knows that the complete blessedness of his posterity consists in the inheritance of the covenant that God had made with him [Abraham].[88]

86. *Institutes* 1.6.1.
87. *Institutes* 1.1.1.
88. *Institutes* 3.20.25.

Inasmuch as the covenant made with Abraham applies to his descendants, Christ, to perform and discharge the pledge made once for all by his Father, came for the salvation of the Jewish nation.[89]

Third, the Abrahamic covenant is still in force for Christians as well. Calvin declares:

Indeed, it is most evident that the covenant which the Lord once made with Abraham is no less in force today for Christians than it was of old for the Jewish people.[90]

Fourth, Calvin affirms the Christ-centeredness of the Abrahamic covenant for all nations:

For even if God included all of Abraham's offspring in His covenant, Paul nevertheless wisely reasons that Christ was properly that seed in whom all the nations were to be blessed.[91]

Fifth, there are two great redemptive benefits contained in the Abrahamic covenant, namely, justification and sanctification:

Abraham's circumcision was not for his justification, but for the seal of that covenant of faith in which he had already been justified. [92]

The Lord covenants with Abraham that he should walk before him in uprighteousness and innocence of heart. This applies to mortification, or regeneration.[93]

Thus for Calvin, the entire sweep of the history of redemption is covenantal and finds its center in the Abrahamic covenant as fulfilled in the incarnation and saving work of Jesus Christ.

89. *Institutes* 4.16.15.
90. *Institutes* 4.16.6.
91. *Institutes* 2.6.2.
92. *Institutes* 4.16.5.
93. *Institutes* 4.16.3.

Calvin's Interpretation of the History of Salvation: The Continuity and Discontinuity of the Covenant

Having reviewed the diverse scholarly assessments of Calvin's understanding of the covenant, as well as having summarized his views of the parties of the covenant in general and of the Abrahamic covenant in particular, let us now turn to his locus classicus on the interpretation of the covenant, namely book 2, chapters 10 and 11 of the *Institutes*.

Calvin's Understanding of the Continuity of the Old and New Covenants[94]

In Zwingli's conflict with the Anabaptists, the continuity of the covenants became pivotal for his defense of infant baptism. For Calvin, too, the Anabaptists are the parties most in need of understanding covenant unity:

> Now let us examine the arguments by which certain mad beasts ceaselessly assail this holy institution of God. First of all, since they feel that they are immoderately cramped and constrained by the likeness between baptism and circumcision, they strive to set these two things apart by a wide difference so that there may seem to be nothing in common between them. For they say that these two signify different things, that the covenant in each is quite different, and the calling of children under each is not the same. . . . In asserting a difference between the covenants, with what barbarous boldness do they dissipate and corrupt Scripture! And not in one passage only—but so as to leave nothing safe or untouched! For they depict the Jews to us as so carnal that they are more like beasts than men. A covenant with them would not go beyond the temporal life, and the promises given them would rest in present and physical benefits. If this doctrine should obtain, what would remain save that the Jewish nation was satiated for a time with God's benefits (as men fatten a herd of swine in a sty), only to perish in eternal destruction?[95]

94. See Peter A. Lillback, "Calvin's Covenantal Response to the Anabaptist View of Baptism," in *The Failure of the American Baptist Culture*, vol. 1 of *Christianity & Civilization* (Tyler, TX: Geneva Divinity School, 1982), 185–232.
95. *Institutes* 4.16.10.

Calvin's invective strikes the modern reader as extreme. It nonetheless indicates Calvin's deep feelings on the issue. His concern is not simply for baptism of infants, but for the inevitable danger to all of scriptural doctrine if the Anabaptist argument is accepted. If infant baptism is to be overturned, then the continuity of the old and new covenants must be denied. But this makes the Old Testament saints nothing more than recipients of material blessings at the expense of their salvation. Consequently, the topic has both polemical and practical significance. "Indeed, that wonderful rascal Servetus and certain madmen of the Anabaptist sect, who regard the Israelites as nothing but a herd of swine, make necessary what would in any case have been very profitable for us."[96]

The First Covenantal Continuity

Calvin's fundamental proposition is that God always covenanted his people to himself by the same law and doctrine. Thus he says, "All men adopted by God into the company of his people since the beginning of the world were covenanted to him by the same law and by the bond of the same doctrine as obtains among us."[97] Similarly he states, "The covenant made with all the patriarchs is so much like ours in substance and reality that the two are actually one and the same. Yet they differ in the mode of dispensation."[98] Not even the Mosaic legal system can be seen to be without its necessary conjunction with the one divine covenant:

> I understand by the word "law" not only the Ten Commandments, which set forth a godly and righteous rule of living, but the form of religion handed down by God through Moses. And Moses was not made a lawgiver to wipe out the blessing promised to the race of Abraham. Rather, we see him repeatedly reminding the Jews of that freely given covenant made with their fathers of which they were the heirs. It was as if he were sent to renew it. This fact was very clearly revealed in the ceremonies.[99]

96. *Institutes* 2.10.1.
97. Ibid.
98. *Institutes* 2.10.2. See also *Calvin's Commentaries* on Gal. 4:1 (21:114–16).
99. *Institutes* 2.7.1.

Calvin explains the relationship of Abraham and Moses in terms of the single covenant of God in the progress of redemptive history.

The Second Covenantal Continuity

Since all of God's people have enjoyed the same law and doctrine, albeit in different degrees of revelation and varying administration, it follows that they have always known Christ as Mediator. Speaking of the old covenant saints, Calvin says, "they had and knew Christ as Mediator, through whom they were joined to God and were to share in his promises."[100] Again he asserts, "There are two remaining points: that the Old Testament fathers (1) had Christ as pledge of their covenant, and (2) put in him all trust of future blessedness."[101] Calvin also makes this same point in *Institutes* 2.6.3–4 where he argues that Christ as the fruit of the covenant was known to David in terms of the promise of an eternal kingdom.

The Third Covenantal Continuity

And if the old covenant was blessed with Christ, it is just as certain that those saints also possessed the grace of justification. So Calvin argues:

> For the same reason it follows that the Old Testament was established upon the free mercy of God, and was confirmed by Christ's intercession. For the gospel preaching, too, declares nothing else than that sinners are justified apart from their own merit by God's fatherly kindness; and the whole of it summed up in Christ. Who, then, dares to separate the Jews from Christ, since with them, we hear, was made the covenant of the gospel, the sole foundation of which is Christ?[102]

The Fourth Covenantal Continuity

If the grace of the covenant in the old covenant era was equal to that of the new covenant era, however, then the sacraments must also have equal significance. Calvin contends that Paul held this belief:

100. *Institutes* 2.10.2. See also *Calvin's Commentaries* on Acts 28:23 (19:425).
101. *Institutes* 2.10.23.
102. *Institutes* 2.10.4. See also *Calvin's Commentaries* on 1 Cor. 10:11 (20:329).

187

Indeed, the apostle makes the Israelites equal to us not only in the grace of the covenant but also in the signification of the sacraments. In recounting examples of the punishments with which, according to Scripture, the Israelites were chastised of God, his purpose was to deter the Corinthians from falling into similar misdeeds. So he begins with the premise: there is no reason why we should claim any privilege for ourselves, to deliver us from the vengeance of God, which they underwent, since the Lord not only provided them with the same benefits but also manifested his grace among them by the same symbols.[103]

The Fifth Covenantal Continuity

Because the Word of God was present in the old covenant, eternal life was also a key blessing of the covenant that the old covenant saints shared with the new covenant believers.

The spiritual covenant was also common to the patriarchs.... Now since God of old bound the Jews to himself by this sacred bond, there is no doubt that he set them apart to the hope of eternal life.... Adam, Abel, Noah, Abraham and other patriarchs cleaved to God by such illumination of the Word. Therefore I say that without any doubt they entered into God's immortal kingdom. For theirs was a real participation in God, which cannot be without the blessing of eternal life.[104]

The Sixth Covenantal Continuity

For Calvin, the very formula of the covenant which was possessed by the Old Testament saints demanded that these saints be seen to be possessors of eternal life.

Let us pass on to the very formula of the covenant.... For the Lord always covenanted with his servants thus: "I will be your God, and you shall be my people." The prophets also commonly explained that life and salvation and the whole of blessedness are embraced in these

103. *Institutes* 2.10.5.
104. *Institutes* 2.10.7.

words. . . . He is our God on this condition: that he dwell among us, as he has testified through Moses. But one cannot obtain such a presence of him without, at the same time, possessing life. And although nothing further was expressed, they had a clear enough promise of spiritual life in these words: "I am . . . your God." For he did not declare that he would be a God to their bodies alone, but especially to their souls. Still souls, unless they be joined to God through righteousness, remain estranged from him in death. On the other hand, such a union when present will bring everlasting salvation with it.[105]

Calvin repeats this same point more briefly, "The Old Testament or Covenant that the Lord had made with the Israelites had not been limited to earthly things, but contained a promise of spiritual and eternal life. The expectation of this must have been impressed upon the hearts of all who truly consented to the covenant."[106]

In his commentaries, Calvin also connects the covenant with salvation or eternal life. On Psalm 67:2, he calls the covenant "the source and spring of salvation." On Zechariah 12:1, he says that the "hope of salvation is founded on the covenant."

In light of this evidence, Calvin believes that he has established the spirituality of the covenant of the Old Testament saints, and hence, its continuity with the new covenant. He concludes, "Yet unless we shun the proffered light, we already possess a clear affirmation of the spiritual covenant."[107] Therefore, "when we hear the public oracles of the Holy Spirit, in which he so clearly and plainly discussed spiritual life in the church of the Jews, it would be intolerable stubbornness to relegate them solely to a carnal covenant, wherein mention is made only of the earth and of earthly riches."[108]

Calvin's view of the continuity of the covenant found in chapter 10 of book 2 of the *Institutes* can be presented as follows:

105. *Institutes* 2.10.8.
106. *Institutes* 2.10.23.
107. *Institutes* 2.10.5.
108. *Institutes* 2.10.19. See also *Calvin's Commentaries* on Rom. 15:8 (19:520–21).

1. The old and new covenants are the same in substance: the same law and same doctrine since the beginning of the world.
2. Christ is mediator of the covenants.
3. Both have the grace of justification.
4. Sacraments have equal significance in both.
5. Both have the Word of God, which is to have eternal life.
6. The formula of the covenant common to both includes eternal life.

One can now appreciate the motivation of Calvin's vehement assault on the Anabaptist rejection of infant baptism. This rejection demanded that the old covenant be a material or carnal covenant and circumcision be considered a non-spiritual symbol. As a result, several important doctrines associated with the covenant were severely injured. Hence, the continuity of the covenant is a doctrine of paramount importance. In fact, "the law is not at all superfluous, nor is the Old Testament, but it is a permanent thing, which must always retain its strength, even to the end of the world."[109] Similarly he declares, "St. Peter tells us that the prophets have served us more than them, that that which God has revealed to them was more for our time than for those to whom they were speaking."[110]

Calvin's Explanation of the Discontinuity of the Covenants: The Relationship of Law to Gospel and Letter to Spirit

Having argued ardently for the essential unity of the old and new covenants, Calvin is conscious that his opponents can charge him with failing to come to grips with the numerous biblical testimonies to the differences between them. So in chapter 11 of book 2, Calvin begins his hermeneutic of the diversity of the old and new covenants:

109. "La Loy n'est pas du tant superflue, ni le vieil Testament, mais que c'est une chose permanante, et qui doit toujours retenir sa vigueur jusque en la fin du monde." Sermon 34 on 1 Timothy 4:12–13, in *Ioannis Calvini opera quae supersunt omnia*, CO 52:412.

110. "Sainct Pierre nous dit, que les prophetes ont servi a nous plus qu'a eux, que ce que Dieu leur ha revele ha este pour nostre temps plustost que pour ceux qui les ont oy parler." Sermon 47 on Daniel, CO 42:164. Cf. Sermon 148 on Deuteronomy, CO 28:288.

Table 1: A Summary of Calvin's View of the Differences Between the Old and New Covenants: They Are Distinct in Administration

Old Covenant—Before Christ	New Covenant—After Christ
1. Material & temporal blessings represent spiritual blessings	1. Direct meditation upon spiritual blessings
2. Images & ceremonies as types of Christ	2. Full revelation of Christ in his incarnation
3. The Old Testament law is the letter that kills	3. The New Testament gospel is the Spirit that makes alive
a. The Old Testament law in the narrow sense condemns because it is the demand of law without the Holy Spirit's aid in the gospel	a. In the new covenant the law is written upon the heart by the Spirit and is accompanied by the forgiveness of sins
b. The Old Testament law in the broad sense includes the gospel by borrowing from it the promises of Christ	b. The gospel of the new covenant has been the experience of God's children since the beginning of the world
4. The old covenant was characterized by bondage and fear	4. The new covenant is characterized by freedom and trust
5. The old covenant was limited to Israel	5. The new covenant is extended to all nations

What then? You will ask: will not difference remain between the Old and New Testaments? What is to become of the many passages of Scripture wherein they are contrasted as utterly different?

I freely admit the differences in Scripture, to which attention is called, but in such a way as not to detract from its established unity.[111]

Calvin enumerates five differences between the covenants. They relate only to the externals and not to the substance of the covenant. For a summary see table 1.

The First Difference

The first difference is that the old covenant used material or temporal blessings to represent spiritual blessings, while members of the new covenant directly experience these spiritual blessings. Accordingly, Calvin rejects the materialistic view of the old covenant:

111. *Institutes* 2.11.1.

The point of our quarrel with men of this sort is this: they teach that the Israelites deemed the possession of the land of Canaan their highest and ultimate blessedness, and that after the revelation of Christ it typified for us the heavenly inheritance. We contend, on the contrary, that, in the earthly possession they enjoyed, they looked, as in a mirror, upon the future inheritance they believed to have been prepared for them in heaven.[112]

This difference is one of divine dispensation, explained by God's will for Israel.

But we shall readily dispose of these misgivings if we turn our attention to this dispensation of God which I have noted. He willed that, for the time during which he gave his covenant to the people of Israel in a veiled form, the grace of future and eternal happiness be signified and figured under earthly benefits, the gravity of spiritual death under physical punishments.[113]

The next three differences Calvin summarizes as the differences between the law and the gospel.[114] In this context, Old Testament means "law" and New Testament means "gospel."

The Second Difference

The second difference between the covenants, and the first in this category, is that truth in the Old Testament was conveyed by images and ceremonies as types of Christ. The new covenant has the benefit of the full revelation of Christ's incarnation. Calvin writes, "The second difference between the Old and New Testaments consists in figures: that, in the absence of the reality, it showed but an image and shadow in place of the substance; the New Testament reveals the very substance of truth as present."[115]

---

112. Ibid.

113. *Institutes* 2.11.3. See also the following references in *Calvin's Commentaries* to the material benefits of the human covenant: Gen. 14:13 (1:384–85); Gen. 17:21 (1:462–63).

114. *Institutes* 2.11.10.

115. *Institutes* 2.11.4.

Calvin appears to be making a distinction between the two covenants with respect to substance due to the presence and absence of the reality. He clarifies himself by explaining that the difference is with respect to promise and fulfilment. From the standpoint of the old covenant, Christ's first advent was future. From the standpoint of the new covenant, his coming as man is past.

> Here we are to observe how the covenant of the law compares with the covenant of the gospel, the ministry of Christ with that of Moses. For if the comparison had reference to the substance of promises, then there would be great disagreement between the Testaments. But since the trend of the argument leads us in another direction, we must follow it to find the truth. Let us then set forth the covenant that he once established as eternal and never perishing. Its fulfillment, by which it is finally confirmed and ratified, is Christ.[116]

This difference between the image and the substance is seen in the Old Testament ceremonies that were temporary and hence accidental to the covenant. These could be discarded at Christ's coming without harming the covenant itself.

> While such confirmation was awaited, the Lord appointed, through Moses, ceremonies that were, so to speak, solemn symbols of that confirmation. A controversy arose over whether or not the ceremonies that had been ordained in the law ought to give way to Christ. Now these were only the accidental properties of the covenant, or additions and appendages, and in common parlance, accessories of it. Yet because they were means of administering it, they bear the name "covenant," just as is customary in the case of other sacraments. To sum up, then, in this passage "Old Testament" means the solemn manner of confirming the covenant, comprised in ceremonies and sacrifices.[117]

So the Old and New Testaments were not inherently different. The Old Testament actually *became* the New Testament when Christ came and

116. *Institutes* 2.11.4.
117. Ibid.

ratified the New Testament, for the New Testament had always been symbolized in the shadowy ceremonies of the Old Testament. Calvin explains:

> Or, if you prefer, understand it thus: the Old Testament of the Lord was that covenant wrapped up in the shadowy and ineffectual observance of ceremonies and delivered to the Jews; it was temporary because it remained, as it were, in suspense until it might rest upon a firm and substantial confirmation. It became new and eternal only after it was consecrated and established by the blood of Christ. Hence Christ in the Supper calls the cup that he gives to his disciples, "the cup of the New Testament in my blood." By this he means that the Testament of God attained its truth when sealed by his blood, and thereby becomes new and eternal.[118]

The Third Difference

The third difference between the old and new covenants, the second between the law and gospel, is the letter-spirit distinction. This is an extension of what Calvin has just explained—that the old covenant became the new covenant. In his explanation of covenantal unity, Calvin argues that the change from the old covenant to the new was because of the coming of Christ. The basis for the variation between the covenants is explained by the coming of Christ and the subsequent work of the Holy Spirit in the new covenant. This is the teaching, Calvin avers, of Jeremiah 31:31–34 and 2 Corinthians 3:6–11.

Because of the importance of this third difference for Calvin's hermeneutic and his theology in general, our consideration here will be more extensive, incorporating some of his exposition from his commentaries. These passages are critical for understanding Calvin, since they reveal his interpretation of these foundational biblical texts that contrast the old and new covenants. As these passages appear to deny that there is one divine covenant throughout Scripture, Calvin is forced by Scripture either to concede the argument to the Anabaptists, or to offer an explanation

---

118. Ibid. See also Calvin's Sermon 15 on Daniel: "la doctrine de l'ancien testament . . . qui est contenu en la loy . . . c'est une mesme doctrine, sinon que par l'Evangile Dieu s'est declare a nous plus clairement," CO 41:481. See also in *Calvin's Commentaries* Ezek. 16:60 (12:173).

of the covenantal discontinuity that does not overthrow his emphasis on covenant continuity. Calvin therein explains how the "old" was broken by Israel, and was a covenant only of the letter, whereas the "new" is a spiritual covenant written by God on the heart. Let us now consider his explanation of these covenantal differences that all the while maintains his commitment to the continuity of the covenants.

Calvin begins by explaining the literal character of the law and the spiritual character of the gospel.[119] The common purpose of Jeremiah and Paul is to analyze what is intrinsic to the law, versus what is associated with the law by its borrowing elements from the gospel. Calvin states:

> For example: the law contains here and there promises of mercy, but because they have been borrowed from elsewhere, they are not counted part of the law, when only the nature of the law is under discussion. They ascribe to it only this function: to enjoin what is right, to forbid what is wicked; to promise a reward to the keepers of righteousness, and threaten transgressors with punishment; but at the same time not to change or correct the depravity of heart that by nature inheres in all men.[120]

The law is letter because in itself it can only tell sinful men what to do, and hence point out their sin, but never enable them to overcome their evil. The gospel, however, has the Holy Spirit that enables men to begin to be holy and to do what the law demands. All of their sin is forgiven by Christ's redemptive work; hence the gospel is spirit. This letter-spirit distinction is carefully addressed by Calvin's exegesis, as can be seen in his commentaries on Jeremiah 31, 2 Corinthians 3, and Hebrews 8.

The Third Difference and Jeremiah 31

Calvin explains how one ought to compare law and gospel in his comments on Jeremiah 31:32–34. First, Calvin notes, one must recognize what the law is in itself—a rule of righteousness that only speaks to the

---

119. *Institutes* 2.11.7. See also the following references in *Calvin's Commentaries* to letter-spirit: Jer. 11:1–5 (9.2:69–80); 2 Cor. 3:6 (20.2:170–79); Heb. 4:12 (22:100–104); Heb. 8:10 (22:188–90); James 1:25 (22:297–98); 1 John 5:3 (22:252–53).

120. *Institutes* 2.11.7.

ear as "letter" since it does not have the Spirit. But secondly, Calvin adds, this distinction ceases once the Spirit is joined with the law. It is then no longer letter, but actually *spirit*, or the gospel itself. In fact, the benefits of the new covenant were even present in the law of the old covenant. To illustrate, Calvin mentions John 1:17. If grace and truth have come through Christ and the law was of Moses, does this mean that these benefits were absent from the law? His answer is that even though grace and truth are found in Christ, and the law does not have them as benefits it can actually bestow, they are nonetheless present adventitiously. Simply, they were borrowed from the gospel. In light of this, Moses can be considered in two different senses. If he is considered without Christ in his narrow office as lawgiver,[121] his message was only letter that produced death. But if Moses is considered in his whole teaching, he is a preacher of the gospel which is found in the new covenant.[122]

The Third Difference and 2 Corinthians 3

Calvin's summary of the narrow office of Moses can be seen in his comments on 2 Corinthians 3:6–9, which are summarized in table 2.[123]

Calvin recognizes that there are other scriptural texts that must be considered in light of this relationship of the letter and the spirit. So a

121. See *Calvin's Commentaries* on Rom. 10:4ff. (19:384).

122. Calvin uses the same type of explanation to counter the criticism that the spiritualists brought against the Reformers for their principle of *sola scriptura*:

They censure us for insisting upon the letter that kills, but in this matter they pay the penalty for despising Scripture. For it is clear enough that Paul there [2 Cor. 3:6] contends against the false apostles, who indeed, in commending the law apart from Christ were calling the people away from the benefits of the New Testament, in which the Lord covenants "to engrave his law in the inward parts of believers, and to write it in their hearts" [Jer. 31:33]. The letter, therefore, is dead, and the law of the Lord slays its readers where it is both cut off from Christ's grace, and, leaving the heart untouched, sounds in the ears alone. But if through the Spirit it is really branded upon hearts, if it shows forth Christ, it is the word of life [cf. Phil. 2:16] "converting souls, . . . giving wisdom to little ones," etc. [Ps. 19:7]. . . . And what has lately been said—that the Word itself is not quite certain for us unless it be confirmed by the testimony of the Spirit—is not out of accord with these things. For by a kind of mutual bond the Lord has joined together the certainty of his Word and of his Spirit so that the perfect religion of the Word may abide in our minds when the Spirit, who causes us to contemplate God's face, shines [*Institutes* 1.9.3; see also 2.5.9 and *Calvin's Commentaries* on Rom. 2:29 (19:112)].

123. See *Calvin's Commentaries* on 2 Cor. 3:6–9 (20:172–79).

Table 2: Calvin's Contrast of Law and Gospel in 2 Corinthians 3

Moses' Narrow Ministry of Law Is a Dead Letter Heard Only by the Ear	Christ's Ministry of Gospel Is a Life-giving Spirit Heard by the Soul
1. A ministry of death	1. A ministry of life
2. Written with letters and ink	2. Written with the Spirit
3. Engraved on stones	3. Engraved on human hearts
4. Temporary and fading	4. Forever
5. Condemnation	5. Righteousness

question of no small difficulty arises out of Psalm 19:8. There, David extols the virtues of the law, but Paul, in his epistles, seems to overthrow the commendations of the law that David has cited. Do these two authors agree? Calvin highlights the contrast. The law restores the souls of men, yet it is only a dead and deadly letter. It rejoices men's hearts, yet by bringing in the spirit of bondage (Calvin's fourth difference between the old and new covenants), it strikes men with terror. David says the law enlightens the eyes, yet Paul says that it casts a veil before men's minds, and so excludes the light which ought to penetrate it.

The differences between the covenants, presented by Paul and Jeremiah, actually contradict David's understanding of the old covenant if they are taken in an absolute sense as the Anabaptists insisted. Calvin's answer to the dilemma is similar to his remarks on Jeremiah 31. Just as the law of Moses can be viewed with the Spirit and so be gospel, or without the Spirit and so be the letter that kills, so David must also be seen as speaking not just of the moral law, but of the "whole covenant by which God had adopted the descendants of Abraham." Thus David is joining to the law—the rule of living well—the free promises of salvation, or Christ himself.

On the other hand, Paul must be interpreted in light of his opponents. He was addressing persons who abused and perverted the law by making it a basis of meritorious salvation. Paul's point was to show that the law without the Spirit was unprofitable and deadly to men's souls. The law without Christ could only be inexorable rigor which consequently cursed all mankind with the wrath of God. So Paul is rehearsing what the law can do by itself without the promise of grace. In this capacity, the law strictly and vigorously exacts men's duty owed to God, which none fulfils. David's praise of the law, however, stems from his consideration of the whole doctrine of the law, which includes the gospel. Thus Calvin concludes, "under the law he comprehends Christ." Calvin does not see the law as antithetical to the gospel since it includes Christ. It is antithetical only when Christ is excluded from it as the Judaizers had done, and as was consequently considered by Paul in his refutation of their doctrine of salvation by human merit.

The Third Difference and Hebrews 8

Commenting on the eighth chapter of Hebrews, Calvin presents another important difference between the covenants in terms of the comparison of the lesser to the greater. The Spirit's regeneration and Christ's forgiveness of sins were enjoyed by the Old Testament saints ("the two main parts in this covenant"). But these benefits of the covenant were available in the Old Testament administration of the covenant of grace to a lesser extent than for the New Testament saint. Accordingly, Calvin points to three ways in which the new covenant is greater than the old. First, the power of the Spirit is greater. God the Father has more fully put forth the power of the Spirit under the kingdom of Christ. Second, he has poured forth more abundantly his mercy on mankind, such that in comparison, the grace of God on the fathers is insignificant. Third, while the promises of God with respect to salvation were known in the old covenant, they were obscure and intricate in comparison to the clarity of revelation of the new covenant. Calvin likens this contrast to the light of the moon and stars in comparison to the clear light of the sun.

But this interpretation can be challenged by the case of Abraham, where in comparison to him, new covenant believers are lesser, and he is the greater. Calvin's response is that this comparison is not to be made of specific persons, but with respect to the economical condition of the church. Under the old economy of the covenant of grace the fathers' spiritual gifts were accidental to their age. They had to direct their eyes to Christ in order to possess them. So Calvin says that the apostle's comparing of the law to the gospel as two different covenants was taking away from the law what was peculiar to the gospel. Nevertheless, Calvin asserts, "There

Table 3: Calvin's Comparison of the Covenants in Hebrews 8 Showing the Superiority of the Economy of the New Covenant

The Old Covenant before Christ Is Lesser	The New Covenant after Christ Is Greater
A. The power of spirit is less	A. The power of spirit is greater
B. Grace & mercy are insignificant among the fathers	B. Grace & mercy are poured forth on the Fathers more abundantly in the gospel age
C. Obscure & intricate promises with respect to salvation	C. Clarity of God's revelation of the promises of salvation
D. Spiritual gifts were accidental to the fathers	D. Spiritual gifts are peculiar to the gospel age
E. Yet true believers have belonged to the the new covenant since the world began	E. New Testament Christians share with the Old Testament saints the same blessings of eternal salvation

is yet no reason why God should not have extended the grace of the New Covenant to the fathers." This then is the "true solution of the question."[124] Calvin's views of the lesser to greater comparison between the covenants are represented in table 3.

The Fourth Difference

With this more extensive consideration of Calvin's third difference, let us return to his thoughts in the *Institutes*, book 2, chapter 11. The fourth difference between the old and the new covenants and the third between law and gospel for Calvin is the bondage of the old and the freedom of the new. Calvin explains: "The fourth difference arises out of the third. Scripture calls the Old Testament one of 'bondage' because it produces fear in men's minds; but the New Testament, one of 'freedom' because it lifts them to trust and assurance."[125]

This understanding of the Old Testament seems, however, to take away the blessings of the Spirit that Calvin has already argued properly belonged to the holy patriarchs. Did they not have the same freedom and joy? Calvin again appeals to the new covenant as the place of salvation in all of redemptive history. Moreover, the comparison of the covenants in

124. *Calvin's Commentaries* on Heb. 8:10 (22:191).
125. *Institutes* 2.11.9.

199

terms of the lesser to the greater would indicate that the Old Testament saints did not have freedom and joy to the same extent as did the New Testament saints.

> But when through the law the patriarchs felt themselves both oppressed by their enslaved condition, and wearied by anxiety of conscience, they fled for refuge to the gospel. It was therefore a particular fruit of the New Testament that, apart from the common law of the Old Testament, they were exempted from those evils. Further, we shall deny that they were so endowed with the spirit of freedom and assurance as not in some degree to experience the fear and bondage arising from the law. For, however much they enjoyed the privilege that they had received through the grace of the gospel, they were still subject to the same bonds and burdens of ceremonial observances as the common people. They were compelled to observe those ceremonies punctiliously, symbols of tutelage resembling bondage. . . . Hence, they are rightly said, in contrast to us, to have been under the testament of bondage and fear.[126]

The Fifth Difference

The fifth and final difference between the covenants is that the old covenant was limited to the nation of Israel while the new covenant is extended by God to all nations.

> The fifth difference, which may be added, lies in the fact that until the advent of Christ, the Lord set apart one nation within which to confine the covenant of his grace. . . . He lodged his covenant, so to speak, in their bosom; he manifested the presence of this majesty over them; he showered every privilege upon them. But—to pass over the remaining blessings—let us consider the one in question. In communicating his Word to them, he joined them to himself, that he might be called and esteemed their God. In the meantime, "he allowed all other nations to walk" in vanity, as if they had nothing whatsoever to do with him.[127]

126. Ibid.
127. *Institutes* 2.11.11.

Because God changed his administration of the gospel by opening it up to all nations, Calvin sees this as a superiority of the new covenant over the old. "The calling of the Gentiles, therefore, is a notable mark of the excellence of the New Testament over the Old. Indeed, this had been attested before by many very clear utterances of the prophets, but in such a way that its fulfillment was postponed until the Kingdom of the Messiah."[128]

With these five administrative distinctives between the covenants, Calvin believes he has shown that the substantial unity of the old and new covenants is in no way diminished. Each of the differences deals with the accidents or externals of the covenants. In spite of the very real differences between the covenants, Calvin clearly agrees with Bullinger that there is "one eternal testament or covenant of God."

Clarification of Calvin's Christ-Centered Covenant—Unclear or Complex?

Paul Althaus declares, "Calvin's covenant teaching kept itself generally in a marked lack of clarity."[129] The conclusion reached here, however, is that Calvin's covenantal thought is not unclear although it is complex since he fully and rigorously grounds it in Christ.

Christ and the Narrow and Broad Sense of the Law and of the New Covenant

As we have seen, Calvin employs a twofold use of the covenant of the law. It can be used to describe the Mosaic economy either in the narrow or strict Pauline sense of self-congratulatory works of merit, or in the broad sense of the rule of living well which is coupled with God's gracious enablement and the Messiah's forgiveness. In the first, there is a profound difference between law and gospel. In this second sense, however, there is no longer any difference between the law and gospel since the Spirit has been added to the law along with Christ's forgiveness.

---

128. *Institutes* 2.11.12; cf. Bullinger's *Of the One and Eternal Covenant*, in McCoy and Baker, *Fountainhead of Federalism*, 117–20, 125.
129. Althaus, *Die Prinzipien*, 153–54.

Similarly, Calvin uses the term "new covenant" in two distinct senses. In the narrow or strict sense of redemptive history, he understands the new covenant as the gospel era brought to pass by Christ's redemptive work and his apostolic sending of the Holy Spirit. Yet Calvin also views the new covenant in a broader sense. The new covenant is also the saving relationship between God and his elect throughout the ages. It either looked forward in promise to Christ's coming or it harks back to his accomplishment of redemption. Calvin is consciously indebted to Augustine at this point. Referring to the ancient bishop, he writes:

> In the same passage he very aptly adds the following: the children of the promise, reborn of God, who have obeyed the commands by faith working through love have belonged to the New Covenant since the world began. This they did, not in hope of spiritual, heavenly, and eternal benefits. For they believed especially in the Mediator; and they did not doubt that through him the Spirit was given to them that they might do good, and that they were pardoned whenever they sinned. It is that very point which I intended to affirm: all the saints whom Scripture mentions as being peculiarly chosen of God from the beginning of the world have shared with us the same blessing unto eternal salvation.[130]

For Calvin, and Augustine before him, the new covenant has always been the place of salvation. This further elucidates, as we saw above, why Calvin includes all the parties of the covenant throughout redemptive history in the context and scope of the Abrahamic covenant.

The Inseparable Link between Christ and the Covenant in Calvin's Theology

Calvin's theology and his development of the history of the covenant possess a logical consistency that is tied directly to his Christ-centered exposition of Scripture. To understand Calvin's theology, one must have a firm grasp of his understanding of the unity and

130. *Institutes* 2.11.10; cf. Bullinger's *Of the One and Eternal Testament,* in McCoy and Baker, *Fountainhead of Federalism,* 134–38, where he discusses "The Antiquity of the Christian Religion" and "The Christian or Evangelical Faith, the Oldest of All."

diversity, or the continuity and discontinuity of the covenant as seen in the history of Christ's promised and accomplished salvation for God's people.

We have here considered the two chapters of book 2 of the *Institutes* which are dedicated to his covenantal hermeneutical method. But further, it is significant that Calvin intentionally places this covenantal hermeneutic before book 3. Calvin's second book is pointedly named *The Knowledge of God the Redeemer in Christ, First Disclosed to the Fathers under the Law and Then to Us in the Gospel*. Clearly, book 2 is intended to be the theological foundation for book 3 where he unfolds the application of salvation, appropriately titled *The Way in Which We Receive the Grace of Christ: What Benefits Come to Us from It, and What Effects Follow*. The point is that if one understands the covenant, this in turn better enables one to understand how he receives the grace of Christ.

Because the covenant is "the source and spring of salvation"[131] and the "hope of salvation is founded on the covenant,"[132] the covenant is inseparable from Christ. This is seen in Calvin's repeated coupling of them in the *Institutes*:

> Let us then set forth the covenant that he once established as eternal and never perishing. Its fulfillment, by which it is finally confirmed and ratified, is Christ.[133]

> Who, then, dares to separate the Jews from Christ, since with them, we hear, was made the covenant of the gospel, the sole foundation of which is Christ?[134]

> The apostle contends that it ought to be terminated and abrogated, to give place to Christ, the Sponsor and Mediator of a better covenant.[135]

131. *Calvin's Commentaries* on Ps. 67:2 (5.3:3).
132. *Calvin's Commentaries* on Zech. 12:1 (15.5:340).
133. *Institutes* 2.11.4.
134. *Institutes* 2.10.4.
135. *Institutes* 2.11.4.

This is the new covenant that God in Christ has made with us, that he will remember our sins no more.[136]

To conclude, Calvin not merely stands in accord with the Rhineland Reformers' covenantal perspective; he develops it further into a cogent covenantal hermeneutic of salvation history. Calvin binds the theology of the old and new covenants together by his keen recognition of their simultaneous continuity and discontinuity in terms of God's covenantal revelation in the history of redemption.

Calvin encourages his followers to find Christ in all the Scriptures.[137] To these believers, the great Reformer of Geneva also offers this covenantal encouragement: "We have no reason to be afraid that God will deceive us if we persevere in his covenant."[138] For Calvin believes that as we persevere in the covenant, we find Christ,[139] who is its very foundation.[140] How appropriate, then, that half a millennium after his birth, there are countless believers in Christ around the globe who continue to proclaim the saving truths of Christ found in the biblical theology of the covenant.

136. *Institutes* 3.4.29. See also the following references in *Calvin's Commentaries* to Christ and the covenant: Ex. 24:5 (3.3:319–21); Dan. 9:27 (13.2:224–25); Mal. 3:1 (15.5:567–69); Luke 24:27 (17.3:360); John 19:30 (18.2:237); Heb. 9:16–17 (22:208–9).

137. For Calvin's overview of the unity of God's saving work in the biblical history of salvation, see his "Christ the End of the Law," in *The Practical Calvinist: An Introduction to the Presbyterian and Reformed Heritage*, ed. Peter Lillback (Fearn, Ross-shire: Christian Focus, 2002), 95–113.

138. *Calvin's Commentaries* on Ps. 25:10 (4:424).

139. *Institutes* 2.10.1.

140. *Institutes* 1.6.1; 2.10.4; 3.30.45.

9

THE MEDIATOR OF THE COVENANT

INSTITUTES 2.12–15
DEREK W. H. THOMAS

---

alvin's treatment of the nature and role of the Mediator is firmly set in the logical order and progression of book 2 of the *Institutes*. Having already established that "the whole human race perished in the person of Adam" and that "after the fall of man no knowledge of God apart from the Mediator has had power unto salvation,"[1] Calvin now takes up what has been called "the center of Calvin's Christology"[2]—the office of Christ as Mediator.

---

1. John Calvin, *Institutes of the Christian Religion*, trans. Ford Lewis Battles, 2 vols., Library of Christian Classics 20–21 (Philadelphia: Westminster, 1960), 2.6.1.

2. See Stephen Edmondson, *Calvin's Christology* (Cambridge: Cambridge University Press, 2004), 5. Cf. Heiko Oberman's observation that in Calvin there is a shift of accent from "a natures-Christology to an office-Christology, converging towards a Mediator-theology." "The 'Extra' Dimension in the Theology of John Calvin," *Journal of Ecclesiastical History* 21.1 (Jan. 1970): 60–62.

What forces this discussion of Christology from a theological-systematic point of view has been Calvin's redemptive-historical treatment of Old Testament history subsequent to Adam's fall as federal head of the human race. The Mediator had been known through shadows and types in the old covenant, and the fullness of revelation under the new covenant is not meant to disparage the proleptic role of the Mediator under the old covenant administration: "The covenant made with all the patriarchs is so much like ours in substance and reality that the two are actually one and the same. Yet they differ in the mode of dispensation."[3] There is only one Mediator of "the covenant of his grace."[4] "They participated in the same inheritance and hoped for a common salvation with us by the grace of the same Mediator."[5] Apart from the Mediator, "God never showed favor toward the ancient people."[6] "God cannot without the Mediator be propitious toward the human race."[7] "There is no other remedy for a hopeless condition, no other way of freeing the church, than the appearance of the Mediator."[8]

It should be noted that Calvin's Christology is not a narrowly conceived christocentrism, but part of a trinitarian understanding of the doctrine of God, an issue that has already been discussed in book 1 of the *Institutes*.[9] It is crucial to grasp how much this permeates Calvin's hermeneutical suppositions: "whenever the name of God is mentioned without particularization, there are designated no less the Son and the Spirit than the Father; but where the Son is joined to the Father, then the relation of the two enters in."[10] Therefore, for Calvin, Christology is a subset of a trinitarian consideration of God.

3. *Institutes* 2.10.2.
4. *Institutes* 2.11.11.
5. *Institutes* 2.10.1.
6. *Institutes* 2.6.2.
7. Ibid.
8. *Institutes* 2.6.4.
9. See *Institutes* 1.13.1–29. In this respect, Calvin's trinitarianism is an attempt to solidify the Reformation with the church fathers. See Anthony N. S. Lane, *John Calvin: Student of the Church Fathers* (Grand Rapids: Baker, 1999); T. H. L. Parker, *Calvin: An Introduction to His Thought* (Louisville: Westminster/John Knox, 1995), 31–34, 64.
10. *Institutes* 1.13.20. As Paul Helm notes, this rule that Calvin employs plays a key role in his understanding of the *communicatio idiomatum*, according to which the properties of

The section begins by raising four substantive issues, the first two of which are significantly problematic: the necessity of the atonement and ontological mediatorship.

1. *The Necessity of the Incarnation.* Calvin begins his discussion by stating that there is no simple or absolute necessity for the atonement. "Rather, it has stemmed from a heavenly decree."[11] This suggests that God *could have* saved us by some other means had he so chosen to do so, a view given expression elsewhere in a comment on John 15:13: "God could have redeemed us by a word or a wish, save that another way seemed best for our sakes: that by not sparing His own and only-begotten Son He might testify in His person how much He cares for our salvation."[12] This issue needs to be set against the background of medieval nominalist thought which gives primacy to the will over the intellect. To suggest that God was "bound" to act in a certain way in salvation limits the freedom of his will. This, partly, reflects Calvin's voluntarism and a dependence on the views of Duns Scotus.[13] God's power is limited only by the power of noncontradiction, and he can effect all possibility, constrained only by his own nature.[14]

---

one nature are not predicable of the other. Paul Helm, *John Calvin's Ideas* (Oxford: Oxford University Press, 2004), 36, 58–92.

11. *Institutes* 2.12.1.

12. *Commentary on the Gospel according to St. John 11–21*, ed. David W. and Thomas F. Torrance, trans. T. H. L. Parker (Grand Rapids: Eerdmans, 1959), 100. This was a view held by many in the Reformed Orthodox tradition of the seventeenth century, including the first prolocutor of the Westminster Assembly, William Twisse (c. 1575–1646); the Scottish divine Samuel Rutherford (1600–1661); and, initially at least, John Owen. See Carl Trueman, *The Claims of Truth: John Owen's Trinitarian Theology* (Carlisle: Paternoster, 1998), 105f. On Rutherford's position, see James Walker, *The Theology and Theologians of Scotland, 1560–1750* (Edinburgh: Knox, 1982), 68–69.

13. Dewey J. Hoitenga Jr. has shown some confusion in Calvin's thought on the voluntary/intellectual issue; see *John Calvin and the Will: A Critique and Corrective* (Grand Rapids: Baker, 1997).

14. The issue of what precisely is constrained by God's nature leads to different answers, and even such vigorous intellectualists as Thomas Aquinas did allow for the hypothetical possibility, *de potentia absoluta*, that God could pardon sin without satisfaction. See *Summa Theologia* 3a.46.2 where he argues that mankind could have been rescued apart from satisfaction, and 3a.46.3, where his argument suggests that no better way could be found than through Christ's passion. Cf. "We cannot limit God's power by saying it could not have happened otherwise." Thomas Aquinas, *A Concise Translation*, ed. Timothy McDermott (Chicago: Christian Classics, 1989), 476.

2. *Ontological Mediatorship*. The problematic statement reads, "Even if man had remained free from all stain, his condition would have been too lowly for him to reach God without a Mediator."[15] Man is in need of a Mediator because of his createdness. Calvin returns to this issue again in his discussion of justification, interpreting Job 4:18 as teaching that even the unfallen angels are in need of a Mediator to approach God, adding that "in the Book of Job mention is made of a righteousness higher than the observance of the law."[16] Further, this matter receives fairly extensive treatment in Calvin's sermons on Job.[17] It raises the issue of double justice—that there exists a standard of justice (righteousness) over and above that which is revealed in the law. In Calvin's view, absolute compliance with the demands of the revealed law still renders an individual liable to judgment according to a higher, undisclosed standard. This further raises our understanding of the relationship between spirit and matter, as well as overall uncertainty about the finality of Christ's mediation; for the obedience rendered to the (revealed) moral law cannot guarantee in and of itself final acquittal unless the Mediator also fulfils the requirements of that righteousness that exceeds the law, which in this view, and necessarily for Calvin, remains in the realm of the incomprehensible (and therefore, to us, unknowable).[18]

15. *Institutes* 2.12.1.
16. *Institutes* 3.12.1; see also 3.17.9.
17. See Derek W. H. Thomas, *Calvin's Teaching on Job: Proclaiming the Incomprehensible God* (Geanies House, Ross-shire: Mentor, 2004), 112–13, 118, 376–78; Susan Schreiner, "Exegesis and Double Justice in Calvin's Sermons on Job," *Church History* 58 (1989): 322–38. Also, Calvin's response to Francesco Stancaro: "Thus we understand first that the name of Mediator applies to Christ not only because he took on flesh or because he took on the office of reconciling the human race with God. But already for the beginning of creation he was truly Mediator because he was always the Head of the Church and held primacy even over the angels and was the first-born of all creatures. Whence we conclude that he began to perform the office of Mediator not only after the fall of Adam but insofar as he is the Eternal Son of God, angels as well as men were joined to God in order that they might remain upright." *Corpus Reformatorum* 9:338, quoted and translated by David Willis, in *Calvin's Catholic Christology*, vol. 2 of *Studies in Medieval and Reformation Thought*, ed. H. A. Oberman (Leiden: E. J. Brill, 1966), 70.
18. On the arbitrariness this injects into the doctrine of God, see David C. Steinmetz, *Calvin in Context* (New York: Oxford University Press, 1995), 40–52. It is not without

3. *Adoption and the Fatherhood of God.* Why did God become man? Calvin's answer is Athanasian: "Who could have done this had not the self-same Son of God become the Son of man, and had not so taken what was ours as to impart what was his to us, and to make what was his by nature ours by grace?" The Son of God takes what is ours, "flesh from our flesh, bones from our bones, that he might be one with us . . . to impart to us what was his."[19] Specifically, the Mediator assumed flesh and blood in order to "make of the children of men, children of God." For Calvin, the appearance of the Mediator secured what the old covenant could not—a knowledge of God as our heavenly Father: "because they had no Mediator it was not possible for them truly to taste God's mercy, and thus be persuaded that he was their Father."[20] Indeed it is a point too infrequently understood, that for Calvin "piety" meant recognizing that our lives are nourished by God's fatherly care and that the chief blessing of the new covenant is free (or gratuitous) adoption.[21] It is deeply significant that Calvin included in the subtitle to the 1536 edition of the *Institutes* the words "Embracing almost the whole sum of *piety*,"[22] a term which he defines early in the final edition of the *Institutes* as "that reverence joined with love of God which the knowledge of his benefits induces," adding "until men recognize that they owe everything to God, that they are nourished by his fatherly care [*paterna cura*] . . . they will never yield

significance that John Owen, who changed his view on this matter, regarded the idea that the incarnation was not an absolute necessity as "a half-way house to the Socinians' complete denial of the necessity of the incarnation and atonement." See Trueman, *Claims of Truth*, 105.

19. *Institutes* 2.12.2. Calvin carefully nuances the doctrine of theosis here. Cf. Athanasius, *De Incarnatione* 54 in *Athanasius: Contra Gentes and De Incarnatione*, ed. and trans. Robert W. Thomson (Oxford: Clarendon, 1971), 268–69. Especially, "for he became man that we might become divine."

20. *Institutes* 2.6.4.

21. *Institutes* 2.14.5. Cf. Calvin's remark in 2.14.6 that we receive adoption "as a gift." *Gratuita adoptio* is a frequent expression in this section of the *Institutes*. See B. A. Gerrish, *Grace and Gratitude: The Eucharistic Theology of John Calvin* (Edinburgh: T. & T. Clark, 1993), 89 n. 12.

22. The full title was *Christianae Religionis Institutio totam fere pietatis summam et quidquid est in doctrina salutis cognitu necessarium complectens. Corpus Reformatorum* 1:6.

him willing obedience."[23] The metaphor of God's fatherly care will eventually dominate in the *Institutes*.[24]

4. *Adam-Christ Parallel.* Having become one with man by incarnation, how does the Mediator remove the barrier and bring reconciliation? Calvin's answer is to employ the Pauline doctrine of the first and second Adam: "Accordingly, our Lord came forth as true man and took the person and the name of Adam in order to take Adam's place in obeying[25] the Father, to present our flesh as the price of satisfaction to God's righteous judgment, and in the same flesh, to pay the penalty that we had deserved."[26] Employing Anselmian terms of substitution (Christ did what Adam failed to do and what we cannot do) and satisfaction ("by his act of expiation" the Mediator "appease[d] the Father's righteous wrath."[27] Calvin insists that the Mediator needed to be both human (so as to die and pay sin's penalty) and divine (to ensure victory).[28] Commenting on Romans 5:17, Calvin writes: "The meaning of the whole passage is that since Christ surpasses Adam, the sin of Adam is overcome by the righteousness of Christ. The curse of Adam is overturned by the grace of Christ, and the life which Christ bestows swallows up the death which came from Adam."[29]

These four assertions are set against a background of false teaching: the views of the German Lutheran theologian Andreas Osiander

23. *Institutes* 1.2.1. On Calvin's concept of piety, see Joel Beeke, "Calvin on Piety," in *The Cambridge Companion to John Calvin*, ed. Donald M. McKim (Cambridge: *Cambridge University Press*, 2004), 125–52.

24. "Therefore God both calls himself our Father and would have us so address him. By the great sweetness of this name he frees us from all distrust, since no greater feeling of love can be found elsewhere than in the Father" (*Institutes* 3.20.36).

25. On Calvin's understanding of Christ's redemptive obedience as the second Adam, see Robert A. Peterson, *Calvin's Doctrine of the Atonement* (Phillipsburg, NJ: P&R, 1983), 40–45. Peterson rejects the view of Hans Scholl that Calvin is here reflecting Irenaeus's recapitulation theory of the atonement.

26. *Institutes* 2.12.3.

27. Ibid.

28. Calvin does not employ the terminology of a "covenant of works" in his understanding of Gen. 2:16–17, but it is difficult to deny that all of the elements of such a covenant are present in his thinking.

29. John Calvin, *Commentary on the Epistles of Paul to the Romans and Thessalonians*, trans. R. Mackenzie, ed. David W. and Thomas F. Torrance (Grand Rapids: Eerdmans, 1973), 116.

(1498–1552) on such issues as the image of God, the work of Christ, and justification, and those of the radical Spanish antitrinitarian theologian, Michael Servetus (1511–53). Osiander's Cabalistic views of predestination led him to propound a view suggested earlier by Duns Scotus (in contrast to Thomistic views) that the Son of God would have become incarnate whether or not humanity had fallen into sin. There is nothing accidental in God; therefore, there can be no alteration of God's original creative purposes for mankind. Adam was made for union with the divine nature, and his creation was an anticipation of Christ's incarnation. Justification is the fulfilment of the divine intent behind Adam's original creation—the indwelling of the divine nature of the Logos, Jesus Christ, and the first stage in the deification of man. Calvin's comment on this, in his later treatment of justification, is to regard Osiander's Christology as essentially Nestorian (in its separation of the divine and human natures) and his view of essential righteousness he regarded as a "strange monster," a recatholicization of Protestant theology. [30]

Orthodox Christology

Chapter 13, though largely set against christological heresies, affirms Chalcedonian Christology. This Calvin does by establishing a number of elementary statements.

Christ Assumed the True Substance of Human Flesh

Continuing the trinitarian polemic in book 1 where the divinity of Christ has already been established,[31] Calvin now asserts his true humanity. Manicheism and Marcionism denied the reality or necessity of Christ's enfleshment, the former's dualism viewing the corporeal as essentially

30. *Institutes* 3.11.5. For further discussion see G. C. Berkouwer, *The Work of Christ*, Studies in Dogmatics (Grand Rapids: Eerdmans, 1965), 27–28. Calvin's opposition to Osiander on the issue of Christ's incarnation apart from any consideration of sin is curiously at odds with his positive reception of ontological mediatorship. See also 3.12.1; 3.17.9. Nevertheless, the vocabulary employed against Osiander in these sections (2.12.5–7) is telling enough: "madness," "monstrous," "ignorant babbling," "drunk with the sweetness of his own speculations," "silly."
31. *Institutes* 1.13.7–13.

imperfect and the latter (as with Docetism) asserting Christ's human body was a phantom appearance only, "a body of air."[32] The real target here is the Dutch founder of the Anabaptist movement, Menno Simons (1496–1561).[33] Calvin never met Menno Simons personally but became aware of his views largely through Martin Micron who had entered into debate with Menno's conception of the incarnation of Christ and had asked Calvin for help. Calvin responded with a letter to Micron in 1558 (*Contra Mennonem* [Against Menno]).[34] Calvin had evidently heard of Menno's theology as early as 1545—the year in which John à Lasco wrote a book against Menno.[35] Menno propounded twenty articles on the incarnation, in which he insisted that Christ was incarnate without partaking of Mary's flesh. His was a heavenly humanity, becoming a man in Mary but not of Mary.

Menno's problem with Chalcedonian theology on the incarnation was to answer the question, how, if Jesus partook of Mary's flesh, could he be kept from partaking of Mary's fallenness? His answer was that Mary fed him but gave him nothing of her substance. Calvin's response to this question raised some problematic issues of its own. In the first place, Calvin responds to the view that if Christ is born of Mary, he is necessarily unclean, by asserting the following: "For we make Christ free of all stain not just because he was begotten of his mother without copulation with man, but because he was sanctified by the Spirit that the generation might be pure and undefiled as would have been true before Adam's fall."[36] Calvin, first of all, denies Christ's sinlessness is retained because of the notion that Adamic sin (the contagion) is passed on only though the male seed—a view he describes as childish babble! The fact that Mary was a virgin (a perpetual virgin in Calvin's view!) does not provide the answer to the problem since Calvin did not hold to Mary's impeccability

32. *Institutes* 2.13.2.
33. See W. de Greef, *The Writings of John Calvin: An Introductory Guide* (Grand Rapids: Baker, 1989), 181; Richard Gamble, "Calvin's Controversies," in *The Cambridge Companion to John Calvin*, 198.
34. *Corpus Reformatorum* 10a:167–76.
35. Jan Łaski (Eng., John of Lasco, John the Younger, 1499–1560). See W. Balke, *Calvin and the Anabaptist Radicals*, trans. William J. Heynen (Grand Rapids: Eerdmans, 1981), 202ff.
36. *Institutes* 2.13.4.

(immaculate conception).[37] Nor should the transmission of sin be linked with the libidinousness of sexual intercourse (Augustine's understanding of concupiscence enmeshed the medieval church in a hopeless state of affairs). For Calvin, as interestingly for Augustine,[38] the sinlessness of Christ was due to the secret working of the Holy Spirit. Adam did not beget Christ; the Holy Spirit did.[39]

Donald MacLeod has pointed out the inadequacy of this argument.[40] The suggestion seems to be that Christ took something and then sanctified it by the Holy Spirit.

> What was sanctified, and when? Was it the unfertilized ovum? Surely not. It makes little sense to speak of sanctifying a piece of tissue. Was it the fertilized ovum: the foetus itself? It seems impossible to speak of this being sanctified without implying that prior to such sanctification it was impure or sinful. . . .
>
> It seems best to avoid altogether language which involves us in such difficulties. We need say no more than that the humanity of Christ was created by the Holy Spirit, rather than procreated by sexual intercourse, and that as such it partook of the essential character of all that God creates: it was very good.[41]

Another issue raised by Calvin's treatment was to bring him into conflict with the Lutherans. Menno Simons had asserted that if the Word of God became flesh, then he was "confined within the narrow prison of an earthly body."[42] Calvin's response to this was to assert the

---

37. The feast of the immaculate conception, celebrated on December 8, was established in 1476 by Pope Sixtus IV, who stopped short of defining the doctrine as a dogma of the faith. The immaculate conception was solemnly defined as a dogma by Pope Pius IX in his constitution *Ineffabilis Deus* on December 8, 1854.

38. "For what he took of flesh, he either cleansed in order to take it, or cleansed by taking it." *On the Merits and Remission of Sins* 2.38 in *Nicene and Post-Nicene Fathers*, 1st series, 5:60.

39. Edmondson, *Calvin's Christology*, 212f.

40. Donald MacLeod, *The Person of Christ* (Leicester: Inter-Varsity, 1998), 40.

41. Ibid., 40–41. MacLeod is severely critical of the route taken by W. G. T. Shedd who suggested that the humanity of Christ existed for a while un-united to the Logos and that he was thereby in need of his own atonement!

42. This is a direct citation from Menno, though the *Institutes* avoids saying so. See Menno Simons, *Complete Writings*, trans. Leonard Verduin, ed. John C. Wenger (Scottdale, PA: Herald, 1956), 881, 909. See the comment by Peterson, *Calvin's Doctrine*, 11.

opposite: "Here is something marvelous: the Son of God descended from heaven in such a way, that, without leaving heaven, he willed to be borne in the virgin's womb, to go about the earth, and to hang upon the cross; yet he continuously filled the world even as he had done from the beginning."[43]

From one point of view, this is no more than what Chalcedon confessed—an incarnation by addition rather than subtraction! In addition to being God, he also became a man. In the incarnation, Jesus Christ is fully divine: none of his deity was set aside or diluted as a result. God the Son was wholly incarnate in Jesus of Nazareth while also being wholly outside (*extra*) of him too.[44] For the Lutherans, this amounted to creating a duality in Christ, separating the Christ of history from the Christ who sustains the universe. It created the possibility of a *Logos asarkos*. Lutherans maintained that subsequent to the incarnation Christ's divinity was nowhere outside of his humanity. Indeed there was such closeness between the two that an exchange of attributes (*communicatio idiomatum*) becomes possible between the one nature and the other. Thus, Lutherans argued for the ubiquity of Christ's body in relation to the consubstantial understanding of the Supper. For the Reformed, this threatened the integrity of the natures. Calvin comments: "For we affirm his divinity so joined and united with his humanity that each retains its distinctive nature unimpaired, and yet these two natures constitute one Christ."[45]

43. *Institutes* 2.13.4. Further, "In this way he was also Son of man in heaven (John 3:13), for the very same Christ, who, according to the flesh, dwelt as Son of man on earth, was God in heaven. In this manner, he is said to have descended to that place according to his divinity, not because divinity left heaven to hide itself in the prison house of the body, but because even though it filled all things, still in Christ's very humanity it dwelt bodily (Colossians 2:9), that is, by nature, and in a certain ineffable way" (4.17.30). In this context, Calvin is arguing against Servetus's claim that Christ is constituted "not by the union of the divine nature of the person of the Word and the human nature of his assumed flesh, but by a mixture of divine and human elements such that he became Son of God in reality only at the time of his birth." Edmondson, *Calvin's Christology*, 211.

44. See E. David Willis, *Calvin's Catholic Christology: The Function of the So-called 'Extra Calvinisticum' in Calvin's Theology*, Studies in Medieval and Reformation Thought 2 (Leiden: Brill, 1966); Heiko Oberman, "The 'Extra' Dimension in the Theology of Calvin," *Journal of Ecclesiastical History* 22 (1970): 43–64.

45. *Institutes* 2.14.1.

Some have seen Nestorian tendencies in Calvin at this point.[46] Others have written in denial of any such tendencies, since the same claims were raised against Chalcedon—a point made by G. C. Berkouwer.[47] And there have been those who have seen Calvin's Christology problematic at some points without charging him with Nestorianism.[48]

Calvin's point, all along, has been to assert the real nature of Christ's humanity. Citing Galatians 4:4, and Hebrews 2:16 and 4:15, Calvin insists that Christ was subject to "hunger, thirst, cold, and other infirmities of our nature,"[49] he "manifested himself as a lowly and despised man," and he was "endowed with a human body and soul."[50] He is descended from Abraham and David through both Joseph and Mary. But having distinguished the two natures, even at the risk of the charge of Nestorianism, Calvin is bound now to answer the question as to the exact relationship (*communicatio*) between the two natures.

The Communion of Properties

Granted that the properties of both natures are attributable to the person, the question was raised as to whether or not we can also say that the attributes of the one nature are communicated to the other. This became a matter of sharp dispute between Calvinists and Lutherans, particularly in debates as to the presence of Christ in the Supper, Lutherans advocating ubiquity to the physical body of Jesus by holding that (in some sense at least) he could be physically present in more than one location at one time.[51]

In opposition to the views of the heterodox Italian Reformer, Francisco Stancaro (c. 1501–74), who claimed that Christ was Mediator only in regard to his human nature, Calvin affirmed with greater force

---

46. François Wendel, *Calvin: Origins and Development of His Religious Thought*, trans. Philip Mairet (Durham, NC: Labyrinth, 1963), 225.

47. G. C. Berkouwer, *The Person of Christ*, Studies in Dogmatics (Grand Rapids: Eerdmans, 1954), 286f.

48. Peterson, *Calvin's Doctrine*, and to some extent, Gerrish, *Grace and Gratitude*, 55–57.

49. *Institutes* 2.13.1.

50. *Institutes* 2.13.2.

51. It is striking that the Lutherans, who argued that the incarnation hinges on the *communicatio*, did argue reciprocity; there is no corresponding communication of the human to the divine.

the unity of Christ's person: "he who was the Son of God became the Son of man—not by confusion of substance, but by unity of person."[52] Writing to Stancaro, Calvin would say: "It is also true to say that all the actions which Christ performed to reconcile God and man refer to the whole person, and are not to be separately restricted to only one nature."[53]

Calvin observes that the Scriptures sometimes attribute to Christ what belongs solely to his humanity, sometimes what belongs uniquely to his divinity, and sometimes what embraces both natures but "fits neither alone," in a way similar to our sometimes speaking of the body and soul: united they constitute one person but each retains its own properties. Sometimes, however, the two natures can be spoken of interchangeably, as when Paul addressed the Ephesian elders at Miletus, saying that "God purchased the church with his own blood" (Acts 20:28),[54] or when Christ (in his human flesh) said, "Before Abraham was, I am" (John 8:58). The ancient writers referred to this as the communicating of properties. God does not have blood, and Christ in his body was not in heaven before the existence of Abraham. To cite Calvin:

> Surely God does not have blood, does not suffer, cannot be touched with hands. But since Christ, who was true God and also true man, was crucified and shed his blood for us, the things that he carried out in his human nature are transferred improperly, although not without reason, to his divinity. Here is a similar example: John teaches "that God laid down his life for us" (1 John 3:16). Accordingly, there also a property of humanity is shared with the other nature. Again, when

52. *Institutes* 2.14.1, 3.

53. See Joseph N. Tylenda, "Christ the Mediator: Calvin versus Stancaro," *Calvin Theological Journal* 8 (1973): 14. See also Tylenda, "The Controversy on Christ the Mediator: Calvin's Second Reply to Stancaro," *Calvin Theological Journal* 8 (1973): 131–57; "Calvin's Understanding of the Communication of Properties," *Westminster Theological Journal* 38 (1975–76): 54–65.

54. Commenting on Acts 20:28, Calvin writes: "For there is nothing more absurd than to suppose that God is corporeal or mortal. But by speaking like this [Paul] is commending the unity of the Person of Christ." *The Acts of the* Apostles, vol. 2, trans. John W. Fraser, ed. David W. and Thomas F. Torrance, Calvin's New Testament Commentaries (Grand Rapids: Eerdmans, 1991), 184.

Christ, still living on earth, said: "No one has ascended into heaven but the Son of man who was in heaven" (John 3:13), surely then, as man, in the flesh that he had taken upon himself, he was not in heaven. But because the self-same one was both God and man, for the sake of the union of both natures he gave to the one what belonged to the other.[55]

The closest Calvin perhaps gets to a communication of properties is the intriguing comment he makes on 2 Peter 1:4 that we might be "partakers of the divine nature": "We should notice that it is the purpose of the Gospel to make us sooner or later like God; indeed it is, so as to speak, a kind of deification."[56] But even here Calvin goes on to insist that it is "fanatics" who surmise that we shall "cross over into God's nature, so that his nature absorbs ours." This is a "kind of madness." What Peter means is that "when we have put off all the vices of the flesh we shall be partakers of divine immortality and the glory of blessedness, and thus we shall be in a way one with God so far as our capacity allows."[57]

For Calvin, then, not even the glorification of Christ involves the impartation of divine properties to his human nature. There are clear limits to the patristic notion of theosis, a subject to which Calvin gives a very wide berth. Here, Calvin is merely giving expression to the statement of the Athanasian Creed: "Who although he be God and Man; yet he is not two, but one Christ. One; not by conversion of the Godhead into flesh; but by taking of the Manhood into God. One altogether; not by confusion of Substance [Essence]: but by unity of Person."[58] On that account, he is displaying Thomistic roots.[59] This is not an attempt by Calvin to explain so much as it is an assertion of "a very great mystery."[60]

55. *Institutes* 2.14.2.
56. John Calvin, *Hebrews and I and II Peter*, trans. W. B. Johnston, ed. David W. Torrance and Thomas F. Torrance, Calvin's New Testament Commentaries 12 (Grand Rapids: Eerdmans, 1989), 330.
57. Ibid.
58. P. Schaff, *Creeds of Christendom*, 3 vols. 6th ed. (Grand Rapids: Baker, 1996), 2:69.
59. See Aquinas's discussion in the *Summa Theologiae* at III.18.5.
60. *Institutes* 2.14.1

One Person, Two Natures

Calvin's "one person, two natures" Christology[61] is entirely Chalcedonian. In his sights are the ancient heresies, even if they have found new forms in the likes of Servetus and Stancaro. In particular, Calvin now engages in an unequivocal rejection of (interestingly) (1) Nestorianism, which separated the two natures to an extent that threatened the unity of the Person and was condemned as a heresy at the Synod of Ephesus in A.D. 431, and (2) Eutychianism, which advocated a human nature in Christ that was unlike any other—one overtaken by the divine nature. The latter was condemned by two councils: the Council of Constantinople in A.D. 448 and the ecumenical Council of Chalcedon in A.D. 451. In some ways, Calvin's defense is thoroughly patristic and is aimed at discrediting the Roman charge of the novelty of Protestant religion. But "a deadly monster" has arisen in Calvin's time—Michael Servetus—"who has supposed the Son of God to be a figment compounded from God's essence, spirit, flesh, and three uncreated elements."[62]

Given the animus that exists in relation to Calvin's involvement in the execution of Servetus, it is important to recall that as far as the church was concerned, both Roman Catholic and Protestant, he was a heretic. Had not Geneva put him to death, sixteenth-century Catholicism would have done so elsewhere. He had, after all, been found guilty and sentenced to death by the Catholic authorities of Vienna, but had managed to escape—to Geneva! We may engage more enlightened views of the separation of church and state, but our quarrel is not so much with Geneva, still less with Calvin; our quarrel is with Europe in the sixteenth century.

Servetus believed the doctrine of the Trinity served as an unnecessary stumbling block to the evangelization of Jews and Muslims. God reveals himself to us through a series of names (*El Shaddai, Elohim,*

---

61. "Meanwhile, the church's definition stands firm: he is believed to be the Son of God because the Word begotten of the Father before all ages took human nature in a hypostatic union. Now the old writers defined 'hypostatic union' as that which constitutes one person out of two natures" (*Institutes* 2.14.5).

62. *Institutes* 2.14.5.

Jesus, Holy Spirit), each one designed to convey additional disclosures on the nature of God. Words such as *hypostasis*, person, substance, and essence are not words found in the Bible and should be discarded. Jesus is the divine Savior, even though he was created in time. There was a time when he did not exist. He did not possess any substance until the incarnation.

Calvin's systematic dismissal of Servetus's antitrinitarian views in book 2 of the 1559 edition of the *Institutes* had found amplification five years earlier in his *Defense of the Doctrine of the Trinity against Servetus*.[63] Servetus himself had first written on the topic of the Trinity in 1531, in a book called *De Trinitatis Erroribus*, possibly before Calvin's conversion to Protestantism.[64] Later in that decade, Calvin made a trip to Paris to meet with Servetus, but Servetus failed to show up. Communication via letters continued through the 1540s but it proved futile. T. H. L. Parker even questions Servetus's sanity in his biography of Calvin.[65] When Servetus wrote *Christianismi Restitutio* (*The Restoration of Christianity*) in 1553, his doom was certain. It proved more than a reiteration of previous views; in the *Restitutio*, Servetus presented a coherent, and radical, alternative interpretation of Christian systematics, including a strain of neo-Gnostic dualism.[66]

The *Munus Triplex*

Robert Peterson has written urging that more attention be given to the structural coherence of the *Institutes* in the chapters under review here. Chapters 12–14 cover the person of Christ and chapters 16–17 the work of Christ. Chapter 15 forms a segue from one to the other and "was Calvin's way of telling his readers not to separate the person and work

63. *Defensio Orthodoxae Fidei de Sacra Trinitate contra Prodigiosos Errores Michaelis Serveti Hispani*, published in 1554, a year after Servetus's death. *Corpus Reformatorum* 8:457–644.
64. On the discussion as to the date of Calvin's conversion, and his remark in the Commentary on the Psalms about a "sudden conversion," see Alexandre Ganoczy, "Calvin's Life and Context," in *The Cambridge Companion to John Calvin*, 7–10.
65. T. H. L. Parker, *John Calvin: A Biography* (Philadelphia: Westminster, 1975), 118.
66. See *The Oxford Encyclopedia of the Reformation*, s.v. "Michael Servetus."

of Christ."[67] We have already cited Oberman's observation that in Calvin
there is a move away from a natures-Christology to an office-Christology,[68]
and whatever its merit or demerit, the fact is that Calvin's discussion of
the Mediator culminates in what is perhaps one of the most distinctive
features of Calvin's theology: the employment of the threefold office of
Christ as prophet, king, and priest or the so-called *munus triplex*.[69]

J. F. Jansen's denial that Calvin held firmly to the prophetic office
of Christ is a failure to sufficiently grasp that, for Calvin, Christ exercises his prophetic role by the ongoing illuminating ministry of the
Holy Spirit.[70] Jansen feared that there is asymmetry between the three
offices since both the kingly and priestly offices are shared in the new
covenant by all believers, but the prophetic office finds continuity only
in the ministerial office(s) of the church. Indeed, Jansen's point is that
Calvin raises Christ's prophetic office only to buttress Reformed church
polity against the Anabaptists on the one hand and the Catholics on
the other. This has been shown to be an exaggeration and a view that
insufficiently underlines the role of the Spirit as Christ's ongoing representative agent in the teaching ministry of the church to the individual
believer.[71] To be sure, there is development in Calvin's thinking at this
point as shown by the fact that, as was customary in the church fathers,
in the 1536 and 1539 editions of the *Institutes* Calvin speaks of only
two offices, priest and king.[72]

67. *Calvin's Doctrine of the Atonement*, 39.
68. See n.2.
69. Calvin uses the order prophet, king, priest rather than the more familiar post-refor-
mational order, prophet, priest, king: "the office enjoined upon Christ by the Father consists
of three parts. For he was given to be prophet, king, and priest" (*Institutes* 2.15.1).
70. On Calvin's treatment of the threefold office of Christ, particularly its historical
development, see J. F. Jansen, *Calvin's Doctrine of the Work of Christ* (London: James Clarke,
1956). He maintains that the prophetic office of Christ largely drops from Calvin's attention,
a view that has been upheld by G. C. Berkouwer. It is criticized by others, including Peterson,
Calvin's Doctrine, 27f.; Willis, *Calvin's Catholic Christology*, 86 n. 1; John Murray, *Collected
Writings of John Murray*, 4 vols. (Edinburgh: Banner of Truth, 1982), 4:302f.
71. Edmondson, *Calvin's Christology*, 154–81.
72. The same is true of his commentary on Hebrews. For example, commenting on
Hebrews 3:1, Calvin writes: "As he had before, by naming him a teacher and a priest, briefly
compared him with Moses and Aaron, so he now includes both clauses; for he adorns him
with two titles, as he sustains a twofold character in the Church of God. Moses was a prophet
and a teacher, and Aaron was a priest; but the two offices belong to Christ."

Christ as Prophet

For Calvin, the unbroken line of Old Testament prophets was a fore-shadowing of the one who alone could provide "the full light of understanding."[73] Citing Hebrews 1:1–2, where the author notes that in times past God spoke to our fathers by the prophets, but now in these last days he has spoken to us by his Son, Calvin draws attention to Christ as the one in whom "the fullness and culmination of all revelations was at hand."[74] In the coming of the Mediator in the flesh, "the perfect doctrine he has brought has made an end of all prophecies," so that "outside Christ there is nothing worth knowing."[75] This gives the explanation as to why Calvin subtitles *Institutes* 1.9, "Fanatics, Abandoning Scripture and Flying Over to Revelation, Cast Down All the Principles of Godliness."[76] Former ways of revelation have ceased, but there is a continuing ministry of the Spirit in the preaching of the gospel enabling the prophetic ministry of the Mediator to continue. "He received an anointing, not only for himself but for his whole body that the power of the Spirit might be present in the continuing preaching of the gospel. . . . this anointing was diffused from the Head to the members."[77] Citing Isaiah 61:1–2, "The Spirit of the Lord is upon me because the Lord has appointed me to preach to the humble," Calvin explains that this was an anointing to be a prophet to the people.

It is here that Calvin's trinitarian theology comes to the fore: Christ continues his prophetic role by the Spirit's role in the illumination of Scripture and the preaching of the Word. The fanatics set the Spirit over against the Scripture as appropriate for those who have come of age. But what Spirit are they talking about? The Spirit of Christ led the apostles and early believers to the Scriptures![78] Christ continues to teach the truth of the gospel through the work of the Holy Spirit.

73. *Institutes* 2.15.1.
74. Ibid.
75. *Institutes* 2.15.2.
76. *Omnia pietatis principia evertere fanaticos, qui posthabita scriptura, ad revelationem transvolant. Corpus Reformatorum* 2:69.
77. *Institutes* 2.15.2.
78. T. H. L. Parker, *Calvin's Preaching* (Louisville: Westminster/John Knox, 1992), 4–5; Susan Schreiner, "Calvin as an Interpreter of Job," in *Calvin and the Bible*, ed. Donald K. McKim (Cambridge: Cambridge University Press, 2006), 54–55.

Christ as King

A certain priority is given to Christ's role as king and head of the church: "I recognize that Christ was called Messiah especially with respect to, and by virtue of, his kingship."[79] Several facets rise to the surface in Calvin's exploration of the messianic king, including Christ's protection of the church from her enemies, his beneficence in the supply of an abundance of spiritual blessings, and his discipline in the maintenance of godly obedience.

Protection. "God surely promises here that through the hand of his Son he will be the eternal protector and defender of his church. . . . Whenever we hear of Christ as armed with eternal power, let us remember that the perpetuity of the church is secure in this protection. Hence, amid the violent agitation with which it is continually troubled, amid the grievous and frightful storms that threaten it with unnumbered calamities, it still remains safe."[80]

This rule (kingship, headship) is spiritual, Calvin insists, for in this world, it may not always appear as though God is in control. Furthermore, the purpose of the king is to secure a kingdom for his subjects, one that will endure for eternity: "Christ enriches his people with all things necessary for the eternal salvation of souls and fortifies them with courage to stand unconquerable against all the assaults of spiritual enemies."[81]

Provision. Linking the offices of prophet and king, Calvin expands on the theme of Isaiah 61:1–2: "as the anointed King, Christ bestows spiritual gifts to his people as the fountain from which the Spirit flows abundantly to his members, as from a head to its body."[82]

Pastor. "All the more reason, then, is there that we should one and all resolve to obey, and to direct our obedience with the greatest eagerness to the divine will! Now Christ fulfills the combined duties of king and

79. *Institutes* 2.15.2. Calvin employs "king" and "head" interchangeably. See 2.6.2–3 especially by way of an example of this.
80. *Institutes* 2.15.3.
81. 1:498; CR 2:364.
82. II.xv.5, I:499–500; CR 2: 365.

pastor for the godly who submit willingly and obediently; on the other hand, we hear that he carries a 'rod of iron to break them and dash them all in pieces like a potter's vessel' (Psa. 2:9)."[83]

Because Christ protects, provides, and pastors, Calvin expands with eloquence exhorting his readers to a sense of comfort and well-being:

Thus it is that we may patiently pass through this life with its misery, hunger, cold, contempt, reproaches, and other troubles—content with this one thing: that our King will never leave us destitute, but will provide for our needs until, our warfare ended, we are called to triumph. Such is the nature of his rule, that he shares with us all that he has received from the Father. Now he arms and equips us with his power, adorns us with his beauty and magnificence, enriches us with his wealth. These benefits, then, give us the most fruitful occasion to glory, and also provide us with confidence to struggle fearlessly against the devil, sin, and death. Finally, clothed with his righteousness, we can valiantly rise above all the world's reproaches; and just as he himself freely lavishes his gifts upon us, so may we, in return, bring forth fruit to his glory.[84]

For Calvin, Christ's kingship has an eschatological dimension to it. He is king now, but the full manifestation of his rule awaits the consummation of all things:

This is the reason why he says that he will then assume the title of King; for though he commenced his reign on the earth, and now sits at the right hand of the Father, so as to exercise the supreme government of heaven and earth; yet he has not yet erected before the eyes of men that *throne*, from which his divine majesty will be far more fully displayed than it now is at the last day; for that, of which we now obtain by faith nothing more than a taste, will then have its full effect. So then Christ now sits on his heavenly throne, as far as it is necessary that he shall reign for restraining his enemies and protecting the Church; but *then* he will appear openly, to establish perfect order in heaven and earth, to crush his enemies under his feet, to assemble his believing people to

83. Ibid.
84. *Institutes* 2.15.4.

partake of an everlasting and blessed life, to ascend his judgment-seat; and, in a word, there will be a visible manifestation of the reason why the kingdom was given to him by the Father.[85]

Christ as Priest[86]

As "a pure and stainless Mediator" Christ's function is to "reconcile us to God."[87] He was anointed to this office (as he was to his offices of prophet and king) so that God's anger against us because of our sin might be appeased as he offers himself in our place and thereby reconciles us to God. Calvin's brief treatment of the function of the cross here underlines both substitution and satisfaction, but it is important not to overly narrow on one aspect of Calvin's atonement theory.[88] Consequently, just as the church shares in the prophetic and kingly offices, so too the church shares in the priesthood of all believers: "Christ plays the priestly role . . . to receive us as his companions in this great office (Rev. 1:6). For we who are defiled in ourselves, yet are priests in him."[89]

Three things are worth noting in Calvin's brief treatment of Christ's priestly work here: (1) He views it through the lens of the book of Hebrews, and as a fulfilment of Old Testament types and shadows. Calvin paraphrases an angelic word to Daniel, "When the shadows have been dispelled the true priesthood will shine forth in Christ."[90]

(2) The Mediator had to be both human and divine. Commenting on the necessity of his human nature, Calvin writes: "Although God under the law commanded animal sacrifices to be offered to himself, in Christ

85. Commentary on Matt. 25:31. The translation is that of William Pringle in the 1863 Calvin Translation Society series: *Commentary on a Harmony of the Evangelists, Matthew, Mark, and Luke*, 3 vols. (Grand Rapids: Baker, 1981 reprint), 3:175.

86. Calvin's treatment of the priestly role is limited in this section because it functions as a segue to an extensive discussion of the redemptive work of Christ in chapters 16 and 17.

87. *Institutes* 2.15.6.

88. Paul Van Buren, *Christ in Our Place: The Substitutionary Character of Calvin's Doctrine of Reconciliation* (Edinburgh: Oliver and Boyd, 1957); note should be given the prefatory warning of J. I. Packer to Robert A. Peterson's treatment of the atonement, *Calvin's Doctrine of the Atonement*, vii.

89. *Institutes* 2.15.6. It has been noted that Calvin's treatment of the priesthood of all believers, a concept dear to Luther, is infrequent and unsystematic. See the comment by Ford Lewis Battles, 1:502 n. 15.

90. *Institutes* 2.15.6.

there was a new and different order, in which the same one was to be both priest and sacrifice. This was because no other satisfaction adequate for our sins, and no man worthy to offer to God the only-begotten Son, could be found."[91] But the Mediator must also be divine. Elsewhere, Calvin insists on the divine nature of the Mediator, a point that distinguishes Christ's priesthood from that of his Aaronic predecessors. As he had written in the first letter to Stancaro earlier, "This divinity is a necessary requisite of the office of Priesthood."[92] The hypostatic union of divine and human natures in the person of the Mediator invests his priestly work with an authority the Levitical priesthood could not attain.[93]

(3) Though that aspect of his priestly work in atoning for our sins is now complete, Christ continues in his priestly work as "an everlasting intercessor."[94] In a subsequent chapter Calvin adds: "having entered a sanctuary not made with hands, he appears before the Father's face as our constant advocate and intercessor (Heb. 7:25; 9:11–12; Rom. 8:34)."[95]

We noted earlier Peterson's comments with regard to the bridging nature of chapter 15, a way of suggesting that we should not separate Christ's person (chapters 12–14) from his work (chapters 16–17). It is worth citing Peterson again: "To speak of Christ's person apart from his work is to fall into the perverse speculation of Osiander. To conceive of His work apart from His person would be meaningless—it is *His* work."[96] The next section of the *Institutes* gives particular attention to this issue.

91. Ibid.
92. Tylenda, "Christ the Mediator," 14.
93. Calvin's comments on Hebrews 5 in his commentary expand on this in greater detail.
94. *Institutes* 2.15.6.
95. *Institutes* 2.16.16.
96. Peterson, *Calvin's Doctrine*, 39.

10

CALVIN ON CHRIST'S SAVING WORK

INSTITUTES 2.16–17
ROBERT A. PETERSON

He gave himself. No words can rightly express what this means; for who can find language to declare the excellency of the Son of God? Yet it is He who gave Himself as the price for our redemption. Atonement, cleansing, satisfaction and all the fruit that we receive from the death of Christ are included under the words "gave himself up."[1]

When he adds, *a sacrifice of a sweet smell*; it is first a commendation of the grace of Christ. . . . No language, indeed, can fully express the fruit and efficacy of Christ's death. We hold that this is the only

---

1. John Calvin, *Galatians, Ephesians, Philippians and Colossians*, ed. D. W. Torrance and T. F. Torrance, trans. T. H. L. Parker, Calvin's New Testament Commentaries 11 (Grand Rapids: Eerdmans, 1965), 45 (on Gal. 2:20, emphasis original).

price by which we are reconciled to God. This doctrine of the faith holds the highest rank.[2]

These two quotations from Calvin's commentaries communicate his awe at the person and especially the saving work of Jesus Christ. In this essay, I offer an exposition of the two main chapters of the *Institutes* treating Calvin's view of Christ's work—2.16 and 17—and then deal with four related issues.

Chapter 16: How Christ Has Fulfilled the Function of Redeemer to Acquire Salvation for Us. Here, Also, His Death and Resurrection Are Discussed, as well as His Ascent into Heaven

2.16.1–4. God's Love and Wrath in the Cross

2.16.1. With a few words—"What we have said so far concerning Christ"[3]—Calvin recalls *Institutes* 2.12–15, where he taught the Son of God's incarnation, divine and human natures, unipersonality, and threefold office.[4] In light of our condition before God since the fall, "condemned, dead, and lost in ourselves," we stand in desperate need of the only Redeemer and Savior of the world—Jesus. And we must give Jesus full attention, for "the moment we turn away even slightly from him, our salvation, which rests firmly in him, gradually vanishes away."

Calvin directs his readers to Jesus' saving work: "But here we must earnestly ponder how he accomplishes salvation for us." In desperation the lost sinner must try to do the impossible: "Accordingly, he must anxiously seek ways and means to appease God—and this demands a satisfaction. No common assurance is required, for God's wrath and curse always lie upon sinners until they are absolved of guilt."

---

2. Ibid., 196 (on Eph. 5:2, emphasis original).
3. The translations used in this essay are from John Calvin, *Institutes of the Christian Religion*, ed. John T. McNeill, trans. Ford Lewis Battles, 2 vols. (Philadelphia: Westminster, 1960).
4. For an exposition of Calvin's teaching on Christ's threefold office in relation to his saving work, see my *Calvin and the Atonement*, rev. ed. (Fearn, Ross-shire: Mentor, 1999), 45–60.

Here Calvin introduces his most important theme of the atonement—the legal, penal theme.

2.16.2. Immediately, Calvin raises a theological problem, labeling it "some sort of contradiction": if God's mercy is the cause of his sending his Son to be our Savior, then in what sense does Scripture say that God was our enemy until he was reconciled to us in his Son?

Calvin notes that Scripture frequently declares that God "anticipates us by his mercy" and gives "in his only-begotten Son a singular pledge of his love to us." At the same time, Scripture consistently portrays unsaved human beings as God's enemies, under a curse, and estranged from him. How are we to reconcile these two truths?

> Expressions of this sort have been accommodated to our capacity that we may better understand how miserable and ruinous our condition is apart from Christ. For if it had not been clearly stated that the wrath and vengeance of God and eternal death rested upon us, we would scarcely have recognized how miserable we would have been without God's mercy, and we would have underestimated the benefit of liberation.

Accommodation in Calvin's thought has been investigated.[5] It is sufficient here to note that, although Calvin does not intend to downplay the reality of the wrath of God toward sinners, he uses the idea of accommodation to stress the equally biblical and more ultimate truth that God's free grace moved him to send his Son to die in our place. That is, even when we truly deserved his eternal wrath, he nevertheless loved us and sent our Redeemer to deliver us. His love went before our reconciliation, although for us to properly appreciate it, he had to emphasize his wrath and downplay his precedent love.

> To sum up: since our hearts cannot, in God's mercy, either seize upon life ardently enough or accept it with the gratefulness we owe, unless our minds are first struck and overwhelmed by fear of God's wrath and by dread of eternal death, we are taught by Scripture to perceive that apart from Christ, God is, so to speak, hostile to us, and his hand

5. See Ford Lewis Battles, "God Was Accommodating Himself to Human Capacity," *Interpretation* 31 (1977): 19–38.

is armed for our destruction; to embrace his benevolence and fatherly love in Christ alone.

2.16.3. When Scripture—to show us our need of a Savior—emphasizes God's wrath and downplays his grace, such statements are "tempered to our feeble comprehension" but are "not said falsely." Calvin means that God rightly condemns the wicked. Nevertheless, "because the Lord wills not to lose what is his in us, out of his own kindness he still finds something to love." He stands opposed to us as sinners, but still loves us as his creatures. "Thus he is moved by pure and freely given love of us to receive us into grace." But how can he receive sinners in light of his infinite holiness?

The answer to this question is that, given God's plan to save sinners, the atonement of his Son was necessary: "Therefore, by his love God the Father goes before and anticipates our reconciliation in Christ. . . . But until Christ succors us by his death, the unrighteousness that deserves God's indignation remains in us, and is accursed and condemned before him. Hence, we can be fully and firmly joined with God only when Christ joins us with him."

2.16.4. Calvin revisits the problem of God's wrath and love, appealing to Scripture and Augustine. In sum, God's wrath is real but not ultimate, for "Paul says that the love with which God embraced us 'before the creation of the world' was established and grounded in Christ [Eph. 1:4–5]." This love is mysterious, as Augustine recognized long ago.

> "God's love," says he, "is incomprehensible and unchangeable. For it was not after we were reconciled to him through the blood of his Son that he began to love us. . . . Rather, he loved us before the world was created, that we also might be his sons along with his only-begotten Son—before we became anything at all. . . . Therefore, he loved us even when we practiced enmity toward him and committed wickedness. Thus in a marvelous and divine way he loved us even when he hated us."

2.16.5–7. *Christ's Lifelong Obedience, Condemnation, Crucifixion, Death, and Burial*

2.16.5. Calvin next considers how Christ has accomplished deliverance for us: "He has achieved this for us by the whole course of his obedience." The Reformer adduces Scripture passages and summarizes: "In short, from the time when he took on the form of a servant, he began to pay the price of liberation in order to redeem us."

By affirming that Christ's incarnation and sinless life are essential for our salvation, Calvin does not detract from the cross. "Yet to define the way of salvation more exactly, Scripture ascribes this as peculiar and proper to Christ's death."

Calvin reveals his method of presentation: "The so-called 'Apostles' Creed' passes at once in the best order from the birth of Christ to his death and resurrection, wherein the whole of perfect salvation consists." In the following sections (2.16.5–17), Calvin follows "the best order" of the creed in describing Christ's saving accomplishment: condemnation under Pilate, crucifixion, death and burial, descent into hell, resurrection, ascension, session at God's right hand, and return. After doing so, he specifies his method: "Thus far I have followed the order of the Apostles' Creed . . . [which] contains nothing that is not vouched for by genuine testimonies of Scripture" (2.16.18).

Christ's obedient life prepares him for the chief part of his saving work, his death and resurrection. And the role obedience plays in his death is significant: "Truly, even in death itself his willing obedience is the important thing because a sacrifice not offered voluntarily would not have furthered righteousness." Here Calvin accents Christ's genuine humanity when he teaches, citing eight Scriptures, that Christ saved us through struggle, weakness, and fear.[6]

Surprisingly, Calvin includes Jesus' condemnation under Pontius Pilate in his saving work. Although we were under God's curse, "to deliver us from it, Christ allowed himself to be condemned before a mortal man—even a wicked and profane man." Could Jesus have saved us by a death other than crucifixion? Calvin answers emphatically: "To take away our condemnation, it was not enough for him to suffer any kind of death: to make satisfaction for our redemption a form of death had to be chosen in which he might free us both by transferring our condemnation to himself and by taking our guilt upon himself."

6. See also John Calvin, *Matthew, Mark and Luke*, ed. D. W. Torrance and T. F. Torrance, trans. A. W. Morrison, Calvin's New Testament Commentaries 3 (Grand Rapids: Eerdmans, 1972), 147 (on Matt. 26:37).

Jesus had to be crucified for that was the only way that he could pay our penalty before God. This is legal, penal substitution. Christ "took the role of a guilty man and evildoer . . . that he might die in the place of the sinner." Calvin defines the important term "satisfaction," previously used by Anselm to describe Christ's death. For Calvin, "satisfaction" should be understood in legal terms. It is also important to underscore Christ's sinlessness, which was recognized even by Pilate, because it is tied up with substitution: "Thus we shall behold the person of a sinner and evildoer represented in Christ, yet from his shining innocence it will at the same time be obvious that he was burdened with another's sin rather than his own."

What is the most important way to view Christ's cross, and where does our assurance come from? Calvin's answer to both questions is the same: "This is our acquittal: the guilt that held us liable for punishment has been transferred to the head of the Son of God [Isa. 53:12]. We must, above all, remember this substitution, lest we tremble and remain anxious throughout life—as if God's righteous vengeance, which the Son of God has taken upon himself, still hung over us."

2.16.6. Calvin moves to the word "crucified" from the creed. The cross was regarded as cursed by both God and men. "Hence, when Christ is hanged upon the cross, he makes himself subject to the curse" of the law. This was in accordance with the Old Testament sacrifices, which prefigured Christ's substitution.

Christ in his cross was the divinely ordained spotless sacrifice "who took upon himself the shame and reproach of our iniquities, and in return clothed us with his purity." Here is Calvin's doctrine of double imputation which he finds in 2 Corinthians 5:21: "For our sake he who knew no sin was made sin by the Father, so that in him we might be made the righteousness of God." Our sins are reckoned to the spiritual bank account of the sinless Son of God, who dies on account of them, and his righteousness is transferred to our bankrupt spiritual bank accounts, making us acceptable before God.

Calvin uses the language of victory in this context, but he subordinates victory and sacrifice to the bigger idea of Christ paying our legal debt and satisfying God's righteous anger: "Christ was offered to the Father in death as an expiatory sacrifice that when he discharged all satisfaction through his sacrifice, we might cease to be afraid of God's wrath." As usual, Calvin marshals passages to prove his point.

While still discussing Christ's sacrifice, Calvin highlights the victory that his cross achieved:

> Yet we must not understand that he fell under a curse that overwhelmed him; rather—in taking the curse upon himself—he crushed, broke, and scattered its whole force. Hence faith apprehends an acquittal in the condemnation of Christ, a blessing in his curse. Paul with good reason, therefore, magnificently proclaims the triumph that Christ obtained for himself on the cross, as if the cross, which was full of shame, had been changed into a triumphal chariot [Col. 2:14–15]!

This has great practical value to Calvin, who urges readers to keep Christ and his sacrifice "constantly in mind. For we could not believe with assurance that Christ is our redemption, ransom, and propitiation unless he had been a sacrificial victim."

2.16.7. "There follows in the Creed: 'He was dead and buried.'" In Calvin's eyes this shows the extent to which Christ our Redeemer identified with us. He submitted to death and the burial of his body. "Death held us captive under its yoke: Christ, in our stead, gave himself over to its power to deliver us from it." Calvin enumerates two benefits that accrue to believers from Christ's death. First is victory over our enemies of death, the devil, and the fear of God's wrath. Second is victory over sin in the Christian life. Christ's efficacious death (and burial) put sin to death in us, as Scripture attests. "By these statements Paul not only exhorts us to exhibit an example of Christ's death but declares that there inheres in it an efficacy which ought to be manifest in all Christians, unless they intend to render his death useless and unfruitful."[7]

Calvin summarizes: "Therefore, in Christ's death and burial a twofold blessing is set forth for us to enjoy: liberation from the death to which we had been bound, and mortification of our flesh."

---

7. See also *The Gospel according to St. John, Part Two, and the First Epistle of John*, ed. D. W. Torrance and T. F. Torrance, trans. T. H. L. Parker, Calvin's New Testament Commentaries 5 (Grand Rapids: Eerdmans, 1961), 269 (on 1 John 3:5).

2.16.8–12. Christ's Descent into Hell

2.16.8. The next five sections of the *Institutes* treat Christ's descent into hell, which comes next in the creed. Calvin notes that some of the church fathers omitted this article, but he still thinks "it contains the useful and not-to-be-despised mystery of a most important matter." He remarks that the Fathers all mentioned the descent although they differed in their interpretations of it. Calvin values it, however, as he does every article in the Apostles' Creed:

> The noteworthy point about the Creed is this: we have in it a summary of our faith, full and complete in all details; and containing nothing in it except what has been derived from the pure Word of God. If any persons have scruples about admitting this article into the Creed, it will soon be made plain how important it is to the sum of our redemption: if it is left out, much of the benefit of Christ's death will be lost.

Although the word translated "hell" is sometime rendered "grave," Calvin opposes those who take "He descended into hell" to mean "He descended into the grave." They err, for he doubts whether such a needless repetition would have been allowed to creep into the creed.

2.16.9. Although Calvin accepts the descent clause in the creed, he does not accept every interpretation of it. Specifically, he rejects the view of some (including Thomas Aquinas) who held that Christ descended into the netherworld to free dead believers from limbo and escort them to paradise. Calvin admits that Christ's death was made known to both the righteous and wicked dead, and offers this as a probable explanation for the difficult passage 1 Peter 3:19, but this text does not furnish a basis for believing in the limbo of the Fathers nor a satisfactory explanation of Christ's descent.

2.16.10. Calvin offers his interpretation of the descent. On the cross, Christ not only suffered death in his body, but also suffered the pains of hell in his soul. "If Christ had died only a bodily death, it would have been ineffectual. No—it was expedient at the same time for him to undergo the severity of God's vengeance, to appease his wrath and satisfy his just judgment."[8] Once again Calvin adds the language of victory to describe Christ's death as one of the results of the propitiation he accomplished.

Is it accurate for the creed to include the descent clause? Calvin answers with an emphatic affirmative: "No wonder, then, if he is said to have descended into hell, for he suffered the death that God in his wrath had inflicted upon the wicked!" But does not this reverse the creed's statements by placing what preceded Christ's burial after it? Calvin has a ready response. These objectors are mistaken because they fail to understand the credal order: first it lists "what Christ suffered in the sight of men"—"he was buried." Only then does it speak "of that invisible and incomprehensible judgment which he underwent in the sight of God"—"he descended into hell."

To sum up: it is essential for the Christian faith to maintain that Christ died for his people in both body and soul. And this death in soul is what the Apostles' Creed means when it confesses his descent.

2.16.11. Calvin undertakes to prove from Scripture his interpretation of Christ's descent. His citation of Acts 2:24 is not convincing. It refers to Christ's resurrection, as Peter in Acts 2 makes clear. But Calvin cogently refers to Hebrews 5:7, which speaks of Christ's "loud cries and tears" in Gethsemane as he contemplated drinking the cup of God's wrath. Christ prayed not to be swallowed up by the abyss, "and surely no more terrible abyss can be conceived than to feel yourself forsaken and estranged by God."[9]

Calvin's next proof text is also good: "My God, my God, why hast thou forsaken me?" (Ps. 22:1; Matt. 27:46). Calvin explains that Christ's cry of abandonment on the cross, though "drawn forth from deep anguish within his heart," does not mean "that God was ever inimical or angry toward him. How could he be angry toward his beloved Son, 'in whom his heart reposed' [Matt. 3:17]?" But in the next breath Calvin seems to contradict himself: "This is what we are saying: he bore the weight of divine severity, since he was 'stricken and afflicted' [Isa. 53:4] by God's hand, and experienced all the signs of a wrathful and avenging God."

8. See also *Hebrews and I and II Peter*, ed. D. W. Torrance and T. F. Torrance, trans. W. B. Johnston, Calvin's New Testament Commentaries 12 (Grand Rapids: Eerdmans, 1963), 64 (on Heb. 5:7).

9. *Matthew, Mark and Luke*, 148 (on Matt. 26:37).

How can we reconcile these two ideas? Perhaps Calvin means that the Father was not angry with the Son in himself, with the Son as Son, but nevertheless poured out his wrath on him as our substitute, who bore our sins. The Father never stopped loving his beloved Son, but for a time abandoned him who stood in our place as a criminal and condemned man.

The Reformer rejects the idea of some that Christ's desertion by God was only apparent. No, the abandonment was real and Christ was tormented with the fear of hell.

2.16.12. Calvin takes pains to defend Christ's descent against various misunderstandings. First, opponents accuse him of slandering Christ by ascribing to him genuine fear on the cross. Calvin points out that the Evangelists openly relate "Christ's fear and dread." These opponents miss the fact that "unless his soul shared in the punishment, he would have been the Redeemer of bodies alone." His taking our human weakness "in no wise detracts from his heavenly glory," but qualifies him "the better to succor us in our miseries [Heb. 4:15]."

Calvin's adversaries claim that his view of the descent attributes to Christ a lack of faith which amounts to sin. Calvin chastises them for ignoring Hebrews 4:15—"Christ in every respect has been tempted as we are, yet without sinning"—and failing to see that he voluntarily submitted to weakness out of love for us. The opponents err because they judge Christ by fallen human standards and fail to "recognize in Christ a weakness pure and free of all vice and stain."

Furthermore, Calvin's foes claim that Christ feared death but not God's wrath. But this would make Christ more cowardly than many common criminals, who bear death calmly. No, something more terrible than death caused the Savior in Gethsemane to emit drops of blood (Luke 22:44) and shrink from drinking the cup (Matt. 26:39), and caused the Father to send an angel to aid him (Luke 22:43). Christ feared the wrath of a holy God!

Calvin's opponents' worst mistake is to fail "to feel how much salvation cost the Son of God." He feared far more than death, even "harsh and dreadful torments," knowing "that he stood accused before God's judgment seat for our sake." And this was not contrary to faith, nor was it sin on Christ's part. For even at his lowest ebb, he cried out to God in deep despair in the cry of dereliction (Matt. 27:46).

Moreover, Calvin's view of the descent defeats ancient errors too. Apollinarianism, which denied to Christ a complete humanity, and monothelitism, which denied to him a human will, are both repudiated by Calvin's insistence that the descent involved Christ's genuine experience of spiritual alienation on the cross.

2.16.13–16. Christ's Resurrection, Ascension, Session

2.16.13. Christ's resurrection comes next. This is an essential article of the Christian faith: "Without this what we have said so far would be incomplete." Unlike many Christians today Calvin holds Jesus' resurrection in the same high esteem that Scripture does:[10]

> For since only weakness appears in the cross, death, and burial of Christ, faith must leap over all these things to attain its full strength. We have in his death the complete fulfillment of salvation. . . . Nevertheless, we are said to "have been born anew to a living hope" not through his death, but "through his resurrection" [1 Peter 1:3]. For as he, in rising again, came forth victor over death, so the victory of our faith over death lies in his resurrection alone.[11]

Scripture teaches that Christ's resurrection is as necessary for our salvation as his crucifixion. "Therefore, we divide the substance of our salvation between Christ's death and resurrection as follows: through his death, sin was wiped out and death extinguished; through his resurrection, righteousness was restored and life raised up, so that—thanks to his resurrection—his death manifested its power and efficacy in us."

Next the Reformer lays down an important principle: "Whenever mention is made of his death alone, we are to understand at the same time what belongs to his resurrection," and the same for his resurrec-

10. See Richard B. Gaffin Jr., *Resurrection and Redemption* (Phillipsburg, NJ: P&R, 1985), which extols Christ's resurrection.
11. See also *The Epistles of Paul to the Romans and the Thessalonians*, ed. D. W. Torrance and T. F. Torrance, trans. R. Mackenzie, Calvin's New Testament Commentaries 8 (Grand Rapids: Eerdmans, 1961), 102 (on Rom. 4:25).

tion. This is the figure of speech synecdoche, here meaning the use of a part to refer to the whole. Christ's death and resurrection are so vital to Christianity that when Scripture speaks of either one of them, readers are to infer the other as well.

More benefits accrue to believers because Jesus not only died for them but also lives for them. As Calvin taught believers' mortification in the cross—Christ broke sin's stranglehold over us—so now he teaches their vivification in Christ's empty tomb—Jesus' resurrection enables us to walk in newness of life, as Scripture testifies. Not only do we gain eternal life and vivification because of Christ's resurrection, "We also receive a third benefit . . . : we are assured of our own resurrection by receiving a sort of guarantee substantiated by his."

2.16.14. Calvin, following the creed, comes to Christ's ascension. Although his resurrection displayed his "glory and power more fully" than did his humble earthly life, death, and burial, "yet he truly inaugurated his Kingdom only at his ascension into heaven," as Paul taught in Ephesians 4:10.

Jesus' ascension into heaven prepared him to send the Holy Spirit in a new and powerful manner: "Indeed, we see how much more abundantly he then poured out his Spirit, how much more wonderfully he advanced his Kingdom, how much greater power he displayed both in helping his people and in scattering his enemies." Christ's ascension marked a great expansion of his royal rule: "As his body was raised up above all the heavens, so his power and energy were diffused and spread beyond all the bounds of heaven and earth."

The disciples lamented his leaving, fearing they would be deprived of his presence. Ironically, however, Christ's absence from earth meant his more powerful presence with them: "Carried up into heaven, therefore, he withdrew his bodily presence from our sight [Acts 1:9], not to cease to be present with believers still on their earthly pilgrimage, but to rule heaven and earth by a more immediate power."

2.16.15. "Consequently, these words come immediately after: 'Seated at the right hand of the Father.'" What is the significance of Christ's session, his sitting at God's right hand? "Christ was invested with lordship over heaven and earth, and solemnly entered into possession of the government committed to him—and . . . he not only entered into possession once for all, but continues in it, until he shall come down on Judgment Day," as Scripture testifies.

Calvin eloquently affirms concerning Christ's session, "You see the purpose of that 'sitting': that both heavenly and earthly creatures may look with admiration upon his majesty, be ruled by his hand, obey his nod, and submit to his power." This is why the apostles sought his will after his ascension. In a word, "'to sit' means nothing else than to preside at the heavenly judgment seat."[12]

2.16.16. Calvin enumerates three benefits of Christ's ascension: heaven is open, he intercedes for us, and he displays his might. First, faith "understands that the Lord by his ascent to heaven opened the way into the Heavenly Kingdom, which had been closed through Adam [John 14:3]." This assures us of salvation, for a human being, one of us, has already entered heaven on our behalf, guaranteeing our eventual entrance also.

Second, "having entered a sanctuary not made with hands, he appears before the Father's face as our constant advocate and intercessor [Heb. 7:25; 9:11–12; Rom. 8:34]."[13] In this role Jesus turns the face of a holy God away from his people's sins to Jesus' own righteousness. Once again, Christ's ascension strengthens our assurance of eternal salvation.

"Thirdly, faith comprehends his might, in which reposes our strength, power, wealth, and glorying against hell." Our exalted Lord and Savior gives enabling grace to his people, sanctifies them by his Spirit, gives gifts to his church, protects it from its enemies, restrains those enemies, and wields all power until he comes again as Judge. Thus, a third time Calvin indicates that Christ's ascension fortifies our assurance.

2.16.17. Calvin next treats Christ's second coming. This too is a vital element of the Christian faith because without it God would not be vindicated. Judging by appearances, many would conclude that God does not have a kingdom now, but there will be no confusion on that day. "Yet his Kingdom lies hidden in the earth, so to speak, under the lowness of

---

12. See also Calvin, *Hebrews and I and II Peter,* 9–10 (on Heb. 1:3).

13. See also Calvin, *Gospel according to St. John, Part Two, and the First Epistle of John,* 244 (on 1 John 2:1).

the flesh. It is right, therefore, that faith be called to ponder that visible presence of Christ which he will manifest on the Last Day."

Christ's magnificent return will reveal him in great majesty, glory, might, and pomp: "He will appear to all with the ineffable majesty of his Kingdom, with the glow of immortality, with the boundless power of divinity, with a guard of angels."

Everyone will stand before Christ's judgment throne. "No one—living or dead—shall escape his judgment." His return will mean very different things to two groups of people, as "he will separate the lambs from the goats, the elect from the reprobate [Matt. 25:31–33]."

Calvin insists that the creed's expression "the living and the dead," which confused some church fathers, be taken in its common sense—it means "that living and dead will be called to judgment." Those who remain alive at Christ's return will die in the sense that "their mortal life will perish and be swallowed up 'in a moment,' and be transformed directly into a new nature [1 Cor. 15:52]." Together with resurrected believers they shall "meet the Lord in the air [1 Thess. 4:16–17]."

2.16.18–19. Christ Is the Subject of the Apostles' Creed

2.16.18. Christ will come again, and all will stand before his judgment seat. This suggests a question: Should we fear his wrath? Calvin replies with exuberance and eloquence: "Far indeed is he from mounting his judgment seat to condemn us! How could our most merciful Ruler destroy his people? How could the Head scatter his own members? How could our Advocate condemn his clients? . . . No mean assurance this—that we shall be brought before no other judgment seat than that of our Redeemer, to whom we must look for our salvation!"

The judge of all the earth is our Savior! Calvin rightly calls this truth "a wonderful consolation."

Earlier we noted that Calvin here tells readers that up until this point he has followed the order of the Apostles' Creed. Although he does not wish to defend apostolic authorship, he regards the creed as an accurate summary of the teaching of the Bible.

2.16.19. Calvin then summarizes his exposition of the Apostles' Creed: "We see that our whole salvation and all its parts are comprehended in

Christ [Acts 4:12]." He laments that some are not content with Christ and consequently are unstable and stray spiritually. His answer is to point most emphatically to the all-sufficiency of Christ. Calvin offers a concluding hymn of praise to Christ that is lengthy but wonderful:

> If we seek salvation, we are taught by the very name of Jesus that it is "of him" [1 Cor. 1:30]. If we seek any other gifts of the Spirit, they will be found in his anointing. If we seek strength, it lies in his dominion; if purity, in his conception; if gentleness, it appears in his birth. For by his birth he was made like us in all respects [Heb. 2:17] that he might learn to feel our pain [Heb. 5:2]. If we seek redemption, it lies in his passion; if acquittal, in his condemnation; if remission of the curse, in his cross [Gal. 3:13]; if satisfaction, in his sacrifice; if purification, in his blood; if reconciliation, in his descent into hell; if mortification of the flesh, in his tomb; if newness of life, in his resurrection; if immortality, in the same; if inheritance of the Heavenly Kingdom, in his entrance into heaven; if protection, if security, if abundant supply of all blessings, in his Kingdom; if untroubled expectation of judgment, in the power given him to judge. In short, since rich store of every kind of goods abounds in him, let us drink our fill from this fountain, and from no other.

Chapter 17: Christ Rightly and Properly Said to Have Merited God's Grace and Salvation for Us

2.17.1. In this chapter, the last of book 2 of the *Institutes*, Calvin is largely polemical, answering "certain perversely subtle men who—even though they confess that we receive salvation through Christ—cannot bear to hear the word 'merit,' for they think that it obscures God's grace." Calvin's chief opponent is Laelius Socinus.

Socinus found two ideas irreconcilable: God's mercy and Christ's merit. Consequently, he denied that Christ merited salvation. Following Augustine, Calvin admits that Christ, considered as a mere man, would not have been able to merit anything from God. But Christ is not to be considered apart from God's plan.

Socinus's first mistake is that he fails to distinguish between first causes and subordinate ones:

In discussing Christ's merit, we do not consider the beginning of merit to be in him, but we go back to God's ordinance, the first cause. For God solely of his own good pleasure appointed him Mediator to obtain salvation for us.

Hence it is absurd to set Christ's merit against God's mercy. For this reason nothing hinders us from asserting that men are freely justified by God's mercy alone, and at the same time that Christ's merit, subordinate to God's mercy, also intervenes on our behalf.

God's plan of salvation—not Christ's merit—is the first and ultimate cause of our salvation. But God ordained means to accomplish that salvation, including Christ's lifelong obedience, death, and resurrection. By obeying the Father Christ merited grace and salvation for us.

Affirming Christ's merit does not introduce human works as a basis of salvation: "To sum up: inasmuch as Christ's merit depends upon God's grace alone, which has ordained this manner of salvation for us, it is just as properly opposed to all human righteousness as God's grace is."

2.17.2. Calvin proves these assertions from Scripture. He cites John 3:16, then comments, "We see how God's love holds first place, as the highest cause or origin; how faith in Christ follows this as the second and proximate cause." Someone may object that Christ is associated with salvation but does not actually save. While citing nine passages, Calvin responds, "If we attain righteousness by a faith that reposes in him, we ought to seek the matter of our salvation in him."

Clearly, 2 Corinthians 5:21 teaches that what Christ accomplished in his death makes us right with God: "This means that we, who 'by nature are sons of wrath' [Eph. 2:3] and estranged from him by sin, have, by Christ's sacrifice, acquired free justification in order to appease God."

2.17.3. Moreover, Scripture attributes merit to Christ's obedience. Calvin cannot understand how anyone could miss this: "I take it to be a commonplace that if Christ made satisfaction for sins, if he paid the penalty owed by us, if he appeased God by his obedience—in short, if as a righteous man he suffered for unrighteous men—then he acquired salvation for us by his righteousness, which is tantamount to deserving it." Paul's Adam/Christ parallel in Romans 5:19 witnesses to Christ's merit: "As by the sin of Adam we were estranged from God and destined to perish, so by Christ's obedience we are received into favor as righteous."

2.17.4. Calvin specifically points to Christ's death as meriting grace and salvation. "But when we say that grace was imparted to us by the merit of Christ, we mean this: By his blood we were cleansed, and his death was an expiation for our sins." In fact, Scripture—including John 1:29—abundantly witnesses to this truth.

The Old Testament sacrifices were God's means of atoning for sin. But these all point to Christ's death as the ultimate sacrifice for sin. "The old figures well teach us the force and power of Christ's death." Hebrews repeatedly makes this point, and "this readily shows that Christ's grace is too much weakened unless we grant to his sacrifice the power of expiating, appeasing, and making satisfaction."

Calvin shows from Scripture that Christ took the curse we deserved (Gal. 3:13), paid the penalty that we owed (Isa. 53:5, 8), and bore our sins (1 Peter 2:24) to further underscore that he performed a work to earn our salvation.

2.17.5. "The apostles clearly state that he paid the price to redeem us from the penalty of death." Paul and Peter both present the price of redemption as the death of Christ. Calvin concludes:

> We must seek from Christ what the law would give if anyone could fulfill it; or what is the same thing, that we obtain through Christ's grace what God promised in the law for our works. . . . For if righteousness consists in the observance of the law, who will deny that Christ merited favor for us when, by taking that burden upon himself, he reconciled us to God as if we had kept the law?

2.17.6. Calvin opposes the idea put forth by some medieval theologians that Christ merited something for himself. He labels this "no less stupid curiosity than . . . temerity." Calvin is flabbergasted: "What need was there for God's only Son to come down in order to acquire something new for himself?" To the contrary, Scripture always sets him forth as meriting salvation for others: "He who gave away the fruit of his holiness to others testifies that he acquired nothing for himself."

Related Issues

Although it is impossible to discuss all of the issues surrounding Calvin's understanding of the atonement here, I will address four of the most important ones: love and wrath, Calvin and Anselm, Calvin's pictures of Christ's saving work, and Calvin and limited atonement.[14]

Love and Wrath

The problem of the relation of God's love and wrath in the cross[15] is at least as old as Augustine, and Calvin was not the last to give it expression, as John Stott's summary reveals: "How then can God express his holiness without consuming us, and his love without condoning our sins? How can God satisfy his holy love? How can he save *us* and satisfy *himself* simultaneously?"[16] Henri Blocher aptly concludes: "The duality, though marvelous and mysterious as God's love must always remain in our eyes, does not involve a real difficulty for understanding, as he [Calvin] ... explains ...: 'I admit that the love of God is prior in time and also in order as regards God (*quantum ad Deum*), but from our point of view (*respectu nostri*) the beginning of love is placed in Christ's sacrifice.'"[17]

Unfortunately, Calvin's theological heirs have not always succeeded as well as he in coordinating the two principles of divine love and justice, as H. D. McDonald relates:

> As long as they were thus coordinated, an acceptable penal substitutionary doctrine could be elaborated. But in its development the principle of love came to be subordinated to that of justice, and the theory left itself open to criticism. Thus for example, Turretin and Quenstedt in an earlier date and Shedd and Hodge at a later time

14. Also sometimes debated is Duns Scotus's influence on Calvin's understanding of the intrinsic value of Christ's obedience and the necessity of the atonement. For valuable discussion, see Henri Blocher, "The Atonement in John Calvin's Theology," in *The Glory of the Atonement* (Downers Grove, IL: InterVarsity, 2004), 296–301.

15. See my *Calvin and the Atonement*, rev. ed., 20–24.

16. John Stott, *The Cross of Christ* (Downers Grove, IL: InterVarsity, 1986), 132.

17. Blocher, "Atonement in John Calvin's Theology," 294–95, citing Calvin's Commentary on 2 Cor. 5:19. See also Calvin, *Gospel according to St. John, Part Two, and the First Epistle of John*, 291 (on 1 John 4:10).

elevated the principle of justice and worked out the penal theory in virtual exclusive relation thereto.[18]

Surely it is better to follow Calvin and emphasize God's love as well as his justice when affirming substitution.

Calvin and Anselm

Timothy George helpfully contrasts Calvin and Anselm on the atonement in five points, which we will examine in turn.[19] First, unlike Anselm, who held to "an almost ontological necessity for the incarnation . . . Calvin denied any simple or absolute necessity for the incarnation."[20] Robert S. Paul agrees, "In Calvin the purpose of the Incarnation is the Atonement, that and nothing else."[21] George is basically correct, but matters are more nuanced, as Blocher shows when he speaks of "the multiplicity of levels" of "necessity" and points to "an inner tension in Calvin's thought."[22]

"Second, while Anselm was concerned primarily to show how through the atonement the justice of God was rectified, Calvin's focus is more on the wrath and love of God which are both illustrated in the work of Christ."[23] George correctly points to a greater emphasis on God's love in Calvin's presentation of the atonement than in Anselm's *Cur Deus Homo*.[24] But George errs when he says that the death of Christ satisfied

18. H. D. McDonald, *The Atonement of the Death of Christ* (Grand Rapids: Baker, 1985), 192.

19. Timothy George, *Theology of the Reformers* (Nashville: Broadman, 1988), 220–23. George is mistaken when he labels Anselm's view "the theory of penal, substitutionary atonement" (220), for two reasons. First, Anselm did not hold to Luther's and Calvin's view of satisfaction through punishment, but, instead, put forth the dilemma: either satisfaction or punishment. Secondly, Anselm did not hold that Christ's death satisfied God's justice, as the Reformers did, but God's offended honor.

20. Ibid., 221.

21. Robert S. Paul, *The Atonement and the Sacraments: The Relation of the Atonement to the Sacraments of Baptism and the Lord's Supper* (New York: Abingdon, 1960), 101.

22. Blocher, "Atonement in John Calvin's Theology," 298–301.

23. George, *Theology of the Reformers*, 221.

24. Some find a de-emphasis on God's love in Anselm, on the basis of *Cur Deus Homo* alone. Benedicta Ward's *The Prayers and Meditations of St. Anselm* (New York: Penguin, 1973) shows a warmer, devotional side to Anselm, one which complements the scholastic side evident in *Cur Deus Homo*.

God's justice in Anselm, for he rather taught that Christ's death satisfied God's offended honor.

"Third, in Anselm's theory the life of Christ was of no salvific value since as a human being Christ owed a perfect, sinless life to the Father anyway. Only Christ's death which, because He had not sinned, He did not deserve could accrue merit for human salvation.... But—here is his [Calvin's] unique emphasis—the salvific efficacy of the atonement was not limited to Christ's death. It extended throughout the 'whole course of his obedience.'"[25] George makes a good point here—and adds that, although Calvin emphasized Christ's life, he did not downplay the significance of his death.

George is correct on the next point: "Fourth, although the legal language of penal satisfaction and substitution predominates in Calvin's discussion of atonement, he did not neglect the theme of *Christus Victor*, the motif of atonement as Christ's triumph over the devil."[26] For nuances, see the discussion in the next section.

George incisively concludes, "Fifth, Calvin surely belongs to that family of theologians who stressed the 'objective' character of Christ's atoning work. But he did not leave out the subjective aspect, either of Christ's work on our behalf or of our response to His sacrifice. By our participation in Christ's redeeming work we are called to a life of radical obedience."[27]

Pictures of Christ's Saving Work

I was correct to argue in *Calvin and the Atonement* that Calvin painted six pictures of the atonement in his presentation of Christ's work.[28] But I was mistaken, as Blocher shows, when I failed to give pride of place to penal substitution,[29] a key doctrine that lamentably is under attack today, even by evangelical Christians.[30]

---

25. George, *Theology of the Reformers*, 221–22.

26. Ibid., 222.

27. Ibid., 223. Paul agrees; see *The Atonement and the Sacraments*, 108–9.

28. *Calvin and the Atonement*, rev. ed., 61–113. The pictures are Christ the obedient second Adam, the victor, our legal substitute, our sacrifice, our merit, and our example.

29. Blocher, "Atonement in John Calvin's Theology," 285–86.

30. So J. Denny Weaver, *The Nonviolent Atonement* (Grand Rapids: Eerdmans, 2001), and Joel B. Green and Mark D. Baker, *Recovering the Scandal of the Cross: Atonement in New Testament and Contemporary Contexts* (Downers Grove, IL: InterVarsity, 2000), 23–32, 90–97, 140–52.

Blocher argues correctly that Calvin's two most common atonement metaphors are the legal-penal theme and sacrifice, and that "the satisfaction of justice lies near the heart of sacrificial atonement!"[31] He also cogently argues that Calvin's *Christus Victor* motif seems to be a consequence of sacrifice and punishment: "A likely interpretation emerges: Satan and death, as they draw their power from the administration of divine justice, were disarmed by the satisfaction of that justice."[32]

Limited Atonement?

The question as to whether Calvin taught limited or unlimited atonement has been the matter of considerable debate.[33] It is significant that the *Institutes* is silent on this question. However, appeal can be made to Calvin's commentaries to argue for limited atonement.[34] James W. Anderson argues for unlimited atonement based largely on Calvin's sermons.[35] Jonathan Rainbow makes an impressive historical and theological case for limited atonement in Calvin.[36] In an endnote to his valuable appendix on "The Intent of the Atonement" in *The Work of Christ*, Robert Letham crisply summarizes:

31. Blocher, "Atonement in John Calvin's Theology," 283–85; the quotation is from 285.

32. Ibid., 289–92; the quotation is from 291.

33. For discussion, see my *Calvin and the Atonement*, rev. ed., 115–20.

34. For example, Calvin addresses the question of the extent of the atonement in 1 John 2:2 as follows: "Here a question may be raised, how have the sins of the whole world been expiated? I pass by the dotages of the fanatics, who under this pretence extend salvation to all the reprobate, and therefore to Satan himself. Such a monstrous thing deserves no refutation. They who seek to avoid this absurdity, have said that Christ suffered sufficiently for the whole world, but efficiently only for the elect. This solution has commonly prevailed in the schools. Though then I allow that what has been said is true, yet I deny that it is suitable to this passage; for the design of John was no other than to make this benefit common to the whole Church. Then under the word all or whole, he does not include the reprobate, but designates those who should believe as well as those who were then scattered through various parts of the world. For then is really made evident, as it is meet, the grace of Christ, when it is declared to be the only true salvation of the world." Calvin, *Gospel according to St. John, Part Two, and the First Epistle of John*, 244 (1 John 2:2).

35. "The Grace of God and the Non-elect in Calvin's Commentaries and Sermons" (Th.D. diss., New Orleans Baptist Theological Seminary, 1976).

36. "Redemptor Ecclesiae, Redemptor Mundi: An Historical and Theological Study of John Calvin's Doctrine of the Extent of Redemption" (Ph.D. diss., University of California, Santa Barbara, 1986).

The position of Calvin has been hotly disputed. The following have advocated that he adopted a form of provisional atonement: R. T. Kendall, *Calvin and English Calvinism to 1649* (Oxford: Oxford Univ. Pr., 1979), pp. 13–28; James B. Torrance, 'The Incarnation and Limited Atonement', *EQ*, 55, 1983, pp. 82–94; M. Charles Bell, *Calvin and Scottish Theology: the Doctrine of Assurance* (Edinburgh: Handsel, 1985), pp. 13–40; [Curt D.] Daniel, *op. cit.* ['HyperCalvinism and John Gill' (Univ. of Edinburgh: Ph.D. thesis, 1983)], pp. 777–829. The following argue that Calvin explicitly taught effective atonement or else his theology demanded it: Paul Helm, *Calvin and the Calvinists* (Edinburgh, Banner of Truth, 1982); 'Calvin and the Covenant: Unity and Continuity', *EQ*, 55, 1983, pp. 65–81; W. Robert Godfrey, 'Reformed Thought on the Extent of the Atonement to 1618', *WTJ*, 37, 1975, pp. 137–138; Roger Nicole, 'John Calvin's View of the Extent of the Atonement', *WTJ*, 47, 1985, pp. 197–225.[37]

Although most Calvin scholars take sides in this debate, I share the minority position of Letham: "My position is that Calvin was ambiguous or contradictory on the question but that he maintained the intrinsic efficacy of the atonement."[38] The statement implies that, although Letham and I view Calvin as noncommittal on the extent of the atonement, the position of limited atonement is a logical extension of Calvin's thought.

I pay tribute to my mentor John Calvin by testifying that twenty-five years after I wrote a book on his doctrine of the atonement,[39] that doctrine still influences my own teaching and writing. Beyond that I have most benefited from his example as a theologian in two areas: his eschewing speculation and seeking to base his theology on the exposition of Holy Scripture. It is a privilege to honor him on the five-hundredth anniversary of his birth.

37. Robert Letham, *The Work of Christ* (Downers Grove, IL: InterVarsity, 1993), 266 n. 5; the appendix is on 225–47.

38. Ibid.

39. *Calvin's Doctrine of the Atonement* (Phillipsburg, NJ: P&R, 1983).

II

Justification and Union with Christ

INSTITUTES 3.11–18
Richard B. Gaffin Jr.

In book 3, chapters 11–18 of Calvin's *Institutes* we have a matured treatment of the doctrine of justification from the first generation of the Protestant Reformation. One does not overstate to say that it has few peers and arguably is unsurpassed among numerous other excellent treatments that have appeared subsequently, particularly in the tradition of confessional Reformed orthodoxy, for which Calvin has proven to be such an important fountainhead figure. To provide a synopsis of these chapters that reflects on their contents is a daunting task under any circumstance. That is all the more so with the limited space at my disposal, and dictates something other than a continuous, section-by-section survey.

Addressing these chapters under the title "Justification and Union with Christ" might seem to be an undue narrowing of their scope or blurring of their controlling focus. That is not at all the case. Rather, not only the appropriateness but also the importance of doing so will emerge as we proceed. Nonetheless, this approach does mean that a number of particular issues addressed in this magisterial treatment of justification, each important and worthy of considerable discussion, will not be addressed, other than some of them tangentially. Of that I am keenly aware.

Justification in the *Institutes*—1536 to 1559

A brief overview of the treatment of justification in successive editions of the *Institutes* prior to the definitive 1559 edition provides a helpful perspective on our chapters. It is notable that in the first edition (1536) justification is not a separate topic. It is treated at the close of the opening chapter, on the law, structured primarily by a discussion of the Ten Commandments. This treatment flows out of a discussion of the summary of the law and has interspersed within it a discussion of the threefold use of the law. It is without a title of its own, and in fact can even be read as beginning within a paragraph.[1] I point this out not at all to suggest that at this time justification was not yet important or of only passing concern for Calvin. All one need do is read these pages to be convinced otherwise. But, clearly, at this point and within the overall design of what he had undertaken to do in the *Institutes*, justification had not yet assumed thematic prominence.

This situation changes strikingly with the substantial, roughly fourfold, expansion of the *Institutes* in the second, 1539 edition. Now and in subsequent editions (1543–45 and 1550–54) there is a separate chapter on justification (6 or 10, depending on the edition), positioned between chapters on repentance and the similarity and difference between the Old and New Testaments. This chapter, with its own title, "Concerning Justification by Faith and the Merits of Works" (*De justificatione fidei et meritis operum*), is approximately seven times the length of the treatment

---

1. John Calvin, *Institutes of the Christian Religion*, 1536 edition, trans. and annotated by F. L. Battles (Grand Rapids: Eerdmans, 1975), 29–35, 37–41. The titles of the six chapters are "The Law," "Faith," "Prayer," "The Sacraments," "The Five False Sacraments," and "Christian Freedom, Ecclesiastical Power, and Political Administration." Section headings within the chapters have been added by the translator.

in 1536 and consists of eighty-seven numbered sections, without subtitling or other internal subdivisions.[2]

The final, 1559 edition, in turn, represents an approximately 25 percent increase over the 1539 edition and subsequent Latin editions and printings (appearing between 1539 and 1554), with some variations among them but of basically the same length. Equally, perhaps more, important is the overall restructuring that takes place. What previously, since 1539, had been a single book of approximately twenty chapters (the number varies among the editions between seventeen and twenty-one, without significant changes in content), now for the first time has the multiple book-chapter-section format, familiar since to readers of this definitive Latin edition in its translation into numerous languages.

We are not left to speculate how Calvin himself viewed this substantial reconfiguration. In his prefatory remarks to the reader, he comments that the editing he had done previously, beginning with the second (1539) edition, was such that the work "has been enriched with some additions." But, he continues, "I was never satisfied until the work had been arranged in the order now set forth."[3]

This statement ought to be kept in mind for its likely bearing on his treatment of justification specifically. Apparently, his handling of that doctrine in 1559, in particular both its internal structuring and its placement in relation to other materials, afforded him a measure of satisfaction that had eluded him previously for twenty years. This treatment is expanded by about 15 percent, with the eighty-seven sections of preceding editions being increased to ninety-four and distributed over eight chapters, with titles. The additional material consists in large part of chapter 11, sections 5–12, which deal with the views of Osiander.

As noted above, prior to 1559, beginning with the expanded 1539 edition, justification was treated in a single lengthy chapter titled "Concerning

2. The 1536 edition and the subsequent Latin editions prior to 1559 (the latter presented together with individual variations between them noted) are in I. Calvinus, *Opera Quae Supersunt Omnia*, vol. 1, ed. G. Baum, E. Cunitz, E. Reuss, *Corpus Reformatorum* 29 (Brunswick: C. A. Schwetschke, 1863); see li–lviii for a synopsis, by topics, of all Latin editions; for the chapter on justification, 738–802.

3. John Calvin, *Institutes of the Christian Religion*, ed. J. T. McNeill, trans. F. L. Battles, 2 vols. (Philadelphia: Westminster, 1960), 1:3. All quotations will be from this translation, unless otherwise indicated.

Justification by Faith and the Merits of Works." None of the chapters in 1559 bear this title, though it is reflected in part in the negative reference to "the Merits of Works" in the title to chapter 15. Still, this faith-merit of works theme remains no less dominant and pervasive in 1559. In fact, seen in its entirety, Calvin's discussion of justification is fairly read as set polemically against Roman Catholic teaching that justification has its proximate source or basis in grace-assisted works, deemed meritorious, of the baptized Christian. This late-medieval system of meriting justification, formalized at the Council of Trent in 1547,[4] is ever on the horizon for Calvin, often being opposed implicitly when it is not being confronted directly.

Sections 1–4 of chapter 11 repay careful analysis. Structurally, they are fairly seen as introductory in a way that provides foundations and sets the direction for virtually everything that follows in our chapters. Accordingly, I will examine them, especially the first section, in some detail, by identifying prominent themes and emphases there, and, as space permits, also exploring some of them elsewhere throughout these chapters. Current debates about Calvin on justification as well as about the doctrine of justification more generally are in the background, although, necessarily, connections to these debates will for the most part be more implicit than elaborated. It needs also to be kept in mind that my assignment is justification in this part of the *Institutes*, not in Calvin as a whole. Certainly, I hope my treatment is not in any way at odds with the considerable pertinent material there is elsewhere both in the *Institutes* and in his commentaries, sermons, and numerous other occasional writings. But such materials can come into consideration only incidentally.[5]

4. See the decree and canons on justification (Sixth Session, 1547), e.g., in P. Schaff, "The Canons and Decrees of the Council of Trent," *The Creeds of Christendom*, 3 vols. (New York: Harper, 1983), 2:89–118. Calvin's lengthy response (on justification) is in "Acts of the Council of Trent with the Antidote," *Tracts and Treatises in Defense of the Reformed Faith*, trans. H. Beveridge (Grand Rapids: Eerdmans, 1958), 2:108–62.

In my view it is difficult to overemphasize the close link between Trent on justification and the immediately preceding decree on original sin (Fifth Session, 1546; *Creeds of Christendom*, 2:83–88). The Roman Catholic understandings of sin and justification stand and fall together. An abandonment of its semi-Pelagian position for a biblically sound view of the former would lead to an uncompromised *sola gratia*, thoroughly biblical revision of the latter.

5. Among recent broader treatments of Calvin on justification, though focused largely on our chapters, see A. N. S. Lane, "The Role of Scripture in Calvin's Doctrine

RICHARD B. GAFFIN JR.

Union with Christ and Twofold Grace

Section 1[6] begins with Calvin reminding his readers of what he has previously explained "with sufficient care," namely that "the one sole means of recovering salvation" left for those under the curse of the law is "in faith." He also recalls his discussion of faith and its attendant "benefits" and "fruits." No doubt, in view, at least primarily, are places in book 3 such as 3.2 and 3.3, on faith and regeneration by faith.[7] Then follows a summary of these matters, which needs to be quoted here in its entirety (725):

> Christ was given to us by God's generosity, to be grasped and possessed by us in faith. By partaking of him, we principally receive a double grace: namely, that being reconciled to God through Christ's blamelessness, we may have in heaven instead of a Judge a gracious Father; and secondly, that sanctified by his Spirit[8] we may cultivate blamelessness and purity of life.

This summary (*summa*) involves two accents that should not be missed. First and foremost is the focus on Christ, on his *person*. The saving benefits in view that Christ procures do not accrue to faith apart from his person. Specifically, they are received only as he, himself, by faith (*fide*), is "grasped and possessed." In other words, in view here is the believer's

---

of Justification," in C. Raynal, ed., *John Calvin and the Interpretation of Scripture*, Calvin Studies 10–11 (Grand Rapids: Calvin Studies Society, 2006), 368–84, and, overlapping, A. N. S. Lane, *Justification by Faith in Catholic–Protestant Dialogue* (London/New York: T. & T. Clark, 2002), 17–43, and pertinent literature cited in each.

6. All section headings as well as chapter subdivisions have been added by the editor (J. T. McNeill); the former, for the most part, have been taken over from those provided by Otto Weber in his German edition (see p. xx). Material quoted in the text will be followed by section and/or page number in parentheses.

7. It is not clear why the editor (725, n. 1) includes 2.12.1. It needs to be kept in mind that Calvin regularly uses "regeneration" in a broader sense than does subsequent Reformed theology beginning in the seventeenth century. He includes the ongoing renewal of the believer, equivalent in subsequent theology to sanctification in distinction from regeneration.

8. Battles's translation "Christ's spirit" is to be corrected in light of the original "eius Spiritu" (J. Calvin, *Opera Selecta*, ed. P. Barth and W. Niesel [Munich: Chr. Kaiser Verlag, 1959], 4:182—hereafter *OS* 4). "Spirit" should be capitalized, and the antecedent of "his" is more likely the Father than Christ (both the Allen and Beveridge translations have "his Spirit"). The reference is surely to the Holy Spirit.

union with Christ, about which we hear, emphatically and repeatedly, as Calvin's treatment of justification unfolds.

Secondly, by this union, this sharing of him,[9] believers "principally" or, as we might also translate, "above all" (*potissimum*) receive "a double grace" (*duplicem gratiam*). This twofold grace, Calvin will presently make clear, consists, each in a word, of justification and regeneration (= sanctification), each being described in this summary statement in terms of its outcome. For the former, justification, in place of an unreconciled heavenly judge believers have a gracious or propitious (*propitium*) Father. Since this twofold grace is "principal," apparently for Calvin it encompasses all other saving benefits of union with Christ.

This summary, with which Calvin opens his treatment of justification, expresses what may be described as "his triangulation of union with Christ, justification, and sanctification."[10] These three elements are fairly taken as points of reference that largely determine the framework of Calvin's thinking, all told, on the application of redemption, the personal appropriation of the finished salvation accomplished by Christ, with which he is formally occupied in book 3 of the *Institutes*. In particular, as we are seeing from the opening of chapter 11, they determine the framework of his thinking on justification.

This raises the large and important question of how these three elements relate to each other, a question that will occupy us, directly or indirectly, throughout the rest of this synopsis. But already, from Calvin's beginning summary, on this relational issue at least two things stand out. For one, union with Christ has precedence in the sense that the twofold grace is rooted in union and flows out of it. This grace is derivative; that is, it is received "by partaking of him." Secondly, as the twofold benefit of union, justification and sanctification are inseparable. As such, however, they are not confused but distinguished. Accenting inseparability, Calvin speaks not of two graces but of "twofold grace," in the singular, although later in this section he does refer to regeneration as "the second of these

---

9. *Cuius participatione* (OS 4:182).

10. M. A. Garcia, "Life In Christ: The Function of Union with Christ in the *Unio-Duplex Gratia* Structure of Calvin's Soteriology with Special Reference to the Relationship of Justification and Sanctification in Sixteenth-Century Context" (Ph.D. diss., University of Edinburgh, 2004), 236.

gifts" or, better, this "second grace,"[11] signaling distinction and a certain priority to justification. The nature of both this difference and inseparability, as well as the nature of the underlying union involved, Calvin will clarify as his discussion unfolds. But these observations already prompt us to speak of the basic union-twofold grace (*unio-duplex gratia*) structure of Calvin's applied soteriology.[12]

Directly following this summary statement Calvin, still in section 1, draws attention to a noteworthy feature of the overall structure of book 3, a feature present from 1539 on.[13] Prior to taking up justification, he has discussed regeneration (sanctification) at considerable length, saying what he deemed "sufficient" on the topic and mentioning justification only in passing. This way of proceeding is apparently counterintuitive, even contrary, to Reformation instincts, for which, in the face of Rome's suspending of justification on an ongoing process of sanctification, stressing the priority of justification to sanctification would appear to be crucial. It also seems at odds with what he himself will presently say about the pivotal importance of justification.

This way of ordering material in book 3, deciding to treat sanctification fully (chapters 3–10) before justification, has provoked considerable discussion about Calvin's motive(s) in doing so.[14] Here we may note that, whatever other factors may have been at work, his primary motivation, at least as he saw it, is plain enough from what he immediately goes on to say. He has proceeded as he has "because it was more to the point to understand first how little devoid of good works is the faith through which alone we obtain free righteousness by the mercy of God; and what is the nature of the good works of the saints, with which part of this question is concerned" (725–26). This clause bears careful scrutiny. First, Calvin says that he has discussed sanctification at length before justification in order to show that

11. *Secunda gratia* (*OS* 4:182).

12. See the penetrating discussion of M. A. Garcia, *Life in Christ: Union with Christ and Twofold Grace in Calvin's Theology* (Paternoster, 2008), chapter 1 and other pertinent literature cited there.

13. Notations in the text of the Battles translation, a valuable feature, indicate the origin of material by edition; see 1:xxvii.

14. See, most recently, the overview of K. Wübbenhorst and the literature cited there in "Calvin's Doctrine of Justification," in B. L. McCormack, ed., *Justification in Perspective: Historical Developments and Contemporary Challenges* (Grand Rapids: Baker, 2006) 117 n. 53.

faith does not lack good works. It was "to the point" (*ad rem*) to make clear the nature of saving faith "first," that is, before discussing justification. Why? One consideration is no doubt polemical. The constantly echoing charge from Rome at that time (and ever since) is that the Protestant doctrine of justification, of a graciously imputed righteousness received by faith alone, ministers spiritual slothfulness and indifference to holy living.

Calvin effectively counters that charge by dwelling at length (133 pages) on the nature of faith, particularly its inherent disposition and concern for holiness. This material is distinct (not separate) from the issue of justification and prior to discussing it in any length. He concerns himself extensively with sanctification and faith in its sanctified expressions, largely bypassing justification and saying little about the role of faith in justification. Calvin destroys Rome's charge by showing that faith, in its Protestant understanding, entails a disposition to holiness without explicit reference to its sole instrumental function in justification. This concern for godliness, an ongoing, ever-present concern in the life of the already justified believer, obviously follows justification, but it is not simply a consequence of justification. Calvin can proceed as he has in this fashion, treating sanctification at length before justification, because for him, as will presently be clear, "justification and sanctification were given to faith simultaneously and inseparably, though also variously, so that the order of their presentation was discretionary."[15]

In addition to this polemical strategy, another, more positive consideration is in view. It should not be missed that the faith "through which alone we obtain free righteousness by the mercy of God" is "little devoid of good works." In other words, sanctifying faith, faith functioning for holy living, is the same faith that justifies. Certainly, this does not mean that faith justifies because it sanctifies or as it functions in sanctification; the role of faith as the sole instrument in receiving justification, he makes clear elsewhere,[16] differs from its role in sanctification. But faith as justifying and faith as sanctifying are not different faiths, nor are these

15. G. Hunsinger, "A Tale of Two Simultaneities: Justification and Sanctification in Calvin and Barth," in Raynal, ed., *John Calvin and the Interpretation of Scripture*, 224 n. 5; see also my "Biblical Theology and the Westminster Standards," *Westminster Theological Journal* 65 (2003): 175–77.

16. Within our chapters: 11.7—733–34; 14.17—784; 14.21—787; 18.8—830.

exercises somehow separable. Further, to understand this and, correlatively, "the nature of the good works of the saints" is a part of the concern of "this question"—the question of *justification*. Pertinent to discussing justification, Calvin is saying here, is to clarify what place the believer's good works have, a question that he will discuss in some depth especially in chapter 16.

These observations prompt a further comment on a point already noted. As twin components of the grace received by being united to Christ, justification and sanctification are inseparable. Now it appears that they are simultaneous as well; inseparability involves a *simul*, simultaneity. Calvin knows nothing of a justification that is first settled and then is only subsequently followed by sanctification. Rather, given with this settled and irreversible justification, from the moment it takes place, is a disposition to godliness and holy living, no matter how weak and sin-plagued that disposition and how imperfectly manifested subsequently. This is so, as we have seen here, because of the nature of justifying faith and, more importantly, because of who Christ is, to whom faith unites.

If it needs to be said again, plainly, by the nature of the case, for Calvin sanctification as an ongoing, lifelong process follows justification, and in that sense justification is "prior" to sanctification, and the believer's good works can be seen as the fruits and signs of having been justified. Only those already justified are being sanctified. But this is not the same thing as saying, what Calvin does *not* say, that justification is the source of sanctification or that justification causes sanctification. That source, that cause is Christ by his Spirit, Christ, in whom, Calvin is clear in this passage, at the moment they are united to him by faith, sinners simultaneously receive a twofold grace and so begin an ongoing process of being sanctified just as they are now also definitively justified.

With this prefatory mix of considerations introduced, flowing out of matters previously treated, Calvin begins, toward the close of section 1, to give justification the thorough treatment due it. What needs to be kept in mind throughout, he says, is that justification is "the main hinge on which religion turns" (726).[17] Several comments are in order on this often-quoted statement. While the Battles translation provides an evocative image (the

17. *Praecipuum . . . sustinendae religionis cardinem* (OS 4:182).

"turning hinge"), it appears to give the original an unintended turn (or perhaps I should say, twist!). Over a wide range of uses, the verbal idea in view (*sustineo*) has the force of "support," "sustain," "maintain," or "bear."[18] The Allen translation probably has it most accurately, "the principal hinge by which religion is supported."[19]

However one decides the exact translation, Calvin plainly intends to highlight the central importance of justification. What figures prominently in Calvin's mind about that importance here appears from what he goes on to say immediately, right at the close of section 1. Without justification, expressed as the believer's settled and, by implication, favorable judicial relationship to God, and knowledge of that relationship, there is lacking a "foundation" (*fundamentum*) for salvation and piety.

With that noted, it is easy enough to lift this "principal hinge" and the following "foundation" statements out of context in the interests of maintaining the view that for Calvin justification is the cardinal and most basic blessing in the application of salvation, the fundamental blessing that gives rise to all others. But neither the wider context of his teaching in the *Institutes* and elsewhere, as we will sample the former, nor even the immediate context of section 1 will tolerate such a reading. The terms of the next to last sentence in section 1 must be noted. In possessing salvation, justification is a sine qua non, not the sole foundational consideration or even the chief article. However crucial, it is not the stand-alone foundation of salvation. As foundation, Calvin is clear from the outset in section 1, justification is a component, with regeneration, of the principal "twofold grace" that flows from the believer's underlying union with Christ. The "hinge" of justification, if I may put it this way, is not a "skyhook." It is anchored firmly, without in any way diminishing its pivotal importance, in that union.

This critical point is reinforced by noting that while the material in section 1 (apart from a single variant in wording) is intact from 1539 on,

18. *Oxford Latin Dictionary* (Oxford: Clarendon, 1968), 1892.
19. Calvin's own French edition (1560) reads, "le principal article de la religion Chrestienne" ("the principal article of the Christian religion"). The German translation of O. Weber has "den hauptsächlichen Pfeiler . . . auf dem unsere Gottesverehrung ruht" ("the main pillar on which our religion rests") and, similarly, the Dutch of A. Sizoo, "de voornaamste pijler . . . waarop de godsdienst rust" ("the main pillar on which religion rests").

in 1559 it is put in a fresh and deepened, though certainly not unexpected, light. This happens from the way in which it and chapters 11–18 as a whole are now, for the first time, to be read within the larger context of book 3. In particular, what we have been considering in section 1 is to be read in light of the outlook, as clearly sweeping as it is controlling, expressed at the very beginning of book 3, in particular chapter 1, sections 1–2, material that is new in 1559.[20] This reading given with the new disposition of material in book 3, we may say with little fear of undue speculation, is one reason why the 1559 edition gave Calvin his expressed measure of settled satisfaction, noted earlier, that he did not have with prior editions. On the point we are considering, Calvin, in his own estimation, expresses himself more adequately than he had previously.

Book 3 is titled "The Way in Which We Receive the Grace of Christ: What Benefits Come to Us from It, and What Effects Follow." This plainly shows that, having dealt, especially in the latter half of book 2 (chapters 9–17), with the finished work of Christ, the once-for-all accomplishment of salvation, Calvin understands himself to be concerned throughout book 3 with the application or personal appropriation of salvation ("the grace of Christ"), its "benefits" and consequent "effects." All told, his concern now is with "the way" (modo, "mode," "manner," "method") in which believers "receive" this grace, in which this salvation is appropriated. With this concern restated in the opening words of 3.1.1, the very next sentence reads, "First, we must understand that as long as Christ remains outside of us, and we are separated from him, all that he has suffered and done for the salvation of the human race remains useless and of no value to us" (537).

In my view it is difficult to exaggerate the importance of this sentence for Calvin's soteriology as a whole. Positioned as it is at the opening of book 3, it expresses what is most fundamental for him, the consideration underlying all others within the application of redemption. This most deeply decisive consideration, put negatively here, is that Christ not remain "outside us," that we not be "separated from him." Or, to

---

20. Barth and Niesel (OS 4:1), followed in the Battles translation, propose that this material stems from the 1536 edition, but the connection is of the loosest and most general sort, especially so far as wording and sentence composition are concerned. To see this, one need only compare 3.1.1–2 (537–39) with Institutes of the Christian Religion, 1536 edition, 57–58.

express it positively, as he presently does, that "we grow into one body (*in unum*[21]) with him." Here Calvin, as his point of departure for all that he has to say in book 3, brings into view and highlights the union that exists between Christ and believers. So central and pivotal is this union for the application of redemption that, again expressing it negatively, he can even say that without it the saving work of Christ "remains useless and of no value."

This union, he immediately goes on to make clear, is "obtained by faith" (*fide*), as it does not exist apart from or prior to faith but is given with, in fact is inseparable from, faith. This mention of faith, and the key role accorded to it, prompts Calvin, still within this opening section, to touch on what would become a central question in subsequent discussions about the *ordo salutis*, namely the origin of faith, giving rise eventually in Reformed theology to the doctrine of regeneration in a narrower sense. We observe "that not all indiscriminately embrace that communion with Christ which is offered through the gospel." Why? Not because of some differentiating factor on our side. The answer is not to be found by looking into ourselves or contemplating the mystery of human freedom and willing. Rather, consistent with his uniform teaching elsewhere about the total inability of the will because of sin, we must "climb higher" and consider "the secret energy of the Spirit" (*arcana Spiritus efficacia*). Faith is Spirit-worked, sovereignly and efficaciously.

Union with Christ, then, is forged by the Spirit's working faith in us, a faith that "puts on" Christ (citing Gal. 3:27), that embraces Christ as he is offered to faith in the gospel. Faith is the bond of that union seen from our side. "To sum up, the Holy Spirit is the bond by which Christ effectually unites us to himself" (538). Subsequently, within our chapters, as we will see (3.11.10—737), he will categorize this union as "spiritual" and "mystical."

This, at its core, is Calvin's *ordo salutis*: union with Christ by Spirit-worked faith. From the overall vantage point provided at the opening of book 3, justification is by faith (alone) because union with Christ is by faith (alone), and that union brings with it justification. Section 1 of 3.11, as we have seen, also begins to make that clear enough.

21. *OS* 4:1.

In sections 2–4 Calvin proceeds by defining and further explaining the basic concept of justification by faith, with support from Scripture. An accent throughout is on the purely forensic character of justification. In principle, justification is either by faith or by works, and justified *coram Deo* is the person "who is both reckoned righteous in God's judgment and has been accepted on account of his righteousness" (726). Since for sinners justification by their works is now excluded, "justified by faith is he who, excluded from the righteousness of works, grasps the righteousness of Christ through faith, and clothed in it, appears in God's sight not as a sinner but as a righteous man" (726–27). "Therefore, we explain justification simply as the acceptance with which God receives us into his favor as righteous men. And we say that it consists in the remission of sins and the imputation of Christ's righteousness" (727). Again, accenting the forensic, "Therefore, 'to justify' means nothing else than to acquit of guilt him who was accused, as if his innocence were confirmed" (728).

These defining statements, from the opening of Calvin's treatment of justification, set its direction. Toward its close, in 3.17.8, he offers what appears to be the single fullest definition, at least within the *Institutes*, drawing together not all but significant threads in the discussion that has preceded: "But we define justification as follows: the sinner, received into communion with Christ, is reconciled to God by his grace, while, cleansed by Christ's blood, he obtains forgiveness of sins, and clothed with Christ's righteousness as if it were his own, he stands confident before the heavenly judgment seat" (811). In the light of these definitions and basic explanatory statements, we can explore further the relationship between union and justification.

Union, Imputation, and Justification

The explanatory statement at the very end of 11.2 (727), quoted in the next to last paragraph above, is the first occurrence in our chapters of the word "imputation." Previously in that section Calvin has spoken, as he will repeatedly subsequently, of righteousness being "reckoned," and, beginning in section 3, again repeatedly thereafter, of righteousness being "imputed" to believers. These two ideas, "reckoning" and "imputing,"

260

"imputation," are close, even overlapping, in their meaning. However, for Calvin they are not simply identical. In their close affinity he distinguishes them. That—a noteworthy distinction—is clear just beyond the middle of section 3. God's justifying action, he says, "absolves us . . . by the imputation of righteousness,[22] so that we who are not righteous in ourselves may be reckoned as such in Christ" (728).

Here, and throughout his discussion, imputation is antecedent to reckoning. The imputation of righteousness, Christ's righteousness as imputed, is the immediate ground or basis of the reckoning of righteousness, of being reckoned as righteous. It seems fair to say, then, that for Calvin justification, the justifying act itself, involves the distinct moments of imputation and reckoning, related to each other as just indicated. This seems to approach closely the notion emerging in later Reformed theology of justification as a constitutive declaration—it should be accented, for both Calvin and others subsequently, a *forensically* constitutive declaration.[23]

In view of Calvin's distinguishing as he does between imputation and (judicial) reckoning, it might be supposed that for him imputation is in fact nonforensic, that "the matter of imputation was participationist not forensic," that Calvin (like Luther) "saw clearly that 'imputation' was a nonforensic term with forensic consequences."[24] Now certainly, it is true to say that for Calvin union with Christ is "the precondition for imputation."[25] For him justification is ever in view, as we have already seen from the outset in 3.11.1, as a component benefit of the "twofold grace"

22. From the immediate and broader context, plainly this imputed righteousness is Christ's specifically.

23. E.g., J. Murray, *The Epistle to the Romans* (Grand Rapids: Eerdmans, 1959), 1: 352–53: "It is declarative in such a way that it is also imputative. . . . The justifying act is constitutive. . . . Hence we may sum up by saying that justification of the ungodly is constitutively and imputatively declarative." On this understanding, the constitutive does not import a nonforensic or transformative element into justification.

24. G. Hunsinger, "Calvin's Doctrine of Justification: Is It Really Forensic?" (unpublished paper delivered at the Twelfth Biennial Calvin Colloquium, Erskine Theological Seminary, January 27–28, 2006; cited here with the author's permission), 7, 22; "Imputation through participation formed the nonforensic center that governed his doctrine of justification" (9). My comments here address a possible, even plausible construal of this language. They should not be read as a fair or adequate response to the case carefully argued in Hunsinger's paper. To interact with that argumentation would require more space than I have at my disposal and, more importantly, the reader would need to have access to the paper.

25. Ibid., 8.

that stems from union. So, then, imputation, included in justification, is likewise given with that union. That is clear throughout. Further, we may fairly say that "For Calvin *participatio Christi* was prior to imputation, and imputation prior to judgment."[26]

But, in putting matters this way, the question needing to be asked is, How exactly does he understand these priorities? It is true, as we have seen (3.1.1—537–38), that the union Calvin has in view is a Spirit-worked bond between the believer and Christ. It is a "spiritual bond" (3.11.10—737) in the sense of being effected and maintained by the Holy Spirit. It is unwarranted, however, to draw the conclusion that because, as we have seen, *within justification* the imputation of righteousness is antecedent to the reckoning of righteousness, therefore imputation is nonforensic. This intrudes into justification a nonforensic element that Calvin is everywhere intent on excluding. The twin benefits of the *duplex gratia* that stem from (Spirit-worked) union, justification and sanctification/ongoing Spirit-worked renewal, are as distinct from each other and unconfused as they are undeniably inseparable. In fact, it seems fair to Calvin to say that this twofold distinction (between justification and sanctification) is, in effect, the distinction between grace as forensic and nonforensic, a distinction that as such is irreducible. Justification, imputation included, is purely forensic. As such, stemming from union with Christ, it is also participationist.

"Participationist not forensic" suggests a disjunction that, as a reading of what he has written, Calvin, I suspect, would likely find puzzling to say the least. The basic *unio-duplex gratia* structure of his applied soteriology is such that the participatory (union) has both forensic (justifying) and nonforensic (sanctifying, renovative) dimensions or aspects, without any confusion or interpenetration of these two aspects. To view union/the participatory as introducing, by imputation, a non-forensic and so presumably Spirit-worked element into an otherwise forensic justification is to blur a basic distinction that Calvin was intent on maintaining, a blurring, further, that he would see as undermining the stability of a fully gracious justification.[27]

26. Ibid., 9.

27. "Nonforensic" is a negative description. To say only that, other than that imputation is "participationist," and given the spiritual character of that participation or union, seems to suggest that, as a transitive reality, imputation is pneumatic and effects a work of the Spirit

A good test passage in this regard, it seems, is the last section (23) of chapter 11, one that serves to summarize important elements developed throughout the chapter as a whole. Justification, characterized here as being "by the intercession of Christ's righteousness" (cf. 3.11.3—728; 3.14.9—776), it is "worth carefully noting," amounts to saying that "man is not righteous in himself but because the righteousness of Christ is communicated to him by imputation" (753). This communication or sharing therefore excludes, he states in the very next sentence, a "frivolous notion."[28] This is the notion "that man is justified by faith because by faith[29] he shares the Spirit of God, by whom he is rendered righteous." This juxtaposition could hardly be more pointed, or its sense clearer. Set in opposition are two notions of being counted or rendered righteous—by the imputation of Christ's righteousness or by sharing[30] in the Spirit. The latter is dismissed decisively, with the further comment, "This [the frivolous notion] is too contrary to the above doctrine ever to be reconciled to it." Here the thought that imputation is nonforensic or somehow a nonjudicial transfer or communication is plainly excluded. The transfer effected by imputation, specifically "the righteousness of Christ . . . communicated . . . by imputation," is nonpneumatic and purely forensic.

At issue here is that "our righteousness is not in us but in Christ." This, as much as any formulation of as few words, captures what is at the heart of Calvin's understanding of justification: "not in us but in Christ." Certainly, as he immediately adds, "we possess it only because we are partakers in Christ," accenting once again the underlying and controlling union. But this "it," the righteousness of those who are "sharers of Christ,"[31] is, for each of them, "righteousness outside himself" and as he is "destitute of righteousness in himself" (with an appeal to 2 Cor. 5:21). He has made that clear in the previous paragraph in denying that it has anything to

---

within the believer. But that appears to verge closely on some sort of infusion, a notion that Calvin everywhere rejects vigorously.

28. *Nugamentum* (*OS* 4:206; Beveridge has "absurd dogma").

29. The antecedent of *illa* is not *Christi iustitia* ("Christ's righteousness") in the preceding sentence (as Battles appears to have taken it), but almost certainly *fide*, two words earlier (so both Allen and Beveridge).

30. *Participat* (ibid.).

31. *Christi . . . participes* (ibid).

do with sharing or participating in the Spirit. The righteousness of the law fulfilled "in us," the "only fulfillment" Paul alludes to (Rom. 8:3–4),[32] to the exclusion of any work of the Spirit in us, is "that which we obtain through imputation."

Calvin walks a fine line here, but in doing so maintains a clear distinction. As we are "in him" (and he "in us"), our righteousness in justification is "outside of us."[33] Union is Spirit-forged, a pneumatic reality, but the imputation given with that union is not. Imputation does not introduce a nonforensic component into justification. It is not a matter of what is pneumatically effected in us. Rather, imputation is a judicial transfer that preserves the purely forensic nature of justification and at the same time ensures that the righteousness reckoned in justification is resident solely in Christ, in his person, and not somehow within the person of the sinner united to him.

In the middle of the second paragraph of section 23, Calvin goes on to say concerning imputation, "For in such a way does the Lord Christ share his righteousness with us that, in some wonderful manner, he pours into us enough of his power to meet the judgment of God." Admittedly, this statement and the language he uses, taken by itself, could be read in a nonforensic, pneumatic-transformative, even infusionist, sense. But that would fly fully in the face of everything else he writes in the immediate context and would attribute to him the view he is intent here on excluding by his appeal, as noted, to Romans 8:3–4 in the sentence preceding, and to Romans 5:19 in the sentence following.

Probably Calvin expresses himself here as he does to accent the forensic power of imputation, the full reality of the judicial transaction it effects, such that, as he goes on to say, "the obedience of Christ is reckoned to us as if it were our own (ac si nostra)."[34] At any rate, his intention is clear from Ambrose's "beautifully stated" illustration, with which he closes this section: the believer's righteousness in justification is like Jacob clothed not

32. Calvin's understanding of these verses here (and in his Romans commentary, *Commentaries on the Epistle of Paul the Apostle to the Romans* [Grand Rapids: Eerdmans, 1948], 283) is probably not correct. But that does not invalidate his theological point here, supported by Scripture, in my view, on other grounds.

33. See the penetrating discussion of these and related matters in W. van't Spijker, "'Extra nos' en 'in nobis' bij Calvijn in pneumatologisch licht," in *Geest, woord en kerk* (Kampen: Kok, 1991), 114–28. My thanks to Ron Gleason for alerting me to this essay.

34. *OS* 4.207.

in his own but his brother's garments that he might receive the blessing of Isaac. An "alien" righteousness indeed! "And we in like manner hide under the precious purity of our first-born brother, Christ, so that we may be attested righteous in God's sight" (753–54).

Within our chapters, in the midst of his treatment of the views of Osiander (3.11.10), is the fullest single passage, and certainly the most striking, in expressing the relationship between union, justification, and imputation, a passage that also serves to focus key aspects of this relationship. It begins with "I confess that we are deprived . . ." (736, bottom) and continues to ". . . fellowship of righteousness with him" (737). Consulting it will be helpful for the comments that follow.

Here justification could not be valued more highly; it is an "utterly incomparable good." Yet it is not that in splendid judicial isolation, as it were, involving a solitary imputative act. Rather, we are left "deprived" of it, "until Christ is made ours." Unmistakable is the echo of the second sentence in 3.1.1 ("as long as Christ remains outside of us, and we are separated from him, all that he has suffered and done . . . remains useless and of no value to us"). In the actual possession of justification this union is what is deeply and ultimately decisive, and so it has "the highest degree of importance."

The union in view is described in a full multiplicity of other ways. It is the "joining together of Head and members," the "indwelling of Christ in our hearts," our being "sharers with him in the gifts with which he has been endowed." It is to "put on Christ," to be "engrafted into his body," in short, to be made "one with him." It is, categorically, "mystical union" and, as such, just beyond this passage, a "spiritual bond."

This Spirit-worked union or bond, however, does not exclude imputation or make it somehow redundant. Rather, on its forensic side, union is a "fellowship of righteousness," and it is that by imputation. "We do not, therefore, contemplate him outside ourselves from afar in order that his righteousness may be imputed to us." Here Christ's righteousness imputed is alien or other in the sense that it is his doing, his obedience, not ours. But in another sense, in union with him, it is not alien at all. Union brings justification as a forensic fellowship, a sharing in Christ's righteousness, and it does so by imputation.

Some further comment, necessarily brief here, is in order at this point on Calvin's treatment of Osiander on justification. As noted earlier, the new material on justification in the 1559 *Institutes* consists in large part of this treatment in 3.11, sections 5–12. Noteworthy is the placing of this lengthy critique directly following the introductory sections 1–4. With the preliminary groundwork for his entire treatment of justification in place, the very first matter of substance he chooses to take up is the position of Osiander. Why? Why before giving attention in depth to anything else, attention to the views of a deceased (putative) Lutheran rather than, say, to Roman Catholic teaching, Trent, for instance, that necessitated the Reformation? In answer, several factors are no doubt at work, but they all have in common that they point to the controlling importance Calvin places on union with Christ and on properly understanding that union, particularly in its relationship to justification.

Osiander's views on justification appeared in late 1550 and sparked immediate controversy.[35] This was Calvin's first opportunity to respond to these views in the *Institutes*, since the previous (fourth) edition had appeared earlier in 1550. This response may have had a measure of added urgency because of a perceived similarity in viewpoint, by some in the meantime, between him and Osiander. But primarily it afforded him the opportunity positively, in contrast, to set out his own views.

Briefly stated, in Calvin's words, Osiander's view of justification is that "we are substantially righteous in God by the infusion both of his essence and of his quality" (730). This is a fair representation. Justifying righteousness is, in Osiander's own words, "essential righteousness." In his view, union with Christ is sharing in Christ's essence, by which his righteousness, specifically the righteousness of his divine nature, is communicated.

Calvin's critique is relentless. This is not because he stresses to the point of exaggeration his distance from a view about which he is forced to recognize, to his anxious discomfort, agreement at a number of points. Rather, he is clearly driven here by the conviction, *corruptio optimi pes-*

---

35. The secondary literature is extensive; see Lane, "Role of Scripture," 368 n. 2, par. 2, and Battles, 729 n. 5; for more detailed discussions of Calvin's interaction, see, e.g., Hunsinger, "Calvin's Doctrine," 10–21, and Garcia, *Life in Christ*, 197–252, with the literature each cites.

sima ("the corruption of the best is the worst"). Any appearance of agreement is no more than formal. Osiander's misunderstanding of union and justification is thoroughly vitiated by the most serious and pernicious errors. From the opening sentence of section 5 the notion of "essential righteousness" is, in Battles's somewhat colorful translation, "some strange monster."[36] This is so, ontologically, because the underlying view of union, akin to Manichaeism, breaks down the Creator-creature distinction (730). No less seriously, soteriologically—and this is where the emphasis falls in Calvin's critique—this view denies the value and even the necessity of "Christ's obedience and sacrificial death," done in his human nature. Further, Osiander's "essential righteousness" bases justification on something done within or transfused into the Christian. Accordingly, his attendant notion of double righteousness breaks down the irreducible distinction between justifying and sanctifying righteousness by confusing pardoning and regenerating grace (732, 738–41). All told, the "strange monster" in the opening sentence of section 5 leads eventually to the closing sentence of section 12: "In short, whoever wraps up two kinds of righteousness in order that miserable souls may not repose wholly in God's mere mercy, crowns Christ in mockery with a wreath of thorns."

Calvin's critique is so unsparing because he recognizes in the position of Osiander an abandonment of the Reformation understanding of justification. It is essentially the Roman Catholic doctrine in other garb—the proximate suspension of justification on righteousness resident in the believer. And he recognizes that the answer to both is the "free imputation" (731, 738) of Christ's righteousness, wrought in his death and resurrection. That imputed righteousness Osiander "despises" and Rome has anathematized. But it is critically necessary to preserve a purely forensic justification. The settled security and "happiness" of believers are the result of their being "righteous, not intrinsically but by imputation" (739).[37] All told, as the result of imputation, "This is a wonderful plan of justification that, covered by the righteousness of Christ,

36. *Monstrum nescio quod* (OS 4:185); Allen has, "I know not what monstrous notion of . . ."; Beveridge, "a kind of monstrosity termed . . . ."
37. *Iustus . . . non re ipsa, sed imputatione* (OS 4:193).

they should not tremble at the judgment they deserve, and that while they rightly condemn themselves, they should be accounted righteous outside themselves" (740–41).[38]

The root error of Osiander on justification lies in his understanding of union with Christ, already noted. Opposing that error affords Calvin the opportunity to elaborate his own view of union, as we have already seen he does in section 10. Early on in his critique, in section 5, he observes that Osiander's self-deception comes from misconceiving "the bond of this unity," and that "all his difficulties" are easily resolved by recognizing that we are "united with Christ by the secret power of his Spirit" (730). In rejecting the view of Osiander, Calvin makes clear that Spirit-worked union is such that it preserves the personal distinction between Christ and the believers. Thus it is a union that insures that justifying righteousness is his accomplishment, not theirs, and is theirs solely by being imputed to them.

In the context of this rebuttal of Osiander, Calvin uses a metaphor for the union—twofold grace structure of his applied soteriology that seems difficult to improve on (3.11.6—732): Christ, our righteousness, is the sun; justification, its light; sanctification, its heat. The sun is at once the sole source of both such that its light and heat are inseparable. At the same time, only light illumines and only heat warms, not the reverse. Both are always present, without the one becoming the other; "reason itself forbids us to transfer the peculiar qualities of the one to the other."

The nature of our union with Christ is such that justification and sanctification coexist, without the "confusion of the two kinds of grace that Osiander forces upon us," and yet "in a mutual and indivisible connection." Why? Again, not simply because as a consequence of forgiving sinners, a consequence that might otherwise be separable from that forgiveness, God has decided that, in addition and subsequently, he will also renew them. Rather, justification and sanctification are inseparable because "Christ cannot be torn into parts." Or as Calvin puts these considerations later (3.16.1—798), "Do you wish, then, to attain righteousness [justification] in Christ? You must first possess Christ; but you cannot possess him without being made partaker in his sanctifica-

38. *Iusti extra se censeantur* (OS 4:195).

tion, because he cannot be divided into pieces." The "triangulation" of union, justification, and sanctification could hardly be expressed more clearly; the controlling priority of Spirit-worked union is plain ("you must first possess Christ"), involving the integral inseparability, without confusion, of justification and sanctification. There is no partial union with Christ, no sharing in only some of his benefits. If believers do not have the whole Christ, they have no Christ; unless they share in all of his benefits they share in none of them.

It is striking that in rejecting Osiander's view of justifying righteousness, rooted, as he sees it, in a seriously false understanding of union, Calvin is not led to reconsider or even tone down on his own understanding of union in relation to justification. Rather, he asserts that union all the more resolutely and emphatically. He could do no other. For he recognized—because he understood Scripture so well, especially the apostle Paul—that the Reformation understanding of justification—justification based exclusively on the forensically imputed righteousness of Christ and received by faith alone—stands or falls with the believer's underlying union with Christ, properly understood.

12

APPROPRIATING SALVATION: THE SPIRIT, FAITH AND ASSURANCE, AND REPENTANCE

INSTITUTES 3.1–3, 6–10
JOEL R. BEEKE

B ook 3 of the *Institutes* has a fascinating title: "The Way in Which We Receive the Grace of Christ: What Benefits Come to Us from It, and What Effects Follow." In the opening three chapters Calvin answers the fundamental question of how we can appropriate salvation personally. François Wendel summarizes the question this way: "The Christ having made satisfaction for our sins, and having by his merits won salvation for us, how can we appropriate this salvation and receive the grace that accompanies it?"[1] Calvin answers this question about the basics of subjective, experiential sal-

1. François Wendel, *Calvin* (London: Collins, 1963), 234.

vation by addressing three subjects: the Holy Spirit as the bond that unites us to Christ (3.1), the nature of faith and assurance (3.2), and the doctrine of repentance (3.3).

The Holy Spirit (3.1)

John Calvin's *Institutes* has earned him the title "the preeminent systematician of the Protestant Reformation." His reputation as an intellectual, however, is too often disassociated from the vital spiritual and pastoral context in which he wrote his theology. For Calvin, theological understanding and practical piety, truth, and usefulness, are inseparable. Theology primarily deals with knowledge—knowledge of God and of ourselves—but there is no true knowledge where there is no true piety.[2]

Calvin's concept of piety (*pietas*) is rooted in the knowledge of God and includes attitudes and actions that are directed to the adoration and service of God. Right attitudes include heartfelt worship, saving faith, filial fear, prayerful submission, and reverential love.[3] "I call 'piety' that reverence joined with love of God which the knowledge of his benefits induces," Calvin concludes (3.2.14).[4]

This love and reverence for God is a necessary concomitant to any knowledge of him and embraces all of life and its actions. As Calvin says, "The whole life of Christians ought to be a sort of practice of godliness."[5] Thus, for Calvin *pietas* includes a host of related themes,

2. The opening paragraphs of this section are a condensed summary of my chapter on "Calvin's Piety," in *The Cambridge Companion to John Calvin*, ed. Donald K. McKim (Cambridge: University Press, 2004), 125–52.

3. Lucien Joseph Richard, *The Spirituality of John Calvin* (Atlanta: John Knox, 1974), 100–101; Sou-Young Lee, "Calvin's Understanding of *Pietas*," in *Calvinus Sincerioris Religionis Vindex*, ed. W. H. Neuser and B. G. Armstrong (Kirksville, MO: Sixteenth Century Studies, 1997), 226–33; H. W. Simpson, "*Pietas* in the *Institutes* of Calvin," in *Reformational Tradition: A Rich Heritage and Lasting Vocation* (Potchefstroom: Potchefstroom University for Christian Higher Education, 1984), 179–91.

4. John Calvin, *Institutes of the Christian Religion*, ed. John T. McNeill and trans. F. L. Battles (Philadelphia: Westminster, 1960), book 3, chapter 2, section 14. For Calvin's Latin works, see *Opera quae supersunt omnia*, ed. Guilielmus Baum, Eduardus Cunitz, and Eduardus Reuss, vols. 29–87 in *Corpus Reformatorum* (Brunswick: C. A. Schwetschke et filium, 1863–1900) hereafter, CO.

5. *Institutes* 3.19.2.

such as filial piety in human relationships, and respect and love for the image of God in human beings.

The goal of piety, as well as the entire Christian life, is the glorifying of God—perceiving and reflecting the glory that shines in God's attributes, in the structure of the world, and in the death and resurrection of Jesus Christ (3.2.1). Glorifying God supersedes personal salvation for every truly pious person.[6] This goal of glorifying God is possible, however, only if one is united with Jesus Christ. Such piety is evident in those who recognize through experiential faith that they have been accepted in Christ and engrafted into his body by the grace of God. In this "mystical union" (*unio mystica*), the Lord claims them as his own in life and in death. They become God's people and members of Christ's body by the power of the Holy Spirit.

Since, for Calvin, piety is rooted in the believer's union with Christ, this union must be our starting point in understanding salvation.[7] None of the subsequent elements of the *ordo salutis*, such as justification, sanctification, and perseverance, are possible without the union with Christ that the Spirit effects through faith. Calvin says, "We must understand that as long as Christ remains outside of us, and we are separated from him, all that he has suffered and done for the salvation of the human race remains useless and of no value for us" (3.1.1). Such a union is possible, however, because Christ took on our human nature, filling it with his virtue. Union with Christ in his humanity is historical, ethical, and personal, but not essential. There is no crass mixture (*crassa mixtura*) of human substance between Christ and us. We are not absorbed into Christ nor united to him in such a way that our human personalities are annulled even in the slightest degree. Nonetheless, Calvin states, "Not only does he cleave to us by an indivisible bond of fellowship, but with a wonderful communion, day by day, he grows more and more into one body with us, until he becomes completely one with us" (3.2.24). This union is one of the gospel's greatest mysteries.[8] Because of the

6. CO 26:693.

7. Howard G. Hageman, "Reformed Spirituality," in *Protestant Spiritual Traditions*, ed. Frank C. Senn (New York: Paulist, 1986), 61.

8. Dennis Tamburello points out that "at least seven instances occur in the *Institutes* where Calvin uses the word *arcanus* or *incomprehensibilis* to describe union with Christ" (2.12.7;

fountain of Christ's perfection in their nature, the pious may, by faith, draw whatever they need for their sanctification.

The heartbeat of Calvin's practical theology and piety is communion (*communio*) with Christ. This involves participation (*participatio*) in his benefits, which are inseparable from union with Christ.[9] The concepts of *communio* and *participatio* helped shape Calvin's understanding of regeneration, faith, justification, sanctification, assurance, election, and the church. He could scarcely speak of any doctrine apart from union and communion with Christ. David Willis-Watkins notes: "Calvin's doctrine of union with Christ is one of the most consistently influential features of his theology and ethics, if not the single most important teaching that animates the whole of his thought and his personal life."[10]

Union and communion with Christ is realized only through Spirit-worked faith. It is actual union and communion not because believers participate in the essence of Christ's nature,[11] but because the Spirit of Christ unites believers so intimately to Christ that they become as flesh of his flesh and bone of his bone (Eph. 5:30). Indeed, the spiritual union with Christ that the Holy Spirit forges within us is even closer than physical union. Calvin writes,

> Let us know the unity that we have with our Lord Jesus Christ; to wit, that he wills to have a common life with us, and that what he has should be ours: nay, that he even wishes to dwell in us, not in imagination, but in effect; not in earthly fashion but spiritually; and that whatever may

---

3.11.5; 4.17.1, 9, 31, 33; 4.19.35); *Union with Christ: John Calvin and the Mysticism of St. Bernard* (Louisville: Westminster/John Knox, 1994), 89, 144. See also William Borden Evans, "Imputation and Impartation: The Problem of Union with Christ in Nineteenth-Century American Reformed Theology" (Ph.D. diss., Vanderbilt University, 1996), 6–68.

9. Willem van't Spijker, "*Extra nos* and *in nos* by Calvin in a Pneumatological Light," in *Calvin and the Holy Spirit*, ed. Peter DeKlerk (Grand Rapids: Calvin Studies Society, 1989), 39–62; Merwyn S. Johnson, "Calvin's Ethical Legacy," in *The Legacy of John Calvin*, ed. David Foxgrover (Grand Rapids: Calvin Studies Society, 2000), 63–83.

10. David Willis-Watkins, "The *Unio Mystica* and the Assurance of Faith according to Calvin," in *Calvin: Erbe und Auftrag: Festschrift für Wilhelm Heinrich Neuser zum 65. Geburtstag*, ed. Willem van't Spijker (Kampen: Kok, 1991), 78.

11. Calvin roundly defeats Osiander's doctrine of essential righteousness with Christ in *Institutes* 3.11.5–12.

befall, he so labors by the virtue of his Holy Spirit that we are united with him more closely than are the limbs with the body.[12]

The culmination of this complete and entire union with Christ in both body and soul will be fully realized in our resurrection from the dead on the judgment day.[13]

Thus, Christ and the Spirit colabor for our salvation. Though distinct, they are inseparable. Calvin moves easily from saying "The Spirit dwelling in us" to "Christ dwelling in us" (3.2.39). Jesus Christ is the unique bearer and bestower of the Spirit. Every action of the Spirit is, in essence, the action of Christ. The Spirit bestows nothing of a saving nature upon us apart from Christ, and Christ bestows on us nothing of a saving nature but through the Spirit.[14] This is hinted at already in Calvin's title for 3.1, "The Things Spoken concerning Christ Profit Us by the Secret Working of the Spirit." Christ works salvation through the Spirit, and the Holy Spirit works salvation for Christ in sinners' hearts (3.1.1).

This collaboration between Christ and the Spirit is reflected in 3.1.2 and 3.1.3. The Spirit himself, in his "whole fullness," is given by the Father to Christ in a "special way," so that we, through the "Spirit of sanctification," might each be given the Spirit "according to the measure of Christ's gift" (3.1.2). The Spirit's work in us then results in our separation from the world and in our being brought by faith and hope into our eternal inheritance (3.1.2). All this is reflected in the very titles Scripture gives the Holy Spirit, such as the "spirit of adoption," "the guarantee and seal" of our inheritance, "water," "oil," and "anointing" (3.1.3).

Only the Spirit can unite Christ in heaven with the believer on earth. This is the Spirit's principal work—a work that he accomplishes in those who believe (3.1.4; 3.2.8). Just as the Spirit united heaven and earth in the incarnation, so in regeneration the Spirit raises the elect from earth to commune with Christ in heaven and brings Christ into the hearts and

---

12. Cited in Wendel, *Calvin*, 235.

13. *Commentary* on 1 Cor. 6:15, in *Calvin's Commentaries*, 22 vols. (Grand Rapids: Baker, 1979).

14. Jelle Faber, "The Saving Work of the Holy Spirit in Calvin," in *Calvin and the Holy Spirit*, ed. Peter DeKlerk (Grand Rapids: Calvin Studies Society, 1989), 3.

lives of the elect on earth.[15] Communion with Christ is always the result of the Spirit's work—a work that is astonishing, albeit not comprehensible.[16] The Holy Spirit is thus the link that binds the believer to Christ and the channel through which Christ is communicated to the believer (3.1.1). Calvin writes to Peter Martyr: "We grow up together with Christ into one body, and he shares his Spirit with us, through whose hidden operation he has become ours. Believers receive this communion with Christ at the same time as their calling. But they grow from day to day more and more in this communion, in proportion to the life of Christ growing within them."[17]

Calvin moved beyond Luther in this emphasis on communion with Christ. Calvin stressed that, by his Spirit, Christ empowers those who are united with him by faith. Being "engrafted into the death of Christ, we derive from it a secret energy, as the twig does from the root," he writes. The believer "is animated by the secret power of Christ; so that Christ may be said to live and grow in him; for as the soul enlivens the body, so Christ imparts life to his members."[18]

From God's perspective, the Spirit is the bond between Christ and believers, whereas, from our perspective, faith is the bond. Calvin asserts that these perspectives do not clash with each other, since one of the Spirit's principal operations is to work faith in a sinner: "Faith itself has no other source than the Spirit" (3.1.4). Human initiative, therefore, cannot contribute to this work; rather, faith is an entirely supernatural gift given by the Spirit. Without the Spirit's work in us through the creation of faith in Christ, all our knowledge would be worthless. Only by the Spirit's faith-creating work can we truly come to know the Redeemer. Thus, "the virtue and the hidden working of the Holy Spirit is the cause of our enjoyment of Christ and of all his benefits."[19]

The Holy Spirit always uses the faith he gives us to unite us with Christ and to give us freedom to appropriate Christ's benefits. This faith

15. *Institutes* 4.17.6; *Commentary* on Acts 15:9.
16. *Commentary* on Eph. 5:32.
17. "Calvinus Vermilio" (#2266, 8 Aug 1555), CO 15:723–24.
18. CO 50:199. See also Barbara Pitkin, *What Pure Eyes Could See: Calvin's Doctrine of Faith in Its Exegetical Context* (New York: Oxford University Press, 1999).
19. Cited in Wendel, *Calvin*, 239.

derives all its value from its object, Jesus Christ. Without Christ, faith is of "no dignity or value," for it is "only instrumental."[20] But, when focused on Christ, faith is of inestimable value because by faith we receive Christ himself and all his benefits, including both justification and sanctification. In 3.11.1, Calvin returns to the subject of faith and summarizes what faith does for us:

> Christ was given to us by God's generosity, to be grasped and possessed by us in faith. By partaking of him, we principally receive a double grace: namely, that being reconciled to God through Christ's blamelessness, we may have in heaven instead of a Judge a gracious Father; and secondly, that sanctified by Christ's Spirit we may cultivate blamelessness and purity of life.

Calvin exalts the power of faith. Faith is able to rise "from the flesh of Christ to his divinity" to penetrate "above all the heaven, even to those mysteries which the angels behold and adore."[21] The Holy Spirit uses faith to bring the heavenly graces of Christ down into the human soul and to raise our souls up to heaven in return. This communion with Christ through faith is so real and so profound that, even though Christ remains in heaven, he is so firmly grasped by faith and so fully possessed by us that he can actually be said to dwell in our hearts.[22] In summary, by faith we "come to possess the Heavenly Kingdom" (3.2.1).

The Nature of Faith and Assurance (3.2)

Calvin's doctrine of the assurance of faith is replete with paradoxes that have often been misunderstood by Calvin scholars. For example, William Cunningham (1805–61) writes, "Calvin never contradicted himself so plainly and palpably as this [when], in immediate connection with the definition given from him of saving faith, he had

20. *Institutes* 3.11.7.
21. *Commentary* on John 12:45 and 8:19.
22. *Commentary* on Acts 15:9.

276

made statements, with respect to the condition of the mind that may exist in believers, which cannot well be reconciled with the formal definition."[23]

How are we to grapple with Calvin's paradoxes on assurance? We must begin by describing and defining Calvin's view of faith, and then set it in the context of his doctrine of assurance. Various principles Calvin sets forth will then come to the fore, revealing a scriptural doctrine of assurance that confirms initial and ongoing spiritual experience in the life of faith.[24]

Faith Defined and Described

Calvin's doctrine of faith affirms the basic tenets of Martin Luther and Ulrich Zwingli and also discloses emphases of his own. Like Luther and Zwingli, Calvin says faith is never merely assent (*assensus*), but involves both knowledge (*cognitio*) and trust (*fiducia*). He affirms that knowledge and trust are saving dimensions of the life of faith rather than notional matters. Faith is not historical knowledge plus saving assent, but a saving and certain knowledge joined with a saving and assured trust (3.2.14). Calvin held that knowledge is foundational to faith. Knowledge rests upon the Word of God, the Holy Scriptures in general as well as the gospel in

23. William Cunningham, *Reformers and the Theology of the Reformation* (London: Banner of Truth Trust, 1967), 120. Cf. Robert L. Dabney, *Lectures in Systematic Theology* (Grand Rapids: Zondervan, 1972), 702; Paul Helm, *Calvin and the Calvinists* (Edinburgh: Banner of Truth Trust), 25–26; Cornelis Graafland, *De zekerheid van het geloof: Een onderzoek naar de geloofsbeschouwing van enige vertegenwoordigers van reformatie en nadere reformatie* (Wageningen: H. Veenman & Zonen, 1961), 21–22n. A portion of this section on 3.2 is rewritten from my *The Quest for Full Assurance: The Legacy of Calvin and His Successors* (Edinburgh: Banner of Truth Trust, 1999).

24. Works that deal exclusively with Calvin's doctrine of faith and assurance include Harry Booth Hazen, "Calvin's Doctrine of Faith" (Ph.D. diss., University of Chicago, 1903); S. P. Dee, *Het geloofsberijp van Calvijn* (Kampen: J. H. Kok, 1918); W. E. Stuermann, "A Critical Study of Calvin's Concept of Faith" (Ph.D. diss., University of Tulsa, 1952); Paul Sebestyén, "The Object of Faith in the Theology of Calvin" (Ph.D. diss., University of Chicago, 1963); K. Exalto, *De Zekerheid des Geloofs bij Calvijn* (Apeldoorn: Willem de Zwijgerstichting, 1978); Victor A. Shepherd, *The Nature and Function of Faith in the Theology of John Calvin* (Macon, GA: Mercer University Press, 1983); Jon Balserak, "Toward an Understanding of Calvin's View of Faith: The Two-Fold Presentation of the Believer's Reception of the Word" (Th.M. thesis, Reformed Theological Seminary, 1996); Pitkin, *What Pure Eyes Could See*.

particular.[25] Faith originates in response to the Word of God. Faith rests firmly upon God's Word; it always says amen to the Scriptures.[26] Hence assurance must be sought *in* the Word and flows *out of* the Word.[27] Assurance is as inseparable from the Word as sunbeams are from the sun.

Calvin is eager to show how his understanding of faith differs from the scholastic understanding of his day. He argues, first, that the Roman Catholic emphasis on faith as mere assent to the gospel is weak, for it denies the personal, relational knowledge of Christ that faith appropriates.[28] Second, the scholastic doctrine of implicit faith is entirely fictional; it "utterly destroys" true faith. Calvin asks: "Is this what believing means—to understand nothing, provided only that you submit your feeling obediently to the church?" (3.2.2). Salvation is not appropriated by mere assent to whatever the church teaches, for such assent does not bring us beyond the magisterium of the church. Rather, salvation is known by "direct experiential *intuitive knowledge* of God as he offers himself to us in Jesus Christ."[29]

Calvin acknowledges that there is an implicit element in faith, that is, a person must be teachable. But that is a far cry from the scholastic understanding of implicit faith. For Calvin, faith is not concerned so much with merely believing in one's mind that the Bible is true (3.2.9) and assenting to sound doctrine (3.2.13), nor about merely knowing that God exists or about knowing who God is in himself (3.2.6). More than that, faith is concerned about attaining to the practical, useful knowledge of God as he is to us—that is, by the illumination of the Spirit, perceiving "what he wills to be toward us" (3.2.6).

Faith is also inseparable from Christ and the promise of Christ, for the totality of the written Word is the living Word, Jesus Christ, in whom

25. For Calvin, the "word of the Lord" can also refer to the spoken word, especially to the "proclamation of the grace of God manifested in Christ" (*Institutes* 2.9.2; *Commentary* on 1 Peter 1:25). See David Foxgrover, "John Calvin's Understanding of Conscience" (Ph.D. diss., Claremont, 1978), 407ff.

26. *Commentary* on John 3:33; Ps. 43:3. See also Exalto, *De Zekerheid des Geloofs bij Calvijn*, 24.

27. *Commentary* on Matt. 8:13; John 4:22.

28. Stephen Thorson, "Tensions in Calvin's View of Faith: Unexamined Assumptions in R. T. Kendall's *Calvin and English Calvinism to 1649*," *Journal of the Evangelical Theological Society* 37.3 (1994): 416–17.

29. M. Charles Bell, *Calvin and Scottish Theology: The Doctrine of Assurance* (Edinburgh: Handsel, 1985), 23; see *Institutes* 1.4.1; 2.6.4; 2.16.9.

all God's promises are "yea and amen."[30] Faith rests on scriptural truth and on promises that are Christ-directed and Christ-centered. True faith receives Christ as he is clothed in the gospel and graciously offered by the Father (3.2.32).

Thus, true faith focuses on the Scriptures in general, and particularly seizes the promises of the grace of God in Christ (3.2.6, 15). Calvin makes much of the promises of God as the ground of assurance, for these promises depend on the very nature of God, who cannot lie. Since God promises mercy to sinners in their misery, faith relies on such promises (3.2.29, 41). The promises are fulfilled by Christ; therefore, Calvin directs sinners to Christ and to the promises as if they were synonymous (3.2.32).

Since faith takes its character from the promise on which it rests, it takes on the infallible stamp of God's very Word. Consequently, faith possesses assurance in its very nature. Assurance, certainty, and trust—such is the essence of faith.

This assured and assuring faith is the Holy Spirit's gift to the elect. The Spirit persuades the elect sinner of the reliability of God's promise in Christ and grants faith to embrace that Word (3.2.16).

In short, for Calvin, assuring faith necessarily involves saving knowledge, the Scriptures, Jesus Christ, God's promises, the work of the Holy Spirit, and election. In the end, God himself, in his truth and trustworthiness, is the assurance of the elect. Assurance is thus founded upon God.[31]

Consequently, Calvin's formal definition of faith reads like this: "Now we shall possess a right definition of faith if we call it a firm and certain knowledge of God's benevolence toward us, founded upon the truth of the freely given promise in Christ, both revealed to our minds and sealed upon our hearts through the Holy Spirit" (3.2.7). Calvin stresses that faith is assurance of God's promise in Christ and involves the whole man in the use of the mind, the application to the heart, and the surrendering of the will (3.2.8).[32] Assurance is of the essence of faith.

30. *Commentary* on Gen. 15:6; Luke 2:21.
31. *Commentary* on Rom. 8:16; 1 Peter 1:4; Heb. 4:10.
32. *Institutes* 1.15.7; A. N. S. Lane, "Calvin's Doctrine of Assurance," *Vox Evangelica* 11 (1979): 42–43, 52n; Robert Letham, "Saving Faith and Assurance in Reformed Theology: Zwingli to the Synod of Dort" (Ph.D. diss., University of Aberdeen, 1979), 2:70n.

Assurance as the Essence of Faith

More specifically, Calvin argues that faith involves more than objective certainty in the promise of God; it involves personal, subjective assurance. In believing God's promise to sinners, the true believer recognizes and celebrates that God is gracious and benevolent to him in particular. Faith is an assured knowledge "of God's benevolence toward *us* ... revealed to *our* minds ... sealed upon *our* hearts" (3.2.7; emphasis added). Faith embraces the gospel promise as more than impersonal abstraction; it is inseparable from personal certainty. Calvin writes, "Here, indeed, is the hinge on which faith turns: that we do not regard the promises of mercy that God offers as true only outside ourselves, but not at all in us; rather, that we make them ours by inwardly embracing them" (3.2.16; cf. 3.2.42).

Thus, Calvin repeatedly describes faith as "certainty (*certitudino*), a firm conviction (*solida persuasio*), assurance (*securitas*), firm assurance (*solida securitas*), and full assurance (*plena securitas*)" (3.2.6, 16, 22).[33] While faith consists of knowledge, it is also marked by heartfelt assurance that is "a sure and secure possession of those things which God has promised us" (3.2.41; cf. 3.2.14).

Calvin also emphasizes throughout his commentaries that assurance is integral to faith.[34] He holds that anyone who believes but lacks the conviction that he is saved by God is not a true believer after all:

> Briefly, he alone is a true believer, who convinced by a firm conviction that God is a kindly and well-disposed Father toward him, promises himself all things on the basis of his generosity; who, relying upon the promises of divine benevolence toward him, lays hold on an undoubted expectation of salvation.... No man is a believer, I say, except him who, leaning upon the assurance of his salvation, confidently triumphs over the devil and death. [3.2.16]

True believers must and do know themselves to be such: "Let this truth then stand sure—that no one can be called a son of God, who does not know himself to be such.... This so great an assurance, which dares

33. Robert T. Kendall, *Calvin and English Calvinism to 1649* (New York: Oxford University Press, 1979), 19.
34. *Commentary* on Acts 2:29 and 1 Cor. 2:12.

to triumph over the devil, death, sin, and the gates of hell, ought to lodge deep in the hearts of all the godly; for our faith is nothing, except we feel assured that Christ is ours, and that the Father is in him propitious to us."[35] Calvin even states that those who doubt their union with Christ are reprobates: "[Paul] declares that all are *reprobates*, who doubt whether they profess Christ and are a part of His body. Let us, therefore, reckon *that* alone to be right faith, which leads us to repose in safety in the favour of God, with no wavering opinion, but with a firm and steadfast assurance."[36] That kind of statement prompted a charge of incautiousness by William Cunningham and Robert Dabney.[37] A culling of Calvin's *Institutes*—particularly in 3.2—however, also presents a formidable number of equally intense, qualifying statements, which, in turn, are buttressed in his commentaries and sermons.

Faith and Assurance versus Unbelief

Throughout his lofty doctrine of faith, Calvin repeats these themes: unbelief dies hard; assurance is often contested by doubt; severe temptations, wrestlings, and strife are normative; Satan and the flesh assault faith; trust in God is hedged with fear (3.2.7).[38] Calvin freely acknowledges that faith is not maintained without a severe struggle against unbelief, nor is it left untinged by doubt and anxiety. He writes: "Unbelief is, in all men, always mixed with faith. . . . For unbelief is so deeply rooted in our hearts, and we are so inclined to it, that not without hard struggle is each one able to persuade himself of what all confess with the mouth, namely, that God is faithful. Especially when it comes to reality itself, every man's wavering uncovers hidden weakness" (3.2.4, 15).

According to Calvin, faith ought to be assuring, but no perfect assurance exists in this life. The believer will not be fully healed of unbelief until he dies. Though faith itself cannot doubt, faith is constantly harassed

---

35. *Commentary* on Rom. 8:16, 34; see also *Institutes* 3.2.2.

36. *Commentary* on 2 Cor. 13:5.

37. Cunningham, *Reformers*, 119ff.; Robert L. Dabney, *Discussions: Evangelical and Theological* (London: Banner of Truth Trust, 1967), 1:216ff.; idem, *Systematic Theology*, 702, 709.

38. See also *Commentary* on Matt. 8:25; Luke 2:40.

with the temptation to doubt (3.2.18–20). The Christian strives for, but never wholly attains, uninterrupted assurance.

Calvin does allow for varying degrees of faith. Though secondary sources often downplay them, Calvin uses such concepts as "infancy of faith," "beginnings of faith," and "weak faith" even more frequently than does Luther (3.2.17–21). All faith begins in infancy, Calvin says: "The forbearance of Christ is great in reckoning as disciples those whose faith is so small. And indeed this doctrine extends generally to us all; for the faith which is now full grown had at first its infancy, nor is it so perfect in any as not to make it necessary that all to a man should make progress in believing."[39]

In expounding faith's maturation process, Calvin asserts that assurance is proportional to faith's development. More specifically, he presents the Holy Spirit not only as the initiator of faith, but also as the cause and agent of its growth (3.2.33ff–36). Faith, repentance, sanctification, and assurance are all progressive (3.2.14; 3.3.9).[40]

In writing on John 20:3, Calvin seems to contradict his assertion that true believers know themselves as such when he testifies that the disciples were scarcely or possibly not at all aware of their faith as they approached the empty tomb:

> There being *so little faith, or rather almost no faith*, both in the disciples and in the women, it is astonishing that they had so great zeal; and, indeed, it is not possible that religious feelings led them to seek Christ. *Some seed of faith, therefore, remained in their hearts, but quenched for a time, so that they were not aware of having what they had.* Thus the Spirit of God often works in the elect in a secret manner. [cf. 3.2.12; emphasis added]

How can Calvin say that assertions of faith are characterized by full assurance, yet still allow for the kind of faith that lacks nearly all assurance? The two concepts appear antithetical. Assurance is free from

39. *Commentary* on John 2:11.
40. See also *Commentary* on John 2:11; 1 John 5:13. Stuermann correctly notes that though Calvin was no perfectionist, the idea of growth and development is ubiquitous in his writings ("A Critical Study of Calvin's Concept of Faith," 117).

doubt, yet not free. It does not hesitate, yet it can hesitate; it contains security, but it may be beset with anxiety. The faithful have assurance, yet they waver and tremble.

Making Sense of Antinomies

Calvin operated from four principles that address the complex issue of antinomies. Each principle helps make sense of his apparent contradictions.

Faith and Experience

First, consider Calvin's need to distinguish between the definition of faith and the reality of the believer's experience. After explaining faith in the *Institutes* as embracing "great assurance," he writes:

> Still, someone will say: "Believers *experience* something far different: In recognizing the grace of God toward themselves they are not only tried by disquiet, which often comes upon them, but they are repeatedly shaken by gravest terrors. For so violent are the temptations that trouble their minds as not to seem quite compatible with that certainty of faith." Accordingly, we shall have to solve this difficulty if we wish the above-stated doctrine to stand. Surely, while we teach that faith *ought* to be certain and assured, we cannot imagine any certainty that is not tinged with doubt, or any assurance that is not assailed. [3.2.16–17; emphasis added]

Later, Calvin says: "And I have not forgotten what I have previously said, the memory of which is repeatedly renewed by experience: faith is tossed about by various doubts, so that the minds of the godly are rarely at peace" (3.2.51).

Those quotations and other writings (most notably when dealing with the sacramental strengthening of faith)[41] indicate that, though Calvin is anxious to define faith and assurance together, he also recognizes that the Christian gradually grows into a fuller faith in God's promises. This recognition is implicit in his expressions such as "full faith in God's promises,"

---

41. See especially *Institutes* 4.14.7.

as though he is distinguishing between the exercise of faith and what he calls "full faith." In short, Calvin distinguishes between the "ought to" of faith and the "is" of faith in daily life. He writes:

> By these words Paul obviously shows that there is no *right faith* except when we dare with tranquil hearts to stand in God's sight. This boldness arises only out of a sure confidence in divine benevolence and salvation. This is so true that the word *faith* is very often used for confidence. . . . When anything is defined we should . . . seek its very integrity and perfection. This, of course, is not to deny a place for growth. [3.2.15; 3.3.8]

Calvin's definition of faith serves as a recommendation about how his readers ought "habitually and properly to think of faith."[42] To define faith in terms of experience would be to confuse the experiencing of two realities (faith and unbelief) in defining one of them (namely, faith). Moreover, that would impune faith's object, Jesus Christ.

Calvin was convinced that a true look at the gospel effects an assured confidence in the beholder, though that assurance may be small. In this way, his approach predates the more sophisticated Puritan notions of assurance without necessarily contradicting them. For Calvin, assurance is derived from what the believer sees by faith. That sight may be dim, or inchoate, but it still results from the smallest act of faith. "When first even the least drop of faith is instilled in our minds, we begin to contemplate God's face, peaceful and calm and gracious toward us. We see him afar off yet we see him clearly enough to know we are not at all deceived" (3.2.19).

For Calvin, the believer is expected to live *coram evangelio*, as one "beholding the gospel face to face." As the Puritans worked out the casuistry of faith and experience more thoroughly, they began to elaborate on the teaching of Calvin and other Reformers. Yet even a reading of the Westminster Standards does not lead to a denial of what Calvin taught. Rather, by explaining that "this infallible assurance is not *so* of the essence of faith" (Westminster Confession, 18.3), they are only qualifying Calvin. Calvin also taught that faith should always aim at full assurance, even if it

---

42. Helm, *Calvin and the Calvinists*, 26.

cannot reach it in experience. In principle, faith gains the victory (1 John 5:4); in practice, it recognizes that it has not yet fully apprehended (Phil. 3:12–13). In writing on Mark 9:24, Calvin said that the two statements "I believe" and "help my unbelief" "may appear to contradict each other, but there is none of us that does not experience both of them in himself. As our faith is never perfect, it follows that we are partly unbelievers; but God forgives us and exercises such forbearance towards us as to reckon us believers on account of a small portion of faith."[43]

The Puritans would fully concur with Calvin here. One difference between them, however, would be that Calvin usually insists that even in the weakest act of faith the believer is conscious of some degree of assurance. Most Puritans did not deny that but would tend to think of fuller measures of assurance when they spoke of assurance, and, therefore, would be less inclined to say that a believer possesses assurance when his consciousness of his own faith is very weak.[44]

Nevertheless, for both Calvin and the Puritans, the practice and experience of faith—weak as it may be at times—validates that faith which trusts in the Word. Calvin is not as interested in experiences as he is in validating Word-grounded faith. Experience confirms faith, Calvin says. Faith "requires full and fixed certainty, such as men are wont to have from things experienced and proved" (3.2.15). Both the object of faith and the validation of faith by experience are gifts of God that confirm his gracious character by means of his Word.

Thus, bare experience (*nuda experientia*) is not Calvin's goal, but experience grounded in the Word, flowing out of the fulfilment of the Word. Experimental knowledge of the Word is essential.[45] For Calvin, two kinds of knowledge are needed: knowledge by faith (*scientia fidei*) that is received from the Word, "though it is not yet fully revealed," and the knowledge of experience (*scientia experientiae*) "springing from the fulfilling of the Word."[46] The Word of God is primary to both, for experience teaches us

43. Charles Partee, "Calvin and Experience," *Scottish Journal of Theology* 26.2 (1973): 172.
44. Cornelis Graafland, "'Waarheid in het Binnenste': Geloofszekerheid bij Calvijn en de Nadere Reformatie," in *Een vaste Burcht voor de Kerk der eeuwen* (Kampen: Kok, 1989), 67–68.
45. *Institutes* 1.7.5.
46. See Charles Partee, "Calvin and Experience," *Scottish Journal of Theology* 26 (1973): 169–81, and W. Balke, "The Word of God and *Experientia* according to Calvin," in *Calvinus*

to know God as he declares himself to be in his Word.[47] Experience that is not constant with Scripture is not an experience of true faith. In short, though the believer's experience of true faith is far weaker than he desires, there is an essential unity in the Word between faith's perception (the "ought to" dimension of faith) and experience (the "is" dimension of faith).

Flesh versus Spirit

The second principle that helps us understand Calvin's "ought to/is" tension in faith is the principle of flesh versus spirit. Calvin writes:

> It is necessary to return to that division of flesh and spirit which we have mentioned elsewhere. It most clearly reveals itself at this point. Therefore the godly heart feels in itself a division because it is partly imbued with sweetness from its recognition of the divine goodness, partly grieves in bitterness from an awareness of its calamity; partly rests upon the promise of the gospel, partly trembles at the evidence of its own iniquity; partly rejoices at the expectation of life, partly shudders at death. This variation arises from imperfection of faith, since in the course of the present life it never goes so well with us that we are wholly cured of the disease of unbelief and entirely filled and possessed by faith. Hence arises those conflicts, when unbelief, which reposes in the remains of the flesh, rises up to attack the faith that has been inwardly conceived. [3.2.18]

Like Luther, Calvin sets the "ought to/is" dichotomy against the backdrop of spirit/flesh warfare.[48] Christians experience this spirit/flesh tension acutely because it is instigated by the Holy Spirit.[49] The paradoxes that permeate experiential faith (e.g., Rom. 7:14–25 in the classical Reformed interpretation) find resolution in this tension: "So then, I myself serve the law of God with my mind [spirit], but with my flesh I serve the law of

---

Ecclesiae Doctor (Kampen: Kok, 1978), 23ff., for Calvin's understanding of experience. Balke points out that Calvin's writings are full of expressions such as "*experientia docet, ostendit, clamat, confirmat, demonstrat, convincit, testator*" (20).

47. *Institutes* 1.10.2.

48. C. A. Hall, *With the Spirit's Sword: The Drama of Spiritual Warfare in the Theology of John Calvin* (Richmond: John Knox, 1970).

49. Shepherd, *Faith in the Theology of John Calvin*, 24–28.

sin" (v. 25). Hence Calvin writes: "Nothing prevents believers from being afraid and at the same time possessing the surest consolation. . . . Fear and faith [can] dwell in the same mind. . . . Surely this is so: We *ought* not to separate Christ from ourselves or ourselves from him. Rather we *ought* to hold fast bravely with both hands to that fellowship by which he has bound himself to us" (3.2.24; emphasis added).

Calvin sets the sure consolation of the spirit side by side with the imperfection of the flesh, for these are what the believer finds within himself. Since the final victory of the spirit over the flesh will be fulfilled only in Christ, the Christian finds himself in a perpetual struggle in this life. His spirit fills him "with delight in recognizing the divine goodness" even as his flesh activates his natural proneness to unbelief (3.2.18, 20). He is beset with "daily struggles of conscience" as long as the vestiges of the flesh remain.[50] The believer's "present state is far short of the glory of God's children," Calvin writes. "Physically, we are dust and shadow, and death is always before our eyes. We are exposed to a thousand miseries . . . so that we always find a hell within us."[51] While still in the flesh, the believer may even be tempted to doubt the whole gospel.

The unregenerate do not have these struggles, for they neither love God nor hate sin. They indulge their own desires "without fear of God," Calvin says. But the more sincerely the believer "is devoted to God, he is just so much the more severely disquieted by the sense of his wrath."[52] Assurance of God's favor and a sense of his wrath only appear contrary. In reality, a reverential spirit of fear and trembling helps to establish faith and to prevent presumption, for fear stems from a proper sense of unworthiness while confidence arises from God's faithfulness.[53] This spirit/flesh tension keeps the believer from indulging in the flesh and from yielding to despair (3.2.17). The believer's spirit will never utterly despair; rather, faith grows on the very brink of despair. Strife strengthens faith. It makes the believer live circumspectly, not despondently (3.2.22–23). With the help of the Holy Spirit, heavenly faith rises above all strife, trusting that God will be faithful to his own Word.

50. *Commentary* on John 13:9.
51. *Commentary* on 1 John 3:2.
52. *Commentary* on Ps. 6:6.
53. *Institutes* 3.20.11.

Even as he is tormented with fleshly doubts, the believer's spirit trusts God's mercy by invoking him in prayer and by resting upon him through the sacraments. By these means, faith gains the upper hand in its struggles with unbelief. "Faith ultimately triumphs over those difficulties which besiege and . . . imperil it. [Faith is like] a palm tree [that] strives against every burden and raises itself upward" (3.2.17).

In short, Calvin teaches that from the spirit of the believer rise hope, joy, and assurance; from the flesh, fear, doubt, and disillusionment. Though spirit and flesh operate simultaneously, imperfection and doubt are integral only to the flesh, not to faith. The works of the flesh often attend faith but do not mix with it. The believer may lose spiritual battles along the pathway of life, but he will not lose the ultimate war against the flesh. Prayer and the sacraments help the spirit of faith gain the ultimate victory.

Germ of Faith versus Consciousness of Faith

Thirdly, despite the tensions between definition and experience, spirit and flesh, Calvin maintains that faith and assurance are not so mixed with unbelief that the believer is left with probability rather than certainty.[54] The smallest germ of faith contains assurance in its very essence, even when the believer is not always able to grasp much of this assurance because of his weakness. The Christian may be tossed about with doubt and perplexity, but the seed of faith, implanted by the Spirit, cannot perish. Precisely because it is the Spirit's seed, faith retains assurance. Calvin says: "The root of faith can never be torn from the godly breast, but clings so fast to the inmost parts that, however much faith seems to be shaken or to bend this way or that, its light is never so extinguished or snuffed out that it does not at least lurk as it were beneath the ashes" (3.2.21).

Calvin thus explains "weak assurance in terms of weak faith without thereby weakening the link between faith and assurance."[55] Assurance is normative but varies in degree and constancy in the believer's conscious-

---

54. Graafland, *Zekerheid van het geloof*, 31n.

55. A. N. S. Lane, "The Quest for the Historical Calvin," *Evangelical Quarterly* 55 (1983): 103.

ness of it. Therefore, in responding to weak assurance, a pastor should not deny the organic tie between faith and assurance, but should urge the pursuit of stronger faith through the use of the means of grace in reliance upon the Spirit.

Trinitarian Framework

Through a fourth sweeping principle, namely, a trinitarian framework for the doctrine of faith and assurance, Calvin spurs the doubt-prone believer toward greater degrees of assurance. As surely as the election of the Father must prevail over the works of Satan, the righteousness of the Son over the sinfulness of the believer, and the assuring witness of the Spirit over the believer's infirmities, so surely faith must and will conquer unbelief.

Calvin's arrangement of book 3 of the *Institutes* reveals the movement of the grace of faith from God to man and man to God. The grace of faith is from the Father, in the Son, and through the Spirit, by which, in turn, the believer is brought into fellowship with the Son by the Spirit, and reconciled to the Father.

For Calvin, a complex set of factors establishes assurance, not the least of which is the Father's election and preservation in Christ. Hence he writes that "predestination duly considered does not shake faith, but rather affords the best confirmation of it,"[56] especially when viewed in the context of our calling. "The firmness of our election is joined to our calling [and] is another means of establishing our assurance. For all whom [Christ] receives, the Father is said to have entrusted and committed to Him to keep to eternal life."[57]

Decretal election is a sure foundation for preservation and assurance; election is not coldly causal. As Gordon Keddie notes:

Election is never seen, in Calvin, in a purely deterministic light, in which God . . . is viewed as "a frightening idol" of "mechanistic deterministic causality" and Christian experience is reduced to either cowering passivity or frantic activism, while waiting some "revelation" of God's hidden

56. *Institutes* 3.24.9.
57. *Institutes* 3.24.6.

decree for one's self. For Calvin, as indeed in Scripture, election does not threaten, but rather undergirds, the certainty of salvation.[58]

Such a foundation is possible only in a christocentric context; hence, Calvin constantly lifts up Christ as the mirror of election "wherein we must, and without self-deception may, contemplate our own election."[59] Election turns the believer's eyes from his hopeless inability to meet any conditions of salvation to focus on the hope of Jesus Christ as God's pledge of undeserved love and mercy.[60]

Through union with Christ "the assurance of salvation becomes real and effective as the assurance of election" (3.1.1).[61] Christ becomes ours in fulfilment of God's determination to redeem and resurrect us. Consequently, we ought not to think of Christ as "standing afar off and not dwelling in us" (3.2.24). Since Christ is for us, truly contemplating him is seeing him form in us what he desires to give us, himself above all. God has made himself "little in Christ," Calvin states, so that we might comprehend and flee to Christ who alone can pacify our consciences.[62] Faith must begin, rest, and end in Christ. "True faith is so contained in Christ, that it neither knows, nor desires to know, anything beyond him," Calvin says.[63] Therefore, "we ought not separate Christ from ourselves nor separate ourselves from him" (3.2.24).

Union with Christ merges objective and subjective assurance; to look to Christ alone for assurance means also to look to ourselves in Christ as his body. As Willis-Watkins notes, "It would be entirely hypothetical for

58. Gordon J. Keddie, "'Unfallible Certenty of the Pardon of Sinne and Life Everlasting': The Doctrine of Assurance in the Theology of William Perkins," *Evangelical Quarterly* 48 (1976): 231; see also G. C. Berkouwer, *Divine Election*, trans. Hugo Bekker (Grand Rapids: Eerdmans, 1960), 10ff.

59. *Institutes* 3.24.5; also John Calvin, *Sermons on the Epistle to the Ephesians* (Edinburgh: Banner of Truth Trust, 1973), 47; idem, *Sermons from Job* (Grand Rapids: Eerdmans, 1952), 41ff.; CO 8:318–21; 9:757.

60. *Institutes* 3.24.6; William H. Chalker, "Calvin and Some Seventeenth Century English Calvinists" (Ph.D. diss., Duke, 1961), 66; David Neeld Wiley, "Calvin's Doctrine of Predestination: His Principal Soteriological and Polemical Doctrine" (Ph.D. diss., Duke, 1971), 260–69.

61. Wilhelm Niesel, *The Theology of Calvin*, trans. Harold Knight (Grand Rapids: Baker, 1980), 196. See also Shepherd, *Faith in the Theology of John Calvin*, 51.

62. *Commentary* on 1 Peter 1:20.

63. *Commentary* on Eph. 4:13.

faith to focus on ourselves apart from Christ—and it would be entirely hypothetical for faith to focus on Christ apart from his body. . . . Assurance of salvation is a derivative self-knowledge, whose focus remains on Christ as united to his body, the church of which we are members."[64]

In this christological manner, Calvin reduces the distance between God's objective decree of election and the believer's subjective lack of assurance that he is elect. For Calvin, election answers, rather than raises, the question of assurance. In Christ, the believer sees his election; in the gospel, he hears of his election.

Nevertheless, Calvin is acutely aware that one may think that the Father has entrusted him to Christ when such is not the case. It is one thing to underscore Christ's task in the trinitarian salvific economy as the recipient and guardian of the elect; the center, author, and foundation of election; and the guarantee, promise, and mirror of the believer's election and salvation. But it is quite another to know how to inquire about whether a person has been joined to Christ by a true faith. Many appear to be Christ's who are strangers to him. Says Calvin: "It daily happens that those who seemed to be Christ's fall away from him again. . . . Such persons never cleaved to Christ with the heartfelt trust in which certainty of salvation has, I say, been established for us."[65]

Calvin never preached so as to mislead his flock into false assurance of salvation.[66] Many scholars minimize Calvin's emphasis on the need for a subjective, experiential realization of faith and election by referring to Calvin's practice of approaching his congregation as saved hearers. They misunderstand him. Though Calvin practiced what he called "a judgment of charity" (i.e., addressing as saved those who maintain a commendable external lifestyle), he also frequently asserted that only a minority (often he speaks of 20 percent) receive the preached Word with saving faith. Sometimes his statements are even stronger: "For though all, without exception, to whom God's Word is preached, are taught, yet scarce one in

64. David Willis-Watkins, "The Third Part of Christian Freedom Misplaced, Being an Inquiry into the Lectures of the Late Rev. Samuel Willard on the Assembly's Shorter Catechism," in *Later Calvinism: International Perspectives*, ed. W. Fred Graham (Kirksville, MO: Sixteenth Century Journal, 1994), 484–85.

65. *Institutes* 3.24.7.

66. Graafland, "Waarheid in het Binnenste," 65–67.

ten so much as tastes it; yea, scarce one in a hundred profits to the extent of being enabled, thereby, to proceed in a right course to the end."[67]

For Calvin, much that resembles faith lacks a saving character. He thus speaks of unformed faith, implicit faith, the preparation of faith, temporary faith, an illusion of faith, a false show of faith, shadow-types of faith, transitory faith, and faith under a cloak of hypocrisy (3.2.3, 5, 10–11).[68]

Self-deception is a real possibility, Calvin says. Because the reprobate often feel something much like the faith of the elect (3.2.11), self-examination is essential. He writes: "Let us learn to examine ourselves, and to search whether those interior marks by which God distinguishes his children from strangers belong to us, viz., the living root of piety and faith."[69] Happily, the truly saved are delivered from self-deception through proper examination directed by the Holy Spirit. "In the meantime, the faithful are taught to examine themselves with solicitude and humility, lest carnal security insinuate itself, instead of the assurance of faith" (3.2.7).

Even in self-examination, Calvin emphasizes Christ. He says we must examine ourselves to see if we are placing our trust in Christ alone, for this is the fruit of biblical experience. Anthony Lane says that Calvin's self-examination is not so much "Am I *trusting* in Christ?" as it is "Am I trusting in *Christ*?"[70] Self-examination must always direct us to Christ and his gospel promise. It must never be done apart from the help of the Holy Spirit, who alone can shed light upon Christ's saving work in the believer's soul. Apart from Christ, the Word, and the Spirit, Calvin says, "if you contemplate yourself, that is sure damnation" (3.2.24).

67. *Commentary* on Ps. 119:101. More than thirty times in his *Commentary* (e.g., Acts 11:23 and Ps. 15:1) and nine times within the scope of *Institutes* 3.21–24, Calvin refers to the fewness of those who possess vital faith.
68. For Calvin on temporary faith, see "'Temporary Faith' and the Certainty of Salvation," *Calvin Theological Journal* 15 (1980): 220–32; Lane, "Calvin's Doctrine of Assurance," 45–46; Exalto, *De Zekerheid des Geloofs bij Calvijn*, 15–20, 27–30.
69. *Commentary* on Ezek. 13:9. David Foxgrover shows that Calvin relates the need for self-examination to a great variety of topics, such as the knowledge of God and ourselves, judgment, repentance, confession, affliction, the Lord's Supper, providence, duty, and the kingdom of God ("John Calvin's Understanding of Conscience," 312ff.). See also J. P. Pelkonen, "The Teaching of John Calvin on the Nature and Function of the Conscience," *Lutheran Quarterly* 21 (1969): 24–88.
70. Lane, "Calvin's Doctrine of Assurance," 47.

Thus Calvin's line of reasoning proceeds like this: (1) The purpose of election embraces salvation. (2) The elect are not chosen for anything in themselves, but only in Christ. (3) Since the elect are in Christ, the assurance of their election and salvation can never be found in themselves or even in the Father apart from Christ. (4) Rather, their assurance is to be found in Christ; hence communion with him is vital.

The question remains, however: how do the elect enjoy such communion, and how does that produce assurance? Calvin's answer is pneumatological: the Holy Spirit applies Christ and his benefits to the hearts and lives of guilty, elect sinners, assuring them that Christ belongs to them and they to him. The Holy Spirit especially confirms within them the reliability of God's promises in Christ. Thus, personal assurance is never divorced from the election of the Father, the redemption of the Son, the application of the Spirit, and the instrumental means of saving faith.

The Holy Spirit has an enormous role in the application of redemption, Calvin says. As personal comforter, seal, and earnest, the Holy Spirit assures the believer of his adoption: "The Spirit of God gives us such a testimony, that when he is our guide and teacher our spirit is made sure of the adoption of God; for our mind of itself, without the preceding testimony of the Spirit, could not convey to us this assurance."[71] The Holy Spirit's work underlies all assurance of salvation, without detracting from the role of Christ, for as the Spirit *of Christ* he assures the believer by leading him to Christ and his benefits, and by bringing those benefits to fruition in the believer (3:2, 34).

The unity of Christ and the Spirit has sweeping implications for the doctrine of assurance. Most recent scholars minimize Calvin's emphasis on the necessity of the Spirit's work in assuring a believer of God's promises. The *ground* of assurance supposedly is God's promises, in Christ and/or in the Word of God, whereas the *cause* of assurance is the Spirit, who works it in the heart. Cornelis Graafland argues, however, that this distinction is too simplistic, since the Spirit always works as the Spirit of Christ. Hence the objective and subjective elements in assurance cannot be so readily

---

71. *Commentary* on Rom. 8:16. See also *Institutes* 3.2.11, 34, 41; *Commentary* on John 7:37–39; Acts 2:4; 3:8; 5:32; 13:48; 16:14; 23:11; Rom. 8:15–17; 1 Cor. 2:10–13; Gal. 3:2; 4:6; Eph. 1:13–14; 4:30; *Tracts and Treatises*, 3:253ff.; J. K. Parratt, "The Witness of the Holy Spirit: Calvin, the Puritans and St. Paul," *Evangelical Quarterly* 41 (1969): 161–68.

separated; objective salvation in Christ is bound to subjective sealing by the Spirit. Graafland concludes that "Christ in and through his Spirit is the ground of our faith."[72]

Moreover, for Calvin, a believer's objective reliance upon God's promises as the primary ground for assurance must be subjectively sealed by the Holy Spirit for true assurance. The reprobate may claim God's promises without experiencing the feeling (*sensus*) or consciousness of those promises. The Spirit often works in the reprobate, but in an inferior manner. Calvin says the minds of the reprobate may be momentarily illumined so that they may seem to have a beginning of faith; nevertheless, they "never receive anything but a confused awareness of grace" (3.2.11).

On the other hand, the elect are regenerated with incorruptible seed (3.2.41). They receive subjective benefits that the reprobate will never taste. They alone receive the promises of God as truth in the inward parts; they alone receive the testimony that can be called "the enlightening of the Spirit"; they alone receive experiential, intuitive knowledge of God as he offers himself to them in Christ.[73] Calvin says the elect alone come to "be ravished and wholly kindled to love God; [they] are borne up to heaven itself [and] admitted to the most hidden treasures of God" (3.2.41). "The Spirit, strictly speaking, seals forgiveness of sins in the elect alone, so that they apply it by special faith to their own use" (3.2.11). The elect alone come to know special faith and a special inward testimony.

When distinguishing the elect from the reprobate, Calvin speaks more about what the Spirit does *in us* than what Christ does *for us*, for here the line of demarcation is sharper. He speaks much of inward experience, of feeling, of enlightenment, of perception, even of "violent emotion."[74] Though aware of the dangers of excessive introspection, Calvin also recognizes that the promises of God are efficient only when they are brought by the Spirit within the scope, experience, and obedience of faith (cf. 3:1.1).[75]

72. Graafland, "Waarheid in het Binnenste," 58–60.

73. *Institutes* 1.4.1; 2.6.4, 19.

74. "Too few scholars have been willing to recognize the intensely experiential nature of Calvin's doctrine of faith" (M. Charles Bell, *Calvin and Scottish Theology: The Doctrine of Assurance* [Edinburgh: Handsel, 1985], 20).

75. Randall C. Zachman, *The Assurance of Faith: Conscience in the Theology of Martin Luther and John Calvin* (Minneapolis: Fortress, 1993), 198–203.

To summarize Calvin's position, all three members of the Trinity are involved in the believer's assurance of faith. The election of the Father, the work of Christ, and the application of the Holy Spirit are complementary. When Calvin replies to Pighius that "Christ is a thousand testimonies to me," he is saying that Christ is an overwhelming, foundational, and primary source of assurance for him precisely because of the Spirit's application of Christ and his benefits to him as one elected by the Father. No one can ever be assured of Christ without the Spirit (3.2.35). The Holy Spirit reveals to the believer through his Word that God is a well-disposed Father, and enables him to embrace Christ's promises by faith and with assurance.

The Doctrine of Repentance (3.3)

Calvin defines repentance as "the true turning of our life to God, a turning that arises from a pure and earnest fear of him; and it consists in the mortification of our flesh and of the old man, and in the vivification of the Spirit" (3.3.5). Thus, repentance involves four things: (1) turning to God from the heart, (2) fearing God purely and earnestly, (3) dying to self and sin (mortification), and (4) being made alive (vivification) in Christ through the Spirit (3.3.3, 5, 9).

Turning to God

Calvin does not limit repentance to an inward grace, but views it as the redirection and transformation of a believer's entire being from sin to righteousness (3.3.6). Nevertheless, repentance is essentially a matter of the heart; it must be done with "all the heart" and "all the soul" (Deut. 6:5). The sinner who turns to God wholeheartedly grieves over sin, casts it out, and pursues righteousness from his "inmost heart" (3.3.6).

Unlike the Roman Catholic Church's emphasis on the outward aspects of repentance rather than the inward renewal of the heart and mind, Calvin underscored the inward aspects of repentance and paid less attention to its external dimensions. To be sure, external dimensions of repentance must be present, but these are but fruits of inward repentance as one turns fully to God (3.3.18). This turning to God, therefore, may not be hardened into mere externalism so as to foster an "outward repentance in

JOEL R. BEEKE

ceremonies." It is not a mere legal repentance motivated primarily by fear
of punishment, but a sorrowful repentance that flows primarily from the
filial fear of God (3.3.6).

Fear of God

One of the greatest "signs and accompaniments of repentance" is the
fear of God. Without a pure, earnest fear of God, a person will not be
aware of the heinousness of sin or want to turn from it and die to it. For
Calvin, the essence of the fear of God is esteeming God's smiles and frowns
to be of greater value than the smiles and frowns of men.

The fear of God stirs within the believer other accompanying emotions
and attitudes as well, including carefulness, indignation, desire, and zeal
(3.3.15)—or perhaps at times, even dismay, anguish of soul, and despair,[76]
though these stronger emotions are primarily reserved for times of "special
repentance" when the believer has stumbled badly (3.3.17–18).

Mortification

For Calvin, to repent is to turn to God from a fear of his judgment,
which involves both mortification of the flesh and vivification in the
Spirit—both of which are experienced by Spirit-worked faith (3.3.5).
Mortification and vivification are both indicatives and imperatives.[77]

Mortification is essential because, although sin ceases to reign in the
believer, it does not cease to dwell in him. Concupiscence abides within
so long as we abide in the flesh, that is, "the totality of man's nature in
the state of moral corruption resulting directly from the sin of Adam."[78]
Consequently, the believer is never free from sin in this life; he must
always battle against it. Calvin writes, "In the saints, until they are divested
of mortal bodies, there is always sin; for in their flesh there resides that
depravity of inordinate desiring which contends against righteousness"
(3.3.10). Romans 7:14–25 shows that mortification is a lifelong activity

76. CO 46:498.
77. Peter J. Leithart, "Stoic Elements in Calvin's Doctrine of the Christian Life: Part
II. Mortification," *Westminster Theological Journal* 55 (1993): 194.
78. Randall C. Gleason, *John Calvin and John Owen on Mortification* (New York: Peter
Lang, 1995), 60.

and process that advances, through Christ, to completion only gradually (3.3.20). The Spirit gives grace to persevere in mortification, enabling us to circumcise the foreskin of our hearts (Jer. 4:4) so that we die daily to sin and to any righteousness of our own.[79]

The believer must put sin to death every day, using the sword of the Spirit. Two critical aspects of mortification are self-denial and cross-bearing. Self-denial is the inward dimension of mortification. It involves suppressing and killing evil desires, affections, and thoughts of the sinful flesh and sacrificing ourselves and all that we own to God. This uproots our love of strife and self and replaces it with a spirit of gentleness and helpfulness. Self-denial is the foundation of neighbor-love. Ultimately, when sanctified by the Spirit, it helps us find true happiness because it helps us do what we were created for—namely, to love God above all and our neighbor as ourselves.[80]

Cross-bearing is the outward dimension of mortification. Because Christ's life was a perpetual cross, our life must also include suffering.[81] Suffering affliction willingly helps wean us from this world. Through cross-bearing we are trained in patience, chastened for our pride, instructed in obedience, and roused to hope. Cross-bearing is strong medicine; it reveals the feebleness of our flesh and teaches us to suffer for the sake of righteousness.[82]

Self-denial conforms us to Christ inwardly and directly, whereas cross-bearing centers on outward Christlikeness. Together, they teach us to esteem Christ and the blessings of heaven far above this present life.[83]

Vivification

Repentance is also characterized by walking in newness of life. Mortification is not an end in itself, but is the necessary prelude to vivification, which Calvin defines as "the desire to live in a holy and devoted manner, a desire arising from rebirth; as if it were said that man dies to himself that he may begin to live to God" (3.3.3).[84]

---

79. *Commentary* on Col. 2:11.
80. *Institutes* 3.7.
81. *Institutes* 3.8.1
82. *Institutes* 3.8.
83. Leithart, "Stoic Elements," 191–96.
84. Gleason, *John Calvin and John Owen on Mortification*, 61.

Vivification involves three things: First, participation in Christ unto righteousness. Through repentance, believers bow in the dust before their holy Judge, and then are raised to participate in the life, death, righteousness, and intercession of their Savior. Calvin writes, "For if we truly partake in his death, 'our old man is crucified by his power, and the body of sin perishes' (Rom. 6:6), that the corruption of original nature may no longer thrive. If we share in Christ's resurrection, then we are raised to newness of life to correspond with the righteousness of God" (3.3.8–9).

Second, vivification involves a Spirit-governed life. Vivification involves living a life "in which the Spirit of God lives and rules."[85] Calvin writes, "The death of the flesh is the life of the Spirit. If the Spirit of God lives in us, we must let him govern our actions."[86] Vivification, then, is being made alive to righteousness, so that the believer increasingly gives himself to possessing and exhibiting the fruits of the Spirit.

Third, vivification involves doing good works. A Spirit-governed life conforms the believer ethically to the will of God so that he is inclined to do good works. Such a life bears positive fruits. Vivified believers operate by an inner impulse to fulfil the law of God by loving God and their neighbor. They deny themselves and are devoted to justice and mercy. They strive against the power of sin and Satan. They both "cease to do evil" and "learn to do well." Walter Stuermann points out that "Calvin is led to assert very strenuously the ethical aspect of repentance, because he wishes to clear his doctrine of justification by faith of the charge of being morally sterile. There is no faith (or repentance, in the sense of inner renewal of life) which is without good works."[87]

Relation to the Image of God, Faith, Conversion, and Sanctification

For Calvin, repentance is a lifelong process, rooted in the redemption accomplished by Christ's death and resurrection, that aims for the restoration of the image of God in the believer (3.3.9). Repentance is not achieved merely by imitating Christ, but only by participating in his

85. John H. Leith, *John Calvin's Doctrine of the Christian Life* (Louisville: Westminster/John Knox, 1989), 75.
86. CO 50:256.
87. Walter Stuermann, *A Critical Study of Calvin's Concept of Faith* (Tulsa: n.p., 1952), 218.

death through faith.[88] The Spirit conforms us to the death of Christ.[89] John Leith concludes: "The reconstruction of the image of God is the achievement of the process we call Christian life and is one of the most frequent notes in Calvin's theology."[90]

For Calvin, repentance is not merely the start of the Christian life; together with faith, repentance *is* the Christian life (3.3.1–2). Calvin writes: "We must strive toward repentance itself, devote ourselves to it throughout life, and pursue it to the very end if we would abide in Christ" (3.3.20). Daily repentance, by which the believer grieves over and forsakes his sins, and the exercise of daily faith, by which he takes refuge in Christ for forgiveness, are two sides of one coin. The Holy Spirit is the author of both; one cannot be experienced without the other.

Repentance and faith must be distinguished, however: "Repentance is a turning to God, as when we frame ourselves and all our life to obey him, but faith is a receiving of the grace offered us in Christ."[91] Repentance is the inevitable result of faith (3.3.5). It must never be viewed as preceding faith, any more than the fruit of a tree precedes the planting and growth of the tree (3.3.1). Calvin writes, "No one will ever reverence God but him who trusts that God is propitious to him" (3.3.2). That does not mean that a period of time needs to elapse, however, before faith gives birth to repentance (3.3.2); rather, repentance naturally and immediately flows out of faith. To place repentance before faith can produce the erroneous doctrine of preparationism, akin to Roman Catholic theology, which views works of penance as contributing to the believer's justification.

As Ronald Wallace has pointed out, Calvin most commonly relates faith as a response to the Bible's more gracious aspects and repentance to its sterner aspects, including a "sincere and serious fear of God" (3.3.5) and grief over sin in reflecting upon God's judgment and wrath upon it.[92] This cannot be taken up as an exclusive rule for Calvin, however, since Calvin can also say that "fear and faith are mutually connected" (3.2.23). Wallace concludes: "We are here dealing with a realm of personal encounter

---

88. *Commentary* on Rom. 6:6.
89. *Commentary* on 1 Peter 4:1.
90. Leith, *John Calvin's Doctrine of the Christian Life*, 70.
91. *Commentary* on Acts 20:21.
92. See *Commentary* on 2 Cor. 7:10.

and personal response where the action of God and the response of man cannot possibly be systematically analyzed and neatly summarized, and Calvin is too great a thinker to attempt such exact systematization."[93]

For Calvin, repentance is a more inclusive term than for Reformed theologians in subsequent centuries. It is nearly synonymous with conversion and sanctification. In fact, Calvin describes repentance as deriving from "conversion or return." It involves confession of sin as well as growth in holiness. Repentance is the lifelong response of the believer to the gospel in his outward life, mind, heart, attitude, and will (3.3.1–2, 6, 18, and 20).

Grace and Means

For Calvin, receiving or appropriating salvation is possible only by God's sovereign grace. In exercising saving grace, however, God uses means. The first three chapters of book 3 of Calvin's *Institutes* present us with the basic means: the Holy Spirit, faith and assurance, and repentance—all working by and through the Word. Calvin's exposition of how these means work in the lives of believers is Christ-centered and God-honoring as well as biblically and experientially nuanced, clear, and profound. In particular, 3.2 is one of the greatest chapters ever written on the relationship of faith and assurance, and perhaps one of the greatest in the entire field of soteriology. If these three chapters were carefully read, studied, and prayed over by Christians today, the Christian church would be freed from many errors and would escape the clutches of both easy believism and hyper-Calvinism.

93. Ronald S. Wallace, *Calvin's Doctrine of the Christian Life* (Grand Rapids: Eerdmans, 1959), 97.

13

THE LAW AND THE
SPIRIT OF CHRIST

INSTITUTES 2.6–9
DAVID CLYDE JONES

Calvin is famous for many things, not least of which is the distinctive contribution to soteriology that earned him the title "theologian of the Holy Spirit."[1] The subject is broached early in the *Institutes* in connection with the exposition of the Ten Commandments (2.8), book-ended in the final edition with new chapters on Christ the Mediator (2.6–9). Calvin's well-known analysis of the use of the law (2.7) now precedes rather than follows his exposition of the Decalogue, and it provides an illuminating gateway for understanding the doctrine of salvation by grace. The law under discussion

---

1. I. John Hesselink, "Appendix: Calvin, Theologian of the Holy Spirit," in *Calvin's First Catechism: A Commentary* (Louisville: Westminster, 1997), 177–87. Hesselink laments that so little has been written on the subject, especially in English, since Warfield first made the (widely acknowledged) acclamation nearly a century ago.

is the moral law, the universal norms of love, the precepts of piety and justice that reflect God's nature and his purpose for human beings created in his image. This law is implanted in human nature (*lex indita*), so that as creatures endowed with reason, human beings both aspire after truth and have some universal impressions of civic fairness and political order (2.2.12–13). In the end, however, natural knowledge of the moral law serves to render human beings inexcusable for not putting it into practice, blinded as they are by self-love. God intervenes in the sinful entail of ignorance and arrogance by revealing his covenant to his chosen people and promulgating the moral law in writing (*lex scripta*). On Calvin's analysis, the use or function of the moral law in its scriptural setting is threefold, which may be conveniently characterized as *preparative*, *preservative*, and *restorative*.

The first use of the law is to prepare sinners to seek salvation in Christ, and particularly justification, through faith alone; the second use is to preserve order in society and the elect prior to their conversion; the third use represents Calvin's breakout understanding and deserves to be quoted in full: "The third and principal use, which pertains more closely to the proper purpose of the law, finds its place among believers in whose hearts the Spirit of God already lives and reigns" (2.7.12). Luther had also used the terms "principal and proper" but with respect to preparative use of the law to convict and condemn sinners. That Calvin is tacitly correcting Luther is debatable, but it is clear that a difference in emphasis has emerged. This is true even to some extent for Calvin, who in the first edition of the *Institutes* (where the use of the law is inserted in the middle of the doctrine of justification) had said only that to Spirit-indwelt believers the law provides "no unimportant use, warning them as it does, more and more earnestly what is right and pleasing in the Lord's sight." From "no unimportant use" to "principal and proper use" is a remarkable advance in strength of expression, and Calvin made the change in the 1539 edition.[2] Calvin's rhetorical coup underscores his distinctive understanding of the role of the law within the covenant of grace. With the work of Christ as the ground of justifica-

2. Byung-Ho Moon, *Christ the Mediator of the Law* (Waynesboro, GA: Paternoster, 2006), 72.

tion and the Holy Spirit as the dynamic of sanctification, the Decalogue is finally appreciated for its true function in Christian discipleship. It was a long time in coming.

The Ten Commandments in Church History

So accustomed are we to the use of the Ten Commandments along with the Apostles' Creed and the Lord's Prayer as the three major forms of Christian catechesis that we may forget this was a rather late development in the history of the church's discipleship of her members. While Irenaeus (130–200) defended the permanence of the Ten Commandments as "natural precepts" which God gave humanity from the beginning and which were written in the hearts of the patriarchs before Sinai, he proposed their use for only the very earliest stage of Christian instruction, to be followed by the Sermon on the Mount as Christians mature in their faith and obedience.[3] By the time of Cyril of Jerusalem (315–86) even that minimal role seems to have been neglected. In his Lenten *Catecheses*, preparatory to baptism on Holy Saturday, Cyril expounded the Creed and the Lord's Prayer. He included some moral instructions, but not as an exposition of the Ten Commandments.[4]

As the catechumenate developed in the Western church, those undergoing progressive instruction in the Christian faith were divided into four groups: (1) *accedentes*, candidates for instruction in the faith; (2) *catechumeni*, candidates for baptism; (3) *competentes*, those approved for baptism; (4) *neophyti*, the newly baptized. Augustine's *First Catechetical Instruction* (c. 405) is the only surviving work dealing with the *accedentes*, consisting of pagans and heretics (covenant children were taught at home). The instruction, appropriately, is in the form of narrative: creation-fall-redemption. It was given in a single lesson, after which the candidate is asked whether he believes these things and desires to observe them. Augustine provides this admirable summary of Christian practice:

3. Irenaeus, *Proof of the Apostolic Preaching*, trans. Joseph P. Smith (New York: Paulist, 1952), 86–96.

4. *The Works of Saint Cyril of Jerusalem*, vol. 1, trans. Leo P. McCauley and Anthony A. Stephenson (Washington, DC: Catholic University of America Press, 1968), 130–38.

[Jesus] sent to [his disciples] the Holy Spirit (for so He had promised), that through the love poured forth in their hearts by Him, they might be able to fulfill the law not only without its being a burden but even with delight. Now this law was given to the Jews in ten commandments, which they call the Decalogue. And these again are reduced to two, namely, that we should love God with our whole heart, and with our whole soul, and with our whole mind; and that we should love our neighbor as ourselves. For that on these two commandments depend the whole law and the Prophets the Lord Himself has both said in the Gospel and made manifest by His own example.[5]

Augustine certainly gives the *accedentes* the right perspective on grace and law. The ideal place for him to have expounded the Ten Commandments is the small treatise he wrote in the last decade of his life in response to the request of one Laurentius, a lay Christian who wanted a portable handbook containing the answers to some key questions of apologetics. Augustine interprets the request as a desire for a summary of the true wisdom which consists in the service of God, the short answer to which is, "God is to be served in faith, hope, and love." Augustine jests that this might be too brief even for Laurentius, so he proposes a mini-treatise on the three theological virtues. He gave it the Greek title *Enchiridion* ("handbook"), intending it to function as a comprehensive summary of the Christian way of life.[6] Having spent 113 sections on Faith expounding the Apostles' Creed (with many digressions), lest the *Enchiridion* become the doorstop Laurentius was not looking for, Augustine wraps it up with three on Hope, the substance of which is contained in the Lord's Prayer, and five on Love, which fulfils the law by grace and the power of the Holy Spirit.

Augustine is very clear on the necessity of grace and the Holy Spirit, without whom "the law may bid but it cannot aid" (119). The law as law exposes sin, but God graciously bestows the Holy Spirit through whom the love that fulfils the law is shed abroad in our hearts. Augustine alludes

5. Augustine, *The First Catechetical Instruction*, trans. Joseph P. Christopher (Westminster, MD: Newman, 1962), 41.

6. *Augustine: Confessions and Enchiridion*, trans. Albert C. Outler (Philadelphia: Westminster, 1955).

to the Ten Commandments, which are "rightly obeyed only when they are measured by the standard of our love of God and our love of our neighbor" (121), but he misses the opportunity to incorporate the Ten Commandments along with the Creed and Lord's Prayer as the foundational materials for Christian discipleship. Augustine's sound understanding of the law and the Spirit of Christ will require reiteration and elaboration by Calvin in view of the theological declension of the church over the next several centuries.

Following the division of the church East and West in 1054, there was a revival of interest in the Decalogue among Western theologians. The *Institutiones* of Hugh of St. Victor (1096–1141) gave a brief exposition of each commandment and of love as the fulfilment of the law. Hugh directly influenced Peter Lombard (1100–1160), whose inclusion of a section on the Decalogue in the *Sentences*, the prime textbook of systematic theology in the Middle Ages, was an agenda-setting precedent. However, except for the commandment against false witness (perjury was a significant contemporary issue), Lombard's exposition is only sketchy and perfunctory. As a recent interpreter of Lombard remarks, "It is obvious that the commandments must stand at the periphery of the Lombard's ethics of charity. In their predominantly negative mode, they do nothing more than to indicate the 'other' of charity, as it were, its outside, the spaces of human conduct where it has broken down."[7]

This negative thrust dominates the use of the Ten Commandments prior to the Reformation, particularly in connection with the sacrament of penance, defined by the Fourth Lateran Council in 1215. Convened by Pope Innocent III, the council's twenty-first canon, known by its incipit *Omnis utriusque sexus*, was a landmark in the history of the church dogma, destined to become a flashpoint of theological debate some three hundred years later in the first of Luther's ninety-five theses. The controversial provision reads as follows:

> *Omnis utriusque sexus fidelis* . . . All the faithful of both sexes, after they
> have reached the age of discretion, must confess all their sins at least
> once a year, to their own parish priest, and perform to the best of their

7. Philipp W. Rosemann, *Peter Lombard* (New York: Oxford, 2004), 143.

abilities the penance imposed, reverently receiving the sacrament of the Eucharist at least on Easter Sunday. . . . Otherwise they shall be cut off from the Church during their lifetime and shall be without a Christian burial in death.[8]

Calvin devotes an entire chapter (3.4) to the scholastic doctrine of penance, according to which forgiveness of sins is conditioned on three elements: contrition, confession, and satisfaction. If one is truly contrite, so the theory goes, one will have the desire to confess to a priest and to perform the work he prescribes as a penalty in order to receive absolution. Forgiveness is thus conditioned on works and not received by faith alone. The result is pure misery. Of course, Calvin says, forgiveness of sins presupposes repentance. "But it makes a great difference whether you teach forgiveness of sins as deserved by just and full contrition, which the sinner can never perform; or whether you enjoin him to hunger and thirst after God's mercy to show him . . . where he ought to seek refreshment, rest, and freedom" (3.4.3, alluding to Matt. 11:28). In the background is Lombard's dual foundation of the hope of eternal life in the grace of God *and* the merit of works. The crucial issue is thus synergism. Calvin quotes Lombard by name, "If you dare to hope for anything without merit, that ought not be called 'hope' but rather 'presumption'" (3.2.43). For Calvin the exact opposite is the case: to ground hope in good works to any degree is the height of presumption and an insult to God's free grace.

As for the requirement to "confess all your sins," Calvin writes: "I shall sum up what sort of law this is. First, it is simply impossible; therefore it can only destroy, condemn, confound, and cast into ruin and despair. Then, depriving sinners of a true awareness of their sins, it makes them hypocrites, ignorant of God and of themselves" (3.4.18). Nor is amendment of life a sufficient sequel to contrition and confession, according to the Roman theologians: "But they say there are many helps by which we may redeem sins: tears, fasting, offerings, and works of charity. With these we must propitiate the Lord. With these we must pay our debts to God's righteousness. With these we must compensate for our transgressions.

---

8. *The Medieval Sinner: Characterization and Confession in the Literature of the English Middle Ages*, trans. Mary Flowers Braswell (London: Associated University Presses, 1983), 26. Calvin cites the language of the canon in 3.4.15.

With these we must merit his pardon" (3.4.25). There are two issues here. One is theological, the other is pastoral: "that Christ's honor be kept whole and undiminished; that consciences assured of pardon for sin may have peace with God" (3.4.27).[9]

As a follow-up to Lateran IV, Archbishop John Peckham of Canterbury in 1281 bound the English clergy to teach "four times a year, on one or more holy-days," the articles of faith, the commandments of the Decalogue, the two precepts of the gospel, the seven works of mercy, the seven capital sins ("with their progeny"), the seven principal virtues, and the seven sacraments of grace. On the continent, the Ten Commandments figured prominently in the popular exposition of the Christian faith offered by Jean Gerson (1363–1429), chancellor of the University of Paris. The highly influential *Opusculum tripartitum* was a Latin translation of Gerson's popular catechetical-pastoral works: *Le miroir de l'âme; Examen de conscience selon les péchés capitaux; La science de bien mourir.* "The Mirror of the Soul" is a concise exposition of the Ten Commandments.

To this growing body of literature in the wake of Lateran IV, Franciscan Brother Dietrich von Münster (Dietrich Kolde, 1435–1515) contributed *A Fruitful Mirror or Small Handbook for Christians* (1470). The first printed catechism in German, it received the imprimatur of the theological faculties of Cologne and Louvain and proved immensely popular, being reprinted nineteen times before 1500 and at least twenty-eight times afterward.[10] The preface advises Christians to have it at hand at all times "since it contains everything that is necessary for the well-being and salvation of the soul." A run-down of the contents provides a window on what medieval theology considered essential for spiritual well-being: the Creed; the Decalogue; the five commandments of the church; the seven deadly sins; the nine alien sins; the openly discussed sins and the mute sins against nature; the six sins against the Holy Spirit; the great sins of the tongue; six conditions of forgiveness; seven signs of the state of grace; repentance, confession, and satisfaction; various devotional instructions

---

9. Calvin, like Luther, commends confession to one's own pastor for persons struggling with forgiveness, with this qualification: "that where God prescribes nothing definite, consciences be not bound with a definite yoke" (3.4.12).

10. Denis Janz, ed., *Three Reformation Catechisms: Catholic, Anabaptist, Lutheran* (New York: Edwin Mellen, 1982). 8.

and prayers, including the Paternoster and Ave Maria; and finally, how to die. Brother Dietrich is especially concerned that Christians understand the meaning of penitential satisfaction:

> You should know that according to canon law the penance we receive from the priest is not sufficient even for the least mortal sin that we have committed. Therefore it is necessary for us to do even more penance, for example by groaning, crying out, begging help, giving alms, private mortification of the flesh, sharp clothes or belts around the body, or by disciplines, or vigils, or humbly going on pilgrimages. [ch. 22].

The only way out of this depressing morass, Luther concluded, was by recovery of the biblical doctrine of justification by faith alone, for which a new catechetical approach was necessary. In 1520 Luther published his three main pastoral works as *A Short Form of the Ten Commandments, of the Creed, and of the Lord's Prayer.* The logic of Luther's order is (1) conviction of need, (2) where to find aid, and (3) how to ask for it: "A man who is sick needs first to know what his illness is and what he can and cannot do. Then he needs to know where the medicine is that can help him live the life of a well man. Third, he must desire this medicine and look for it until he finds it or have it brought to him."[11]

These materials became the basis for Luther's justly famous Small Catechism (*Der Kleine Katechismus*), first published in 1529 in the form of placards or posters for display in churches, schools, and homes, and snapped up immediately by a spiritually hungry public.[12] The parts of Luther's Small Catechism, which is presented as an enchiridion especially for pastors and preachers, are as follows: the Ten Commandments, the Creed, the Lord's Prayer, the sacrament of baptism, and the sacrament of the altar. The latter is preceded by "A Short Method of Confessing" intended especially for those about to receive communion. This provides the model for the first edition of the *Institutes*, which Calvin similarly

11. Martin Luther, cited in Carl Volz, ed., *Teaching the Faith: Luther's Catechisms in Perspective* (River Forest, IL: Lutheran Education Association, 1967), 47.
12. The larger *Deutsch Catechismus* was published later the same year; in 1580 both it and the Small Catechism were made official church doctrine by inclusion in the Book of Concord.

intended as a kind of enchiridion, as he explains in the prefatory letter to King Francis I. The first five chapters of the original *Institutes* follow the standard catechetical format: Ten Commandments, Creed, Lord's Prayer, sacraments (with a fifth chapter on false sacraments).[13] The sixth chapter, unique to Calvin, is an apologia in three parts: Christian freedom, ecclesiastical power, civil government. This landmark work was then developed in two directions: a more simplified catechism and a much more amplified systematic theology in which the Ten Commandments are finally understood as an integral part of God's covenantal revelation.

The Ten Commandments in the History of Redemption

Calvin made a number of key hermeneutical moves in connection with his exposition of the Ten Commandments that enabled him to articulate as never before their proper office in the doctrine of salvation.[14] The most far-reaching of these moves is Calvin's location of the Ten Commandments within the history of redemption, preparing the way for his distinctive understanding of the relationship between the moral law and the indwelling Spirit of Christ. For Calvin the definitive text is Romans 10:4: "For Christ is the end (*telos*) of the law unto righteousness to every one that believes." Taking *telos* in the sense of "completion or perfection," Calvin understands that the law was given to "lead us by the hand" to Christ. By "law" he understands the whole scriptural revelation (*lex scripta*): "Indeed, every doctrine of the law, every command, every promise, always points to Christ."[15] In short, the purpose of the Holy Scriptures, including the Ten Commandments, is to make us "wise for salvation through faith in

---

13. Cf. the classic statement of Henrician Anglo-Catholicism (1537): *The Institution of a Christian Man*, which contained the Creed, the seven sacraments, the Ten Commandments, the Lord's Prayer and Ave Maria, plus an article on justification and a brief notice on prayers for the dead and purgatory. Charles Lloyd, ed., *Formularies of Faith* (Oxford: Clarendon, 1825). The revised edition, *A Necessary Doctrine and Erudition for Any Christian Man* (1543), added articles on freewill and good works.

14. Calvin's preferred terminology for the third use of the law as the norm of Christian obedience was *usus in renatis*. I. John Hesselink, *Calvin's Concept of the Law* (Allison Park, PA: Pickwick, 1992), 251.

15. *Commentary on Romans*, trans. Ross Mackenzie (Grand Rapids: Eerdmans, 1960), 221. See also *Institutes* 2.6.4 and 2.7.2.

Christ Jesus." In achieving that purpose, the Spirit-inspired Scripture is profitable "for teaching, for reproof, for correction, and for training in righteousness" as the Spirit works by and with God's Word to renew believers in the image of Christ (2 Tim. 3:15–16).

Calvin's hermeneutical breakthrough is reflected in the new chapters that precede and follow the exposition of the Ten Commandments in the final edition of the *Institutes*, significantly advancing the organizing principle of book 2, "The Knowledge of God the Redeemer." The chapter that precedes the exposition of the Decalogue (2.6, "Fallen Man Ought to Seek Redemption in Christ") provides the narrative context for its authentic interpretation. The original excellence and nobility of God's handiwork in creating humankind in his image have been corrupted and defiled by sin to the point of nonrecognition. "The natural order was that the frame of the universe should be the school in which we were to learn piety, and from it pass over to eternal life and perfect felicity." No more. After the revolt of Adam and Eve, wherever we turn we encounter God's curse, so that we cannot infer that God is our Father from the natural order. "Dullness and ingratitude follow, for our minds, as they have been blinded, do not perceive what is true." Conscience serves to make us aware of our alienation from God, no longer worthy to be called his sons. The only hope of salvation is through Christ the mediator, the seed of Abraham, the son of David.

From these two covenants of promise it is clear that "under the law Christ was always set before the holy fathers as the end to which they should direct their faith" (2.6.2). Promulgation of the moral law was necessary in view of human ignorance and arrogance, but it must be fully appreciated that the written law is "graced with the covenant of free adoption" (2.7.2). The preface or preamble to the Ten Commandments forever establishes the proper relationship between enabling grace and obedient love (2.8.13).

The chapter that follows the exposition of the Decalogue bears the lengthy title (made even longer here!), "Christ, Although He Was Known to the Jews under the Law [i.e., the Mosaic administration of the covenant of grace], Was at Length Clearly Revealed Only in the Gospel [i.e., the culminating revelation of the incarnation]" (2.9). The bracketed insertions

310

serve to clarify Calvin's use of "law and gospel" to characterize the major epochs of redemptive history: promise and fulfilment, attested respectively by the prophetic word and the apostolic witness to Christ in the fullness of his saving work, including the outpouring of the Holy Spirit.

The corollary to Calvin's Christ-centered understanding of the Ten Commandments within the one covenant of grace is his analysis of how the moral law functions when abstracted from that context. Calvin distinguishes between the promise of the law as law—eternal life as recompense for observance—and the promise in the law as covenant—eternal life through faith alone. The law as law promises eternal life for the perfect practice of righteousness, which translates as "an unwavering and unwearying observance of the divine will" (3.19.10), and threatens death for a single act of unrighteousness. As Augustine observed, "If the Spirit of grace is absent, the law is present only to accuse and kill us" (cited, 2.7.7). Calvin's opponents invariably define observance down, making artificial distinctions between legal duties and evangelical counsels (2.8.56–57) and between mortal and venial sins (2.8.58–59). Calvin insists that when it comes to the law, it is all or nothing, and sinners need a divine physician to make them well, not a scholastic lawyer to get them off the hook (2.5.18).

Calvin puts the "mirror of the soul" use of the law popularized in medieval handbooks of devotion in its proper context by observing that "righteousness is taught in vain by the commandments until Christ confers it by free imputation and by the Spirit of regeneration" (2.7.2). The law was promulgated to convict sinners of their just condemnation, the true and only preparative for seeking salvation by grace. "The law of the Lord slays where it is cut off from Christ's grace." But if it is branded on the heart and shows forth Christ, then it is the word of life through the Spirit of Christ (1.9.3). In other words, adopting the language of Paul, "Christ is the Spirit who quickens the letter that of itself is death-dealing" (2.7.2). The law in its covenantal context teaches that the power to obey comes from God's goodness; in humbling sinners, the commandments point them to grace (2.5.7).

Calvin provides help in understanding the consistency of the Scriptures on salvation by grace through faith by making the hermeneutical observation that Paul, to refute the error that human beings merit righteousness by works of law, sometimes takes "law" in his opponents' sense. Calvin appeals to Deuteronomy 30:14 ("The word is near you, in your mouth and in your heart") as interpreted by Romans 10:8 ("that is, the word of faith that we proclaim") to illustrate the point. Moses refers to the promise of the gospel, not the precepts which Paul underscores would have been ruinous. The reference is to "the covenant of mercy" that was promulgated as the redemptive context of the stipulations of the law (2.5.12). The passage does not refer to the impossible condition of the law—perfect observance—but the readily accessible condition of the gospel—trust in Christ alone. The perennial stumbling stone of taking the Ten Commandments out of context is the pursuit of righteousness "as if it were based on works" rather than by faith alone (Rom. 9:32).

It is characteristic of Calvin to emphasize that this gospel-evoked, Spirit-given, grace-of-adoption faith embraces Christ "not only for righteousness, forgiveness of sins, and peace, but also for sanctification" (3.2.8). Justification by free imputation of the righteousness of Christ and sanctification by the Spirit of regeneration are inseparable benefits of union with Christ. On this point Calvin is most emphatic: "Christ cannot be known apart from the sanctification of the Spirit" (3.2.8). The point is established early in the *Institutes*: "The end of regeneration is that Christ should reform us to God's image" (1.15.4). The standard of righteousness, "the straightedge to which we must be shaped," is thus none other than the Lord himself who created humankind in his image to reflect his righteousness, wisdom, and holiness (1.2.2). The object of sanctification is to manifest the harmony between God's righteousness and the obedience of believers to confirm their adoption (3.6.1). As Christ is the bond of our adoption, conformity to the likeness of Christ is the goal; his example is the pattern believers are to express in their life (3.6.3). God's grace in regeneration is "the rule of the Spirit to direct and regulate man's will" (2.5.15), correcting, reforming, renewing, moving, acting, impelling, bearing, keeping. The Spirit works by and with the Word, God's revealed will, which Calvin describes positively as "a way in which we ought to walk in safety and a lamp to guide our feet, the light of life, and the school of sure and clear truth" (1.17.2).

The Ten Commandments are the comprehensive summary of the will of God, but for their proper interpretation they must be read in the light of the whole of Scripture, and particularly the teaching and example of Christ. Here Calvin makes another hermeneutical move; for the Decalogue to be viable as a teaching tool, certain rules have to be observed (2.8.6–11). Firstly, the law is spiritual. The reason is the character of the Lawgiver; his will reaches to the innermost recesses of the human heart. Obedience consists not only of external acts of conformity, but inward dispositions, habits of heart and mind. The Ten Commandments are to be understood as interpreted by Jesus in the Sermon on the Mount and in his own obedience to the Father.

Secondly, the precepts embody principles and convey more than the literal words, which are "manifest synecdoches," by which a part stands for the whole. Thus, adultery is not limited to sexual violation of marriage but extends to all forms of sexual sin. In addition, the rule of opposites applies; the negative sets the boundary, but the positive is open-ended in the requirement of love.

Thirdly, since "the law sounds in our ears without effect unless God inspires in our hearts the whole sum of the law" (2.5.6), the commandments are delivered in two tables to underscore the wholeness of the twofold expression of love toward God and our neighbor. As for self-love, Calvin famously remarked, "there was no need of a law that would increase or rather enkindle this already excessive love" (2.8.54). The point is well taken—love requires "the other" for expression, which is why "God is love" eternally is coherent only given the doctrine of the Trinity. But when Calvin posits as the basis of the commandment the emotion of love that stems from our natural depravity (2.8.54), surely he goes wide of the mark. Instead of reading the commandment as, "You shall love your neighbor as you [*now sinfully*] love yourself," he could have made his point (of self-love not being directly commanded) by reading, "You shall love your neighbor as [*a person like*] yourself."

For all its deontological features, Calvin's positive understanding of the role of the law derives from his teleological framework. The perfection of human happiness is to be united with God and to be loved by him (2.1.5). The Lawgiver expresses his personal will by way of precepts or commandments, which in turn are reflective of who he is and his ideal purpose for human beings in their calling as his vicegerents in creation. Since God has delineated his own character in the law, it is unthinkable that it should not be observed by those whom he has graciously adopted as his children (2.8.51). Jesus is the full and final expression of the character and will of God; the law is thus personalized in Christ, the Mediator. Character is ultimately Christlikeness and is formed by the Holy Spirit through the means of grace and the practice of the truth.

Calvin carefully distinguishes between the power of the law (to condemn) and the instruction of the law (to be observed). For those who are united to Christ by faith, the law is a teacher, but not an enforcer (2.7.15). The law continues to exhort believers, "to pinch them awake to their imperfection," but "it may no longer condemn and destroy their consciences by frightening and confounding them" (2.7.14). The law has no power to bind the consciences of believers by a curse because Jesus has fully endured the curse of the law on the cross.

In this connection, Calvin firmly rejected the law-gospel dialectic in which the (typically Lutheran) formula *simul iustus et peccator* is interpreted to mean: "Christ indeed has life in himself; but you, as you are sinners, remain subject to death and condemnation." Calvin puts his finger on the pastoral problem: "In brief, they so set conscience between hope and fear that it alternates from one to the other intermittently and by turns."[16] The antidote to this unworkable dialectic, in which despair and hope reign in the mind by turns, is the doctrine of union with Christ. Being ingrafted into his body through the effectual work of the Holy Spirit, believers become partakers of Christ himself. The decisive and determinative work of renewal in Christ has already begun. To be sure, "it pleases God gradually to restore his image in us, in such a manner that some taint always remains in our flesh" (3.20.45). But that is a far different thing from being both old Adam and new Adam, which would be equivalent to being both unregenerate and regenerate, old creation and new creation. For those who are united to Christ, the law has no power to condemn.

---

16. Without naming names, Calvin is characteristically vehement in his critique: "Yet we do not thus accept that most pestilent philosophy which certain half-papists are furtively beginning to fashion today" (3.2.24).

The dialectical approach to law and gospel takes as a given the proposition that the law always accuses, meaning the law always convicts and condemns; guilt and punishment are its stock-in-trade. In Calvin's view, condemnation is off the table for believers, but inasmuch as they are still in the process of being renewed, the law always humbles by exposing their imperfection and inability, directing them to the Spirit and the means of grace. The gospel brings both freedom from guilt, wrath, curse, and freedom to the obedience of faith. The privilege of the elect is that "regenerated through the Spirit of God, they are moved and governed by his leading" (2.3.10). The readiness to obey righteousness is the work of the Holy Spirit, to nourish the new inclination of the heart (*habitus*) and to "strengthen its constancy to persevere" (2.3.11). Calvin does not conclude from free justification that the law is superfluous for believers; it teaches and exhorts and urges believers to do good, "though before God's judgment seat it has no place in their consciences" (3.19.2).

The promulgation of the law at Sinai, Calvin asserted with particular clarity and force, was in the context of God's covenant, alternatively referred to as the covenant of mercy and the covenant of free adoption. This paves the way for Calvin's most distinctive insight: the law was never intended to be a rule of life apart from the gift of the Spirit. The law itself teaches that "for the fulfillment of all God's commands the grace of the Lawgiver is both necessary and is promised to us" (2.5.9). Calvin admits that the time-worn formula "ability limits obligation" has a certain surface plausibility, but argues that to measure what human beings are capable of by the precepts they are commanded to obey rests on "the crassest ignorance of the law" whose purpose and fulfilment are Christlike love (2.5.6). Thus, the Spirit of Christ is necessary for fulfilment of the covenant precepts, and the covenant Lord graciously promises the illumination and enablement of his Spirit to bring it to fruition.

Nor is this characteristic of only the "new law"; the covenant with the patriarchs is one and the same as ours in substance and reality, differing only in mode of dispensation (2.10.2). The same grace is common to both dispensations; they had a slight taste of what we richly enjoy, a glimpse of what is clearly revealed to us with the incarnation of Christ and its attendant redemptive events. Though there is an important comparative difference between the testaments, the basic principle is one and the same:

> God works in his elect in two ways: within, through his Spirit; without, through his Word. By his Spirit, illuminating their minds and forming their hearts to the love and cultivation of righteousness, he makes them a new creation. By his Word, he arouses them to desire, to seek after, and to attain that same renewal. [2.5.5]

It is the Spirit alone who sanctifies, but as human beings are not sticks or stones their activity is elicited to the fullest extent. The key text is Philippians 2:12–13. Paul assigns tasks so as not to indulge the sluggishness of the flesh, but to correct sloth. "But enjoining fear and carefulness, he so humbles them that they remember what they are bidden to do is God's own work." To avoid any semblance of synergism, Calvin notes that "believers act passively, so to speak," by which he means capacitated from heaven so as to be able to claim no credit to themselves. As for the "reward" of good works, Calvin repeatedly cites Augustine's maxim: "God does not crown our merits but his own gifts" (2.5.2). Thus, "[God] rewards, as if they were our own virtues, those graces which he bestows upon us because he makes them ours" (2.5.2).

We do the things for which God receives praise because (1) "whatever God out of his loving-kindness does in us is ours" and (2) "ours is the mind, ours the will, ours the striving, which he directs toward the good" (2.5.15). God's grace in regeneration works efficaciously: correcting, reforming, renewing, moving, acting, impelling, bearing, keeping the human will. The idea of human merit is thus radically excluded, though human beings are significantly engaged in participation in the renewal process.

Calvin's figures of speech for the functions of the law are for the most part straightforward and easily understood. As a preparative for faith, the law is a mirror to show sinners their sin and their need of a Savior. As a preservative in a fallen world, the law is a halter to restrain the godless in civil society and a bridle to keep the unconverted elect in check pending regeneration. As the instrument of the Spirit in sanctification, the law is a lantern to guide believers in their new obedience, to enable them to grow in wisdom and knowledge of the will of God. The Word is God's revealed will, "a way in which we ought to walk in safety and a lamp to guide our feet, the light of life, and the school of sure and clear truth" (1.17.2). Calvin notes how often in the Psalms (e.g., Ps. 119) the believing approach to the law is accompanied with constant prayer for illumination as well as enablement. "Without the illumination of the Holy Spirit, the Word can do nothing" (3.2.33). The efficacy of the Word at every point depends on the grace of the Spirit.

Though Calvin's primary metaphor for the third use of the law is that of a lantern, since the law not only instructs but exhorts believers, Calvin introduces an additional metaphor: "The law is to the flesh like a whip to an idle and balky ass, to arouse it to work" (2.7.12). This seems to attribute to the law a motivating power that is inconsistent with the gospel, and indeed some Lutheran theologians have seized on it to charge Calvin with legalism. But Calvin is speaking to the usefulness of exhortation in the Christian life, a subject he had dealt with in answering the typical objections to the doctrine of the bondage of the will (2.5.5). Exhortations have a particular value for believers in whom the Spirit makes effective use of the instrument of the Word: "with the Spirit acting within, they are perfectly able to kindle in us the desire for the good, to shake off sluggishness" (2.5.5). The law is thus an instrument of the Spirit, if not to whip us into shape, at least to "pinch us awake" to our imperfection and to spur us on to love and good works motivated and enabled by grace.

Although the "balky ass" simile may seem over the top in a theological context where the emphasis overwhelmingly falls on the freedom of the gospel, it nevertheless fits with Calvin's realistic appraisal of indwelling sin and the consequent sluggishness of the flesh. It may help to realize that Calvin is speaking out of his own experience, that he regarded himself as lazy.[17] If that self-assessment is to be taken at face value, then Calvin's productivity is all the more remarkable as a triumph of God's grace. What really propelled Calvin was his extraordinary sense of calling as a teacher in Christ's church. This he felt duty-bound at all times to fulfil, even against his natural inclinations, in obedience to and empowered by the Spirit of Christ.[18]

17. Jean-François Gilmont documents Calvin's confessed "laziness" in *John Calvin and the Printed Book*, trans. Karin Maag (Kirksville, MO: Truman State University Press, 2005), 92.

18. The largely unappreciated existential aspect of Calvin's doctrine of the Spirit is explored by I. John Hesselink in a groundbreaking article, "Governed and Guided by the

Preaching the Ten Commandments

The surest proof of a grace-based understanding of the law is a theologian's exposition of the Ten Commandments for a popular audience.[19] Here Calvin exceeds expectations, at least for those who have no prior knowledge of his pastoral heart. Contrary to the way he is usually typecast—it is no secret that Calvin could be difficult, even irascible—in these sermons he is warm, personal, gracious, embodying in his language and appeal the overtures of the gospel that he knows provide the only viable motivation for obedience. A couple of examples will suffice. First, on the condescension of God in entering into covenant with his people, Calvin says,

> For if God only demanded his due, we should still be required to cling to him and to confine ourselves to his commandments. . . . [But it pleased God] by his infinite goodness to enter into a common treaty . . . [he] mutually binds himself to us . . . enumerates that treaty article by article . . . chooses to be our father and savior . . . receives us as his flock and his inheritance. It is as if God said, "I set aside my right. I come here to present myself to you as your guide and savior. I want to govern you. You are like my little family. And if you are satisfied with my Word, I will be your King." Besides, the purpose is not "to take anything from you." Rather, "I procure your well-being and your salvation."[20]

This draws on Calvin's exposition of the prologue in the *Institutes* where Calvin emphasizes the personal pronoun, "I am the Lord *your* God."

On motivation in the Christian life, Calvin says,

> The beginning of obedience, as well as its source, foundation, and root, is [the] love of God . . . this love cannot exist until we have tasted the

---

Spirit," in *Reformiertes Erbe*, vol. 2, ed. Heiko A. Oberman et al. (Zurich: Theologischer Verlag, 1993), 161–71.

19. Edmund P. Clowney, *How Jesus Transforms the Ten Commandments* (Phillipsburg, NJ: P&R, 2007), provides a contemporary model of exposition in the best Calvinistic tradition.

20. John Calvin, *John Calvin's Sermons on the Ten Commandments*, ed. and trans. Benjamin W. Farley (Grand Rapids: Baker, 1980), 45.

goodness of our God. For as long as we conceive of God as being opposed to us, of necessity we will flee from him. Therefore do we wish to love him? Do we wish to be reformed by being obedient to him that we might receive all of our pleasure in his service? Then we must realize that he is our Father and Savior, that he only wants to be favorable to us. Thus once we have tasted his mutual love which he reserves for us, then we will be motivated to love him as our Father. For if this love is in us, then there will be no doubt that we will obey him and that his law will rule in our thoughts, our affections, and in all our members.[21]

Finally, there is Calvin's take on the comparison God makes between his anger and his mercy (Deut. 5:9–10):

Now by that he shows what is still better explained in other texts of Scripture, that he is slow to anger, inclined toward mercy, patient, and that, if his anger burns for a minute, his lovingkindness is for life and permanent. Thus there you have the true character of God; that he only wants to draw men in all gentleness and does so through his goodness. When he punishes them it is almost (*quasi*) against his nature. Not that it is any more improper for God to punish than it is for him to be gracious, but he wishes to show us that his goodness is much greater, and, in brief, that he is not harsh. Rather he only wants to open his heart to us if we will permit him. In fact, he wills to be known as good and merciful; and it is in that that his glory principally shines.[22]

Here Calvin directs his hearers away from being motivated by servile fear, which "obeys" only out of dread of punishment, to filial piety, which yields willing obedience out of love and reverence for one's heavenly Father. "Even if there were no hell," Calvin says, the pious mind "would still shudder at offending him alone" (1.2.2; 3.2.26). Similarly, in rejecting the Roman doctrine of penance, Calvin distinguishes between God's retributive justice, fully satisfied for the elect by Christ on the cross, and his corrective love by which God chastens his erring children (3.4.31–35). Calvin's preaching of the Ten Commandments is directed toward producing the fruit of the Spirit in the lives of God's children by the covenant of free adoption.

21. Ibid., 76.
22. Ibid., 78.

14

ETHICS: THE CHRISTIAN LIFE AND GOOD WORKS ACCORDING TO CALVIN

INSTITUTES 3.6–10, 17–19
WILLIAM EDGAR

W hile not explicitly trinitarian, the structure of the *Institutes* can certainly be understood generally to move from themes that relate to the first, the second, and the third persons of the Godhead. Thus the entire work begins with the Father ("The Knowledge of God the Creator," book 1), then moves to the Son ("The Knowledge of God the Redeemer in Christ . . .," book 2), finally to the Holy Spirit (in two parts, "The Way in Which We Receive the Grace of Christ," book 3, and "The External Means . . .," book 4. Chapters 6 to 8 of book 3 concern the Christian life, which for Calvin is effected by the secret working of the Holy Spirit. As he puts it, "I say that no uprightness can be found except where that Spirit reigns that Christ received to communicate to his members" (3.3.2). This point could not be more important. Calvin would never consider such matters as the cultivation of righteousness, self-denial, and the rule of love, without grounding them in the same grace of God through Christ in the Spirit by which we were introduced to the reality of salvation. Thus, in the immediately preceding chapters, he goes to great lengths showing the nature of faith, and the manner in which at every point it is awakened in us by the Spirit himself.

This synopsis considers two related but nonsequential sections in Calvin's *Institutes*. The section in book 3, chapters 6–10 addresses the Christian life, while the section in book 3, chapters 17–19 addresses good works. One oft-noted feature of this portion of Calvin's *Institutes* immediately leaps out. Sandwiched into these two sections on the Christian life is a full discussion of justification by faith (chapters 11–16). Why would this be? Calvin, the Reformer, certainly accords justification a primary place. He calls it the "main hinge," and says that "unless you first of all grasp what your relationship to God is, and the nature of his judgment concerning you, you have neither a foundation on which to establish your salvation nor one on which to build piety toward God" (3.11.1). Again, justification is the "soil out of which the Christian life develops."[1] So, would it not be confusing to place this topic in the middle of a larger discussion on sanctification, especially since his Roman Catholic opponents tended to confuse the two?

Perhaps there is no single answer to this question. But surely at least two can be adduced. First, Calvin places the discussion of sanctification (he often calls it regeneration) before justification precisely because it heads off possible objections from the Roman Catholics who would accuse him of antinomianism (*libertinage*).[2] Ever the polemicist, he wants to show his opponents that he cares deeply about sanctification. In that way he is somewhat different from the Lutherans, who were perceived so to emphasize justification as not to recognize the importance of piety. Indeed, Calvin is so concerned for piety, the holiness of life, the knowledge of God and true sanctification, that he sees justification here as a means

---

1. John H. Leith, *John Calvin's Doctrine of the Christian Life* (Louisville: Westminster/John Knox, 1989), 87.

2. See the very helpful analysis of Wilhelm Niesel, *The Theology of Calvin*, trans. Harold Knight (Philadelphia: Westminster, 1956), 130ff.

as much as an end. Second, Calvin's arrangement of material drives home the point that the two are inseparable, both being part of the larger topic of union with Christ. In *Institutes* 3.3.1 he announces that he will discuss the effects of faith in Christ, which comports two things, the newness of life (sanctification) and free reconciliation (justification) that are given to us. They are inseparable. Calvin is not underplaying justification, but showing it for its true value, in the context of the whole. So as not to minimize justification, he says that by discussing repentance first, it will "better appear how man is justified by faith alone." Holiness of life cannot be separated from the free imputation of righteousness (3.3.1).

There is a primacy in Calvin's understanding of living for the glory of God. In his view we are being claimed by God for his own glory in such a way that both justification and sanctification are "members" of the same covenant of grace, through our union with Christ. They are inseparable though distinct. To separate them is to "tear Christ in pieces," as he says in his commentary on 1 Corinthians (1:30). As John Leith elegantly puts it, "[For Calvin] it must be constantly borne in mind that the pardon of sins is the prerequisite and milieu in which sanctification takes place."[3]

The general term that encompasses the Christian life for Calvin is "regeneration." Unlike our modern tendency to reduce regeneration to the moment of the new birth, Calvin sees it as a process which moves the believer forward from sin and vice to eternal life. And, in contrast with the place regeneration came to occupy among the Puritans, which was the way of access producing faith, here it more broadly refers to the entire process of the Christian life. Similarly, he uses the term "repentance" to indicate the natural outcome of faith, which in turn is grounded in the gospel. That outcome is to depart from oneself and to turn to God. These two terms are virtually synonymous, perhaps the one stressing God's initiative and the other human effort. They both apply to the entire process of conversion: "Therefore, in a word, I interpret repentance as regeneration, whose sole end is to restore in us the image of God" (3.3.8).

Although there is a once-for-all aspect to this rebirth in Christ, restoration does not take place in an instant, but over a period of time, over

3. Leith, *John Calvin's Doctrine*, 65. See also Peter A. Lillback, *The Binding of God: Calvin's Role in the Development of Covenant Theology* (Grand Rapids: Baker, 2001), 180–85.

an entire lifetime. So concerned is Calvin to ground this process in the free grace of God, and to keep it clear from human corruption, that he spends a good deal of time, with sharp polemics, defining true repentance over against penance, indulgences, and the like (3.3.5).

The Christian Life: Book 3, Chapters 6–10

Our first section, 3:6–8, forms a unit. Calvin calls it a treatise.[4] He sets forth the basic purpose in the first sentence: "The object of regeneration, as we have said, is to manifest in the life of believers a harmony and agreement between God's righteousness and their obedience, and thus to confirm the adoption that they have received as sons [Gal. 4:5; cf. 2 Peter 1:10]." Notice the basic goal is to wed together human obedience with divine righteousness. Calvin argues that the Christian life (regeneration) is a striving to conform increasingly to the image of Christ, after having corrupted our natures in Adam. But it is never a matter of starting from scratch. Rather, it is an outworking of our adoption. "For we have been adopted as sons by the Lord," he says, "with this one condition: that our life express Christ, the bond of our adoption" (3.6.3). This stress on showing ourselves to be children accomplishes the same purpose that moves Calvin throughout, namely that in the Christian life we are paradoxically becoming what we are. And what we are is entirely the product of God's love. Thus, we will see him appeal for our sanctification as our beginning point, expressed in numerous ways: dwelling in the New Jerusalem (3.6.2), being God's sons by adoption (3.6.3), having the gospel in our hearts (3.6.4), all of which exhibit that we function in terms of our most basic, God-given identity. We strive *from* this identity, and not *unto* it.

Book 3, Chapter 6

To begin with, it is worth noting a stylistic feature of this section, one that Calvin cares deeply about, one that characterizes his work as a whole. It is a commitment to brevity. "Brevity and clarity" were themes that

---

4. The section is sometimes published separately and titled *The Golden Booklet of the True Christian Life* (Grand Rapids: Eerdmans, 1985).

gripped Calvin throughout his life.[5] Here he is concerned not to distract his readers with the vain inanities of the philosophers. Whereas they strove for nimbleness of wit, the Spirit of God teaches "without affectation." Calvin also muses on the curious need felt by many, including the Fathers, to wax prolix when describing the virtues of the Christian life. He admits he loves brevity by nature, but adds that he would fail were he to go on at length, because the Scriptures themselves love this kind of powerful concision (3.6.1).

His entire instruction in these chapters can be summed up as twofold: the love of righteousness from our hearts, and a discipline to guide us in our zeal for this righteousness (3.6.2). In our first section he particularly delves into the love of righteousness. He will take up the discipline, or rule, more in chapters 17–19. But here Calvin stresses motive. There is no better way to begin than the reminder that we must be made holy because our God is holy. As God gathers us lost people to himself he joins us to himself, with the bond of holiness. Not our holiness, but his, which is the fundamental reason for our calling. If we are to dwell in the holy city of Jerusalem, then we may not profane the place with any impurity.

In 3.6.3 Calvin reflects upon the difference between the biblical idea of conformity to Christ's likeness and the philosopher's notion of virtue, in accordance with nature.[6] As adopted children of God and as those baptized in Christ, we must no longer "befoul ourselves with new pollutions." And since we are destined for heavenly incorruption with an unfading crown, we must live our lives in the light of our goal. None of this perspective is found in the philosophers, whose notion of virtue never rises above the natural dignity of man.

Continuing the theme of motives, in 3.6.4 Calvin attacks those who live their lives externally, and not from the heart. The knowledge of Christ cannot be apprehended merely intellectually, but "it is received only when it possesses the whole soul, and finds a seat and resting place in the inmost

5. A historical fact not without significance is that this mentality, which stresses brevity and clarity, has a background in Renaissance humanism. And it also would be influential on the rise of modernity in many forms. Calvin, like Luther for German, was a chief agent in modernizing the French language.

6. He would appear to be thinking of Cicero's and Seneca's views. In his *Moral Essays* Seneca declares that "To live happily is to live according to nature" (2.116f.).

affection of the heart." Here he is echoing what he has said in other places, especially in his reflections on the nature of faith. True faith does not "flit about in the top of the brain," but takes root in the depths of the heart (3.2.36; see also 1.5.9 and 3.2. 8, 33). Again, none of this depth is found in the philosophers.

Finally, in 3.6.5, Calvin warns against perfectionism. This is comforting after the very high standards he has just set. No Christian has yet attained evangelical perfection. If utter perfection were the only measure of our faith, we would have to clear the church of everyone. Instead, what we are after is integrity, sincerity, the cultivation of holiness. Although we must be wary of perfectionism, we may all hope to make some progress. "No one shall set out so inauspiciously as not daily to make some headway, though it be slight" (3.6.5). Indeed, we are on a journey, and while we are still in the "earthly prison of the body," we do not have the strength we need to move any faster. The image of the body as a prison, which Calvin often employs, owes something to Plato.[7] There is no doubt that for him the soul is the most essential and characteristic component of our natures, capable of the knowledge of God, and thus of immortality. In that regard, the body is but a prison (1.15.2). However, Calvin is aware that Plato is less than helpful when describing the components of the soul. In an extended discussion of human anthropology, he reviews the views of several philosophers only to suggest the reader pass them over (1.15.6–8).

Book 3, Chapter 7

With this chapter Calvin begins a strong discussion of self-denial. Significantly, he begins in 3.7.1 by praising the law, but then by showing that God has given an even more explicit plan than that provided by the law, a plan to conform us to him in reasonable worship. Following Paul's words in Romans 12:1–2, he stresses that our identity is in God. Being his possession, we have been dispossessed of our own autonomy and pressed into God's service. Characteristically, he terms service to mean obedience to God's Word, but also emptying the mind of its carnality

7. See, for example, 3.9.4 and 3.25.1. A considerable body of literature on the influence of Plato on Calvin's anthropology can be found. See, for example, Dewey Hoitenga, *John Calvin and the Will: A Critique and Corrective* (Grand Rapids: Baker, 1997).

and turning it to the bidding of the Holy Spirit. Of this turning, again, the philosophers were ignorant. But "the Christian philosophy" bids our reason submit entirely to the Holy Spirit, "so that the man himself may no longer live but hear Christ living and reigning within him [Gal. 2:20]." The expression "Christian philosophy" is used several times by Calvin to mean conformity to the Scriptures, in contrast to the work of the philosophers, which means ordering one's thought merely by human wisdom.[8]

It is striking to note how much Calvin is concerned with the psychology of conversion in these pages. In denying the self and yielding to God, we leave off an unhealthy desire for power, ambition, and "other secret plagues" (3.7.2). Whereas the philosophers can pursue virtue only for its own sake, the Christian is so focused on seeking God's will that he is truly able to rid himself of all evil vices in order to get on with righteousness as a way to join "in true holiness to God." Calvin has a brief section on self-renunciation according to Titus 2 (3.7.3). At the heart of this Pauline ethic is a twofold move, a repudiation of ungodliness and worldly lusts, and the embrace of true godliness and holiness, which can be accomplished only by recalling the hope of blessed immortality. Again, he describes our sanctification as a journey: we are pilgrims in this world, traveling on to our celestial destination.

In 3.7.4 Calvin directs our attention to proper relations with our neighbors. What he attacks most in his admonitions to properly respect others is pride. Following tradition, he recognizes this greatest vice as the mother of all sins. Throughout the *Institutes* Calvin stresses the importance of considering our tendency to arrogance and merit.[9] He reminds us that any talent we have received is from the Lord, a gift, not a meritorious accomplishment. When we realize that we have nothing that we have not received, then we may bestow to others the honor they are due, being properly reverent and lowly toward them. He goes on in 3.7.5 to

8. While the concept of a Christian philosophy can be traced back to the Fathers, and throughout the Middle Ages, it came into its own in this Renaissance sense in the works of Erasmus. See Erasmus, *Responsio ad Stunicam*, LB 10:367C. Also, Jean-Claude Margolin, *Érasme, précepteur de l'Europe* (Paris: Julliard, 1995), chapter 10.

9. Early in book 2, while reminding the reader about the nobility of the human race and our free will, he explains that original sin has damaged our grandeur through pride. In his long and thoughtful defense of free will, his chief concern is that we distinguish between our natural free will and the part of freedom which has been lost through sin (see 2.1.4).

remind us that any gift we have is for the sake of the church. Following Paul in his letters to the Corinthians, and many other biblical passages, he explains that every good gift we have is meant not for ourselves, but to be distributed for our neighbor's good. He introduces the notion of stewardship, which is so strongly present in his many works, and which would become so central to later Reformed theology.[10] We have received our gifts as a trust, for the sake of others, and we shall be held accountable for our stewardship of them.

In 3.7.5–7 Calvin further develops the theme of self-renunciation, especially in relation to our responsibility to our neighbor. Here he leans on Paul's description of love from 1 Corinthians 13, and then on his metaphor of the body in the previous chapter. He eloquently reminds the reader of the need to put others first, and use all of one's gifts for their benefit. Even when there is advantage for ourselves, that is of secondary importance to the benefit of neighbor. Thus, everything is subjected to the rule of love. Ultimately, though, our gifts come from God, "the Author himself," without whom our gifts are not sanctified, though we fool ourselves into thinking our generosity benefits their Author. Calvin is at pains to explain that while our gifts are of little value in themselves, yet if we consider their beneficiary to be God's image-bearers, then we will have less difficulty in sharing them. Indeed, we may be called to benefit our very enemies. And because God himself has had their crimes charged to his own account, then we are free to look, not at their evil intentions, but at the image residing in them, with its beauty and dignity.

Although not the focus of his discussion here, earlier Calvin asks who this neighbor might be. In his extensive treatment of the Ten Commandments he often remarks on the identity of our neighbor, and the need always to promote his dignity, no matter who he may be (2.8.13–50). At the end, discussing the law in relation to the teachings of Christ, he asks outright who our neighbor is (2.8.55). His answer, based on the parable of the good Samaritan (Luke 10:25–37), is that the neighbor includes "even the most remote person." In sharp contrast to our modern sensibility, he

---

10. For example, in his second sermon on Job, he has an extended section on Job's conscientious and generous use of his riches. John Calvin, *Sermons on Job* (Edinburgh: Banner of Truth, 1993).

argues that we must embrace the entire human race with no distinction in a single feeling of love, so that we see everyone in God, not in themselves. Thus, Calvin does not make a basic distinction between the household of faith and the rest of the world, even though he acknowledges that we will have friends that are closer than others.

Continuing his discussion of self-denial and love of neighbor, he advocates giving material gifts freely and without contempt (3.7.7). True love requires that we put ourselves in the place of him who is in need. If we see ourselves as debtors to our neighbors, we will be combining Christian virtue with the law of nature. Again in 2.8.1, before going into the Ten Commandments, he discusses the relation of the written moral law of God to natural law. Most often, as here, Calvin speaks of the natural law as centered on our conscience. Throughout the *Institutes* we find various discussions on the conscience.[11] For Calvin, it means that "inward law" which is engraved upon the hearts of all, and thus, "in a sense asserts the very same things that are to be learned from the two Tables." Accordingly, the ancients could be well aware of the requirements of the natural law. Thus Calvin goes on to quote Seneca's dictum that we are "born to help one another."[12] But the ethic of Christian love will extend this principle so that we should be limited in its expression only by coming to the end of our resources.

In the final section (3.7.8–10) self-denial is elaborated in relation to God. So resignation of ourselves goes hand in hand with the full acceptance of the Lord's will. Calvin rails against our evil desire of pomp and vanity, because it robs us of true happiness, which may be found only in God. However severe our trials, in the end honor and riches will only lead to misery, while abandonment to God will bring blessedness (3.7.8). Here Calvin is particularly severe against the pursuit of riches and honor (3.7.9).

In the light of his admonition to rest only upon the Lord and renounce the vainglorious pursuit of gain, it is surprising that an idea about a simple

11. His most extensive treatment of conscience is in 3:19, where he discusses the theme of Christian freedom. Although the law objectively prescribes the conditions for true freedom, the conscience is the inward sense of the law's requirements. So conscience is "a sense of divine judgment" (3.19.15). And a good conscience is "nothing but inward integrity of heart" (3.19.16). Above all, he is anxious to let the Word of God rather than any set of man-made rules rule the conscience (3.10.1).

12. *Homo in adiutorum* (to assist, to help) *mutuum genitus est*, from *De ira* 1.5.2.

relation between Calvinism and capitalism has become popular. According to the Weber thesis, God's love by election is absolutely free, and so in the search to find out whether or not one is elect, one must work hard to amass tangible signs of blessing. Thus, profit-making, charging interest, and generating wealth are encouraged, and a free market economy is the structural result.[13] While it is true that Calvin allowed for interest within certain boundaries, it is mistaken to find the source for market capitalism in his views of election and assurance of salvation, which say nothing about making sure one produces visible signs of material blessing.[14] And it is certainly true that Calvin commended diligence and hard work, yet he would never equate those with the assured outcome of wealth. Quite the contrary, from this passage and many others (see 3.10.3–6) we find him warning most severely against seeking any solace in fortune. Again, like Seneca, Calvin recommends not trusting in "blind fortune" who wounds the deserving and undeserving alike, but instead trusting in God alone who may prosper or deprive us, but will always be orderly and just (3.7.10).[15]

Book 3, Chapter 8

Here Calvin takes up the subject of suffering. Though succinct, in keeping with his intentions as mentioned above, this chapter includes some of the most beautiful and profound thoughts about the subject penned by any Christian. It flows directly out of the previous material on self-denial. Sections 1–6 center around the theme of the cross. Then, building on this, he treats the larger issue of persecution, then compares

13. Max Weber, in *The Protestant Ethic and the Spirit of Capitalism* (New York: Scribner, 1958), argues that Calvin never taught this directly, but by implication his theology led to a close psychological association between being elect and the pursuit of tangible manifestations of the glory of God. For a thorough discussion of the Weber thesis, see *Protestantism and Capitalism: The Weber Thesis and Its Critics*, ed. Robert Green (Boston: Heath, 1959).

14. In his 1545 letter to his friend Claude de Sachin on usury Calvin argues that one could lend with interest to businessmen who would make a profit, but not to the working poor, who stood no chance of making any profit. *Opera Quae Supersunt Omnia*, 10:245–49. In English, see Oliver O'Donovan and Joan Lockwood O'Donovan, *From Irenaeus to Grotius* (Grand Rapids: Eerdmans, 1999), 682–69. Compare Calvin's commentaries on Ex. 23:25; Lev. 25:35–38; Deut. 23:19–20; and Ps. 15:5.

15. See Seneca, *On Tranquility of Mind*, 8–11.

the biblical approach to that of the philosophers. One cannot read these pages without the keen sense that Calvin himself suffered a great deal in his life.[16] However, unlike our modern practice, he virtually never referred to himself, and not even here where it might have added credence to his case. Instead, he focuses on the cross and union with Christ.

Sections 3.8.1–2 set forth the ground rules. We must suffer because Christ our Redeemer was called to a life of suffering. Indeed, "his whole life was nothing but a sort of perpetual cross." If this Son of God who was loved above any other should have to suffer, why should we be exempt? But this is ultimately a great comfort, since just as he passed through "a labyrinth of all evils into heavenly glory," so may we share in his sufferings so as to share in his glory. Calvin is so confident in this union that he declares the very sufferings to be blessed and to help promote our salvation. As usual, Calvin is greatly concerned to keep away pride. And so he argues that Christ's sufferings had only one purpose, to show his obedience to the Father, whereas ours have several purposes, especially to restrain our arrogance. When we are truly humble, then we are truly able to call upon the Lord and be established in his strength, rather than our own.

In 3.8.3–6 Calvin develops the theme of patience and obedience. Basing his arguments on the cross, he shows in how many ways good things come from this instrument of death. By it we are given hope (Rom. 5:3–4). By it we, like Abraham, are made patient. By it our virtues, conferred by God, are stirred up. By it we learn obedience. In 3.8.5 Calvin compares the cross to medicine. By our natural complacency we become flabby, and so to make us healthier the Lord confronts us with the cross.[17] In 3.8.6 the cross is deemed the instrument by which the Father chastens us. Even in the harshest of tribulations we can thus know the kindness of the Lord,

---

16. Calvin was almost never well. He suffered stomach difficulties. He was an insomniac. He had gallstones, and lung troubles, most likely tuberculosis. He was stricken by the quartan fever of 1558–59, and was so delicate toward the end that he had to be carried about. Moreover he was often in bereavement over friends and relatives. His son lived only a few months after a premature birth, and Idelette, his dear wife, was constantly ill, and died after less than nine years together: "Truly mine is no common grief," he related, "I have been bereaved of the best friend of my life." And, of course, Calvin was hated by many, persecuted, once banished from Geneva, and never quite safe from opposition.

17. This must have struck some of his readers as nearly comical, in that Calvin was so thin as to be emaciated.

since all of it contributes to our salvation. When we fall away from him, he either destroys us or recalls us by reproof. For the unbeliever chastisement results in hardening. For the believer it leads to repentance. Calvin urges the reader to choose in which group he would prefer to be numbered.

Now the focus changes to address persecution (3.8.7–8). As he puts it, persecution for the sake of righteousness is a "singular comfort." Calvin includes a broad spectrum within the notion of persecution, but reminds us we must see it as a blessing, as do the beatitudes (Matt. 5:10). Poverty, exile, contempt, prison, disgrace, and death itself are so many examples of such blessedness. Touchingly, he tells us that if we are cast out of our own house, we are yet received more intimately into God's family. He goes on to relate that disgrace is one of the worst forms of suffering, but that following Paul we can take comfort in our reproaches, for such was Christ's call as well.

Calvin would never glorify the pain itself, nor does he fall into a Stoical stiff upper lip (3.8.9–11). Our cheerfulness does not take away bitterness and pain. The Stoics and the "new Stoics" among Christians are wrong to teach their "iron philosophy," since Christ himself groaned and wept over his own and others' suffering.[18]

Throughout these discussions one must note the pastoral approach taken by Calvin. He is concerned that believers not be plunged into despair because of the natural feeling of sorrow engendered by suffering. The remedy is the cultivation of patience. In this Christians will be torn because of both their inclination to flee adversity and their godly desire to submit to God's will (3.10.10). Calvin cites the case of Peter's martyrdom, predicted by Jesus (John 21:18). When the time

---

18. Calvin's interactions with the ancient Stoics are complex. On the one hand he often agreed with them on individual doctrines. For example, on the concept of the creation the Stoics taught (against the Epicureans) that the purpose for making the world was so that mankind could use it. (See, for example, *Institutes* 1.14.22.) On the other hand, as here, Calvin faults them for their view of *apatheia*, and for their belief in fate. While Calvin agreed with them that suffering was sent by God, he denies their cold, passionless approach to human misery. See Charles Partee, *Calvin and Classical Philosophy* (Louisville: Westminster/John Knox, 2005), chapter 8. The so-called new Stoics (the term *novi Stoici* was likely coined by Calvin) refers to a sixteenth-century movement, led by Justus Lipsius (1547–1606) and eventually including Pierre Charron (1541–1603) and Michel de Montaigne (1533–92), which revived the Stoic idea of *apatheia*. They ultimately denied the reality of suffering altogether.

for his death would come, Peter would be unlikely to resist it. Otherwise his martyrdom would not have been praised.

On the subject of martyrdom Calvin takes the standard Protestant position. On the one hand the testimony of martyrs is vital for establishing the credibility of the Scriptures (1.8.12–13). On the other hand we need to guard against any undue glorification of martyrs, since only Christ's blood can atone for sin (3.5.3). Calvin of course had firsthand acquaintance with the call to martyrdom. So many French Huguenots would go into their ministries in order to be put to death. Calvin held a large correspondence with the persecuted church. He saw an intimate connection between believers shedding their blood and the shed blood of Christ. In his discussion on the Lord's Supper Calvin argues against the Roman practice of reserving the cup only for the priest. Citing Cyprian, he contends for lay people needing to partake of the cup: "How do we teach or call upon them to shed their blood in confession of Christ, if we deny Christ's blood to those about to fight? Or how do we make them fit for the cup of martyrdom, if we do not first in the church by the right of communion admit them to drink the cup of the Lord?"[19]

Finally, here, Calvin brings all these thoughts together and reiterates his plea that we neither resist our trials, nor simply yield to them as though they were a grim necessity, but instead "bear patiently," knowing that they are for our good (3.8.11). For "in the very act of afflicting us with the cross [the Father] is providing for our salvation."

Book 3, Chapters 9–10

We should consider these final two chapters on suffering and the Christian life together. For they treat of the balance between a wrong and a right kind of attachment to this world. If one does not read the entire section, then one could get the impression that Calvin is preaching detachment. He does begin strongly with reminders that an unbalanced love for this life will be disastrous (3.9.1–2). One of the chief purposes

19. On the attitude toward martyrdom in the French Reformation, see Nikki Shepardson, *Burning Zeal: The Rhetoric of Martyrdom and the Protestant Community in Reformation France, 1520–1570* (Lehigh, PA: Lehigh University Press, 2007).

of tribulation is to keep us focused on heavenly immortality. Following Christian tradition, Calvin reminds us that our aspiration to immortality is what makes us different from the animals. Calvin compares man and beast in several places in the *Institutes*. Our aspiration to immortality is one of our unique traits, not shared with animals (1.4.3). Reason and conscience testify to our immortal spirit (1.15.2).

In 2.2.12, in the midst of a discussion of the vestiges of natural gifts in human beings, he notes that while we are corrupt, there is still enough left of human reason so as to distinguish us from the animals.[20] Here we clearly detect the influence of Plato. The question is, however, whether he received Plato's anthropology uncritically or not. In his treatment of the image of God (1.15) we find him interacting with Plato a fair amount. In 1.15.6, for example, he approves Plato over others, because he attaches the image of God to the soul. He goes on to discuss the five senses, the cognitive faculties of the soul, and the appetitive faculties; in this he is quite obviously supported by Plato and, to a lesser extent, Aristotle. But then he turns around and declares these distinctions obscure, preferring the simpler distinction between understanding and will (1.15.7). The reason the philosophers are not sure guides, as was earlier mentioned, is that they ignore the corruption of human nature.[21]

What seems certain about Calvin's anthropology is that while to some degree it works with the Greek view of a separation of body and soul, with the soul being prone to immortality, yet he is breaking away from the Platonic idea of the body as a prison for the soul (3.6.5) as well as the idea that the soul is somehow deathless by nature. In the New Testament, immortality belongs only to God, and is conferred to man, in all his attributes, body, soul, mind, heart, as a gift (1 Tim. 6:16). Calvin's strong view of the physical resurrection is one of the indicators that he is moving away from a purely Platonic notion.[22]

---

20. This entire section in 2.2 has valuable insights into the natural and the supernatural gifts of God. In 2.2.14–16 Calvin discusses what we would call common grace. All of these natural gifts tell us that the faculty of reason distinguishes us from both beasts and inanimate things (2.2.17).

21. See n. 7. For a helpful discussion of Calvin's approach to immortality, see Paul Helm, *John Calvin's Ideas* (New York: Oxford University Press, 2006), 129–56.

22. See Murray J. Harris, *Raised Immortal* (Grand Rapids: Eerdmans, 1985), 201–5.

Thus here Calvin argues that because of the vanity of the human heart, and a wrongheaded search for earthly happiness, the Lord sends his people proof of the miseries of the present life, precluding an unhealthy attachment to it. Under the "discipline of the cross," we learn that this life is troubled, and "in no respect clearly happy" (3.9.1). There is no immortality for us on earth, so we need constantly to be reminded that here we are but a vapor and a shadow (3.9.2).

But now, so as not to state all of this too strongly, Calvin exhorts believers not so to hate the present life that it leads to an improper disdain for its benefits. Characteristically, his chief concern is for gratitude toward God (3.9.3). If we had the wrong kind of contempt for the world, we would ignore its testimony to God's goodness. So good is the world, in this way, that it becomes an appetizer, whetting our hope, for God's full revelation.

Calvin finally returns to the theme of longing for eternal life (3.9.4–6). He endorses the pessimism of unbelievers, since they have nothing to hope for. Again, he tells believers that if heaven is our true home, then earth must be seen to be a place of exile (3.9.4). But still, there is the balance: this earthly life is never to be hated except in that it holds us subject to sin. He eloquently exhorts us to rejoice at the prospect of death and final resurrection, for which we long with groaning and sighs (3.9.5). Finally, in the most rhapsodic section of this text, he reminds us of the comfort and joy that are to come, and the vanity of hoping in anything less than the peace of God's kingdom. "To conclude in a word: if believers' eyes are turned to the power of the resurrection, in their hearts the cross of Christ will at last triumph over the devil, flesh, sin, and wicked men" (3.6.6).

Calvin then extends his discussion of the balance between the denial and the enjoyment of the things of this life in 3.10. But here, the emphasis is clearly on the enjoyment of life. In 3.10.1 he critiques those who would only grudgingly indulge in physical goods. No doubt thinking of Augustine, who allowed for marriage only out of necessity, Calvin worries about the unnecessary severity of mere concession.[23]

23. For example, Augustine's treatise *On the Good of Marriage*, 1.9, has it that "cohabitation . . . should not be a matter of will but of necessity." To which he adds that without this union there could be no children. For Calvin, this is "a godly counsel," but "far too severe."

Instead, we ought to be guided by our conscience, rather than restraining our freedom.[24]

In 3.10.2 we have one of the most succinct and powerful statements of Calvin's ethics: "Let this be our principle: that the use of God's gifts is not wrongly directed when it is referred to that end to which the Author himself created and destined them for us, since he created them for our good, not for our ruin. Accordingly, no one will hold to a straighter path than he who diligently looks to this end." From here he waxes eloquent on the good things of the earth: food is not only for need but for delight; clothing is not only necessary but comely; in grass, trees, and fruit there are beauty of appearance and pleasantness of odor; wine is for gladdening the heart. His argument is that God gave us things to enjoy, and not simply for their utility. For those who may think Calvin has no aesthetic sense these passages together with many others throughout his writings should lay such a view to rest.[25]

Calvin continues his teleological approach to ethics in 3.10.3–6. And it is always with that balance that we see him strike throughout. He is as exercised over the inhuman philosophy that disallows taking pleasure in God's good gifts as he is against the lust of the flesh. Following Christian tradition, particularly the Fathers, he rails against "banqueting" and gluttony.[26] He returns to the theme of contempt for the world, and desire for heavenly immortality. To put this in modern terms, Calvin is concerned for priorities. Quoting Cato, he affirms, "There is great care about dress, but great carelessness about virtue" (3.10.4).[27] And he sets forth three basic rules, based on 1 Corinthians 7:29–31, not fixed formulae but general guidelines. (1) If you use the things of this world do not overindulge. (2) If you are called to a life of few means, be patient about it. (3) Remember

24. On the conscience, see n. 11.

25. See, for example, his *Commentary on Genesis*, Gen. 4:20. Also, while it is somewhat dated, consult the excellent French study by Léon Wencelius, *L'Esthétique de Calvin* (Paris: Les Belles Lettres, 1937). See also William Dyrness, *Reformed Theology and Visual Culture: The Protestant Imagination from Calvin to Edwards* (Cambridge: Cambridge University Press, 2004).

26. Among the many Fathers who wrote on such excesses, none is more eloquent than Augustine, whose *Confessions*, especially 10.30–34, is likely in his mind here.

27. McNeill traces this quote to an attribution to Cato by Ammianus Marcellinus, *Calvin: Institutes of the Christian Religion*, ed. John T. McNeill, 2 vols. (Philadelphia: Westminster, 1960), 1:722 n. 6.

the one to whom we shall render account, the God who enjoins moderation. As was mentioned above (3.7.8–10), it is hard to see how so many, following a certain interpretation of Weber, can attach credence to the connection between Calvinism and the quest for prosperity.

Finally, in 3.10.6, significantly the last part in this section on sanctification, Calvin discusses calling.[28] Again he places this grand notion in the context of human rashness and the need to quell one's ambitions for the sake of staying within certain divinely established limits. As many have noted, Calvin is both conservative and progressive on human vocation. He is conservative because he insists that we stay by our sentry post and not wander around heedlessly through life.[29] And he inserts a brief word forbidding regicide. Progressive, though, because there is no hierarchy of callings in God's view. So that it is a noble thing to free one's country of tyrants, although not by the individual citizen. He ends this whole section with eloquent words about handling our frustrations because of our calling. If we know the burden was placed upon us by God, then we will have this singular consolation: "that no task will be so sordid and base, provided you obey your calling in it, that it will not shine and be reckoned as precious in God's sight."

About Good Works: Book 3, Chapters 17–19

Now, then, after his magisterial treatment of justification in 3.11–16,[30] Calvin takes up ethics again. He is not just picking up from 3.3.6–10, since the discussion on justification is foundational to all of sanctification.

---

28. There exists a considerable body of literature on Calvin's view, and the Reformed view, of calling. See André Bieler, *The Social Humanism of Calvin* (Louisville: John Knox, 1964); Georgia Harkness, *John Calvin: The Man and His Ethics* (New York: Henry Holt, 1931); R. S. Wallace, *Calvin's Doctrine of the Christian Life* (Edinburgh: Oliver & Boyd, 1959); Bernard Cottret, *Calvin*, M. trans. Wallace McDonald (Grand Rapids: Eerdmans, 1995), see esp. 136, 165; and Alister E. McGrath, *A Life of John Calvin: A Study in the Shaping of Western Culture* (Oxford: Blackwell, 1993). To put calling in the larger context, see Douglas J. Schuurman, *Vocation: Discerning Our Callings in Life* (Grand Rapids: Eerdmans, 2004).

29. Alluding to Cicero's *On Old Age*, he tells us we are each assigned a sentry post which we should not leave.

30. The remainder of this essay may be consulted after reading Richard Gaffin's treatment of justification (ch. 11, pp. 248–69).

This time, however, having fully explained justification, he will focus on the relation of the law to the gospel. This is a perennial issue in theology, but it was specially critical in the sixteenth century. Controversies had arisen, not only from the Roman Catholic Church, but also within Protestantism, about the relation of good works to grace, and thus law and gospel. In general, for the Roman Catholic Church keeping the law was an essential part of being reconciled to God. Martin Luther opened up a fresh way to understand the relationship of law to gospel.

Protestants generally agreed that the law was given to Adam as a way of life. Not that law was anything but a gift, nor was it anything but the blessing of a good God. But the covenant of works, as it would be called, was valid for our first parents, but was terminated when they fell. By God's mercy, another arrangement was instituted, the covenant of grace. The law, good in itself, now shows us our sinfulness and our need for a Savior who could free us from guilt. Because he perfectly kept the law, and died in the place of his people, Christ became this Savior, and imputed his righteousness to us. For Luther and his followers the distinction of law and gospel is quite pronounced, and forms a basic structural foundation to their theology. For Calvin and the Reformed tradition the relation of law and gospel is more complex. Three uses of the law are identified: the first, to restrain and guide society; the second, for conviction of sin; and the third, to direct believers in the life of righteousness.

Two principal threats exist to keeping these things straight. The first is moralism, or legalism. When law is stressed to the detriment of gospel, piety becomes drudgery, and assurance wanes.[31] The opposite danger is antinomianism, which so emphasizes the freedom of the gospel that it becomes careless about sin and the need for the law. Lutherans especially were accused of antinomianism by Roman Catholics.[32] The Reformers had challenged the prevailing view that penance was a sacrament involving

31. On this tendency within the Puritans, see C. Fitzsimmons Allison, *The Rise of Moralism: The Proclamation of the Gospel from Hooker to Baxter* (Vancouver: Regent College, 2003).

32. Although less concerned with the third use of the law, Luther was nevertheless critical of some in his own movement for antinomianism. The most notable case is his disagreement with Johann Agricola, with whom he and Melanchthon had disputes. See Thomas M. McDonough, *The Law and Gospel in Luther: A Study of Martin Luther's Confessional Writings* (New York: Oxford University Press, 1963); and Timothy J. Wengert, *Law and Gospel: Philip Melanchthon's Debate with John Agricola of Eisleben over* Poenitentia (Grand Rapids: Baker, 1997).

contrition, confession, and satisfaction. So the Catholics were able to retort that they were not committed to repentance, nor really to the Christian life, especially as it is represented in the law. Here, then, Calvin begins a significant section in which he addresses these issues.

Book 3, Chapter 17

In 3.17.1–5 Calvin conducts a frontal attack on those who would accuse Protestants of denying good works. He is quite combative, no doubt because this issue is of critical importance for the integrity of the Christian faith. He gives numerous memorable aphorisms and elegant statements here. For example, "For justification is withdrawn from works, not that no good works may be done, or that what is done may be denied to be good, but that we may not rely upon them, glory in them, or ascribe salvation to them" (3.17.1).

As Calvin interacts with critics of the Reformation, he demonstrates considerable knowledge of their arguments. One line of reasoning was advanced by some of Luther's opponents: if the law is not simply nullified, then why should it not be effective? They cite scores of passages which tell us that keeping the law will result in God's blessing.[33] Calvin answers with the distinction mentioned above: true, the law promises blessings to those who keep it, but if we, sinners, cling to the law, we will now only discover its curse, because God requires perfect keepers of the law, and none can be found. The function of the law is to convict of sin, not to give us salvation. Salvation, indeed, means freedom from the bondage of the law (3.17.1). However, this is not to say all the promises of the law are void, because in the gospel we are so restored as to rediscover the righteousness of the law. So, another aphorism, "our depravity makes us experience no benefit [from the law] until we have obtained another righteousness from faith" (3.17.2).

Basically Calvin argues that the promises of the law are still in effect, only they must be understood through the gospel. The law by itself only

33. The best-known of these critics was Erasmus, who worried that if the gospel simply trumps the law, then what is to prevent wanton immorality? But according to Luther, he lacked a basic knowledge of the true law-gospel distinction and thus was in danger of "confounding everything." See *Luther and Erasmus: Free Will and Salvation*, ed. Ernest G. Rupp (Philadelphia: Westminster, 1969), 197.

condemns our pretended good works. But the law as lived-out because of the gospel enables us to walk in righteousness without having to earn our salvation (3.17.3). He gives three reasons. (1) God reproves any good works in themselves, but accepts them when they are done through Christ by faith. (2) Because of his generous love, God raises our poor works to a place of some honor and value. (3) He receives our works in a spirit of forgiveness, knowing they are imperfect. Calvin rails against the "Sophists" who claim that within the covenant, somehow good works are of great value.[34] Although he somewhat repeats his arguments from 3.11.13–20, here he is still focused on the law.

In 3.17.4 Calvin begins to present his well-known doctrine of double acceptance. Over against the Sophists he argues that there is not one ounce of righteousness in us by nature. But once we are accepted by the pure mercy of God, then the Spirit begins to work in us good things, his fruit, which God also accepts. Thus, there is a sense, after justification, in which we may be accepted for our good works. "God 'accepts' believers by reason of works only because he is their source" (3.17.5).[35] Calvin is careful to explain that all of the biblical passages that teach that we are approved because we keep God's commandments refer to an obedience generated only by the same God who has forgiven us (Heb. 3:1; 1 Peter 2:5; Rom. 9:21; Deut. 7:9).

Moving on, in 3.17.6–15 Calvin discusses in considerable detail exactly how good works relate to justification by faith. The many promises indicating that God is merciful to those who love him make sense only if we understand we are adopted as children, and the sign of being children is the good fruit of righteousness. Doing righteousness is never the foundation by which believers have their acceptance, but the means whereby we are gradually formed and strengthened in his fellowship (3.7.6). Calvin

---

34. Calvin no doubt is referring to the schoolmen from the Sorbonne, a steady target of his disagreements, rather than to all scholastics. He clearly makes a distinction between the "Sophists" and the "sounder schoolmen," such as Thomas Aquinas and Abelard, toward whom he was more sympathetic (see 2.2.6).

35. The occurrences of justification and sanctification are not sequential, though distinct in character. Peter Lillback convincingly argues that we have here the framework of the covenant. For in the covenant of grace we may receive a double benefit, justification *and* sanctification. In this Calvin overcomes the exaggerated Lutheran disjunction of law and gospel. Lillback, *Binding of God*, 192ff.

delves deep into those passages where good works are titled righteousness, which to the "Pharisees of our day" appear to be the way of justification (e.g., Deut. 6:25; Ps. 106:30–31). He admits that the precepts of the law are called righteousness, yet he insists that this is in no way an access to God's first acceptance, but only a true description: in the law perfect righteousness is represented, though it cannot save us.[36]

Other passages appear to teach that somehow works are needful to complete our righteousness (3.17.8). For example, Abraham's faith was reckoned to him as righteousness. Here again Calvin argues that we are not justified by works. By justification is meant "the sinner, received into communion with Christ, is reconciled to God by his grace; while cleansed by Christ's blood, he obtains forgiveness of sins, and clothed with Christ's righteousness as if it were his own, he stands confident before the heavenly judgment seat." But then after this forgiveness, the good works of believers are counted righteous because all is covered in Christ's perfection. Good works are evaluated "otherwise than on their own merits." Indeed this kind of works righteousness only makes the power of justification shine stronger (3.17.9). Blessedness is promised throughout Scripture, but it has no benefit to us unless our sins are forgiven in the foundation of justification (3.17.10).

Naturally, Calvin pauses to discuss the relation of James to Paul (3.17.11–12). The issue is that James says a person is justified by works, and not by faith alone (James 2:24), whereas Paul never uses such language.[37] Significantly, Calvin begins not with a harmonization, but with a presupposition. The Holy Spirit who inspired all of Scripture is not going to be in conflict with himself. That being the case, then how should one go about reconciling the apparent contradictions? Furthermore, Calvin continues his pastor's concern. His adversaries would deprive people of

36. As an example of Calvin's careful scholarship, he explains that the Hebrew word *huqim* would have better been translated "edicts" rather than "righteousnesses" in the Septuagint, though he adds that his argument remains the same. He accepts this weaker translation, among other reasons, because Luke does so in describing Zechariah and his wife who "walked in the righteousness of the Lord" [Luke 1:6] (3.17.7).

37. Calvin cites James 2:24, which states that Abraham was "justified by works." Not only are Roman Catholic opponents in view, who thought James supported a role for good works as a foundation, but on the opposite side there was Luther who worried the other way about James's message, calling it a "right strawy epistle."

a peaceful conscience because they would snuff out the light of the truth (3.17.11). He sees James himself as an ally in combating these troubles of souls. They make two simple mistakes, a faulty understanding of "faith" and a faulty understanding of "justify." Nonsaving faith merely believes formally. True faith leans on God's mercy. In 3.17.12 Calvin contrasts James's use of justification with Paul's. James, he contends, is using the term to describe heavenly approval of works that follow true faith, so as to avoid antinomianism, whereas Paul is defining it as the entrance point, where there can be no place for good works.[38]

Calvin next takes up another difficult passage, Romans 2:13, which says it is the doers of the law, not the hearers, who are justified (3.17.13). He rejects Ambrose's solution, to the effect that to fulfil the law requires faith in Christ.[39] Rather, he says, Paul is simply telling the Jews that if they claim the law, they had better be true observers of it, not hypocritically knowing it while despising it. Paul is saying that there is righteousness by the law if one can perfectly keep it. Since no one does, there is no righteousness through the law.

Another issue surrounds the numerous passages that appeal to God to approve good works (for example, Pss. 7:8; 17:1, 3; 18:20, etc.). In effect these passages appear to commend the believer on the basis of works: "Judge me, O Lord, for I have walked in my innocence [Ps. 26:1]." Calvin had previously discussed the relation of assurance to good works (see 3.14.18–20). Here he pleads for respecting the context. These saints are not claiming perfection or freedom from all guilt. Rather, they are asking God to compare the level of their righteousness with that of their enemies. The same psalmist who appeals to innocency in another context asks God

38. While such a harmonization is quite plausible, Calvin may have missed some of James's reasons for the language he used, which, among other things, is meant to be provocative. Although likely the earliest of the New Testament epistles, before Paul had written, there appeared to be a perversion of Paul's message by antinomians. The two uses of the two terms may not have been as far apart as Calvin is contending.

39. He calls this a "mere evasion," the severity of his rejection no doubt owing to the fact that Ambrose's solution was the favorite of opponents of the Reformation, such as Johannes Eck, in the *Enchiridion*, chapter 5, fo. 23a. A good modern edition of this is *Enchiridion locorum communium adversus Lutherum et alios hostes ecclesiae*, ed. Pierre Fraenkel (Münster: Aschendorff, 1979). For an English translation see Johannes Eck, *Enchiridion of Commonplaces against Luther and Other Enemies of the Church* (Grand Rapids: Baker, 1979).

not to enter into judgment, for if God should mark iniquity, who could stand [Pss. 143:2; 130:3]? In 3.17.15 Calvin concludes the chapter by inveighing against perfectionism, yet all the while trying to encourage the practice of good works. So, he says, the uprightness of believers, though imperfect, is indeed a step toward immortality. At the same time in no way can such uprightness give access to salvation.[40] Paul prays that believers may be blameless and irreproachable on the day of the Lord (Col. 1:22; 1 Cor. 1:8, etc.). But only when we have finally put off the flesh may we fully claim such blamelessness.[41]

Book 3, Chapter 18

Now Calvin has a special section on the notion of reward. Associating merit with reward was common in Roman Catholic theology at the time. Calvin is concerned here to fight against any idea that our works have merit.[42] Yet he recognizes that the concept of reward is real enough, and quite present throughout Scripture. To note only one, "God will render to every man according to his works" (Rom. 2:6). Calvin argues again that Paul is talking of a sequence, rather than a cause. Only by mercy are we received into God's glory. But then, we will go on to work for his sake, always by the same grace that began our journey (3.18.1). The same goes for the term "inheritance." Though it is ours, it comes from that same grace of God which freely gave us our benefits in Christ (3.18.2). Now rehabilitating Ambrose, Calvin agrees with him that the parable of the eleventh hour is a strong reminder of God's showering the "riches of his goodness upon those whom he has chosen apart from works" (3.18.3).[43] Our translation from death to life is the true reward, and it is done by

40. Again, the schoolmen made a distinction between works for salvation, which cannot be done, and works given value by God's "accepting grace," which Calvin rejects. Developed by Duns Scotus and Ockham, this idea of accepting grace found its way into Eck's *Enchiridion*, chapter 5.

41. Because of his great respect for Augustine, he allows quoting his phrase "the perfection of the saints," but only in the context of Augustine's strong refutation of Pelagius's friend Coelestus, in *On Man's Perfection in Righteousness*, 9.20.

42. In 3.14.14 he rails against the doctrine of works of supererogation, which suggests that we can do extra good works, when in fact we are basically unworthy servants, doing the minimum, which is already quite a high standard.

43. These comments appear in Pseudo-Ambrose, *The Call of the Gentiles*, 1.5, but not in J.-P. Migne, *Patrologia Latina* 51.

adoption alone. And the reason for the promise of reward is not to puff us up, but to direct us to the greater goal of eternal life. The discipline of the cross prevents us from investing wrongly in the present (3.18.4).

In 3.18.5–10 Calvin takes up various objections against the views he has set forth. Section 5 replies to those who would adduce the reward of a crown of righteousness for God's people. Following Augustine, he answers that the crown is a gift from the same grace as did justify us.[44] In section 6 he takes up the notion of "treasures in heaven." This phrase (Matt. 6:19–21, etc.) refers not to the value of works but to the proper investment of our priorities: "But if we believe heaven is our country, it is better to transmit our possessions thither than to keep them here where upon our sudden migration they should be lost to us." In section 7 he asks whether tribulations are not sent in order to measure the worthiness of those who suffer. On the surface, this is what is conveyed by 2 Thessalonians 1:5. Again, he replies that this is not to attribute worth to our works, but to strengthen our hope in the divine promise. In section 8 he addresses the objection that love can justify us, based on such passages as 1 Corinthians 13. Here he answers in the same vein, but stresses that faith, not love, justifies, because faith is the proper instrument by which to obtain the free righteousness of Christ. In section 9 he responds to the "stupid Sorbonnists" who contend that because Jesus says, "If you would enter into life, keep the commandments" (Matt. 19:17), our obedience has merit. But keeping them is impossible unless we flee to Christ over the brink of death. Finally, in section 10 he makes the interesting point that although in one sense one can weigh good works and evil works on a sort of scale, making death the result of a number of sins and life the result of a number of good deeds, in another it matters greatly how we position ourselves. He notes, as have his opponents, that faith is sometimes called a work (John 6:29). Again, he argues that faith is an instrument, an embrace of mercy, not a good work per se. The force of his argument is that to fail in one place in the law is to fail in all (following James 2:10–11). He disagrees with Luther, who solves the problem by saying condemnation is not the result of an accumulation of sins but merely of unbelief.[45]

44. Calvin continues to interact with Johannes Eck's *Enchiridion*, chapter 5.
45. Typically, Calvin agrees that unbelief is the root of all evil, but he is cautious not to minimize the actual transgression of the law. Good works are therefore quite necessary, but

Book 3, Chapter 19

Finally, we have a splendid chapter on freedom. It is here more than anywhere else that Calvin treats of the conscience.[46] He calls it an "appendage of justification," and considers it impossible to summarize the gospel without a strong mention of the power of freedom. And of course, this is one of the clarion calls of the Reformation.[47] Again he is concerned both to avoid antinomianism and to promote a proper sense of Christian liberty. "Unless this freedom be comprehended, neither Christ nor gospel truth, nor inner peace of soul, can be rightly known" (3.19.1).

Calvin explains that Christian freedom is in three parts. (1) Conscience must rise above all law righteousness. Justification is a matter of God's mercy alone. And while the law retains its (third) use, that has nothing to do with being in Christ alone (3.19.2). This, he reckons, is the entire argument of Galatians (3.19.3). Here Calvin argues against the imposition of anything unnecessary (*in rebus non necessariis*).

(2) True freedom is to obey without compulsion. That is, the conscience must obey the law not by constraint but because now that we are free from its yoke, we readily embrace its teachings (3.19.4). Again, he stresses adoption. Those who are sons will obey imperfectly, but freely, knowing they are already approved by the Father (3.19. 5). Touchingly, he adds that we need no longer fear the remaining effects of sin. Even though we do not feel that sin is fully conquered, being emancipated by grace we are truly free (3.19.6).

(3) The third subject is the *adiaphora*, or "things indifferent." This is a crucial concern in the Reformation, one which was already addressed by Luther, but here made much tighter.[48] Calvin's pastoral concern emerges

---

can be experienced by God's children only because of grace. Luther tends to put everything to the account of unbelief versus faith.

46. He had briefly discussed it before; see 2.7.14–15 and 3.11.17–18.

47. Certainly, Luther's treatise *On the Freedom of the Christian* stands as a landmark document. But the whole Reformation in a forceful way ushered in the modern notion of freedom, with implications for every area of life. See Steven Ozment, *Protestants: The Birth of a Revolution* (New York: Image, 1991).

48. With Luther one of the issues was whether certain ceremonies or rites neither expressly commanded nor forbidden in Scripture could be practiced in good conscience. Melanchthon believed that in times of distress one could practice some of these, so as not to add fuel to the fire of persecution. See his *Apology of the Augsburg Confession* 15.52, where he argues

throughout. He does not want believers to be in doubt, but free of conscience (3.19.7). Here he elaborates on what he had said in 3.10.1–4. He takes up one of the classic texts, Romans 14, and gives extensive comments. (He briefly refers to the other significant passage on the adiaphora, 1 Cor. 8–10, in 3:19, 16.) He argues that not by daring all things, but by using them for the purpose given by God, we may truly be free in practicing things indifferent. In a way, therefore, nothing is quite indifferent, since every practice ought to be subject to God (3.19.8). Always seeking a balance, Calvin cautions against opulence in the name of freedom (3.19.9). Though we have never been forbidden to laugh, eat well, gain wealth, enjoy music, or drink wine, yet when desire gives way to gluttony, then we lose all sense of propriety in the exercise of freedom.

In 3.19.10–13 Calvin discusses how freedom must rightly guard the conscience of the weaker brother. Here he carefully distinguishes between proper respect for the weak and the need to declare our freedom before men. We must distinguish between the truly weaker brother and the legalistic Pharisee, and make our decision accordingly. Care for neighbor should always guide our conscience. "Nothing is plainer than this rule: that we should use our freedom if it results in the edification of our neighbor, but if it does not help our neighbor, then we should forgo it" (3.19.12). He reminds the reader we are not talking about absolute matters, on which there is no room to move, but things indifferent. For example, the papal mass is not something indifferent. To practice it is not a matter of being immature, or feeding on milk (1 Cor. 3:2), but of taking poison (3.19.13)!

Finally (3.19.14–16) Calvin has some words on civil government, a topic he more fully treats in book 4. Still addressing the matter of conscience, he here wants the Christian to be free in the right way with regard to laws and constitutions.[49] He explains that we are under a

---

that love requires freedom in the adiaphora. Matthias Flacius, on the other hand, argued that never could one give in to such practices with a clear conscience. In the *Formula of Concord* (1577), a middle way is proposed in Article 10. On Calvin's approach, see Thomas Watson Street, "John Calvin on Adiaphora: An Exposition and Appraisal of His Theory and Practice" (Th.D. thesis, Union Theological Seminary, 1954); see also *Church History* 27.1 (March 1958): 70–71.

49. It appears by "constitutions" Calvin is not referring to governmental documents but to ecclesiastical constitutions which are burdensome. See 4.10.8–18.

twofold government, the one spiritual and the other political. Is Calvin here teaching the two-kingdoms view of the Lutherans? It would appear that his position is very close, particularly when he argues that there are two worlds over which different kings and laws have authority. But a closer look reveals that Calvin is simply maintaining that we are no less subject to the government, though it be ruled by magistrates, than to the church.[50]

Calvin's main concern here is for the place of conscience. As mentioned above (our comments on 3.7.7), the conscience for Calvin is a tribunal in the heart. Quoting Quintilian, he calls it an awareness of "a thousand witnesses" (3.19.15).[51] "Therefore, as works have regard to men, so conscience refers to God. A good conscience, then, is nothing but inward integrity of heart" (3.19.16). As always, spirituality for Calvin has a Godward reference. Whereas it is perfectly proper to claim, as did Paul, that we need to take pains to walk with a clear conscience "toward God and men" (Acts 24:16), the fundamental concern is for conscience to respect God alone. Were there no people on earth, our conscience would still be bound to God's bidding.

50. Abraham Kuyper and the so-called Neo-Calvinists further developed this idea. When Christ remarks that we ought to render unto Caesar the things of Caesar, he is not suggesting that such obedience is outside of Christ's Lordship. When he says, render to God that which is God's, the clear implication is that everything belongs to God, not only so-called spiritual things.

51. A popular proverb from Quintilian, *Institutes of Oratory*, 5.11.41. Seneca has a similar statement.

15

PRAYER: "THE CHIEF EXERCISE OF FAITH"

INSTITUTES 3.20

DAVID B. CALHOUN

George S. Hendry employed a simple device in evaluating the systematic writings of theologians new and old. He read what they had to say about prayer, and noted how much space they devoted to the subject. It was not that the amount of space was important in itself, Hendry believed, but that it served as an index of how seriously the theologian took prayer.[1]

Integral to John Calvin's thought from his earliest writings is an emphasis on prayer. He begins chapter 3 of the first edition (1536) of the *Institutes of the Christian Religion* with an ample exposition of the

---

1. George S. Hendry, "The Life Line of Theology," *Princeton Seminary Bulletin* 65.2 (Dec. 1992): 25–26.

Lord's Prayer, preceded by a discussion of "Prayer in General" and followed by "The Practice of Prayer."[2]

One of the longest chapters in Calvin's 1559 *Institutes* is about prayer; it extends for seventy pages in the English translation. "This thoughtful and ample chapter, with its tone of devout warmth, takes its place in the forefront of historically celebrated discussions of prayer."[3] One thinks of writings on prayer by the church fathers, especially Tertullian, Origen, Gregory of Nyssa, Augustine, and Hugh of St. Victor, as well as Luther's *A Simple Way to Pray*, Matthew Henry's *A Method for Prayer*, J. C. Ryle's *A Call to Prayer*, and C. S. Lewis's *Letters to Malcolm: Chiefly on Prayer*. Calvin's treatment is to be placed high in this list for its balance, clarity, scriptural faithfulness, and pastoral tone—although in my opinion it lacks something of Calvin's usual care in organization.[4]

It is important to note where Calvin's chapter on prayer comes in the 1559 *Institutes*. After "The Knowledge of God the Creator" in book 1 and "The Knowledge of God the Redeemer in Christ" in book 2, Calvin turns in book 3 to "The Way in Which We Receive the Grace of Christ; What Benefits Come to Us from It; and What Effects Follow." Beginning with a new chapter on the Holy Spirit, Calvin follows with treatments of faith, sanctification, justification, prayer, election, and eschatology. T. H. L. Parker comments that "a hasty reading" might conclude that these topics were "a mixed bag thrown in here because they had to go somewhere. But if we pay careful attention to the 'stage-directions' we shall see that there is good reason for the ordering. We might even say that the *Institutio* reaches its climax here."[5] A Christian on his or her knees praying can be seen as the goal

2. John Calvin, *Institutes of the Christian Religion* (1536), trans. Ford Lewis Battles (Grand Rapids: Eerdmans, 1975), 68–86. For a strophic translation of this chapter, see Ford Lewis Battles, *The Piety of John Calvin* (Grand Rapids: Baker, 1978), 91–116.

3. John Calvin, *Institutes of the Christian Religion*, ed. John T. McNeill, trans. Ford Lewis Battles, 2 vols. (Philadelphia: Westminster, 1960) 2:850 n. 1.

4. In *Praying: Finding Our Way through Duty to Delight* by J. I. Packer and Carolyn Nystrom (Downers Grove, IL: InterVarsity, 2006), Calvin's treatment of prayer in the *Institutes* is described as "a classic minitreatise on the proper mindset for praying and the Lord's Prayer as a pattern for so doing" (308). Most of *Institutes* 3.20 has been recently published as a booklet with the title *On Prayer: Conversation with God*, with an introduction by I. John Hesselink (Louisville: Westminster/John Knox, 2006).

5. T. H. L. Parker, *Calvin: An Introduction to His Thought* (Louisville: Westminster/John Knox, 1995), 107.

to which Calvin's *Institutes* has been moving from page 1 (although book 4 will stress that our Christian identity is found in the life and fellowship of the church). Also Calvin's chapter on prayer is excellent preparation for his long-delayed treatment of election that follows!

The importance that the subject of prayer has for Calvin is obvious, not only in its extent and location, but also in his title for chapter 20 of book 3: "Prayer, Which Is the Chief Exercise of Faith, and by Which We Daily Receive God's Benefits." Book 3 is about faith—"the way in which we receive the grace of Christ"—and prayer is the chief exercise of faith. God, writes Calvin, "has laid down this order: just as faith is born from the gospel, so through it our hearts are trained to call upon God's name" (3.20.1).

Calvin introduces the subject of prayer (3.20.1–2)[6] by looking back to "those matters so far discussed" in the *Institutes*—reviewing in a few words book 1 ("how destitute and devoid of all good things man is") and book 2 (how God in Christ "offers all happiness in place of our misery"). Recognizing then that "whatever we need and whatever we lack is in God," we in prayer draw from him as from "an overflowing spring" (3.20.1). Changing the image, Calvin says that it is "by the benefit of prayer that we reach those riches which are laid up for us with the Heavenly Father" (3.20.2). Calvin's favorite picture of prayer is that of God's adopted children calling upon him as their heavenly Father (3.20.2). Prayer is simply conversation with God our Father (3.20.4–5). It is the unburdening of ourselves in God's presence.[7] By prayer we cast our "desires, sighs, anxieties, fears, hopes, and joys into the lap of God."[8] Prayer is properly "an emotion of the heart within, which is poured out and laid open before God" (3.20.29).

Given the riches and blessing available to us through prayer, for Christians not to pray is as senseless as it would be for "a man to neglect a treasure, buried and hidden in the earth, after it had been pointed out to

6. I will follow the order of *Institutes* 3.20 in this chapter, supplementing and illustrating the material there with Calvin's other writings, especially the commentaries and sermons.

7. John Calvin, *Commentary on the Book of Psalms*, trans. James Anderson (Grand Rapids: Eerdmans, 1949), 3:448. References to this 5–volume set will appear in the text as follows (*Psalms* volume:page).

8. *Calvin's Commentaries*, ed. David W. Torrance and Thomas F. Torrance (Grand Rapids: Eerdmans, 1980), 3:149. These New Testament commentary translations will be referenced in the text as follows (*NT* volume:page).

him" (3.20.1). Not only is prayerlessness foolish, it is idolatry. By it people defraud God "of his due honor [just as much] as if they made new gods and idols, since in this way they deny God is the author of every good thing" (3.20.14).

Calvin quickly deals with the question of why we should pray when God already knows everything (3.20.3). His short answer is that God ordained prayer "not so much for his own sake as for ours" (3.20.3). David Crump states that "John Calvin provides an especially ardent exposition of petition's purely therapeutic powers when he defends the importance of praying to an all-knowing sovereign Lord because 'he ordained [prayer] not so much for his own sake as for ours.'" The importance of prayer for Calvin, argues Crump, is that it "reorients the believer's mind and heart." Therefore, "any apparent impetratory [procuring by petition] effects are merely illusory misinterpretations of providence."[9] Crump focuses on an important aspect, indeed the major point, of Calvin's understanding of prayer, but fails to give full weight to Calvin's "not so much for his own sake as for ours." Neither in the *Institutes* nor elsewhere in his writings does Calvin assert that prayer is not at all for God's own sake, but only for ours.

Herman J. Selderhuis correctly asserts that Calvin believes that God, by means of our prayers, does what he planned all along to do. As Selderhuis puts it, for Calvin "prayer has a greater interest in honoring God than in changing him." Even though Selderhuis finds in Calvin's commentary on the Psalms "various indications that [Calvin] thinks prayer does somehow *affect* God," he questions "whether Calvin's opinions are in conformity with the biblical view of God when, in his opinion, prayer is not so much about moving God to a responsive action as it is given to bring a believer to greater confidence."[10]

"Holy Scripture gives us authority," writes Ronald S. Wallace, "to speak as if by prayer we can in some way prevail upon God to do things He would not have done unless we had prayed."[11] Calvin attempts to give full

9. David Crump, *Knocking on Heaven's Door: A New Testament Theology of Petitionary Prayer* (Grand Rapids: Baker Academic, 2006), 297.
10. H. J. Selderhuis, *Calvin's Theology of the Psalms* (Grand Rapids: Baker Academic, 2007), 224–26.
11. Ronald S. Wallace, *Calvin's Doctrine of the Christian Life* (Grand Rapids: Eerdmans, 1959), 290.

meaning to such biblical passages, while maintaining his view that God's perfect will is just that—perfect, and so unchangeable.

Calvin writes that God permits us to urge him "to make haste" (*Psalms* 3:454), and he is "stirred up by our prayers" (3.20.3). He "so tempers the outcome of events according to his incomprehensible plan that the prayers of the saints . . . are not nullified," Calvin asserts (3.20.15). In his comments on Elijah's prayer in James 5:17, Calvin writes that "it was a notable event for God to put heaven, in some sense, under the control of Elijah's prayers, to be obedient to his requests. By his prayers, Elijah kept heaven shut for two years and a half. Then he opened it, and made it suddenly pour with a great rain, from which we may see the miraculous power of prayer" (*NT* 3:317). Moses' resisting God's desire to destroy the rebellious Israelites, Joshua's prayer for the sun to stand still, and Elijah's prayer for drought and rain—all answered by God—were not utterly unique and exceptional instances, Calvin argues, but vivid illustrations of the privilege that is open in prayer to all God's children.[12] Preaching on Deuteronomy 9:13–14, Calvin states that Moses' prayer appears to set bounds to God's liberty to destroy the people. But, he explains, out of his goodness God "does so bind himself to our praying and supplications, that they be as it were restraints of his wrath: so that whereas diverse times he would destroy all, he is as it were changed, if we come and humble ourselves before him."[13]

Commenting on Psalm 145:19, Calvin writes that

the Holy Spirit, by the mouth of David, tells us, that God will accommodate himself to the desires of all who fear him. This is a mode of expression of which it is difficult to say how much it ought to impress our minds. Who is man, that God should show complaisance to his will, when rather it is ours to look up to his exalted greatness, and humbly submit to his authority? Yet he voluntarily condescends to these terms, to obtemper [comply with] our desires. [*Psalms* 5:282]

Calvin's statements such as "it is *as if* He were changed" and "for God to put heaven *in some sense* under the control of Elijah's prayers" are not

---

12. John Calvin, *Sermons on Deuteronomy* (Edinburgh: Banner of Truth Trust, 1987), 395.
13. Calvin, *Sermons on Deuteronomy*, 394.

meant to deny or weaken the scriptural passages but to remind us, as Calvin does so often, that God's word to us is an accommodated word, in which God speaks in a manner suitable to our finitude and frailty. A full and complete understanding will always be beyond our grasp, but, in this way, an adequate and useful revelation can be provided.

Bruce A. Ware correctly sums up Calvin's thought:

> It was surely Calvin's perspective that prayer . . . does make a difference to the work of God. While prayer never coerces God to act other than his infinite wisdom has willed, it nevertheless is one important and necessary condition which must be present for certain aspects of God's work to be carried out. Prayer, then, is not contrary to divine sovereignty but a divinely ordained instrument functioning within the sphere of God's sovereign wisdom and power in carrying out his will.[14]

In some sense, then, our prayers do affect God and make a difference to his work. Furthermore, our prayers, Calvin claims, help others. He writes: "The Lord commands that believers shall pray for one another. It is then no small comfort for each of them to hear that the care of his salvation is enjoined on the rest, and to be told by God Himself that the prayers of others on his behalf are not poured out in vain" (*NT* 11:222–23). For Calvin, the prayers of believers are not "purely therapeutic"; they in some real way affect God and they help other people, while they benefit the one who prays.

In his brief treatment in the *Institutes* of the above questions (so perplexing and troubling to many modern commentators), Calvin does not avoid a difficult problem (for, as we have seen, he deals with these matters when they come up in his commentaries) but reflects his attitude toward similar questions. Calvin is not concerned to give a rational explanation of how the unchangeable God can be changed by our prayers. It is important for him (and for us) to believe that the Bible teaches that God is omniscient, good, and sovereign, and that he works all things according to his perfect will. And it is important to know that in the Bible God repeatedly assures us that he will hear and answer

14. Bruce A. Ware, "The Role of Prayer and the Word in the Christian Life according to John Calvin," *Studia Biblica et Theologica* 12 (1982): 90.

our prayers. Logically, one cannot have it both ways, but, according to Calvin, scripturally we can.

In our praying, Calvin teaches that we can safely follow Christ's example in Gethsemane. Christ did not "turn His eyes to the divine plan but rested His desire that burned within Him upon His Father's knees." So we "in pouring out [our] prayers do not always rise to speculate upon the secret things of God" (*NT* 3:150). "As various musical sounds, different from each other, make no discord but compose a tuneful and sweet harmony," Calvin writes by way of illustration, "so in Christ there exists a remarkable example of balance between the wills of God and of man; they differ from each other without conflict or contradiction" (*NT* 3:151). There is room in prayer for tension between the human will and the will of God, Calvin maintained, "a kind of indirect disagreement." For example, we pray rightly that the church may flourish and have peace when, indeed, at times it pleases God to make it quite otherwise (*NT* 3:150–51).

Calvin, concerned more with the practice of prayer than its theory, gives six reasons why we should pray (3.20.3). His six points overlap and reinforce one another, exhorting us to pray to God, bringing to him our love and our concerns, with thanksgiving for his kindness, with delight in his goodness, and with confidence in his faithfulness. Calvin is content to end this short discussion of why we should pray by quoting 1 Peter 3:12: "For the eyes of the Lord are upon the righteous, and his ears toward their prayers" (3.20.3). "One might resolve the question of prayer thus," Calvin writes in his commentary on James 5:16, "it is of great benefit, because it is effective" (*NT* 3:317).

Calvin next turns to an extended discussion of four rules of right prayer (3.20.4–14). Calvin's practical guidance and exhortation given here "presuppose a clear view of the essence of prayer,"[15] coming as they do deep in book 3 of the *Institutes*. François Wendel describes Calvin's instructions as setting forth "the general attitude required of the faithful rather than precise and clearly-distinguishable rules."[16] We could sum up Calvin's points by saying that we must strive to pray

15. Wilhelm Niesel, *The Theology of Calvin* (Philadelphia: Westminster, 1956), 157.
16. François Wendel, *Calvin: The Origins and Development of His Religious Thought* (Glasgow: Collins, 1963), 254.

reverently, with a deep sense of need and a zeal for God's glory, with humility, and with confident hope.

The first rule is reverence. "Moved by God's majesty," we pray with careful thought and deep devotion (3.20.5). "Earnestness of soul," "sincerity of heart," and "pure simplicity" are "the finest rhetoric that we can bring to God," Calvin writes (*Psalms* 1:236). Preaching on Ephesians 6:18–19, Calvin says that our prayers must "proceed from a well-disposed and earnest mind" and should not only be made with our mouth, but also come from "the bottom of our heart."[17] In another sermon Calvin reminds the congregation that

> we not only must serve God and call on him with only our mouth and voice, but that it is necessary that our heart be lifted up so that our melody rises above the heavens and comes right before the majesty of God. Now it is true that to attain this, it is not necessary that the tongue labors too much. For they who have spoken not a word have sometimes really called out to God, and he has heard and answered them. . . . He knows what we need before we ask it of him. He thus looks into our heart and gives it more attention than he does to the voice of the mouth. For there are many who cry out enough, but it is nothing more than a voice sounding in the air. All this is of no use unless the heart is touched. For if we desire that God hears us and answers our prayers, it is necessary that the heart speaks and is burning with a strong desire to pray to him and praise him.[18]

The second rule is repentance and a sense of need. Calvin writes in the *Institutes*: "Lawful prayer . . . demands our repentance" (3.20.7). And in the preface to his Psalms commentary he states: "Genuine and earnest prayer proceeds first from a sense of our need" (*Psalms* 1:xxxvii). Wallace summarizes Calvin's point: "Prayer is the genuine cry of the human heart for help in the midst of circumstances that cannot be met by merely human resources."[19]

17. John Calvin, *Sermons on the Epistle to the Ephesians* (Edinburgh: Banner of Truth Trust, 1973), 679. Many of Calvin's thoughts on prayer are summed up in his sermon on Eph. 6:18.
18. "A Fragment from a Sermon of John Calvin," ed. and trans. Erik A. de Boer, *Calvin Theological Journal* 34.1 (April 1999): 178.
19. Wallace, *Calvin's Doctrine of the Christian Life*, 280.

The third rule is humility. Here Calvin reiterates the importance of repentance. He writes: "To sum up: the beginning, and even the preparation, of proper prayer is the plea for pardon with a humble and sincere confession of guilt" (3.20.9).

The fourth rule is confident hope. We are "encouraged to pray by a sure hope that our prayer will be answered" (3.20.11). We must not "provoke God" by asking for blessings "that we do not expect" (3.20.11). Calvin develops at some length the implications of this rule. "If we would pray fruitfully," he writes, "we ought therefore to grasp with both hands this assurance of obtaining what we ask. . . . For only that prayer is acceptable to God which is born, if I may so express it, out of such presumption of faith, and is grounded in unshaken assurance of hope" (3.20.12).

Calvin sets a high standard for prayer, but he recognizes our weakness and failure (3.20.15–16). He assures us that God will not "reject those prayers in which he finds neither perfect faith nor repentance, together with a warmth of zeal and petitions rightly conceived" (3.20.16). In David's prayers, for example, there "come forth—sometimes, rather boil up—turbulent emotions, quite out of harmony with the first rule that we laid down" (3.20.16). "Even in our best formed prayers, we have always need of pardon. There always escapes from us some language or sentiment chargeable with excess, and therefore it is necessary for God to overlook or bear with our infirmity" (*Psalms* 3:455). God tolerates "even our stammering and pardons our ignorance" (3.20.16). God allows us to plead with him in a "babbling manner" (*Psalms* 2:171) and to deal "familiarly" with him (*Psalms* 3:447). In his commentary on Psalm 102:2, Calvin writes that

> when God permits us to lay open before him our infirmities without reserve, and patiently bears with our foolishness, he deals in a way of great tenderness towards us. To pour out our complaints before him after the manner of little children would certainly be to treat his Majesty with very little reverence, were it not that he has been pleased to allow us such freedom. [*Psalms* 4:98]

Calvin notes that God granted the petitions of Jotham, Samson, and others—even though their prayers were "not framed to the rules of the

Word." "The prayers that God grants," Calvin explains, "are not always pleasing to him." Psalm 107 clearly teaches "that prayers which do not reach heaven by faith still are not without effect." In answering such prayers God bestows "mercy even upon the unworthy," but their prayers are not "a valid example for imitation" (3.20.15).

In developing his chapter on prayer up to this point, Calvin has touched on several points (and will repeat them later) that we will review before coming to Calvin's next major section in the *Institutes*. We pray—Calvin teaches in many places—invited by God, stirred up by faith, instructed by the Word, and guided by the Holy Spirit.

God's many invitations in Scripture are "as so many banners set up before our eyes to inspire us with confidence" (3.20.13). God "opens a way for us in his own words" and invites and bids us "not to fear for the sweetness of the melody that he himself dictates" (3.20.13). "How gently God attracts us to himself" (3.20.14). He draws "near us as a father."[20] He is "easily entreated and readily accessible" (3.20.13).

Prayer is the evidence, the proof, "the chief exercise" of faith. It is "the inevitable outcome of the presence of faith in the human heart."[21] "To sum up," Calvin writes, "it is faith that obtains whatever is granted to prayer" (3.20.11). In his comments on Christ's healing the epileptic boy, Calvin explains that not only does faith lead to prayer, but also faith is "stirred up by prayer" (*NT* 2:210).

"Prayer rightly begun springs from faith, and faith, from hearing God's Word" (3.20.27). "We dig up by prayer the treasures that were pointed out by the Lord's gospel, and which our faith has gazed upon" (3.20.2). "Faith . . . breaks into prayer and reaches for the riches of the grace of God which are revealed in the Word" (*NT* 3:9). God, "in all His promises, is set before us as if he were our willing debtor" (*Psalms* 4:444). Our prayers are simply a summing up of God's promises.[22] In a sermon on 2 Samuel 7:25–29, Calvin comments that God's opening of our ears to hear his word "opens our mouths as well. When we have heard God speak, then we respond mutually to him, so that there is

---

20. John Calvin, *A Commentary on Daniel* (Edinburgh: Banner of Truth Trust, 1966), 262.
21. Wallace, *Calvin's Doctrine of the Christian Life*, 271.
22. Calvin, *Sermons on Deuteronomy*, 915.

harmony and accord between his promises by which he draws us to himself, and these prayers through which we come to him."[23]

It is the Word of God, then, that shapes and controls the content of our prayers.

Calvin notes how often in the Psalms the "thread of prayer" is broken by meditations on various aspects of God's character (3.20.13). David "interlaces his prayers with holy meditations for the comfort of his own soul" (*Psalms* 2:362). "As one must frequently lay on fuel to preserve a fire, so the exercise of prayer requires the aid of such helps" (*Psalms* 1:422).

Throughout the Bible we find examples and patterns for our prayers. In the introduction to his commentary on the Psalms, Calvin wrote that "a better and more unerring rule for guiding us in this exercise [of prayer] cannot be found elsewhere than in the Psalms" (*Psalms* 1:xxvii). Meditation upon the promises of Scripture furnishes us with words and expressions for prayer (*Psalms* 3:371).

The Lord's Prayer is also a model for our prayers, and Calvin will come in sections 34–49 of chapter 20 to a lengthy discussion of its meaning and use. We are not bound to the words of the prayers of the Psalms, the Lord's Prayer, and other biblical prayers, as long as we pray according to the patterns they provide. Our words may be "utterly different, yet the sense ought not to vary" (3.20.49). The Holy Spirit not only inspired the biblical prayers, but the same Spirit repeatedly suggests to believers other prayers. Calvin wrote his own prayers and prayed extemporaneously on many occasions, but his words were taken directly from Scripture or biblically enriched.

Not only do we have the words of Scripture to guide us in our praying, we have the help of the Holy Spirit. "God gives us the Spirit as our teacher in prayer" (3.20.5). It is the Spirit of God who "stirs up in our hearts the prayers which it is proper for us to address to God" (*NT* 8:178). "God teaches us in His word what He wants us to ask, and He also set over us His Spirit as our leader and ruler to restrain our affections, that we may not let them stray beyond due bounds" (*NT* 5:309). "We have a rule, for our prayers prescribed to us in the Word of God,"

---

23. John Calvin, *Sermons on 2 Samuel*, trans. Douglas Kelly (Carlisle, PA: Banner of Truth Trust, 1992), 393–94.

but "our affections remain oppressed with darkness in spite of this, until the Spirit guides them by His light" (*NT* 8:178). The Holy Spirit not only directs the contents of our prayer, he "affects our hearts in such a way that these prayers penetrate into heaven itself by their fervency" (*NT* 8:178). We are not to wait, however, until the Spirit moves us to pray, but "flee to God and demand" that we be "inflamed with the fiery darts of his Spirit, so as to be rendered fit for prayer."[24]

In our praying we have the promises of Scripture and the presence of the Holy Spirit. We also have Christ as our teacher and mediator (3.20.17–20). Christ not only teaches us to pray (Calvin will come to this in his treatment of the Lord's Prayer) but he enables us, sinful creatures, to come to a righteous and holy God in prayer. He is our "advocate," "mediator," "intercessor," "intermediary," who transforms God's "throne of dreadful glory into the throne of grace" (3.20.17). "The Father cannot look upon His Son without at the same time having before His eyes His whole body," Calvin writes in his commentary on John 17:26 (*NT* 5:152).

Christ is the "only Mediator, by whose intercession the Father is for us rendered gracious and easily entreated" (3.20.19). He not only enables us to come to God without fear, he also by his priestly work cleanses our prayers "by sprinkled blood" (3.20.18). "Let us learn to wash our prayers with the blood of our Lord Jesus Christ," Calvin told the people in a sermon on Genesis 26:23–25.[25] "Having entered the heavenly sanctuary," Christ "alone bears to God the petitions of the people, who stay far off in the outer court" (3.20.20). T. H. L. Parker sums up Calvin's thought when he writes that "it is, then, not simply a matter of praying *through* Christ, but rather *with* Christ, of our prayers being united with his intercession for us." In an illustration that will appeal especially to Scottish Presbyterians, Parker adds, "Thus Christ becomes the precentor who leads the prayers of his people."[26]

---

24. *Calvin: Theological Treatises*, trans. J. K. S. Reid (Philadelphia: Westminster, 1954), 121. The quotation is from the Geneva Catechism, question 245.

25. John Calvin, *Sermons on Election and Reprobation*, trans. John Field (Audubon, NJ: Old Paths Publications, 1996), 210.

26. Parker, *Calvin*, 110. Calvin expresses this idea in his commentary on Hebrews 2:12, when he writes that Christ is "the chief Conductor of our hymns" (*NT* 12:27). The centrality of Christ for Calvin is illustrated in his daily prayers, which, Elsie McKee writes, demonstrate that for Calvin "the passion and death of Christ should be remembered every day, and the

Calvin follows his treatment of the intercession of Christ with a rejection of the erroneous doctrine of the intercession of saints (3.20.21–27). In this highly polemical section Calvin accuses the Roman Catholic Church of transferring to the saints "that office of sole intercession which … belongs to Christ" (3.20.21). The saints are our examples in prayer, Calvin argues, but we do not pray to them or through them. In some detail Calvin vehemently rejects Catholic practice as unscriptural and superstitious.

Calvin next describes various kinds of prayer: private, public, spoken, sung, and silent (3.20.28–33).

In discussing private prayer, Calvin returns to many of the points that he has already made. Prayer includes, he maintains, petition, thanksgiving, and praise. It embraces both our seeking the extension of God's glory and our asking for our own needs.

For Calvin there are three important elements of public worship: preaching, prayers, and the administration of the sacraments. In the *Institutes* he writes that "the chief part" of public worship "lies in the office of prayer" (3.20.29). Calvin titled his liturgy *The Form of Prayers.*[27] Public prayers should take place at certain convenient stated times, but also at special times because of "some major need" (3.20.29). Although there ought to be church buildings in which public prayers can be offered to God, "we ourselves are God's true temple" (3.20.30). Prayer should be in the common language of the people and avoid ostentatious show and artificial eloquence. Prayer should be characterized by perseverance and constancy but not with "vain repetition," although the frequent repetition of the same request is not vain, "for hereby the saints, by little and little, discharge their cares into the bosom of God, and this importunity is a sacrifice of a sweet savour before Him" (*Psalms* 3:384).

"As for the bodily gestures customarily observed in praying, such as kneeling and uncovering the head, they are exercises whereby we try to rise to a greater reverence for God" (3.20.33). Noting that Paul "knelt down" when he prayed with the elders at Ephesus, Calvin wrote:

hope of eternal life born of Christ's resurrection should light each day's journey through this world" (*John Calvin: Writings on Pastoral Piety* [New York: Paulist, 2001], 26–27).

27. See W. de Greef, *The Writings of John Calvin: An Introductory Guide* (Grand Rapids: Baker, 1989), 126–31.

The inward attitude certainly holds first place in prayer, but outward signs, kneeling, uncovering the head, lifting up the hands, have a two-fold use. The first is that we may employ all our members for the glory and worship of God; secondly, that we are, so to speak, jolted out of our laziness by this help. There is also a third use in solemn and public prayer, because in this way the sons of God profess their piety, and they inflame each other with reverence of God. But just as the lifting up the hands is a symbol of confidence and longing, so in order to show our humility, we fall down on our knees. [NT 7:190]

Singing, which is a form of public prayer, "both lends dignity and grace to sacred actions and has the greatest value in kindling our hearts to true zeal" (3.20.32).[28] By singing we "with one common voice, and as it were, with the same mouth . . . glorify God together" (3.20.31). Our singing must "spring from deep feeling of heart" (3.20.31), giving careful attention to the words and with appropriate music suitable to "the majesty of the church" (3.20.32). Not only does our singing express our praise and thanksgiving to God, it also helps other people. It is not enough, Calvin writes, for each Christian "individually to be grateful to God for the benefits he has received, without giving public evidence of our gratitude and thus mutually encouraging each other to the same purpose" (NT 12:27). Furthermore, our singing in public worship should "be an impetus and a means to praise God even in our houses and fields, and for raising our hearts to him, for consoling us in meditating on his virtue, goodness, wisdom, and justice—a thing more necessary than we can express."[29]

A lengthy exposition of the Lord's Prayer follows (3.20.34–49). In this prayer which "the Heavenly Father has taught us through his beloved Son" (3.20.34), we learn "what is worthy of him, acceptable to him, necessary for us" (3.20.48).

When we begin our prayer with the words "our Father," we are moved by "the great sweetness of this name." "In calling God 'Father,'

28. For discussion of this topic in Calvin, see Ross J. Miller, "Calvin's Understanding of Psalm-Singing as a Means of Grace" and "Music and the Spirit: Psalm-Singing in Calvin's Liturgy," in *Calvin Studies VI* (Colloquium on Calvin Studies at Davidson College, 1992), 35–58.

29. John Calvin, "Preface to the Strassburg Psalter," *Joannis Calvini Opera Selecta*, ed. Peter Barth and Wilhelm Niesel (Munich: Chr. Kaiser, 1952), 2:15–16.

we put forward the name 'Christ' " (3.20.36). In his name we come boldly into the presence of God our Father.

Praying to God as *our* Father shapes our attitude and conduct because if God is our Father, "there ought not to be anything separate among us that we are not prepared gladly and wholeheartedly to share with one another" (3.20.38). "Strife shuts the gate to prayers," Paul warns, and thus Christians should strive to "offer their petitions in common with one accord" (3.20.39). Christians have "a special affection" for those "of the household of faith" and also concern and care for "all men who dwell on earth" (3.20.38). Calvin writes that "we are thus stirred up by the Holy Spirit to the duty of prayer in behalf of the common welfare of the church. Whilst each man takes sufficient care of his own individual interests, there is scarcely one in a hundred affected as he ought to be with the calamities of the church" (*Psalms* 4:97). Each of us in suffering our "private miseries and trials" should extend our "desires and prayers to the whole Church" (*Psalms* 1:436). In his own prayers and in those he prepared for the congregation Calvin was aware of being linked with other members of Christ's body, near or far, and prayed often for those who were tried by any afflictions of spirit, mind, or body, for all who suffered, everywhere.

On November 4, 1545, at the weekly day of prayer in Geneva, the prayers centered on intercession for the Protestants in Germany who were defending themselves against their Catholic opponents. In his sermon, Calvin reminded the people that if they were the church they had

> a spiritual connection with all the faithful. As there is only a single God, a single Redeemer, a single true teaching, a single faith, one baptism, so we ought to be one body. So we should have a union each with the others. If one member suffers, we all ought to have compassion. . . . Should we say: "Those [people in Germany] are far from us"? Not at all. They are of the church, and we are its members; because we have the same Father in heaven, let us have a brotherhood together which is indeed more than fraternal! Let us reflect that what happens to one member of the church happens to us. . . . We cannot help [the German Protestants] with our hands, but we ought to pray to God for them as for ourselves.[30]

30. McKee, *Pastoral Piety*, 166–67.

When we pray to God who is "in heaven," we understand that "heaven and earth are ruled by his providence and power" and so remember not to measure God "by our small measure" being assured that he is able to answer our prayers and provide for those who come to him (3.20.40).

There are six petitions in the Lord's Prayer, grouped in two parts, each containing three points. The first part is concerned with God's glory and the second with our human needs. Both parts, however, Calvin states, are ultimately concerned with both God's glory and our benefit. The first three petitions are similar (because of our apathy, we need the triple list)—the hallowing of God's name is always attached to his reign, the chief feature of which is to be acknowledged in the doing of his will.

When we pray "hallowed be thy name," we wish God to have "the honor he deserves" in our lives and among all people, so that "God may shine forth more and more in his majesty" (3.20.41).

In praying "thy kingdom come," we ask that God cast down all his enemies and humble "the whole world" and that "he shape all our thoughts in obedience to his rule" (3.20.42). There is a shift of emphasis between the first and last editions of the *Institutes* from individual obedience in 1536 to the planting of churches in 1559—"We must daily desire that God gather churches unto himself from all parts of the earth" (3.20.42). Calvin notes that this prayer instructs us "in bearing the cross. For it is in this way that God wills to spread his Kingdom" (3.20.42).

In his commentary on Matthew 6:10, Calvin comments: "So we pray that God will show His power both in Word and in Spirit, that the whole world may willingly come over to Him" and that he will "bring our hearts to obey His righteousness by the breathing of His Spirit, and restore to order at His will, all that is lying waste upon the face of the earth" (*NT* 1:208). Calvin was impressed that the "godliness and the sincerity" of the early Christians in Acts are evident in their prayers "not so much for their personal safety as for the advancement of the Kingdom of Christ" (*NT* 6:124).

When we pray "thy will be done," we ask not only that what is opposed to God's will may not be done, but also that "we may learn to love the things that please him and to hate those which displease him" (3.20.43). A little later, Calvin warns us not to impose any condition on God but "leave to his decision to do what he is to do, in what way, at what time, and in what place it seems good to him" (3.20.50). In his commentary on 2 Corinthians 12:8, Calvin writes that we must be careful not to specify too closely the means that God should use in answering our prayers and the exact manner and time in which his answer should come. We ask for those things that God has promised "with full confidence and without reserve," Calvin asserts, "but it is not for us to prescribe the means, and if we do specify them, our prayer always has an unexpressed qualification included in it" (*NT* 10:160). "This is faith's due limit," Calvin writes concerning Christ's prayer in Gethsemane, "to allow God to decide differently from what we desire" (*NT* 3:151).

In praying the first three petitions of the Lord's Prayer we "keep God's glory alone before our eyes" (3.20.43), but in descending "to our own affairs" in the second three petitions we do not "bid farewell to God's glory" (3.20.44).

Calvin understands the prayer "give us this day our daily bread" as a request for physical bread (against Erasmus who felt that it was inappropriate to pray for something so ordinary as food). To pray to God for everything, including the least things, is the ultimate test of faith, because "by this we give ourselves over to his care, and entrust ourselves to his providence" (3.20.44). We ask God for our daily bread, even when we think we have enough to see us through. "Unless God feeds us," Calvin writes, "no amount of accrued capital will mean anything. Although grain, wine, and everything else be there to overflowing, if they do not have the dew of God's unseen benediction, these all vanish on the spot, or that enjoyment is taken away, or the power they have to nourish us is lost, and we starve in the midst of great supply" (*NT* 1:210).

When we pray "forgive us our debts, as we forgive our debtors," Calvin recognizes that forgiveness on our part can be accomplished only by the power of the Holy Spirit, whose presence in our hearts is the witness of our adoption. God's children forgive; if we do not, we show ourselves not to be his. Not only does this prayer require us to forgive others, it comforts "the weakness of our faith" by assuring us God "has granted forgiveness of sins to us just as surely as we are aware of having forgiven others" (3.20.45).

In the prayer "lead us not into temptation" we "seek to be equipped with such armor and defended with such protection that we may be able to win the victory" (3.20.46). With this petition, Calvin states, Christ has put forth "the objects of our soul's eternal salvation and spiritual life. . . . He offers us free reconciliation, by not imputing our sins to us, and He promises the Spirit, to engrave upon our hearts the righteousness of the Law" (*NT* 1:211).

Calvin notes that the conclusion of the Lord's Prayer—"which it fits so well"—does not appear in the earliest New Testament manuscripts, but "was added not only to warm our hearts to press towards the glory of God, and warn us what should be the goal of all our supplications, but also to tell us that all our prayers . . . have no other foundation than God alone" (*NT* 1:213).

By the "amen" our hope is "strengthened" that God hears and answers our prayers, our confidence stemming "solely from God's nature" (3:20, 47).

Calvin states that not only should we pray "without ceasing" (or with steady "constancy" as he interprets 1 Thessalonians 5:17 [*NT* 8:375]), we should also "set apart certain hours" for prayer (3.20.50). Just as Israel had fixed times in which to present sacrifices, we, since we are "naturally indisposed for the duty of prayer," should also have specific times for prayer (*NT* 2:339). Noting that Daniel prayed three times a day, Calvin warns that "unless we fix certain hours in the day for prayer, it easily slips from our memory."[31] Calvin recommended special times of prayer throughout the day and wrote sample prayers for people to use on those occasions: in the morning, when rising; before school or work; before eating; thanksgiving after eating; and before going to sleep at night.[32]

Calvin closes his long chapter on prayer by encouraging us to "learn to persevere in prayer . . . and patiently wait for the Lord" (3.20.51–52). When we do not experience the benefits we seek, we must not fall into despair or become indignant with God, but

> our faith will make us sure of what cannot be perceived by sense, that we have obtained what was expedient. For the Lord so often and so certainly promises to care for us in our troubles, when they have once been laid upon his bosom. And so he will cause us to possess abundance in poverty, and comfort in affliction. For though all things fail us, yet

31. Calvin, *Commentary on Daniel*, 362.
32. For these prayers, see McKee, *Pastoral Piety*, 211–15.

God will never forsake us, who cannot disappoint the expectation and patience of his people. (3.20.52)

God, "even when he does not comply with our wishes, is still attentive and kindly to our prayers" (3.20.52). "The only legitimate proof of trust is when anyone who is disappointed of his desire does not lose heart," Calvin says (*NT* 2:125). We learn from Daniel that "our prayers may be already heard while God's favor and mercy is concealed from us."[33] We learn from Christ's experience in Gethsemane that "God often hears our prayers, even when it is least apparent" (*NT* 12:65). We learn from Paul's prayer in 2 Corinthians 12:8 that

> just as there are many kinds of asking, so there are two kinds of obtaining. We ask without qualification for those things about which we have a sure promise, such as the perfecting of God's kingdom and the hallowing of His name, the forgiveness of sins and everything profitable to us. But when we imagine that God's kingdom can and indeed must be furthered in such and such a way, or that this or that is necessary for the hallowing of His name, we are often mistaken, just as, in the same way, we are often deluded as to what in fact tends to our own welfare. Thus we ask for these things that are certainly promised with full confidence and without reserve, but it is not for us to prescribe the means, and if we do specify them, our prayer always has an unexpressed qualification included in it. Now Paul was well aware of this, and as far as the intention and purpose of his prayer was concerned, he was without doubt answered, even if the form in which he made his request was refused. From this we should be warned not to be despondent, when God does not meet or satisfy our requests, as though prayer were wasted effort. For His grace ought to be sufficient for us, that is, it should be enough that He has not forsaken us. This is why He sometimes withholds from the godly in His mercy things that He grants to the ungodly in His wrath, because He Himself can foresee better than our minds what is good for us. [*NT* 10:160–61]

Even though we are disappointed in our expectations in our prayers, we can make known to God our perplexities about our very prayers—unburdening even this burden to him (*Psalms* 1:362). In the *Institutes*

---

33. Calvin, *Commentary on Daniel*, 251.

and in his commentaries and sermons, Calvin strives to uphold God's people in prayer (like Aaron and Hur holding up the hands of Moses in Ex. 17), continually exhorting them not to become discouraged but to strive "toward a goal not immediately attainable" (3.20.16).

Not only did John Calvin write extensively about prayer, and preach frequently on prayer, he prayed often, both privately and publicly. Elsie McKee notes that "Calvin seems to have accompanied almost every public act with prayer, and many of those words of praise and petition were recorded."[34] One of the most distinctive forms of Calvinist Reformed worship was the regular weekly day of prayer. Begun in Strasbourg, this service spread to other places, especially Geneva. Wednesdays were partial holidays, with businesses closed until after worship, which was held at two times so that everyone could attend. The day of prayer had its own liturgy, including the congregational singing of psalms, but could be shaped to take into consideration special needs for repentance, petition, or thanksgiving. "This day has been established to offer prayers," Calvin told the people. "Therefore, let us be more diligent than is customary, not only to come and present ourselves [here], but let us be moved to humble ourselves before our God, asking Him to convert our hearts and change our lives."[35] Preaching on Psalm 115 for the weekly day of prayer on November 4, 1545, Calvin said:

> After the prayer, let us remember how this thought is given to us, that "our God is in heaven" (Ps. 115:3), in order that it may be for us

34. McKee, *Pastoral Piety*, 29. For Calvin's formal, set prayers, see *Calvin's Tracts and Treatises*, vol. 2, trans. and ed. Henry Beveridge (Grand Rapids: Eerdmans, 1958). Selections from these prayers can be found in A. Mitchell Hunter, *Teaching of Calvin*, 2d ed. (London: James Clarke, 1950), 215–21; and *John Calvin: The Christian Life*, ed. John H. Leith (San Francisco: Harper & Row, 1984), 78–82. The brief prayers that follow Calvin's lectures were apparently given extemporaneously. A representative selection of these prayers is found in *Calvin's Devotions and Prayers of John Calvin*, compiled by Charles E. Edwards (Grand Rapids: Baker, 1954). See McKee, *Pastoral Piety*, for representative "Occasional Prayers from the Catechism and Liturgy" (210–19), "Prayers from Calvin's Sermons" (220–39), and "Prayers from Calvin's Lectures" (240–45). McKee writes that "finding the prayers that Genevans heard from the pulpit requires effort, so the collection here attempts to give a representative selection" (31). Calvin's prayers following his lectures exist only for the Old Testament prophets and are available in the commentaries as translated by the Calvin Translation Society.

35. McKee, *Pastoral Piety*, 167.

a shield to withstand every evil thought—thoughts such as wondering whether our God can aid us. . . . This must be imprinted in our memory: our God will aid us. The reason: nothing can prevent Him. And He has declared to us that it is His good pleasure never to fail us at need. . . . And if God does not help us at first, let us wait on Him; we will not be disappointed. Our God will come, and when? He knows when it will be time.[36]

36. McKee, *Pastoral Piety*, 172.

16

CALVIN, WORSHIP,
AND THE SACRAMENTS

INSTITUTES 4.13–19
W. ROBERT GODFREY

Worship

The reform of the worship of God was a central concern for John Calvin. Indeed in his great defense of the Reformation, "The Necessity of Reforming the Church," addressed to Emperor Charles V, Calvin asked "by what things chiefly the Christian religion has standing existence among us and maintains its truth" and answered: "first . . . the mode in which God is duly worshipped."[1] Throughout his ministry he gave very careful attention to worship, both its practice and its theology. He sought to reform worship according to the teaching of the Bible.

---

1. John Calvin, "The Necessity of Reforming the Church," in *Selected Works*, ed. H. Beveridge and J. Bonnet (Grand Rapids: Baker, 1983), 1:126.

Practice of Worship

In practice Calvin purified church buildings by removing all religious images and symbols, including the cross. He made the reading and preaching of the Bible in the language of the people central to worship. He eliminated rites and ceremonies that were without biblical warrant. He removed musical instruments and introduced the singing of the Psalms by the congregation. He restored the Word of God, the gospel of Christ, and a profound sense of meeting with God to the center of worship.

Theology of Worship

These practical reforms flowed out of Calvin's theology of worship. His study of the Scriptures led him to comprehensive thinking about worship. However, Calvin did not gather his thoughts about worship into one single place in his 1559 edition of the *Institutes of the Christian Religion*.[2] Rather his discussions of worship cluster around three specific contexts in the *Institutes*. Those contexts are first, the doctrine of God; second, the demands of the law, especially the second commandment; and third, the power of the church. Each of these discussions reflects that Calvin's thought on worship forms a coherent whole. Each illumines a different dimension of his theology of worship, and together they show the basic character of worship.

For Calvin the spiritual nature of God was foundational to worship and to every effort to avoid idolatry. Because God is spirit, he should never be portrayed in visible form (1.11.1). Calvin attacked various distinctions that were used before the Reformation to avoid the full implication of this point. First, he insisted, against Eastern Orthodoxy, that the spiritual nature of God led to the rejection of paintings and mosaics as well as statues (1.11.4). Second, citing Galatians 4:8 (1.12.3), he disputed the distinction made by medieval theologians that worship (*latria*) was offered to God alone, but veneration (*dulia*) might be offered to images or saints. Such a distinction was impossible in practice and could not conform to biblical usage of the words. Third, he rejected the notion that images

2. All citations from the *Institutes* in this chapter are from John Calvin, *Institutes of the Christian Religion*, ed. J. T. McNeill, trans. F. L. Battles, 2 vols. (Philadelphia: Westminster, 1960).

could be the books of the uneducated (1.11.7). All of these efforts to find a place for images in Christian churches led Calvin to the conclusion that fallen mankind was perpetually trying to compromise the nature of God by depicting him in images. "From this we may gather that man's nature, so to speak, is a perpetual factory of idols" (1.11.8).

Calvin also discussed worship in relation to the demands of the law in his exposition of the second commandment. The God who is spirit is also the God who alone can reveal his will for his own worship (2.8.5). "The purpose of this commandment, then, is that he does not will that his lawful worship be profaned by superstitious rites .... He makes us conform to his lawful worship, that is, a spiritual worship established by himself" (2.8.17). Christians are forbidden not only images, but all forms of worship invented by the mind of man. The apparent holiness of the medieval church in vestments, rituals, priests, and sacrifices did not please God because he had not ordained it.

Calvin also discussed worship in his reflections on the power of the church. God alone regulates his worship; he has not given to the church the authority to introduce new forms of worship: "he alone (when we seek the way to worship him aright and fitly) has authority over our souls, him we ought to obey, and upon his will we ought to wait" (4.10.8). The temptations to add to or take away from revealed worship are enormous and must be rigorously resisted: "Paul knew that all counterfeit worship in the church was condemned, and that the more it delights human nature the more it is suspected by believers" (4.10.11). Calvin stressed that the church had no power to bind the consciences of members with worship invented by the church and without the warrant of God (4.10.27).

Unbiblical ceremonies are very attractive to fallen human nature (4.10.12). The simple forms of worship instituted by God are very different and "ought to lead us straight to Christ" (4.10.29).

Calvin did not argue that every detail of outward arrangements for worship was revealed in the Bible (4.10.30). The church does have discretion to order externals which are not essential elements of worship such as times of worship on Sunday or physical postures in worship (standing, sitting, or kneeling).

Calvin's approach to worship would later be called the regulative principle of worship and be seen as a distinctive of Reformed theology. In its simplest terms the regulative principle holds that the Word of God alone regulates, directs, and warrants all elements of worship. Some scholars have tried to argue that the regulative principle is a Puritan doctrine developed in the seventeenth century and foreign to the thought of Calvin. Such an argument fundamentally misunderstands Calvin. While there are some relatively minor differences between Calvin and most Puritans on the application of the regulative principle, the principle itself is common to them: we may worship God only as he has commanded us to do in the Bible.

Calvin's last chapter on the church in book 4 (ch. 13) is in part a transition to the subject of the sacraments. This chapter is titled "On Vows, through Which Each One Miserably Entangled Himself by a Rash Commitment."[3] Calvin showed that the medieval church had imposed many unbiblical requirements on Christians, especially priests, monks, and nuns, and tied them to those requirements by unbiblical vows. Such vows produced only legalism and bondage to human inventions.

On the matter of vows, as in other subjects related to the church, Calvin made clear the freedom that Christ had bought for his people, freedom from all forms of human invention and tyranny in matters of religion. The law of God alone shows Christians how they should please him (4.13.1). Particularly in worship, church invention is an imposition both dangerous to man and offensive to God. "For, however the flesh may judge it, God hates nothing more than counterfeit worship" (4.13.7). True worship includes the true sacraments which, in part, Calvin understood to be vows that Christians make to God (4.13.6).

Sacraments

For Calvin the sacraments were a central and vitally important part of worship. For this reason Calvin gave a great deal of attention to the subject of the sacraments of the church in the fourth book of his

---

3. The title of each of the chapters cited in this essay is translated literally from Calvin's Latin title.

Institutes. About 45 percent of that fourth book and about 14 percent of the entire *Institutes* is on the sacraments. This close study reflected Calvin's conviction about the spiritual importance of the sacraments in the life of the Christian and the church. The sacraments were not an academic wrangling point for Calvin. They were vital to the well-being of the faithful. For Calvin the sacraments were one of the most important helps or aids that the Spirit of God uses for his people in their weakness (4.1.1). Although faith is personal and internal, as Calvin shows in book 3, the believer must have external helps to begin and sustain that faith.

Calvin also gave much attention to the sacraments because of all the Reformation controversies; those surrounding the sacraments in general and the Lord's Supper in particular were the most emotional and intense. The sacraments stood at the center of the worship and life of the medieval church. The work of the priests at the altar was at the heart of worship. Also the Fourth Lateran Council in 1215—regarded as an authoritative ecumenical council by the Western medieval church—had officially defined the doctrine of seven sacraments and the doctrine of transubstantiation as binding dogma for every Christian. For defenders of the Roman Church these doctrines were essential to the life and authority of the church.

In addition to the divide between the Roman Catholics and Protestants, the Protestants found themselves significantly divided, especially over the doctrine of the Lord's Supper. Lutherans, Calvinists, and Zwinglians took rather different approaches to the subject. Luther had seen the great error of Rome in the doctrine of eucharistic sacrifice and turning the Supper into a human work rather than a divine gift. The Zwinglians had seen the great error of Rome in the doctrine of transubstantiation and the idolatry of bread and wine that flowed from it. Calvin believed the two sides were not fundamentally different. Although he had more sympathy with Luther and the moderate Lutherans, he labored tirelessly to bring the two sides together.

Calvin believed that two errors must be avoided. One error, that of the radical Zwinglians in his day, gave too little meaning and power to the sacraments. The other, the dominant error of Calvin's day and of the medieval church, gave too much power to the sacraments. For Calvin both errors missed the true teaching of the Bible and weakened or destroyed the church. A correct understanding of the sacraments was critical for Christians. That correct understanding used the sign of the sacrament to lift the heart above that sign and thus to Christ (4.14.16).

Calvin's opponents, and even some of his followers, have not always considered his sacramental theology to be clear or even comprehensible. In part this reflects the greatly diminished importance the sacraments have in the theology and lives of many later Protestants. In part this reflects the complexity of the issues that Calvin had to address in his *Institutes*. Calvin's sacramental theology was not inherently difficult, but so many alternative theologies had to be analyzed and answered that the subject as a whole became difficult. He wanted to show that while his views were not identical to those of the ancient church fathers, he did agree with them substantially. He also had to examine the medieval and sixteenth-century Roman Catholic theology of the Supper as well as Lutheran and Zwinglian Protestant interpretations. Finally he needed to elaborate the theology and piety of his own position. No wonder that his discussion at times became complex.

In particular Calvin wanted to take full account of various scriptural texts and their interpretations. Calvin sought to be faithful to the biblical revelation and to be pastoral in communicating to the church. He recognized that the language of the Bible is at times very strong with reference to the sacraments: "Baptism . . . now saves you" (1 Peter 3:21); "Take, eat; this is my body" (Matt. 26:26); "For my flesh is true food, and my blood is true drink" (John 6:55). Calvin did not want to attribute too much or too little to this language.

Practice of the Sacraments

Calvin believed that the ceremonies related to the administration of the sacraments should be simple. For example, in relation to baptism he rejected the accretions that had grown up around the practice of baptism such as candles and chrisms. He argued that it was a matter of indifference whether baptism was by immersion or sprinkling, although he acknowledged that the ancient church practiced immersion (4.15.19).

He rejected all forms of emergency baptism by unordained persons. Baptism was the ministry of the church and to be performed only by her ministers. Even if the children of believers were to die before they could be brought to the church for baptism, they were not at any spiritual risk because they were already part of God's covenant (4.15.20, 22).

In regard to the Lord's Supper, Calvin believed that many of the details of administration were a matter of indifference: "whether they hand the cup back to the deacon or give it to the next person; whether the bread is leavened or unleavened; the wine red or white—it makes no difference" (4.17.43). Still he believed that the unbiblical, complicated ceremonies of the medieval church that had been added as holy elements to the rite should be eliminated and the whole service have a simple form. He summarized that form in terms of prayers, a sermon, the Lord's Supper, singing of Psalms, and the benediction (4.17.43).

Calvin utterly rejected the infrequent communion of the Roman system, which required the reception of communion only once a year. He preferred weekly communion (4.18.46). The Lord's Supper, which God designed to help Christians in their weakness, ought to be administered frequently.

Theology of the Sacraments

As sacraments are a part of worship for Calvin, his basic approach to worship is clearly reflected in his approach to the sacraments. In relation to the nature of God he saw the sacraments reflecting God's benevolence and saving intention to his own people. In relation to the law Calvin stressed the need to understand the sacraments only as God had taught about them in his Word. In relation to the power of the church he insisted that the sacraments must not be added to or reinterpreted by the church.

Sacraments and the Nature of God: Sacraments Revealing the Goodness of God

Calvin developed his full sacramental theology in chapters 14–19 of book 4. In chapter 14 ("On the Sacraments") he presented a general

374

overview of the subject of sacraments. He began with a brief definition of a sacrament: "an outward sign by which the Lord seals on our consciences the promises of his good will toward us in order to sustain the weakness of faith; and we in turn attest our piety toward him in the presence of the Lord and of his angels and before men" (4.14.1). Sacraments are visible signs through which God acts and to which his people respond.

In working out the implications of this definition, first, Calvin clarified the relationship between the sacraments and the Word of God. Because the sacraments are signs and seals of a promise, the Word of God must precede and create the sacrament. Without a clear statement of the promise the sign has no meaning or power: "the sacrament requires preaching to beget faith" (4.14.4).

The sacraments do not bring any blessings different from those brought by the Word. Their function is to guarantee the reliability of that Word. Because sacraments guarantee the promises of the Word, they are called seals (4.14.5). Calvin also particularly embraced the phrase of Augustine that the sacraments are "visible words." They are promises that can be seen, but never function independently of the spoken word (4.14.6).

Divine institution and divine promise are what establish a sacrament. Calvin insisted that because of the importance of sacraments in the Christian life, God alone could make a sacrament. The promise is God's and only God can appoint a sign to ratify that promise. In the new covenant the Bible shows that God has established only two sacraments, baptism and the Lord's Supper.

A second critical element for Calvin's understanding of the sacraments is that the sacrament brings no blessing ultimately except where it is received in faith. The Word and the sacrament minister salvation only where they are believed. "It is therefore certain that the Lord offers us mercy and the pledge of his grace both in his Sacred Word and in his sacraments. But it is understood only by those who take Word and sacraments with sure faith, just as Christ is offered and held forth by the Father to all unto salvation, yet not all acknowledge and receive him" (4.14.7).

A third critical point for Calvin is that the Spirit of God makes the sacrament efficacious for the people of God. As the Spirit must empower the Word and give the gift of faith, so he connects the sign to the thing signified (4.14.9). For Calvin, power always remains in God. To place that power intrinsically in the sign would dishonor God and distract from him.

After his general discussion of the sacraments, Calvin proceeded in chapter 15 ("On Baptism") to an examination of the first Christian sacrament. In the first six sections of this chapter Calvin showed how baptism expressed the benevolence of God to his people. Calvin saw baptism as "the sign of initiation by which we are received into the society of the church, in order that, engrafted in Christ, we may be reckoned among God's children" (4.15.1). This initiation has two purposes: "first, to serve our faith before him; secondly, to serve our confession before men" (4.15.1). In other words, baptism has two functions. One is for the person baptized to build up faith. The other is as a testimony to the world that the person baptized belongs to Christ.

For Calvin, baptism built up faith in the Christian and in the church because it came with three rich promises. The first promise is cleansing, or the forgiveness of sins. Calvin is clear that the water of baptism does not contain in itself "the power to cleanse, regenerate, and renew." Rather "in this sacrament are received the knowledge and certainty of such gifts" (4.15.2). Baptism assures the Christian that the promise of forgiveness held out in the gospel is true and reliable.

The second promise of baptism is mortification and renewal (4.15.5). The God who promises to justify his people also promises in baptism to sanctify them both in progressively putting to death the life of the flesh and in establishing the life of the Spirit.

The third promise of baptism is that we are "so united to Christ himself that we become sharers in all his blessings." Baptism is "the firmest bond of the union and fellowship which he has deigned to form with us" (4.15.6). Christians are united to Christ as their Head so that all of the benefits of his work are theirs.

In chapter 17 ("On the Sacred Supper of Christ: and What It Confers on Us") Calvin turned to the subject of the second sacrament in this theology. In the first eleven sections of this chapter he showed how the Lord's Supper expressed the benevolence of God toward his people. In these first sections he presented his doctrine simply and positively for the "unlearned." Calvin gave very careful attention to this matter because it was so important to him: God has given the Lord's Supper "to nourish us throughout the course of our life" and to be "his pledge, to assure us of this continuing liberality" (4.17.1).

For Calvin the simple way to understand the Lord's Supper was as food that God gave to nourish his people as the words of the institution of the Supper and as John 6 testified (4.17.1). In God's gift of this food Christians were to delight. The sacrament assured that what Christ promised was surely theirs: "Godly souls can gather great assurance and delight from this Sacrament; in it they have a witness of our growth into one body with Christ such that whatever is his may be called ours. . . . This is the wonderful exchange which, out of his measureless benevolence, he has made with us; that, becoming Son of man with us, he has made us sons of God with him" (4.17.2). God has bountifully provided this sacrament to help believers in their weakness and doubt.

How can Christians feed on the body and blood of Christ when Christ is in heaven? Calvin answered that the Spirit of God unites to Christ. Christ does not descend into the bread, but the Spirit lifts the believer up to heaven: "What, then, our mind does not comprehend, let faith conceive: that the Spirit truly unites things separated in space" (4.17.10). For Calvin the Supper is a spiritual communion, not in the sense that Christians commune with a disembodied Christ, but in the sense that by the action of the Spirit they commune with the whole, real Christ.

The promise of God and the work of the Spirit are certain to all who come to the table in faith (4.17.10). Faith does not create the promise or cause the Spirit to work. But only faith receives the blessing of the promise and the Spirit.

A firm principle of Calvin for the simple (and the sophisticated) was that the sacrament presented to the believer what was represented there: "And the godly ought by all means to keep this rule: whenever they see symbols appointed by the Lord, to think and be persuaded that the truth of the thing signified is surely present there" (4.17.10). Therefore for Calvin, through the Lord's Supper Christians receive the whole Christ—including his body and blood—and all his benefits.

Sacraments and the Law: Sacraments as Defined by the Word

❖ Baptism

After Calvin presented his positive teaching on the meaning of baptism (chapter 15, sections 1–6), Calvin turned his attention to answering several ideas about this sacrament that were contrary to the Word of God. First, he argued vigorously that the baptism of John the Baptist and of Jesus and his apostles was fundamentally the same, both testifying to repentance and forgiveness of sin. Here Calvin was particularly concerned to undercut any argument that some disciples were baptized first by John and later by the church. Calvin insisted that baptism in the Bible was never done twice. He probably had the Anabaptists and the Roman Catholics in mind with this argument, rejecting both the idea of rebaptism and the idea that rites before the establishment of the church were not true sacraments.

Second, Calvin rejected the doctrine that baptism removed original sin—a doctrine taught by the medieval church. Such teaching, Calvin believed, made both too much and too little of baptism. This medieval teaching promised too much in saying that the water of baptism removed the original sin of everyone baptized. But it also promised too little by reducing baptism to dealing only with original sin and having little significance for the rest of life. Instead Calvin taught that baptism promised the believer the forgiveness of all sins for the whole of life (4.15.10). In the lifelong and sometimes discouraging fight against sin, baptism always remained a present promise and encouragement to Christians that God was at work in them to sanctify (4.15.11).

Third, Calvin recognized that his teaching—that baptism blesses only when received by faith—might seem to encourage the Anabaptists with their teaching that faith must precede baptism. His response to the Anabaptists was very important:

> We indeed, being blind and unbelieving, for a long time did not grasp the promise that had been given us in baptism; yet that promise, since it was of God, ever remained fixed and firm and trustworthy. . . . We therefore confess that for that time baptism benefited us not at all, inasmuch as the promise offered us in it—without which baptism is

nothing—lay neglected. . . . But we believe that the promise itself did not vanish. Rather, we consider that God through baptism promises us forgiveness of sins, and he will doubtless fulfill his promise for all believers. This promise was offered to us in baptism; therefore, let us embrace it by faith. [4.15.17]

Faith does not make or even complete baptism. Rather, faith receives baptism and its promises.

In chapter 16 ("Infant Baptism as Best Agreeing with the Institution of Christ and the Nature of the Sign") Calvin continued his argument in more detail that the sacrament and the promise could precede faith. Calvin defended the practice of infant baptism against "certain frantic spirits" (4.16.1). He called this chapter an "appendix" and seemed to recognize that it might "seem too long." But he hoped that his analysis would clarify the doctrine of baptism as well as protect the pure doctrine and practice of the church. He certainly was answering a very powerful attack on the ancient practice of the church by the Anabaptists.

Calvin acknowledged that the Anabaptist argument was "seemingly quite plausible" (4.16.1) in the claim that God's Word did not teach the baptism of infants. Calvin responded that Christians must begin with the promises of Christ in baptism, not with the ceremony itself. He summarized the promises of baptism that he discussed at more length in chapter 15. His key argument for infant baptism began with showing that the promises of forgiveness as well as of mortification of the flesh and renewal of life in Christ that were attached to baptism were also attached to circumcision in the Old Testament. Circumcision was not a promise only of physical and temporal blessings to the Jews, but also was a promise of spiritual and eternal blessings. The children in the old covenant "were called a holy seed [Ezra 9:2; Isa. 6:13]" (4.16.6). If the children of the old covenant had spiritual promises sealed to them in the sacrament of circumcision, then the children of the new covenant must have the same.

Calvin extended the argument from circumcision by examining the relationship between Jesus' blessing of the children and baptism. He argued that Jesus' blessing showed clearly that the kingdom of God belonged to children of the covenant. So Calvin asked, if the kingdom belonged to them, how could the sign of the kingdom be denied them (4.16.7).

Further Calvin argued that the record of household baptisms in Acts clearly implied infant baptism. The Anabaptist rejection of this implication suggested an approach to exegesis that would equally conclude that women might not receive the Lord's Supper since there was no explicit command or example of women receiving the Lord's Supper in the New Testament (4.16.8).

Next Calvin turned to the question: if baptism did not regenerate infants, what real value did it have? First, it had value for parents. The baptism of children gives to their parents "a surer confidence" that God cares for his posterity. It also encourages parents to teach the faith to their children (4.16.32).

Second, infant baptism has value for the children. In it they are commended to the care of all church members, and as they grow up "they are greatly spurred to an earnest zeal for worshipping God, by whom they were received as children through a solemn symbol of adoption before they were old enough to recognize him as Father" (4.16.9). Further Calvin insisted that elect children who died in infancy would be saved by the work of the Holy Spirit. If they belonged to God in this way, they should receive the sign of his covenant (4.16.21).

Calvin also carefully considered the Anabaptist objection that if infants could receive the sacrament of baptism, they should also receive the sacrament of the Lord's Supper (4.16.30). It is particularly worth following Calvin's line of thought here since today some hyper-Reformed theologians have raised this same question and concluded that infants in fact should receive the Supper. Calvin noted that in the ancient church, Cyprian and Augustine defended the practice of infant communion. He did not seem aware that it continued in Eastern Orthodoxy.

Calvin saw the Supper as "solid food" which was not to be given to infants. He argued that according to the apostolic instruction only those might come to the table who could discern the body and blood of Christ there (1 Cor. 11:29). He insisted this was a very serious matter: "If only those who know how to distinguish rightly the holiness of Christ's body are able to participate worthily, why should we offer poison instead of life-giving food to our tender children?" (4.16.30).

He extended this argument, reflecting on the other apostolic directions: Christians are individually to examine themselves; they are to remember the work of Christ for them; they are to proclaim his death in their communing.

> None of these is prescribed in baptism. Accordingly, there is a very great difference between the two signs, as we have noted in like signs also under the Old Testament. Circumcision, which is known to correspond to our baptism, had been appointed for infants [Gen. 17:12]. But the Passover, the place of which has been taken by the Supper, did not admit all guests indiscriminately, but was duly eaten only by those old enough to be able to inquire into its meaning [Ex. 12:26]. If these men [the Anabaptists] had a particle of sound brain left, would they be blind to a thing so clear and obvious? [4.16.30]

He concluded the chapter reflecting again on the blessing of infant baptism: "how sweet is it to godly minds to be assured, not only by word, but by sight, that they obtain so much favor with the Heavenly Father that their offspring are within his care?" (4.16.32).

✦ The Lord's Supper

After laying out the simple meaning of the Lord's Supper in the first eleven sections of chapter 17, Calvin then turned in the rest of the chapter to some of the difficult controversies about the Supper that needed to be resolved by the teaching of the Word. Specifically he discussed, first, issues about the relationship of the bread of the sacrament to the body of Christ (sections 12–37); second, issues about faith and love in communing (sections 38–42); and third, issues about the ceremony of the administration of the sacrament (sections 43–50).

On the question of the relationship of the bread of the Supper to the body of Christ, Calvin began by examining the Roman Catholic doctrine that the bread and wine were miraculously transformed into the body and blood of Christ, so that the elements only appeared to be bread and wine, but in reality were entirely Christ's body and blood (sections 12–19). Calvin called this "superstition" and mocked it: "as if the body of Christ, by a local presence, were put there to be touched by the hands, to be chewed by the teeth, and swallowed by the mouth" (4.17.12). Theologically Calvin rejected the Roman idea as a denial that the body of Christ was a real body and as a violation of the reality of his ascension into heaven.

Calvin recognized that this doctrine of transubstantiation was one "for which today they fight more bitterly than for all the other articles of their faith" (4.17.14). Calvin rejected their view utterly, showing that it was not taught in the ancient church. He labeled their novelty "magic" and pointed out that by it they destroyed any analogy to baptism. Even Rome did not claim that the water of baptism was turned into the blood of Christ (4.17.15). Rome also did not understand the work of the Spirit in the Lord's Supper as the one who truly united the believer with Christ (4.17.16).

As Calvin turned to consider the Lutheran doctrine of the Lord's Supper (sections 20–34), he responded particularly to the Lutheran doctrine of ubiquity. The word "ubiquity" is derived from the Latin "ubique," meaning everywhere. The doctrine states that the human nature of Christ shares in his divine attribute of omnipresence and therefore his body can be everywhere. While the Lutheran confessions did not require a belief in ubiquity, it became the standard way in which Lutherans explained how Christ's body could be in, with, and under the bread. In particular Calvin had debated in lengthy treatises the Lutheran theologian Joachim Westphal, and much of the discussion in these sections draws on that debate. Calvin had concluded that he agreed substantially with the moderate Lutherans including Melanchthon, but differed strongly with the hyper-Lutherans such as Westphal.

Westphal and others, following Luther's argument with Zwingli at Marburg in 1529, insisted that they simply accepted the words of Jesus, "This is my body," literally while the Reformed rejected them rationalistically (see 4.17.20, 22, 24, 26). Calvin mocked this claim as he had Rome's: "But it is intolerable blasphemy to declare literally of an ephemeral and corruptible element that it is Christ" (4.17.20). Rather, sound exegesis would look to Christ's words about the wine as "the testament in my blood" to show the meaning of his briefer words about the bread (4.17.20). Calvin declared that he believed the words of Christ, but insisted that it was not rationalistic to ask what they mean: "The only question is whether it is a crime to investigate the true sense of his words" (4.17.22).

Calvin argued that a proper interpretation of all that the Bible teaches shows that the words of Jesus must be seen as a metonymy (4.17.21). A metonymy is a term used in rhetorical analysis of language to identify a figure of speech in which one word is substituted for another with which it is in some way associated. For example, the statement that Jesus is the lamb of God is a metonymy. That statement is literally true, not in the sense that Jesus has been transformed into a sheep, but as a figure of speech in which Jesus is seen, like a lamb, as a sacrifice for sin. The bread of the Lord's Supper is called Christ's body as a metonymy which says that the sacrament nourishes Christians with the whole Christ and all the benefits of his sacrifice (4.17.23).

Calvin's chief argument against the doctrine of ubiquity was that it denied the ascension and thereby turned the body of Christ into something other than a body, namely a spirit. "Not Aristotle, but the Holy Spirit teaches that the body of Christ from the time of his resurrection was finite" (4.17.26). Calvin believed the Bible whereas the hyper-Lutherans did not: "they make a spirit out of Christ's flesh" (4.17.29). This doctrine, Calvin declared, was worse than the Roman (4.17.30).

Calvin was very agitated by the doctrine of ubiquity not only because he believed that it was absurd and unbiblical, but also because it destroyed Protestant unity over a minor matter. He agreed with the Lutherans about what was received in the Supper, namely the body and blood of Christ, and saw their difference only over the way in which Christ was given in the Supper: "The question is therefore only of the manner, for they place Christ in the bread, while we do not think it lawful for us to drag him from heaven. . . . Only away with that calumny that Christ is removed from his Supper unless he lies hidden under the covering of bread! For since this mystery is heavenly, there is no need to draw Christ to earth that he may be joined to us" (4.17.31).

Far from constructing a rationalistic doctrine of the Supper, Calvin saw himself as simply taking account of all that the Scripture taught. He recognized that the mind of man could not fully comprehend it all: "Now, if anyone should ask me how this takes place, I shall not be ashamed to confess that it is a secret too lofty for either my mind to comprehend or my words to declare. And, to speak more plainly, I rather experience it than understand it" (4.17.32). He recognized that far from a rationalistic doctrine, his was full of miracles: "We say Christ descends to us both by the outward symbol and by his Spirit, that he may truly quicken our souls by the substance of his flesh and blood. He who does not perceive many miracles are subsumed in these few words is more than stupid" (4.17.24). Above all he simply wanted to confess that in the Supper he received Christ: "In his Sacred Supper he bids me take, eat, and drink his body and blood under the symbols of bread and wine. I do not doubt that he himself truly presents them, and that I receive them" (4.17.32).

Calvin continued to stress against the hyper-Lutherans that only believers—not the unworthy—received the body of Christ in the Supper. Calvin believed that one could not separate in the Supper the body of Christ from his blessings. This insistence on faith did not undermine the objective promise of the sacrament, but rather remembered that "it is one thing to be offered, another to be received" (4.17.33). Christ was as truly offered to all in the sacrament as he was in the preaching of the gospel, but he was received only by faith: "I hold that men bear away from this Sacrament no more than they gather with the vessel of faith" (4.17.33).

Calvin summarized this point in a particularly telling and clear statement: "And this is the wholeness of the Sacrament, which the whole world cannot violate: that the flesh and blood of Christ are no less truly given to the unworthy than to God's elect believers. At the same time, it is true, however, that, just as rain falling upon a hard rock flows off because no entrance opens into the stone, the wicked by their hardness so repel God's grace that it does not reach them" (4.17.33).

In the final sections dealing with the bread and the body (sections 35–37) Calvin turned to the Roman practice of displaying the consecrated elements to be worshiped. He argued that the false Roman doctrine of transubstantiation led to this damnable idolatry: "For what is idolatry if not this: to worship the gifts in place of the Giver himself?" (4.17.36).

The second complex of issues that Calvin addressed was the need of faith and love in those who would commune (sections 38–42 of chapter 17). Rome stressed the importance of purifying the soul before coming to communion. Calvin responded that even those who had most pursued holiness were not worthy of coming to the table in themselves (4.17.41). Rather it was those who knew themselves to be sinners and their need of Christ who should come:

> Let us remember that this sacred feast is medicine for the sick, solace for sinners, alms to the poor.... Therefore, this is the worthiness—the best and only kind we can bring to God—to offer our vileness and (so to speak) our unworthiness to him so that his mercy may make us worthy of him; to despair in ourselves so that we may be comforted in him; to abase ourselves so that we may be lifted up by him; to accuse ourselves so that we may be justified by him. [4.17.42]

Christians can come to the table if they have faith in Christ and see in themselves evidence of the beginning of the sanctifying work of the Holy Spirit.

Sacraments and the Church: Sacraments Showing the Limits of Church Power

In chapter 18 ("On the Papal Mass, by Which Sacrilege the Supper of Christ Was Not Only Profaned, but Reduced to Nothing") Calvin focused more particularly on the Roman doctrine of the mass as a eucharistic sacrifice. He seemed to see this error as worse than the error of transubstantiation. This Roman doctrine is "the height of frightful abomination" and "a most pestilential error—the belief that the Mass is a sacrifice and offering to obtain forgiveness of sins" (4.18.1). For Calvin the idea that the mass was a propitiatory sacrifice was a human invention and abuse of church power without a hint of biblical warrant, whereas transubstantiation was a serious misunderstanding of a biblical text.

The doctrine of eucharistic sacrifice was so offensive for Calvin because it destroyed the finished and complete sacrifice of Christ on the cross for sinners. The mass "inflicts signal dishonor upon Christ, buries and oppresses his cross, consigns his death to oblivion, takes away the benefit which came to us from it, and weakens and destroys the Sacrament by which the memory of his death was bequeathed to us" (4.18.1).

Christ needed no fellow priests as partners in the offering of propitia-tory sacrifices (4.18.2), and his sacrifice on the cross could not be repeated (4.18.3). In Calvin's day some Roman theologians such as John Eck called the mass a repetition of Christ's sacrifice. Since that time Rome insists that the mass is not a repetition, but a continuation of the one sacrifice on the cross. But Calvin had heard that argument in his day too and rejected it (4.18.3). Any language that continued to make of the mass a propitiatory sacrifice offered to God, in any sense, destroyed the finished work of Christ on the cross.

Calvin was adamant—and correct—that the idea of the Lord's Sup-per as a propitiatory sacrifice fundamentally distorted and destroyed the meaning of the sacrament. It turned the sacrament upside down, changing it from a gift that God gives, into an offering given to God (4.18.7).

Calvin recognized the antiquity of aspects of the error of eucharistic sacrifice (4.18.11). But he insisted that the ancient church was not at all as bad as the medieval. Most often the ancient church called the Lord's Supper a sacrifice in the sense of a sacrifice of praise or thanksgiving which the church offered to him in worship (4.18.13, 16). This sense of sacrifice is not propitiatory and does not undermine the finished work of Christ on the cross.

In summary Calvin reiterated that the "sacraments have been appointed by God to instruct us concerning some promise of his, and to attest to us his good will toward us" (4.18.19). This conviction led Calvin on to his next chapter (chapter 19: "On the Five Sacraments Falsely So-called: Where It Is Declared That These Five Are Not Sacraments, Although They Are Com-monly Held to Be Sacraments until Now, and It Is Shown What They Are"). His last chapter on the sacraments is an examination of the other five rites that the Roman church had recognized as sacraments.

Calvin began by again warning against a human curiosity that would extend sacraments to ceremonies that have neither a divine command nor a divine promise. He particularly complained that Peter Lombard, the author of the foundational medieval theology text *The Sentences*, had taken the name "sacrament" away from the divine institutions of the Old Testament and applied it to gross human inventions in the church which have neither command nor promise (4.19.2).

Calvin again stressed the witness of the ancient church on this point: "If they would like to press us with the authority of the ancient church, I say that they are deceiving. For nowhere among the ecclesiastical writers is this number 'seven' found" (4.19.3). He showed that Augustine explicitly listed only baptism and the Lord's Supper as sacraments (4.19.3).

Calvin analyzed each of the five Roman ceremonies: confirmation, penance, extreme unction, ordination, and marriage. Nearly two-thirds of his discussion focuses on confirmation and ordination.

✦ Confirmation

Calvin saw the origin of confirmation in the ancient practice of a public recognition that a child baptized in the church has personally embraced the faith. Calvin saw real value in some such practice, but denied that it was a sacrament (4.19.13):

> How I wish that we might have kept the custom which, as I said, existed among the ancient Christians. . . . A catechizing, in which children or those near adolescence would give an account of their faith before the church. . . . A child of ten would present himself to the church to declare his confession of faith. . . . If this discipline were in effect today, it would certainly arouse some slothful parents, who carelessly neglect the instruction of their children as a matter of no concern to them; for then they could not overlook it without public disgrace." [4.19.13]

Rome invented the idea that confirmation was a sacrament, claiming that it increased grace and equipped for living the Christian life. But those claims in fact denigrated baptism, which provided precisely those blessings (4.19.8).

✦ Penance

On penance Calvin noted that the origins of this pseudosacrament were to be found in the ancient practice of public acts of penance to demonstrate sincere repentance for serious sins. Later, private acts of penance were also introduced into the life of the church. These practices were not evil in themselves, but the medieval church turned them into a sacrament even though the character of the sacrament remained unclear and no definite sign accompanied it. Most seriously this so-called sacrament also detracted from baptism, which is a perpetual call to repentance (4.19.17).

✦ Extreme Unction

Next Calvin examined extreme unction, arguing that Rome had confounded the extraordinary ministry in the time of the apostles, described in James 5, with the ordinary ministry of the church. "Therefore, they make themselves ridiculous when they boast that they are endowed with the gift of healing. The Lord is indeed present with his people in every age; and he heals their weaknesses as often as necessary, no less than of old; still he does not put forth these manifest powers, nor dispense miracles through the apostles' hands" (4.19.19). Also for Rome this rite had become a sacrament of dying, not a sacrament of healing.

✦ Ordination

Calvin gave even more attention to ordination than to confirmation. He began noting a great muddle in Rome on exactly how many offices there were in the church and how the various ceremonies connected with the different offices can form one sacrament. He argued that Rome did not take the minor orders very seriously and yet had invented a variety of ceremonies to surround them.

On the ordination of priests or presbyters he again noted that the laying on of hands might be seen as sacramental, but probably should not be regarded as a sacrament since it was not given to the whole church (4.19.28, 31). He utterly rejected the notion that by ordination priests could offer expiatory sacrifices. He especially ridiculed the Roman claim that their priests had received their anointing from the sons of Aaron (4.19.30). Rome clearly was unacquainted with the Letter to the Hebrews where Christ's priesthood is derived from Melchizedek, not Aaron (4.19.30).

✦ Marriage

Finally Calvin considered marriage, which again he believed was not designated a sacrament in Scripture. "Marriage is a good and holy ordinance of God; and farming, building, cobbling, and barbering are lawful ordinances of God, and yet are not sacraments" (4.19.34). In fact, he argued that although Rome appeared to exalt marriage by making it a sacrament, in fact it had a low view of marriage. He showed how medieval theologians saw the married state as filled with sin and uncleanness (4.19.36). For Calvin a key motive in Rome's approach to marriage was as a way to advance its power and control in society, making marriage a church rather than state matter (4.19.37).

Conclusion

Calvin recognized that he had spent much time in criticizing the erroneous views of Rome and others (4.19.37). But his real purpose was not ultimately to criticize and correct. He wanted to exalt the positive value of the sacraments as a central part of worship and faith for the Christian. He taught that, properly used and understood, the sacraments "are to nourish, refresh, strengthen, and gladden" (4.17.3). The true meaning and ministry of the sacraments leads Christians to "hunger for, seek, look to, learn, and study Christ alone" (4.18.20).

Bibliography

Bromiley, Geoffrey. *Sacramental Teaching and Practice in the Reformation Churches*. Grand Rapids: Eerdmans, 1957.

Davis, Thomas. *The Clearest Promises of God: The Development of Calvin's Eucharistic Theology*. New York: AMS, 1995.

Gerrish, Brian. *Grace and Gratitude: The Eucharistic Theology of John Calvin*. Minneapolis: Fortress, 1993.

Mathison, Keith. *Given for You: Reclaiming Calvin's Doctrine of the Lord's Supper*. Phillipsburg, NJ: P&R, 2002.

Marcel, Pierre. *Baptism: Sacrament of the Covenant of Grace*. Cherry Hill, NJ: Mack, 1973.

Riggs, John W. *Baptism in the Reformed Tradition*. Louisville: Westminster/ John Knox, 2002.

Wallace, Ronald S. *Calvin's Doctrine of the Word and Sacrament*. Edinburgh: Oliver and Boyd, 1953.

17

JOHN CALVIN'S VIEW OF CHURCH GOVERNMENT

INSTITUTES 4.3–9
JOSEPH H. HALL

The necessity for biblical church government was cogently brought home to the present writer by Westminster Seminary professor Paul Woolley's consideration of the reason for the great demise of biblical faithfulness in the Presbyterian Church, U.S.A., in the late nineteenth and twentieth centuries. Professor Woolley laid it largely at the feet of a theologically uninformed and uninterested eldership which failed to oppose the increasingly liberal professors and ministers. Certainly biblical church government is a vital part of a healthy church. Indeed, if preaching the pure Word of God faithfully is the lifeblood of the congregation, then biblical church government affords the sinews holding the church in unity and faithfulness. Governed by faithfulness to Scripture and a love for Christ and his church, Calvin presents a rich and foundational government for the church with Christ at the helm, a body of church officers, and the Scriptures, correctly interpreted, the standard to which we will do well to take heed.

Calvin himself was ejected from Geneva in 1538 by the Geneva council that controlled the church. Having sought exile in South German Strasbourg with Martin Bucer, Calvin found a ready place of service by ministering to French refugees, teaching theology in the renowned Johann Sturm's Strasbourg Academy, and writing. Calvin had firsthand opportunity to observe the Strasbourg Reformed church government and to consider the necessity of such for a God-honoring church. In God's providence, the Geneva council overtured Calvin to return to Geneva, due in measure to his response to Roman Catholic Cardinal Sadoleto's efforts to reclaim Geneva again for Catholicism. Calvin found the call to return to Geneva very traumatic. In a letter to his former fellow Reformer, Pierre Viret, Calvin remarked concerning Geneva, "there is no place under heaven of which I have greater dread … because I see so many difficulties presented … which I do feel myself far from being equal to mount."[1] Nevertheless, believing it to be God's will, the Reformer conceded to go and, writing to his former Geneva colleague, William Farel, stated, "when I remember that I am not my own, I offer up my heart, presented as a sacrifice to the Lord."[2] Motivated by the dual consideration of God's call and his own love for the Geneva church, Calvin returned in September 1541 with some apprehension but a firm trust the call was in God's providential will.

Having seen firsthand a Reformed model of church government operative in Bucer's Strasbourg church, Calvin presented to the Geneva council the necessity of settling the issue of church government, without which, he concluded, the Geneva church could not "hold together."[3] He believed it necessary to divide the duties of church and civil government. Whereas the church was to wield the "spiritual sword," the civil government had the biblical mandate to legislate for and govern the state.

The Geneva council agreed to the formation of an ecclesiastical order written jointly by the Geneva pastors and several members of the council. The result of this was the completion of the "Ecclesiastical Ordinances" in

---

1. John Calvin, *Selected Works* (Grand Rapids: Baker, 1983), 4:231.
2. Ibid., 4:280.
3. Ibid., 4:284.

November 1541, having a prefatory conclusion that in Protestant Geneva each estate (civil and ecclesiastical) would attend to the "duty of its office."[4] The work concluded with the mandate that discipline cases administered by the church consistory would be reported to the Geneva council.[5] Nevertheless, the wording was ambiguous so that Calvin interpreted it as a separation of church and the council.[6] Thus these ordinances became the concrete mandate for the functioning of the church of Geneva. Nevertheless, the council would later revise the "Ecclesiastical Ordinances," thus creating greater control over the church, especially in church discipline requirements. The council's changes effectively brought church discipline into the council's hands and caused Calvin perpetual difficulty until the situation was resolved in 1555 in favor of the biblical role of autonomous church discipline. Thus far the background of the thematic presentation of church government found in Calvin's *Institutes of the Christian Religion.*

Calvin presented the raison d'etre of church government more thoroughly in book 4 of the *Institutes* than in any of his other writings. In chapters 1–2 Calvin sets forth the nature of the church and contrasts it with the false church, mainly the Roman Catholic Church. Chapters 3–4 present the church officers, their calling, number, and duties, and how, under the aegis of Christ, they are placed in office. Chapters 5–7 masterfully outline the history of the ancient church and its complete overthrow by the elevation of the monarchical papal bishop and the restraint of earlier ecclesiastical freedoms. Calvin then presents in chapter 8 how church power is limited by the Word of God in contrast with the Roman Catholic Church's locating its power in the hierarchical bishops. Finally, in chapter 9 Calvin deals with the true authority of church councils in contrast with the intrusion of the dual authority of both Scripture and tradition found in Roman Catholicism.

Church order, or the government of the church, is not, for Calvin, an end in itself. Rather, it always must serve the high biblical purposes of both the glory of God and the welfare of the church. But what are the means for achieving those ends? Calvin everywhere points, first, to

4. "Ecclesiastical Ordinances" (hereafter EO), in *The Register of the Company of Pastors of Geneva in the Time of Calvin,* ed. P. E. Hughes (Grand Rapids: Eerdmans, 1968), 35.

5. Ibid., 49.

6. François Wendel, *Calvin* (London: W. Collins, 1965), 74.

the pure preaching of the Word as the primary means of realizing God's honor and the welfare of the church. The ministry of the Word is ordered by God and is "the most excellent of all things" in benefiting the church. Indeed, Calvin declared, there exists "nothing more notable or glorious in the church than the ministry of the gospel, since it is the administration of the Spirit and of righteousness and eternal life."[7]

The question next arises, "How is this primary means of achieving the welfare of the church realized?" Thus Calvin introduced church government as, under Christ, the means of both securing and maintaining the faithful preaching of the Word. Therefore, while Calvin teaches the primacy of preaching for the well-being of the church, he in no way denigrates God-ordained church government order. Indeed, since church government is God's ordination for the church's establishment and continuation, Calvin declared that "whoever discounts it as not necessary, is striving for the undoing, or rather, the ruin and destruction of the church."[8] Church government, then, becomes the God-given means of both securing gifted, equipped, faithful preachers of the Word and maintaining them for the preservation of the church.

Officers in the Church: Their Election and Duties

In the seminal *Institutes* book 4, chapter 3, Calvin introduced the four offices: doctors (teachers), pastors, disciplinary elders, and deacons. Calvin placed these four offices under two genres: teachers, pastors, and elders under the genus *presbyteros/episkopos* and deacons under the single genus of *diakonos*.[9] That Calvin held these two genres of governmental church offices as the biblical order and the order of the ancient church is indisputably clear. Disputation of the subject will await the final section on critiquing Calvin's church government. Further, Calvin plainly asserted that the teaching office requires neither disciplinary labors nor administration of the sacraments, but rather the maintenance of the pure interpretation

---

7. John Calvin, *Institutes of the Christian Religion*, ed. John T. McNeill, trans. Ford Lewis Battles (Philadelphia: Westminster, 1960), 4.3.3.

8. Ibid., 4.3.2.

9. Ibid., 4.3.8.

of the Word. The pastors' duties include preaching, administration of the sacraments, and discipline, jointly with the body of disciplinary elders of the church. Most certainly, then, the pastor/elder and the disciplinary elder are included in one genus and, therefore, are the governing body (senate or consistory) of the local church, while the teacher does not share the elder duties of the former. Nevertheless, in practice, both Calvin and Theodore Beza, his successor, and perhaps others, shared the offices of teacher, pastor and disciplinary elder.

Pastor and Teacher Presbyters (Presbyteroi)

Calvin began chapter 3 by posing the question, "Why doesn't the Lord rule His church immediately and directly?" He answered by simply stating that, since God is now not visible to us, he is pleased to use men to declare his will, very much as an ambassador declares the will of the king. Thus, when the ambassadors (pastors, teachers) speak in faithfulness to the Word, God speaks, just as though he himself speaks in person. Should God himself speak from heaven, who would not be completely undone by his majesty? Therefore, when puny man, as pastor or teacher, speaks to the church, it calls for an exercise in humility to receive God's Word through the weak, human instrument. Thus, relying on God speaking through the pastor, the church members are brought together in a bond of unity and spirit as they obey God's voice.

Who is the man called to ministry of the Word? Calvin answered the question by declaring him to be a man who sincerely feared God and desired to build up the church. Moreover, he must embrace sound doctrine, live a holy life, and be of good reputation, so as not to disgrace the ministry.[10] God, therefore, Calvin declared, gifts and calls men to the church for the purposes of both calling forth his church and instructing the church toward obedience and, thereby, through the Holy Spirit, enabling the members of the church to love and glorify God and love one another. In New Testament times, Calvin stated, those called to govern the church were, in order, apostles, prophets, evangelists, pastors, and teachers. In the post-New Testament era only the latter two remain as ordinary offices related to the ministry of the Word.

10. Ibid., 4.3.11–12.

In reading chapter 3, it becomes very obvious that Calvin placed more emphasis upon the duties of the pastor than the other three offices. Why did he so do? A close reading reveals Calvin's purpose. He did so because the faithful pastor is God's very own voice to the local church in the preaching of the Word. And, indeed, since biblical preaching is the means by which the Holy Spirit brings righteousness and new life, the crucial nature of the preaching office becomes apparent. Calvin declared, then, that the gospel ministry is both most notable and most glorious.[11] The absolute necessity of ministry of the Word in the church may be shown by God's use of men to instruct the church. Calvin adduced the example of Ananias teaching Paul, called to be an apostle. Indeed, declared Calvin, "Who, then, would dare despise that ministry or dispense with it as something superfluous, whose use God willed to attest with such proofs?"[12]

Whereas Calvin greatly emphasized the pastoral office of preaching in the local church, it might be concluded that the teaching office is of less benefit to the church since the teacher is not called to pastoring nor to joint disciplinary duties. Not so, since it is Christ who has ordained the teacher as well as the pastor. Christ calls the teacher to the duty of keeping "doctrine whole and pure among the believers." While pastors correspond to the apostles, Calvin declared the teachers comparable to the Old Testament prophets whose office was to speak forth their gift of revelation. And although the teacher does not have the gift of revelation, Calvin declared that the teacher's office "is very similar in character and has exactly the same purpose." Thus, while Calvin says little more in book 3 about the teacher, in no way does he denigrate or lower the office of teaching. Indeed, quite the contrary, it is Christ's called and gifted teacher who labors in training pastors for the glorious ministry of the Word.[13] The teachers were those appointed to the theological department of the Academy of Geneva.

Governing, or Disciplinary, Elders (Presbyteroi)

Calvin taught that the office of governing, disciplinary elder was a continuation of the Old Testament office into the New Testament and

11. Ibid., 4.3.3.
12. Ibid., 4.3.3.
13. Ibid., 4.3.5.

afterward, perpetually necessary for every age. Moreover, elders must be "godly, grave, and holy men" chosen from the membership of the church to work alongside the pastor in censoring the morals of the church members.[14] Together, the minister and elders, both of whom were designated elders, formed the senate in the ancient church that was appointed by Christ to offer spiritual jurisdiction in the affairs of the church. Such joint governing of the church precludes the office of one man as obtained in the bishopric of the Roman Catholic Church.[15]

Deacons (Diakonoi)

The second genus of the church officers is that of deacon. The diaconate, like the office of elder, is a perpetual office in the church. Deacons are also called by Christ to care for the poor in the church. Deacons are to receive alms from church members and distribute them to the poor and so to serve as stewards of the people's gifts to the poor. This duty was the special scriptural designation for the deacon and his enduring office. However, Calvin found a wider designation of diakonoi, that is, widows whom Scripture gave the duty of caring for the poor and sick, since the apostle Paul mandated that true widows should care for the poor. Calvin concluded this function was the only public office women could fill. Nevertheless, the enduring office of deacon was for men chosen to show Christ's mercy for the financial need of the poor as described in Acts 6 in the care exercised for the Greek widows.[16] Thus, in the 1541 "Ecclesiastical Ordinances" the mandate for Geneva provided for the establishment of two kinds of deacons, one to handle finances and distribution to the poor and a second deacon with the duty of caring for the sick.[17]

Manner of Choosing Officers of the Church

Calvin, then, concluded that two genres of offices exist by Christ's mandate: the office of elder (presbyter) of whom there were three kinds, teachers (doctors), pastors, and governing elders, and the office of deacon.

14. Ibid., 4.2.8.
15. Ibid., 4.11.6.
16. Ibid., 4.3.8–9.
17. EO 42.

Calvin scorned the Roman Catholic prelates' method of appointment of ministers (elders) and deacons. By ordaining these officers, they created not presbyters "to lead and feed the people, but priests to perform sacrifices. Similarly, when they consecrate deacons, they . . . ordain them only for certain rites concerned with chalice and paten."[18] Rather, the members of the church are to choose their officers for the biblical purposes for which each office is called. Only then will there exist order in the church and the honor of Christ the head observed.[19]

The Power of the Church: Affirmative and Negative

One frequently hears it said that "power corrupts; absolute power corrupts absolutely." Not so with God's power, which is perfect in absolute righteousness, justice, mercy, and consummate wisdom! Calvin's doctrine of power in the church may be briefly summarized by his constant insistence that, since Christ redeemed the church, it belongs to him. Therefore, Christ must have the love, honor, and obedience that his revealed Word requires from members of the church. Finally, Christ's power is perfected in the well-being of his church, which requires delegated, operative spiritual power in humble obedience to his Word.

Affirmative: Calvin's Reformed View

Ecclesiastical power is not, declared Calvin, inherent in the church, nor an end in itself. Rather, the operative power is found in Christ, the head of the church, who guides the church in obedience to the Word for God's glory and the welfare of the church. Moreover, it has pleased Christ to delegate power, gifts, and calling to men worldwide. Therefore, Calvin concluded the church's power resides partly in the local elders, partly in councils, whether provincial or general.[20] Finally, the church's power is spiritual, unlike civil power; therefore, his delegated officers in the church wield a spiritual sword.

18. Calvin, *Institutes* 4.5.4.
19. Ibid., 4.3.15; 4.5.2–4; see also Calvin, *The True Method of Giving Peace in Christendom and Reforming the Church*, in his *Selected Works*, 3:240, and especially, 294–99.
20. Calvin, *Institutes* 4.8.1.

Calvin maintained three aspects of the power of the church: power to bring forth biblical doctrine faithfully, power in implementing jurisdiction, and power to legislate in the church. Next, the Geneva Reformer adduced operative principles Christ gave in the use of these powers. First, those to whom power is delegated must use it according to Christ's purposes, according to his Word. Therefore, church officers are to hear Christ, for he is the schoolmaster of the church. Moreover, the power must be used for building up the saints and not for their destruction. To achieve the welfare of the church, officers of the church must always preserve the authority for Christ himself.[21]

Power with Respect to Doctrine

Christ has given to the presbyters, the elders of the church, power to preach and maintain biblical doctrine and articles of faith. "Faithful ministers are now not permitted to coin any new doctrine . . . but simply to cleave to that doctrine to which God has subjected all men without exception."[22] Keeping in mind that the purpose of church government is the welfare of the saints, ministers and governing elders must, of necessity, preserve the authority of Christ for himself. To achieve this, church officers must be taught by Christ, from the Word of God. Therefore, church power is not arbitrary or whimsical but, rather, preserves Christ's direction in the church for his honor and the welfare of the saints.[23]

Calvin presented the biblical development of church power from the Old Testament forward, from Moses, priests, and prophets to the New Testament apostles. Moses, the prince of prophets, declared to Israel only that which God gave him orally. All other prophets had to follow Moses in so doing. Priests also were messengers of the Lord to communicate only his commands; likewise, the apostles, his sent ones, were to report faithfully the commands of Christ who sent them.[24] In due time, when God raised up a more visible form of his church, he caused his Word to be written.

21. Ibid.
22. Ibid.
23. Ibid.
24. Ibid., 4.8.2.

Thus his law became the substance of priestly teaching. Later, prophets added to the law God's fuller revelation, after which came the promised Messiah, when the Word became flesh. In Christ, God the Father spoke his final testimony, admonishing the apostles, "Hear him!" Therefore, declared Calvin, we are led away from all merely human doctrines to the Word made flesh. From the apostolic writings, then, we have the final Word from God, inspiring them through the Holy Spirit. Moreover, the apostles themselves did not go beyond the revealed Word of God.[25] Since the apostles did not go beyond God's revealed will in his Word, ministers and teachers in the post-apostolic age and later are not permitted to coin new doctrine, but must "cleave to that doctrine to which God has subjected all men without exception."[26] In so stating, Calvin followed Luther, Zwingli, and others in proclaiming Scripture alone (*sola scriptura*) as the sole procedural foundation of the Reformation.

Power with Respect to Jurisdiction

The power of the church consistory to exercise its own discipline apart from the intervention of the Geneva council was incontrovertibly the major jurisdiction of church power, and also the greatest obstacle for the Geneva Reformed Church. Indeed, Calvin deemed corrective discipline (or, as he called it, "spiritual polity") as the most important exercise of jurisdiction in a well-ordered church. Moreover, the church courts were established for the censure of morals among the people, and have their power from the keys of the kingdom given to the apostles, and by extension, to presbyters, by Christ in Matthew 18:15–18. These keys were given to the presbyters to "bind and loose" people through God's Word to either the possession of heaven or its denial.[27]

When a believer gave a credible profession, he or she had the door of the kingdom opened for membership in the church. Conversely, when a member was found living in sin and unrepentant, he or she was excommunicated and the kingdom was shut. While Calvin taught that such persons should be excommunicated, he appealed to the presbyters to labor

25. Ibid., 4.8.7–8.
26. Ibid., 4.8.9.
27. Ibid., 4.11.1–2.

for their restoration.[28] Contrary to the Roman Catholic Church whose disciplinary exercises were for the benefit of the organized hierarchical church, Calvin maintained that church discipline is for the well-being of church members and the glory of Christ. Moreover, church discipline is a prototype of what should exist for each church member: he or she must exercise self-discipline. Indeed, by the Spirit of God, who brings softness to our heart, "we do also try daily in ourselves" for personal discipline.[29]

Negative Power: That of the Roman Catholic Church

Calvin then turned from presenting the biblical foundation of church power to its derogation by the Roman Catholic Church, whose claim is that, since universal councils image or constitute the true church in a larger context, such councils are infallibly guided by the Holy Spirit. Therefore, the Roman Church contends it has power to frame new articles of faith, and by so doing, Calvin concluded, they stand in contempt of God's Word as they construct new doctrines after their own whim.[30]

Calvin agreed that when the Roman Catholic Church speaks on matters of salvation its statements are true "insofar as the church, having forsaken all its own wisdom, allows itself to be taught by the Holy Spirit through God's Word." Their great error is declaring doctrine apart from God's Word and proclaiming the new doctrine infallible because, they claim, they have been guided by the Holy Spirit. In so doing they effectively separate God's Word from the Holy Spirit, whereas, Calvin maintained, Word and the Holy Spirit are inseparable. Therefore, the church must always speak according to the Word of God. However, Calvin maintained, no church is infallible as the Roman Catholic Church teaches; it continues to err, as do all churches, which should present cause to humble themselves before God, causing them to return to God's Word alone as the only necessary and infallible guide into all truth.[31]

28. Ibid., 4.12.10.

29. Calvin, *Commentary on the Acts of the Apostles*, Calvin's Commentaries 20 (Grand Rapids: Baker, 1989), 373.

30. Calvin, *Institutes* 4.8.10.

31. Ibid., 4.8.12–13.

Calvin then proceeded to inquire how the Roman Catholic Church arrived at its teaching of being infallible, even when creating doctrine apart from the Word of God, which doctrine then becomes tradition, equal with the Word of God. The Roman Catholic Church, Calvin maintained, clearly misinterpreted such passages as John 16:12, where Christ addressed the apostles: "I have many things to say to you, which you cannot hear now." Roman Catholics maintain that "the many things" of which Christ spoke are "decrees which, apart from Scripture, have been accepted only by use and custom." On the contrary, declared Calvin, the disciples prior to committing their doctrine to writing had already been prepared by the Holy Spirit for later writing. Therefore, asked Calvin, "What hindered them from embracing and leaving in written form a perfect and distinct knowledge of gospel doctrine?"[32]

Finally, Calvin concluded Roman Catholic attempts to prove tradition equal to Scripture were simply absurd. They afford examples notoriously weak. For example, where does one find the key word "consubstantial" in Scripture, declared by the Council of Nicaea? Roman Catholics then maintained that the council's declaration, even though not found in Scripture, must be accepted as tradition, and infallible, apart from the Scripture. Although the word "consubstantial" is nonscriptural, Calvin did admit that "when it is so often asserted in Scripture that there is one God, and when Christ is called so often the true and eternal God one with the Father—what else are the Nicene fathers doing when they declare them of one essence but simply expounding the real meaning of Scripture?"[33]

Councils and Their Authority

The nature of councils and their authority had been in contention for two centuries prior to Calvin's writing. However, the issue had remained in the Roman Catholic context, where the question was posed: where does the primal authority reside, in the papacy or in the council? Papal supremacy won the day by the mid-fifteenth century, although not without continued contention.

32. Ibid., 4.8.14.
33. Ibid., 4.8.16.

In chapter 9, Calvin presented the basic principles and the power of the graded courts of the church basic to the Reformed system beginning with the foundational and prototype congregational council (session, consistory) and then proceeding to the synod or to the general assembly, representative gatherings of the church. Calvin also repudiated the Roman Catholic councils on several principal counts: failing to recognize Christ as the head of the church, failing to recognize the necessity of following Scripture, and failing to seek enlightenment through the Holy Spirit's illuminating the Word. Calvin concluded that Christ is the central authority in the church and brooks no rivals for his position. Moreover, Christ presides in the church only when it is governed by both his Word and Spirit. Therefore, there exists no need to require additional authority such as the papacy and Roman Catholic Church council. Indeed, when one reviews the work of the general councils of the first four centuries (from Nicaea through Chalcedon, 325–451), one finds theological conclusions honoring to God and sufficient to discount subsequent councils.[34]

True and False Councils

A true council may be small or large, according to Christ's definition that he is present where even two or three are met in his name. Moreover, it must be governed by his Word and Spirit. Calvin maintained that this is true in both the Old and New Testament. For example, in the Old Testament church the Levitical priests had to teach only from "God's lips." How much more in the New Testament and post-New Testament era, where we are enjoined never to add to nor take away from God's Word![35]

Roman Catholic Departure from True Councils

According to Calvin, the Roman Catholic Church taught that the church is nonexistent unless there is agreement among the pastors and, secondly, that the church becomes visible only when the general councils meet. The Geneva Reformer rebutted this, declaring that the church existed even in Isaiah's day when the pastors in the church were blind

34. Ibid., 4.9.1.
35. Ibid., 4.9.2.

to the truth. Moreover, in the New Testament, Peter asserted that the church and truth will exist even when false teachers/pastors arise within the church. Therefore, one must discriminate whether pastors are faithful to the Word. However, the "pope" and the "whole troupe of bishops" have "shaken off obedience to God's Word" and tumbled and tossed "everything at their pleasure." Little did they realize, said Calvin, that they were "singing the same song that those once sang [in Zechariah's time] who were fighting against God's Word."[36]

The Geneva Reformer was equally concerned to maintain the truth apart from Roman Catholic general councils that pervert the truth. The truth will stand despite such perversion. Witness in the Old Testament when Ahab gathered in council four hundred priests who desired to flatter their king. God sent Satan, a lying spirit, among them. Or, more significantly, in the New Testament, even when the Jewish council condemned the Son of God, the truth and the true church continued to exist. Indeed, Calvin said, one must not conclude the church "consists in the assembly of pastors, whom the Lord nowhere assumes to be forever good, but has declared will sometimes be evil."[37]

Indeed, synods and councils may err. How, then, can one discover the validity of a council's declarations? Calvin declared his agreement with Augustine when the ancient father declared that councils must always stand the test of Scripture with respect to their validity. Should the councils be in conformity with Scripture, Calvin concluded, "councils would come to have majesty that is their due; yet in the meantime Scripture would stand out in a higher place." Calvin then declared the first four councils were the "golden age" of councils, because of their faithfulness to Scripture.[38]

The history of councils reveals that some councils have contravened others. For example, Calvin showed how the Eutychean heresy which denied Christ's true human nature was approved at the Second Council of Ephesus in 449, but denied at the Council of Chalcedon in 451.[39] Therefore, Calvin declared, the Roman Catholic Church wrongly required submission to the pronouncements of some councils, even while they

36. Ibid., 4.9.5.
37. Ibid., 4.9.7.
38. Ibid., 4.9.8.
39. Ibid., 4.9.9.

admitted that councils may err in things not pertaining to salvation. Then Calvin asked the question, Why does God allow councils to make errors? Simply, said Calvin, to show that one should not place too much confidence in men.[40] Councils after Chalcedon, in 451, do not stand the test of Scriptures, but have opposed Scripture with their decisions. Therefore, we must, according to Scripture, beware of false prophets among those later councils. Calvin concluded by declaring that the church has no power to formulate new doctrines.

The True Power of Church Councils

What power, then, do the councils have? How is it possible to return to the principles observed by the early faithful councils of the first four centuries? Calvin outlined the proper method of so doing. First, a synod of true bishops (or, presbyters) must be assembled. Second, upon meeting, these bishops must call upon Christ's Spirit to guide their discussion regarding doctrine. Third, they must deliberate in common, always seeking to follow the teaching of Scripture and conclude in conformity with God's Word. That is the way the ancient churches declared doctrine in the face of heresy. Should the church fail to follow God's way of guidance into truth, however, one should conclude, as did Calvin, that the truth of God shall never fail nor be extinguished.

Critique of Calvin's Presbyterian Government: A Biblical Mandate?

If, indeed, Calvin held to presbyterianism as the divinely prescribed (*ius divinum*) form of the church, why did he offer an apparently positive historical assessment of the early episcopal church government prior to A.D. 600? J. T. McNeill concluded that Calvin affirmed the structure of the episcopal government, but did so placing emphasis upon its functioning effectiveness rather than the form of government.[41] However, rather than concluding that the early church government was episcopal, Calvin viewed

40. Ibid., 4.9.11.
41. John T. McNeill, "Calvin and Episcopacy," *Presbyterian Tribune*, 57:14.

the rise of the metropolitan bishop very much in the context of an elected presbyter who had continued to perform all the duties of a minister and who was considered the first among equals (*primus inter pares*), so as to maintain order and unity in the church. There is another level of Calvin's historical acceptance of this structure, that is, in context he argued that the form and functioning were far purer than what followed beginning with Roman Bishop Gregory the Great's successors and the development of the papacy.[42]

McNeill pressed further, claiming that Calvin affirmed episcopal government also in his correspondence to leaders in various countries in which episcopacy was established: England, Poland, Sweden, and Denmark. Moreover, McNeill pointed as well to the office of superintendent in the French Reformed Church, which was also established and lasted for more than a decade in Scotland. In all these letters to leaders, McNeill showed that not once did Calvin attempt to change the episcopal form of government. Indeed, Calvin's several letters to England's Archbishop Thomas Cranmer do reveal ample opportunity to speak to the issue of Calvin's twofold governmental position. In Calvin's initial letter to Cranmer, in response to attempts to call a convocation of Reformation leaders, Calvin did, indeed, address Cranmer as "most illustrious Archbishop," while at the same time he presented his wish that various churchmen "eminent for their learning" might convene as Cranmer wished. However, Calvin's purpose in that wish was that these men might discuss the "main points of belief one by one," and that they should "from their united judgments, hand down to posterity the true doctrine of Scripture." May one interpret the "true doctrine of Scripture" as including also the proper biblical form of government? Indeed, it would seem so. Calvin's willingness to "cross ten seas" in an effort to assist churches would surely be incomplete if he did not speak to the issue of biblical church government.[43]

Moreover, on the issue of McNeill's conclusion that Calvin affirmed episcopacy, one may arguably assess the letters as a temporary ecumenical accommodation to episcopacy with the hope of amelioration in the

42. Calvin, *Institutes* 4.4.3.
43. Calvin, "Letter to Cranmer," in *Selected Works*, 5:345.

future, since Calvin did, indeed, embrace a *ius divinum* form of church government. One may point to Calvin's own temporary accommodation to the Geneva Council's rather Erastian control of church discipline, as well as to his patient, obedient, prayerful awaiting God's providence to bring about the change that occurred, over a decade, for the benefit of the church.

However, above all, for proof of Calvin's *ius divinum* form of church government one must look to his writings. Calvin's exegesis of the biblical words for elder (*presbyteros/episkopos*) is at the very heart of ecclesiastical unity and order.[44] Moreover, the 1541 "Ecclesiastical Ordinances," of which Calvin was the mover and most certainly one of the writers and subscribers, declared in the preface: "it has seemed to us advisable that the spiritual government of the kind our Lord demonstrated and instituted by His Word should be set out in good order so that it may be established and observed among us."[45]

Mention might be made of certain passages in the *Institutes* and Calvin's commentaries that ostensibly contravene Calvin's *ius divinum* view of presbyterian government on both the level of the local church and the broader councils. An example is found in 1 Corinthians 11:2, where the apostle Paul praises the Corinthians that they have kept the traditions he delivered to them. This passage has been interpreted as though every church has the right to choose its own form of government. Calvin commented: "we know that every church has the liberty to frame for itself a form of government that is suitable and profitable for it, because the Lord has not prescribed anything definite."[46] Benjamin Milner has aptly shown that Calvin here is not speaking of the presbyterian form of government, but rather the local church constitutions that should guide it, while abiding in the God-ordained form of presbyterian government.[47]

44. Calvin, *Institutes* 4.3.8.
45. EO 35; see also Peter Lillback, "The Reformers' Rediscovery of Presbyterian Polity," in *Pressing toward the Mark*, ed. Charles G. Dennison and Richard C. Gamble (Philadelphia: Orthodox Presbyterian Church, 1986), 63–81; also, *The Divine Right of Church Government*, ed. David W. Hall (Dallas: Naphtali, 1995).
46. Calvin, *Commentary on the First Epistle of Paul to the Corinthians*, Calvin's Commentaries 20 (Grand Rapids: Baker, 1989), 353.
47. Benjamin J. Milner, *Calvin's Doctrine of the Church* (Leiden: E. J. Brill, 1970), 173.

The Councils of the Church

Concerning the local church consistory, one need not seek far for criticism of Calvin's twofold genre of elder and deacon, from the redoubtable conservative nineteenth-century Presbyterians, the American Charles Hodge and the Scottish Peter Colin Campbell, to the twentieth-century broad Presbyterian, T. F. Torrance. The former pair, although agreeing with Calvin's goals in church government, differ with him in terms of disparity between the ordained pastor and the layman, the non-theologically trained, governmental elder. However, both pastor and elder have equal authority in church courts.[48] T. F. Torrance, on the other hand, is widely discursive in, first, charging Calvin with adopting a fourth- and fifth-century church practice and then proceeding to Scripture to validate it. Second, Torrance attempts to redefine the office of ruling elder in terms of an elder/deacon role by declaring the elder charged primarily with sacramental duties. In so doing Torrance has virtually discarded the ruling and disciplinary function that characterized the Presbyterians of former times.[49]

We have seen that Calvin taught that, for each local church, there should exist the two foundational governmental genres that Christ established in the post–New Testament church, comprising four kinds of offices within the genres of elder (*presbyteros/episkopos*) and deacon (*diakonos*). In the former were found teacher, pastor, and ruling elder, and in the latter deacon alone. Moreover, all of them are to be elected by the members of the church.[50] Although the elders are equal in office, the roles of each calling differ: the teacher (doctor) is responsible for maintaining the purity of biblical interpretation; the pastor for purity of preaching the Word of God and, together with the elders, ruling and encouraging church members in their faith and life and applying censures when necessary. By establishing this church government in the Genevan churches, Calvin obviated Roman Catholic papal and sacerdotal bishops, Anglican

48. Charles Hodge, *The Church and Its Polity* (London: Thomas Nelson, 1879), 130; Peter C. Campbell, *The Theory of Ruling Eldership* (Edinburgh: William Blackwood, 1846), 5–8.

49. Thomas F. Torrance, *The Eldership in the Reformed Church* (Edinburgh: Handsel, 1984), 1, 4, 8.

50. Calvin, *Institutes* 4.3.7–10, 15.

episcopal government, Congregational church government, and Independent church government. Thus, Calvin's system of church government has been denominated Presbyterian.

Councils and Their Power

Calvin maintained that Christ alone is the source of all power in the church and that he is pleased to delegate the power of the keys of the kingdom to the presbyters of the church as they meet jointly to determine doctrine, jurisdiction, and legislation on the sole basis of the Word of God. Moreover, the graded courts of the church begin with the foundational local consistory, followed by the presbytery, and then the synod or general assembly. The graded courts of the church are all biblically founded, and all have power to determine the threefold functions above.[51] Calvin concluded the power in these graded courts is established because Christ promised to be present where two or three meet in his name and where the Holy Spirit guides according to the Word of God.[52]

Because men still err, even in councils, Calvin is a bit chary of placing absolute confidence in the labors of councils. Nevertheless, Calvin maintains that God can work with or without the councils. Indeed, he concluded that "truth does not die in the church, even though it be oppressed by one council, but is wonderfully preserved by the Lord so that it may rise up and triumph again in its own time."[53]

Concluding Notes

In many respects, the separation of form and substance of Calvin's church government is the most devastating of current criticisms. The argument is that Calvin is not too concerned with the form of church government (whether presbyterian, episcopal, or congregational) but rather the end result of a supposed pious ministry and people.[54] The arguments

51. Ibid., 4.8.1.
52. Ibid., 4.9.2; *Commentary on Acts*, ch. 15.
53. Calvin, *Institutes* 4.9.13.
54. McNeill, "Calvin and Episcopacy," 15; G. S. Sunshine, "Reformed Theology and the Origins of Synodical Polity: Calvin, Beza and the Gallican Confession," in *Later Calvin-*

are pragmatic, to say the least, while most certainly avoiding the necessity of asking the hard question, "Is this form of government biblical?" Thus contemporary criticism of Calvin is extremely vulnerable concerning biblical religion, since God in true religion supplies the means for church government as well as the end result of biblical government, that is, the welfare of the church and his glory. Indeed, grace (God's unmerited favor) is the means of our salvation, the end result of securing and maintaining through biblical church government what perpetuates faithful pastors, teachers, and elders.

Calvin's high view of Scripture and the absolute necessity of the illumination of the Holy Spirit is foundational for all his theology. Just as in the Old Testament the priests were to regulate the worship of God prescriptively according to God's directions, so in the New Testament how much more are we to be faithful to God's Word, since we have the substance as well—God incarnate in Christ and his perfect obedience for sinners.

Why the need for a particular form of church government? First, Calvin declares, it must be the biblical form. Presbyters are the biblical foundation of church government. Moreover, Calvin is wary of allowing men freedom in choosing their preferred form of church government, because of our residual sinfulness. Therefore, we need God's Word to guide us in the proper form of church government. Calvin would reject a purely philosophical argument to attempt to prove the validity of the presbyterian form of government. Rather, he points us to God's Word.

Why does Calvin conclude that church power "resides partly in individual bishops [synonymous with presbyters], and partly in councils, either provincial or general," a definition, arguably, that is the key to Calvin's church government?[55] Simply because Calvin finds the bishop/presbyter (as pastor and ruling elders, the governing body of the church) in Scripture, for both the local congregation and the broader structures in provincial and general councils. Thus the local church government with its foundational plurality of elders is biblically prescribed as the God-ordained means of

---

ism: International Perspectives, ed. W. F. Graham, Sixteenth Century Essays & Studies 23 (Kirksville, MO: Sixteenth Century Journal, 1994), 148.

55. Calvin, *Institutes* 4.8.1.

achieving the end of his glory and the welfare of the church. Moreover, church members are used by God to achieve this end, since they have as their duty to choose both a faithful pastor and elders who are godly, grave, and of good testimony in the church.

Beyond the local church exists the plurality of churches abroad. In Acts 15 Calvin finds the regulative principle of councils broader than the local church council or consistory. Therefore, this larger form contravenes the purely local, or congregational, church government as the sole locus of authority with no accountability to or participation in the broader provincial or general councils as Acts 15 teaches. Calvin, then, in faithfulness to Scripture, rather than philosophy, brings the local church with its foundational, prototype government by the plurality of elders elected by the people, into the larger governmental administration of broader councils. Therefore, Calvin stresses both the prototype and the larger councils as the truly catholic Christian government which should be recognized as the biblical form of church government.

18

CALVIN ON HUMAN GOVERNMENT AND THE STATE

INSTITUTES 4.20
DAVID W. HALL

ompared with the heft of its international and multigenerational influence, John Calvin's commentary on political matters in his magnum opus is relatively diminutive. However, seldom have so few words inspired so much political impact. While many later theologians would scarcely brave a comment on matters of state in a systematic theology text, John Calvin (1509–64) addressed political topics without trepidation. The resulting forty pages of discussion on the civil government in the *Institutes* would blaze a trail for others.

Numerous scholars have traced Calvin's political ideas.[1] Among the various evaluations, Douglas Kelly identifies the "sober Calvinian assessment

1. Among the scholars who have set their hand to explicating Calvin's political thought and impact are: Harro Höpfl, *The Christian Polity of John Calvin* (Cambridge: Cambridge University Press, 1982); Quentin Skinner, *The Foundations of Modern Political Thought:*

of fallen man's propensity to seize, increase, and abuse power for personal ends rather than for the welfare of the many." He further explains: "Governmental principles for consent of the governed, and separation and balance of powers are all logical consequences of a most serious and Calvinian view of the biblical doctrine of the fall of man."[2] Although historian Franklin Palm mistakenly classified Calvin as "wholly medieval" and as favoring an "aristocratic theocracy in which he was dictator," nevertheless, he recognized Calvin's contribution as "emphasizing the supremacy of God and the right of resistance to all other authority. . . . [H]e did much to curb the powers of kings and to increase the authority of the elected representatives of the people."[3] Further, Palm noticed Calvin's belief in the "right of the individual to remove the magistrate who disobeys the word of God. . . . Consequently, he justified many revolutionary leaders in their belief that God gave them the right to oppose tyranny."

Recently, John Witte Jr. has noted how "Calvin developed arresting new teachings on authority and liberty, duties and rights, and church and state that have had an enduring influence on Protestant lands." Adaptability "rendered early modern Calvinism one of the driving engines of Western constitutionalism. A number of our bedrock Western understandings of civil and political rights, social and confessional pluralism, federalism and social contract, and more owe a great deal to Calvinist theological and political reforms."[4]

The Age of Reformation, vol. 2 (Cambridge: Cambridge University Press, 1978); Abraham Kuyper, *Lectures on Calvinism* (Grand Rapids: Eerdmans, 1953); Robert Kingdon, *Calvin and Calvinism: Sources of Democracy* (Lexington, MA: D. C. Heath, 1970); Ralph C. Hancock, *Calvin and the Foundations of Modern Politics* (Ithaca, NY: Cornell University Press, 1989), 62-81; John Witte Jr., *The Reformation of Rights: Law, Religion and Human Rights in Early Modern Calvinism* (Cambridge: Cambridge University Press, 2007); John T. McNeill, "Calvin and Civil Government," in Donald McKim, ed., *Readings in Calvin's Theology* (Grand Rapids: Baker, 1984); Herbert D. Foster, *Collected Papers of Herbert D. Foster* (privately printed, 1929); John T. McNeill, "John Calvin on Civil Government," in *Calvinism and the Political Order*, ed. George L. Hunt (Philadelphia: Westminster, 1965); Douglas Kelly, *The Emergence of Liberty in the Modern World* (Phillipsburg, NJ: P&R 1992); Franklin Charles Palm, *Calvinism and the Religious Wars* (New York: Henry Holt, 1932); Karl Holl, *The Cultural Significance of the Reformation* (Cleveland: Meridian, 1959); and Keith L. Griffin, *Revolution and Religion: American Revolutionary War and the Reformed Clergy* (New York: Paragon House, 1994).

2. Kelly, *Emergence of Liberty*, 18.
3. Palm, *Calvinism and the Religious Wars*, 32.
4. Witte, *Reformation of Rights*, 2.

The final chapter of the *Institutes* is also, in some ways, the culmination of a tradition. It followed decades of Renaissance thought and sat perched atop centuries of medieval and scholastic theological reflection on political principles. Calvin was not alone in addressing these matters; in fact, it was not uncharacteristic for leading theologians of the period to expound on matters of state. However, the subsequent expansion and replication of his thought by his followers virtually created a new trajectory of political discourse. It is no exaggeration to observe that before Calvin, certain political principles were viewed as radical, while after him they became widely acceptable.

Any proper analysis of Calvin's political thought should begin with his discussion in the *Institutes*; however, an accurate understanding of Calvin will also take into account his other writings and, importantly, the manner in which his disciples codified his teachings into a school of political thought. The elaboration below thus highlights his other commentaries and the concerted effort of many other orchestra members—Peter Viret, Christopher Goodman, John Ponet, Theodore Beza, among others—but first one should acquaint himself with the maestro's score.

Calvin's *Institutes*: Blueprint for Civil Government

Calvin's political thought found in the *Institutes of the Christian Religion* is, even by critics, still credited with immense political impact. Asserting that the state was not merely a necessary evil for Calvin, Karl Holl recognized that Calvinism, even more than Lutheranism, provided a theological basis to oppose unjust governments.[5] Everywhere Calvinism spread, so did its impulse to limit government. Later Calvinist and prime minister of the Netherlands Abraham Kuyper summarized the essence of Calvin's theocentric emphasis:[6]

It is therefore a political faith which may be summarily expressed in these three theses: 1. God only, and never any creature, is possessed

5. Holl, *Cultural Significance*, 65–66.
6. Hancock, *Calvin and the Foundations*, asserts that the Protestant Reformation was "an essentially modern movement that in some way laid the foundations for our modern openness."

of sovereign rights, in the destiny of nations, because God alone created them, maintains them by his Almighty power, and rules them by
his ordinances. 2. Sin has, in the realm of politics, broken down the
direct government of God, and therefore the exercise of authority, for
the purpose of government, has subsequently been invested in men,
as a mechanical remedy. And 3. In whatever form this authority may
reveal itself, man never possesses power over his fellow man in any
other way than by the authority which descends upon him from the
majesty of God.[7]

Calvinism, Kuyper continued, "protests against State omni-compe-
tence, against the horrible conception that no right exists above and beyond
existing laws, and against the pride of absolutism, which recognizes no
constitutional rights." Calvinism "built a dam across the absolutistic stream,
not by appealing to popular force, nor to the hallucination of human
greatness, but by deducing those rights and liberties of social life from
the same source from which the high authority of government flows, even
the absolute sovereignty of God."[8]

Such thoughts are indeed contained in Calvin's *Institutes of the Christian Religion*,[9] which underwent considerable evolution between editions.
The original 1536 edition composed in Basel combined the chapter on
civil government with Calvin's treatment of Christian liberty and ecclesiastical power.[10] Calvin believed that civil government was the second
part of a twofold government, properly chartered to "establish civil justice
and outward morality" (4.20.1).

Calvin's major sections addressed these topics:

1. The magistrate, who is "the protector and guardian of the laws"
   (4.20.3)
2. The laws, which provide objectivity for governors

7. Kuyper, *Lectures on Calvinism*, 85.
8. Ibid.
9. John Calvin, *The Institutes of the Christian Religion*, ed. John T. McNeill, trans. Ford
Lewis Battles (Philadelphia: Westminster, 1960). Unless otherwise referenced, all quotations
in this essay from the *Institutes* 4.20 are from this edition.
10. Skinner, *Foundations of Modern Political Thought*, 2:192, suggests that by 1559 Calvin had
begun to change his views, permitting at least a discussion of the propriety of active resistance.

3. The people—an early statement of the contract theory later rightly associated with Ponet, Beza, the *Vindiciae*, Buchanan, and Althusius[11]

Calvin believed that civil government supplied an example of how God had compassionately provided for mankind; the sphere of human government thus was a gracious token for human culture much like the law itself. The task of the civil ruler was to ensure "that a public manifestation of religion may exist among Christians, and that humanity be maintained among men." If no civil government existed or if depraved men perceived that they could go "scot-free" (4.20.2), they surely would opt for sin, and society would deteriorate into chaos. On one occasion, Calvin likened such anarchy to living "pell-mell, like rats in straw."[12] He argued that God does not bid persons to "lay aside their authority and retire to private life, but submit to Christ the power with which they have been invested, that he alone may tower over all." Calvin believed that

> powers are from God, not as pestilence, and famine, and wars, and other visitations for sin, are said to be from him; but because he has appointed them for the legitimate and just government of the world. For though tyrannies and unjust exercise of power, as they are full of disorder, are not an ordained government; yet the right of government is ordained by God for the well-being of mankind.[13]

Calvin, in marked contrast to the Anabaptists of his day, recognized service in a political office as entirely appropriate, even going so far as to speak of civil service as the most sacred and honorable of

11. A more detailed outline of Calvin's chapter on civil government for students:
20.1–2: Separation of governments
20.3–8: Tasks and ordination of magistrates
20.9–13: The magistrates' prerogatives and duties
20.14–16: The rule of law
20.17–21: Courts
20.22–29: Obedience and deference from citizens
20.30–32: Constitutional mechanisms
12. *Institutes* 2:1490 n. 15.
13. John Calvin, *Calvin's Commentary on Romans*, Calvin's Commentaries 19 (Grand Rapids: Baker, 1979), 479.

human callings. Calvin referred to civil rulers favorably as "vicars of God" (4.20.6), "the highest gift of [God's] beneficence to preserve the safety of men" (4.20.25), and as "ordained protectors and vindicators of public innocence, modesty, decency, and tranquility [whose] sole endeavor should be to provide for the common safety and peace of all" (4.20.9). Calvinism, thus, did not inspire an inherently negative view of civil government. Elsewhere he stated that the appointed goal of the civil government was "to cherish and protect the outward worship of God, to defend sound doctrine of piety and the position of the church, to adjust our life to the society of men, to form our social behavior to civil righteousness, to reconcile us with one another, and to promote general peace and tranquillity" (4.20.2).

By early 1553 Calvin had summoned the magistrates of Geneva to be "the vindicators, not the destroyers, of sacred laws."[14] The use of the sword was the necessary corollary to human depravity. Civil magistrates were to be honored as superiors in keeping with the commandment to honor one's superiors. Even evil rulers kept God's law to some degree, and disobedience was justified only in response to actions contrary to God's law. The task of civil government according to Calvin's commentary on Romans was prescribed as follows:

> Magistrates may hence learn what their vocation is, for they are not to rule for their own interest, but for the public good; nor are they endued with unbridled power, but what is restricted to the well-being of their subjects; in short, they are responsible to God and to men in the exercise of their power. For as they are deputed by God and do his business, they must give an account to him: and then the ministration which God has committed to them has a regard to the subjects; they are therefore debtors to them.[15]

Calvin believed that both politics and providence were operative; indeed, he suggested that the kingdom of God was already present, albeit not completely realized: "For spiritual government, indeed, is

14. Theodore Beza, *Life of John Calvin* (in John Calvin, *Tracts and Treatises on the Reformation of the Church* [Grand Rapids: Eerdmans, 1958], vol. 1), c.
15. Calvin, *Commentary on Romans*, 481.

already initiating in us upon earth certain beginnings of the Heavenly Kingdom, and in this mortal and fleeting life affords a certain forecast of an immortal and incorruptible blessedness" (4.20.2). He advised, "Let no man be disturbed that I now commit to civil government the duty of rightly establishing religion" (4.20.3). Few would be greatly disturbed by such a statement, since it was the common notion of Calvin's time for government to uphold religion. Calvin acknowledged this: "All have confessed that no government can be happily established unless piety is the first concern" (4.20.9). He also stated that the civil magistrate should care for both tables of the law (4.20.9). Later conflicts between church and state, however, would beg for re-evaluations of this maxim. Furthermore, he included a limitation for his theory: no administration was permitted to tailor the worship of God to its own imaginations or to prohibit the practice of true religion (4.20.3).

Lest, however, we brand Calvin a theocrat, his comments on a gospel passage (John 18:36) in which Jesus stated that his servants did not strive for enforcement of an earthly kingdom may reassure. His view of the separation of jurisdictions, enunciated in the mid-sixteenth century, is still helpful. Discussing the conditions under which it is appropriate to defend "the kingdom of Christ by arms," Calvin wrote:

> Though godly kings defend the kingdom of Christ by the sword, still it is done in a different manner from that in which worldly kingdoms are wont to be defended; for the kingdom of Christ, being spiritual must be founded on the doctrine and power of the Spirit. In the same manner, too, its edification is promoted; for neither the laws and edicts of men, nor the punishments inflicted by them, enter into the consciences.... It results, however, from the depravity of the world that the kingdom of Christ is strengthened more by the blood of the martyrs than by the aid of arms.[16]

For Calvin, serving in civil government could be "the most sacred and by far the most honorable of all callings in the whole life of mortal men" (4.20.4). He wrote that if civil rulers properly understood their callings,

16. John Calvin, *Calvin's Commentary on John*, Calvin's Commentaries 18 (Grand Rapids: Baker, 1979), 210.

that is, to be "occupied not with profane affairs or those alien to a servant of God, but with a most holy office, since they are serving as God's deputies" (4.20.6), they would serve with more equity. Echoing Aristotle's morphology of the state and its tendency toward deterioration from monarchy to tyranny and from democracy to anarchy, Calvin advocated "a system compounded of aristocracy and democracy" (4.20.8). He also saw a legitimate place for checks and balances, realizing the need for "censors and masters to restrain his [the monarch's] willfulness" (4.20.8).

The civil magistrate does not act on his own, but "carries out the very judgments of God" (4.20.10) in bearing the sword to punish lawbreakers. Calvin even cited King David as condoning the destruction of the wicked in the land as an example of the right to wage war. But, far from legitimating vengeance, violence, or undue cruelty, the magistrate was to avoid both exorbitant severity and "superstitious affectation of clemency." Alluding to the proverb from Seneca, Calvin concurred, "It is indeed bad to live under a prince with whom nothing is permitted; but much worse under one by whom everything is allowed" (4.20.10). He argued: "Now if their [rulers'] true righteousness is to pursue the guilty and the impious with drawn sword, should they sheathe their sword and keep their hands clean of blood, while abandoned men wickedly range about with slaughter and massacre, they will become guilty of the greatest impiety, far indeed from winning praise for their goodness and righteousness thereby!" (4.20.10).

In a phrase that would become incendiary, Calvin noted that not only kings but also "people must sometimes take up arms to execute public vengeance" (4.20.11). The same basis for waging war was used both to justify revolution and to put down sedition. If the magistrates were to punish private evildoers, then they could certainly punish mobs and protect the country from an external foe (4.20.11). Regardless of class, the noble governor was to protect the people equally from robbers and invaders. If he did not, he would be considered a robber and worthy of censure. Calvin rested his logic that the governor has the right to wage war, as he saw it, on "both natural equity and the nature of the office" (4.20.11). If additional grounds were needed to reject pacifism, Calvin would argue that governors could still defend their subjects, that an exclusively New Testament basis was not necessary, and that Christ did not compel soldiers to resign (4.20.12).

That Calvin gave attention to a far-ranging set of civic concerns is evidenced by his discussion of the magistrate's right to tax in the *Institutes*. He recommended prudent limits, arguing that taxes should only support public necessity; for "to impose them upon the common folk without cause is tyrannical extortion" (4.20.13). Obedience was a Christian duty in this area; however, princes were not to indulge in "waste and expensive luxury," lest they earn God's displeasure. Excessive taxation was alluded to in his comment later: "Others drain the common people of their money, and afterward lavish it on insane largesse" (4.20.24).

Another major topic of discussion for Calvin is the use of the Old Testament judicial law, which Calvin called "the silent magistrate." In a proper republic, laws were "the stoutest sinews of the commonwealth" (4.20.14). Not as theocratic as some might expect, Calvin affirmed that just as the Old Testament ceremonial laws (laws regulating ritual and diet, not viewed as permanent like the moral law; see Calvin's own definitions of this tripartite taxonomy in 4.20.15) had been "abrogated while piety remained safe and unharmed, so too, when these judicial laws were taken away, the perpetual duties and precepts of love could still remain" (4.20.15). He admitted that different nations were free to make laws as they saw best, but with this qualification: "Yet these must be in conformity to that perpetual rule of love, so that they indeed vary in form but have the same purpose" (4.20.15). And while some of his own day thought that a commonwealth could be "duly framed" only if it included a theonomic approach, Calvin called that idea "perilous," "seditious," "false and foolish" (4.20.14).

Calvin taught, however, that even if all the specifics and particulars of the Mosaic judicial law were not binding, the moral principle within each command continued. The moral law,[17] which Calvin viewed as nothing

---

17. R. Scott Clark has recognized the formal identity between Calvin and Aquinas on natural law. However, believing that original sin corrupted moral and intellectual capabilities, Calvin constricted the sweep of natural law. Like Thomas, notes Clark, Calvin was "influenced by the classics, but unlike Aquinas, he defined natural law very precisely by identifying it with the decalogue or moral law." R. Scott Clark, "Calvin on the *Lex Naturalis*," *Stulos Theological Journal* 6.1–2 (May-Nov. 1998): 3. Further attempting to correct the claims of earlier Calvin scholar J. T. McNeill, Clark notes that Abelard, Luther, and others equated natural law with the Ten Commandments (9, 11) rather than appealing to strict moral neutrality. Calvin, according to Clark, identified the Decalogue with natural law, as was "the general custom

other than a "testimony of natural law" and conscience (4:20, 16), was never abrogated, contrary to the ceremonial and judicial codes:

> Consequently, the entire scheme of this equity of which we are now speaking has been prescribed in it. Hence, this equity alone must be the goal and rule and limit of all laws. Whatever laws shall be framed to that rule, directed to that goal, bound by that limit, there is no reason why we should disapprove of them, howsoever they may differ from the Jewish law or among themselves. [4.20.16]

Notwithstanding, Calvin did not teach that the Mosaic law was to be in force everywhere (4.20.16). Since Calvin is seldom accused of laxness, his own comments must be taken seriously. So taken, they do not call for disavowal of the equitable principles of the Old Testament judicial law but merely for the adaptation of nonessential and nonmoral aspects. It was, as Calvin realized, possible to maintain the applicability of God's law while not necessarily advocating all the cultural specifics of the original Hebrew code. Some of his political descendants would adhere to this notion more than others.

Derivative of the proper understanding of laws and the magistracy, Calvin acknowledged that Christians could certainly avail themselves of public courts (4.20.17). Access to legal process was not evil in itself, and the right to sue was a logical corollary of Calvin's refutation of pacifism, this time applied to the personal right to defend property legally. However, Calvin warned against greed, revenge, and an excessive reliance on litigation (4.20.18–21). Typical of his ethic, he recommended moderation, sometimes taking an economic loss; to summarize: "love will give every man the best counsel" (4.20.21).

In his third section, Calvin enumerated the duties of the Christian citizen, beginning with a call to honor the office as established by God as the first duty. Moreover, subjects should prove their obedience by paying taxes,

---

in Protestantism" in the early seventeenth century. Clark concludes: "For Calvin and for his successors . . . it was a given that God had entered into a probationary, federal-covenantal relationship with Adam, and that the *lex moralis* . . . is the same law which he codified at Sinai and which Calvin called the *lex naturalis*. It was part of the warp and woof of 16th and 17th century Reformed theology to think of these things synonymously as components of the creational order" (20).

obeying proclamations, and serving to protect the nation. Furthermore, Calvin warned Christians not to intrude excessively into the authority of the magistrate as long as he honored the office (4.20.23).

Calvin's discussion of governmental largesse led him to acknowledge the common reaction that called oppressive governors tyrants (4.20.24). Still he warned that the mere existence of some overtaxation or misappropriation was not the same as divine warrant to overthrow the tyrant. There was still a scriptural priority on submitting to the governors who "have their sole authority from him" (4.20.25). Moreover, Calvin devoted several sections (26–29), relying heavily upon narratives in Daniel and Jeremiah, to discussing how God's providence presumptively called for submission to civil rulers.

However, despite such clarion calls to submit to the civil ruler, in some cases the lesser magistrates were justified in overturning a wicked ruler. That, however, was not to be carried out merely by private individuals. Calvin's argument, which was drawn upon by his disciples, was that rulers (whether in home, church, or civil spheres) also had obligations. The abuse of such obligations could negate their authority and relegate them to tyrant status.

Calvin acknowledged that, at times, divine providence was satisfied in the overthrowing of wicked rulers (4.20.30), but he still preferred to allow the Lord to correct unbridled despotism. Calvin urged believers to consider that through prayer God might change the hearts of rulers (4.20.29). Concerning revolution, he advocated a peaceful, incremental revolution via the intermediate magistrates:

> For if there are now any magistrates of the people, appointed to restrain the willfulness of kings (as in ancient times the ephors . . .), I am so far from forbidding them to withstand, in accordance with their duty, the fierce licentiousness of kings, that, if they wink at kings who violently fall upon and assault the lowly common folk, I declare that their dissimulation involves nefarious perfidy, because they dishonestly betray the freedom of the people, of which they know that they have been appointed protectors by God's ordinance. [4.20.31]

The obvious exception to any of these rules, however, was that persons were not only free but also obligated to resist the magistrate who compelled ungodly activity. Calvin taught not only that there were exceptions to the above considerations, but also that obedience to God was primary: "Obedience [to a ruler] is never to lead us away from obedience to Him" (4.20.32), a good illustration of qualified absolutism.[18] He reasoned: "How absurd would it be that in satisfying men you should incur the displeasure of him for whose sake you obey men themselves!" (4.20.32). Still, this argument is balanced with Calvin's conclusion that we should "comfort ourselves with the thought that we are rendering that obedience which the Lord requires when we suffer anything rather than turn aside from piety" (4.20.32).

The other aspect of Calvin's argument that resistance was appropriate under certain conditions was his argument from relative authorities. In this contention, he maintained that a lower authority (an elder, a father, or a magistrate) could not contradict the rule or norms of a higher authority. Calvin expressed it: "As if God had made over his right to mortal men, giving them the rule over mankind! Or as if earthly power were diminished when it is subjected to its Author" (4.20.32). A blend of necessary factors, then, determined whether revolution was in order. The following factors were necessary: (a) a tyrant who exceeded his divinely charted boundaries; (b) a tyrant who in so doing contradicted some other divine mandate; and (c) lower magistrates to bring constitutional correction.

Calvin's Political Theology in Other Works

Geneva's premier Reformer, though, was more than the sum of precise theology. He was also an able commentator and communicator. Driven by the need to record biblical insights for posterity, Calvin composed com-

---

18. "Qualified absolutism" is the term I use in *Savior or Servant: Putting Government in Its Place* (Oak Ridge, TN: Kuyper Institute, 1996). See also Ralph Keen, "The Limits of Power and Obedience in the Later Calvin," *Calvin Theological Journal* 27. 2 (Nov. 1992): 252–77, for a good harmonization between the earlier and later statements by Calvin on the propriety of resistance. Although Calvin is sometimes accused of shifting toward a more republican posture, as if influenced by Beza, Keen summarizes: "It is simply necessary to recognize that the position is not pro-monarchical in itself (that is, as a political doctrine) but pro-monarchical in the theological sense of being an endorsement of the divine presence in governments" (259).

mentaries on most biblical books. His commentaries contained practical discussions as well as doctrinal treatises, expounding on subjects ranging from human relationships to work ethic concerns. Several parts of Calvin's commentaries develop certain significant themes more broadly than either his sermons or the *Institutes* permitted. Representative samples, concentrating on several key texts (Ex. 18; 1 Sam. 8; Dan. 6), along with other illuminating glosses, are provided below in order to present a more rounded vignette of Calvin's thought.

Old Testament Texts

In his comments on Genesis 49, Calvin noted: "In order to make the distinction between a legitimate government and tyranny, I acknowledge that counselors were joined with the king, who should administer public affairs in a just and orderly manner."[19] Calvin also expressed his approval of classical republican traditions:

> In as much as God had given them the use of the franchise, the best way to preserve their liberty for ever was by maintaining a condition of rough equality, lest a few persons of immense wealth should oppress the general body. Since, therefore, the rich, if they had been permitted constantly to increase their wealth, would have tyrannized over the rest, God put a restraint on immoderate power by means of this law.[20]

Calvin's resistance theory is further exhibited in his commentary on the rebellion of the Hebrew midwives.[21] He characterized any obedience to the murderous command of Pharaoh as "preposterously unwise," a detestable effrontery, and ill-conceived in its attempt to "gratify the transitory kings

19. Hopfl, *Christian Polity*, 162.
20. John Calvin, *Harmony of Moses* (Edinburgh: Calvin Translation Society, 1843–59), 3:154.
21. James Smylie notes that King James VI did not approve of the Geneva Bible's note on Ex. 1, seeing all too clearly that the Marian exiles in Geneva felt quite free to recommend resistance. See James H. Smylie, "America's Political Covenants, the Bible, and Calvinists," *Journal of Presbyterian History* 75.3 (Fall 1997): 156, 163. The marginal note on Ex. 1:19 of the 1560 Geneva Bible reads: "Their disobedience her[e]in was lawful, but their dissembling evil."

of earth" while taking "no account of God."[22] Most clear in that context, Calvin wrote that God did not delegate his rights to princes, "as if every earthly power, which exalts itself against heaven, ought not rather most justly to be made to give way."

Exodus 18

Calvin's commentary on Exodus 18 displays his appreciation for the robust Hebrew contributions to republicanism.[23] In between Nimrod[24] and Moses, the notion of a republic vanished or seemed unknown. Calvin realized that all that the Israelites had known for four centuries was the monarchical rule by the Pharaohs. Thus, the republican-type plan suggested by Jethro appears as an innovation that did not originate in the mind of man, thought Calvin.

Rather than commending either a democracy or a monarchy, Jethro advised Moses and the people to select a plurality of prudent representative leaders (Ex. 18:21).[25] Moses instituted a graduated series of administrations with greater and lesser magistrates, and Calvin asserted that the earliest Hebrew republican government devolved from the divine mind long before the golden age of Greco-Roman governance, the Enlightenment, or other modern revolutions.

The early federal scheme adopted in Exodus 18 seemed, to Calvin and his followers (as it had to Aquinas and Machiavelli), to be republicanism. Commenting on a similar passage in Deuteronomy 1:14–16, Calvin stated:

22. John Calvin, *Calvin's Commentary on Exodus*, Calvin's Commentaries 2 (Grand Rapids: Baker, 1979), 33.

23. See Daniel Elazar, *Covenant and Polity in Biblical Israel* (New Brunswick, NJ: Transaction Publishers, 1998), 1:437–47, for a full treatment of the progressive and enduring features of the early Israeli republic.

24. Even prior to Algernon Sidney, Lambert Daneau called Nimrod the first true monarch.

25. For an example of early American exposition on the character needed for office holders, complete with a discussion similar to Calvin's on this Exodus passage, see Simeon Howard's 1780 Election Sermon, in *Sermons for Election Days*, ed. David W. Hall (Oak Ridge, TN: Kuyper Institute, 2002). Charles Chauncy addressed the requisite character of civil rulers in his 1747 election day sermon (contained in *Election Day Sermons* [Oak Ridge, TN: Kuyper Institute, 1996], 143–68). T. H. Breen provides one of the most thorough studies of American expectations for civil rulers in *The Character of the Good Ruler: A Study of Puritan Political Ideas in New England, 1630–1730* (New York: W. W. Norton, 1970).

Hence it more plainly appears that those who were to preside in judgment were not appointed only by the will of Moses, but elected by the votes of the people. And this is the most desirable kind of liberty, that we should not be compelled to obey every person who may be tyrannically put over our heads; but which allows of election, so that no one should rule except he be approved by us. And this is further confirmed in the next verse, wherein Moses recounts that he awaited the consent of the people, and that nothing was attempted which did not please them all.

Thus, Calvin viewed the Hebrew republic as being led by elected representatives who ruled by the consent of the governed.

Later, Calvinist Johannes Althusius (1557–1638) agreed: "I consider that no polity from the beginning of the world has been more wisely and perfectly constructed than the polity of the Jews." Part of what he believed was unimprovable was an early form of republican-federal government. As Emile Doumergue noted, Calvin was the "founder of stable and powerful democracies, a defender not of 'egalitarianism,' but of 'equality before the law.'"[26] Whether Calvin was the founder of modern democratic governments or not, as Doumergue suggested, his sermons on these passages from the Pentateuch illustrated God's inestimable gift to the Jewish commonwealth, specifically the "freedom to elect judges and magistrates."

A century after Calvin, Samuel Rutherford used this same Mosaic pattern in his 1644 *Lex Rex* to argue for a republican form of civil polity. Indeed, most of the Reformation era political tracts (e.g., those by Calvin, Beza, Bucer, Knox, Buchanan, Ponet, Althusius, etc.) devoted extensive commentary to the Old Testament patterns of government. These Reformers viewed Old Testament precedents as applicable to the politics of their own settings, and these same ideas were drawn upon later by an American tradition that nourished its founders. Ideas like those that Calvin espoused furthered these arguments and Western political discourse.

1 Samuel 8

Calvin's sermon on 1 Samuel 8, one of the most widely expounded political passages in Scripture, provides more insight into his political

---

26. Cited by Hancock, *Calvin and the Foundations of Modern Politics*, 66.

matrix. His 1561 exposition discusses the dangers of monarchy, the need for proper limitation of government, and the place of divine sovereignty over human governments. It is an example of Calvinism at its best, carefully balancing individual liberty and proper government.

Calvin began his sermon on 1 Samuel 8 by asserting that the people of Israel were not required to elect a king.[27] Warning against hierarchical "plundering and robbery," Calvin reasoned that

> the Lord does not give kings the right to use their power to subject the people to tyranny. Indeed, when the liberty to resist tyranny seems to be taken away by princes who have taken over, one can justly ask this question: since kings and princes are bound by covenant to the people, . . . if they break faith and usurp tyrannical power by which they allow themselves everything they want: is it not possible for the people to consider together taking measures in order to remedy the evil?

Calvin preached that "there are limits prescribed by God to their power, within which they ought to be satisfied: namely, to work for the common good and to govern and direct the people in truest fairness and justice; not to be puffed up with their own importance, but to remember that they also are subjects of God." Leaders were always to keep in mind the purpose (i.e., the glory of God) for which they had been providentially appointed.

From Samuel's warning citizens about "the royal domination they will have to bear, and that their necks will have to be patiently submitted to his yoke," Calvin inferred something very significant: intervening magistrates, not citizens themselves, should seek to correct abuses and tyranny. His doctrine was that "there are legitimate remedies against such tyranny, such as when there are other magistrates and official institutions to whom the care of the republic is committed, who will be able to restrict the prince to his proper authority so that if the prince attempts wrong action, they may hold him down." He counseled that, if the intervening magistrates did not free the people from tyranny, perhaps the people were being disciplined by God's providence.

27. Quotations are from the translation of Calvin's Sermon on 1 Sam. 8 by Douglas Kelly in *Calvin Studies Colloquium*, ed. Charles Raynal and John Leith (Davidson, NC: Davidson College Presbyterian Church, 1982).

Even though Calvin was more permissive of monarchy than most of his successors, his calls to submit to the governor were not without limit. God established magistrates properly "for the use of the people and the benefit of the republic." Accordingly, royal powers were circumscribed "not to undertake war rashly, nor ambitiously to increase their wealth; nor are they to govern their subjects on the basis of personal opinion or lust for whatever they want." Kings had authority only insofar as they met the conditions of God's covenant. Accordingly, he proclaimed from the pulpit of St. Peter's, "Subjects are under the authority of kings; but at the same time, kings must care about the public welfare so they can discharge the duties prescribed to them by God with good counsel and mature deliberation."

Anticipating the later teaching of Beza and Knox, Calvin taught in this sermon that lawful obedience to a ruler "does not mean that it is ever legitimate for princes to abuse [their subjects] willfully.... This authority is therefore not placed in the hands of kings to be used indiscriminately and absolutely." In an early statement of limitations on political power, he noted that private property was not "placed under the power and will of kings." Kings, too, were to obey the laws, lest they convince themselves that they may do anything they wish. Rather, rulers should employ "all their ingenuity for the welfare of their subjects," considering themselves bound by God's law. Calvin had the foresight to explain that magistrates were instituted to be "ministers and servants of God and the people."

This Genevan beacon, whose sermonic ideas later reached the shores of America, enumerated the ways kings abuse their power from the Samuel narrative, and he distinguished a tyrant from a legitimate prince in these words: "a tyrant rules only by his own will and lust, whereas legitimate magistrates rule by counsel and by reason so as to determine how to bring about the greatest public welfare and benefit." Calvin decried the oppressive custom of government servants "taking part in the plundering to enrich themselves off the poor."

In this sermon, Calvin forewarned about the price associated with hierarchical government and warned that if political consequences resulted from poor political choices, perhaps that was an instance of God's judging a nation. Calvin did not call for rebellion, as Knox later did. However, similar sermons, along with reactions to the real depravity witnessed in the Saint Bartholomew's Day Massacre, demanded that Calvinistic political theory progress to the next level and more directly address the propriety of resistance to oppressive government.

Daniel 6

Although some theologians claim to see discrepancies between Calvin's early thought in the *Institutes* and his later commentaries and sermons on the matter of resistance, a review of his commentary on Daniel 6:21–23 reveals no radical discontinuity. Admittedly, certain events, such as the 1572 Saint Bartholomew's Day Massacre,[28] forced development and clarification within the Calvinistic political tradition, but Calvin's own view about the legitimacy of reforming bad government need not be considered internally inconsistent.

Calvin expected his commentary on Old Testament Daniel to become a handbook for princes. [29] His belief that "the throne of [God's] sceptre is nothing else but the doctrine of the gospel" shows that God's conquest was not to be one of physical coercion. Meanwhile, not only were governors limited, but they were also expected to be virtuous, avoiding pride, bridling their lusts, and supporting piety. Whenever rulers and governors did not "willingly submit to the yoke of Christ," societal turbulence ensued. Calvin's commentary also decried corrupt judges who only gratified their own appetites.

Except for a few comments (e.g., on Dan. 6:22), Calvin consistently discouraged rebellion unless sound reasons demanded it and legitimate measures were employed. Both Luther and his understudy, Philipp Melanchthon (whom Calvin knew from his Strasbourg exile), allowed resistance to the superior magistrate to be carried out by the inferior magistrate in a Roman Catholic establishment.[30] This Lutheran claim was applicable, in their view, if a superior magistrate "undertook by force

---

28. For more on this historically significant event see chapter 4 of my *Genevan Reformation and the American Founding* (Lanham, MD: Lexington, 2003).

29. References are to John Calvin, *Calvin's Commentary on Daniel,* Calvin's Commentaries 12 (Grand Rapids: Baker, 1979), lxiv–lxxv.

30. Griffin, *Revolution and Religion,* 5. From 1550 on, Lutherans from Magdeburg acknowledged this.

to restore popish idolatry and to suppress or exterminate the pure teaching of the Holy Gospel. . . . Then the lower Godfearing magistrate may defend himself and his subjects."[31] Thus, tyrants were to be removed by the intermediating magistrates.

Calvin taught similarly that princes "who are not free agents through being under the tyranny of others, if they permit themselves to be overcome contrary to their conscience, lay aside all their authority and are drawn aside in all directions by the will of their subjects."[32] Calvin's frequent disparagement of ungodly kings in his sermons on Job and Deuteronomy in 1554–55 and in his lectures on Daniel in 1561 indicate that he was not, in principle, a monarchist. Accordingly, the distinctive Calvinistic contribution was phrased: "Men's vices and inadequacies make it safer and better that the many hold sway. In this way may rulers help each other, teach and admonish one another, and if one asserts himself unfairly, they may act in concert to censure, repressing his willfulness."[33]

Calvin's commentary on Daniel 6 virtually enshrines all the major principles contained in the *Institutes*, yielding a consistency to be reckoned with.[34] Calvin displayed his suspicion of aggregate power in that commentary, to wit: "In the palaces of kings we often see men of brutal dispositions holding high rank, and we need not go back to history for this." Of the low and contemptible character of some rulers, he wrote, "But now kings think of nothing else than preferring their own panders, buffoons, and flatterers; while they praise none but men of low character."

Calvin also alluded to the necessity for fixed laws and universal norms, warning that "many are necessarily injured, and no private interest is stable unless the law be without variation; besides, when there is a liberty of changing laws, license succeeds in place of justice. For those who possess the supreme power, if corrupted by gifts, promulgate first one edict and then another. Thus justice cannot flourish where change in the laws allows of so much license." Of the need for resistance against a totalitarian power that wrongly attempts to command the conscience,

31. Ibid.
32. John Calvin, "Commentaries on Daniel," in *On God and Political Duty* (Indianapolis: Bobbs-Merrill, 1956), 100–101.
33. *Institutes* 4.20.8.
34. Calvin, *Calvin's Commentary on Daniel*, 350–87.

Calvin noted that "Daniel could not obey the edict [making public prayer a crime] without committing an atrocious insult against God and declining from piety."

Calvin most clearly articulated his doctrine of contingent submission to the governor in his gloss on Daniel 6:22. Daniel, he wrote, "was not so bound to the king of the Persians when he [the king] claimed for himself as a god what ought not to be offered to him." Earthly regimes were "constituted by God, only on the condition that he deprives himself of nothing, but shines forth alone, and all magistrates must be set in regular order and every authority in existence must be subject to his glory." Daniel did not err when he disobeyed an illegitimate request from the king. As to duty, Calvin commented on this verse: "For earthly princes lay aside their power when they rise up against God, and are unworthy to be reckoned among the number of mankind. We ought, rather, utterly defy them than to obey them."

Commenting on Micah 5:5, Calvin suggested that rulers should be elected, interpreting the Hebrew word for "shepherds" as synonymous with "rulers." He asserted:

> In this especially consists the best condition of the people, when they can choose, by common consent, their own shepherds; for when any one by force usurps the supreme power, it is tyranny. And when men become kings by hereditary right, it seems not consistent with liberty. *We shall then set up for ourselves princes*, says the Prophet: that is, the Lord will not only give breathing time to his Church, he will also cause that she may set up a fixed and well-ordered government, and that by the common consent of all."[35]

This election by common suffrage is advocated elsewhere when Calvin recognizes, "it is tyrannous if any one man appoint or make ministers at his pleasure." Election by members adequately balanced the mean between tyranny and chaotic liberty.[36]

35. John Calvin, *Calvin's Commentary on Micah*, Calvin's Commentaries 4 (Grand Rapids: Baker, 1979), 309–10.
36. John Calvin, *Calvin's Commentary on Acts*, Calvin's Commentaries 18 (Grand Rapids: Baker, 1979), 233.

These examples illustrate the fullness of Calvin's commentary on political subjects as well as illuminate certain nuances of his theory that extend beyond the *Institutes*.

New Testament Passages

Calvin's doctrine of contingency, that is, that governors should be supported contingent upon their ruling as divinely instituted, was also manifest in his explanation of Acts 4:19–20. He stated that, regardless of titles employed, we should obey officials only "upon this condition, if they lead us not away from obeying God."[37] Commenting a chapter later, he summarized: "Therefore, we must obey rulers so far that the commandment not be broken."[38] His balance is displayed in a related comment: "If a magistrate do his duty as he ought, a man shall in vain say that he is contrary to God. . . . We must obey God's ministers and officers if we will obey him." However, if rulers lead away from obedience to God, they are dishonorable and "darken his glory." Using a parallel analogy: should a father order something unlawful in the home, he forfeits honor and "is nothing else but a man." Similarly, "if a king or ruler or magistrate becomes so lofty that he diminishes the honor and authority of God, he is but a man. . . . For he who goes beyond his bounds in his office must be despoiled of his honor, lest, under a color or visor, he deceive."[39]

Commenting on Jesus' teaching to "render to Caesar what is Caesar's and to God what is God's," Calvin stated that obedience to a poor magistrate did not "prevent us from having within us a conscience free in the sight of God," and also concluded this: "Those who destroy political order are rebellious against God, and therefore, . . . obedience to princes and magistrates is always joined to the worship and fear of God; but . . . on the other hand, if princes claim any part of the authority of God, we ought not to obey them any farther than can be done without offending God."

Even in view of the later New Testament teaching to "fear God, honor the king," certain priorities must not be forgotten. Calvin

37. Ibid., 178.
38. Ibid., 214.
39. Ibid., 215.

commented: "The fear of God ought to precede, that kings may obtain their authority. For if any one begins his reverence of an earthly prince by rejecting that of God, he will act preposterously, since this is a complete perversion of the order of nature." Calvin noted that "earthly kings lay aside all their power when they rise up against God, and are unworthy of being reckoned in the number of mankind." Rather than fulfilling unjust laws, although care in this determination was commended as well, the Geneva Reformer advised the following: "We ought rather utterly to defy than to obey them whenever they are so restive and wish to spoil God of his rights, and, as it were, to seize upon his throne and draw him down from heaven."

Romans 13

Calvin's discussion of Romans 13 began by explaining that all civil power originates with the sovereign God—not with man, as later secular schemes suggested. He then discussed the role of civil government and the duty of the Christian to submit to that government except in extreme circumstances. The civil government was given, wrote Calvin, to prevent the damage of human sinfulness. Albeit restraining, it was a gracious institution for society. Calvin, it should be remembered, believed that any government was better than no government at all: "further, some kind of government, however deformed and corrupt it may be, is still better and more beneficial than anarchy."[40]

In sum, he concluded: "Now this passage confirms what I have already said, that we ought to obey kings and governors, whoever they may be, not because we are constrained, but because it is a service acceptable to God; for he will have them not only to be feared, but also honored by a voluntary respect."[41] In addition, his comments called for magistrates to protect religion and public decency ("endeavor to promote religion and to regulate morals by wholesome discipline").[42]

40. John Calvin, *Calvin's Commentary on I Peter*, Calvin's Commentaries 22 (Grand Rapids: Baker, 1979), 83. He also commented on Romans: "there can then be no tyranny which does not in some respects assist in consolidating the society of men." *Calvin's Commentary on Romans*, 480.
41. *Calvin's Commentary on Romans*, 483.
42. See his comments on 1 Timothy 2:2.

Calvin called for ethical and religious considerations to be included in good government, argued for republicanism on an authoritative basis, pleaded with believers to exemplify virtue and be submissive as a norm, and paved the way for later political developments by stating that the governor could be resisted under certain conditions. His disciples later augmented and expanded the conditions under which such revolution was acceptable.

With the scriptural survey above, Harro Hopfl's recognition of the signatures of political Calvinism may be appreciated:

- Calvin detested rulers who acted as if their will made right (*sic volo sic iubeo*).
- Because no single individual possessed "power and breadth of vision enough to govern" unilaterally, a council was needed.
- Even in a monarchy, a council was required.
- Tyranny was exhibited in a ruler's unwillingness to tolerate restraint or live within the law. Any ruler should be *sub Deo et sub lege* (under God and under law).[43]

Hopfl views Calvin's notion of order as necessitating law. Law then required enforcement, and different agencies with differing gifts and tools must each "adhere to his station and perform its duties willingly." Hopfl's summary is worth repeating:

> There is an unmistakable preference for an aristocratic form with popular admixtures of sorts, and for small territorial units. Monarchy is explicitly rejected for ecclesiastical polity on scriptural grounds; in civil polity no such outright rejection was possible because of the earlier *parti pris* in favor of the divine authorization of all forms of government and Calvin's almost inflexible opposition to political resistance. Nonetheless, the animus against monarchs is clear enough, and civil monarchy remains a discrepant and disturbing element in an otherwise carefully synchronized arrangement of mutual constraints.[44]

43. Hopfl, *Christian Polity*, 112, 162, 164, 165, 166.
44. Ibid., 171. In this and other sections, Hopfl notes "a very clear but imperfect homology" between church government and civil polity in Calvin.

With the foregoing review of Calvin's own teaching, let us briefly illustrate how it grew and expanded.

Calvin's Thought Disseminated through His Political Disciples

It is frequently though inappropriately implied that Calvin wished to unite church and state. In fact, he persistently advocated a difference of jurisdiction as noted above. François Wendel has corroborated that neither church nor state was to be annexed or collapsed into the other formally. This distinction or separation of jurisdictions "was the fountain of the entire edifice. Each of these autonomous powers, State and Church, was conceived as issuing from the Divine Will."[45] Wendel recognized that Calvin advocated the complementarity of the civil and ecclesiastical powers, even if many modern interpreters do not sense his preservation of that key distinction. Moreover, Douglas Kelly suggests that this distinction, even with a close cooperation between church and state, was an important factor in the diffusion of Calvinism.[46] Calvin himself stated the relationship succinctly in a 1538 letter: "As the magistrate ought by punishment and physical restraint to cleanse the church of offenses, so the minister of the Word should help the magistrate in order that fewer may sin. Their responsibilities should be so joined that each helps rather than impedes the other."[47] Calvin did not merge church and state into a theocratic monster.[48] He had no desire to advance the Reformation's political tradition on the back of coercion. Instead, Calvin wished to energize the church to become a world-changing community.[49]

45. François Wendel, *Calvin*, trans. Philip Mairet (London: Collins, 1963), 79.
46. Kelly, *Emergence of Liberty*, 14.
47. Cited in Kelly, *Emergence of Liberty*, 15.
48. William Naphy raises three key points to rebut the idea that Calvin was a repressive theocrat. First, he notes that the Genevan ministers focused on religious issues and did not seek to gain the civil magistrate's sword to punish crime. Second, the theoretical ideal for church government was not always followed, even at the height of Reformist zeal. Third, Naphy suggests that by the 1570s, the influence of the church had begun to wane. *Calvinism in Europe, 1540–1610: A Collection of Documents*, selected, translated, and edited by Alistair Duke, Gillian Lewis, and Andrew Pettegree (Manchester: Manchester University Press, 1992), 15.
49. See Kelly, *Emergence of Liberty*, 23.

Calvinists developed a knack for distilling theo-political thought. Theodore Beza, for example, wrote widely on political theory. His 1574 *Rights of the Magistrates* became a classic supporting republicanism and limited submission to governors. Although Calvin and Beza had discouraged rebellion before Calvin's death, even recommending support of existing rulers if at all possible, with the treacherous slaughter and virtual extinction of Reformed religion in France, Beza led efforts to reassess that formulation. The result was a tradition that included the likes of Knox, Viret, Ponet, and others. Beza's argument to normalize resistance to evil governments on biblical bases transformed Calvinist political theory.[50]

After beginning with a historical review, Beza's *Rights of the Magistrates* argued for a circumscribed resistance to tyrannical rulers. Organizing his work around ten questions, he affirmed that scriptural obedience did not categorically deny revolution in some cases. Toward the end of this tract, he articulated three axioms to clarify conditions warranting armed resistance: "(1) That the tyranny must be undisguised and notorious; (2) That the recourse should not be had to arms before all other remedies have been tried; (3) Nor yet before the question has been thoroughly examined, not only as to what is permissible, but also as to what is expedient, lest the remedies prove more hazardous than the very disease."[51]

From studying the Hebrew monarchy in the Old Testament, Beza, like Calvin, called for popular election. Moreover, Beza championed a double-covenant idea, similar to later Protestant tracts. In what amounted to a sweeping survey of the history of Western civilization, Beza found support for resistance to tyranny not only in Swiss republicanism, but also in the political histories of Denmark, England, Scotland, Poland, Sweden, Venice, Spain, France, and the Roman Empire itself. It is difficult to imagine a more informed or comprehensive history of resistance. The case Beza made was compelling.

---

50. The summaries of Beza and Goodman below are taken, in part, from my *Genevan Reformation*, chapters 4–5; used with permission.

51. For a good summary of these ideas, see Patrick S. Poole, "The Development of the Reformational Doctrine of Resistance in the Sixteenth Century," at: http://fly.hiwaay.net;~pspoole/Defense.htm.

Other Calvinistic disciples such as Christopher Goodman,[52] a Gene-van exile with John Knox and William Whittingham, authored a system-atic defense of ideas close to Knox's heart in 1558: *How Superior Powers Ought to Be Obeyed by Their Subjects: And Wherein They May Lawfully by God's Word Be Disobeyed and Resisted.*[53] Arguing against custom and negligence as twin sisters of error, Goodman, Knox, and Whittingham united (on January 1, 1558, from Geneva) to declare:

> Obedience is necessary where God is glorified, but if God is dishon-ored, your obedience is abominable in the sight of God, be it never so beautiful in man's eyes.... When it [Scripture] commands us to obey God, we must disobey man to the contrary: for no man can serve two masters.... Obedience to God's Laws by disobeying man's wicked laws is very commendable, but to disobey God for any duty to man is all together damnable.

Goodman (with Knox's hardy concurrence) argued that had the apostles obeyed the government when it prohibited their free exercise of religion, "the foundation of the Church should have been shaken, and the whole assembly discouraged." On the basis of that historical precedent, Goodman awarded both power and discretion to the people (prefiguring explicit formulations of "the consent of the governed") as he wrote: "the residue of the common people, seeing their superiors of all degrees and estates, by whom they should be governed with godly laws, and to whom they ought to obey in the fear of God only, thus cowardly forsake their obedience to God" if they fail to resist a tyrant. Thus, Goodman insisted that "to obey man in anything contrary to God, or His precepts though he be in highest authority, or never so orderly called there unto is no obedience at all, but disobedience."

Whether conscious of its revolutionary implications or not, Good-man was pioneering a new concept that would achieve wide currency

52. As a sign of the long continuity, in 1603 a Geneva diplomat attended to the estate debts of Christopher Goodman, one of Knox's compatriots. E. William Monter, *Studies in Genevan Government, 1536–1605* (Geneva: Librairie Droz, 1964), 55.

53. This document is available in Patrick S. Poole, "Reformation Political Works," at http://fly.hiwaay.net/~pspoole/Goodman1.HTM. Searches for the citations I have used may be conducted from phrases on that page.

centuries later: the election of princes and kings. Rulers who are elected can of course be recalled or unelected. Picking up on the growing swell of a Reformation chorus, Goodman essentially denied that kingship was hereditary. He succinctly stated, "Obedience is to hear God rather than man, and to resist man rather than God." Moreover, he proclaimed, "there is no obedience against God, which in His judgment is not manifest rebellion." Resistance to wicked kings is not rebellion. It is difficult not to see the seeds of Thomas Jefferson's motto, "Rebellion to Tyrants Is Obedience to God," in Goodman's Calvinistic manifesto.

Following Calvin's teaching but predating the final edition of the *Institutes*, in good Calvinistic style, John Ponet delineated when tyrannicide itself would be legitimate: either if the tyrant was an overt criminal or when lower-level political officials became involved. With a passionate style, Ponet's *Short Treatise* (1556) argued for the following:

- The people could hold a ruler, who was to be viewed as the servant of citizens, accountable.
- Overthrow, even if forceful, was permitted under certain conditions.
- The basis for just governance was transcendental as well as universal.
- Government was to be limited in scope and in force.
- Authority was to be diffused among various spheres, not concentrated in one office.
- Checks and balances, via ephors or tribunes, were necessary.[54]

These and other tenets of Calvinism would become standard fare in lands where the Reformed faith spread.[55] The ideas (1) that God is the Superior Governor, (2) that man is a fallen sinner, and (3) that law, fixed constitutions, and decentralization of power are all necessary to limit human aggression became the signature of Calvinism in

---

54. John Adams commended Calvinist theorist John Ponet for promulgating "all the essential principles of liberty, which were afterward dilated by Sidney and Locke." Later Adams specifically endorsed several other works from the Puritan period, including those by Milton and the *Vindiciae contra Tyrannos*.

55. Skinner, *Foundations of Modern Political Thought*, 2:221–24, provides a helpful comparison of the thought of Ponet and Christopher Goodman.

political forums. Later Hotman, Daneau, and Althusius expanded these themes as the tradition developed.

Most knowledgeable historians spot a definite evolution in political theology from Calvin's early disciples (Knox, Goodman, Ponet) to his later disciples (Beza, Hotman, Daneau). Two major linchpins, however, changed after the 1570s: (a) submission was *limited* and (b) representation was *absolute*. These dynamics began to be publicized from pulpits and academies.

By the early seventeenth century, a new tradition was congealing. A summary from Dartmouth historian Herbert Foster about a century ago noted the following as hallmarks of Calvin's political legacy,[56] and most are exhibited by the works of his closest disciples referenced above:

(1) The absolute sovereignty of God entailed that universal human rights (or Beza's "fundamental law") should be protected and must not be surrendered to the whim of tyranny.

(2) These fundamental laws, which were always compatible with God's law, are the basis of whatever public liberties we enjoy.

(3) Mutual covenants, as taught by Beza, Hotman, and the *Vindiciae*, between rulers and God and between rulers and subjects were binding and necessary.

(4) As Ponet, Knox, and Goodman taught, the sovereignty of the people flows logically from the mutual obligations of the covenants above.

(5) The representatives of the people, not the people themselves, are the first line of defense against tyranny.[57]

I have summarized the five points of political Calvinism slightly differently:

+ Depravity as a perennial human variable to be accommodated
+ Accountability for leaders provided via a collegium

---

56. *Collected Papers of Herbert D. Foster*, 163–74.

57. Ibid., 174. Besides Calvin, this idea was reiterated in Buchanan, Beza, Peter Martyr, Althusius, Hotman, Daneau, *Vindiciae*, Ponet, William the Silent, and others.

+ Republicanism as the preferred form of government
+ Constitutionalism needed to restrain both the rulers and the ruled
+ Limited government, beginning with the family, as foundational

The resulting mnemonic device, DARCL (though not as convenient as TULIP), seems a more apt summary if placed in the context of the political writings of Calvin's disciples.

The evolution was real, it was philosophically significant, it was politically revolutionary, and it would last for centuries, providing a true turning point in history. Whether one agrees with all of Calvin's theology or not, the subsequent altered terrain is clear. And Calvin, whether it is in his *Institutes*, or in his commentaries and sermons, stood at the font of a new, or renewed, political tradition.

There is abundant evidence that Goodman, Ponet, Beza, and Knox all had discussions with Viret, who also likely discussed these notions with Calvin. Inasmuch as his *Remonstrances aux Fidèles* (1547) was published a full generation before the Saint Bartholomew's Day Massacre, and his 1561 *The World and the Empire* was available (and unrefuted by Calvin) more than a decade before that tragic event, it may be that an older theory was correct after all—namely that the Calvinist and Huguenot resisters did not merely react in the throes of crisis and then recast their theory after the fact. They had precedents and a history of understanding the propriety of resistance under certain conditions even before Calvin's death.

That being the case, Calvin's commentaries fit into a consistent paradigm, and the reason that Calvin devoted no more attention to explicit development of resistance theory is best understood as a combination of two important facts: (1) resistance theory based on the priority of the commandments was a philosophical given during Calvin's day, needing little further proof; and (2) with the tensions of the times, Calvin did not want to stoke revolutionary fervor unnecessarily, nor did he wish to attract royalist criticism from France and elsewhere for espousing anarchical views. The later works of Beza and Hotman, as well as the *Vindiciae contra Tyrannos* in the 1570s, thus were not radical departures from the previous tradition that spanned from Farel to Viret to Calvin; rather, they were applications of the same seminal principles. Or as Robert Linder puts it: after 1547, anyone "looking for an ideology to justify revolution could have found many choice and useful ideas in the writings of Peter Viret."[58] The result, as one non-Protestant scholar put it, is that "in the political domain, Calvinist ideas are at the origin of the revolution which from the eighteenth to the nineteenth centuries gave birth and growth to the parliamentary democracies of Anglo-Saxon type."[59]

Few, if any, postcanonical theologians made broader societal impact than Calvin on the public square. Interestingly, everywhere Calvinism spread, so did its views of both respecting government and limiting it. Calvinism, in fact, "placed a solid barrier in the path of the spread of absolutism"[60] and helped make the world safer from tyrants. Furthermore, Karl Holl claimed that even though ancestors of human rights were found in the Middle Ages, nonetheless, their "formal acceptance into political theory is not completed until this period [Calvin's day] and only under the impact of religion. . . . The acceptance of universal human rights into the constitution was, however, not just the modification of a single point; it included in itself the transformation of the whole concept of the state."[61] Calvin's pen, particularly through the *Institutes*, and personal genius spawned that revolution.

58. Robert Dean Linder, *The Political Ideas of Pierre Viret* (Geneva: Librairie Droz, 1964), 178.

59. Cited by Paul T. Fuhrmann, "Philip Mornay and the Huguenot Challenge to Absolutism," *Calvinism and the Political Order*, ed. Hunt, 50.

60. Holl, *Cultural Significance*, 68.

61. Ibid., 72–73.

19

CALVIN'S DOCTRINE OF THE LAST THINGS: THE RESURRECTION OF THE BODY AND THE LIFE EVERLASTING

INSTITUTES 3.25 ET AL.
CORNELIS P. VENEMA

I n the introduction to his study of Calvin's doctrine of the last things, Heinrich Quistorp observes that "the theology of the reformers is not primarily concerned with questions of eschatology. . . . Their chief concern is with the problem of justification and the matters immediately relevant to it."[1] Quistorp's claim that Calvin was not particularly interested

---

1. Heinrich Quistorp, *Calvin's Doctrine of the Last Things*, trans. Harold Knight (London: Lutterworth, 1955), 11. See also Eric A. De Boer, "The Book of Revelation in Calvin's Geneva," in *Calvin's Books: Festschrift for Peter De Klerk*, ed. Wilhelm H. Neuser et al. (Heerenveen: J. J. Groen en Zoon, 1997), 23: "One interesting feature of Peter DeKlerk's annual *Calvin Bibliography* is that it lists the subsections where few books or articles appear. In this way it

in the subject of eschatology is apparently shared by many interpreters of Calvin's theology. In the burgeoning secondary literature on virtually every facet of Calvin's reformatory labor, there are relatively few studies of Calvin's eschatology. If the size of chapter 25 of book 3 of Calvin's *Institutes*, which is the subject of this chapter, is taken as a measure of Calvin's interest in questions of eschatology, this claim appears to be confirmed. In the span of only twenty-five pages, Calvin offers a brief exposition of the concluding articles of the Apostles' Creed, an exposition that adheres closely to the classical consensus of Christian theology on these topics.

Even though it might appear from this brief section of Calvin's *Institutes* that his interest in the subject of eschatology is rather perfunctory and unexceptional, this is more a matter of appearance than reality. Calvin's theology represents a comprehensive exposition of the knowledge of God as Creator and Redeemer that is mediated through divine revelation or the Word of God. In his exposition of this knowledge, Calvin exhibits a keen interest in the course of redemptive history under the sovereign superintendence of the triune Creator and Redeemer. Eschatology, or a consideration of the goal or telos of the works of the triune God, constitutes a pervasive thread that is interwoven throughout the entirety of the *Institutes* as well as Calvin's other writings. For this reason, our analysis of Calvin's exposition of two of the key topics of Christian eschatology in chapter 25 of book 3 of the *Institutes* will include an additional treatment of a number of key eschatological themes that recur throughout his theological writings. Our treatment of these themes will exhibit the extent to which Calvin's understanding of the knowledge of God includes an emphasis on the consummation of God's gracious purposes in Christ at the end of history.

In order to summarize key elements of Calvin's eschatology, we will begin with a exposition of and commentary on chapter 25 of book 3 of the *Institutes*. In the course of this exposition, we will occasionally refer to other places in Calvin's writings where some of the themes of this chapter are also addressed. After providing an exposition of this chapter, we

---

underlines subjects which Calvinscholars [sic] tend to neglect. To me the most prominent example is the subsection 'Doctrine of the Last Things' (IV,F) or, since 1979, 'Eschatology.' In the early volumes of the Calvinbibliography [sic] this section is sometimes left out completely. In later volumes DeKlerk printed the heading, even if no titles could be listed."

will also identify a number of important aspects of Calvin's eschatology, some of which have been the special focus of discussion in the secondary literature. Since our exposition will necessarily be brief at a number of points, we will also identify the most important sources in the literature for further study of Calvin's eschatology.[2]

An Analysis of Book 3, Chapter 25: The Resurrection of the Body and the Life Everlasting

Location within the Structure of the Institutes

Before we survey Calvin's chapter on the resurrection of the body and the life everlasting, it will be helpful to note the location of this chapter within the structure of the *Institutes*.[3]

An analysis of the various editions of the *Institutes* shows that this chapter was completely rewritten and significantly enlarged in the 1559, or final, Latin edition.[4] Only a small fragment of the chapter stems from

---

2. In addition to the studies of Quistorp and De Boer, the following are among the most important general studies of Calvin's eschatology: T. F. Torrance, *Kingdom and Church* (Edinburgh: Oliver & Boyd, 1956), ch. 4, "The Eschatology of Hope: John Calvin"; Martin Schultze, *Meditatio vitae futurae: Ihr Begriff und ihre herrschende Stellung im System Calvin's* (Leipzig, 1901); David E. Holwerda, "Eschatology and History: A Look at Calvin's Eschatological Vision," in *Exploring the Heritage of John Calvin*, ed. David E. Holwerda (Grand Rapids: Baker, 1976), 110–39; J. H. Van Wyk, "John Calvin on the Kingdom of God and Eschatology," *In die Skriflig* 35.2 (2001): 191–205; Andrew Martin Davis, "A New Assessment of John Calvin's Eschatology," (Ph.D. diss., Southern Baptist Theological Seminary); François Wendel, *Calvin: The Origins and Development of His Thought*, trans. P. Mairet (Grand Rapids: Baker, 1997) 284–90; Charles E. Raynal, "John Calvin's Teaching about Eternal Life: Its Reformation Setting and Religious Significance," in *Calvin Studies V*, ed. John H. Leith (Davidson, NC: Davidson College Presbyterian Church, 1990), 73–93; and W. Balke, "Some Characteristics of Calvin's Eschatology," in *Christian Hope in Context*, ed. A. van Egmond and D. van Keulen (Zoertermeer: Meinema, 2001), 1:30–64.

3. For an extended discussion of the structure of the *Institutes*, see Edward Dowey Jr., *The Knowledge of God in Calvin's Theology*, 3d ed. (Grand Rapids: Eerdmans, 1994, 41–49, 243–60; Cornelis P. Venema, *Accepted and Renewed in Christ: The "Twofold Grace of God" and the Interpretation of Calvin's Theology* (Göttingen: Vandenhoeck & Ruprecht, 2007), chapter 3; and Richard A. Muller, *The Unaccommodated Calvin: Studies in the Foundation of a Theological Tradition* (New York: Oxford University Press, 2000), 118–39.

4. See Ford Lewis Battles, *Analysis of the Institutes of the Christian Religion of John Calvin* (Phillipsburg, NJ: P&R, 1980), 156–59, for a diagrammatic representation of the various editions and outlines of the *Institutes*. See also Jean-Daniel Benoît, "The History and

the first edition of 1536. A larger portion of the chapter derives from material that was first included in the 1539 edition under the topic of faith. In the 1539 and subsequent editions of the *Institutes*, Calvin treats the topics of the resurrection and the life everlasting at the conclusion of his exposition of the content of the Christian faith, which is itself based upon the summary provided in the Apostles' Creed. Prior to the final Latin edition of 1559 and the French edition of 1560, the earlier editions of the *Institutes* follow a structure that roughly parallels the classical plan of Christian catechisms with the sequence of topics: the Decalogue, the Apostles' Creed, the Lord's Prayer, and the sacraments.[5] Only in the final editions of the *Institutes* do we find chapter 25 in its present form, which represents a substantial expansion of his comments in earlier editions, and is now located, not in a section on the Christian faith as summarized in the Apostles' Creed, but in book 3, which bears the title "The Way in Which We Receive the Grace of Christ: What Benefits Come to Us from It, and What Effects Follow."

Though there has been much dispute in the secondary literature regarding the structure of Calvin's *Institutes*, the arrangement of material seems to be governed by at least three broad considerations: the distinction between the "twofold knowledge of God" (*duplex cognitio Dei*) as Creator (book 1) and Redeemer (books 2–4); the trinitarian arrangement of the articles of the Apostles' Creed (book 1: God the Father; book 2: God the Son; books 3–4: God the Holy Spirit); and the influence of Calvin's commentaries, particularly his commentary on Romans.[6] None of these considerations can explain all of Calvin's decisions regarding where to treat a common topic of Christian theology. However, they do give us a sense of the overall structure of Calvin's theology as it is summarized in his *Institutes*, and provide a help to understanding the interpretive context for Calvin's exposition. Though Calvin treats the last two articles of the

Development of the *Institutio*: How Calvin Worked," in *John Calvin: A Collection of Distinguished Essays*, ed. G. E. Duffield (Appleford, Abingdon, Berkshire: Sutton Courtenay Press, 1966), 102–17, for a treatment of the development of the *Institutes* in its various editions.

5. Benoît, "History and Development," 109.

6. Muller, *Unaccommodated Calvin*, 118–39, suggests that the structure of Calvin's *Institutes* reflects a variety of factors, including Melanchthon's *Loci Communes*, which follows the outline of Paul's Letter to the Romans, and Calvin's exegetical commentaries.

creed in chapter 25 at the end of book 3, before taking up the topic of the church in book 4 (reversing the sequence of the creed's final articles), he clearly understands the topics he considers in book 3 to anticipate the doctrine of the church. Only within the society of the church does Christ unite believers to himself by his Spirit and Word, and grant them a full participation in all the saving benefits of his mediation.

The significance of this location for Calvin's treatment of the resurrection of the body and the life everlasting is not difficult to discern. The redemptive work of Christ as Mediator is imparted to believers by the ministry of the Holy Spirit, who unites believers to Christ and grants them all the benefits of redemption. Through union with Christ, believers enjoy principally a double benefit of free justification or acceptance with God and renewal after the image of God. The purpose of God the Father in redemption is to restore believers to acceptance and favor, and to conform them to the image of Christ in true knowledge, righteousness, and holiness. The work of the triune Creator and Redeemer aims to bring those who are united to Christ to glory, and to repair the brokenness and disorder of sin in human life. Calvin's treatment of the resurrection of the body and the life everlasting represents, accordingly, his account of the *telos* of the believer's union with Christ. In union with Christ, believers are justified, sanctified, and ultimately glorified. Considering the location of chapter 25 in the *Institutes*, it might well be titled "The Believer's Glorification in Union with Christ."

The Resurrection of the Body

As the title of chapter 25 indicates, Calvin intends to provide an exposition of the two traditional subjects of the resurrection of the body and the life everlasting. The actual distribution of material in the chapter, however, suggests that it is best divided into three parts: (1) an affirmation of the Christian doctrine of a final resurrection; (2) a rebuttal of several objections to the doctrine of the resurrection; and (3) a brief discourse on the nature of the final state of glorification.

Calvin begins his treatment of the subject of the resurrection by noting the importance of the hope of the resurrection for the entirety of the Christian life. Echoing themes that were emphasized in his earlier treatise on the Christian life in book 2, and his prior description of redemption through union with Christ, Calvin insists that believers must always cling to Christ in hope. The expectation of believers for the fullness of redemption in union with Christ will not be fulfilled in this life and world. Rather, believers must walk with their "minds lifted up to heaven," pressing onward toward the hope of their calling in Christ.[7]

Employing language reminiscent of his description of the Christian pilgrimage as a "meditation upon the future life" (*meditatio futurae vitae*), Calvin notes that "he alone has fully profited in the gospel who has accustomed himself to continual meditation (*continuam . . . meditationem*) upon the blessed resurrection."[8] Even though among the ancient philosophers, Plato enjoys the distinction of having recognized that "man's highest good . . . is union with God," none of the philosophers understood that the achievement of this good depends on the "sacred bond" of union with Christ.[9] Only in Christ, whose resurrection from the dead is "already completed," do believers have the promise of the fullness of redemption. The life of the Christian is one of hope, a continual anticipation of the day of Christ's coming when Christ's work already begun in the believer will reach "its completion."[10]

In the remainder of this opening section on the resurrection of the body, Calvin appeals to two grounds for the believer's confidence and hope for resurrection. The first of these grounds is Christ's resurrection, which constitutes a type of the believer's resurrection. The second of these grounds resides in the power of God, who alone is able to raise and glorify the bodies of believers in conformity to Christ. Because many of the philosophers had no knowledge of Christ, they were able to teach the immortality of the soul but they were unable to affirm the resurrection of the flesh. On the principle that believ-

7. *Institutes* 3.25.1 (OS 4:432–33; OS = *Calvini opera selecta*, ed. P. Barth and G. Niesel, 5 vols. [Munich: Kaiser, 1926–52]).

8. *Institutes* 3.25.1 (OS 4:433).

9. *Institutes* 3.25.2 (OS 4:433).

10. *Institutes* 3.25.2 (OS 4:433). Though the language is "anachronistic" when applied to Calvin, this understanding of what is "already" the believer's possession but "not yet" his in completion resembles what some contemporary biblical theologians term the "already-not yet" structure of biblical eschatology.

ers through union with Christ have a full participation in all that is his, as members enjoy the privileges of their Head, we may be confident that the Holy Spirit will "quicken" believers in union with him. "Christ rose again that he might have us as companions in the life to come. He was raised by the Father, inasmuch as he was Head of the church, from which the Father in no way allows him to be severed. He was raised by the power of the Holy Spirit, the Quickener of us in common with him."[11] Furthermore, even though the prospect of the believer's resurrection in union with Christ exceeds the ordinary course of nature, it does not exceed the greatness and power of God who is able to grant life from the dead and ensure the believer's inheritance in Christ.

Objections to the Doctrine of the Resurrection

After a brief and positive presentation of the doctrine of the resurrection of the body, Calvin turns in the middle part of chapter 25 to several objections that are raised against the doctrine. These objections include not only traditional denials of the resurrection but also errors of Calvin's contemporaries, some of which are addressed at greater length in his other treatises and commentaries. In the course of rebutting these objections, Calvin also expands and clarifies his own understanding of the nature of the resurrection of believers. He then closes this part of the chapter with a brief reflection on the nature of the resurrection of the ungodly at the time of Christ's second coming.

Calvin begins and ends his consideration of various objections to the doctrine of the resurrection by noting that a denial of the resurrection is common within paganism, and even at times among the people of God (e.g., the Sadducees). However, this denial is countered by the ancient practice of burial, which is before the eyes of all men a kind of "earnest of new life" (*effigiem resurrectionis*).[12] The meticulous care and interest that are devoted to the preparation of bodies for burial is a kind of testimony to the expectation of resurrection and new life. Indeed, the etymology

---

11. *Institutes* 3.25.3 (OS 4:436): "Suscitatus est virtute Spiritus, qui nobis ad vivificandi munus communis est."
12. *Institutes* 3.25.5 (OS 4:439).

of the word for "cemetery" suggests that it is a "sleeping place," which is a kind of anteroom for the body as believers await the resurrection of the last day.[13]

The first significant error that Calvin identifies in this part of chapter 25 is the error of the "chiliasts, who limited the reign of Christ to a thousand years."[14] In his rejection of this particular error, Calvin notes that it has expressed itself throughout the history of the church from the time of the apostles and has appealed to the teaching of the Apocalypse of John (Rev. 20). The appeal to Revelation on the part of the chiliasts is only a "pretext," however, since the language of "one thousand" does not "apply to the eternal blessedness of the church but only to the various disturbances that awaited the church, while still toiling on earth."[15] The principal objection that Calvin raises to the teaching of chiliasm is that it limits the "inheritance of the life to come" in the kingdom of God to a period of one thousand years. Such a restriction in the temporal duration and blessedness of Christ's future kingdom casts "reproach upon Christ" and fails utterly to do justice to the biblical teaching regarding the undying glory and perpetuity of Christ's kingdom in its consummation.[16] Moreover, among the contemporary advocates of chiliasm, there are some who deny the doctrine of the eternal punishment of the wicked, arguing that such punishment would be excessive when compared with the temporal nature of human sin. In his rebuttal of this objection, Calvin notes that it fails to reckon with the truth of God's majesty and justice, which are too little esteemed.[17]

In addition to the errors of chiliasts, Calvin identifies two further errors that are taught by "perversely curious men."[18] The first of these errors is the claim that the soul of man dies with the body, only to be

13. *Institutes* 3.25.8 (OS 4:439).
14. *Institutes* 3.25.5 (OS 4:439). For general treatments of Calvin's criticism of chiliasm, see Quistorp, *Calvin's Doctrine of the Last Things*, 158–62; and Davis, "A New Assessment of John Calvin's Eschatology," 240–47.
15. *Institutes* 3.25.1 (OS 4:440).
16. *Institutes* 3.25.5 (OS 4:440).
17. *Institutes* 3.25.5 (OS 4:440). Among his contemporaries, a number of Anabaptists may have taught the views Calvin is here condemning, for example, John Denck, Balthasar Hubmaier, Sebastian Franck, and Melchior Hoffman.
18. *Institutes* 3.25.6 (OS 4:441–42).

resurrected at the last day. The second is the claim that the resurrection bodies of believers are radically new, not the renewed and glorified bodies of the saints.

With respect to the first of these errors, Calvin observes that he has addressed the subject of the distinction between the soul and the body in the context of his treatment of the doctrine of creation.[19] Though he does not explicitly refer to his early treatise *Psychopannychia*, which constitutes a more extensive rebuttal of the doctrine of "soul sleep," he offers a short summary of its argument.[20] Those who deny an intermediate state, teaching that the soul dies with the body or falls asleep prior to the resurrection, fail to distinguish between the soul and the body, and deny the truth that the soul is "that part of us in which the divine especially shines, and in which there are such clear tokens of immortality."[21] They also fail to acknowledge the clear scriptural teaching of a conscious intermediate state in which believers enjoy communion with Christ in the period between death and resurrection.[22] Admittedly, we are not free to speculate about the nature of the soul's intermediate state, as some have done in the history

19. See *Institutes* 1.5.5 (OS 3:48–50); 1.15 (OS 3:173–87).

20. For a critical edition of this work, which was first published in 1542 and then in a revised edition in 1545, see *Psychopannychia*, ed. Walther Zimmerli (Leipzig: Deichert, 1932). An English translation of the work by Henry Beveridge is provided in *Selected Works of John Calvin* (Grand Rapids: Baker, 1983), 3:413–90. In a recent study of this early work (*The Starting Point of Calvin's Theology* [Grand Rapids: Eerdmans, 2000]), George H. Tavard argues that it illustrates the catholicity and dependence upon church tradition evident in Calvin's theological work (contrary to the biblicism of later Protestantism). Richard A. Muller, in a review of Tavard's book ("The Starting Point of Calvin's Theology," *Calvin Theological Journal* 36.2 [2001]: 314–41), properly notes that the catholicity of Calvin's thinking in this treatise, as well as the absence of antipapal rhetoric, is because of the literary genre and theological topic of the work. Since Calvin is not focusing upon a doctrinal theme that was controversial in the debates between Protestant and Roman Catholic in the sixteenth century, his sentiments are catholic in nature, as is true of much of his theological program (and that of his Protestant contemporaries).

21. *Institutes* 3.25.6 (OS 4:441).

22. Perhaps this is the place to observe that Calvin's understanding of the intermediate state excludes the Roman Catholic dogma of purgatory. According to Calvin, the dogma of purgatory has no scriptural warrant and belies the believer's union with Christ, whose atoning death fully satisfies for the eternal and temporal penalty of the sins of his people. For Calvin's evaluation of this dogma, see *Institutes* 3.5.6–10 (OS 4:138–46), and his *Canons and Decrees of the Council of Trent, with the Antidote*, in *Selected Works of John Calvin*.

of Christian theology. But we must affirm what the Scriptures teach without inquiring "too curiously" beyond its boundaries.[23]

Calvin's response to the second of these errors—that the bodies of the saints are altogether new and not the glorified form of their present bodies—is drawn largely from his letter to Laelius Socinus written in June 1549.[24] This error, which is reminiscent of the ancient error of the Manichaeans who disparaged the body and earthly created existence, fails to acknowledge that believers as members of Christ will enjoy the same glorification/resurrection that he enjoyed. The resurrection of the body does not promise the bestowal of another body, but rather the renewal and glorification of the present body of believers. In an important statement, which provides a general principle regarding the relation between creation and redemption, Calvin notes that "if death, which takes its origin from the fall of man, is accidental, the restoration which Christ has brought belongs to that self-same body which began to be mortal."[25] The corruption and weakness of the body or the flesh is an adventitious or accidental quality that does not belong intrinsically to the body as God first created it.[26] Redemption restores what sin has corrupted and deformed, but it does not displace what God created good. Consequently, Calvin insists that there is a unity or continuity between the present body and the resurrected body, though he simultaneously insists on the discontinuity that follows from the glorification of the believer's body in union with Christ.

In a brief concluding section of this part of chapter 25, Calvin addresses a question that often arises in the context of discussing the resurrection of believers: what about the resurrection of the ungodly? To speak of the resurrection of believers and unbelievers seems, Calvin observes, to suggest that the resurrection is a sort of common benefit of Christ's work that accrues to both.[27] In his reply to this question, Calvin

23. *Institutes* 3.25.6 (OS 4:442).
24. *Institutes* 3.25.7–8 (OS 4:443–51). Socinus taught the doctrine that Calvin here opposes. For an English translation of this letter, see *Selected Works of John Calvin*, 3:415.
25. *Institutes* 3.25.7 (OS 4:447).
26. *Institutes* 3.28.8 (OS 4:449): "as to substance (*substantiam*) we shall be raised again in the same flesh we now bear, but ... the quality will be different (*qualitatem aliam*)."
27. *Institutes* 3.25.9 (OS 4:451).

argues that there is a radical difference between these resurrections. The resurrection of the ungodly is not, strictly speaking, a benefit of Christ's redemptive mediation. It is rather a "resurrection of judgment," which manifests the power, justice, and prerogatives of Christ as the One whom the Father has appointed as the Judge of all flesh. This resurrection is an "incidental resurrection in which [the wicked] are haled before the judgment seat of Christ."[28] Most often, however, when the Scriptures speak of the resurrection, they mean to refer to the heavenly glory that will properly belong to those who are members of Christ. Since Christ came "properly not for the destruction of the world but for its salvation," this is the chief emphasis to be found in the Word of God.[29]

The Life Everlasting

The most remarkable feature about Calvin's concluding observations on the life everlasting is the emphasis on the fruitlessness of undue speculation about the final state. Calvin affirms that the final state will be one "filled with splendor, joy, happiness, and glory."[30] But he insists that these things are so far removed from our present perception as to remain largely obscure and hidden from us. We know that believers will enjoy the most intimate and direct communion with God, which is the highest blessedness and joy. Yet Calvin strongly cautions his reader to "keep sobriety, lest forgetful of our limitations we should soar aloft with the greater boldness, and be overcome by the brightness of the heavenly glory."[31] In this connection, Calvin criticizes indirectly the discussions among many medieval theologians about the final state that amount to little more than "dangerous speculations" that exceed the limits of the Word of God. One question that he does acknowledge to be legitimate is the question of a diversity of rewards in the kingdom of God. In addition to the gift of eternal life, which will be the common inheritance of all believers, God will variously distribute particular gifts to his servants in acknowledgment of their service in his name.

28. *Institutes* 3.25.9 (OS 4:451).
29. *Institutes* 3.25.9 (OS 4:452).
30. *Institutes* 3.25.10 (OS 4:452).
31. *Institutes* 3.25.10 (OS 4:453).

In a final section on the future of the reprobate, Calvin exhibits similar restraint. Though we must affirm the scriptural teaching of the doctrine of eternal punishment, we must also recognize that the biblical descriptions of hell utilize physical metaphors that should not be pressed unduly. The focus of our understanding, so far as the doctrine of hell is concerned, should be upon what it means to be "cut off from all fellowship with God" (*alienari ab omni Dei societate*).[32]

Key Aspects of Calvin's Eschatology in His Writings and the Secondary Literature

The relative brevity of Calvin's treatment of the topic of eschatology in this section of his *Institutes* might suggest that the claim of Quistorp and others, namely, that Calvin gives short shrift to biblical eschatology, is accurate. Calvin's interest in eschatology, however, cannot be measured simply by considering what he says on the subject in the *Institutes*. Since he intends the *Institutes* to be a kind of handbook that accompanies his commentaries and other treatises, a fair assessment of Calvin's eschatology requires that we also take note of related themes or aspects of his view that are treated more extensively elsewhere in the corpus of his theological writings. Several of these aspects of Calvin's view, which may be only briefly discussed in the *Institutes*, require further elaboration. Though our discussion will have to be limited to a general sketch or overview of some of the more important themes in Calvin's eschatology, we will especially consider those that have been the focus of some debate in the literature.

Calvin's Aversion to Speculative Approaches

One feature of Calvin's approach to eschatology that stands out in chapter 25 of book 3 is his aversion to speculative approaches to the subject of the future. On several occasions, Calvin speaks critically of those who exceed the boundaries of biblical revelation in speculating about the future state of the individual believer after death or the precise nature of the final state of glory. When he treats the believer's fellowship with Christ

32. *Institutes* 3:25.12 (OS 456).

in the state intermediate between death and resurrection, he affirms a form of conscious fellowship with Christ and rejects the alternatives of soul sleep and mortalism. But he is unwilling to say anything more about this state. The limits of scriptural revelation, which teaches the believer's communion with Christ subsequent to death without enlarging on the nature of that state, must be respected. Similarly, in his brief comments on the final state, Calvin is unwilling even to entertain the kind of questions that often occupied the attention of medieval theologians.[33] Here too the boundaries of scriptural teaching must be respected. Undue speculation regarding curious questions is a temptation that Calvin insists must be rejected.

In resisting the temptation to speculate beyond the limits of scriptural revelation, Calvin is simply echoing a basic methodological claim of his theology. In the early chapters of the *Institutes*, Calvin provides an account of his theological epistemology. All true knowledge of God and ourselves, which comprises the sum of Christian wisdom, depends upon God's sovereign initiative in making himself known through his revelatory Word. Such knowledge as we have must be born of a faithful listening to the Word of God, who is his own best witness and interpreter. Throughout the *Institutes*, Calvin repeatedly employs the metaphor of a labryrinth to describe the predicament that theologians find themselves in when they indulge their curiosity and exceed the boundaries of divine revelation. In the context of his treatment of the doctrine of creation, for example, Calvin sets forth the rule that must govern all theological reflection: "Let us remember here, as in all religious doctrine, that we ought to hold to one rule of modesty and sobriety: not to speak, or guess, or even to seek to know, concerning obscure matters anything except what has been imparted to us by God's Word."[34] This rule applies especially to the

---

33. For an example of his opposition to speculation regarding the final state in his commentaries, see his Commentary on Rom. 8:21 in *Calvin's New Testament Commentaries*, ed. David W. Torrance and Thomas F. Torrance (Grand Rapids: Eerdmans, 1979), 8:174. See also Davis, "A New Assessment of John Calvin's Eschatology," 159–73.

34. *Institutes* 1.14.4. For similar statements, see *Institutes* 1.13.21 (OS 3:135–37); 1.14.4 (OS 3:156–57); 3.21.4 (OS 4:372–73); 3.25.11 (OS 4:454–55). Interestingly, Calvin cites the doctrine of the intermediate state as an example of a "non-fundamental" article of the Christian faith. Differences of opinion regarding this state do not constitute a basis for division among Christians. See *Institutes* 4.1.12 (OS 5:15–16).

subject of eschatology, which considers topics that can be known only on the basis of the prophecies of Scripture.

Among interpreters of Calvin's theology, it has been suggested that Calvin's aversion to speculation in the area of eschatology accounts for his failure to write a commentary on the book of Revelation. Calvin's failure to write a commentary on Revelation is especially striking, since he wrote commentaries on most of the books of the Old and New Testaments and throughout his life gave special attention to the preparation of his commentaries.[35]

Opinions vary as to why Calvin never wrote such a commentary, but a common opinion is that it reflects his wariness of speculation in this area and uncertainty how best to interpret the apocalyptic portions of Scripture. T. H. L. Parker, who devotes some attention to this question, maintains that Calvin's failure to write a commentary on the book of Revelation stems from his conviction that "apocalyptic is foreign to the New Testament's complete revelation of Christ."[36] According to Parker, the unsubstantiated claim that Calvin regarded Revelation as an obscure book whose interpretation was beyond his mien, is little more than scholarly "gossip." In his dissertation on Calvin's theology, Andrew Martin Davis concludes that Calvin's failure to write a commentary on Revelation probably stemmed from his aversion to speculation and represents a deliberate omission on his part.[37]

In perhaps the most extensive treatment of the question regarding Calvin's decision not to write a commentary on Revelation, Eric De Boer offers the hypothesis that this simply resulted from Calvin's failure to complete all his commentaries before his death. Noting that Calvin wrote commentaries on a number of Old Testament apocalyptic writings, including Ezekiel and Daniel, that influenced significantly the apocalypse of John, De Boer suggests that Calvin was preparing to write a commentary on Revelation, but was never able to realize this intention.[38] According

35. T. H. L. Parker, *Calvin's New Testament Commentaries* (Grand Rapids: Eerdmans, 1971), 4.

36. Ibid., 78.

37. Davis, "A New Assessment of John Calvin's Eschatology," 174–81.

38. De Boer, "The Book of Revelation in Calvin's Geneva," 40. It is worth noting that De Boer bases his case in part on the number of instances where Calvin refers to the book

to De Boer, Calvin broke off his exposition of the New Testament books later in his life and devoted his attention to the prophetic books of the Old Testament in order to prepare for his anticipated exposition of the only prophetic book in the New Testament, the book of Revelation.

Of all the hypotheses regarding Calvin's omission of commentary on Revelation, De Boer's seems to me the most plausible. Though it is true, as we have noted, that Calvin was averse to speculation in the area of eschatology, this aversion was not directed against interpreting the apocalyptic portions of Scripture. Since Calvin draws no sharp line of distinction between the prophetic and apocalyptic books of the Bible, his convictions regarding the canonicity of the book of Revelation and his substantial commentaries on many of the Old Testament prophecies suggest that a commentary on the book of Revelation would have been desirable, were there opportunity to write one. Furthermore, there are sufficient clues in Calvin's commentaries on those Old Testament books, especially Daniel, that form an important background for the interpretation of Revelation, for anticipating what would likely have been the broad themes of Calvin's approach. Calvin's aversion to speculation was always directed against theologies that exceeded the boundaries of scriptural revelation, and not against the proper interpretation of Scripture itself.

The Debate regarding Calvin's View of the Intermediate State

Among interpreters of Calvin's eschatology, perhaps the most common criticism is that Calvin's view of the intermediate state betrays an unbiblical overemphasis on individual, in distinction from cosmic, eschatology. Furthermore, since Calvin's conception of the nature of the intermediate state depends on his doctrine of the immortality of the soul, Calvin's eschatology at this juncture owes as much or more to the influence of Greek philosophy than to biblical revelation. Indeed, despite Calvin's insistence that Christian theology must eschew speculation and remain with the limits of scriptural revelation, his doctrine of the intermediate

---

of Revelation in his early work *Psychopannychia* and in his other writings. Davis, "A New Assessment of John Calvin's Eschatology," reaches an opposite conclusion on the basis of the same evidence, arguing that the relative number of references to Revelation in Calvin's writings indicates that he was uncertain as to its interpretation.

state departs from his own strictures regarding how a true knowledge of God and ourselves is to be achieved. Rather than echoing the scriptural emphasis on the resurrection of the body as the primary promise for the believer's future in union with Christ, Calvin places an undue emphasis on the immortality of the soul and disparages the body as a kind of prison house of the soul.

An examination of Calvin's teaching in the area of anthropology confirms that he does insist on a sharp distinction between the soul and the body, and he ascribes a kind of preeminence to the soul.[39] Calvin is a dichotomist in his anthropology, and does employ expressions on occasion that do disparage the body and reflect a more philosophical, even Platonic, emphasis. When Calvin treats the subject of the human nature as it was created by God, he notes that "man consists of a soul and a body" and defines the soul as "an immortal, yet created essence."[40] The soul is said to indwell the body as a kind of house, and death is described as release of the soul from the "prison house of the body."[41]

While Calvin acknowledges that all of man's faculties and gifts, both of the soul and the body, belong to man's creaturely integrity as he was first created by God, he also maintains that the soul is the principal part of the human constitution and the proper seat of the image of God. He even acknowledges that, with respect to our understanding of the soul, Plato alone among the philosophers had a keen understanding of its immortal substance. In his treatment of the intermediate state, Calvin appeals to the distinction between the soul and the body to undergird his opposition to the "soul sleep" and mortalism views that were taught in the history of the church and by some of his contemporaries. Death brings about a separation between the body and the soul, and the soul of the believer continues to enjoy conscious fellowship with Christ until the time of the general resurrection at the last day.

39. See Quistorp, *Calvin's Doctrine of the Last Things*, ch. 2, 55–107, for a general discussion of Calvin's teaching regarding the soul.
40. *Institutes* 1.15.2 (OS 3:174).
41. *Institutes* 1.15.2 (OS 3:175). Calvin uses the language of the body as a prison house in his *Psychopannychia* (*Selected Works of John Calvin*, 3:443): "If the body is the prison of the soul, if the earthly habitation is a kind of fetters, what is the state of the soul when set free from this prison, when loosed from these fetters?"

Though there may be some unbiblical accents in Calvin's treatment of the distinction between the soul and the body, critics of Calvin's view need to put in proper perspective his understanding of the distinction and its implications for our understanding of the intermediate state. Calvin's distinction between the body and the soul is one that is expressly drawn in the Scriptures, and it is to the Scriptures that Calvin ultimately appeals in arguing for a conscious intermediate state. A principal part of Calvin's argument is that the doctrines of soul sleep and mortalism are in conflict with the scriptural assurances that even death cannot separate believers from Christ. Moreover, Calvin's disparaging use of the language of the body as a kind of prison house for the soul is mitigated by a number of clear themes in his theology. The whole of man's constitution in the state of integrity, soul and body, owes its existence to God's creative action. For Calvin, this is a basic assumption that undergirds the biblical hope for the resurrection of the body.

As we noted in our survey of chapter 25 of book 3, Calvin carefully distinguishes between sin and its consequences, which are accidental features of man's nature, and the original goodness of man's creatureliness, which will be restored, even surpassed, in the future state of glory. Calvin's eschatology includes a clear affirmation of the renewal and restoration of the fullness of the believer's creaturely constitution, body and soul. Therefore, it is incorrect to argue that Calvin's teaching regarding the intermediate state commits him to an individualistic eschatology that terminates upon the soul's communion with Christ, and largely overlooks the biblical themes of the resurrection of the body and the renewal of the created cosmos.[42]

Calvin's Emphasis on Meditation on the Future Life

While we are addressing the criticism that Calvin's eschatology tends to be individualistic and disparages the created order, it is necessary to consider also Calvin's emphasis on the eschatological nature of the

---

42. See Holwerda, "Eschatology and History," 116–22, who argues the same point, and appeals to an express statement of Calvin in his "Reply to Cardinal Sadolet's Letter" (*Selected Works of John Calvin*, 1:33–34). In this letter Calvin explicitly denies that he teaches that the Christian life consists only in the quest of the soul for salvation in heaven.

Christian life in union with Christ. One of the principal themes in Calvin's description of the Christian life is that it is characterized by a "meditation on the future life." In Calvin's understanding of the Christian life, which is set forth at length in book 3, chapters 6–10, of the *Institutes*, he describes the life of the Christian as an imitation of or conformity to Christ. Believers who are united to Christ by faith and the office of the Holy Spirit are summoned in conformity to Christ to deny themselves and bear their cross. In the context of his description of what such self-denial and cross-bearing entails, Calvin maintains that a principal feature of the Christian life is that it is governed by an eschatological hope for the life to come. As believers experience the tribulation and struggle that characterize life short of eschatological glory, they are moved forward and sustained by an eager anticipation of the life to come. In the course of his description of this feature of the Christian life, Calvin speaks of the cultivation of a "contempt for the present life" that is born of a contemplation of the future.[43]

In his study of Calvin's view of the believer's meditation on the future life, Martin Schultze has argued that Calvin's view amounts to a kind of monastic and otherworldly asceticism.[44] As the title of his study of Calvin's position suggests, Schultze ascribes a dominating place in Calvin's theology to this theme of an otherworldly contempt for the present life and a longing for the life to come. In this sense, Calvin's theology is thoroughly eschatological, but it reflects an eschatology that repudiates any substantial interest in the transformation of this life and its orders by the norms of the law of God.

There are several problems with Schultze's interpretation of Calvin's view of meditation on the future life. First, Schultze ascribes what he regards as Calvin's otherworldly asceticism to the influence of Erasmian humanism and the philosophy of Plato. The problem with this claim is that Calvin views meditation on the future life in distinctly christological terms, as an implication of what it means to live in conformity to Christ.[45]

43. *Institutes* 3.9.1 (OS 4:170).

44. Schultze, *Meditatio vitae futurae*: Quistorp, *Calvin's Doctrine of the Last Things*, 51–54, offers a cogent rebuttal of Schultze's interpretation.

45. Holwerda, "Eschatology and History," 118–19, notes that the phrase "contempt for the world" did not originate with Calvin, but is borrowed from the devotional literature of

Second, it must be observed that Calvin correlates what he means by "contempt for the world" with a related emphasis on the proper use of this life and its helps.[46] For Calvin, contempt for the world is only so far as the world has been negatively corrupted through human sinfulness and disobedience. It is certainly not contempt for the world as God created it, or as it is being renewed by the Spirit of Christ. For this reason, Calvin speaks of how the believer should receive all of God's good gifts in this life with gratitude, and use them in the service of God and others who bear his image.

And third, the interpretation of Schultze fails to discriminate between an eschatological orientation that is world-denying and one that is governed by the theme of union with Christ. It is particularly significant, as we noted in our summary of chapter 25, that Calvin parallels meditation on the future life with what he terms "meditation on the resurrection of Christ." The whole of the Christian life is dominated by the motif or theme of hope. This hope is not for the ultimate release of the Christian from worldly engagement or life in the body, but for the renewal of life, even the resurrection of the body, in the life to come.

Christology and Eschatology

A proper evaluation of Calvin's eschatology requires a consideration of certain features of his Christology. The prominence of the theme of hope in the Christian life in Calvin's theology stems from his understanding of Christ's person and work as the Mediator of creation and redemption. Because believers embrace Christ "clad in his own promises," they live in a constant state of expectation and anticipation.[47] There are two dimensions of Calvin's Christology that are of particular importance to the subject of eschatology. The first dimension is Calvin's understanding of Christ's mediatorial work in creation and redemption. The second dimension is Calvin's conception of the believer's union with Christ, a

---

his time, the classic example of which is Thomas à Kempis's *On the Imitation of Christ and Contempt for the World*. Whereas a Kempis's use of the phrase calls for withdrawal from worldly engagements, Calvin's use of it calls for seeking a new form of life in the world in union with Christ.

46. *Institutes* 3.10 (OS 4:177–81).

47. *Institutes* 2.9.3 (OS 3:401).

union that bestows a double benefit of free justification before God and sanctification or the restoration of the image of God. Each of these dimensions of Calvin's Christology has far-reaching implications for the doctrine of the last things.

Among more recent interpreters of Calvin's theology, reference is sometimes made to what is termed the "extra dimension" of Calvin's theology.[48] This language means to call attention to the way Calvin distinguishes between the work of Christ as Mediator of creation and as Mediator of redemption. Contrary to the trajectory of the neoorthodox interpretation of Calvin that governed Calvin studies in the early and middle twentieth century, more recent studies of Calvin's theology have noted the importance of Calvin's distinction between the knowledge of God as Creator and as Redeemer. The presupposition for Calvin's treatment of redemption in Christ is the biblical doctrine of the creation and ordering of all things by the Word and Spirit of God. According to Calvin, the knowledge of God as Redeemer can be understood only within the framework of the doctrine of creation. The eternal Son through whom all things were made is the One through whom all things are being redeemed. Redemption, accordingly, amounts to nothing less than the restoration of all things to proper order through the mediation of Christ and the work of his Spirit.

Because Christ is the Mediator of creation and redemption, Calvin views the first advent of Christ as a decisive moment in the realization of God's redemptive purposes. With Christ's coming, the promises of the old covenant are being fulfilled and the purpose of God to renew all things has commenced. In describing the significance of Christ's coming and his saving work, Calvin is fond of speaking of the comprehensive purpose of God as a restoration of all things to proper order. In his commentary on John 13:31, for example, Calvin offers a comprehensive statement of the purpose of Christ's advent and crucifixion:

> For in the cross of Christ, as in a splendid theatre, the incomparable goodness of God is set before the whole world. The glory of God shines,

48. See Heiko A. Oberman, "The 'Extra' Dimension in the Theology of Calvin," *Journal of Ecclesiastical History* 21 (1970): 43–64. By the "extra" dimension of Calvin's theology, Oberman means to refer to the "mutuality" and "discontinuity" (48) between the created order and redemption in the work and purposes of God.

indeed, in all creatures on high and below, but never more brightly than in the cross, in which there was a wonderful change of things—the condemnation of all men was manifested, sin blotted out, salvation restored to men; in short, the whole world was renewed and all things restored to order.[49]

Calvin uses similar language in his comments on John 12:31:

> The word *judgment* is taken as "reformation" by some and "condemnation" by others. I agree rather with the former, who expound it that the world must be restored to due order. For the Hebrew word *mishpat* which is translated as *judgment* means a well-ordered constitution. Now we know that outside Christ there is nothing but confusion in the world. And although Christ had already begun to set up the kingdom of God, it was His death that was the true beginning of a properly-ordered state and the complete restoration of the world.[50]

In these and similar statements, Calvin clearly views the work of Christ to issue in nothing less than the renovation of the whole creation, a reversal of the consequence of human sin and disobedience. In his threefold office as prophet, priest, and king, Christ reveals the fullness of the Word of God, reconciles a new humanity to God, and by means of the scepter of his kingdom, subdues all things to new obedience. Calvin's conception of the person and work of Christ, accordingly, represents a compelling eschatological vision in which the whole of the course of history is brought to its appointed end, the renewal or glorification of the fallen creation in service to the triune God.

When Calvin describes the believer's participation in the redemptive benefits of Christ's mediation, he especially calls attention to the double benefit of justification and sanctification by faith. Through fellowship with Christ, believers enjoy through faith an anticipation of the final verdict of free acceptance and favor with God. Justification in Calvin's conception is, therefore, a thoroughly eschatological benefit. By virtue of

49. Commentary on John 13:31, in *Calvin's New Testament Commentaries*, 5:68.
50. Commentary on John 12:31, in *Calvin's New Testament Commentaries*, 5:42. See also Commentary on 2 Thess. 1:5 (8:388–90) and on Isa. 65:25, in *Calvin's Commentaries* (Grand Rapids: Baker, 1979), 8:405–6.

461

Christ's atoning death and resurrection, believers who are united to him enjoy the gospel pronouncement of free acceptance with God, which is no less than the present declaration of what will be publicly confirmed at the last judgment. Furthermore, those who are joined to Christ by faith simultaneously enjoy the working of the Spirit of sanctification, whose work in renewal will restore the image of God and bring the believer to a future condition of full sanctity and glory. The goal of redemption is the full conformity of believers to Christ in indefectible holiness. This goal is not yet fulfilled, but its firstfruits are evident in the lives of all true believers who share in Christ's victory over the power of sin and death.

Biblical Prophecy, Millennial Questions, and the Signs of the Times

While Calvin does not address some of the familiar questions of eschatology in the brief compass of chapter 25, this should not mislead readers into concluding that he does not address these questions elsewhere, especially in his commentaries. Though there is always the danger of reading Calvin outside the context of his sixteenth-century setting, we will conclude our summary description of important aspects of his eschatology with a consideration of some of these familiar questions. In broad terms, we are interested here in Calvin's approach to the interpretation of biblical prophecy, the nature of the millennium and related questions, and the expectation of Christ's coming in association with what are known as the signs of the times.

We have already had occasion to comment on Calvin's interpretation of biblical prophecy when we commented on his not writing a commentary on the book of Revelation. This omission certainly cannot be taken to mean that Calvin shied away from or was unwilling to offer extensive exposition of scriptural prophecy that promises the coming of Christ or that foretells the course of the history of redemption leading up to its consummation in the new heaven and new earth. Since Calvin's commentaries or lectures treat most of the books of the Old and New Testaments, students who are interested in his interpretation of biblical prophecy in respect to questions of eschatology will find a rich body of material to mine.

A fine illustration of the pattern of Calvin's handling of biblical prophecy and apocalyptic can be seen in his commentary on the Old Testament book of Daniel. That Calvin wrote a commentary on this book belies the claim that he chose not to comment on the book of Revelation because of its presumed obscurity or difficulty of interpretation. Several features of Calvin's commentary on Daniel are especially noteworthy.

First, Calvin frequently criticizes exegetes, including Jewish commentators, who indulge in needless speculation or entertain curious questions that exceed the limits of a responsible interpretation of Daniel's prophecies.[51] When it comes to the interpretation of Daniel, it is especially important that the interpreter resist the attraction of fanciful and imaginative exegesis.

Second, the prophecies of Daniel regarding the future coming of God's kingdom are invariably associated by Calvin with the complex of events that occurred at the time of Christ's first advent. Calvin's basic hermeneutical commitment to a christological reading of the Scriptures is clearly evident throughout his exposition of the book.[52] God's purposes in history for the redemption of his people and the establishment of his kingdom all terminate upon the person and work of Christ.

And third, Calvin frequently argues that the future fulfilment of Daniel's prophecies will not be immediate or encompassed within the limits of the events that occurred within the context of Christ's first coming.[53] The perspective on the future unfolding of God's purposes in Christ, which is revealed by means of Daniel's prophecies, includes the entire period of history between the first and second advents of Christ. What begins at Christ's first coming is brought to completion only at his second coming. The fullness of the kingdom, which commenced at Christ's first coming, will be realized only through the administration of the gospel of the kingdom. The kingdom purposes of God, though already realized in some measure through the ministry of Christ and his church, will ultimately be fulfilled only at the last day.

---

51. See, e.g., Commentary on Dan. 2:44–46, in *Calvin's Commentaries*, 12:181–95.

52. Commentary on Dan. 2:44–45, in *Calvin's Commentaries*, 12:186–88.

53. Cf. Commentary on Matt. 24:1–34, in *Calvin's New Testament Commentaries*, 3:73–99. In his handling of this difficult passage, Calvin allows that the prophecy of Daniel concerning the temple's destruction in Jerusalem may be fulfilled on several occasions, and describes events that are "typical" of the entire period between Christ's first and second advents.

The pattern of interpretation that marks Calvin's comments on the book of Daniel is evident as well in the way he handles millennial questions. In our review of chapter 25, we noted that Calvin rejects chiliasm, or the teaching of a future one-thousand-year reign of Christ on the earth, as a childish fiction hardly requiring rebuttal.[54] In Calvin's eschatology, the idea of a future reign of Christ on the earth militates against some of the most fundamental features of his understanding of the kingdom of God and the realization of that kingdom in the course of redemptive history. The kingdom of God is not simply a future period, but a present reality that commenced with the first advent of Christ, which was itself a fulfilment of a long period of preparation under the administration of the old covenant. This kingdom, which not only spans the period between the first and second advents of Christ but also includes the glorious future of consummate blessedness, cannot be restricted in temporal duration to a period of one thousand years. Furthermore, this kingdom is a spiritual kingdom whose coming and ultimate realization will transpire through the proclamation of the gospel of Christ and the work of the Holy Spirit.[55]

Though Calvin does not identify the kingdom exclusively with the church, he insists that the church is the principal instrument that Christ uses to effect God's purposes for redemption. Since the ultimate achievement of God's redemptive purposes entails no less than the renewal and renovation of the whole created order, Calvin regards chiliasm in all of its forms to be subeschatological. Such a one-thousand-year reign of Christ would represent a kind of interregnum in the course of history that fails

54. See Commentary on Dan. 7:27, in *Calvin's Commentaries*, 13:225–31, for a similar assessment. In his rejection of chiliasm, Calvin regards it as a peculiar Jewish heresy. This opinion was generally shared by the other Reformers, including Heinrich Bullinger. See the Second Helvetic Confession, ch. 11, section 14: "We further condemn Jewish dreams that there will be a golden age on earth before the Day of Judgment, and that the pious, having subdued all their godless enemies, will possess all the kingdoms of the earth." Calvin's opposition to chiliasm places him in a long tradition of interpretation of Revelation, which was represented among the church fathers by Tyconius and Augustine. For a treatment of the influence of Augustine and Tyconius on Calvin's interpretation of Revelation 20, see Davis, "A New Assessment of John Calvin's Eschatology," 28–57.

55. See, e.g., Commentary on Rom. 14:11, in *Calvin's New Testament Commentaries*, 8:295–96; on 1 Cor. 4:20, in *Calvin's New Testament Commentaries*, 9:1–2; and on Isa. 11:4, in *Calvin's Commentaries*, 7:379–82.

to acknowledge the reality of Christ's present kingship or the perfected glory of the future consummation of the kingdom.

Calvin's approach to the interpretation of biblical prophecy and the nature of the coming of God's kingdom in Christ is illustrated by his treatment of biblical passages that speak of the signs of the times that will precede Christ's second coming. In his handling of these passages, Calvin consistently rejects the propriety of seeking to ascertain the date or proximate time of Christ's return. In his extensive comments on Matthew 24, which describes the events that will occur in conjunction with the destruction of the temple and Jerusalem and prior to Christ's coming, Calvin follows the pattern that we identified in his interpretation of the biblical prophecy of Daniel. According to Calvin, Christ's words in this passage describe not only events that coincide with his first coming, including the destruction of the temple, but also the entire period of fulfilment from the time of his first coming until the end of the present age. The interpretation of Christ's words in this passage must acknowledge that prophecies are often fulfilled at earlier and later points in the course of redemptive history.

An especially important passage for understanding Calvin's interpretation of Christ's coming and the events that will precede it is 2 Thessalonians 2.[56] In his exposition of this passage, which speaks of a future period of apostasy and lawlessness as well as the appearance of the man of lawlessness, Calvin places it in the broad context of his conception of the conflict in history between the kingdom of Christ and the kingdom of the antichrist. Though he refuses to use this passage as a basis for determining a timetable regarding future events, Calvin regards its depiction of such apostasy and the emergence of the antichrist as a description of a falling away that will occur among the people of God, the church, prior to the return of Christ at the end of the age.

Unlike many of his medieval predecessors, he does not identify "that which restrains" such apostasy in the present with the Roman Empire. Rather, Calvin identifies the present restraint on apostasy and lawlessness with the work of Christ through the preaching of his Word in the power

56. Commentary on 2 Thess. 2:1–12, in *Calvin's New Testament Commentaries*, 8:396–408. The following paragraph is a brief summary of Calvin's interpretation of this passage.

of the Holy Spirit. One feature of his interpretation of this passage is well known and of particular significance, namely, his identification of the man of lawlessness with the papacy.[57] According to Calvin, this mysterious figure represents the spirit of opposition to Christ's kingdom and gospel that has come to expression in the papacy. Although Calvin shared this view with many of his Reformation contemporaries, he stopped short of identifying this mysterious figure with any particular pope or using it to ascertain whether the return of Christ was imminent at the time of the Reformation. Even the language in this passage regarding Christ's return may not be restricted to his second advent, since "Paul does not think that Christ will accomplish this in a moment."

Conclusion

With this cursory sketch of some aspects of Calvin's eschatological viewpoint, we must draw our summary to a close. The purpose of our treatment of these various features of Calvin's eschatology was not to provide anything like a complete statement of his view. Students of Calvin's eschatology are obliged to read all of his substantial corpus of writings—his commentaries, treatises, and lectures as well as his *Institutes*—to obtain an accurate portrait of the comprehensiveness of his eschatological reflections. Those who take the trouble to read extensively in his writings will discover that Calvin treats virtually all of the topics traditionally associated with the doctrine of the last things. They will also discover, as we have attempted to demonstrate in a limited way, that it is not accurate to represent Calvin as a theologian for whom eschatology was a relatively minor or peripheral interest. Calvin's theology exhibits a strongly eschatological cast, and articulates a comprehensive perspective on the work of God in creation and in redemption, culminating in the restoration of all things to proper order through the mediation of Jesus Christ.

There are two broad motifs in Calvin's eschatology that require special emphasis, and that are of abiding importance to Christian theology. The first is his hermeneutically restrained interpretation of biblical prophecy and teaching regarding the last things. In an area of Christian theology

57. Commentary on 2 Thess. 2:3, in *Calvin's New Testament Commentaries*, 3:399.

that has always tempted interpreters to adopt fanciful and speculative views, Calvin represents a model of restraint in his biblical and theological exposition on eschatological topics. The second is Calvin's focus on the person and work of Christ in his redemptive mediation as the central theme of all Christian and biblical theology. All of redemptive history prior to Christ's first advent is viewed as a kind of "preparation for Christ" (*preparatio Christi*). With the coming of Christ in the fullness of time, the promise of future redemption and consummate blessedness in the kingdom of God has commenced its fulfilment. Believers in union with Christ live, therefore, in hope and expectation that the blessings of salvation that are now enjoyed will be theirs in indefectible fullness in the future of Christ at the last day. The same triune God who first created all things and declared them to be good, will certainly realize all of his saving purposes in Christ, when the whole of the created order is renewed, and every accidental feature of human sin and rebellion is eradicated. For Calvin, who enjoys properly the reputation of being a theologian of God's sovereignty, all things are of, from, and *unto* God's glory.

20

ESSENTIAL CALVIN BIBLIOGRAPHY

RICHARD C. GAMBLE AND
ZACHARY JOHN KAIL

For the last quarter century there has been heightened interest in Calvin. That interest within the academic community can be quantified by the breadth and depth of presentations that are made at the International Calvin Congress—which meets at different places in the world every four years.[1]

With heightened interest has come a commensurate flood of annual publications. The literature on Calvin is enormous! Each year the *Calvin Theological Journal* produces a bibliographic article on publications touching on Calvin and Calvinism, organized under a list of topics. This invaluable resource is available both in print and on line.

---

1. Usually there is a volume published from the papers presented at those meetings. One of those papers concerns this chapter's topic. See Richard C. Gamble, "Current Trends in Calvin Research, 1982–90," *Calvinus Sacrae Scripturae Professor*, ed. W. Neuser (Grand Rapids: Eerdmans, 1994), 91–112. The same author has provided a summary of important articles organized by topics: *Articles on Calvin and Calvinism*, 14 vols. (New York and London: Garland, 1992).

The *Calvin Theological Journal* summary is over twenty pages long; thus, our "Essential Calvin Bibliography" has to take a different approach. It will be rather narrow in focus, underlining literature that is found in English and generally published within the last five to ten years. Also, it will focus on books and articles that are more readily available to Western readers. Practically speaking, that means that a host of excellent English-language literature produced in South Africa and Asia will be omitted.

Primary texts are the most important means to Calvin's thought. The best way to understand Calvin is to read Calvin! Since Calvin wrote in Latin and French, primary texts will not be limited to English. From a presentation of recent primary publications, we will move to relevant bibliography organized by topic.

Primary Texts

Battles, Ford Lewis, and John R. Walchenbach. *Analysis of the Institutes of the Christian Religion of John Calvin.* Phillipsburg, P&R, 2001.

Calvin, John *Calvini Opera Database 1.0.* Edited by Herman J. Selderhuis et al. Apeldoorn: Instituut voor Reformatieonderzoek, 2005. DVD Database.

———. *Calvin's Commentary on Seneca's* De Clementia. Edited and translated by F. L. Battles and André Hugo. Leiden: Brill, 1969.

———. *Calvin's Institutes 1536.* Edited and translated by F. L. Battles. Grand Rapids: Eerdmans.

———. *Calvin's Institutes.* Abridged Edition. Edited by Donald K. McKim. Louisville: Westminster/John Knox, 2001.

———. *Calvin's Institutes of the Christian Religion.* Edited by Mark DeVries. Shepherd's Notes—Christian Classics. Nashville: Broadman & Holman, 1998.

———. "Calvin to All Ministers of Christ in the Churches of Saxony and Lower Germany (1556)." In *Documents from the History of Lutheranism, 1517–1750,* edited by Eric Lund, 210–12. Minneapolis: Fortress, 2002.

———. *Come Out from Among Them: "Anti-Nicodemite" Writings of John Calvin.* Translated by Seth Skolnitsky. Dallas: Protestant Heritage Press, 2001.

———. *Commentariorum in Acta Apostolorum Liber Posterior.* Edited by Helmut Feld. *Ioannis Calvini Opera Omnia.* Series II. Vol. XII/2. *Opera Exegetica Veteris et Novi Testamenti.* Geneva: Droz, 2001.

———. *Commentariorum in Acta Apostolorum Liber Primus.* Edited by Helmut Feld. *Ioannis Calvini Opera Omnia,* Series II. Vol. XII/1. Geneva: Droz, 2001.

———. *The Complete Recueil des opuscules of John Calvin* [CD-ROM]. Geneva: Droz, 2003.

———. *Contre les Libertins Spirituelz; Epistre contre un Cordelier; Response à un Certain Holandois.* Edited by Mirjam G. K. van Veen. Vol. 1, *Ioannis Calvini Scripta Didactica et Polemica.* Series 4 of *Ioannis Calvini Opera Omnia.* Geneva: Droz, 2005.

———. "Correction to Impose Silence on a Certain Scoundrel Named Antoine Cathelan, Former Gray Friar of Albigeois." Translated by Rob Roy McGregor. *Calvin Theological Journal* 35.1 (2000): 66–75.

———. *Epistolae—1530–Sep. 1538.* Edited by Frans Pieter Van Stam and Cornelius Augustijn. Vol. 1 of *Epistolae.* Series 6 of *Ioannis Calvini Opera Omnia.* Geneva: Droz, 2005.

———. *La Famine spirituelle: Sermon inédit sur Esaïe 55, 1–2.* Eglise Française de Londres, Ms. VIII. F. 2. Edited by Max Engammare et al. Geneva: Droz, 2000.

———. *La Famine spirituelle: Sermon inédit sur Esaïe 55.* Sermon on Isaiah 55:1–2. Edited by Max Engammare. Geneva: Droz, 2000.

———. "From *Institutes of Christian Religion,* Book 1, Chaps. 1–6, 10." In *Christianity and Plurality: Classic and Contemporary Readings,* edited by Richard J. Plantinga, 137–62. Oxford: Blackwell, 1999.

———. *Heart Aflame: Daily Readings from Calvin on the Psalms.* Edited by Sinclair B. Ferguson. Philadelphia: P&R, 1999.

———. "Human Nature and Free Will." In *The Renaissance,* edited by Raymond Obstfeld. San Diego: Greenhaven, 2002.

———. *Ioannis Calvini Opera Omnia II.* Edited by T. H. L. Parker. *Opera Exegetica Veteris et Novi Testamenti.* Geneva: Droz, 1999.

———. "John Calvin (1509–64)." In *From Irenaeus to Grotius: A Sourcebook in Christian Political Thought, 100–1625,* edited by Oliver O'Donovan et al., 662–84. Grand Rapids: Eerdmans, 1999.

———. "John Calvin: *Institutes of the Christian Religion* 3.7.1, 2 & 5; 3.10.2, 5 & 6; 3.24.8, 9." In *Callings: Twenty Centuries of Christian Wisdom on Vocation*, edited by William C. Placher, 232–39. Grand Rapids: Eerdmans, 2005.

———. "Response to a Certain Dutchman Who under the Guise of Making Christians Very Spiritual Permits Them to Defile Their Bodies in All Idolatries: Written by Mr. John Calvin to the Faithful in the Low Countries." Translated by Rob Roy McGregor. *Calvin Theological Journal* 34.2 (1999): 291–326.

———. "The Sensus Divinitatis." *Institutes of the Christian Religion 1.111.1–3. Faith and Reason*, edited by Paul Helm, 143–45. Oxford: Oxford University Press, 1999.

———. *Sermons on Melchizedek & Abraham: Justification, Faith & Obedience*. Willow Street, PA: Old Paths, 2000.

———. *Sermons on the Book of Micah*. Translated by Benjamin Wirt Farley. Phillipsburg: P&R, 2003.

———. *Steward of God's Covenant: Selected Writings*. Edited by John F. Thornton and Susan B. Varenne. New York: Vintage, 2006.

———. *Supplementa Calviniana; Sermons inédits*. Part I: *Sermons sur la Genèse chapitres 1, 1–11, 4*; Part II: *Sermons sur la Genése chapitres 11, 5–20, 7*. Edited by Max Engammare. Neukirchen: Neukirchener, 2000.

———. "'The Testimony of the Holy Spirit.' *Institutes of the Christian Religion 1:7*." In *Faith and Reason*, edited by Paul Helm, 146–48. Oxford: Oxford University Press, 1999.

———. *Tracts Containing the Antidote to the Council of Trent*. Vol. 3. Translated by Henry Beveridge. Eugene, OR: Wipf and Stock, 2002.

———. *Tracts Containing Treatises on the Sacraments, Catechism of the Church of Geneva, Forms of Prayer, and Confessions of Faith*. Vol. 2. Translated by Henry Beveridge. Eugene, OR: Wipf and Stock, 2002.

———. *Tracts Relating to the Reformation*. Vol. 1. Translated by Henry Beveridge. Eugene, OR: Wipf and Stock, 2002.

———. *Treatises on the Sacraments: Catechism of the Church of Geneva, Forms of Prayer, and Confessions of Faith*. Translated by Henry Beveridge. Fearn, Scotland: Christian Heritage, 2002.

———. *The Word and Prayer: Classic Devotions from the Minor Prophets.* Edited by Charles E. Edwards. Birmingham: Solid Ground Christian Books, 2005.

———, and Jacob Sadoleto. *A Reformation Debate.* Edited by John C. Olin. Grand Rapids: Baker, 2000.

McKee, Elsie Anne. "Excerpts from 'The Necessity of Reforming the Church.'" In *A Journey through Christian Theology.* With Texts from the First to the Twenty-First Century, edited by William P. Anderson, 114–22. Minneapolis: Fortress, 2000.

———. ed. *John Calvin: Writings on Pastoral Piety.* New York: Paulist, 2001.

White, Robert. "Calvin and the Nicodemite Controversy: An Overlooked Text of 1541." *Calvin Theological Journal* 35 (2000): 282–96.

Calvin's Biography

Augustijn, Cornelis, et al. "Calvin in the Light of the Early Letters." In *Calvinus Praeceptor Ecclesiae*, edited by Herman J. Selderhuis, 139–58. Geneva: Droz, 2004.

Beza, Theodore. *The Life of John Calvin.* Durham: Evangelical, 1997.

Ganoczy, Alexandre. "Calvin's Life and Context." In *The Cambridge Companion to John Calvin*, edited by Donald K. McKim, 3–24. Cambridge: Cambridge University Press, 2004.

Kingdon, Robert M. "Calvin, John (1509–1564)." In *Encyclopedia of Protestantism*, edited by Hans J. Hillerbrand, 328–31. New York: Routledge, 2003.

———. "Calvin's Last Years." In *Calvinus Praeceptor Ecclesiae*, edited by Herman J. Selderhuis, 179–88. Geneva: Droz, 2004.

Lindner, William. *John Calvin.* Minneapolis: Bethany, 1998.

Naphy, William G. "Calvin and Geneva." In *The Reformation World*, edited by Andrew Pettegree, 309–22. New York: Routledge, 2000.

Piper, John. "The Divine Majesty of the Word. John Calvin: The Man and His Preaching." In *The Legacy of Sovereign Joy: God's Triumphant Grace in the Lives of Augustine, Luther, and Calvin*, 114–48. Wheaton: Crossway, 2000.

Puckett, David Lee. "Calvin, John (1509–1564)." In *Historical Handbook of Major Biblical Interpreters*, edited by Donald K. McKim, 171–79. Downers Grove, IL: InterVarsity, 1998.

Reymond, Robert L. *John Calvin: His Life and Influence*. Christian Focus, 2004.

Wilkinson, John. "The Medical History of John Calvin." In *The Medical History of the Reformers: Martin Luther, John Calvin, John Knox*, edited by John Wilkinson, 51–84. Edinburgh: Handsel, 2001.

Calvin's Cultural Context—Social and Intellectual History

Douglass, E. Jane Dempsey. "Calvin in Ecumenical Context." In *The Cambridge Companion to John Calvin*, edited by Donald K. McKim, 305–16. Cambridge: Cambridge University Press, 2004.

Gamble, Richard C. "Calvin's Controversies." In *The Cambridge Companion to John Calvin*, edited by Donald K. McKim, 188–203. Cambridge: Cambridge University Press, 2004.

Ganoczy, Alexandre. "Calvin, Jean: Theologian and Reformer." In *Dictionary of the Reformation*, edited by Klaus Ganzer and Bruno Steimer, 44–48. New York: Crossroad, 2004.

Gilmont, Jean François. *John Calvin and the Printed Book*. Translated by Karin Maag. Kirksville, MO: Truman State University Press, 2005.

Hochuli Dubuis, Paule, ed. *Registres du Conseil de Genève à l'époque de Calvin*. Geneva: Droz, 2003.

Kingdon, Robert M. "Confessionalism in Calvin's Geneva." *Archive for Reformation History* 96 (2005): 109–16.

———. "The Protestant Reformation as a Revolution: The Case of Geneva." *Journal of the Historical Society* 1.2–3 (2000): 101–8.

———. "Worship in Geneva before and after the Reformation." In *Worship in Medieval and Early Modern Europe: Change and Continuity in Religious Practice*, edited by Karin Maag and John D. Witvliet, 41–60. Notre Dame: University of Notre Dame Press, 2004.

Kingdon, Robert M., et al. *Registres du Consistoire de Genève au temps de Calvin*. Vol. 2. Geneva: Droz, 2001.

———. eds. *Registers of the Consistory of Geneva in the Time of Calvin.* Vol. 1: *1542–1544.* Grand Rapids: Eerdmans, 2000.

Lambert, Thomas A., et al., eds. *Registres du Consistoire de Genève au temps de Calvin.* Geneva: Droz, 2004.

Maag, Karin. "Calvin in Context: Current Resources." In *The Cambridge Companion to John Calvin,* edited by Donald K. McKim, 317–29. Cambridge: Cambridge University Press, 2004.

Naphy, William G. *Calvin and the Consolidation of the Genevan Reformation.* Louisville: Westminster/John Knox, 2003.

———. "Calvin's Geneva." In *The Cambridge Companion to John Calvin,* edited by Donald K. McKim, 25–37. Cambridge: Cambridge University Press, 2004.

Nijenhuis, Willem N. "The Limits of Civil Disobedience in Calvin's Latest Known Sermons: The Development of His Ideas of the Right of Civil Resistance." In *The Reformation: Critical Concepts in Historical Studies* 3, edited by Andrew Pettegree, 71–91. London: Routledge, 2004.

Puckett, David Lee. "Calvin, Jean (1509–1564)." In *Historical Handbook of Major Biblical Interpreters,* edited by Donald K. McKim, 171–79. Downers Grove, IL: InterVarsity, 1998.

Watt, Jeffrey R. "Childhood and Youth in the Geneva Consistory Minutes." In *Calvinus Praeceptor Ecclesiae,* edited by Herman J. Selderhuis, 43–64. Geneva: Droz, 2004.

Wright, David F. "Calvin's Role in Church History." In *The Cambridge Companion to John Calvin,* edited by Donald K. McKim, 277–88. Cambridge: Cambridge University Press, 2004.

Calvin's Theology

Balserak, John. "The God of Love and Weakness: Calvin's Understanding of God's Accommodating Relationship with His People." *Westminster Theological Journal* 62.2 (2000): 177–95.

Carpenter, Craig B. "A Question of Union with Christ? Calvin and Trent on Justification." *Westminster Theological Journal* 64.2 (2002): 363–86.

Greenbury, James. "Calvin's Understanding of Predestination with Special Reference to the *Institutes.*" *Reformed Theological Review* 54.3 (1995): 121–34.

Griffith, Howard. "The First Title of the Spirit: Adoption in Calvin's Soteriology." *Evangelical Quarterly* 73.2 (2001): 135–53.

Helm, Paul. "John Calvin on 'Before All Ages.'" *Tyndale Bulletin* 53.1 (2002): 143–48.

———. *John Calvin's Ideas*. Oxford: Oxford University Press, 2004.

Hesselink, I. John. "Calvin, Theologian of Sweetness." *Calvin Theological Journal* 37.2 (2002): 318–32.

———. "Calvin's Theology." In *The Cambridge Companion to John Calvin*, edited by Donald K. McKim, 74–92. Cambridge: Cambridge University Press, 2004.

Kroon, Marijn de. *The Honour of God and Human Salvation: A Contribution to an Understanding of Calvin's Theology according to His Institutes*. New York: T. & T. Clark, 2001.

Lane, A. N. S. (Anthony). "Calvin and Article 5 of the Regensburg Colloquy." In *Calvinus Praeceptor Ecclesiae*, edited by Herman J. Selderhuis, 233–64. Geneva: Droz, 2004.

———. "Traditional Protestant Doctrine: John Calvin." In *Justification by Faith in Catholic-Protestant Dialogue*, edited by A. N. S. Lane, 17–43. London: T & T Clark, 2002.

Lillback, Peter A. *The Binding of God: Calvin's Role in the Development of Covenant Theology*. Texts and Studies in Reformation and Post-Reformation Thought. Edited by Richard A. Muller. Grand Rapids: Baker, 2001.

———. "The Early Reformed Covenant Paradigm: Vermigli in the Context of Bullinger, Luther and Calvin." In *Peter Martyr Vermigli and the European Reformations*, edited by Frank A. James III, 70–96. Leiden: Brill, 2004.

Muller, Richard A. "The Starting Point of Calvin's Theology: An Essay-Review." *Calvin Theological Journal* 36.2 (2001): 314–41.

Olson, Roger E. "Zwingli & Calvin Organize Protestant Thought." In *The Story of Christian Theology: Twenty Centuries of Tradition & Reform*, 397–413, 630. Downers Grove, IL: InterVarsity, 1999.

Pitkin, Barbara. *What Pure Eyes Could See: Calvin's Doctrine of Faith in Its Exegetical Context.* Oxford Studies in Historical Theology, series editor David C. Steinmetz. New York: Oxford University Press, 1999.

Steinmetz, David C. "The Theology of John Calvin." In *The Cambridge Companion to Reformation Theology*, edited by David C. Steinmetz and David Bagchi, 113–29. Cambridge: Cambridge University Press, 2004.

Analysis and Critique

Battles, Ford Lewis, and John R. Walchenbach. *Analysis of the Institutes of the Christian Religion of John Calvin.* Phillipsburg, NJ: P&R, 2001.

Currid, John D. "Calvin as Hebraist: Guarding the Sacred Deposit." *Reformed Theological Review* 63.2 (2004): 61–71.

De Boer, E. A. *John Calvin on the Visions of Ezekiel: Historical and Hermeneutical Studies in John Calvin's "Sermons Inédits," Especially on Ezekiel 36–48.* Leiden: Brill, 2004.

Edmondson, Stephen. "The Biblical Historical Structure of Calvin's *Institutes*." *Scottish Journal of Theology* 59.1 (2006): 1–13.

Greef, Wulfert de. "Calvin's Writings." In *The Cambridge Companion to John Calvin*, edited by Donald K. McKim, 41–57. Cambridge: Cambridge University Press, 2004.

Thomas, Derek W. H. *Proclaiming the Incomprehensible God: Calvin's Teaching on Job.* Ross-shire, Scotland: Mentor, 2004.

Zachman, Randall C. "What Kind of Book Is Calvin's 'Institutes'?" *Calvin Theological Journal* 35.2 (2000): 238–61.

Piety, Worship, and Ecclesiology

Beeke, Joel R. "Calvin on Piety." In *The Cambridge Companion to John Calvin*, edited by Donald K. McKim, 125–52. Cambridge: Cambridge University Press, 2004.

———. "Overcoming the World through Piety: Calvin's Answer for Worldliness." In *Overcoming the World: Grace to Win the Daily Battle*, 39–74. Phillipsburg, NJ: P&R, 2005.

de Boer, Erik A. "Calvin and Colleagues: Propositions and Disputations in the Context of the Congrégations in Geneva." In *Calvinus Praeceptor Ecclesiae*, edited by Herman J. Selderhuis, 331–42. Geneva: Droz, 2004.

DeVries, Dawn. "Calvin's Preaching." In *The Cambridge Companion to John Calvin*, edited by Donald K. McKim, 106–24. Cambridge: Cambridge University Press, 2004.

Gaffin, Richard B. *Calvin and the Sabbath*. Fearn, Ross-shire: Mentor, 1998.

Gamble, Richard C. "Sacramental Continuity among Reformed Refugees: Peter Martyr Vermigli and John Calvin." In *Peter Martyr Vermigli and the European Reformations*, edited by Frank A. James III, 97–112. Leiden: Brill, 2004.

Holder, R. Ward. "Ecclesia, Legenda atque Intelligenda Scriptura: The Church as Discerning Community in Calvin's Hermeneutic." *Calvin Theological Journal* 36.2 (2001): 270–89.

Kim, Jae Sung. "Prayer in Calvin's Soteriology." In *Calvinus Praeceptor Ecclesiae*, edited by Herman J. Selderhuis, 265–74. Geneva: Droz, 2004.

Kingdon, Robert M. "Catechesis in Calvin's Geneva." In *Educating People of Faith*, edited by John Van Engen, 294–313. Grand Rapids: Eerdmans, 2004.

———. "The Genevan Revolution in Public Worship." In *The Long Reformation*, edited by Jeffrey R. Watt, 106–15. Boston: Houghton Mifflin, 2006.

———. "The Genevan Revolution in Public Worship." *Princeton Seminary Bulletin* 20.3 (1999): 264–80.

Lane, Anthony N. S. *John Calvin: Student of the Church Fathers*. Grand Rapids: Baker, 1999.

Mathison, Keith A. *Given for You: Reclaiming Calvin's Doctrine of the Lord's Supper*. Phillipsburg, NJ: P&R, 2002.

McKee, Elsie Anne. "Calvin and His Colleagues as Pastors: Some New Insights into the Collegial Ministry of Word and Sacraments." In *Calvinus Praeceptor Ecclesiae*, edited by Herman J. Selderhuis, 9–42. Geneva: Droz, 2004.

Old, Hughes Oliphant. "Calvin's Theology of Worship." In *Give Praise to God: A Vision for Reforming Worship*, edited by Philip Graham Ryken, et al., 412–35. Phillipsburg, NJ: P&R, 2003.

——. "The Reformation: John Calvin (1509–1564)." In *The Reading and Preaching of the Scriptures in the Worship of the Christian Church*, 90–133. Grand Rapids: Eerdmans, 2002.

Ward, Peter. "Coming to Sermon: The Practice of Doctrine in the Preaching of John Calvin." *Scottish Journal of Theology* 58.3 (2005): 319–32.

Calvin's Exegesis and Hermeneutics

Holder, R. Ward. *John Calvin and the Grounding of Interpretation: Calvin's First Commentaries*. Leiden: Brill, 2006.

Leahy, Frederick S. "Calvin and the Inerrancy of Scripture." *Reformed Theological Journal* 17 (2001): 44–56.

Manetsch, Scott. "Historical and Theological Studies. Problems with the Patriarchs: John Calvin's Interpretation of Difficult Passages in Genesis." *Westminster Theological Journal* 67.1 (2005): 1–21.

Paddison, Angus. "John Calvin and I Thessalonians." In *Theological Hermeneutics and 1 Thessalonians*, 100–35. Cambridge: Cambridge University Press, 2005.

Selderhuis, Herman. "Calvin's Theology of the Psalms." In *Calvin Studies IX: Papers Presented at the Ninth Colloquium on Calvin Studies*, edited by John H. Leith, 1–15. Decatur, GA: Columbia Theological Seminary, 2000.

Zachman, Randall C. "Expounding Scripture and Applying It to Our Use: Calvin's Sermons on Ephesians." *Scottish Journal of Theology* 56.4 (2003): 481–507.

Calvin and Social, Ethical, and Political Issues

Biéler, André. *Calvin's Economic and Social Thought*. Translated by James Greig. Geneva: World Alliance of Reformed Churches, WCC, 2005.

Haas, Guenther H. "Calvin's Ethics." In *The Cambridge Companion to John Calvin*, edited by Donald K. McKim, 93–105. Cambridge: Cambridge University Press, 2004.

Naphy, William. "Sodomy in Early Modern Geneva: Various Definitions, Diverse Verdicts." In *Sodomy in Early Modern Europe*, edited by Tom Betteridge, 94–111. Manchester: Manchester University Press, 2002.

Olson, Jeannine E. "Calvin and Social-ethical Issues." In *The Cambridge Companion to John Calvin*, edited by Donald K. McKim, 153–72. Cambridge: Cambridge University Press, 2004.

Parsons, Michael. *Reformation Marriage: The Husband and Wife Relationship in the Theology of Luther and Calvin*. Edited by David Wright and Donald Macleod. Edinburgh: Rutherford House, 2005.

Spierling, Karen E. "Making Use of God's Remedies: Negotiating the Material Care of Children in Reformation Geneva." *Sixteenth Century Journal* 36.3 (2005): 785–807.

Stevenson, William R., Jr. "Calvin and Political Issues." In *The Cambridge Companion to John Calvin*, edited by Donald K. McKim, 173–87. Cambridge: Cambridge University Press, 2004.

VanDrunen, David. "The Two Kingdoms: A Reassessment of the Transformationist Calvin." *Calvin Theological Journal* 40.2 (2005): 248–66.

Watt, Jeffrey R. "Calvinism, Childhood, and Education: The Evidence from the Genevan Consistory." *Sixteenth Century Journal* 33.2 (2002): 439–56.

Witte, John, Jr., and Robert M. Kingdon. *Sex, Marriage, and Family in John Calvin's Geneva*. Vol. 1. *Courtship, Engagement, and Marriage*. Grand Rapids: Eerdmans, 2005.

Wykes, Michael. "Devaluing the Scholastics: Calvin's Ethics of Usury." *Calvin Theological Journal* 38.1 (2003): 27–51.

479

Index of Scripture

482

John—30
1–10—125n10, 149
1:1—73, 89
1:3—89
1:4—29
1:5—29
1:17—196
1:29—242
2:11—282n39, 282n40
3:13—214n43, 217
3:16—241
3:33—278n26
4:22—278n27
4:24—68
5:17—140
6—377
6:29—343
6:55—373
7:37–39—293n
8:14—51n5
8:19—276n21
8:58—216
11–21—207
12:31—461, 461n50
12:41—80, 86
12:45—276n21
13:9—287n50
13:31—460
14:3—238
15:13—207
16:12—401
17:3—66, 89
17:26—358
18:36—417
19:30—204n136
20:3—282
21:18—331

Acts
1:9—237
2—234

2:4—293n
2:23—147
2:24—234
2:29—280n34
3:8—293n
3:25—104
4:12—240
4:19–20—431
4:28—147
5:32—293n
6—396
7:14–16—62
7:53—131
11:23—292n67
12:15—132
13:48—293n
15—410
15:9—275n15, 276n22
16:14—293n
17—38
17:16–34—26
17:28—24, 137, 140
17:34—130
20:21—299n91
20:28—216, 216n54
23:11—293n
24:16—346
28:23—187n100

Romans—19, 40, 95, 102–3, 116, 118, 121, 444
1—21, 31, 162, 165
1:18—24n22, 25–26, 31
1:18–20—23
1:18–21—27–28
1:18–23—28
1:18–25—23
1:19—24n22, 25
1:19–21a—25
1:20—32
1:21—28

1:21–25—31
1:21b–23—25
1:22—31
1:25—35
2—162
2:6—342
2:13—341
2:25—106
2:28—106
2:29—196n122
3:4—62
4:25—236
5—157
5:3–4—330
5:17—210
5:19—241, 264
6:6—298, 299n88
7:14–25—286, 296
8:3–4—264
8:15–17—293n
8:16—279n31, 281n35, 293n
8:21—453n33
8:34—225, 238, 281n35
9—98, 103, 107, 111, 119
9:6—106
9:10—62
9:11—106
9:12—107
9:13—121
9:20–21—114
9:21—339
9:32—312
10:4—309
10:4ff.—196
10:8—312
11:12—62
11:36—66
12:1–2—325
13—432
14—345
14:1—62

14:11—464n55
15:8—189n108

1 Corinthians
1:8—342
1:30—240, 322
2:10–13—293n
2:12—280n34
2:16—70n23
3:2—345
4:20—464n55
6:15—274n13
7:29–31—335
8–10—345
10:11—187n102
11:2—406
11:29—380
12:11—81, 87
13—327, 343
15:52—239

2 Corinthians
3—195–97
3:6—195n119, 196n122
3:6–9—196, 196n123
3:6–11—194
4:4—135
5:19—243n17
5:21—231, 241, 263
7:10—299n92
12:2—131
12:4—131
12:8—363, 365
13:5—281n36

Galatians
2:20—226, 326
3:2—293n
3:13—240, 242
3:19—131
3:27—259

4:1—186n98
4:4—215
4:5—323
4:6—293n
4:8—369
4:28—104

Ephesians—116, 121–22
1:1–3—117
1:3–4—117
1:4–5—229
1:13–14—293n
2:3—241
4:8—62
4:10—237
4:13—290n63
4:30—293n
5:2—227n2
5:30—273
5:32—275n16
6:18—354n17
6:18–19—354

Philippians
2:12–13—316
2:16—196n122
3:12–13—285

Colossians
1:16—133
1:20—133
1:22—342
2:9—214n43
2:11—297n79
2:14–15—232

1 Thessalonians
4:16—131
4:16–17—239
5:17—364

2 Thessalonians
1:5—343, 461n50
2—465
2:1–12—465n
2:3—466n
2:9–10—135

1 Timothy
2:2—432n42
4:12–13—190n109
5:21—131
6:16—333

2 Timothy
3:15–16—310
3:16—59, 62

Hebrews—388
1:1–2—221
1:2—180
1:3—74, 77, 140, 238n12
1:4—131
2:5—131, 180
2:12—358n26
2:16—131, 215
2:17—240
3:1—220n72, 339
4:10—279n31
4:12—195n119
4:15—215, 235
5—225
5:2—240
5:7—234
5:9—180
6:13—51, 51n5
6:17—181n51
7:25—225, 238
8—195, 198–99
8:10—181n51, 181n57, 195n119, 199n124
9:11–12—225, 238

9:16–17—204n136
11:3—161
11:21—62

James
1:25—195n119
2:10–11—343
2:24—340, 340n37
5—388
5:16—353
5:17—351

1 Peter
1:3—236
1:4—279n31
1:20—290n62
2:5—339
2:9—181n51
2:24—242
3:12—353
3:19—233
3:21—373
4:1—299n89

2 Peter
1:4—217

1:10—323
1:20—59

1 John
1:1—180
2:1—238n13
2:2—246n34
3:2—287n51
3:16—216
4:10—243n17
5:3—195n119
5:4—285
5:13—282n40

Jude
5—181n51
9—131

**Revelation—454–55,
  462–63**
1:6—224
5:11—131
19:10—133
20—448, 464n54
22:8–9—133

Index of Subjects and Names

490

semi-Pelagians, 91, 251n4

Seneca, 324n6, 328, 329, 418

sensus deitatis, 45n2

sensus divinitatis, 19, 26-31, 45n2, 159-60

Septuagint, 79

Sermon on the Mount, 303, 313

Servetus, Michael, 100, 211, 214n43, 218-19

servile fear, 319

session, 402

Shedd, W. G. T., 213n41

shepherds, rulers as, 430

Simons, Menno, 100, 212, 213

sin, 155, 157-63

    corrupted whole person, 160

    eradication of, 467

    and grace, 165-67

    indwelling, 317

    restrained by civil government, 432

Sixtus IV, Pope, 213n37

Skinner, Quentin, 414n10, 437n54

Smith, Christian, 166

Smylie, James, 423n21

social contract, 412, 415

Socinians, 96, 209n18

Socinus, Laelius, 100, 240, 450

Socrates, 5

sola scriptura, 52, 121, 196n122, 399

Son

    deity of, 125

    eternally begotten, 88-89

    sonship of, 87

song, as form of prayer, 360

Sophists, 100, 107, 165, 339

Sorbonnists, 100, 107, 165, 339n34, 343

soul, 325, 333, 449, 456-57

    as image of God, 456

    immortality of, 455-56

soul sleep, 449, 453

Sozomen, 5

space, 127

special providence, 139

special revelation, 137

speculation, 162

    futility of, 164

    regarding eschatology, 451-55, 463, 467

spiritual blessings, 191

spiritualists, 54

Stancaro, Francisco, 215-16, 218, 225

state. *See* civil government

Staupitz, John von, 93

Steinmetz, David, 98, 99

stewardship, 327

Stoicism, 331

Stott, John, 243

Strasbourg, 99, 366, 391

Strehle, Stephen, 175-77

strife, stengthens faith, 287

Stuermann, Walter, 282n40, 298

Sturm, Johann, 391

subordinationism (in Trinity), 81-84, 86, 89

subsistence, 73-74

substitution, 210, 224, 231, 244-46

suffering, 329-32

supererogation, 342n42

superstition, 139, 160-62, 166

suppression

    of image of God, 158

    of truth, 25, 31-32, 162

synecdoches, in law, 313

synergism, 316

synod, 402, 404, 408

Synod of Dort, 96, 155-56, 164

Tamburello, Dennis, 272n8

Tandy, Jean, 5

taxation, 419-21

teaching office, 393-95, 407

temple, destruction of, 463n53

temporary faith, 292

Contributors

William S. Barker has served as professor of church history at Westminster and Covenant Theological Seminaries.

K. Scott Oliphint is professor of systematic theology at Westminster Theological Seminary, Philadelphia.

Robert L. Reymond is professor of systematic theology at Knox Theological Seminary.

Douglas F. Kelly is professor of systematic theology at Reformed Theological Seminary, Charlotte, North Carolina.

R. Scott Clark is professor of church history at Westminster Seminary, California.

Joseph A. Pipa Jr. is president and professor of historical and systematic theology at Greenville (SC) Presbyterian Theological Seminary.

Michael S. Horton is professor of church history at Westminster Seminary, California.

Peter A. Lillback is president and professor of historical theology at Westminster Theological Seminary, Philadelphia.

Derek W. H. Thomas is professor of systematic theology at Reformed Theological Seminary, Jackson, Mississippi.

Robert A. Peterson is professor of systematic theology at Covenant Theological Seminary, St. Louis.

Richard B. Gaffin Jr. is professor of systematic theology at Westminster Theological Seminary, Philadelphia.

Joel R. Beeke is president and professor of historical theology at Puritan Reformed Theological Seminary, Grand Rapids, Michigan.

David Clyde Jones is professor of systematic theology at Covenant Theological Seminary, St. Louis.

William Edgar is professor of systematic theology at Westminster Theological Seminary, Philadelphia.

David B. Calhoun is professor of historical theology at Covenant Theological Seminary, St. Louis.

W. Robert Godfrey is president and professor of church history at Westminster Seminary, California.

Joseph H. Hall has served as librarian and professor of church history at Covenant, Knox, and Mid-America Reformed Seminaries.

David W. Hall is senior pastor at Midway Presbyterian Church in Powder Springs, Georgia.

Cornelis P. Venema is president and professor of doctrinal studies at Mid-America Reformed Seminary, Dyer, Indiana.

Richard C. Gamble is professor of historical theology at Reformed Presbyterian Theological Seminary in Pittsburgh.

Zachary John Kail has been a teaching assistant in the systematic theology department at Reformed Presbyterian Theological Seminary for the past two years.